A THEOLOGY OF THE NEW TESTAMENT

Other Books by George E. Ladd:

Crucial Questions About the Kingdom of God; The Blessed Hope; The Gospel of the Kingdom; The New Testament and Criticism; The Pattern of New Testament Truth; A Commentary on The Revelation of John; The Presence of the Future.

A THEOLOGY OF THE NEW TESTAMENT

by

GEORGE ELDON LADD

William B. Eerdmans Publishing Company
Grand Rapids
Michigan

Reprinted, June 1991

Printed in the United States of America

Library of Congress Cataloging in Publication Data

Ladd, George Eldon, 1911-
A theology of the New Testament.

Includes bibliographical references.
1. Bible. N.T.—Theology. I. Title.
BS2397.L33 225.6'6 74-766
ISBN 0-8028-3443-4

PREFACE

This book is intended to introduce seminary students to the discipline of New Testament theology. It does not purport to be an original contribution or to solve difficult problems, but to give a survey of the discipline, to state its problems, and to offer positive solutions as the author sees them. Since all theology is a human undertaking and no man's position can be considered final, the author has continually engaged in interaction with the most important recent literature, sometimes to gain support, sometimes to debate solutions to problems. Sometimes the discussion is primarily a dialogue with other outstanding theologians. In this task, the author has deliberately imposed upon his words several restrictions. He has limited bibliographical references largely to materials available in English, since the book is designed for seminary students and not for research; and he has limited the bibliographical materials for the most part to modern works. Valuable materials will be found in the three Hastings encyclopedias, but he has not drawn upon such older works, with a few exceptions. It is his hope that the student will find guidance into the most important recent literature on all the main topics of New Testament theology.

The reader should note that sometimes, especially in the case of commentaries, abbreviated titles are used. When two dates appear after a given work, they represent two different printings, or, in the case of works by German scholars, the date of the German and of the English translation, unless these dates are close together. Common abbreviations are used for periodical and encyclopedia literature.

The author approaches his task feeling that New Testament theology must be primarily a descriptive discipline. However, he is convinced that any man's presuppositions distinctly influence his approach. For this reason, while the primary objective is to outline what the various New Testament authors teach, critical questions are not neglected, even though they obviously cannot be thoroughly discussed. The author has often learned most from those with whom he disagrees, and he trusts he has represented other scholars accurately and treated them with respect. It is his hope that the initiate to the study of New Testament theology will not only find a positive exposition, but will be stimulated to wrestle with the problems for himself.

A debt of gratitude is due Professor David Wallace, who carefully read the entire manuscript and offered many helpful suggestions.

The author would express his appreciation to the Trustees and Administration of Fuller Theological Seminary whose generous sabbatical program made possible the writing of this book.

Some of the material on the Kingdom of God appeared in my book, *Jesus and the Kingdom.* A second revised edition of this book has now appeared under the title *The Presence of the Future,* published by the Eerdmans Publishing Company. Part of Chapter 28 appeared in *Apostolic History and the Gospel,* edited by W. Ward Gasque and Ralph P. Martin, published by Paternoster Press. Chapter 35 was published in *Soli Deo Gloria,* edited by J. McDowell Richards, from John Knox Press. These sections are used by permission of the publishers.

George E. Ladd

CONTENTS

PART III: THE PRIMITIVE CHURCH

PART IV: PAUL

PART V: THE GENERAL EPISTLES

PART VI: THE APOCALYPSE

ABBREVIATIONS

ATR	*Anglican Theological Review*
BJRL	*Bulletin of the John Rylands Library*
CBQ	*Catholic Biblical Quarterly*
CJTh	*Canadian Journal of Theology*
DCG	*Dictionary of Christ and the Gospels* (Hastings)
EQ	*Evangelical Quarterly*
ET	*Expository Times*
EvTh	*Evangelische Theologie*
HDB	*Hastings' Dictionary of the Bible*
HERE	*Encyclopedia of Religion and Ethics* (Hastings)
HTR	*Harvard Theological Review*
HUCA	*Hebrew Union College Annual*
IB	*Interpreter's Bible*
ICC	*International Critical Commentary*
IDB	*Interpreter's Dictionary of the Bible*
Int	*Interpretation*
ISBE	*International Standard Bible Encyclopedia*
JBL	*Journal of Biblical Literature*
JBR	*Journal of Bible and Religion*
JR	*Journal of Religion*
JTS	*Journal of Theological Studies*
NT	(in titles) New Testament
NT	*Novum Testamentum*
NTS	*New Testament Studies*
OT	(in titles) Old Testament
Rev and Exp	*Review and Expositor*
RGG	*Religion in Geschichte und Gegenwart*

SJTh	*Scottish Journal of Theology*
StEv	*Studia Evangelica*
StTh	*Studia Theologica*
TDNT	*Theological Dictionary of the New Testament* (Kittel)
ThSt	*Theological Studies*
TLZ	*Theologische Literaturzeitung*
TT	*Theology Today*
TZ	*Theologische Zeitschrift*
Vig Chr	*Vigiliae Christianae*
WThJ	*Westminster Theological Journal*
ZNTW	*Zeitschrift für die neutestamentliche Wissenschaft*
ZSysTh	*Zeitschrift für Systematische Theologie*

PART 1

THE SYNOPTIC GOSPELS

1

INTRODUCTION

A. THE HISTORY OF NEW TESTAMENT THEOLOGY

Literature:

R. Bultmann, "The History of NT Theology as a Science," *Theology of the NT* (1955), II, 241-51; A. Richardson, "Present Issues in NT Theology," *ET* 75 (1964), 109-12; K. Stendahl, "Biblical Theology," *IDB* A-D (1962), pp. 418-32—see extensive bibliography; O. Betz, "History of Biblical Theology," *IDB* A-D (1962), pp. 432-37; R. C. Dentan, *Preface to OT Theology* (1963²)—valuable for parallel movements in the Old Testament; D. H. Wallace, "Biblical Theology: Past and Future," *TZ* (1963), pp. 88-105; S. Neill, *The Interpretation of the NT 1861-1961* (1964), contains much material relevant for theology; A. M. Hunter, "Modern Trends in NT Theology" in *The NT in Historical and Contemporary Perspective,* ed. by H. Anderson and W. Barclay (1965), pp. 133-48; G. E. Ladd, "History and Theology in Biblical Exegesis," *Int* 20 (1966), 54-64; G. E. Ladd, "The Problem of History in Contemporary NT Interpretation," *StEv* V (1968), 88-100; H. Conzelmann, "History of the Discipline," *An Outline of the Theology of the NT* (1969), pp. 3-8; M. Dibelius, "Biblical Theology and the History of Biblical Religion," *Twentieth Century Theology in the Making*, J. Pelikan, ed., I (1969), 23-31; G. E. Ladd, "The Search for Perspective," *Int* 25 (1971), 41-62—a defense of *Heilsgeschichte;* B. S. Childs, *Biblical Theology in Crisis* (1970); W. J. Harrington, *The Path of Biblical Theology* (1973).

THE MIDDLE AGES. During the Middle Ages, biblical study was completely subordinated to ecclesiastical dogma. The theology of the Bible was used only to reinforce the dogmatic teachings of the church, which were founded upon both the Bible and church tradition. Not the Bible alone, historically understood, but the Bible as interpreted by church tradition was the source of dogmatic theology.

THE REFORMATION. The reformers reacted against the unbiblical character of dogmatic theology and insisted that theology must be founded on the Bible alone. Dogmatics should be the systematic formulation of the teachings of the Bible. This new emphasis led to a study of the original languages of Scripture and to a consciousness of the role of history in biblical theology. The reformers insisted that the Bible should be interpreted literally and not allegorically, and this led to the beginnings of a truly biblical theology. However, the reformers' sense of history was imperfect, and the Old Testament was often interpreted not in its own historical setting but in terms of New Testament truth. For instance, Calvin writes as though the Jews knew and understood the New Testament doctrine of Christ (*Institutes* II, vi, 4).

ORTHODOX SCHOLASTICISM. The gains in the historical study of the Bible made by the reformers were soon lost in the post-reformation period, and the Bible was once again used uncritically and unhistorically to support orthodox doctrine. The Bible was viewed not only as a book free from error and contradiction but also without development or progress. The entire Bible was looked upon as possessing one level of theological value. History was completely lost in dogma, and philology became a branch of dogmatics.

THE RATIONALIST REACTION. Biblical theology as a distinctive discipline is a product of the impact of the Enlightenment upon biblical studies. A new approach to the study of the Bible emerged in the eighteenth century that gradually freed itself altogether from all ecclesiastical and theological control and interpreted the Bible with "complete objectivity," viewing it solely as a product of history. Several interrelated influences produced this movement. The rise of rationalism with its reaction against supernaturalism, the development of the historical method, and the rise of literary criticism led to the treatment of the biblical records viewed no longer as the Word of God, given by the inspiration of the Spirit, but as human historical records like any other ancient literature.

These influences, focused upon the study of theology, led to the conclusion that scholarship was not to seek a theology in the Bible but only the history of religion. The Bible is a compilation of ancient religious writings that preserves the history of an ancient Semitic people, and is to be studied with the same presuppositions with which one studies other Semitic religions. This conclusion was first clearly articulated by J. P. Gabler, who in an inaugural address in 1787 distinguished sharply between biblical theology and dogmatic theology. The former must be strictly historical and independent of dogmatic theology, tracing the rise of religious ideas in Israel and setting forth what the biblical writers thought about religious matters. Dogmatic theology, on the other hand, makes use of biblical theology, extracting from it what has universal relevance and making use of philosophical concepts. Dogmatic theology is that which a particular theologian decides about divine matters, considered philosophically and rationally in accordance with the outlook and demand of his own age, but biblical theology is concerned solely with what men believed long ago.

Gabler was essentially a rationalist, and his approach to biblical theology prevailed for some fifty years. Works on the theology of the Bible were written by Kaiser (1813), De Wette (1813), Baumgarten-Crusius (1828), and von Cölln (1836). Some scholars of this period were extremely rationalistic, finding in the Bible religious ideas that were in accord with the universal laws of reason. Others tried to reconcile Christian theology with the thought forms of the modern period. While rationalism as such is long since passé, it is obvious that this basic approach to the study of the Bible is still used by modern scholarship; and even the evangelical scholar employs the historical method, although with limitations.

THE RISE OF THE PHILOSOPHY OF RELIGION. Rationalism was superseded under the influence of the idealist philosophy of Hegel (d. 1813), who saw the Absolute Idea or Absolute Spirit eternally manifesting itself in the universe and in human affairs. Hegel taught that the movement of human thought followed the dialectic pattern from a position (thesis) to an opposite position (antithesis); and from the interaction of these two emerged a new insight or aspect of reality (synthesis). Hegel saw in the history of religion the evolution of Spirit in its dialectical apprehension of the divine, from nature religions, through religions of spiritual individuality, to the Absolute Religion, which is Christianity.

Under the influence of Hegel, F. C. Baur abandoned the rationalistic effort to find timeless truth in the New Testament, but in its stead found in the historical movements in the early church the unfolding of wisdom and spirit. The teaching of Jesus formed the point of departure. Jesus' teachings were not yet theology but the expression of his religious consciousness. Theological reflection began over the question of the Law. Paul, the first theologian, took the position that the Christian was freed from the Law (thesis). Jewish Christianity, represented particularly by James and Peter, took the opposite position, that the Law was permanently valid and must remain an essential element in the Christian church (antithesis). Baur interpreted the history of apostolic Christianity in terms of this conflict between Pauline and Judaistic Christianity. Out of the conflict emerged in the second century the Old Catholic Church, which effected a successful harmonization between these two positions (synthesis).

Baur was less concerned with the truth of the Scriptures than with the effort to trace historical development. He has made a lasting contribution, for the principle that biblical theology is inseparably related to history is sound, even though Baur's application of this principle is not. Baur's interpretation gave rise to the so-called "Tübingen School," which had great influence in German New Testament studies.

THE CONSERVATIVE REACTION. These new approaches to the study of the Bible naturally met with strong resistance in orthodox circles, not only from those who denied the validity of an historical approach but from those who tried to combine the historical approach with a belief in revelation. Influential was E. W. Hengstenberg's *Christology of the OT* (1829-35) and *History of the Kingdom of God Under the OT* (1869-71). Hengstenberg saw little progress in revelation and made little distinction between the two testaments, and interpreted the prophets spiritually with little reference to history. A more historical approach was structured by J. C. K. Hofmann in a series of writings beginning in 1841 (*Prophecy and Fulfillment*). He attempted to vindicate the authority and inspiration of the Bible by historical means, developing his *Heilsgeschichte* theology. Hofmann found in the Bible a record of the process of saving or holy history that aims at the redemption of all mankind. This process will not be fully completed until the eschatological consummation. He tried to assign every book of the Bible to its logical place in the scheme of the history of redemption. These scholars (see also J. A. Bengel, J. T. Beck), who comprised the so-called "Erlangen School," did not regard the Bible primarily as a collection of proof texts or a repository of doctrine but as the witness to what God had done in saving history. They held that the propositional statements in Scripture were not meant to be an end in themselves nor an object of faith, but were designated to bear witness to the redemptive acts of God.

The Erlangen school had great influence in conservative circles upon such scholars as Tholuck, T. Zahn, and P. Feine, and is represented in the theologies of F. Büchsel (1937), A. Schlatter (1909), and Ethelbert Stauffer (1941).[1] Stauffer rejects the "systems of doctrine" approach and does not try to trace the development of the Christian understanding of the person and work of Jesus. Rather, he presents a "Christocentric theology of history in the New Testament," i.e., the theology of the plan of salvation enacted in New Testament history. The book has the defects of not distinguishing between canonical and noncanonical writings and of ignoring the variety of the several interpretations of the meaning of Christ in the New Testament.

A new form of the *Heilsgeschichte* theology has emerged in recent years, for there is a widespread recognition that revelation has occurred in redemptive history, and that *Heilsgeschichte* is the best key to understand the unity of the Bible. This will be developed later.

LIBERAL HISTORICISM IN NEW TESTAMENT THEOLOGY. Bultmann has pointed out that the logical consequence of Baur's method would have been a complete relativism,[2] for the liberal mind could not conceive of absolute truth in the relativities of history. This was avoided by the influence of romanticism, by which personality is interpreted as a history-forming power. Under the influence of Ritschlian theology, the essence of Christianity was interpreted as a pure spiritual-ethical religion, which was proclaimed by and embodied in the life and mission of Jesus. The Kingdom of God is the highest good, the ethical ideal. The heart of religion is personal fellowship with God as Father.

This theological interpretation was reinforced by the solution of the Synoptic problem with its discovery of the priority of Mark and the hypothetical document, Q. Scholars of this "old liberalism" believed that in these most primitive documents, historical science had at last discovered the true

[1] Only Stauffer has been translated into English (1955).
[2] R. Bultmann, *Theology of the NT* (1951), I, 245.

Jesus, freed from all theological interpretation. Biblical theologians of this school began with this "historical" picture of the ethical religion of Jesus and then traced the diverse systems of doctrine (*Lehrbegriffe*) that emerged as the result of later reflection and speculation. The great classic of this school is H. J. Holtzmann's *Lehrbuch der NT Theologie* (1896-97, 1911[2]). Paul Wernle's *The Beginnings of Our Religion* (1903-4) is another illustration. Adolf von Harnack's *What Is Christianity?* (1901) is a classic statement of this liberal view.

This "old liberal" approach influenced even conservative writers. Both B. Weiss (*Theology of the NT,* 1868, Eng. 1903) and W. Beyschlag (*NT Theology,* 1891, Eng. 1895) interpreted Jesus primarily in spiritual terms, placing great emphasis upon the centrality of the Fatherhood of God. These men are conservative in that they recognize the reality of revelation and the validity of the canon; but their picture of Jesus shares the features of liberalism. They also employ the "systems of doctrine" method, Weiss going so far as to discover four different periods of theological development in Paul, which he treats separately. This approach is found in English in the writings of Orello Cone, *The Gospel and Its Earliest Interpreters* (1893); G. B. Stevens, *The Theology of the NT* (1899); E. P. Gould, *The Biblical Theology of the NT* (1900); and A. C. Zenos, *The Plastic Age of the Gospel* (1927). The same method is used by even more conservative writers in Germany, such as T. Zahn, *Grundriss der NT Theologie* (1932) and P. Feine, *Theologie des NT* (1910, 1950).

THE VICTORY OF RELIGION OVER THEOLOGY. Along with liberalism developed the *religionsgeschichtliche Schule*. Liberalism found the distinctive element in biblical theology in the simple ethical teachings of Jesus. While its representatives paid some attention to the influence of the religious environment of early Christianity (Holtzmann's theology devoted 120 pages to sketching Jewish and Hellenistic backgrounds), yet the essence of Christianity was treated as something unique. Holtzmann does recognize Hellenistic influences on Paul.

Otto Pfleiderer presaged a new approach. The first edition of *Das Urchristentum* (1887) took the same position as Harnack and Holtzmann; but in the second edition (1902, Eng. 1906, *Primitive Christianity*), he interpreted many elements in New Testament theology in terms of their religious environment. The program for this new approach was sounded by W. Wrede in 1897 in a little book entitled "Concerning the Task and Method of the So-called NT Theology."[2a] He attacked the prevailing method of interpreting New Testament theology as a series of doctrinal systems, for the Christian faith is religion, not theology or a system of ideas. New Testament theology has the task, not of formulating timeless truths, whether these be mediated by a supernatural revelation or discovered by rational thought, but of formulating expressions of the living religious experiences of early Christianity understood in the light of the religious environment.

[2a] Translated by R. Morgan in *The Nature of NT Theology* (1973), pp. 68-116.

Therefore the theology of the New Testament must be displaced by the history of religion in primitive Christianity.

This new approach had distinct centers of interest: the interpretation of New Testament ideas in terms of expressions of religious experience, and the explanation of the rise of these religious experiences and ideas in terms of the religious environment. One of the first to attempt the former task was H. Weinel in his *Biblische Theologie des NT* (1913, 1928[4]). Weinel had no interest in the value or truth of Christianity but only in its nature in comparison with other religions. He set forth types of religions against which Christianity is to be understood as an ethical religion of redemption. Books in English that reflect this influence are S. J. Case, *The Evolution of Early Christianity* (1914); E. W. Parsons, *The Religion of the NT* (1939); and E. F. Scott, *The Varieties of NT Religion* (1943).

The basic assumptions of this approach led to very different treatments of Jesus and Paul. In 1892, J. Weiss published a slim little booklet of sixty-seven pages on *The Preaching of Jesus About the Kingdom of God*[3] in which he interpreted Jesus' message of the Kingdom in terms of the milieu of Jewish apocalyptic. This approach was made famous by Albert Schweitzer's *The Quest of the Historical Jesus* (1906, Eng. 1910), which gives a history of the interpretation of Jesus and then in a hundred pages interprets Jesus in terms of "Consistent Eschatology," i.e., as a Jewish apocalyptist who belongs to first-century Judaism and has little relevance for the modern man. This preacher of eschatology is diametrically opposed to the ethical teacher of the pure religion of the Fatherhood of God of Harnack and Holtzmann, and it has become clear that the "old liberal" Jesus was a distinct modernization. Eschatology, instead of being the husk (Harnack), was shown to be the very kernel of Jesus' message.

If Jesus was interpreted in terms of the milieu of Jewish apocalyptic, Paul was interpreted in terms of Hellenistic Judaism or the Hellenistic cult and mystery religions. Some scholars, like Bousset, still interpreted Jesus along the lines of liberalism but applied the *religionsgeschichtliche Methode* to Paul. Brückner argued that Paul found a ready-made doctrine of a heavenly man in Judaism, which he applied to Jesus. Günkel held that there had sprung up in the Orient a syncretistic religion, gnostic in character, with faith in the resurrection as its central doctrine. This pre-Christian gnosticism had penetrated Judaism, and through this medium influenced Christianity, even before Paul. W. Bousset put this view on a firmer basis by arguing that gnosticism was not an heretical new formation in Christianity, as Harnack had supposed, but was a pre-Christian pagan phenomenon, oriental rather than Greek, and religious and mystical rather than philosophical. In his *Kyrios Christos*[4] Bousset traced the history of belief in Jesus in the early church, and sharply distinguished between the religious consciousness of Jesus, the faith of primitive Christianity that held Jesus to

---

[3] Eng. ed. *Jesus' Proclamation of the Kingdom of God* (1971).

[4] 1913, 1921[2]; Eng. ed. 1970.

be the transcendental Son of Man of Jewish apocalyptic, and the view of the Hellenistic church and Paul, who held Jesus to be a divinity, like the Greek cult lords.

The most important theology embodying this approach is that of Rudolf Bultmann (1951). Bultmann differs from Bousset in that he interprets Jesus in terms of Jewish apocalyptic; but he follows him in his understanding of the Hellenistic church and Paul. However, Bultmann added a new feature in his existential understanding of these New Testament myths that will be discussed below.

THE CONTEMPORARY RETURN TO BIBLICAL THEOLOGY. During the 1920s a new viewpoint began to make itself felt that resulted in a revival of biblical theology. Dentan suggests three factors that contributed to this end: a loss of faith in evolutionary naturalism; a reaction against the purely historical method that claimed complete objectivity and believed in the adequacy of bare facts to disclose the truth of history; and the recovery of the idea of revelation.[5] This led to the conviction that the Bible contained both history and a word concerning the ultimate meaning of history. This new approach to theology has changed the complexion of New Testament studies. The historical assurance of liberalism had been challenged by Martin Kähler in a far-seeing book that was ahead of its times but which has proven to be crucial for the modern debate. Kähler structured the problem in terms of "The So-called Historical (*historische*) Jesus and the Historic (*geschichtliche*) Biblical Christ."[6] The *historische* Jesus was the picture of Jesus reconstructed by the liberal critical method. Kähler argued that this Jesus never really existed in history but only in the critical reconstruction of scholarship. The only Jesus who possesses reality is the Christ pictured in the Bible, whose character is such that he cannot be reconstructed by the methods of modern scientific historiography. The Gospels are not historical (*historische*) documents in the scientific sense of the term, but witnesses to the Christ. They are kerygma, not "history"; and it is impossible to get behind the kerygma. Indeed, the "historical Jesus" serves only to obscure from us the living biblical Christ. The real *geschichtliche* Christ is the Christ who is attested in the Gospels and preached by the church.

Another signpost pointing in the same direction was the book by W. Wrede, *The Messianic Secret in the Gospels* (1901).[7] Wrede shattered the liberal portrait of the historical Jesus by showing that the Jesus of Mark was not the inspired prophet but a messianic (divine) being. Wrede differed from Kähler in that he did not accept the Markan portrait of Jesus as true but attempted to explain historically how the nonmessianic, historical Jesus became the messianic Christ of the Gospels.

In the years that followed, gospel criticism turned to the study of the

---

[5] R. C. Dentan, *Preface to OT Theology* (1963^2), p. 59.
[6] 1896, 1956. Eng. ed. 1964.
[7] Eng. tr. 1971.

oral stage of the gospel tradition (*Formgeschichte*) to try to discover the laws controlling the tradition that could explain the transformation of the "historical" Jesus into the kerygmatic (divine) Christ. One outstanding positive result of this study is the admission that form criticism could not find in any stratum of the gospel tradition a purely historical (i.e., human) Jesus. This has issued in two different results. On the one hand is the agnosticism of such form critics as Rudolf Bultmann, who feels that the historical Jesus has been so hidden beyond the Christ of faith that we can now know almost nothing concerning the life and personality of Jesus. Bultmann sees only discontinuity between the Jesus of history and the Christ of the kerygma, and he has excluded Jesus from the subject matter of New Testament theology. R. H. Lightfoot in England has taken a similar position.

On the other hand, E. H. Hoskyns and Noel Davey in *The Riddle of the NT* (1931) show that all of the evidence of the New Testament converges on a single point: that in Jesus God revealed himself for man's salvation. The critical method has revealed most clearly the living unity of the New Testament documents. The historian is compelled to state that both the unity and uniqueness of this claim are historical facts. This claim, while occurring in history, transcends history, for it demands of the historian what he as an historian may not give: a theological judgment of ultimate significance.

This "kerygmatic" interpretation of New Testament theology received its greatest impetus through the writings of C. H. Dodd. In his inaugural lecture at Cambridge University, Dodd called for a new emphasis on the unity of New Testament thought in place of the analytic approach that had prevailed throughout the preceding century. In the same year he implemented his own suggestion in *The Apostolic Preaching and Its Developments.* Dodd finds the unity of the New Testament message in the kerygma, the heart of which is the proclamation that the New Age has come in the person and mission of Jesus. Here, for the first time, a single biblical concept was used to relate all the New Testament materials into a unified development. Dodd has enlarged upon this thesis in *The Parables of the Kingdom* (1935) and *The Interpretation of the Fourth Gospel* (1953), interpreting both the message of Jesus and of the Gospel of John in terms of the inbreaking of the Age to Come. While this approach is sound in principle, Dodd's work has the defect of understanding the Age to Come in terms of platonic thought rather than biblical eschatology. The Age to Come is the wholly other, the eternal breaking into the temporal, instead of the future age breaking into the present age.

This kerygmatic approach has produced an extensive literature. The outstanding American protagonist has been F. V. Filson. His *One Lord, One Faith* (1943) defends the unity of the New Testament message, and his *Jesus Christ the Risen Lord* (1956) argues that New Testament theology must understand New Testament history from the theological point of view, i.e., of the living God who acts in history, the most notable event being the resurrection of Christ. Filson interprets the entire New Testament theology in the light of the resurrection.

A. M. Hunter expounded *The Unity of the NT* (1944; published in America under the title *The Message of the NT*) in terms of One Lord, One Church, One Salvation. More recently, in a slim volume *Introducing NT Theology* (1957), he has interpreted the "Fact of Christ," including in this term "the totality of what Jesus Christ's coming involved, his person, work and words, of course, but also the Resurrection, the advent of the Spirit and the creation of the new Israel . . ." (p. 9).

Oscar Cullmann also follows the *Heilgeschichte* interpretation, and provides an excellent corrective for Dodd's platonic approach. In *Christ and Time* (1946, Eng. 1950), he argued that the New Testament finds its unity in a common conception of time and history rather than in ideas of essence, nature, eternal or existential truth. Theology is the meaning of the historical in time. In Cullmann's work, *Heilsgeschichte* theology has emerged in a new form; and the principle of *Heilsgeschichte* as the unifying center of New Testament theology has been widely recognized. We can accept the basic validity of Cullmann's approach without agreeing with him that the New Testament shows no interest in questions of nature and being but only in "functional Christology."[8] Cullmann has published a second volume, *Salvation in History* (1967), in which he contrasts *Heilsgeschichte* with existential theology.

Alan Richardson in his *Introduction to the Theology of the NT* (1958) assumes the kerygmatic approach by accepting the hypothesis that the "brilliant re-interpretation of the Old Testament scheme of salvation which is found in the New Testament" goes back to Jesus himself and is not the product of the believing community. In an essay on "Historical Theology and Biblical Theology," Richardson argues that biblical theology cannot use a purely objective, scientific, neutral approach, but must interpret the biblical history from the standpoint of a biblical faith.[9]

W. G. Kümmel's *The Theology of the New Testament According to Its Major Witnesses* (1969, Eng. tr. 1973) may well be characterized within the *Heilsgeschichte* school. In this first volume he deals only with Jesus, the Primitive Church, Paul, and John, and he is particularly concerned to find the central message of the chief witnesses. He finds this in the saving act of God in Jesus Christ. In Christ, God has begun his salvation promised for the end of the world, and in this Christ event, God encounters us to rescue us from imprisonment in this world and free us to love. This divine activity is expressed differently by the several witnesses, but all four in different ways attest to the central redeeming event in the history of Jesus Christ.

THE BULTMANNIAN SCHOOL. The exponents of this "kerygmatic" approach assume that the Christ proclaimed in the kerygma is continuous

---

[8] *The Christology of the NT* (1959), pp. 326-27. See Cullmann's defense in *SJTh* 15 (1962), 36-43.

[9] See *CJTh* 1 (1955), 157-67.

with the historical Jesus. The "kerygmatic" factor is the interpretive element that necessarily accompanies the event. This position has been radically rejected by the most influential living German New Testament scholar, Rudolf Bultmann. Bultmann is also a "kerygmatic" theologian, but he uses the concept of the kerygma and of *Geschichte* very differently from the scholars discussed above. The historical Jesus, for Bultmann, has been quite obscured behind the layers of believing tradition, which reinterpreted the significance of the historical Jesus in terms of mythology. Historically, Jesus was only a Jewish prophet who proclaimed the imminent apocalyptic end of the world and warned people to prepare for the catastrophe of judgment. He conceived of himself neither as Messiah nor as Son of Man. He did, however, possess an overwhelming sense of the reality of God, and he realized that he was the bearer of the Word of God for the last hour, which placed men under the demand for decision. His death was an incomparable tragedy, which was, however, redeemed from meaninglessness by the Christian belief in his resurrection. The early church reinterpreted Jesus, first in terms of the Jewish apocalyptic Son of Man, and then in terms of a conflated apocalyptic Son of Man and gnostic heavenly man. All of this is, however, mythological kerygma by which the early church reinterpreted the meaning of Christ for them. The kerygma, i.e., the early church's proclamation of Christ, is an historical fact in the life of early Christianity, and therefore there is continuity between the historical Jesus and the kerygma. It was Jesus who gave rise to the kerygma. If there had been no Jesus, there would have been no kerygma. However, the Christ who is proclaimed in the kerygma is purely a mythological construction and had no existence in history, for mythology by definition is nonhistorical. Therefore, there can be no continuity between the historical Jesus and the Christ of the kerygma. The kerygma is the expression of the meaning Christ had for the early Christians, formulated in mythological terms.

Bultmann's interpretation of New Testament theology is controlled by three facts. First, historical reality must be understood in terms of unbroken historical causality. If God is thought to act in history, the action must always be hidden in historical events and evident only to the eye of faith.[10] All ideas of supernatural acts—real incarnation, virgin birth, miracles, bodily resurrection, etc.—are *ipso facto* unhistorical but mythological. Second, the Synoptic Gospels give us such a theological picture of Jesus that they cannot be historical. The *historische* Jesus is nearly lost from sight behind the *geschichtliche* Christ of the church's faith. Third, this is no loss for theology, for faith cannot rest itself upon the security of historical research but must trust only the bare Word of God in the kerygma. However, the kerygma itself is expressed in mythological terms and must therefore be "demythologized" to yield its existential meaning. Man can achieve "authentic existence"—freedom from the past and openness to

---

[10] See also J. D. Smart, *The Strange Silence of the Bible in the Church* (1970), for the same position.

the future—only by faith in the demythologized kerygma, not in the Jesus of history. Bultmann sees no continuity between the Jesus of history and the Christ of faith—only between the Jesus of history and the kerygma.

Bultmann's followers have been disturbed by the extremeness of his position, which divorced the historical Jesus from Christian faith and removed him from Christian theology. They have therefore initiated a new quest for the historical Jesus, who will stand in a measure of continuity with the Christ of the kerygma. This has been accomplished by postulating the same authentic existence in response to the historical Jesus as to the kerygma. The most notable products of this "post-Bultmannian" school to date have been James Robinson's *A New Quest of the Historical Jesus* (1959), G. Bornkamm's *Jesus of Nazareth* (1960), and Hans Conzelmann's *An Outline of the Theology of the NT* (1969).

Joachim Jeremias represents an independent position. He does not consider himself one of the "new questers," for he has never given up the old quest. He thinks that by form criticism he can strip off the layers of accretion in the gospel tradition and discover the *ipsissima vox* if not the *ipsissima verba* of the historical Jesus. Here alone is revelation to be found—in the message of Jesus. The epistles are not revelation but the response of the believing community to the revelation in Jesus. Jesus possessed unique authority as the Son of God to reveal the Father. In the historical Jesus, we find ourselves confronted by God himself. Jesus proclaimed the imminent Kingdom of God and anticipated his own exaltation as the heavenly Son of Man. He saw himself as the Suffering Servant giving his life for the sins of men. In the resurrection, his disciples experienced his parousia, which meant his enthronement in heaven and the coming of the eschaton. His most notable works in this connection are *The Problem of the Historical Jesus* (1964) and *NT Theology* (1971), Vol. I.

THE AMERICAN SCENE. American scholarship has not been noted for its creative contribution to New Testament theology. The last full-scale textbook that treated the discipline in a comprehensive manner was that of George Barker Stevens, *The Theology of the NT* (1906).

The last twenty-five years have witnessed a debate between a theological approach to New Testament interpretation and a strictly "scientific" approach that insists that considerations of faith belong to the discipline of systematic theology. New Testament theology must interpret the Scriptures by the thoroughgoing application of the "historical-critical" method. C. C. McCown argued that history is the result of the complex interaction of natural and social forces and the actions and reactions of men. God acts only through men (*JBL* 75 [1956], 12-18; see his book, *The Search for the Real Jesus* [1940]). Cadbury labeled the "theology of history" approach as archaizing and therefore unscientific (*Int* 3 [1949], 331-37). This "scientific" approach was more interested in religion than in theology.[11] Millar Burrows wrote *An Outline of Biblical Theology* (1946) in which he

[11] See above, pp. 17-18.

defines theology as the elements in biblical religion that are of timeless worth and abiding significance. As we might expect, this school, if it can be called such, has been little interested in trying to produce works in New Testament theology.

Other scholars have espoused a theological approach to the interpretation of the New Testament, insisting that so-called scientific objectivity was neither desirable nor attainable, and maintaining that revelation has truly occurred in history, but is recognizable only by the eyes of faith.[12] This has been the most notable movement in American New Testament theology, and it has been documented in Connolly Gamble, Jr., "The Literature of Biblical Theology," *Int* 7 (1953), 466-80, and in G. E. Ladd, "The Search for Perspective," *Int* 25 (1971), 41-43. A. N. Wilder, surveying the scene in New Testament theology, considered *Heilsgeschichte* or *Geschichtstheologie* to be the most promising approach to the contemporary task.[13] While this approach is to be found in numerous periodical articles, it has produced only a few books. Among these are Otto Piper's *God in History* (1939), which explicitly defends *Heilsgeschichte;* Floyd V. Filson's *Jesus Christ, the Risen Lord* (1956), a brief New Testament theology as seen through the perspective of the resurrection; and John Wick Bowman's *Religion of Maturity* (1948) and *Prophetic Realism and the Gospel* (1955). Bowman strongly defends the position that revelation has occurred on the plane of history, but he appears to go altogether too far in rejecting "the religion of the throne," namely, apocalyptic.[14] Even F. C. Grant recognizes the concept of *Heilsgeschichte*.[15]

One of the characteristics of most of these books is that they use the topical or synthetic rather than the historical or analytical approach. W. D. Davies has produced an excellent survey that deals with the Synoptics, Paul, and John,[16] but its level is more for laymen than for students. Ralph Knudsen and Frank Stagg have both written topical surveys in New Testament theology,[17] but they are both too limited in scope to serve theological students.

Although this movement of "biblical theology" has recently been pronounced dead,[18] Brevard Childs surveys it in *Biblical Theology in Crisis* (1970). The crisis, he feels, is due to the fact that the biblical theology movement tried to combine a liberal critical methodology with a normative biblical theology. They failed to bridge the gap between exegesis and

---

[12] See P. S. Minear, *Eyes of Faith* (1946).

[13] "NT Theology in Transition" in *The Study of the Bible Today and Tomorrow*, ed. by H. R. Willoughby (1947), p. 435.

[14] See G. E. Ladd, "Why Not Prophetic-Apocalyptic?" *JBL* 76 (1957), 192-200.

[15] F. C. Grant, *An Introduction to NT Thought* (1958), p. 41.

[16] W. D. Davies, *Invitation to the NT* (1966).

[17] R. E. Knudsen, *Theology in the NT* (1964); F. Stagg, *NT Theology* (1962).

[18] See the editorial in *Interpretation,* 23 (1969), 78-80. R. Grant pronounced the movement a failure and has summoned "New Testament scholars to come to themselves, stop trying to feed on pods, and return to the father's house." Cf. "American NT Study, 1926-1956," *JBL* 87 (1968), 43.

theology. This can be done, Childs thinks, only by viewing the Bible in its own context, that of canonical literature. The Bible must be recognized as the normative vehicle of revelation, and therefore as inspired.

Gerhard Hasel has given us an excellent survey of Old Testament theology in *OT Theology: Basic Issues in the Current Debate* (1972) in which he deals with the same issues that confront us in New Testament theology. He insists that there is "a transcendent or divine dimension in Biblical history which the historical-critical method is unable to deal with" (p. 85). Biblical theology must be done from a starting-point that is biblical-historical in orientation. Only this approach can deal adequately with the reality of God and his inbreaking into history. This is the methodology employed by the present writer in the study of New Testament theology.

With the exception of dispensational writers,[19] American evangelicals have made little contribution to New Testament theological literature. The only comprehensive work is that of Geerhardus Vos, *Biblical Theology* (1948), but it breaks off abruptly in the middle of Jesus' ministry, and is more a long essay on revelation in the Old Testament than a biblical theology. His *Self-Disclosure of Jesus* (1926), long out of date, has some chapters that are still of great value for the christological problem of the New Testament. One of Evangelicalism's spokesmen has said, "If evangelical Protestants do not overcome their preoccupation with negative criticism of contemporary theological deviations at the expense of the construction of preferable alternatives to these, they will not be much of a doctrinal force in the decade ahead."[20] It is to meet this challenge that the present book was written.

B. BIBLICAL THEOLOGY, HISTORY, AND REVELATION

Biblical theology is that discipline which sets forth the message of the books of the Bible in their historical setting. Biblical theology is primarily a descriptive discipline.[21] It is not initially concerned with the final meaning of the teachings of the Bible or their relevance for today. This is the task of systematic theology.[22] Biblical theology has the task of expounding the theology found in the Bible in its own historical setting, and its own terms, categories, and thought forms. It is the obvious *intent* of the Bible to tell a story about God and his acts in history for man's salvation. For Bultmann the idea of revelation in *history* is mythological. He argues that the real intent of the New Testament is to describe man's existential situation. However, this is modernization. Mythology or not, the intent of the Bible

---

[19] See J. F. Walvoord, *The Millennial Kingdom* (1959); J. D. Pentecost, *Things to Come* (1959); A. J. McClain, *The Greatness of the Kingdom* (1959). Dispensationalism is refuted in G. E. Ladd, *Crucial Questions About the Kingdom of God* (1952).

[20] C. F. H. Henry in *Jesus of Nazareth: Saviour and Lord*, ed. by C. F. H. Henry (1966), p. 9.

[21] K. Stendahl, "Biblical Theology," *IDB* A-D, pp. 422f.

[22] O. Piper, "Biblical Theology and Systematic Theology," *JBR* (1957), pp. 106-11.

is to tell a story about what God has done, which also affects human existence. However, biblical theology cannot be blind to the second question: the truthfulness of the biblical story.

The problem is that presuppositions about the nature of history have continued to interject themselves into the reconstruction of the biblical message. For instance, the Gospels represent Jesus as a divine man and as being conscious of his divine power. Can this be true to history? For scholars who feel bound by a secularistic historical method, history has no room for divine men. Therefore, back of the Jesus of the Gospels must be hidden an historical Jesus. The New Testament pictures the church as being founded by the resurrection of Christ. Did Jesus actually rise from the dead? In ordinary historical experience, dead men do not rise. Such presuppositions affect the methodology of biblical theologians.

However, since biblical theology is concerned with the self-revelation of God and with the redemption of men, the very idea of revelation and redemption involves certain presuppositions that are everywhere implicit and often explicit in the Bible. These presuppositions are God, man, and sin. The reality of God is everywhere assumed. The Bible is not concerned to prove God or to discuss theism in a philosophical manner. It assumes a personal, powerful, self-existent being who is creator of the world and of man, and who is concerned about man. The divine concern is caused by man's sin, which has brought him into a state of separation from God and carries with it the doom of death. The human plight has affected not only individual existence, but also both the course of history and the world of nature in which man is placed. Redemption is the divine activity whose objective is the deliverance of men, both as individuals and as a society, from their sinful predicament and their restoration to a position of fellowship and favor with God.

Biblical theology is neither the story of man's search for God, nor is it a description of a history of religious experience. Biblical theology is *theo*logy: it is primarily a story about God and his concern for men. It exists only because of the divine initiative realizing itself in a series of divine acts whose objective is human redemption. Biblical theology therefore is not exclusively, or even primarily, a system of abstract theological truths. It is basically the description and interpretation of the divine activity within the scene of human history that seeks man's redemption.

BIBLICAL THEOLOGY, REVELATION, AND HISTORY. The bond that unites the Old and the New Testaments is this sense of the divine activity in history. Orthodox theology has traditionally undervalued or at least underemphasized the role of the redemptive acts of God in revelation. The classic essay by B. B. Warfield acknowledges the fact of revelation through the instrumentality of historical deeds but subordinates revelation in acts to revelation in words.[23] A contemporary evangelical has

[23] See B. B. Warfield, "The Biblical Idea of Revelation," *The Inspiration and Authority of the Bible* (1948), pp. 71-104.

defined "revelation, in the biblical sense of the term, [as] the communication of information."[24] Such a view does not require history, but only communication via thought or speech. It is more accurate to say that "revelation moves in the dimension of personal encounter. . . . This is indeed the end of all revelation, to see the face of God!"[25] What God reveals is not only information about himself and human destiny; he reveals *himself,* and this revelation has occurred in a series of historical events.

This is why Henry has written, "Revelation cannot . . . be equated simply with the Hebrew-Christian Scriptures; the Bible is a special segment within a larger divine activity of revelation. . . . Special revelation involves unique historical events of divine deliverance climaxed by the incarnation, atonement, and resurrection of Jesus Christ."[26]

The greatest revelatory act of God in the Old Testament was the deliverance of Israel from bondage in Egypt. This was no ordinary event of history like the events that befell other nations. It was not an achievement of the Israelites. It was not attributed to the genius and skillful leadership of Moses. It was an act of God. "You have seen what I did to the Egyptians, and how I bore you on eagles' wings" (Exod. 19:4).

This deliverance was not merely an act of God; it was an act through which God made himself known and through which Israel was to know and serve God. "I am the Lord, and I will bring you out from under the burdens of the Egyptians, and I will deliver you from their bondage . . . , and *you shall know that I am the Lord your God*" (Exod. 6:6-7).

In the later history of Israel, the Exodus is recited again and again as the redemptive act by which God made himself known to his people. Hosea appeals to Israel's historical redemption and subsequent experiences as evidence of the love of God. "When Israel was a child, I loved him, and out of Egypt I called my son. . . . I led them with the cords of compassion, with the bands of love" (Hos. 11:1, 4).

History also reveals God in wrath and judgment. Hosea goes on immediately to say that Israel is about to return to captivity because of her sins. Amos interprets Israel's impending historical destruction with the words: "Therefore thus I will do to you, O Israel; because I will do this to you, prepare to meet your God, O Israel!" (Amos 4:12). The revelation of God as the judge of his people in historical events is sharply reflected in the designation of Israel's historical defeat by the Assyrians as the Day of the Lord (Amos 5:18).

Israel's history is different from all other history. While God is the Lord of all history, in one series of events God has revealed himself as he has nowhere else done. German theologians have coined the useful term *Heilsgeschichte* to designate this stream of revelatory history. In English we speak

---

24 E. J. Young, *Thy Word Is Truth* (1947), p. 41.

25 P. K. Jewett, "Special Revelation as Historical and Personal," in *Revelation and the Bible,* ed. by C. F. H. Henry (1958), pp. 52, 56.

26 C. F. H. Henry in *Inspiration and Interpretation,* ed. by J. Walvoord (1957), pp. 254f.

of "redemptive history" or "holy history." To be sure, God was superintending the course of Egypt and Assyria and Babylon and Persia. There is a general providence in history, but only in the history of Israel had God communicated to men personal knowledge of himself.

The New Testament stands in this stream of "holy history." The recital of God's acts in history is the substance of Christian proclamation. The earliest semblance of a creedal confession is found in I Corinthians 15:3ff., and it is a recital of events: Christ died, he was buried, he was raised, he appeared. The New Testament evidence for God's love does not rest on reflection on the nature of God but upon recital. God so loved that he gave (Jn. 3:16). God shows his love for us in that Christ died for us (Rom. 5:8). The revelation of God in the redemptive history of Israel finds its clearest word in the historical event of the life, death, and resurrection of Christ (Heb. 1:1-2).[27]

New Testament theology therefore does not consist merely of the teachings of the several strata of the New Testament. It consists primarily of the recital of what God has done in Jesus of Nazareth. Furthermore, the redemptive act of God in Jesus is but the end term in a long series of redemptive acts in Israel. The message of the prophets places great emphasis on hope—what God will yet do in the future. The New Testament constantly sounds the note that what God had promised, he was now doing. Mark summarizes Jesus' message with the words, "The time is fulfilled" (Mk. 1:15). Luke strikes this key by citing the words, "Today this prophetic scripture has been fulfilled in your hearing" (Lk. 4:21). Matthew frequently cites the Old Testament prophecies to show that what God was doing in Jesus is what he had promised through the prophets. The Gospels record the works and words of Jesus; the Acts relates the establishment and extension of the movement set up by Jesus' ministry; the epistles explicate further the meaning of Jesus' redemptive mission; and the Revelation outlines the consummation of the redemptive work of Christ for the world and human history, which is made possible because of what he has done in history (Rev. 5).

BIBLICAL THEOLOGY AND THE NATURE OF HISTORY. The biblical view of *Heilsgeschichte* raises two difficulties for the modern thinker. First, is it conceivable that history can receive a revelation of God? Plato viewed the realm of time and space as one of flux and change. History by definition involves relativity, particularity, caprice, arbitrariness, whereas revelation must convey the universal, the absolute, the ultimate. History has been called "an abyss in which Christianity has been swallowed up quite against its will."

How can the Infinite be known in the finite, the Eternal in the temporal, the Absolute in the relativities of history? From a purely human perspec-

[27] K. Stendahl recognizes that *Heilsgeschichte* is more accurate than existential philosophy in describing the theology of the Bible. "Biblical Theology," *IDB* A-D, p. 421.

tive, this seems impossible; but at precisely this point is found perhaps the greatest miracle in the biblical faith. God is the living God, and he, the Eternal, the Unchangeable, has communicated knowledge of himself through the ebb and flow of historical experience. This, as Cullmann has pointed out, is the supreme scandal of Christian faith.[28]

It is at this point that scholars like Rudolf Bultmann take offense. It is to them incredible that God could act in history in the terms in which the New Testament represents it. To Bultmann, "mythology" includes not only ideas of God and his acts, but also the acts of God within the phenomena of world history. Bultmann thinks that "we must speak of God as acting only in the sense that He acts with me here and now."[29] For Bultmann, by definition there can be no *Heilsgeschichte* in the sense in which we have described it, and he has tried to reinterpret the meaning of God's redemptive activity in terms of personal human existence. However, he has done this only at the sacrifice of the gospel itself, which proclaims a redemptive history of which Christ is the end term. The fundamental issue at stake is not the nature of history but the nature of God.

A second difficulty must be faced. Not only is the Bible conscious that God has been redemptively active in one stream of history in a way in which he is not active in general history; it also is conscious that at given points God has acted in history in ways that transcend ordinary historical experience.

This can best be appreciated by a brief consideration of the nature of "history." The layman thinks of history as the totality of past events; but a moment's reflection will show that we have no access whatever to vast areas of past human experience. There can be no history unless there are documents—records of past events. However, ancient records do not themselves constitute "history." The writings of Herodotus are a sort of history, but they are replete with fancy, imagination, and errors. "History" therefore must be understood as the modern historian's reconstruction of the events of the past by the critical use of ancient documents. In such a reconstruction, there must be accepted critical procedures, "ground-rules." When one reads in Greek literature of the alleged activities of the gods among men, he does not consider this to be history but mythology.

Many historians feel that this same critical definition of history must be applied to the study of biblical history.[30] This, however, runs head on into a difficult problem. Frequently, the Bible represents God as acting through "ordinary" historical events. The course of events that brought Israel into captivity in Babylon and later effected their restoration to Palestine were "natural" historical events. God used the Chaldeans to bring defeat to the chosen people and banishment from the land; but it was nonetheless a divine judgment. He also used Cyrus, "his anointed" (Isa. 45:1),

---

[28] Cullmann, *The Christology of the NT,* pp. 315-28.

[29] Bultmann, *Jesus Christ and Mythology* (1958), p. 78. See also *Kerygma and Myth* (1961), p. 196.

[30] See C. C. McCown, "In History or Beyond History?" *HTR* 38 (1945), 151-75.

as an agent to accomplish the divine purpose of restoring his people to the land. In such events, God was active in history, carrying forward his redemptive purposes through the nation Israel. This one stream of history carries a meaning that sets it apart from all others in the river of history. Within the historical events, the eye of faith can see the working of God.

Frequently, however, God is represented as acting in unusual ways. Sometimes the revelatory event assumes a character that the modern secular historian calls unhistorical. The God who reveals himself in redemptive history is both Lord of creation and Lord of history, and he is therefore able not only to shape the course of ordinary historical events but to act directly in ways that transcend usual historical experience.

The most vivid illustration of this is the resurrection of Christ. From the point of view of scientific historical criticism, the resurrection cannot be "historical," for it is an event uncaused by any other historical event, and it is without analogy. God, and God alone, is the cause of the resurrection. It is therefore causally unrelated to other historical events. Furthermore, nothing like it ever occurred elsewhere. The resurrection of Christ is not the restoration of a dead man to life but the emergence of a new order of life—resurrection life. If the biblical record is correct, there can be neither "historical" explanation nor analogy of Christ's resurrection. Indeed, its very offense to scientific historical criticism is a kind of negative support for its supernatural character.

The underlying question is a theological one. Is such an alleged supernatural event consistent with the character and objectives of the God who has revealed himself in holy history? Is history as such the measure of all things, or is the living God indeed the Lord of history? The biblical answer to this question is not in doubt. The Lord of history is transcendent over history yet not aloof from history. He is therefore able to bring to pass in time and space events that are genuine events yet which are "supra-historical" in their character. This merely means that such revelatory events are not produced by history but that the Lord of history, who stands above history, acts within history for the redemption of historical creatures. The redemption of history must come from outside of history—from God himself. This does not mean the abandonment of the historical method in studying the Bible. It does mean that at certain points the character of God's acts is such that it transcends the historical method, and that the historian *qua* historian can say nothing about them.

HISTORY AND REVELATION. While revelation has occurred in history, revelatory history is not *bare* history. God did not act in history in such a way that historical events were eloquent in and of themselves. The most vivid illustration of this is the death of Christ. Christ died. This is a simple historical fact that can be satisfactorily established by secular historical criticism. But Christ died for our sins. Christ died showing forth the love of God. These are not "bare" historical facts. The cross by itself did not speak of love and forgiveness. Proof of this may be found in the experience of those who watched Jesus die. Was any of the witnesses overwhelmed with a sense of the love of God, conscious that he was beholding the awesome spectacle of atonement being made for his sins? Did John, or Mary, or the centurion, or the High Priest throw himself in choking joy upon the earth before the cross with the cry, "I never knew how much God loved me!"

The historical events are revelatory *only when they are accompanied by the revelatory word.* This, however, is not an accurate formulation if it suggests two separate modes of revelation. The fact is that God's word is his deed, and his deed is his word. We would therefore be more accurate if we spoke of the deed-word revelation.

God's deed is his word. Ezekiel describes the captivity of Judah with the words, "And all the pick of his troops shall fall by the sword, and the survivors shall be scattered to every wind; and you shall know that I, the Lord, have spoken" (Ezek. 17:21). Captivity was itself God's word of judgment to Israel. The event is a word of God.

Yet the event is always accompanied by words, in this case the spoken words of the prophet Ezekiel. The event is never left to speak for itself, nor are men left to infer whatever conclusions they can draw from the event. The spoken word always accompanies and explains the revelatory character of the event. Therefore, not the deed by itself, but the deed-word is revelation.

This is equally true in the New Testament. *Christ died* is the deed; Christ died *for our sins* is the word of interpretation that makes the act revelatory. It was only after the interpretive word was given to the disciples that they came to understand that the death of Christ was revelatory of the love of God.

We must go yet a step further. God's word not only follows the historical act and gives it a normative interpretation; it often precedes and creates the historical act. The test of whether a prophet speaks the word of the Lord is whether his word comes to pass (Deut. 18:22). For when God speaks, something happens. Events occur. "I, the Lord, have spoken; surely this will I do to all this wicked congregation . . . they shall die" (Num. 14:35). "I the Lord have spoken; it shall come to pass, I will do it" (Ezek. 24:14). "You shall die in peace. . . . For I have spoken the word, says the Lord" (Jer. 34:5).

The revelatory word may be both spoken and written. Jeremiah both spoke and wrote down the word of the Lord. Both his spoken and written utterances were "the words of the Lord" (Jer. 36:4, 6). It is against this background that the New Testament refers to the Old Testament Scriptures as "the word of God" (Jn. 10:35). It is for this reason that the theologian is justified, indeed required, to recognize the Bible as the word of God.

Revelation has occurred in the unique events of redemptive history. These events were accompanied by the divinely given word of interpretation. The word, both spoken and written, is itself a part of the total event.

The Bible is both the record of this redemptive history and the end product of the interpretive word. It is the necessary and normative explanation of the revelatory character of God's revealing acts, for it is itself included in God's revelation through the act-word complex that constitutes revelation.

BIBLICAL THEOLOGY AND THE CANON. The question will arise why the study of biblical theology is limited to the sixty-six canonical books of the Bible. Ought we not include the Jewish intertestamental literature? Is not Enoch as important a book as Daniel? IV Ezra as the Revelation of John? Judith as Esther? In fact, Stauffer insists that the "old biblical tradition" upon which biblical theology draws should include this noncanonical Jewish literature.[31] However, Stauffer neglects a very important fact. The canonical writings are conscious of participating in redemptive history while the noncanonical writings lack this sense of redemptive history.

Antiquity is replete with literary records that preserve the historical experiences, the religious aspirations, the literary exploits of the times. In one sense of the word the canonical Scriptures are like other ancient writings in that they are the historical and literary products of men living in a distinct historical milieu to serve specific immediate objectives. Yet there is a difference: the writings of the canonical Scriptures partake of the character of holy history. They are those records which embody for us the story of God's activity in history. There are many elements shared in common by canonical and noncanonical books. Jubilees and Genesis cover much of the same ground, and Enoch and Daniel share many traits of apocalyptic literature. But the books outside the canon lack the sense of holy history found in the canonical books. The Apocalypse of Baruch and the Apocalypse of John were written at about the same time and both deal with apocalyptic eschatology; but one reflects Jewish hopes for a happy future, and the other forms a conclusion to the entire biblical narrative in which the purposes of God, expressed in the prophets, manifested in the incarnation of Christ, and explained in the epistles, are brought to a consummation. These divine purposes, which have been operative within holy history, finally are perfectly accomplished in a consummation that brings history in its entirety to its divinely ordained end. The canonical books thus share in a unity of redemptive history that is intrinsic within them rather than superimposed upon them from without.[32] No collection of sixty-six books drawn from the Jewish apocryphal writings and from the Christian apocryphal literature can be assembled that will share in any sort of inner unity such as that which we find in the books of Scripture.

UNITY AND DIVERSITY. Since biblical theology traces the divine acts in redemptive history, we must expect progression in the revelation. The various stages of the prophetic interpretation of redemption history are equally inspired and authoritative, but they embody differing degrees of

[31] E. Stauffer, *NT Theology* (1955), ch. 1.
[32] See B. S. Childs, *Biblical Theology in Crisis* (1970), pp. 70ff.

apprehension of the meanings involved. The Old Testament interpretation of the divine redemption gives the broad outlines of the consummation of God's ultimate purpose. Some students make much of the fact that the prophets have little if anything explicit to say about the church age. However, the perspective from which God granted the prophets to see the great redemptive events is that of their own environment—the history of the nation Israel. Again, some students distinguish sharply between the "gospel of the Kingdom" proclaimed by Jesus and the "gospel of grace" preached by Paul as though they were different gospels. However, the gospel of the Kingdom is essentially the same as the gospel of grace; the seeming differences are due to the different points of perspective along the line of redemptive history. It should be obvious that if our Lord experienced great difficulty in conveying to his disciples that the messianic death was a *fact* in the divine purpose (Mt. 16:21-23), he could hardly instruct them in the gracious and redeeming *significance* of that death. It was unavoidable that the gospel, the good news of redemption, should be couched in different terms before the event than those used by the apostles after the event of the messianic death and resurrection had become a part of redemptive history.

For the same reason, we must expect diversity within a basic unity; and, in fact, this is what we find. A generation ago, it was customary for some scholars to find in biblical theology diversity so radical as to destroy any real unity. However, recent criticism gives larger recognition to the fundamental unity.[33] In fact, A. M. Hunter goes so far as to express the desire that all future textbooks in New Testament theology be written from the synthetic rather than the analytic point of view.[34] We feel, however, that this synthetic approach, which is followed by Richardson, Filson, Stauffer, and even F. C. Grant, ignores the important fact of historical development within the New Testament. There is great richness in the variety of New Testament theology which must not be sacrificed. The teachings of the Kingdom of God in the Synoptic Gospels, eternal life in John, justification and the life in Christ in Paul, the heavenly High Priest in Hebrews, and the Lamb who is a Lion and a conquering Son of Man in the Revelation are diverse ways of describing various aspects and depths of meaning embodied in the one great redemptive event—the person and work of Jesus Christ. Great loss is incurred when this variety is not recognized. Our procedure therefore will not be a monochromatic treatment of the several redemptive themes, but will attempt to set forth the development, progress, and diversity of meanings that are embodied in the redemptive events of New Testament theology.

---

[33] Cf. F. V. Filson, *One Lord, One Faith* (1943); E. Stauffer, *NT Theology;* C. H. Dodd, *The Apostolic Preaching* (1936); H. H. Rowley, *The Unity of the Bible* (1955).

[34] A. M. Hunter, *The Message of the NT* (1944), p. 121.

2

JOHN THE BAPTIST

Literature:

H. H. Rowley, "Jewish Proselyte Baptism," *HUCA* 15 (1940), 313-34; C. H. Kraeling, *John the Baptist* (1951); T. W. Manson, *The Servant Messiah* (1953), pp. 36-58; T. W. Manson, "John the Baptist," *BJRL* 36 (1953-54), 395-412; W. F. Flemington, *The NT Doctrine of Baptism* (1953), pp. 13-24; H. H. Rowley, "The Baptism of John and the Qumran Sect" in *NT Essays,* ed. by A. J. B. Higgins (1959), pp. 218-29; E. Best, "Spirit-Baptism," *NT* 4 (1960), 236-44; G. R. Beasley-Murray, *Baptism in the NT* (1962), pp. 31-44; J. A. T. Robinson, "The Baptism of John and the Qumran Community," *Twelve NT Studies* (1962), pp. 11-27; J. A. T. Robinson, "John the Baptist," *IDB* E-J (1962), pp. 955-62; C. Scobie, *John the Baptist* (1964); W. Wink, *John the Baptist in the Gospel Tradition* (1968); J. D. G. Dunn, *Baptism in the Holy Spirit* (1970), pp. 8-22; J. Steinmann, *Saint John the Baptist and the Desert Tradition* (n.d.); J. Jeremias, *NT Theology,* I (1971), 43-49.

A NEW PROPHET. The significance of the ministry of John the Baptist can be appreciated only against the historical setting of the times. For centuries the living voice of prophecy had been stilled. No longer did God speak directly through a human voice to his people to declare his will, to interpret the reason for the oppression of Israel by the Gentiles, to condemn their sins, to call for national repentance, to assure judgment if repentance was not given and to promise deliverance when the nation responded.

In place of the living voice of prophecy were two streams of religious life, both deriving from a common source: scribal religion, which interpreted the will of God strictly in terms of obedience to the written Law as interpreted by the scribes, and the apocalyptists, who in addition to the Law embodied their hopes for the future salvation in apocalyptic writings usually cast in a pseudepigraphical mold.[1] We possess no evidence that any of the apocalyptists who produced such an extensive literary corpus ever moved among the people as heralds of the coming eschatological deliverance, as

[1] Cf. IV Ez. 14:37-48 where reference is made to seventy such books that partake of the same inspiration as the canonical Scriptures.

preachers of salvation, i.e., as prophetic voices announcing to the people, "Thus saith the Lord." There is also no evidence that their writings created popular eschatological movements among the people, stirring them up to expect the imminent intervention of God to bring his Kingdom. Such would have been the inevitable result had the apocalyptists embodied the true prophetic spirit. The Qumranians looked for an early apocalyptic consummation, but they withdrew into the wilderness and did not try to prepare the people for the end.

The movements of which we do have evidence were rather political and military rebellions against Rome, and these were not a few. To strike a blow against Rome meant to strike a blow for the Kingdom of God. Again and again, large groups of the people took up arms, not merely in the interests of national independence, but to achieve the Kingdom of God, that God alone rather than Rome might reign over his people.[2]

Some scholars have interpreted the Qumran community as a prophetic eschatological movement. These sectarians did indeed believe they were inspired by the Holy Spirit; but this inspiration led them to find new meanings in the Old Testament Scriptures, not to speak a new prophetic word, "Thus saith the Lord." In the real sense of the word, the Qumran community was a legalistic movement. Further, it had no message for Israel, but withdrew by itself into the desert, there to obey the Law of God and to await the coming of the Kingdom.

The historical significance of the unexpected appearance of John will be appreciated against this background. Suddenly, to a people who were chafing under the rule of a pagan nation that had usurped the prerogative belonging to God alone, who were yearning for the coming of God's Kingdom, and yet who felt that God had become silent, appeared a new prophet with the announcement, "The kingdom of God is near."

As he approached maturity, John felt an inner urge thrusting him forth from the centers of population into the wilderness (Lk. 1:80).[3] After a number of years, apparently of meditation and waiting on God, "The word of God came to John" (Lk. 3:2), in response to which John appeared in the valley of the Jordan announcing in prophetic manner that the Kingdom of God was near.

John's garb—the hairy mantle and the leathern girdle—appears to be a deliberate imitation of the external marks of a prophet (cf. Zech. 13:4; II Kings 1:8, LXX). Some scholars think that John by this means indicated

---

[2] See T. W. Manson, *The Servant-Messiah* (1953), and W. R. Farmer, *Maccabees, Zealots, and Josephus* (1956), for Jewish religious nationalism.

[3] The theory of C. H. Kraeling that John's withdrawal to the wilderness requires for its explanation a catastrophic experience (*John the Baptist,* p. 27) with the priestly order, creating in John a violent revulsion for the established cultic order, is nothing but conjecture. Far better explain it in Kraeling's own words by "the essential mystery of prophetic insight and divine inspiration" (p. 50). Other more recent scholars (Brownlee, J. A. T. Robinson, Scobie) are sure that John was a member of the Qumran sect "in the wilderness." This is an obvious possibility, but it must remain in the realm of speculation.

that he thought himself to be Elijah,[4] but according to John 1:21 John denies this.

John's entire bearing was in the prophetic tradition. He announced that God was about to take action, to manifest his kingly power; that in anticipation of this great event men must repent; and as evidence of repentance must submit to baptism. This he does on his own prophetic authority, because of the word of God that had come to him. It is not difficult to imagine the excitement that the appearance of a new prophet with such a thrilling announcement would create. God, who for centuries, according to current Jewish thought, had been inactive, now was at last taking the initiative to fulfill the promises of the prophets and to bring the fullness of the Kingdom. Apparently news of this appearance of a new prophet spread like wildfire throughout Judea and moved throngs of people to flock to the Jordan River where he was preaching (Mk. 1:5) to listen to his message and submit to his demands. At long last, God had raised up a prophet to declare the divine will (Mk. 11:32; Mt. 14:5).

THE APPROACHING CRISIS. John's announcement of the impending divine activity in the Kingdom involved two aspects. There was to ensue a twofold baptism: with the Holy Spirit and with fire (Mt. 3:11=Lk. 3:16). Mark in his greatly condensed account of John's ministry mentions only the baptism with the Spirit (Mk. 1:8).

This announcement of John has been subject to diverse interpretations. The majority view is that John announced only a baptism of fire. He proclaimed an imminent judgment of purging fire. The idea of baptism with the Spirit is seen as a Christian addition in the light of the experience of Pentecost.[5] An alternate view is that the baptism of *pneuma* is not the Holy Spirit but the fiery breath of Messiah that will destroy his enemies[6] (Isa. 11:4; IV Ez. 13), or the wind of divine judgment that will sweep through the threshing floor to carry away the chaff.[7]

A third view is that John announces a single baptism that includes two elements, punishing the wicked but purging and refining the righteous.[8]

A further view is suggested by the context. The Coming One will baptize the righteous with the Holy Spirit and the wicked with fire. John announces, as Dunn insists, a single baptism, but it is a baptism that involves two elements. The word "baptism" is, of course, used metaphorically and has nothing to do with water baptism. It is true that the Old Testament and

---

[4] Cf. J. Klausner, *Jesus of Nazareth* (1952), p. 243.

[5] See V. Taylor, *Mark* (1952), p. 157; W. F. Flemington, *Baptism*, p. 19; T. W. Manson, *The Servant-Messiah*, p. 42. For further references see G. R. Beasley-Murray, *Baptism*, p. 36; J. D. G. Dunn, *Baptism in the Holy Spirit*, p. 8.

[6] See C. H. Kraeling, *John the Baptist*, pp. 61-63.

[7] C. K. Barrett, *The Holy Spirit and the Gospel Tradition* (1947), p. 126. For further literature, see J. D. G. Dunn, *Baptism in the Holy Spirit*, pp. 8-9.

[8] J. D. G. Dunn, *Baptism in the Holy Spirit*, pp. 12-13.

Judaism did not expect the Messiah to bestow the Spirit,[9] but there is no reason to deny to John a novel element.[10]

The expectation of an eschatological outpouring of the Spirit finds a broad base in the Old Testament. In one of the "servant" prophecies of Isaiah, God promises to pour out his Spirit on the descendants of Jacob in quickening and life-giving power (Isa. 44:3-5). Such an outpouring of God's Spirit will be a basic element in effecting the transformation of the messianic age when the messianic King will reign in righteousness and prosperity, and justice and peace will prevail (Isa. 32:15). Ezekiel promises the resurrection of the nation when God will put his Spirit within them to give them life (Ezek. 37:14). God will then give to his people a new heart and a new spirit by putting his Spirit within them, enabling them to walk in obedience to God's will (Ezek. 36:27). A similar promise is reiterated in Joel (2:28-32). The great and terrible Day of the Lord is to be attended by a great outpouring of the Spirit and by apocalyptic signs in heaven and on earth. John announces that these promises are about to be fulfilled, not through himself, but through one who is to follow him. The Coming One will baptize with the Holy Spirit. The great messianic outpouring of the Spirit is about to take place. Against this background of prophetic expectation there is no valid reason to insist that John announced only a baptism of judgment.

John also announces a baptism of fire. That this refers to judgment is clear from the context of the saying. The meaning of the twofold baptism with the Spirit and fire is further described in the clearing of the threshing floor: the wheat will be gathered into the granary but the chaff will be burned up with unquenchable fire (Mt. 3:12; Lk. 3:17).[11] The description of the fire as "unquenchable" points to an eschatological judgment, for it extends the limits of the ordinary means of consuming chaff (cf. Isa. 1:31; 66:24; Jer. 7:20). The coming of the Kingdom, the impending divine visitation, will affect all men. A separation is to take place: some will be gathered into the divine granary—theirs will be a baptism of the Spirit; others will be swept away in judgment—theirs will be a baptism of fire. This prospect of coming judgment is further emphasized in John's warning: "Who warned you to flee from the wrath to come?" Judgment is impending and unfruitful trees will be cut down and thrown into the fire (Mt. 3:7-10; Lk. 3:7-9). The drastic character of this announcement may be understood from the fact that in a poor country like Palestine, unfruitful trees would normally not be destroyed by burning but would be saved that the wood might be used for domestic and manufacturing purposes.[12] In John's

---

[9] V. Taylor, *Mark,* p. 157.

[10] The possibility of a twofold baptism is suggested by G. Bornkamm, *Jesus of Nazareth* (1960), p. 46; J. A. T. Robinson in *Twelve NT Studies,* p. 19; C. Scobie, *John the Baptist* (1964), pp. 70-71. Robinson bases his view on similar ideas in the Qumran literature which are very impressive.

[11] Cf. Isa. 17:13; Jer. 23:28f.

[12] Cf. C. H. Kraeling, *John the Baptist,* p. 44.

announcement such fruitless trees will be consumed in a flaming holocaust of judgment.

John's announcement of the Kingdom anticipated the fulfillment of the Old Testament expectation in a twofold direction. God is to act in his kingly power for the salvation of the righteous and the judgment of the wicked—the two central themes that run throughout the Old Testament. The character of judgment falls in the "apocalyptic" category. The judgment of fire does not contemplate an historical visitation when God would act through an historical nation, an "anointed" agent (Isa. 45:1) to visit Israel as a nation with an historical judgment of war. It is rather a judgment of individuals carried out by a messianic personage in apocalyptic fire. Such a judgment is anticipated in the Old Testament (Mal. 4:1; Nah. 1:6; Isa. 30:33),[13] and the idea is developed at great length in the intertestamental literature.

It is clear that John, like the prophets of the Old Testament, views these two messianic acts as two aspects of a single visitation, even though there is no explicit affirmation of that fact. Undoubtedly John thought of them as taking place simultaneously.[14] They were to be carried out by a messianic personage whom John describes merely by the rather colorless phrase, the Coming One (Mt. 3:11), which was not a contemporary messianic title. The character of this messianic deliverer and judge in John's thought is not clear. John uses neither "Messiah" nor "Son of Man" nor "Servant" to describe him. The fact that he would be the *agent* of apocalyptic judgment suggests that he will be a superhuman person, far more than a Davidic king. The Psalms of Solomon, written less than a hundred years before, anticipates a Davidic king, the Lord's Anointed, who will establish the Kingdom by destroying the wicked "with the word of his mouth" (Ps. Sol. 17:27), i.e., by supernatural power. Something more than this is involved in John's expectation. The fiery judgment would suggest an event terminating this age and initiating the Age to Come. It is notable that John's announcement transcends the usual Old Testament expectation in that the messianic personage is to be both Savior and Judge, whereas in the Old Testament he is a Davidic king who is not the agent for establishing the Kingdom.

JOHN'S BAPTISM. To prepare the people for the coming Kingdom John calls on them to repent and to submit to water baptism. Repentance (*metanoia*) is an Old Testament idea and means simply to turn (*shub*) from sin to God. God called upon apostate Israel to "repent and turn away from your idols; and turn away your faces from all your abominations" (Ezek. 14:6; see 18:30; Isa. 55:6-7). The idea of conversion is expressed in the idiom of turning or returning to the Lord (Isa. 19:22; 55:7; Ezek. 33:11; Hos. 14:1; Joel 2:13). "Conversion" expresses the idea better than repentance. "Repentance" suggests primarily sorrow for sin;

[13] See especially Zeph. 1:2-6, 14-15, 18.
[14] Cf. G. Vos, *Biblical Theology* (1948), p. 339.

metanoia suggests a change of mind; the Hebrew idea involves the turning around of the whole man toward God.

Apocalyptic literature placed little emphasis on conversion. Israel was the people of God because they alone of all nations had received the Law (IV Ez. 7:20, 23). God made the world for Israel's sake (IV Ez. 6:55; 7:11) and gave to them the Law so that they might be saved (Apoc. Bar. 48:21-24). When God brings the Kingdom, Israel will be gathered together to enjoy the messianic salvation (Ps. Sol. 17:50), and to witness the punishment of the Gentiles (Ass. Mos. 10:7-10). The problem of the apocalyptic writers was that God's people were obedient to the Law but still suffered grievous evil.

In rabbinic writings, there is an apparent contradiction about repentance. On the one hand, the sons of Abraham believed that the faithfulness of Abraham provided a treasury of merit that was available to all Jews.[15] On the other hand, the rabbis placed great value on repentance—so much so that repentance has been called the Jewish doctrine of salvation.[16] The reason for this is that repentance is understood in the light of the Law. The prevailing view of *teshuba* is legal.[17] Conversion means turning to the Law in obedience to the expressed will of God. It means, therefore, the doing of good works. Conversion can be repeated when one breaks the commandments and then turns again in obedience.[18]

The idea of repentance is also emphasized in the Qumran literature, where the sectarians called themselves "the converts of Israel" (CD 6:5; 8:16), and stressed both ceremonial purity and inner conversion. "Let not (the wicked) enter the water to touch the purification of the holy, for a man is not pure unless he be converted from his malice. For he is defiled as long as he transgresses His word" (IQS 5:13-14). The sectarians practiced daily repeated bodily lustrations to achieve ceremonial purity. But these waters of purification were meaningful only when there was a corresponding moral uprightness (IQS 3:4-9). However, the whole context of Qumranian conversion meant social separation from "the sons of darkness" and rigid obedience to the sectarian interpretation of the Law. Their view has been summarized as a "legalistic understanding of conversion," when a man "turns away from sin and separates himself radically from sinners in order to observe the Law in its purest form."[19]

John's baptism rejected all ideas of nationalistic or legal righteousness and required a moral-religious turning to God. He refused to assume a righteous people. Only those who repent, who manifest this repentance in changed conduct, will escape the impending judgment. It will be futile

---

15 A. Edersheim, *The Life and Times of Jesus the Messiah* (1896), I, 271; S. Schechter, *Some Aspects of Rabbinic Theology* (1909), ch. 12; Strack and Billerbeck, *Kommentar zum NT,* I, 117-19.

16 G. F. Moore, *Judaism* (1927), I, 500.

17 J. Behm, *TDNT* IV, 997.

18 *Ibid.,* pp. 997-98.

19 J. B. Bauer, "Conversion," *Sacramentum Verbi* (1970), I, 138.

to rely on descent from Abraham as a ground of experiencing the messianic salvation. Unfruitful trees will be cut down and burned up, even though they are, according to contemporary belief, the planting of the Lord.[20] The basis of messianic salvation is soundly ethico-religious and not nationalistic. In violent terms, John warned the religious leaders in Israel (Mt. 3:7) to flee, like snakes before a fire, from the coming wrath. This again is eschatological language with an Old Testament background.[21] Current Jewish thought looked for a visitation of God's wrath, but it would fall upon the Gentiles. John turns the wrath upon Jews who will not repent.

Luke gives illustrations of the change John demanded. Those who have an abundance of possessions are to help those in need. Tax collectors, instead of gouging the people for all they could get, must collect no more than is appointed. This demand would "set them at odds with the social and economic structures of which they were a part."[22] Soldiers were told to be satisfied with their wages and not to engage in unwarranted pillaging.

A difficult question rises as to the precise relationship between John's baptism and the forgiveness of sins. Many scholars read a sacramental meaning into his baptism; it is "a sacramental act of purification which effects both remission of sins . . . and conversion."[23] Mark (1:4) and Luke (3:3) speak of "a baptism of repentance for (*eis*) the forgiveness of sins." Luke 3:3 shows that "repentance for (*eis*) the forgiveness of sins" is a compact phrase, and we should probably understand the whole phrase in Luke 3:3 as a description of baptism, with *eis* dependent only on repentance. It is not a repentance *baptism* that results in forgiveness of sins, but John's baptism is the expression of the *repentance* that results in the forgiveness of sins.[24]

THE SOURCE OF JOHN'S BAPTISM. Scholars are not agreed as to the source of John's baptism. Some (Robinson, Brown, Scobie) think that John adapted the lustrations of the Qumranians for his baptism of repentance. Scobie makes a great deal of a passage in the Manual of Discipline (IQS 2:25-3:12) where he finds an initiatory lustration (baptism).[25] However, it is not at all clear that the Qumranians had a distinct initiatory baptism. The context of this passage suggests the daily lustrations of those already members of the sect.[26] It is still possible that John adapted the daily lustrations of the Qumranians to a single, unrepeatable, eschatological rite.

Others see the background in the baptism of proselytes. When a Gen-

---

20 En. 10:16; 83:2, 5, 10.

21 Isa. 13:9; Zeph. 1:15; 2:2f.; Mal. 3:2; 4:1.

22 J. A. T. Robinson, "John the Baptist," *IDB* E-J, p. 960.

23 J. Behm, *TDNT* IV, 1001.

24 J. D. G. Dunn, *Baptism in the Holy Spirit,* p. 15. See C. Scobie, *John the Baptist,* pp. 112f.

25 C. Scobie, *John the Baptist,* pp. 104f.

26 See H. H. Rowley, "The Baptism of John and the Qumran Sect," *NT Essays* (1959), pp. 220f. A. Dupont-Sommer, *The Essene Writings from Qumran* (1961), p. 76, heads this section with the caption "The Annual Census."

tile embraced Judaism, he had to submit to a ritual bath (baptism) and to circumcision, and offer sacrifice. The problem is whether proselyte baptism is as early as New Testament times. This is sometimes denied,[27] but affirmed by experts in Jewish literature.[28] Since the immersion of proselytes is discussed in the Mishnah by the schools of Hillel and Shammai,[29] we have the practice carried back very close to New Testament times.

Some scholars have argued that it would be too paradoxical for John to treat Jews as though they were pagans,[30] but it may well be that this is precisely the point of John's baptism. The approach of God's Kingdom means that Jews can find no security in the fact that they were sons of Abraham; that Jews, apart from repentance, had no more certainty of entering the coming Kingdom than did Gentiles; that both Jews and Gentiles must repent and manifest that repentance by submitting to baptism.

There are certain points of similarity between John's baptism and proselyte baptism. In both rites, John's and proselyte baptism, the candidate completely immersed himself or was immersed in water. Both baptisms involved an ethical element in that the person baptized made a complete break with his former manner of conduct and dedicated himself to a new life. In both instances, the rite was initiatory, introducing the baptized person into a new fellowship: the one into the fellowship of the Jewish people, the other into the circle of those who were prepared to share in the salvation of the coming messianic Kingdom. Both rites, in contrast to ordinary Jewish lustrations, were performed once for all.

There are, however, several distinct differences between the two baptisms. John's baptism was eschatological in character, i.e., its *raison d'être* was to prepare men for the coming Kingdom. It is this fact which gives to John's baptism its unrepeatable character. The most notable difference is that, while proselyte baptism was administered only to Gentiles, John's baptism was applied to Jews.

It is possible that the background for John's baptism is neither Qumranian nor proselyte baptism, but simply the Old Testament ceremonial lustrations. The priests were required to wash themselves in preparation for their ministry in the sanctuary, and the people were required to engage in certain lustrations on various occasions (Lev. 11-15; Num. 19). Many well-known prophetic sayings exhort to moral cleansing under the figure of cleansing with water (Isa. 1:16ff.; Jer. 4:14), and others anticipate a cleansing by God in the last times (Ezek. 36:25; Zech. 13:1). Furthermore, Isaiah 44:3 conjoins the gift of the Spirit with the future purification. Whatever the background, John gives a new meaning to the rite of immersion in calling to repentance in view of the coming Kingdom.

---

27 T. M. Taylor, "The Beginnings of Jewish Proselyte Baptism," *NTS* 2 (1956), 193-97.

28 See H. H. Rowley, "Jewish Proselyte Baptism," *HUCA* 15 (1940), 313-34. See also T. F. Torrance, "Proselyte Baptism," *NTS* 1 (1954), 150-54.

29 Pes. 8:8. See H. Danby, *The Mishnah* (1933), p. 148.

30 G. Bornkamm, *Jesus of Nazareth,* p. 47.

JESUS AND JOHN. The significance of John's ministry is explained by Jesus in a difficult passage in Matthew 11:2ff. After he was imprisoned, John sent disciples to ask Jesus whether he was the Christ or not. Many have interpreted this to mean that in his imprisonment at the hands of Herod Antipas, John became despondent and began to question the reality of his own call and message. However, the clue is found in Matthew 11:2, "When John heard . . . about the deeds of the Christ." The point is that they were not the deeds John expected. There was neither a baptism of Spirit nor of fire. The Kingdom had not come. The world remained as before. All Jesus was doing was preaching love and healing sick people. This was not what John expected. He never questioned his own call and message; he only questioned whether Jesus was indeed the one who was to bring the Kingdom in apocalyptic power.

In answer, Jesus asserted that the messianic prophecy of Isaiah 35:5-6 was being fulfilled in his mission. The days of the messianic fulfillment had arrived. Then he uttered an accolade of praise for John; no greater man had ever lived, yet he who is least in the Kingdom of heaven is greater than he. "From the days of John the Baptist until now the kingdom of heaven *biazetai*. . . . For all the prophets and the law prophesied until John" (Mt. 11:11, 13). Then Jesus asserted that John was the Elijah who was to herald the Day of the Lord (Mal. 4:5). It is impossible to decide with certainty whether the expression "from the days of John" is meant inclusively or exclusively: beginning with the days of John, or *since* the days of John. Wink makes a great deal of this passage, arguing that the preposition *apo* in temporal expressions is always inclusive. He argues that the language includes John in the era of the Kingdom.[31] However, this does not seem to be accurate. In Matthew 1:17 "from David to the deportation" is exclusive; David belongs to the period from Abraham to David. The expression, "nor from that day did anyone dare to ask him any more questions" (Mt. 22:46) means "after that day," with the exclusive sense. They were asking Jesus questions on that day. Furthermore, in the context John is not in the Kingdom although he was the greatest of the prophets. The least in the Kingdom is greater than John (Mt. 11:11).[32] We conclude that Jesus means to say that John is the greatest of the prophets; in fact, he is the last of the prophets. With him, the age of the Law and the prophets has come to its end. Since John, the Kingdom of God is working in the world, and the least in the new era knows greater blessings than John did, because he enjoys personal fellowship with the Messiah and the blessings this brings. John is the herald, signaling that the old era has come to its end, and the new is about to dawn.

JOHN IN THE FOURTH GOSPEL. The account of John's ministry in

---

[31] W. Wink, *John the Baptist,* p. 29. See also J. Jeremias, *NT Theology,* I (1971), 47.

[32] Wink meets this problem by viewing this verse as a later addition of the church. *Ibid.,* p. 25.

the Fourth Gospel is quite different from that in the Synoptics, for John describes the Coming One as the Lamb of God who will take away the sin of the world (Jn. 1:29). It is customary for modern criticism to see in the Johannine account a radical reinterpretation of John's ministry by the Christian church in the light of the actual ministry of Jesus. The apocalyptic announcement is set aside in favor of soteriology. John's account therefore is not history but theological reinterpretation.[33] However, this conclusion is quite unnecessary and ignores certain important facts. The record is historically consistent and psychologically sound as it stands. The account in John's Gospel presupposes the events of the Synoptic Gospels. This is indicated clearly in John 1:32-33 where the baptism of Jesus has already taken place, and by the fact that the mission of the priests and Levites to challenge John as to his authority must have been occasioned by some such events as those described in the Synoptic Gospels. The Fourth Gospel does not purport to give a different story from that of the Synoptics but represents an independent tradition.

This further proclamation of the messianic ministry by the Baptist is to be understood as John's own interpretation of his experience at the baptism of Jesus, illuminated by further prophetic inspiration. It should be remembered that while the Baptist's ministry in the Synoptics has several points of contact with contemporary eschatological and apocalyptic thought, it has even more striking elements of divergence. "The essential mystery of prophetic insight and divine inspiration" cannot be explained by the limitations of a naturalistic methodology.[34] The Christian historian will not therefore deny its reality, for it is one of the basic facts of biblical history. The same prophetic inspiration that drove John to announce the imminence of the divine activity for the messianic salvation now, in the light of his experience with Jesus, impels him to add a further word. When Jesus came to John for baptism, John recognized that he stood in the presence of a person of different quality from other men. Jesus neither had sins to confess nor a sense of guilt to lead him to repentance. Whether John's recognition of the sinlessness of Jesus was based upon a conversation in which he directed to him searching questions, or solely upon prophetic illumination, we cannot say. Probably both elements were involved. In any case, John was convicted of his own sinfulness in comparison with the sinlessness of Jesus. Nevertheless, Jesus insisted on baptism that he might thereby "fulfill all righteousness" (Mt. 3:15). In the act of baptism, God showed to John that Jesus was not only a sinless man but was indeed the Coming One whom John had heralded (Jn. 1:31-33). As John further meditated on the significance of these events, he was led by the prophetic Spirit to add a new feature to his message that the Coming One is to be the Lamb of God who takes away the sin of the world.[35]

---

[33] Cf., for instance, C. J. Wright, *Jesus the Revelation of God* (1950), pp. 112-13.

[34] Cf. C. H. Kraeling, *John the Baptist*, p. 50. "What John knew of the Christ, he knew by way of revelation." L. Morris, *John* (1971), p. 149.

[35] If this language were due to Christian reinterpretation, we would expect it to be

Another element in John's description of the Coming One, according to the RSV, is that he is the Son of God (1:34). However, the NEB renders it, "This is God's Chosen One," and this reading is followed by both Brown and Morris.[36] This is based on a rather strong textual variant found possibly in a third-century papyrus and definitely in the original hand of Sinaiticus, in the Old Latin and Old Syriac versions, and in several fathers. As both Brown and Morris point out, it is easy to account for changing the text from "God's Chosen" to "God's Son" but not easy to account for the reverse process. If we accept this reading, John is saying that Jesus is the object of the divine call, and it presents no theological problem.

more explicit in referring to Jesus' death. The verb *airō* does not emphasize the means of removal of sin as *pherō* would have done (I Pet. 2:24; cf. Isa. 54:4); it means "to take away," not "to bear." For the theology of "the Lamb of God" see Ch. 18. There is a notable tendency in recent critical scholarship to recognize the possible historicity of the Fourth Gospel at this point. J. A. T. Robinson, *Twelve NT Studies* (1962), p. 25. R. E. Brown thinks that the Baptist uttered these words, but with a different meaning from that which the Evangelist saw in them. Cf. *CBQ* 22 (1960), 292-98.

[36] R. E. Brown, *John*, p. 55; L. Morris, *John*, pp. 153-54.

3

THE NEED OF THE KINGDOM:
The World and Man

Shortly after his baptism by John the Baptist, Jesus entered upon a ministry of proclaiming the Kingdom of God. Mark describes the initiation of this ministry with the words, "Now after John was arrested, Jesus came into Galilee, preaching the gospel of God, and saying, 'The time is fulfilled, and the kingdom of God is at hand'" (Mk. 1:14-15). Matthew summarizes his ministry with the words, "He went about all Galilee, teaching in their synagogues and preaching the gospel of the kingdom, and healing every disease and every infirmity among the people" (Mt. 4:23). Luke records an incident in Nazareth when Jesus read a prophecy about the coming of one anointed by the Spirit of the Lord who would proclaim the coming of the acceptable year of the Lord, and then announced, "Today this scripture has been fulfilled in your hearing" (Lk. 4:18-21). We cannot understand the message and miracles of Jesus unless they are interpreted in the setting of his view of the world and man, and the need for the coming of the Kingdom.

Literature: See footnotes.

ESCHATOLOGICAL DUALISM. The Old Testament prophets looked forward to the Day of the Lord and a divine visitation to purge the world of evil and sin and to establish God's perfect reign in the earth. We find, then, in the Old Testament a contrast between the present order of things and the redeemed order of the Kingdom of God.[1] The difference between the old and the new orders is described in different terms, with differing degrees of continuity and discontinuity between the two; Amos (9:13-15) describes the Kingdom in very this-worldly terms, but Isaiah sees the new order as new heavens and a new earth (Isa. 65:17).

---

[1] The term "the Kingdom of God" is not used in the Old Testament to describe the new order that is introduced by the Day of the Lord, but the idea runs throughout the prophets. See J. Bright, *The Kingdom of God* (1953).

The idea of a new redeemed order is described in different terms in the literature of late Judaism. Sometimes the Kingdom of God is depicted in very earthly terms, as though the new order meant simply the perfection of the old order;[2] sometimes it involves a radical transformation of the old order so that the new order is described in transcendental language.[3] In some later apocalypses, there is first a temporal earthly kingdom, followed by a new transformed eternal order.[4]

Somewhere in this historical development emerged a new idiom—this age and the Age to Come.[5] We are unable to trace with precision the history of this idiom. The first extant evidence of it is Enoch 71:15, which refers to the "world to come," probably representing the Hebrew *olam haba*—the coming age.[6] The idiom emerges into full expression in Jewish literature only in the first century A.D. in the books of IV Ezra and Apocalypse of Baruch.[7]

The idiom of two ages became common in rabbinic literature, beginning with Pirke Aboth, which contains sayings of the rabbis dating back to the third century B.C.[8] The earliest of these references do not seem to be earlier than the late first century A.D.[9]

Whatever be the origin of the specific idiom, the idea expressed by it goes back to the Old Testament contrast between the present world and the future redeemed order. It provides the framework for Jesus' entire message and ministry as reported by the Synoptic Gospels. The full idiom appears in Matthew 12:32: "Whoever speaks against the Holy Spirit will not be forgiven, either in this age or in the age to come." While the idiom at this place may be a Matthean formulation,[10] the idiom also appears in the request of the rich young ruler for the way to eternal life. In the following discussion with his disciples, Jesus contrasts their situation "in this time" with the eternal life that they will experience "in the age to come" (Mk. 10:30). The idiom "this time" (*en tō kairō toutō*) is a synonym for "this age" (see Rom. 8:18).

Cullmann has correctly expounded the view that the eschatological dual-

---

2 See En. 1-36; Ps. Sol. 17, 18.

3 En. 37-71.

4 IV Ez. 7:28ff.; Apoc. Bar. 40:3.

5 Unfortunately, the concepts involved in this terminology are often obscured because the term *aiōn* (Heb. *olam*) is translated "world" instead of "age." The AV is guilty of this mistranslation throughout.

6 H. Sasse, *TDNT* I, 207. Sasse thinks that En. 48:7, "this world of unrighteousness," also embodies this same idiom. See also En. 16:1, "The age shall be consummated."

7 See IV Ez. 7:50, "The Most High has made not one Age but two" (G. H. Box's translation); 8:1, "This age the Most High has made for many, but the age to come for few." See also IV Ez. 7:113; Apoc. Bar. 14:13; 15:7.

8 See Pirke Aboth 4:1, 21, 22; 6:4, 7.

9 P. Volz, *Die Eschatologie der jüdischen Gemeinde* (1934), p. 65. Aboth 2:7, which speaks of "the life of the age to come," may go back to Hillel in the first century B.C. See G. Dalman, *The Words of Jesus* (1909), p. 150.

10 Mk. 3:29 has, he "is guilty of an eternal sin."

ism is the substructure of redemptive history.[11] There is no New Testament word for "eternity," and we are not to think of eternity as the Greeks did, as something other than time. In biblical thought eternity is unending time. In Hellenism men longed for release from the cycle of time in a timeless world beyond,[12] but in biblical thought time is the sphere of human existence both now and in the future. The impression given by the AV at Revelation 10:6, "there should be time no longer," is corrected in the RSV, "there should be no more delay." The entire New Testament expresses the idea of eternity by the idiom *eis ton aiōna,* translated "forever" (Mk. 3:29), or *eis tous aiōnas* (Lk. 1:33, 55), and sometimes *eis tous aiōnas tōn aiōnōn* (Gal. 1:5; I Pet. 4:11; Rev. 1:18)—"unto the ages of the ages," translated "forever and ever."

The Age to Come and the Kingdom of God are sometimes interchangeable terms. In response to the rich young ruler's request about the way to eternal life, Jesus replied that eternal life is the life of the Age to Come (Mk. 10:30). The Age to Come is always looked at from the viewpoint of God's redemptive purpose for men, not from the viewpoint of the unrighteous. The attaining of "that age," i.e., the Age to Come, is a blessing reserved for God's people. It will be inaugurated by the resurrection from the dead (Lk. 20:35), and is the age when death will be no more. Those who attain to that age will be like the angels in that they will become immortal. Only then will they experience all that it means to be sons of God (Lk. 20:34-36). Resurrection life is therefore eternal life—the life of the Age to Come—the life of the Kingdom of God.

Not only resurrection marks the transition from this age to the coming age; the parousia of Christ will mark the close of this age (Mt. 24:3). The Son of Man will come with power and great glory and will send his angels to gather the elect together from the four corners of the earth into the Kingdom of God (Mt. 24:30-31).

Matthew's version of the parables of the Kingdom speaks three times of the end of the age (Mt. 13:39, 40, 49), but the concept is consistent throughout the Gospels. The parable of the wheat and the weeds (Mt. 13:36-43) contrasts the situation in this age with that which will exist in the Kingdom of God. In this age, the wheat and the weeds—sons of the Kingdom and sons of the evil one—live together in a mixed society. The separation of the wicked from the righteous will take place only at the harvest—the judgment. Then "all causes of sin and all evildoers" will be excluded from the Kingdom of God and will suffer the divine judgment, while "the righteous will shine like the sun in the kingdom of their Father" (Mt. 13:42-43).

The character of this age is such that it stands in opposition to the Age to Come and the Kingdom of God. This is shown in the parable of the soils. The sower sows the seed, which is "the word of the kingdom" (Mt. 13:19).

---

[11] O. Cullmann, *Christ and Time* (1950), pp. 37ff.

[12] E. Jenni, "Time," *IDB* R-Z, p. 648.

The word seems to take root in many lives, but the cares of the age (Mk. 4:19; Mt. 13:22) choke out the word and it becomes unfruitful. From this point of view, this age is not in itself sinful; but when the concerns of the life of this age become the major object of interest so that men neglect the message about the Kingdom of God, they become sinful.

Paul goes further than do the reported sayings of Jesus and speaks about "this present evil age" (Gal. 1:4). The wisdom of this age cannot attain to God (I Cor. 2:6). He exhorts the Romans not to be conformed to this age but to be transformed by a new power working in those who believe in Christ (Rom. 12:2). All this is consistent with the concept of the two ages appearing in the Synoptics.

In this eschatological dualism, Jesus and Paul shared the same world view that prevailed in Judaism. It is essentially the apocalyptic view of history. Some scholars defend the view that this was not a natural development of the true Hebrew prophetic hope, which looked for an earthly kingdom within history. However, it can be argued that the Old Testament prophetic hope of the coming of the Kingdom always involved a catastrophic inbreaking of God and always involved both continuity and discontinuity with the old order.[13] Vos believed that this eschatological dualism which was developed in Judaism was incorporated by divine revelation into the writers of the New Testament era.[14] If so, it was a natural development of the Old Testament prophetic hope.

In brief, this age, which extends from creation to the Day of the Lord, which in the Gospels is designated in terms of the parousia of Christ, resurrection and judgment, is the age of human existence in weakness and mortality, of evil, sin, and death. The Age to Come will see the realization of all that the reign of God means, and will be the age of resurrection into eternal life in the Kingdom of God. Everything in the Gospels points to the idea that life in the Kingdom of God in the Age to Come will be life on the earth—but life transformed by the kingly rule of God when his people enter into the full measure of the divine blessings (Mt. 19:28).

Therefore, when Jesus proclaimed the coming of the Kingdom of God, he did so against the background of Hebrew-Jewish thought, which viewed men living in a situation dominated by sin, evil, and death, from which they needed to be rescued. His proclamation of the Kingdom includes the hope, reaching back to the Old Testament prophets, that anticipates a new age in which all the evils of the present age will be purged by the act of God from human and earthly existence.

THE SPIRIT-WORLD

Literature:

A. Fridrichsen, "The Conflict of Jesus with the Unclean Spirits," *Theology,* 22 (1931), 122-35; W. Foerster, "Diabolos," *TDNT* II (1935,

---

[13] This is one of the main arguments in the chapter on the Old Testament promise in the author's *Jesus and the Kingdom* (1964).

[14] G. Vos, *The Pauline Eschatology* (1952), p. 28.

1964), 72-81; W. Foerster, "Daemon," *TDNT* II (1935, 1964), 1-20; T. W. Manson, *The Teaching of Jesus* (1935), pp. 151-57; W. O. E. Oesterley, "Angelology and Demonology in Early Judaism" in *A Companion to the Bible,* ed. by T. W. Manson (1939), pp. 332-47; E. Langton, *Essentials of Demonology* (1949); G. H. C. MacGregor, "Principalities and Powers," *NTS* 1 (1954), 17-28; G. B. Caird, *Principalities and Powers* (1956); J. Kallas, *The Significance of the Synoptic Miracles* (1961); T. Ling, *The Significance of Satan* (1961); H. Schlier, *Principalities and Powers in the NT* (1961); T. H. Gaster, "Satan," *IDB* R-Z (1962), pp. 224-28; T. H. Gaster, "Demon," *IDB* A-D (1962), pp. 812-23; D. S. Russell, "Angels and Demons," *The Method and Message of Jewish Apocalyptic* (1964), pp. 235-62; W. Manson, "Principalities and Powers: The Spiritual Background of the Work of Jesus in the Synoptic Gospels," *Jesus and the Christian* (1967), pp. 77-90.

SATAN. After his baptism, Jesus was led by the Spirit into the wilderness to be tempted by the devil (Mt. 4:1). One of the temptations consisted of being taken to a very high mountain—probably in imagination—and being shown all the kingdoms of the world with their glory. Then the devil said to Jesus, "To you I will give all this authority and their glory; for it has been delivered to me, and I will give it to whom I will" (Lk. 4:6). Throughout the Synoptic Gospels, Satan[15] is pictured as a supernatural evil spirit at the head of a host of inferior evil spirits called demons. As such he is "the prince of demons" (Mk. 3:22).

The background of this concept stems from the Old Testament, which pictures God as surrounded by a heavenly host of spirits who serve him and do his bidding (Ps. 82:1; 89:6; Dan. 7:10). Many scholars see in Deuteronomy 32:8, where the RSV has "sons of God," a reflection of the idea that God superintended the nations through subordinate spiritual beings.[16] In Job 1-2 Satan is one of these "sons of God" who appears before God to accuse Job and to receive permission to put him to the test. In I Chronicles 21:1, Satan incited David to sin.[17]

Intertestamental Judaism proliferated the concept of evil spirits. Seldom is the chief of spirits called Satan; instead such names as Mastema, Azazel, Semjaza, Beliar, and Asmodaeus appear. Belial is the most common term in the Qumran writings. The term "demons" does not often appear, but there are hosts of evil spirits who are subject to the chief of spirits. In

---

[15] "Satan" comes from a Hebrew verb meaning "to oppose, obstruct." In the LXX the word is uniformly translated *diabolos,* which means "the slanderer." From the Hebrew background it carries the meaning "the adversary" (I Pet. 5:8). The two words are used interchangeably, both in the Gospels and throughout the New Testament. He is also called Beelzebul (Mk. 3:22; the spelling is uncertain), "the tempter" (Mt. 4:3), "the evil one" (Mt. 13:19), "the enemy" (Mt. 13:39).

[16] See also Dan. 10:13, 20-21.

[17] On Satan and the heavenly assembly in the Old Testament, see E. Jacob, *Theology of the OT* (1958), pp. 70-72; T. H. Gaster, "Satan," *IDB* R-Z, pp. 224-25; G. E. Wright, "The Faith of Israel," *IB* I, 359-62; J. Kallas, *The Significance of the Synoptic Miracles* (1961), ch. 4.

Enoch, these evil spirits were the spirits of giants who were the offspring resulting from the mating of fallen angels, called "watchers," with women (En. 15). These evil spirits are the source of all kinds of evil on earth. The fall of these angels is described in Enoch 6, with the names of eighteen leaders, all under the headship of Semiazaz. They came down from heaven to earth because they lusted after women and mated with them. These angels taught men all kinds of practices; and the whole earth was corrupted through the works of these fallen angels, particularly Azazel, to whom all sin is ascribed (En. 10:8). Sometimes in Enoch the evil spirits are called satans who accuse men as in the Old Testament (En. 40:7; 65:6) and who tempt men to sin (En. 69:4ff.).[18] A single chief, Satan, is mentioned twice (En. 54:3, 6).

The chief function of Satan in the Gospels is to oppose the redemptive purpose of God. In the temptation narrative he claims a power over the world that Jesus does not question. The temptation consists of the effort to turn him aside from his divinely given mission as the Suffering Servant and to gain power by yielding to Satan. This same idea is even more vividly expressed by Paul when he calls Satan the "god of this age" (II Cor. 4:4). The same theology of a kingdom of evil is found in Judaism. The Testament of Dan describes the present as "the kingdom of the enemy" (Test. Dan. 6:4). The Manual of Discipline speaks of this age as the time of "the dominion of Belial" (IQS 1:17, 23; 2:19), as does the War Scroll (IQM 14:19). The same idea is reflected in Matthew 12:29 where Jesus invades the "strong man's house"—this age—to despoil him.

Neither in Judaism nor in the New Testament does this antithetical kingdom of evil opposing the Kingdom of God become an absolute dualism. The fallen angels are helpless before the power of God and his angels. In the New Testament, all such spiritual powers are creatures of God and therefore subject to his power. In the apocalyptic literature, they will meet their doom in the day of judgment.

The doctrine of Satan and demons has several distinct theological implications. Evil is not imposed upon men directly by God, nor is evil blind chance or capricious fate. Evil has its roots in personality. Yet evil is greater than men. It can be resisted by the human will, although the human will can yield to it. Yet evil is not a disorganized, chaotic conflict of powers, as in animism, but is under the direction of a single will whose purpose it is to frustrate the will of God. Furthermore, a rationale for the creation of spiritual powers that were allowed to become hostile to God is not lacking. "When once the fantastic and mythological trappings of the apocalyptic scheme are removed, there remains the central postulate which is the foundation of all attempts to find a satisfactory solution for the problem of evil, namely, that it is the price that must be paid for freedom."[19]

---

[18] For demonology in Judaism, see D. S. Russell, *The Method and Message of Jewish Apocalyptic* (1964), pp. 235-62. That Satan is a fallen angel is nowhere explicitly taught in biblical literature, except Jude 6 and II Pet. 2:4.

[19] T. W. Manson, *The Teaching of Jesus* (1935), p. 158.

In the Synoptics, the activity of Satan is seen in several aspects. In one case, a woman who had been a cripple for eighteen years is spoken of as bound by Satan (Lk. 13:16). But Satan's activities are mainly ethical. In the parable of the weeds and the wheat, which represents the mixed society in this world, the wheat represents the "sons of the kingdom" while the weeds are "the sons of the evil one" (Mt. 13:38). Here society is divided into two antithetical classes: those who hear and receive the word of the Kingdom and those who either do not know it or reject it. Furthermore, it is Satan's purpose where he can to snatch away the word of the Kingdom from hearts that are too hard to receive it (Mk. 4:15). He tried to divert Jesus from his redemptive mission in the temptation, and he spoke through Peter urging that it could not be the role of Messiah to suffer and die (Mk. 8:33). Satan entered into Judas, leading him to betray Jesus to the priests (Lk. 22:3). He also desired to lay his hands upon Peter to prove the unreality of his faith (Lk. 22:31), to show that in truth he was nothing but chaff. The satanic purpose in this instance was frustrated by Jesus' prayer.

This background of satanic evil provides the cosmic background for the mission of Jesus and his proclamation of the Kingdom of God. As to whether such an evil spiritual personage exists, neither science nor philosophy has anything to say. There is really no more difficulty in believing in the existence of a malevolent spirit behind the evils in human history than to believe in the existence of a good spirit—God. Our purpose is primarily to show that the theology of the Kingdom of God is essentially one of conflict and conquest over the kingdom of Satan.

One fact is very significant. Neither the Synoptics nor the rest of the New Testament shows any speculative interest in either Satan or demons as do some of the Jewish apocalypses. This is seen in the diverse names given to Satan in the apocalypses. The New Testament interest is altogether practical and redemptive. It recognizes the supernatural power of evil, and its concern is the redemptive work of God in Christ delivering men from these malignant forces.

DEMONS. In the Synoptics, the most characteristic evidence of the power of Satan is the ability of demons to take possession of the center of men's personalities. Clearly, demons are represented as evil supernatural spirits. At the very outset of his ministry in Capernaum, Jesus came face to face with demonic power. Immediately, the demon recognized Jesus by direct intuitive insight and said, "What have you to do with us, Jesus of Nazareth? Have you come to destroy us? I know who you are, the Holy One of God" (Mk. 1:24). In Judaism, the destruction of satanic powers was expected at the end of the age when the Kingdom of God should come. The demon recognizes a supernatural power in Jesus that is capable of crushing satanic power here and now.

Demon possession manifested itself in various ways. Sometimes it was associated with other afflictions of a physical nature: with dumbness (Mt.

9:32), with blindness and dumbness (Mt. 12:22), and with epilepsy (Mt. 17:15, 18). There is only one place where demon possession is identified with mental illness. Obviously, the Gadarene demoniac who dwelt in the tombs and was possessed of superhuman strength was insane. The record says that after his healing the man was found clothed and in his right mind (Mk. 5:15). While this suggests that the man had been insane, we need not conclude that his illness was a case of simple insanity. Rather the derangement was due to the center of personality falling under the influence of foreign powers.[20]

It is not accurate, however, simply to explain away demon possession by saying it is an ancient interpretation for what we now know to be various forms of insanity. Frequently in the Synoptics demon possession is distinguished from other diseases. Jesus healed both the sick and those possessed by demons (Mk. 1:32). Demon possession is distinguished from epilepsy and paralysis (Mt. 4:24), from sickness and leprosy (Mt. 10:8). However, demon exorcism was one of the most characteristic of Jesus' acts of power. There were, to be sure, men who practiced magic arts and incantations, and claimed to exorcise demons.[21] However, belief in demons and their exorcism in the ancient world at large was intertwined with magic of a crude sort. By contrast, the amazing factor in Jesus' ministry was the power of his mere word: "What is this? A new teaching! With authority he commands the unclean spirits, and they obey him" (Mk. 1:27).

The role that demon exorcism plays in the ministry of our Lord has been a stumbling block to modern interpreters. Since biblical theology is primarily a descriptive discipline, our primary task is to set forth the mission of Jesus in its historical setting; and we cannot avoid the conclusion, as we shall see, that Jesus' message of the coming of the Kingdom of God involved a fundamental struggle with and conquest of this spiritual realm of evil. However, we cannot be indifferent to the relevance of New Testament theology for our own age.

Some scholars admit that Jesus appears to have believed in Satan and demons; but this represents a mere adaptation to the concepts of the age and in no way represents the content of Jesus' teachings; nor is his authority as a teacher impaired by a recognition that demons do not exist. Jesus' purpose was ethical, and he used the concepts of his time as symbols to serve ethical ends. He did not purpose to give information about the existence or the conduct of supernatural beings.[22] This explanation is utterly inadequate.[23]

A second interpretation is similar to this. Jesus was a child of his day and was mistaken in his belief about demons. What the ancients call demon possession was, in fact, nothing but mental derangement, and the modern

[20] W. Foerster, *TDNT* II, 19.

[21] See Acts 19:19-20, and the account of the exorcism of demons in Josephus, *Ant.* VIII, 2.5.

[22] G. B. Stevens, *The Theology of the NT* (1906), pp. 86-91.

[23] E. Langton, *Essentials of Demonology* (1949), p. 173.

man would have described the phenomenon of ancient demon possession in terms of mental sickness.[24] McCasland goes on to affirm the wisdom and the high character of Jesus. He was a man of great authority, possessed by the Holy Spirit. However, if this is so, a serious difficulty is raised by the admission that Jesus was mistaken in his belief about demons; for the exorcism of demons was no mere peripheral activity in Jesus' ministry but was a manifestation of the essential purpose of the coming of the Kingdom of God into the evil age. We must recognize in the exorcism of demons a consciousness on the part of Jesus of engaging in an actual conflict with the spirit world, a conflict that lay at the heart of his messianic mission. To say that "demons and angels are for Jesus' Gospel mere surds or irrational elements without obvious functions in his teachings as a whole"[25] does not reflect the facts of the Gospels. The demonic is absolutely essential in understanding Jesus' interpretation of the picture of sin and of man's need for the Kingdom of God. Man is in bondage to a personal power stronger than himself. At the very heart of our Lord's mission is the need of rescuing men from bondage to the satanic kingdom and of bringing them into the sphere of God's Kingdom. Anything less than this involves an essential reinterpretation of some of the basic facts of the gospel.

A third interpretation goes farther than either of the first two. It finds in the biblical concept of demons an essential truth: there is a demonic element in human experience. "As we look at history, what we see is often not merely the impersonal and unmeaning but the irrational and *the mad.* The face that looks through at us is akin often to the insane. Certainly as Jesus looked at men, He saw them not always as rational moral units or self-contained autonomous spirits; He saw their souls as a battle-ground, an arena or theatre of tragic conflict between the opposed cosmic powers of the Holy Spirit of God and Satan."[26]

Certainly the history of the church's belief in demons and witches has been used by superstitious people to bring about much evil and suffering. But in spite of abuses of the concept, neither science nor philosophy can prove or reasonably affirm that superhuman spirits or beings do not exist. If for *a priori* rationalistic reasons we reject Jesus' belief in the existence of a realm of evil spiritual powers, it is difficult to see why Christ's belief in a personal God may not be eliminated also, or why such a process of evaporation might not be successfully applied to all contemporary literature.[27] When theories of accommodation and mental illness and the impact of a powerful personality have been taken into account, "we are left with a kind of mystery and with many unanswered questions."[28]

THE WORLD. While Jesus shared the general New Testament attitude to-

---

[24] S. V. McCasland, *By the Finger of God* (1951).
[25] J. W. Bowman, *The Religion of Maturity* (1948), p. 258.
[26] W. Manson, "Principalities and Powers," *Jesus and the Christian* (1967), p. 87.
[27] O. C. Whitehouse, "Satan," *HDB* IV, 411.
[28] E. Langton, *Essentials of Demonology*, p. 162.

ward this age as the domain of Satan, he does not view the created world as evil. Greek dualism contrasted the noumenal world to which man's soul belongs with the phenomenal world, including man's body. The wise man was he who so disciplined his mind and controlled his bodily appetites that the soul was freed from the clogging, cloying influences of the material world. In later gnostic thought, the material world was itself *ipso facto* the realm of evil. Hebrew thought, on the other hand, regarded the world as God's creation, and even though it was plagued with evils, it was in itself good.

Jesus shared the Hebrew view of the world. He clearly regarded God as the creator, and both man and the world as his creation (Mk. 13:19; Mt. 19:4). Jesus constantly drew upon illustrations from nature to illustrate his teachings, assuming the order and regularity of nature as a proof of the steadfastness and unchanging care of God for his creatures.[29] God not only created but also sustains the world. He clothes the lilies of the field and feeds the ravens (Lk. 12:22ff.). He is even concerned for the sparrows—one of the most insignificant of birds (Lk. 12:4-7). God makes the sun to rise on the evil and the good and sends rain upon the just and unjust (Mt. 5:45). He is Lord of heaven and earth (Lk. 10:21). There is no spirit of world-denial or asceticism either in Jesus' teaching or conduct. Indeed, he drew upon himself the wrath of the religious purists of his day because of his habit of eating together with people considered irreligious (Mt. 9:10; Lk. 15:1-2). He frequently used the metaphor of banqueting and feasting to illustrate the joys of the eschatological Kingdom of God.[30] He was even accused of being "a drunkard and a glutton" (Mt. 11:19). Clearly, while Satan was the ruler of this age, the world was still God's world. Nothing in creation is morally bad, and man's sinfulness does not inhere in the fact that he is a creature with bodily appetites. Jesus taught his disciples to trust God to meet their physical needs.

At the same time man's highest good cannot be found on the level of creation. It will profit a man nothing "to gain the whole world and forfeit his life" (Mk. 8:36). In this context the "world" (*kosmos*) is not the physical world or the world of men, but the whole complex of human earthly experience. To achieve everything one could desire on the human level is not evil, but it does not minister to a man's true life. He can gain everything on the human level but forfeit his true life, which can be found only in relationship to God. When the riches of the world become the chief end of man's interest so that they crowd out the things of God, they become an instrument of sin and death (Lk. 12:16-21, 30). It is easy for those who have much to love their possessions. Only a work of God, enabling them to put God first, can overcome this natural human love for the world (Mk. 10:27).

MAN. The old liberal interpretation of man had wide influence both in

[29] E. C. Rust, *Nature and Man in Biblical Thought* (1953), p. 162.
[30] See G. E. Ladd, *Jesus and the Kingdom,* pp. 172f.

theological and pastoral circles. "In the combination of these ideas—God the Father, Providence, the position of men as God's children, the infinite value of the human soul—the whole Gospel is expressed."[31] "The whole idea of a family—fatherhood, sonship, brotherhood—is the unifying conception in his doctrine of human nature; we do well to classify and test all our resolves by it, including our whole idea of the kingdom of God."[32] Robinson would distinguish between that which is transitory and external and that which is permanent in Jesus' teaching. Eschatology belongs to the transitory elements; the permanent core is the filial relationship between man and God. Four basic teachings are deduced which constitute the main outlines of this permanent core. First is the supreme value of man as the child of God. In the eyes of God human life is of unique and priceless worth. Second is the duty of man as the child of God. Man owes to God a relationship of filial trust and obedience. Third is the natural deduction of the brotherhood of man. This is universal because God's Fatherhood is universal. Fourth, it is recognized that sin has broken the relation of sonship but has in no way impaired God's Fatherhood. The mission of Jesus aims at the restoration of that which ideally belongs to man.[33]

This, however, misrepresents Jesus' view of man. We shall see later[34] that while God's Fatherhood is one of the most important characteristics of Jesus' view about God, he never speaks of God as Father of any but his disciples. Fatherhood is the gift of the Kingdom of God.

Jesus does indeed view man as of more value than the animal world. While man is a creature of God, he is of more worth than the birds of the air or the lilies of the field (Mt. 6:26-30; 10:31). God cares for men; the very hairs of their heads are numbered (Mt. 10:30).

As God's creature, man is bound to serve God. He can make no claim upon his divine Master. When he has done all he possibly can do, he has done no more than is to be expected of a servant who does his duty (Lk. 17:7-10). As God's creature, man is completely dependent on God. He cannot make his hair white or black; he cannot add to his stature; he cannot determine the length of his life (Mt. 5:36; 6:27). A man may seek security in possessions, but God can snatch away the rich farmer from his possessions before he can enjoy them (Lk. 12:16-21). God can condemn a man to hell (Mt. 10:28) and judge him in accordance with his behavior in the face of tasks assigned to him (Mt. 25:41ff.).

Jesus viewed all men as sinful.[35] This is proven by the fact that he addressed his summons to repentance and discipleship to all men. The tragedies of human experience are not laid upon men in proportion to their sinfulness; but all men must repent or they will perish (Lk. 13:1-5). Even

---

31 A. Harnack, *What Is Christianity?* (1901), p. 74.

32 H. Wheeler Robinson, *The Christian Doctrine of Man* (1926), pp. 78-79.

33 *Ibid.*, pp. 80-92.

34 See below, pp. 84ff.

35 See the excellent discussion by W. G. Kümmel, *Man in the NT* (1963), pp. 18ff.

Israel, the people of the covenant, are lost; Jesus came to seek and to save them (Mt. 10:6; 15:24; Lk. 19:10). When Jesus said that he did not come to call the righteous but sinners (Mk. 2:17) or when he speaks of the righteous who have no need of repentance (Lk. 15:7), he does not mean to say that there are some who are actually righteous, who do not need repentance. He is only reflecting the view of religious Jews who considered themselves righteous and did not heed his summons. "It is His intention to tell His opponents who see themselves as righteous rather than sinful, that His call to salvation is directed precisely at those who are ready to listen to Him because they are aware of their sinfulness. His opponents' mistake lies in the fact that they exclude themselves from insight into their own sinfulness, whereas Jesus presupposes that all men, including these 'righteous ones,' are sinful."[36]

Man finds his ultimate value in terms of his relationship to God. The parable of the rich fool teaches that a man cannot satisfy his life with barns of grain and physical comforts; he must also have riches toward God (Lk. 12:15-21). It is folly to gain the whole world and suffer the loss of one's true life (Mt. 16:26), which is realized only in fellowship with God. Man is thus created for sonship with God. God takes delight in man not because of what he is in himself, for he is a lost sinner; but every man is capable of responding to God's love and becoming a child of God. It is only when the sinner repents that there is joy in heaven (Lk. 15:7).

[36] *Ibid.*, p. 20.

4

THE KINGDOM OF GOD

Literature:

J. Weiss, *Jesus' Proclamation of the Kingdom of God* (1892, Eng. ed. 1971); A. von Harnack, *What Is Christianity?* (1901); A. Schweitzer, *The Quest of the Historical Jesus* (1911); R. Bultmann, *Jesus and the Word* (1934); T. W. Manson, *The Teaching of Jesus* (1935); C. H. Dodd, *The Parables of the Kingdom* (1936); G. von Rad *et al.*, "Basileus, Basileia," *TDNT* I (1949, 1964), 565-90; W. G. Kümmel, *Promise and Fulfilment* (1957); R. Schnackenburg, *God's Rule and Kingdom* (1963); H. N. Ridderbos, *The Coming of the Kingdom* (1963); G. E. Ladd, *Jesus and the Kingdom* (1964); R. Hiers, *The Kingdom of God in the Synoptic Tradition* (1970); J. Jeremias, *NT Theology* (1971).

Modern scholarship is quite unanimous in the opinion that the Kingdom of God was the central message of Jesus. Mark introduces Jesus' mission with the words, "Now after John was arrested, Jesus came into Galilee, preaching the gospel of God, and saying, 'The time is fulfilled, and the kingdom of God is at hand; repent and believe in the gospel' " (Mk. 1:14-15). Matthew summarizes his ministry with the words, "He went about all Galilee, teaching in their synagogues and preaching the gospel of the kingdom" (Mt. 4:23). Luke's introductory scene does not mention the Kingdom of God but in its stead quotes a prophecy from Isaiah about the coming of the Kingdom and then relates Jesus' affirmation, "Today this scripture has been fulfilled in your hearing" (Lk. 4:21).

INTERPRETATIONS OF THE KINGDOM OF GOD

Literature:

For surveys of the history of interpretation see G. E. Ladd, *Crucial Questions About the Kingdom of God* (1952), pp. 21-60; H. N. Ridderbos, *The Coming of the Kingdom* (1963), pp. xi-xxxiv; N. Perrin, *The Kingdom of God in the Teaching of Jesus* (1963); G. Lundström, *The Kingdom of God in the Teaching of Jesus* (1963); G. E. Ladd, *Jesus and the Kingdom* (1964), pp. 3-38.

Interpretations of the Kingdom of God have taken several distinct forms, with almost infinite variety in detail. From Augustine to the reformers, the prevalent view was that the Kingdom was in some sense or other to be identified with the church. This view is seldom defended now, even among Catholic scholars. The church is the people of the Kingdom but cannot be identified with the Kingdom.

The old liberal view is represented by Harnack's *What Is Christianity?* and understands the Kingdom of God as the pure prophetic religion taught by Jesus: the Fatherhood of God, the brotherhood of man, the infinite value of the individual soul, and the ethic of love. The obvious apocalyptic element in Jesus' teaching was only the time-conditioned husk that contained the kernel of his real religious message. Non-eschatological interpretations of the Kingdom of God have been legion. Many scholars have understood the Kingdom primarily in terms of personal religious experience—the reign of God in the individual soul.[1]

In 1892, Johannes Weiss published a slim book, entitled "The Preaching of Jesus About the Kingdom of God,"[2] in which he argued that Jesus' view of the Kingdom was like that of the Jewish apocalypses: altogether future and eschatological. The victory of the Kingdom of God over Satan had already been won in heaven; therefore Jesus proclaims its coming on earth. The Kingdom will be altogether God's supernatural act, and when it comes, Jesus will be the heavenly Son of Man.

Albert Schweitzer picked up this idea and interpreted the entire career of Jesus from the point of view of the eschatological understanding of the Kingdom, which Jesus expected to come in the immediate future—an interpretation that he called *konsequente Eschatologie* (Consistent Eschatology). Jesus' ethical teaching was designed only for the brief interval before the end comes (interim ethics), not for the ordinary life of men in society. The Kingdom did not come, and Jesus died in despair and disillusionment. Such to Schweitzer was "the historical Jesus"—a deluded first-century apocalyptist.

Since Weiss and Schweitzer, most scholars have recognized that the apocalyptic element belongs to the kernel and not the husk of Jesus' teachings, but few contemporary scholars view the Kingdom as exclusively eschatological. Richard Hiers is an exception. Rudolf Bultmann has accepted the imminent approach of the eschatological Kingdom as the correct historical interpretation of Jesus' message, but the true meaning must be understood in existential terms: the nearness and the demand of God.

In Great Britain, the most influential interpretation has been the "Realized Eschatology" of C. H. Dodd. Dodd does not simply discard the apocalyptic language as did Harnack; he understands it as a series of symbols standing for realities that the human mind cannot directly apprehend. The Kingdom of God, which is described in apocalyptic language, is in reality the transcendent order beyond time and space that has broken into his-

---

[1] See T. W. Manson, *The Teaching of Jesus* (1935), p. 135.

[2] Eng. ed. *Jesus' Proclamation of the Kingdom of God* (1971).

tory in the mission of Jesus. In him, the "wholly other" has entered into history. This transcendent "wholly other" in Dodd's thought is more platonic than biblical. In this event, all that the prophets had hoped for has been realized in history. This is what Dodd means by "realized eschatology."

Dodd has been criticized for minimizing the futuristic aspect of the Kingdom,[3] and in his latest publication he admits that the Kingdom yet awaits consummation "beyond history."[4] However, many scholars have followed Dodd in his view that the most distinctive thing about Jesus' teaching was the presence of the Kingdom.

If a majority of scholars have approached a consensus, it is that the Kingdom is in some real sense both present and future. W. G. Kümmel understands that the primary meaning of the Kingdom is the eschaton—the new age analogous to Jewish apocalyptic. Jesus proclaimed that the new age was near. But Kümmel holds that it is also present, but only in the person of Jesus, not in his disciples. The future eschatological Kingdom has already begun its activity in Jesus' mission. It is not altogether clear how in Kümmel's view the Kingdom can be both the future eschaton and a present activity in Jesus. Other scholars have solved this problem by holding that the Kingdom was altogether future, but it was so very near that its power could already be felt—as the dawn precedes sunrise;[5] or else the signs of the Kingdom were present but not the Kingdom itself.[6]

Jeremias defends a distinctive position. While commending C. H. Dodd for achieving a real breakthrough in the history of interpretation by his emphasis on the present irruption of the Kingdom, he criticizes him for minimizing the eschatological aspect. In place of Dodd's "realized eschatology" Jeremias suggests "eschatology in process of realization."[7] Jeremias understands Jesus' entire ministry to be an event in which the Kingdom is realized. He even sees John the Baptist as standing in the time of fulfillment, because the Spirit has come upon him and the time of salvation has begun.[8] With Jesus' message of the Kingdom of God and his miracles of exorcism, the Kingdom has broken into history. However, Jesus looked forward to the imminent eschatological consummation of the Kingdom which would involve his own resurrection and parousia. Jeremias follows Dodd's suggestion that Jesus regarded his resurrection, parousia, and the consummation of the Kingdom as a single event in which the triumph of God would be manifested.[9] In the resurrection appearances, the disciples experienced Jesus' parousia.[10] Only after Easter did the early church separate

---

[3] See below.
[4] C. H. Dodd, *The Founder of Christianity* (1970), p. 115.
[5] C. T. Craig, *The Beginning of Christianity* (1943), p. 87.
[6] M. Dibelius, *Jesus* (1949), pp. 68-88.
[7] "Sich realisierende Eschatologie." See J. Jeremias, *The Parables of Jesus* (1963; rev. ed.), pp. 21, 230.
[8] J. Jeremias, *NT Theology*, I (1971), pp. 47, 82.
[9] *Ibid.*, p. 286.
[10] *Ibid.*, p. 310.

the parousia from the resurrection.[11] It is difficult to see any material difference between Jeremias' view and the view of Dodd that he criticizes.

In certain evangelical circles in America and Great Britain, a rather novel view of the Kingdom has had wide influence. Starting from the premise that all Old Testament prophecies to Israel must be fulfilled *literally,* dispensationalists have distinguished sharply between the Kingdom of God and the Kingdom of Heaven. The latter is the rule of heaven (God) on earth and has primary reference to the earthly theocratic Kingdom promised Old Testament Israel. Matthew's Gospel alone gives us the Jewish aspect of the Kingdom. When Jesus announced that the Kingdom of Heaven was at hand, he had reference to the earthly theocratic Kingdom promised Israel. However, Israel rejected the offer of the Kingdom, and instead of establishing the Kingdom for Israel Jesus introduced a new message, offering rest and service for all who would believe, and initiating the formation of a new family of faith that cuts across all racial lines. The mystery of the Kingdom of Heaven in Matthew 13 is the sphere of Christian profession—Christendom—which is the form God's rule over the earth takes between the two advents of Christ. Leaven (Mt. 13:33) always represents evil; in the Kingdom of Heaven—the professing church—true doctrine is to be corrupted by false doctrine. The Sermon on the Mount is the law of the Kingdom of Heaven—the Mosaic Law of the Old Testament theocratic Kingdom, interpreted by Christ, destined to be the governing code of the earthly Kingdom. The Kingdom of Heaven, rejected by Israel, will be realized at the return of Christ when Israel will be converted and the Old Testament promises of the restoration of David's Kingdom literally fulfilled. The basic tenet of this theology is that there are two peoples of God—Israel and the church—with two destinies under two divine programs.[12]

Within a year (1963-64), three books appeared independently of each other that interpreted the Kingdom in basically the same way in terms of the unfolding of redemptive history. The Kingdom is God's kingly rule which has two moments: a fulfillment of the Old Testament promises in the historical mission of Jesus and a consummation at the end of the age, inaugurating the Age to Come.[13]

THE KINGDOM OF GOD IN JUDAISM

Literature:

S. B. Frost, *OT Apocalyptic* (1952); J. Bright, *The Kingdom of God* (1953); S. Mowinckel, *He That Cometh* (1956); G. E. Ladd, *Jesus and the Kingdom* (1964), pp. 41-97.

---

[11] *Ibid.,* p. 286.

[12] Recent literature: J. D. Pentecost, *Things to Come* (1958); A. J. McClain, *The Greatness of the Kingdom* (1959); J. Walvoord, *The Millennial Kingdom* (1959); C. C. Ryrie, *Dispensationalism Today* (1965); *The New Scofield Reference Bible* (1967). A thorough criticism of this view will be found in the present author's *Crucial Questions About the Kingdom of God* (1952).

[13] See the studies by H. N. Ridderbos, R. Schnackenburg, and G. E. Ladd.

While the idiom "the Kingdom of God" does not occur in the Old Testament, the idea is found throughout the prophets. There is a twofold emphasis on God's kingship. He is frequently spoken of as the King, both of Israel (Exod. 15:18; Num. 23:21; Deut. 33:5; Isa. 43:15) and of all the earth (II Kings 19:15; Isa. 6:5; Jer. 46:18; Ps. 29:10; 99:1-4). Although God is now King, other references speak of a day when he shall become King and shall rule over his people (Isa. 24:23; 33:22; 52:7; Zeph. 3:15; Zech. 14:9ff.).[14] This leads to the conclusion that while God *is* the King, he must also *become* King, i.e., he must manifest his kingship in the world of men and nations.

The form of the future Kingdom is expressed differently by different prophets. Many scholars see two distinctly different kinds of hope in the Old Testament and Judaism. The truly Hebraic, prophetic hope expects the Kingdom to arise out of history and to be ruled by a descendant of David in an earthly setting (Isa. 9, 11). When this hope faded after the return from exile, the Jews lost hope of a Kingdom in history. In its place, they looked for an apocalyptic inbreaking of God in the person of a heavenly Son of Man with a completely transcendental Kingdom "beyond history" (Dan. 7). The present author has argued elsewhere that while there is considerable diversity in the description of the Kingdom in the Old Testament, it always involves an inbreaking of God into history when God's redemptive purpose is fully realized. The Kingdom is always an earthly hope, although an earth redeemed from the curse of evil. However, the Old Testament hope is always ethical and not speculative. It lets the light of the future shine on the present, that Israel may be confronted by history in the here and now. For this reason, there is a coalescing of the near and the distant future. God will act in the near future to save or judge Israel, but he will also act in the indeterminate future to bring about the fulfillment of the eschatological hope. The prophets do not sharply distinguish between the near and the distant future, for both will see the act of God for his people.

Apocalyptic Judaism also had diverse hopes. Some writers emphasize the earthly, historical aspect of the Kingdom (En. 1-36; Ps. Sol. 17-18), while others emphasize the more transcendental aspects (En. 37-71). However, the emphasis is always eschatological. In fact, Jewish apocalyptic lost the sense of God's acting in the historical present. At this point, apocalypticism had become pessimistic—not with reference to the final act of God to establish his Kingdom, but with reference to God's acting in present history to save and bless his people. Jewish apocalyptic despaired of history, feeling that it was given over to evil powers. God's people could only expect suffering and affliction in this age until God would act to establish his Kingdom in the Age to Come.[15]

---

[14] See G. von Rad, *TDNT* I, 567-69. Bright's excellent books deal almost exclusively with the Kingdom of God as a future hope.

[15] See G. E. Ladd, *Jesus and the Kingdom*, pp. 72-97.

The Qumran community shared a similar hope for the Kingdom. In the eschatological consummation, they expected the angels to come down and join battle with them—"the sons of light"—against their enemies—"the sons of darkness"—and to give victory to the Qumranians over all other peoples, whether worldly Jews or Gentiles.[16]

The rabbinic literature developed a similar eschatology, but made somewhat more use of the term "the kingdom of the heavens." The Kingdom of God was the reign of God—the exercise of his sovereignty.[17] Throughout the course of human history, God exercised his sovereignty through his Law. Anyone who submits to the Law thereby submits himself to the reign of God. When a Gentile turns to Judaism and adopts the Law, he thereby "takes upon himself the sovereignty (kingdom) of God."[18] Obedience to the Law is thus equivalent to the experience of God's Kingdom or rule. It follows that God's Kingdom on earth is limited to Israel. Furthermore, it does not *come* to men; it is there, embodied in the Law, available to all who will submit to it.

At the end of the age, God will manifest his sovereignty in all the world. A very ancient prayer concludes with the wish, "and may He (God) set up His sovereignty in your lifetime, and in your days, and in the lifetime of the whole house of Israel, (yea) speedily, and in a time that is near."[19] The Assumption of Moses reads, "And then His Kingdom shall appear throughout all His creation" (Ass. Mos. 10:1). In this age, God's rule is limited to those who accept the Law; at the end of the age, it will appear to subjugate all that *resists* the will of God. The experience of God's sovereignty in the present is dependent upon the free decision of men;[20] but when it *appears* at the end of the age, "the Heavenly One shall arise from His royal throne" (Ass. Mos. 10:3) to punish the wicked and gather righteous Israel into a redeemed order of blessing.[21]

Another movement in Judaism was quite certainly concerned with establishing the Kingdom of God: the Zealots. In the early decades of the first century A.D., insurrection broke out again and again, promoted by the Zealots, against Rome. The New Testament speaks of insurrection under Judas and Theudas (Acts 5:36, 37), and another revolt under an unnamed Egyptian (Acts 21:38). Josephus speaks of other revolutionary movements not mentioned in the New Testament. He does not label these revolutionaries, but in the last rebellion of A.D. 132 the leader, Bar Kokhba, was styled by the Akiba, most famous rabbi of the time, as the Messiah.[22] The

---

16 See the War Scroll in A. Dupont-Sommer, *The Essene Writings from Qumran* (1961), pp. 164-97; H. Ringgren, *The Faith of Qumran* (1963), pp. 152ff.

17 G. Dalman, *The Words of Jesus* (1909), pp. 91-101.

18 *Loc. cit.*

19 *Ibid.*, p. 99. Probably late first century B.C.

20 See K. G. Kuhn, "Basileus," *TDNT* I, 572.

21 For this twofold emphasis, see J. Jeremias, *NT Theology*, I (1971), 99.

22 E. Schürer, *The Jewish People in the Time of Jesus Christ* (1890), I, ii, p. 299. For newly discovered letters from his hand, see J. T. Milik, *Ten Years of Discovery in the Wilderness of Judaea* (1959), p. 136.

Zealots were Jewish radicals who were not content to wait quietly for God to bring his Kingdom but wished to hasten its coming with the sword.[23] It is possible, and even probable, that the whole series of revolts against Rome were messianic, i.e., that they were not conducted solely for political or nationalistic goals, but were religiously motivated to hasten the coming of God's Kingdom.[24]

In any case, throughout all Judaism, the coming of God's Kingdom was expected to be an act of God—perhaps using the agency of men—to defeat the wicked enemies of Israel and to gather Israel together, victorious over her enemies, in her promised land, under the rule of God alone.

THE MEANING OF BASILEIA TOU THEOU. Scholars are not agreed as to the basic meaning of *basileia* (Heb. *malkuth*). Many have defended the view that the *basileia* is the "eschaton"—the final eschatological order.[25] If this is taken as the point of departure, it is difficult to see how the eschaton can be both future and present; it must be exclusively future. However, the Hebrew word has the abstract dynamic or idea of reign, rule, or dominion. "They shall speak of the glory of thy kingdom, and tell of thy power. . . . Thy kingdom is an everlasting kingdom, and thy dominion endures throughout all generations" (Ps. 145:11, 13). "The Lord has established his throne in the heavens, and his kingdom rules over all" (Ps. 103:19).[26] In late Judaism, the Kingdom of God means God's rule or sovereignty.[27] This is also the best point of departure for understanding the Gospels. Several times the RSV renders *basileia* by the English word "kingship," or "kingly power" (Lk. 19:12; 23:42; Jn. 18:36; Rev. 17:12). The meaning "reign" or "rule" is obvious in other passages.[28] The coming of the Kingdom for which we pray in the Lord's Prayer means that God's will be done on earth, i.e., that his rule be perfectly realized (Mt. 6:10). The "kingdom" that Jesus appointed for his disciples (Lk. 22:29) is "royal rank."[29]

This is important for the interpretation of Jesus' message, for one of the major problems is that of how the Kingdom of God can be both future and present. If the Kingdom is primarily the eschaton—the eschatological era of salvation—it is difficult to see how this future realm can also be present. However, we have seen that both in the Old Testament and in rabbinic Judaism, God's Kingdom—his reign—can have more than one meaning. God *is* now the King, but he must also *become* King. This is the key to the solution of the problem in the Gospels.

THE KINGDOM OF HEAVEN(S). The phrase "the kingdom of the

---

[23] E. Schürer, *The Jewish People,* p. 80.

[24] S. Mowinckel, *He That Cometh* (1956), pp. 284f.

[25] See W. G. Kümmel, *Promise and Fulfilment* (1957).

[26] See G. E. Ladd, *Jesus and the Kingdom* (1964), pp. 43ff.

[27] See G. Dalman, *The Words of Jesus,* pp. 91-101; G. F. Moore, *Judaism* (1927), II, 371-76.

[28] See G. E. Ladd, *Jesus and the Kingdom,* p. 130. See also "The Kingdom of God—Reign or Realm?" *JBL* 31 (1962), 230-38.

[29] Arndt and Gingrich, *A Greek-English Lexicon* (1957), p. 134.

heavens" occurs only in Matthew, where it is used thirty-four times.[30] Several times in Matthew,[31] and everywhere in the rest of the New Testament, the phrase "kingdom of God" is used. "The kingdom of the heavens" is a Semitic idiom, where heavens is a substitute for the divine name (see Lk. 15:18). Since the gospel tradition shows that Jesus did not consistently avoid the word "God," it is possible that "the kingdom of the heavens" is native to the Jewish-Christian milieu, which preserved the gospel tradition in Matthew rather than reflecting the actual usage of Jesus.[32] Possibly he used both phrases, and the Gospels that were addressed to a Gentile audience omitted the Semitic idiom, which would be meaningless to their ears.

As a matter of fact, both "the kingdom of God" and "the kingdom of the heavens" are seldom used in Jewish literature *before* the days of Jesus.[33] Jeremias stresses this fact, that in Jesus' teaching a large number of new phrases about the *basileia* appear that have no parallels in the literature of the world of Jesus—a fact to which sufficient attention has not yet been paid.[34]

THE ESCHATOLOGICAL KINGDOM. We have seen above that the basic structure of Jesus' thought is the eschatological dualism of the two ages. It is the coming of God's Kingdom (Mt. 6:10) or its appearing (Lk. 19:11) that will bring this age to its end and inaugurate the Age to Come. It is important to note, however, that *basileia* can designate both the manifestation or coming of God's kingly rule and the eschatological realm in which God's rule is enjoyed. In this sense, inheriting eternal life and entrance into the Kingdom of God are synonymous with entering into the Age to Come. When the rich young ruler asked Jesus what he must do to inherit eternal life, he was thinking of the eschatological life of Daniel 12:2. Jesus replied that it is hard for a rich man to enter the Kingdom of God.[35] Then, turning to his disciples, he assured them that because they had left house and family to follow him, they would receive eternal life in the Age to Come (Mk. 10:17-31).

The coming of God's Kingdom will mean the final and total destruction of the devil and his angels (Mt. 25:41), the formation of a redeemed society unmixed with evil (Mt. 13:36-43), perfected fellowship with God at the messianic feast (Lk. 13:28-29). In this sense the Kingdom of God is a synonym for the Age to Come.

One of the most distinctive facts that set Jesus' teaching apart from Judaism was the universalizing of the concept. Both in the Old Testament and in Judaism, the Kingdom was always pictured in terms of Israel. In the Old Testament, sometimes the Gentiles would be conquered by Israel

[30] An exception is some manuscripts of Jn. 3:21.
[31] Mt. 12:28; 19:24; 21:31, 43.
[32] J. Jeremias, *NT Theology* (1971), I, 97.
[33] G. E. Ladd, *Jesus and the Kingdom,* pp. 126-27.
[34] J. Jeremias, *NT Theology,* p. 96.
[35] It is significant that the parallel passage in Mt. 19:23-24 has both "kingdom of God" and "kingdom of the heavens."

(Amos 9:12; Mic. 5:9; Isa. 45:14-16; 60:12, 14), sometimes they are seen as converted (Zeph. 3:9, 20; 2:2-4; Zech. 8:20-23). But the Kingdom is always Israel's. Late Judaism had become quite particularistic, and the establishing of God's Kingdom meant the sovereignty of Israel over her political and national enemies: "Then thou, O Israel, shalt be happy, and thou shalt mount upon the necks and wings of the eagle . . . and thou shalt look from on high and shalt see thy enemies in Gehenna, and thou shalt recognize them and rejoice" (Ass. Mos. 10:8-10).

We have seen that John the Baptist rejected this Jewish particularism and looked upon the most religious of the Jews as being in need of repentance to enter the coming Kingdom. Jesus made response to his own person and message the determining factor for entering the eschatological Kingdom. In fact, Jesus affirmed that Israel, the natural "sons of the kingdom," will be rejected from the Kingdom and their place taken by others (Mt. 8:12). The true "sons of the kingdom" are those who respond to Jesus and accept his word (Mt. 13:38). One must receive the present proclamation of the Kingdom of God with a childlike attitude of complete dependence to enter into the eschatological Kingdom (Mk. 10:15).

THE PRESENT KINGDOM. The expectation of the coming of the eschatological Kingdom in Jesus' teaching was nothing new. It goes back to the prophets and was developed in different ways in Judaism. C. H. Dodd is right in affirming that the most characteristic and distinctive of the gospel sayings are those which speak of a present coming of the Kingdom. Such sayings have no parallel in Jewish teaching of prayers of the period.[36]

Jesus saw his ministry as a fulfillment of the Old Testament promise in history, short of the apocalyptic consummation.[37] This is particularly clear in two passages. In the synagogue of Nazareth, Jesus read the messianic prophecy from Isaiah 61:1-2 about the coming of an anointed one to proclaim the acceptable year of the Lord; and he then solemnly asserted, "Today this scripture has been fulfilled in your hearing" (Lk. 4:21). When John the Baptist, in doubt, sent emissaries to ask Jesus if he really was the Coming One, Jesus replied by citing the messianic prophecy in Isaiah 35:5-6 and told them to report to John that the prophecy was indeed being fulfilled (Mt. 11:2-6). Throughout the Synoptic Gospels, Jesus' mission is repeatedly understood as the fulfillment of the Old Testament promises.

The sayings about the Kingdom of God as a present reality must be interpreted against this background. The strongest statement is Matthew 12:28: "But if it is by the Spirit of God[38] that I cast out demons, then the Kingdom of God has come upon you." One of Jesus' most characteristic miracles was the exorcism of demons. Jesus amazed people because he spoke words of command and men were at once delivered from satanic bondage (Mk.

---

[36] C. H. Dodd, *The Parables of the Kingdom* (1935), p. 49.

[37] See G. E. Ladd, "Fulfillment Without Consummation," *Jesus and the Kingdom*, pp. 101-17.

[38] The parallel verse, Lk. 11:20, reads "finger of God."

1:28). When accused of himself exercising satanic power, he replied that he cast out demons by the power of God, and this was proof that the Kingdom of God had come upon them.

A vigorous debate has been waged over the precise meaning of the Greek word *ephthasen,* "has come." Many have interpreted the word to designate proximity, not actual presence. But other uses make it clear that the verb connotes actual presence, not merely proximity.[39]

What was present was not the eschaton, but the kingly power of God, attacking the dominion of Satan, and delivering men from the power of evil. "Or how can one enter a strong man's house and plunder his goods, unless he first binds the strong man? Then indeed he may plunder his goods" (Mt. 12:29). In these words, Jesus declares that he has invaded the kingdom of Satan and has "bound" the strong man.

In these two verses is embodied the essential theology of the Kingdom of God. Instead of waiting until the end of the age to reveal his kingly power and destroy satanic evil, Jesus declares that God has acted in his kingly power to curb the power of Satan. In other words, God's Kingdom in Jesus' teaching has a twofold manifestation: at the end of the age to destroy Satan, and in Jesus' mission to bind Satan. Before Satan's final destruction, men may be delivered from his power.[40]

"Binding" is of course a metaphor and designates in some real sense a victory over Satan so that his power is curbed. Sometimes the metaphorical nature of the idiom is not recognized, and it is thought that the saying must mean that Satan is rendered completely powerless.[41] However, Satan continues to be active: he snatches away the word of the Kingdom when it does not find real acceptance among men (Mt. 13:19); he was able to speak through Peter (Mk. 8:33); he entered into Judas (Lk. 22:3); and he wanted also to take possession of Peter (Lk. 22:31). Cullmann interprets the binding of Satan by his quaint idiom that he is bound, but with a long rope.[42] Satan is not powerless, but his power has been broken. Cullmann again illustrates this by resorting to a military idiom. The decisive battle in a war may be won and the tide of battle turn before the gaining of final victory.[43] The whole mission of Jesus, including his words, deeds, death, and resurrection, constituted an initial defeat of satanic power that makes the final outcome and triumph of God's Kingdom certain. "Every occasion in which Jesus drives out an evil spirit is an anticipation of the hour in which Satan will be visibly robbed of his power. The victories over his instruments are a foretaste of the eschaton."[44]

Scholars have debated *when* the binding of Satan occurred. Many refer

---

[39] See Rom. 9:31; II Cor. 10:14; Phil. 3:16. See G. E. Ladd, *Jesus and the Kingdom,* pp. 137ff.

[40] G. E. Ladd, *Jesus and the Kingdom,* pp. 145-57.

[41] E. Best, *The Temptation and the Passion* (1965), p. 12.

[42] O. Cullmann, *Christ and Time* (1964), p. 198.

[43] *Ibid.,* p. 84.

[44] J. Jeremias, *NT Theology,* p. 95.

it to the specific event of Jesus' victory over Satan in the wilderness;[45] but "the simplest explanation is that the exorcisms themselves are regarded as a victorious combat with the devil and his kingdom. Whenever a demon is cast out from a body it signifies that Satan has been defeated and spoiled of his goods."[46] "In each act of exorcism Jesus saw a defeat of Satan."[47]

The same victory over Satan is seen in the power Jesus gave to his disciples when he commissioned them to travel throughout Galilee preaching the Kingdom of God (Lk. 10:9). When the missioners returned, they reported with joy that even the demons were subject to them in Jesus' name. Then Jesus said, "I saw Satan fall like lightning from heaven" (Lk. 10:18). There is no need to postulate a vision in which Jesus saw Satan cast out of heaven.[48] The context suggests that Jesus saw in the successful mission of the seventy an evidence of the defeat of Satan. Here again is metaphorical language that employs a different idiom to affirm that in the mission of Jesus, a decisive victory has been won. Satan has been bound; he has fallen from his place of power; but his final destruction awaits the end of the age.[49]

Here is an insoluble mystery in New Testament theology, which is found not only in the Synoptics but elsewhere as well. The enemies of God's Kingdom are now seen not as hostile evil nations as in the Old Testament but spiritual powers of evil. The victory of God's Kingdom is a victory in the spiritual world: God's triumph over Satan. Paul affirms the same truth in I Corinthians 15:25: "He must reign until he has put all his enemies under his feet." The interesting question is: Why does the New Testament not picture this as a battle exclusively in the spiritual world? Why can the victory over evil be won only on the plane of history? No explanation is given, but the answer lies in the fact that the fate of men is involved in this struggle. In some way beyond human comprehension, Jesus wrestled with the powers of evil, won a victory over them, that in the end of the age these powers may be finally and forever broken.

This sets the Christian gospel apart from Judaism. Contemporary apocalyptic conceived of the age as under the power of evil while God had retreated from the scene of human history. In the Dream Visions of Enoch, God is pictured as withdrawing his personal leadership from Israel after the captivity. He surrendered his people to wild beasts to be torn and devoured. God "remained unmoved, though He saw it, and rejoiced that they were devoured and swallowed and robbed, and left them to be devoured in the hand of all the beasts" (En. 89:58). In the day of judgment Israel would be delivered and her tormentors punished; but in history God was aloof and unmoved by the sufferings of his people.

Jesus' message is that in his own person and mission God has invaded

---

[45] E. Best, *The Temptation and the Passion*, p. 15.

[46] R. Leivestad, *Christ the Conqueror* (1954), p. 47.

[47] A. Fridrichsen, *Theology*, 22 (1931), 127.

[48] J. Jeremias, *NT Theology*, p. 85.

[49] See G. E. Ladd, *Jesus and the Kingdom*, pp. 150-54.

human history and has triumphed over evil, even though the final deliverance will occur only at the end of the age.

The presence of the Kingdom is asserted in Luke 17:20. When the Pharisees asked *when* the apocalyptic Kingdom was coming, Jesus answered them, rather enigmatically, that the Kingdom was already in their midst, but in an unexpected form. It was not accompanied by the signs and outward display the Pharisees expected and without which they would not be satisfied. The phrase *entos humōn* can mean either "within you," i.e., in your hearts, or "in your midst." While Mark 10:15 makes it clear that the Kingdom is to be received in the inner man,[50] it is unlikely that Jesus would have said to the Pharisees, "the Kingdom of God is within *you*." The translation "in your midst," in Jesus' person, best fits the total context of his teaching.[51]

THE NEW ESCHATOLOGICAL STRUCTURE. Jesus' teaching about the Kingdom of God radically modifies the redemptive time line. The Old Testament and Judaism looked forward to a single day—the Day of the Lord—when God would act to establish his reign on the earth. It can be diagrammed by a straight line:

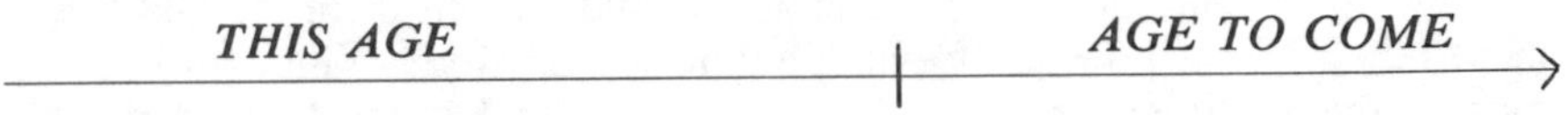

Cullmann argues that Christ has modified the time line by giving it a new center. It retained the same basic structure as in Judaism, but the center shifted.[52] Cullmann has been justly criticized for overemphasizing the midpoint of history at the expense of the end.[53]

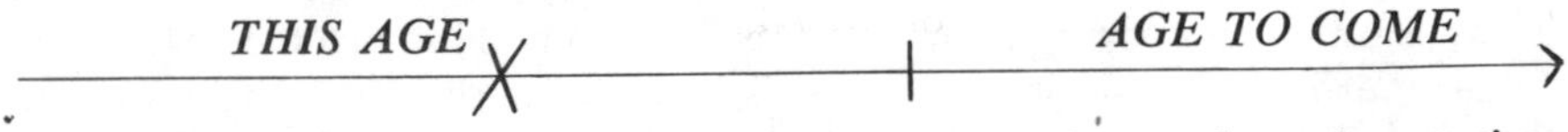

Long ago Geerhardus Vos suggested a similar but perhaps better time line.[54]

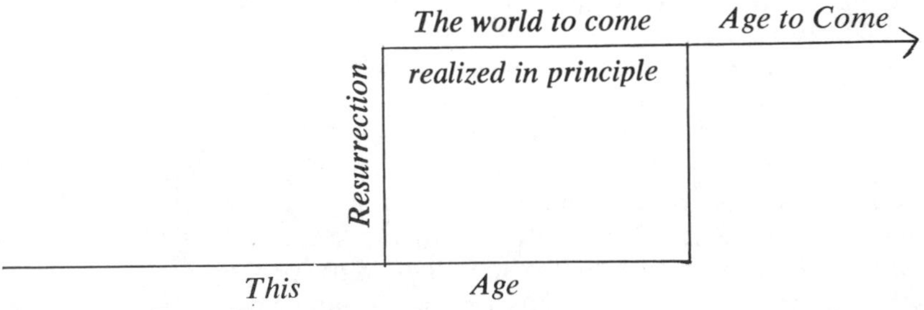

[50] L. H. Marshall takes this idea as "the point of departure for understanding Jesus' message of the Kingdom." *The Challenge of NT Ethics* (1947), pp. 26ff.
[51] For further discussion, see G. E. Ladd, *Jesus and the Kingdom,* p. 224.
[52] O. Cullmann, *Christ and Time,* p. 82.
[53] C. K. Barrett in *ET* 65 (1953-54), 372.
[54] G. Vos, *The Pauline Eschatology* (1952), p. 38.

This scheme has the advantage of illustrating that the Age to Come moves on a higher level than this age, and that the time between the resurrection and the parousia is a time of the overlapping of the two ages. The church lives "between the times"; the old age goes on, but the powers of the new age have irrupted into the old age.

We would suggest a further modification better to illustrate the New Testament time line:

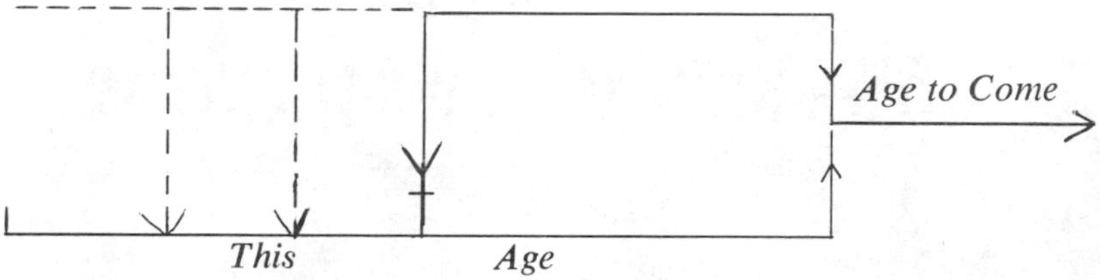

There is a twofold dualism in the New Testament: God's will is done in heaven; his Kingdom brings it to earth. In the Age to Come, heaven descends to earth and lifts historical existence to a new level of redeemed life (Rev. 21:2-3). This is hinted at, although not elaborated on, in the Gospels. Those who "attain to that age and to the resurrection from the dead neither marry nor are given in marriage, for they cannot die any more, because they are equal to angels and are sons of God, being sons of the resurrection" (Lk. 20:35-36). Here is a truly inconceivable order of existence. There are no human analogies to describe existence without the physiological and sociological bonds of sex and family. But this is the will of God: to conquer evil and to bring his people finally into the blessed immortality of the eternal life of the Age to Come.

This diagram also suggests that God's Kingdom was active in the Old Testament. In such events as the Exodus and the captivity in Babylon, God was acting in his kingly power to deliver or judge his people. However, in some real sense God's Kingdom *came* into history in the person and mission of Jesus.

5

THE NEW AGE OF SALVATION

Literature: See Chapter 4.

We saw in the last chapter that the meaning of *basileia* cannot be reduced to a single concept but is a complex concept with several facets. Its root meaning is the reign or rule of God. It can designate the eschatological act of God when God acts in kingly power to destroy his enemies and save his people. It can also designate the future realm of salvation into which God's people will be gathered to enjoy the blessings of his reign. As such, it is interchangeable with the Age to Come.

The most distinctive fact in Jesus' proclamation of the Kingdom was its present inbreaking in history in his own person and mission. We should not be surprised to find *basileia tou theou* used of a new realm of redemptive blessing into which men enter by receiving Jesus' message about the Kingdom of God.

THE KINGDOM AS A PRESENT REALM OF BLESSING. There are several texts that speak of entering the Kingdom as a present reality. Jesus uttered a woe against the scribes and Pharisees because, "You shut the kingdom of heaven against men, for you neither enter yourselves, nor allow those who would enter to go in" (Mt. 23:13). The parallel verse in Luke is even clearer: "Woe to you lawyers! You have taken away the key of knowledge; you did not enter yourselves; and you have hindered those who were entering" (Lk. 11:52). On another occasion Jesus said, "The tax collectors and the harlots go into the kingdom of God before you"—the religious leaders of Israel (Mt. 21:31). The most natural interpretation of such passages is of a present situation. "The outcast classes are entering the Kingdom, and there is no evidence that the outwardly respectable leaders will respond. Even the sight of the outcasts streaming into the Kingdom has not changed their attitude."[1]

The most interesting, and at the same time most difficult, saying is Matthew 11:11-13. In reply to the emissaries of John the Baptist, Jesus

[1] F. V. Filson, *Matthew* (1960), p. 227.

answered their question as to whether or not he was the Messiah by alluding to the messianic prophecy in Isaiah 35:5-6, saying in effect, "This prophecy is now being fulfilled; the age of the messianic salvation is here" (Mt. 11:2-6). Then, speaking of the Baptist, now in Herod's prison, Jesus declared that "among those born of women there has arisen no one greater than John the Baptist; yet he who is least in the kingdom of heaven is greater than he. From the days of John the Baptist until now the kingdom of heaven *biazetai,* and men of violence take it by force. For all the prophets and the law prophesied until John" (Mt. 11:11-13).

This passage involves three difficult problems: the meaning of *biazetai,* of "men of violence," and of "he who is least in the kingdom of heaven."

The verb *biazō* means "to use force or violence," and the form can be either a passive voice, "to be forcibly treated," or a middle, "to exercise force." Elsewhere, we have discussed six different interpretations of this word[2] and can here only present our conclusions. It fits best the dynamic view of the Kingdom of God as God's kingly reign active in the mission of Jesus to take the verb as a middle voice, "The kingdom of heaven has been coming violently" (RSVmg); and there are no philological objections to this interpretation.[3] God's rule makes its way with great force and keen enthusiasts lay hold on it, that is, want to share in it.[4] The mission of Jesus has set up a powerful movement. The power of God is at work mightily among men. It requires an equally powerful reaction. This set Jesus' teaching apart from rabbinic teaching. The rabbis taught that men should take on them the yoke of the Kingdom and accept the Law as the norm of God's will. Jesus taught that this was not enough. On the contrary, God was acting mightily in his own mission; and because the dynamic power of the Kingdom has invaded the world, men are to respond with a radical reaction. Jesus sometimes described this reaction with violent acts. "If your hand causes you to sin, cut it off; . . . and if your eye causes you to sin, pluck it out" (Mk. 9:43, 47). These are acts of violence required of those who would enter the Kingdom.[5] Elsewhere Jesus uses violent language of hating one's family for his sake (Lk. 14:26). He said that he did not come to bring peace but a sword (Mt. 10:34). The presence of the Kingdom demands a radical reaction.

It is clear that Luke understood this passage in this way. He renders this saying, "The good news of the kingdom of God is preached, and every one enters it violently" (*eis autēn biazetai,* Lk. 16:16). Here is the same use of *biazetai* in the middle voice.

---

[2] G. E. Ladd, *Jesus and the Kingdom* (1964), pp. 155-58.

[3] In addition to the reference in *Jesus and the Kingdom,* pp. 158-59, see also M. Black in *ET* 63 (1951-52), 290; R. Schnackenburg, *God's Rule and Kingdom* (1963), p. 131; H. N. Ridderbos, *The Coming of the Kingdom* (1963), p. 54.

[4] R. Schnackenburg, *God's Rule and Kingdom,* p. 132.

[5] For this interpretation see R. Otto, *The Kingdom of God and the Son of Man* (1943), p. 111; T. W. Manson, *The Sayings of Jesus* (1949), p. 134; S. E. Johnson, *IB* VII, 383.

In both of these sayings, the Kingdom of God is the dynamic rule of God active in Jesus; it is also a present realm of blessing into which men enter who receive Jesus' word. Jesus calls John the Baptist the greatest man among men. All the prophets and the Law prophesied until John. He was the last of the prophets. Since the days of John[6] something new has been happening, creating a new situation, with the result that, "great as John was, the least in the dawning Kingdom was greater; not in personal achievement and worth but by God's gift he, unlike John, was in the Kingdom."[7] The contrast is not between John and other people but between the old age of the prophets and the new age of the Kingdom that had begun with Jesus' ministry.[8]

THE KINGDOM AS A PRESENT GIFT. When we ask about the content of this new realm of blessing, we discover that *basileia* means not only the dynamic reign of God and the realm of salvation; it is also used to designate the gift of life and salvation. Here is another original element in Jesus' teaching. The Kingdom of God stands as a comprehensive term for all that the messianic salvation included.[9] Dalman recognized that the Kingdom in Jesus' teaching could be "a good which admits of being striven for, of being bestowed, of being possessed, and of being accepted."[10]

In the eschatological consummation, the Kingdom is something to be freely inherited by the righteous (Mt. 25:34). The word here designates neither the reign of God nor the Age to Come but the blessing of life that is the gift of God's rule in the coming age (Mt. 24:46). In answer to the young man's question about inheriting eternal life (Mk. 10:17), Jesus spoke of entering the Kingdom (10:23-24) and receiving eternal life (10:30) as though they were synonymous concepts. The Kingdom is a gift that the Father is pleased to bestow upon the little flock of Jesus' disciples (Lk. 12:32).

If God's Kingdom is the gift of life bestowed upon his people when he manifests his rule in eschatological glory, and if God's Kingdom is also God's rule invading history before the eschatological consummation, it follows that we may expect God's rule in the present to bring a preliminary blessing to his people. This is in fact what we find. The Kingdom is not only an eschatological gift belonging to the Age to Come; it is also a gift to be received in the old aeon.

This is reflected in numerous sayings. The Kingdom is like a treasure or a costly pearl whose possession outranks all other goods (Mt. 13:44-46). It is something to be sought here and now (Mt. 6:33) and to be received as children receive a gift (Mk. 10:15=Lk. 18:16-17). In this saying the Kingdom is God's rule, but it includes the gift of his rule. The divine reign

---

[6] For the exclusive use of *apo,* see *Jesus and the Kingdom,* p. 197.
[7] F. V. Filson, *Matthew,* p. 138.
[8] See G. E. Ladd, *Jesus and the Kingdom,* p. 197.
[9] R. Schnackenburg, *God's Rule and Kingdom,* p. 94.
[10] G. Dalman, *The Words of Jesus* (1909), p. 121.

is not a fearful power before which men are compelled to bow, but a gift. Children exemplify the trustfulness and receptivity required of the "sons of the Kingdom." The Kingdom belongs to them, not because their humility is a virtue that merits it, but because they are responsive. "The Kingdom belongs to such because they receive it as a gift. . . . [It] is the gift of the divine rule."[11] Matthew 19:14 echoes the same thought that the Kingdom of God is a present possession of the childlike. The promise that those who ask shall receive, and those who seek shall find (Mt. 7:7), is to be understood in this context. "The thing to be sought is the Kingdom of God, which, being found, is the satisfaction of all needs (Lk. 12:31). The door to be knocked at is the door which gives entrance into the Kingdom of God."[12]

The Beatitudes view the Kingdom as a gift. The poor in spirit, those persecuted for righteousness' sake, receive the gift (Mt. 5:3,10). It is not easy to decide whether the Kingdom in these sayings is future or present. The Beatitudes certainly have an eschatological cast. The sayings about inheriting the earth, obtaining mercy (in the day of judgment), and seeing God are primarily eschatological. However, the main objective of the Beatitudes is to teach a present blessedness rather than to promise blessing in the consummation.[13] The comfort for those who grieve because of their spiritual poverty[14] is both present and future, as is the satisfaction of the hungry (Mt. 5:4, 6). The gift of the Kingdom, twice mentioned, probably includes both present and future. The Beatitudes expound both the eschatological salvation and the present blessedness.

THE GIFT OF SALVATION. The Kingdom as God's gift may be further illustrated by a study of the word "salvation." In the Gospels, the words "to save" and "salvation" refer both to an eschatological and to a present blessing.

Salvation is primarily an eschatological gift. In Jesus' answer to the rich young ruler about eternal life, salvation is synonymous with eternal life and entrance into the Kingdom of God in the Age to Come (Mk. 10:17-30). This eschatological salvation is elsewhere described merely as a saving of one's (true) life in contrast with losing one's physical life (Mk. 8:35; Mt. 10:39; Lk. 17:33). This eschatological salvation can be described simply as entrance into (eternal) life (Mk. 9:43; Mt. 25:46) or into the joy of the Lord (Mt. 25:21, 23).

This future salvation means two things: deliverance from mortality, and

---

[11] V. Taylor, *Mark* (1952), p. 423. We differ with Taylor when he eliminates the eschatological significance of the last phrase. See also T. W. Manson, *The Teaching of Jesus* (1935), p. 135. Acceptance of God's present rule is the condition of entrance into the eschatological order.

[12] T. W. Manson, *The Sayings of Jesus,* p. 81.

[13] Even Windisch admits this, although he attributes this meaning to theological exegesis (*The Meaning of the Sermon on the Mount* [1951], pp. 175f.).

[14] See J. W. Bowman and R. W. Tapp, *The Gospel from the Mount* (1957), pp. 31f.

perfected fellowship with God. The Gospels do not say much about resurrection, but the saying in Luke 20:34-36 (cf. Mk. 12:24-27) makes it clear that eschatological salvation includes the whole man. Resurrection life will have something in common with the angels, namely, the possession of immortality. This immortal resurrection life is the life of the Age to Come (Lk. 20:35). The evils of physical weakness, sickness, and death will be swallowed up in the life of the Kingdom of God (Mt. 25:34, 46).

Eschatological salvation means not only the redemption of the body but also the restoration of communion between God and man that had been broken by sin. The pure in heart will see God (Mt. 5:8) and enter into the joy of their Lord (Mt. 25:21, 23). This eschatological consummation is usually described in pictures drawn from daily life. The harvest will take place and the grain will be gathered into the barn (Mt. 13:30, 39; Mk. 4:29; cf. Mt. 3:12; Rev. 14:15). The sheep will be separated from the goats and brought safely into the fold (Mt. 25:32). The most common picture is that of a feast or table fellowship. Jesus will drink wine again with his disciples in the Kingdom of God (Mk. 14:25). They will eat and drink at Jesus' table in the Kingdom (Lk. 22:30). Men will be gathered from all corners of the earth to sit at table with the Old Testament saints (Mt. 8:11-12; Lk. 13:29). The consummation is likened to a wedding feast (Mt. 22:1-14; 25:1-12) and a banquet (Lk. 14:16-24). All of these metaphors picture the restoration of communion between God and men that had been broken by sin.[15]

The religious dimension of the eschatological salvation is set in sharp contrast to what it means to be lost. The one Greek word (*apollumi*) carries two meanings: to destroy or kill, and to lose (passive: to be lost, to die or perish). Both meanings, to be destroyed and to perish, are used of the eschatological destruction (*apōleia,* Mt. 7:13). Not to be saved means to lose one's life (Mk. 8:35; cf. Mt. 10:39; 16:25; Lk. 9:24; 17:33), and to lose one's life is to lose everything (Mk. 8:36), for one has lost himself (Lk. 9:25). Thus to lose one's life is to be destroyed. It is within God's power to destroy not only the body but also the soul; and this destruction is described in terms of the fire of Gehenna (Mt. 10:28; Mk. 9:42-48), eternal fire (Mt. 18:8; 25:41), and darkness (Mt. 8:12; 22:13; 25:30). Since fire and darkness are not homogeneous concepts, the central fact is not the form of this ultimate destruction but its religious significance. This is found in the words, "I never knew you; depart from me, you evildoers" (Mt. 7:23; Lk. 13:27). Here is the meaning of destruction: exclusion from the joys and pleasures of the presence of God in his Kingdom.

Jesus' mission to save the lost sheep of the house of Israel (Mt. 10:6; 15:24) stands against this eschatological background. Their "lostness" is both present and future, for they have strayed from God and forfeited their lives. Because they are now lost, they stand under the threat of eternal

[15] J. Jeremias, *The Parables of Jesus* (1963), p. 222.

destruction. The lost son was in fact dead; his "salvation" or restoration to his father's house meant restoration to life (Lk. 15:24).

Jesus' mission to save the lost has a present as well as a future dimension. He sought the sinner not only to save him from future doom but to bring him into a present salvation. To a repentant Zacchaeus Jesus said, "Today salvation has come to this house. . . . For the Son of man came to seek and to save the lost" (Lk. 19:9-10). Against the background of the meaning of "lost," one can approve of the decision of Arndt and Gingrich, following Bauer, to list "lost" in Luke 19:10 under the meaning "eternal death."[16] The lost have not only gone astray but are in danger of perishing unless rescued. God promised through Ezekiel (34:16, 22), "I will seek the lost. . . . I will save my flock." *This mission Jesus claimed to be fulfilling.* The salvation Jesus brought to Zacchaeus was a present visitation, although its blessings reach into the future.

The parables of the lost sheep, the lost coin, and the lost son are not eschatological but describe a present salvation (Lk. 15). The restoration of the lost son to the joy of his father's house illustrates the blessing of a present salvation that Jesus brought to Zacchaeus and to the tax collectors and sinners who welcomed his fellowship. The elder brother represented the Pharisees and the scribes. As they claimed to be the true Israel who alone obeyed the Law of God, so the elder brother dwelt under his father's roof. But he too was lost, for he knew neither real fellowship with his father nor the joy of his father's house.

This gift of present fellowship in anticipation of the eschatological consummation is the motif illustrated by the acted parable of table fellowship. The scribes were offended because Jesus joined in a dinner party with tax collectors and sinners (Mk. 2:15ff.). This was no ordinary meal but a feast. The Jews did not follow the Gentile custom of reclining at ordinary meals but sat at the table. Only on special occasions—parties, wedding feasts, or royal banquets—did the Jews recline.[17] The metaphor of a feast was a common Jewish picture of the eschatological salvation;[18] and the fellowship of Jesus with his disciples and those who followed them is to be understood as an anticipation of the joy and fellowship of the eschatological Kingdom. The religious significance of this meal is reflected in Jesus' words, "I came not to call the righteous, but sinners" (Mk. 2:17). He was fulfilling his messianic mission when he gathered sinners into fellowship with himself.

That this was no isolated instance is reflected in two other sayings. Luke records that one of the main grounds of criticism by the scribes and the Pharisees was the fact that Jesus received sinners and ate with them (Lk. 15:1-2). All three parables that follow emphasize the fact of joy at the recovery of lost sinners. The central truth is the joy in heaven over one

---

[16] Arndt and Gingrich, *Lexicon* (1957), p. 94.

[17] See J. Jeremias, *The Eucharistic Words of Jesus* (1955), pp. 20-21 and references. The translation of the RSV, "sat at table," renders the idea in modern idiom.

[18] G. F. Moore, *Judaism* (1927), II, 363ff.

sinner who repents (Lk. 15:7); but it is a joy that was anticipated on earth in the table fellowship of Jesus and repentant sinners.

So typical of Jesus' ministry was this joyous fellowship that his critics accused him of being a glutton and a drunkard (Mt. 11:18). The same note of messianic joy is heard in Jesus' answer to the criticism that he and his disciples did not follow the example of the Pharisees in fasting. Fasting does not belong to the time of a wedding. The presence of the bridegroom calls for joy, not fasting (Mk. 2:18-19). While we have no evidence that the metaphor of a bridegroom was applied to the Messiah in Judaism, the wedding feast was a symbol of the Kingdom of God.[19] During the seven days of the wedding festivities, the friends and guests of the bridegroom were excused from the observance of many serious religious duties that they might share in the festivities. Jesus described his presence in the midst of his disciples by this messianic symbol of the wedding. The day of salvation has come, the wedding songs resound; there is no place for mourning, only for joy. Therefore Jesus' disciples cannot fast.[20]

The presence of the messianic salvation is also seen in Jesus' miracles of healing, for which the Greek word meaning "to save" is used. The presence of the Kingdom of God in Jesus meant deliverance from hemorrhage (Mk. 5:34), blindness (Mk. 10:52), demon possession (Lk. 8:36), and even death itself (Mk. 5:23). Jesus claimed that these deliverances were evidences of the presence of the messianic salvation (Mt. 11:4-5). They were pledges of the life of the eschatological Kingdom that will finally mean immortality for the body. The Kingdom of God is concerned not only with men's souls but with the salvation of the whole man.

The limitation of these physical deliverances illustrates the nature of the present Kingdom in contrast to its future manifestations. In the eschatological Kingdom, all "who are accounted worthy to attain to that age" (Lk. 20:35) will be saved from sickness and death in the immortal life of the resurrection. In the present working of the Kingdom, this saving power reached only a few. Not all the sick and crippled were saved, nor were all the dead raised. Only three instances of restoration to life are recorded in the Gospels. Men must come into direct contact with Jesus or his disciples to be healed (Mk. 6:56). The saving power of the Kingdom was not yet universally operative. It was resident only in Jesus and in those whom he commissioned (Mt. 10:8; Lk. 10:9).

However, not even all who came into contact with Jesus experienced the healing life of the Kingdom; this physical salvation required the response of faith. It did not work *ex opere operato*. "Your faith has saved you" (Mk. 5:34; 10:52). A spiritual response was necessary to receive the physical blessing. The miracles of healing, important as they were, were not an end in themselves. They did not constitute the highest good of the messianic

---

19 See J. Jeremias, *TDNT* IV, 1101.

20 J. Jeremias, *The Parables of Jesus*, p. 117; C. H. Dodd, *The Parables of the Kingdom* (1936), pp. 115f.; H. Seesemann, *TDNT* V, 163.

salvation. This fact is illustrated by the arrangement of the phrases in Matthew 11:4-5. Greater than deliverance of the blind and the lame, the lepers and the deaf, even than raising the dead, was the preaching of the good news to the poor.[21] This "gospel" was the very presence of Jesus himself, and the joy and fellowship that he brought to the poor.

That salvation from physical sickness was only the external aspect of spiritual salvation is shown by a saying about demon exorcism. While this miracle was one of the most convincing evidences of the presence of the Kingdom (Mt. 12:28), it was preliminary to God's taking possession of the vacant dwelling. Otherwise, a man is like a house that stands in good order, clean but empty (Mt. 12:44=Lk. 11:25). Unless the power of God enters that life, the demon can return bringing seven other demons with him, and the man will be worse off than he was at first. Healings and demon exorcisms were the negative side of salvation; the positive side was the incoming of the power and life of God.

The bond between physical salvation and its spiritual aspect is illustrated by the healing of the ten lepers. All ten were "cleansed" and "healed" (Lk. 17:14f.). To the one, a Samaritan who returned to express his gratitude, Jesus said, "Your faith has saved you" (Lk. 17:19). These are the same words used elsewhere of healing. Are we to suppose that the other nine were not really healed? Many commentators suspect confusion in the text. However, in view of the fact that these same words are clearly used of "spiritual" salvation (Lk. 7:50), we may agree with those expositors who see a greater blessing bestowed on the Samaritan than on the nine. His "salvation" or wholeness was more than physical healing. It implied a sound spiritual state.[22]

That this present "salvation" is spiritual as well as physical is proved by the incident of the sinful woman in the house of Simon. Her tears and display of affection proved her repentance. To her Jesus said, "Your faith has saved you, go in peace" (Lk. 7:50). No miracle of healing was performed. Her disease was altogether moral and spiritual. The meaning of her "salvation" is expounded in the words, "Your sins are forgiven" (Lk. 7:48).

THE GIFT OF FORGIVENESS. This mention of forgiveness points to the deeper significance of the messianic salvation. According to Mark, the conflict between Jesus and the scribes began when Jesus claimed to forgive sins. Such a claim was nothing less than blasphemy, for only God had the right to forgive sins (Mk. 2:7). On their own presuppositions, the scribes were right (Ps. 103:3; Isa. 43:25). In the prophets, forgiveness will be one of the blessings of the messianic age. The Lord who is judge, ruler, and king will save his people so that there will be no longer any sick, for the Lord will forgive all iniquity (Isa. 33:24). The saved remnant will be pardoned and forgiven, for their sins will be cast into the depths of the

[21] G. Friedrich, *TDNT* II, 718.
[22] See L. Ragg, *St. Luke* (1922), p. 228; W. F. Arndt, *St. Luke* (1956), p. 372.

sea (Mic. 7:18-20). God will make a new covenant and will inscribe his Law in the heart, granting a perfect fellowship with himself and the forgiveness of sins (Jer. 31:31-34; cf. also Ezek. 18:31; 36:22-28). A fountain will be opened for the house of David that will cleanse God's people from all sin (Zech. 13:1).

With one possible exception, this function was limited to God.[23] One prophecy tells of the servant of the Lord who will bear the iniquities of the people and give himself as an offering for sin (Isa. 53:11-12); but Judaism did not apply this prophecy to the Messiah until the third century and later.[24] There is no source known to us in which the Messiah by virtue of his own authority promises to men the forgiveness of sins. Furthermore, while God was believed to forgive sins, Judaism never solved the problem created by the tension between God's justice and his grace.[25] The righteous man was not one who had been freely pardoned by God, but the man whose merit outweighed his debt. Righteousness is the divine acquittal in the day of judgment, but this eschatological acquittal is determined by a theory of merit. A man's standing before God is settled by the balance between his good deeds and his transgressions. If the former outweigh the latter, he will be acquitted.[26]

Against this background, one can readily understand the amazement and dismay among the scribes when Jesus on his own authority pronounced the free forgiveness of sins. John the Baptist had promised forgiveness (Mk. 1:4); Jesus fulfilled this promise. The healing of the paralytic was the external proof that "the Son of man has authority on earth to forgive sins" (Mk. 2:10). The Son of Man was the heavenly figure in Daniel 7:13 representing the saints of the Most High, who would come with the clouds of heaven to bring the Kingdom of God, and to judge men. In this saying, Jesus claimed that he was this heavenly judge, but that he had appeared on earth among men exercising the divine prerogative to forgive sins. This was the sign of the presence of the messianic salvation.

The centrality of the forgiveness of sins in the concept of the Kingdom of God is illustrated by the parable of forgiveness (Mt. 18:23-35). It sets forth the relationship between the divine and human forgiveness in the Kingdom of God. The divine forgiveness precedes and conditions human forgiveness. While Jeremias emphasizes the eschatological element of judgment, he recognizes that the parable teaches primarily God's mercy; for the eschatological judgment will be based on a prior experience of the gift of God's forgiveness.[27] The free gift of God's forgiveness lays upon men the demand of a forgiving spirit.

---

[23] Forgiveness is a prerogative of God that he shares with no other and deputes to none (G. F. Moore, *Judaism,* I, 535).

[24] G. Quell in *TDNT* II, 187.

[25] Note the struggle with this same problem by the modern Jewish scholar, J. Klausner, *Jesus of Nazareth* (1925), p. 379.

[26] See G. Schrenk, *TDNT* II, 196-97; W. O. E. Oesterley and G. H. Box, *The Religion and Worship of the Synagogue* (1907), pp. 244-51.

[27] J. Jeremias, *The Parables of Jesus,* p. 213.

Jesus did not teach a new doctrine of forgiveness; he brought to lost sinners a new experience of forgiveness. He did not tell the woman in the house of Simon that God was forgiving her or explain to her the way she might find salvation; he pronounced her sins forgiven (Lk. 7:48). This was her "salvation." Jesus did what he proclaimed. The presence of the Kingdom of God was not a new teaching about God; it was a new activity of God in the person of Jesus bringing to men as present experience what the prophets promised in the eschatological Kingdom.[28]

THE GIFT OF RIGHTEOUSNESS. Closely related to forgiveness is righteousness. Righteousness is not primarily an ethical quality, but a right relationship, the divine acquittal from the guilt of sin.[29] To seek the Kingdom means to seek God's righteousness (Mt. 6:33); and to receive the Kingdom of God means to receive the accompanying righteousness.

Righteousness in Jewish thought was a human activity.[30] The rabbis taught that it was a human work consisting of obedience to the Law and acts of mercy. Jesus taught that it was both God's demand and God's gift. A righteousness exceeding that of the scribes and the Pharisees was demanded for entrance into the eschatological Kingdom (Mt. 5:20). This righteousness includes freedom from anger, from lust, from retaliation (Mt. 5:21-48). If the attainment of such a perfect righteousness is left to human effort, no one can acquire it; it must be God's gift.

Here is the very heart of Jesus' ethical teaching: the renunciation of self-attained righteousness and the willingness to become like children who have nothing and must receive everything. The scribes were unwilling to lay aside their pride in their righteousness to become nothing that they might receive the gift of God's righteousness. So long as they considered themselves to be righteous (Mk. 2:17; Lk. 18:9),[31] they felt no need of God's gift. In contrast to the self-righteous Pharisee stands the tax collector, who cast himself entirely upon God's mercy. He had nothing: no deeds of righteousness, no acts of merit. He was therefore open toward God. "This man went down to his house justified" (Lk. 18:14), declared righteous by God. Obviously his righteousness was no attainment of his own, but the gift of God. The teaching of this parable is the same as the Pauline doctrine of free justification with the exception that there is no mention of the cross.[32]

The righteousness of the Sermon on the Mount is also God's gift. The promise of satisfaction to those who hunger and thirst after righteousness (Mt. 5:6) is a promise to those who are conscious of their own unrigh-

[28] See the excellent note on forgiveness in V. Taylor, *Mark*, pp. 200f.

[29] G. Schrenk in *TDNT* II, 185-95.

[30] G. Schrenk, *TDNT* II, 196.

[31] While Jesus adopted the usual Jewish terminology of "the righteous" and "the unrighteous," "there is in the Syn. a stern rejection of the hypocrisy of a righteous appearance and of the confidence of the *dikaios* in his own piety." G. Schrenk, *TDNT* II, 190.

[32] G. Schrenk, *TDNT* II, 215.

teousness but hunger and thirst to be right with God. In opposition to the Jewish thought of merit, *dikaiosunē* is plainly regarded as a gift that God gives to those who ask for it.[33]

Thus the unforeseen presence of the eschatological salvation is illustrated in many aspects of Jesus' message and mission and is to be seen far beyond the actual terminology of the Kingdom of God. The mission of Jesus brought not a new teaching but a new event. It brought to men an actual foretaste of the eschatological salvation. Jesus did not promise the forgiveness of sins; he bestowed it. He did not simply assure men of the future fellowship of the Kingdom; he invited men into fellowship with himself as the bearer of the Kingdom. He did not merely promise them vindication in the day of judgment; he bestowed upon them a present righteousness. He not only taught an eschatological deliverance from physical evil; he went about demonstrating the redeeming power of the Kingdom, delivering men from sickness and even death.

This is the meaning of the presence of the Kingdom as a new era of salvation. To receive the Kingdom of God, to submit oneself to God's reign meant to receive the gift of the Kingdom and to enter into the enjoyment of its blessings. The age of fulfillment is present, but the time of consummation still awaits the Age to Come.

[33] G. Schrenk, *TDNT* II, 198.

6

THE GOD OF THE KINGDOM

Literature:

R. Bultmann, *Jesus and the Word* (1926), pp. 133-219; T. W. Manson, *The Teaching of Jesus* (1935), pp. 89-115; G. Schrenk, "Patēr," *TDNT* V, 974-96; H. F. D. Sparks, "The Doctrine of the Divine Fatherhood in the Gospels" in *Studies of the Gospels,* ed. by D. E. Nincham (1955), pp. 241ff.; H. W. Montefiore, "God as Father in the Synoptic Gospels," *NTS* 3 (1956), 31-46; C. F. D. Moule, "Children of God," *IDB* A-D (1962), pp. 558-61; A. W. Argyle, *God in the NT* (1966); J. Jeremias, *The Prayers of Jesus* (1967), pp. 11-65; H. Conzelmann, "The Idea of God," *Theology of the NT* (1969), pp. 99-105; J. Jeremias, *NT Theology* (1971), I, 56-75.

The dynamic understanding of the *basileia tou theou* has been drawn first from a linguistic and exegetical study of the meaning and use of the term itself. This dynamic interpretation is further illustrated by the theology of the Gospels, strictly speaking, i.e., by their doctrine of God.

The Kingdom is God's Kingdom, not man's: *basileia tou theou.* The emphasis falls on the third word, not the first; it is the Kingdom of *God.* "The fact with which we have to reckon at all times is that in the teaching of Jesus his conception of God determines everything, including the conceptions of the Kingdom and the Messiah."[1] If the Kingdom is the rule of God, then every aspect of the Kingdom must be derived from the character and action of God. The presence of the Kingdom is to be understood from the nature of God's present activity; and the future of the Kingdom is the redemptive manifestation of his kingly rule at the end of the age.

This was also true in Judaism. God's Kingdom was God's overall sovereign rule. He never ceased to be the God whose kingly providence ultimately superintended all existence. Furthermore, God's rule could always and everywhere be known through the Law; and God would act to establish his Kingdom at the end of the age. Jesus' proclamation of the presence of the Kingdom means that God has become redemptively active in history on

[1] T. W. Manson, *The Teaching of Jesus* (1935), p. 211.

behalf of his people. This does not empty the eschatological aspect of the Kingdom of its content, for the God who was acting in history in the person and mission of Jesus will again act at the end of the age to manifest his glory and saving power. Both the present and future display God's Kingdom, for both present and future are the scene of the redemptive acting of God.

THE SEEKING GOD. This thesis is supported by a study of the particular concept of God found in Jesus' teachings. Here we find a striking fact: the novel element in Jesus' proclamation of the Kingdom is paralleled by a new element in his teaching about God, namely, that God is the seeking God. We do not mean to suggest that it was Jesus' purpose to impart a new theoretical truth about God. God is one who is to be experienced, not a teaching to be imparted. This does not exclude the question of what concept of God is reflected in and through Jesus' teaching and ministry. In one sense the God of late Judaism was not the God of the Old Testament. The God of the prophets was constantly active in history both to judge and to save his people; the God of late Judaism had withdrawn from the evil world and was no longer redemptively working in history.[2] One final redemptive act was expected at the end of the age; but meanwhile God stood aloof from history.

Jesus' message of the Kingdom proclaimed that God not only will finally act, but that God was now again acting redemptively in history. In fact, God had entered into history in a way and to a degree not known by the prophets. The fulfillment of the Old Testament promises was taking place; the messianic salvation was present; the Kingdom of God had come near. God was visiting his people. In Jesus, God has taken the initiative to seek out the sinner, to bring lost men into the blessing of his reign. He was, in short, the seeking God.

Some scholars interpret Jesus' view of the Kingdom along the lines of rabbinic thought, except that the role of the Law is replaced by Jesus' religious experience. The heart of the Kingdom of God was Jesus' inner experience of God as Father. His mission was to share this experience with men. As men enter into Jesus' experience of God, the Kingdom of God, his rule, "comes" to them. As increasingly large circles of men enter into this experience, God's Kingdom grows and is extended in the world.[3]

While there is an important element in this interpretation that must be preserved, it is inadequate because it overlooks the dynamic character of the Kingdom of God. At the very heart of our Lord's message and mission was embodied the reality of God as seeking love. God was no longer waiting for the lost to forsake his sins; God was seeking out the sinner.

The fact was embodied in Jesus' own mission. When he was criticized

---

[2] See the essay by W. G. Kümmel in *Judaica,* I (1945), 40-68. Bultmann's way of expressing this same phenomenon is "The God of the future is not really God of the present" (*Jesus and the Word* [1934], p. 148).

[3] Cf. H. E. W. Turner, *Jesus Master and Lord* (1953), pp. 256-60.

by the Pharisees for violating their standards of righteousness and associating with sinners, he replied that it was his mission to minister to sinners (Mk. 2:15-17). It is those who know they are sick who need a physician. Jesus must bring the saving good news of the Kingdom to such sinners. He does not deny that they are sinners, nor does he make light of their guilt. Rather he points to their need and ministers to it.

The great truth of God seeking out the sinner is set forth at length in Luke 15 in three parables given to silence the criticism that Jesus welcomed sinners to the intimacy of table fellowship. He said that it was the divine purpose to search out the sheep that had strayed; to seek the coin that had been lost; to welcome the prodigal into the family even though he did not merit forgiveness. In each parable there is a divine initiative: the shepherd searches for sheep; the woman sweeps the house for the coin; the father longs for the prodigal's return. The central character in the parable of the "prodigal son" is not the son but the longing father. The parable illustrates primarily not the prodigality of man but the love and grace of God.

Jewish scholars admit that this concern for the sinner was something new. Abrahams insists that Pharisaism taught that God was always ready to take the first step; yet he admits that the initiative was usually left to the sinner to turn to God.[4] Montefiore recognizes that the "greatness and originality" of Jesus opened "a new chapter in men's attitudes towards sin and sinners" because he sought out sinners rather than avoiding them.[5] This concern for sinners is something entirely unheard of in Judaism and contrasts strikingly with such sentiments as those expressed in IV Ezra, where the author, grieving over the small number of the righteous, is told, "For indeed I will not concern myself about the fashioning of those who have sinned, or about their death, their judgment, or their destruction; but I will rejoice over the creation of the righteous, over their pilgrimage also, and their salvation" (8:38f.). The heart of the "good news" about the Kingdom is that God has taken the initiative to seek and to save that which was lost.

THE INVITING GOD. The God who seeks is also the God who invites. Jesus pictured the eschatological salvation in terms of a banquet or feast to which many guests were invited (Mt. 22:1ff.; Lk. 14:16ff.; cf. Mt. 8:11). Against this background we may understand the frequent table fellowship between Jesus and his followers as an acted parable representing an offer of and summons to the blessings of the Kingdom of God.[6] Table

---

[4] I. Abrahams, *Studies in Pharisaism and the Gospels* (First Series, 1917), p. 58.

[5] C. A. Montefiore, *The Synoptic Gospels* (1927), I, 55. The validity of Montefiore's observation stands even though his view that Jesus looked upon these sinners as the children of God is to be questioned. It is not because men are God's children that Jesus sought out the sinner, but because God would make them his children.

[6] Cf. G. Bornkamm, *Jesus of Nazareth* (1960), p. 81.

fellowship to the Jew was a most intimate relationship, and it played an important role in Jesus' ministry (Mk. 2:15). The Pharisees were offended because he ate with sinners (Lk. 15:2). He was called "a glutton and a drunkard, a friend of tax collectors and sinners" (Mt. 11:19). The word "call" means invite. "To invite sinners to the Great Banquet of the Kingdom was precisely the Lord's mission."[7]

Jesus called men to repentance, but the summons was also an invitation. In fact, the character of Jesus' summons to repentance as invitation sets his call apart from the Jewish teaching. In Judaism, the doctrine of repentance held a place of greatest importance, for it was one of the means by which salvation was to be obtained.[8] Repentance was understood largely in terms of the Law and meant, negatively, breaking off evil works and offenses against the Law and, positively, obedience to the Law as the expression of the divine will. The "yoke of the Law" could also be called the "yoke of repentance." The order of events is: man repents, God forgives. The human action must precede the divine. "According to Jewish teaching, the forgiveness of sins depends upon the sinner, for there is no question of a mediator."[9]

Jesus' demand for repentance was not merely a summons to men to forsake their sins and to turn to God; it was rather a call to respond to the divine invitation and was conditioned by this invitation, which was itself nothing less than a gift of God's Kingdom. This distinguished Jesus' call to repentance from that of John the Baptist. John called upon men to forsake their sins in view of the coming day of judgment; Jesus called on men to accept an invitation.[10]

Jesus' message of the Kingdom of God is the announcement by word and deed that God is acting and manifesting dynamically his redemptive will in history. God is seeking out sinners; he is inviting them to enter into the messianic blessing; he is demanding of them a favorable response to his gracious offer. God has again spoken. A new prophet has appeared, indeed one who is more than a prophet, one who brings to men the very blessing he promises.

THE FATHERLY GOD. God is seeking out sinners and inviting them to submit themselves to his reign that he might be their Father. An inseparable relationship exists between the Kingdom of God and his Fatherhood; and it is particularly notable that this affinity between the two concepts appears most frequently in an eschatological setting. In the eschatological salvation, the righteous will enter into the Kingdom of their Father (Mt. 13:43). It is the Father who has prepared for the blessed this eschatological inheritance

[7] A. E. J. Rawlinson, *Mark* (1925), p. 20.

[8] See W. O. E. Oesterley and G. H. Box, *The Religion and Worship of the Synagogue* (1907), pp. 245ff.; G. F. Moore, *Judaism,* I, 507-34. Moore describes repentance as "the Jewish doctrine of salvation" (p. 500).

[9] Oesterley and Box, *The Religion and Worship of the Synagogue,* p. 247.

[10] See G. Bornkamm, *Jesus of Nazareth*, pp. 82f.

of the Kingdom (Mt. 25:34). It is the Father who will bestow upon Jesus' disciples the gift of the Kingdom (Lk. 12:32). The highest gift of God's Fatherhood is participation in God's sovereignty, which is to be exercised over all the world. In that day Jesus will enjoy a renewed fellowship with his disciples in the Father's Kingdom (Mt. 26:29). Since the greatest joy of children of God is that of sharing the blessings of the Kingdom, Jesus taught his disciples to pray, "Our Father who art in heaven . . . thy kingdom come" (Mt. 6:9, 10). Clearly kingship and Fatherhood are closely related concepts.[11]

These eschatological sayings illustrate one important fact about God's Fatherhood. It is a blessing and a relationship that cannot be enjoyed by all men but only by those who enter the eschatological Kingdom. The concept of Fatherhood is qualified by that of the Kingdom. It is as the Father that God will grant men entrance into the eschatological Kingdom; and it follows that those who do not enter that Kingdom will not enjoy the relationship to God as their Father.

The gift of Fatherhood belongs not only to the eschatological consummation; it is also a present gift. Furthermore, the future blessing of the Kingdom is dependent upon a present relationship. This is shown from the fact that Jesus taught his disciples to call God their Father and to look upon him as such. But even in this present relationship, Fatherhood is inseparable from the Kingdom. Those who know God as their Father are those for whom the highest good in life is the Kingdom of God and its righteousness (Mt. 6:32, 33; Lk. 12:30).

This raises the important question of the source and nature of Jesus' teaching about the Fatherhood of God. The concept has its roots in the Old Testament where Fatherhood is a way of describing the covenant relationship between God and Israel. Israel is God's firstborn son because of this covenant (Exod. 4:22). God is therefore frequently conceived of as the Father of the nation (Deut. 32:6; Isa. 64:8; Mal. 2:10). This is not a relationship that is grounded in nature,[12] but was created by the divine initiative. Although God was the Father of the nation as a whole, when Israel became faithless, God's Fatherhood was limited to the faithful remnant of the righteous within Israel (Ps. 103:13; Mal. 3:17). In the postcanonical literature, God's Fatherhood was particularly stressed with reference to the individual (Sir. 23:1; Wisd. Sol. 2:16). The full meaning of Fatherhood is eschatological and will be experienced in the Kingdom of God (Ps. Sol. 17:30; Jub. 1:24). In the rabbinical literature, the Fatherhood of God is an ethical relationship between God and Israel.[13]

The old liberal view of the Kingdom of God seized upon this concept of Fatherhood in Jesus' teaching and made it the determinative theme, in-

---

[11] G. Schrenk, *TDNT* V, 995.

[12] Paul has a doctrine of God's universal Fatherhood resting upon the fact of creation (Acts 17:28-29), which represents a different line of thought.

[13] See T. W. Manson, *The Teaching of Jesus,* pp. 89-92.

terpreting it in universal terms. Jesus allegedly took up the Jewish teaching of God's Fatherhood, deepened and enriched it, extending it to all men. God is Father to all men because he is perfect in love, and love is the sum of all his moral perfections. God is the universal Father because he always remains what he ought to be.[14]

Recent criticism has recognized that "in spite of what is commonly supposed, there is no ground whatever for asserting that Jesus taught a doctrine of 'the Fatherhood of God and the Brotherhood of man.' "[15] Two facts emerge from a study of the terminology. (a) Jesus never grouped himself together with his disciples as the sons of God. The usage in John 20:17 is only more explicit than that in the Synoptics: "I am ascending to my Father and your Father, to my God and your God." Jesus' messianic sonship is different from the sonship of his disciples. (b) Jesus never applied the category of sonship to any but his disciples. Men became sons of God by recognizing his messianic sonship.[16]

A universal Fatherhood of God has been seen in Jesus' saying, "Love your enemies and pray for those who persecute you, so that you may be sons of your Father who is in heaven; for he makes his sun rise on the evil and on the good, and sends rain on the just and on the unjust" (Mt. 5:44f.). This saying has been interpreted to mean that love for one's enemies is required because God is the universal Father and Jesus' disciples must love all men because God loves all men as his children. This interpretation reads something into the saying. Actually, God is viewed only as the Father of Jesus' disciples. The goodness of God in sending rain to all men, good and evil alike, is not to be confused with the divine Fatherhood. The same exegesis should lead to the conclusion that God is also the Father of all creatures. "Look at the birds of the air; they neither sow nor reap nor gather into barns, and yet your heavenly Father feeds them" (Mt. 6:26). It is not as Father that God cares for the birds, and it is not as Father that God bestows his creaturely blessings on those who are not his children. The Fatherhood of God belongs to those who have responded to the divine seeking love and have submitted themselves to God's Kingdom. God seeks men, not because he is their Father, but because he would become their Father.

The universal Fatherhood of God has also been seen in the parable of the prodigal son (Lk. 15:11-24). The prodigal has been interpreted to teach that every man is by nature a son of God and needs only to return where he belongs. This ignores the fact that a parable is a story drawn from daily

---

[14] W. Beyschlag, *NT Theology* (1895), I, 79ff.; T. Rees, "God," *ISBE* II, 1260ff.; G. H. Gilbert, "Father," *DCG* I, 580ff. See H. W. Montefiore in *NTS* 3 (1956), 31-46.

[15] H. F. D. Sparks in *Studies of the Gospels* (D. E. Nineham, ed., 1955), p. 260.

[16] For this teaching of "limited sonship" see H. F. D. Sparks in *Studies of the Gospels,* pp. 241-62; G. S. Duncan, *Jesus Son of Man* (1949), pp. 43-45; T. W. Manson, *The Teaching of Jesus,* pp. 98, 102; J. Jeremias, *The Prayers of Jesus* (1967), p. 43; C. F. D. Moule, "Children of God," *IDB* A-D, p. 560.

life whose purpose is to set forth a basic truth and whose details cannot be pressed. It is improper exegesis to say that this parable teaches that men are by nature children of God as it would be to say that dumb beasts (Lk. 15:1-7) are also sons of God. The central truth of all three parables is that of the yearning God. God is like one who seeks for lost sheep, who searches for a lost coin, who longs for the return of a prodigal. This is a parable about the Father, not about the son. The one element all three parables embody about the lost is belonging—the lost sheep belongs in the fold; the lost coin belongs in the housewife's possessions; the son belongs in his father's house. Man's proper place is in the house of the Father.

This certainly teaches the potential universal Fatherhood of God but not an actual Fatherhood. While the son was in the strange land, his sonship was an empty thing, void of content. However, he belonged in the Father's house; and "when he came to himself," he returned where he belonged. So is God not only willing but longing to receive all who will come to themselves and turn to the Father, that they may enter into the enjoyment of the Father's blessings.

The meaning of God as Father has been investigated by Jeremias. It is clear that Jesus used the Aramaic word *abba* to address God, and also taught his disciples to do so. This Aramaic form of address appears in Greek clothing in the epistles (Rom. 8:15; Gal. 4:6). The word *abba* was taken from children's speech, and is something like our "Daddy." The Jews did not use this word in their address to God, for it was too intimate and would have seemed disrespectful. Jesus spoke to God like a child and taught his disciples so to speak. He forbade them to use *abba* in everyday speech as a courtesy title (Mt. 23.9), they are to reserve it for God. *Abba* represents the new relationship of confidence and intimacy imparted to men by Jesus.[17]

THE JUDGING GOD. While God seeks the sinner and offers him the gift of the Kingdom, he remains a God of retributive righteousness to those who reject the gracious offer. His concern for the lost does not dissipate the divine holiness into a benign kindliness. God is seeking love, but he is also holy love. He is the heavenly Father. His name is to be hallowed (Mt. 6:9). Therefore those who reject the offer of his Kingdom must stand under his judgment.

Indeed, the very fact that God is seeking love throws man into a predicament. Man must respond to this overture of love; otherwise a greater condemnation awaits him. Bultmann speaks of God as one who has come near to men as "the Demander."[18] When confronted by the person of Jesus a man stands before God and must make a decision. The outcome will be either the salvation of the Kingdom or judgment.

This note of retributive righteousness sounds repeatedly in Jesus' proclamation of the Kingdom. In the preaching of the Baptist, the coming of the

---

[17] J. Jeremias, *The Prayers of Jesus,* pp. 57-61.

[18] *Der Fordernde;* cf. R. Bultmann, *Theology* (1951), I, 24.

eschatological Kingdom will mean salvation for the righteous but a fiery judgment for the unrighteous (Mt. 3:12). Jesus taught the same thing. The obverse of inheriting the Kingdom will be to suffer the punishment of everlasting fire (Mt. 25:34, 41). To those who refused to enter the Kingdom and who tried to prevent others from entering (Mt. 23:13), Jesus said, "You serpents, you brood of vipers, how are you to escape the sentence of hell?" (Mt. 23:33). The power of the Kingdom was present and active in Jesus to deliver men from bondage to evil, and God not only offers free forgiveness to the penitent but even seeks out the sinner to bring him to himself. When a man has become so blind that he cannot distinguish between the power of God's Kingdom and the working of the devil but thinks that the Kingdom of God is demonic, that person can never be forgiven; he is guilty of an eternal sin (Mk. 3:29). A fearful doom awaits those who try to turn believers away from the Kingdom of God (Mt. 18:6). The great truth of God as seeking love does not nullify the righteousness and justice of God. The meaning of God's Kingdom is both salvation and judgment.

This eschatological judgment of God's Kingdom is in principle decided in Jesus' mission among men. As men react to Jesus and his proclamation, their eschatological doom is determined (Mk. 8:38; Mt. 10:32-33). When Jesus' disciples visited various cities proclaiming the Kingdom and were rejected, they were to wipe the dust from their feet in an acted parable of judgment,[19] and their announcement "Nevertheless know this, that the kingdom of God has come near" becomes a threat instead of a promise. Fearful judgment awaits such a town.

Jesus also pronounced judgment upon cities where he had preached and performed the works of the Kingdom: Chorazin, Bethsaida, Capernaum (Mt. 11:20-24; Lk. 10:13-15). The nature of the judgment pronounced on Capernaum is not altogether clear. Luke (10:14) like Matthew (11:22) describes the judgment that will befall Chorazin and Bethsaida in eschatological terms. But both Luke (10:15) and Matthew (11:23) speak of Capernaum's judgment in less eschatological terms, saying merely that this proud city, which was the center of Jesus' Galilean ministry and had heard the message of the Kingdom repeatedly, would be brought down to Hades. Even though Matthew adds an eschatological note (Mt. 11:24), it is evident that he understood this saying to refer to a judgment in history, for he adds that if the works of the Kingdom seen in the streets of Capernaum had been performed in Sodom, "it would have remained until this day" (Mt. 11:23). In this judgment of Capernaum, Jesus uses the taunt

---

[19] This gesture in rabbinic thought indicated that the persons concerned were thereafter to be viewed as heathen and all intercourse broken off (Strack and Billerbeck, *Kommentar,* I, 581). The context of the act seems to suggest that the towns concerned would be forever after aliens to the Kingdom of God and would be no part of the true Israel, the "sons of the kingdom" who accept it. Theirs would be judgment instead of blessing.

song directed against Babylon in Isaiah 14:13-15, even though he does not quote it directly.[20]

Here is an important note recorded by both Matthew and Luke: the judgment for rejecting the Kingdom occurs in history as well as at the eschatological day. Capernaum, which was lifted up with worldly pride, would be dragged down to the lowest level of shame. Capernaum would suffer the same fate as Sodom: extinction. Here is the relevance of the allusion to Isaiah 14: Capernaum, like Babylon, would be dragged down to ruin. Jesus, like the prophets, could view the divine visitation for judgment in historical as well as eschatological terms. The destruction of Capernaum would be the judgment of the Kingdom of God.

This is not the only time Jesus spoke of judgment in historical terms. A number of sayings pronounce judgment upon Jerusalem and its inhabitants for their spiritual blindness and failure to recognize the proffered messianic salvation. Jesus wept over Jerusalem because it had rejected the offer of the Kingdom (Mt. 23:37-39; Lk. 13:34-35). The metaphor of a hen gathering her brood is drawn from the Old Testament (Deut. 32:11; Ps. 17:8; 36:7); and the Jew who converts a Gentile is said to bring him under the wings of the Shekinah (the presence of God).[21] "The sense is the quite simple one of bringing men into the Kingdom of God."[22] Rejection of this invitation will mean that "your house is forsaken and desolate." It is not clear whether "your house" refers to the temple or to the Jewish commonwealth, but the sense is the same, for the temple and the Jewish commonwealth stand and fall together. Because the offer of the Kingdom has been rejected, Jerusalem, which the Jews expected to be the capital of the redeemed world, and the temple, the only sanctuary of mankind, are to be forsaken by God and to become a desolation.

This idea is repeated in Luke 19:41-44. Jesus wept over Jerusalem because she did not recognize "the time of your visitation." In this word (*episkopē*) is reflected the prophetic idea of the God who comes to visit his people.[23] In this saying, God has graciously visited Jerusalem in the mission of Jesus to bring peace. The Kingdom of God had drawn near to Israel in grace and mercy. But Israel rejected the offer of mercy and chose the road that led to disaster.[24] The catastrophe is an historical visitation bringing death and destruction to the city.

We do not need to survey other sayings about the historical judgment that is to overtake Jerusalem (Lk. 21:20-24; 23:27-31) and the temple (Mk. 13:2; cf. 14:58; 15:29). Wilder is right when he says that Jesus can look at the future in two different ways. He can describe the coming visitation sometimes in terms of an imminent historical catastrophe and

---

20 F. V. Filson, *Matthew* (1960), p. 141; T. W. Manson, *Sayings*, p. 77.

21 Strack and Billerbeck, *Kommentar*, I, 943.

22 T. W. Manson, *Sayings*, p. 127.

23 *Episkopē* is used in the LXX in this sense in such passages as Isa. 10:3; 23:17; 24:22; 29:6.

24 T. W. Manson, *Sayings*, pp. 321f.

sometimes as an apocalyptic transcendental event.[25] Both the historical and the eschatological are divine visitations bringing upon Israel judgment for having rejected the Kingdom of God. God has once again become active in history. He has visited his people in the mission of Jesus to bring them the blessings of his Kingdom. But when the offer is spurned, a visitation of judgment will follow: both a judgment in history and an eschatological judgment at the end. Both are judgments of God's kingly rule.

[25] A. N. Wilder, *Eschatology and Ethics in the Teaching of Jesus* (1950), ch. 3.

7

THE MYSTERY OF THE KINGDOM

Literature:

C. H. Dodd, *The Parables of the Kingdom* (1936); W. O. E. Oesterley, *The Gospel Parables in the Light of Their Jewish Background* (1936); B. T. D. Smith, *The Parables of the Synoptic Gospels* (1937); A. E. Barnett, *Understanding the Parables of Our Lord* (1940); G. Bornkamm, "Mystērion," *TDNT* IV, 813-24; O. Piper, "The Mystery of the Kingdom of God," *Int* 1 (1947), 183-200; C. E. B. Cranfield, "St. Mark 4:1-34," *SJTh* 4 (1951), 398-414; 5 (1952), 49-66; N. A. Dahl, "The Parables of Growth," *StTh* 5 (1951), 132-66; A. M. Hunter, *Interpreting the Parables* (1960); M. Black, "The Parables as Allegory," *BJRL* 42 (1960), 273-87; H. N. Ridderbos, *The Coming of the Kingdom* (1963), pp. 121-35; R. Schnackenburg, *God's Rule and Kingdom* (1963), pp. 143-59; I. H. Marshall, *Eschatology and the Parables* (1963); J. Jeremias, *The Parables of the Kingdom* (1963; rev. ed.); G. E. Ladd, *Jesus and the Kingdom* (1964), pp. 214-38; D. O. Via, *The Parables* (1967); R. E. Brown, *The Semitic Background of the Term Mystery in the NT* (1968).

Our central thesis is that the Kingdom of God is the redemptive reign of God dynamically active to establish his rule among men, and that this Kingdom, which will appear as an apocalyptic act at the end of the age, has already come into human history in the person and mission of Jesus to overcome evil, to deliver men from its power, and to bring them into the blessings of God's reign. The Kingdom of God involves two great moments: fulfillment within history, and consummation at the end of history. It is precisely this background which provides the setting for the parables of the Kingdom.

CANONS OF INTERPRETATION. Modern critical study has posited two canons for interpreting the parables that are necessary for a correct historical understanding. The first of these was enunciated by Jülicher, who established the essential principle that parables must not be interpreted as though they were allegories.[1] An allegory is an artificial story created by the author as a teaching medium. Since the details of an allegory are under the control of the author, it can be structured so that every detail bears a distinct and important meaning. A simple allegory is the story of the thistle and the cedar in II Kings 14:9-10.

A parable is a story drawn from everyday life to convey a moral or religious truth. Because the author does not create his story and therefore does not have control over the details, they are often of little importance to the truth conveyed by the story. A parable is designed to convey essentially a single truth rather than a complex of truths.

This principle can be clearly demonstrated in the parable of the unjust steward (Lk. 16:1-13). If the details are pressed, this parable teaches that cleverness is better than honesty; but this is obviously impossible. Such details as *ninety-nine* sheep (Lk. 15:4) and *ten* coins (Lk. 15:8) carry no particular significance. In the parable of the Good Samaritan, the allegorical meaning of the robbers, the priest and the Levite, the significance of oil and wine, the reason for two coins, the meaning of Jerusalem, Jericho, and the hotel are no more to be sought than is the identity of the donkey. We must therefore seek in each of the parables of the Kingdom a central truth.

The second canon of criticism is that the parables must be understood in the historical life setting of Jesus' ministry and not in the life of the church. This means that it is not a sound historical approach to understand the parables as prophecies of the working of the gospel in the world or of the future of the church. Exegesis of the parables must be carried out in terms of Jesus' own mission in Palestine. This admission should not blind us to the fact that if analogies exist between Jesus' mission and the role of the word and the church in the world, important, even necessary, applications of the parables may be made to the later situation. However, we are here concerned to try to find the historical meaning of the parables in Jesus' ministry.

Jülicher's method was defective at this point because he found in the parables religious truths of general and universal application. Recent scholarship, especially the work of C. H. Dodd, has shown that the *Sitz im Leben* of the parables is Jesus' proclamation of the Kingdom of God. Jeremias considers this to be a breakthrough of historical criticism that introduced a new era in the interpretation of the parables.[2] However, he criticizes Dodd's one-sided emphasis which resulted in a contraction of eschatology, emptying it of its futuristic content. Jeremias proposes to correct Dodd's conclusions while accepting his method; and he attempts to discover the original message of the parables by recovering their primitive historical

---

[1] A. Jülicher, *Die Gleichnisreden Jesu* (1910).
[2] *The Parables of Jesus* (1963), p. 21.

form. Jeremias suggests "an eschatology in process of realization."[3] Jesus' mission inaugurated an eschatological process that he expected would shortly carry through to its eschatological consummation. The early church dissolved this single process into two events, and in so doing applied to the parousia parables that originally had a non-eschatological meaning.

However, Jeremias goes too far in taking as his main presupposition that the original meaning of the parables can be recovered only in terms of what they must have meant to Jesus' Jewish hearers. This assumes that the proper *Sitz im Leben* of the parables is Judaism, not the teachings of Jesus. This tends to limit the originality of Jesus. We must make allowance for the possibility that his teachings transcended Jewish ideas. Therefore the proper *Sitz im Leben* of the parables in Jesus' teachings, not Judaism.

THE MYSTERY OF THE KINGDOM. The parables as they stand are susceptible to an adequate historical interpretation in terms of the life setting of Jesus without the assumption of such a radical transformation as Jeremias assumes. The historical *Sitz im Leben* of the parables is summed up in the single word "mystery." Mark summarized the message of the Kingdom parables by reporting the words of Jesus to his disciples: "To you has been given the mystery of the kingdom of God, but for those outside everything is in parables; so that they may indeed see but not perceive, and may indeed hear but not understand; lest they turn again, and be forgiven" (Mk. 4:11-12). The mystery of the Kingdom is the coming of the Kingdom into history in advance of its apocalyptic manifestation. It is, in short, "fulfillment without consummation." This is the single truth illustrated by the several parables of Mark 4 and Matthew 13.[4]

While the word *mystērion* is found in the Old Testament in Daniel, the idea of God disclosing his secrets to men is a familiar Old Testament concept.[5] In Daniel is found the background of the New Testament use of the word. God granted a dream to the king that was meaningless to him and whose meaning could be recognized only by revelation through a vision given to Daniel, God's inspired servant. The dream had to do with the mystery of God's eschatological purpose.[6]

The concept of mystery (*raz*) also appears in the Qumran literature. To the Teacher of Righteousness, "God made known all the mysteries of the words of his servants the prophets."[7] This means that God has given special illumination to the Teacher of Righteousness to find in the prophetic Scrip-

---

[3] Jeremias' words are "sich realisierende Eschatologie." See *Die Gleichnisse Jesu* (1947), p. 114; *The Parables of Jesus,* p. 230.

[4] Mt. 13:11 and Lk. 8:10 speak of the "mysteries" of the Kingdom. Mark's wording suggests a single truth, the others a truth embodied in *several aspects.* Cf. O. Piper in *Int* I (1947), 183-200.

[5] R. E. Brown, *The Semitic Background of the Term "Mystery"* (1968), pp. 1-30.

[6] G. Bornkamm, *TDNT* IV, 814.

[7] Commentary on Habakkuk 7:1-5. The passages have been collected by E. Vogt in *Biblica,* XXXVII (1956), 247-57. See also R. E. Brown, *Semitic Background,* pp. 1-30; Ringgren, *The Faith of Qumran* (1963), pp. 60-67.

tures their true and hidden meaning. These mysteries have to do both with the events the Qumran community expected to occur in the end time[8] and with the "divine unfathomable unalterable" decisions of God.[9]

There is ample background for the idea of mystery in the Old Testament and in Jewish literature. While the term enters upon a new career in the New Testament, it is not altogether novel but further develops the idea found in Daniel. Paul understood "mysteries" to be revealed secrets, divine purposes hidden from men for long ages but finally disclosed by revelation to all men (Rom. 16:25-26). A mystery is not something esoteric, proclaimed only to the initiated. Mystery designates "the secret thoughts, plans, and dispensations of God which are hidden from the human reason, as well as from all other comprehensions below the divine level, and hence must be revealed to those for whom they are intended."[10] However, the mystery is proclaimed to all men even though it is understood only by those who believe. All men are summoned to faith; only those who respond really understand.

This interpretation of mystery reinforces the view of the Kingdom of God supported in this study. The mere fact that God proposes to bring in his Kingdom is no secret; practically every Jewish apocalyptic writing reflects that expectation in one form or another. Those who follow Schweitzer's Consistent Eschatology quite fail to do justice to this fact. That the Kingdom was to come in apocalyptic power was no secret; it was affirmed also by orthodox Jewish theology. The mystery is a new disclosure of God's purpose for the establishment of his Kingdom. The new truth, now given to men by revelation in the person and mission of Jesus, is that the Kingdom that is to come finally in apocalyptic power, as foreseen in Daniel, has in fact entered into the world in advance in a hidden form to work secretly within and among men.[11]

THE FOUR SOILS. The parable of the soils involves allegorical elements, but the authenticity of either the parable or the interpretation may not reasonably be rejected for this reason. There is no *a priori* ground for assuming that Jesus could not have employed allegorical parables.[12] However, this is not a true allegory, for the details are quite secondary to the central teaching of the parable. There are four kinds of soil, only one of which is fruitful. The message of the parable would not be affected in the least if there were only two kinds of soil, or if there were three, or six. Neither

---

[8] See F. F. Bruce, *Biblical Exegesis in the Qumran Texts* (1959), pp. 16, 66f.

[9] J. Licht, *Israel Exploration Journal,* VI (1956), 7-8.

[10] Arndt and Gingrich, *A Greek-English Lexicon* (1957), p. 532.

[11] Essentially this view is held by Flew, Cranfield, Piper, and W. Manson (*Jesus the Messiah* [1946], p. 60). N. A. Dahl (*StTh* V [1952], 156f.) finds this truth in the parables but discounts the validity of Mk. 4:11. J. Jeremias, *Parables,* p. 16: "a particular revelation, namely, the recognition of its present irruption." For the problem in Mk. 4:12, see *Jesus and the Kingdom,* pp. 222ff.

[12] Cf. C. E. B. Cranfield, *SJTh* IV (1951), 405-12, for a detailed study of the authenticity of the parable.

would the message be affected if the three unfruitful soils were unfruitful for entirely different reasons than those illustrated. Some seed might be washed away by an unseasonable cloudburst. Tender shoots of grain might be crushed under the feet of a careless passer-by. Some seeds might be devoured by rodents. Such details would not affect the central message: the Kingdom of God has come into the world to be received by some but rejected by others. The Kingdom is in the present to have only partial success, and this success is dependent on a human response.

While the parable may have an application to the gospel in the world during the church age as older interpreters thought,[13] this is not its historical meaning. The *Sitz im Leben* of the parable is Jesus' announcement that the Kingdom of God had come among men. The Jews thought that the coming of the Kingdom would mean the exercise of God's mighty power before which no man could stand. The Kingdom of God would shatter the godless nations (Dan. 2:44). The dominion of wicked rulers would be destroyed and the Kingdom be given to the saints of the Most High, that all nations should serve and obey them (Dan. 7:27). In apparent disagreement with the Old Testament promises, which were elaborated in great detail in the contemporary apocalyptic expectations, Jesus said that the Kingdom had indeed come upon men, but not for the purpose of shattering evil. It is now attended by no apocalyptic display of irresistible power. Rather, the Kingdom in its present working is like a farmer sowing seed. It does not sweep away the wicked. In fact, the word in which the Kingdom is proclaimed may lie like seed on the roadside and never take root; or it may be superficially received only to die; or it may be choked by the cares of the age, which is hostile to the Kingdom of God.

The Kingdom is working quietly, secretly among men. It does not force itself upon them; it must be willingly received. But wherever it is received, the word of the Kingdom, which is practically identical with the Kingdom itself,[14] brings forth much fruit. There is no emphasis upon the harvest, either in the parable or in its interpetation. The single emphasis is upon the nature of the sowing: the present action of God's Kingdom.

THE TARES. The parable of the tares further illustrates the mystery of the Kingdom, i.e., its hidden, unexpected presence in the world. At the outset we should note that there are details in the parable that do not bear any meaning in its interpretation. The identity of the servants is utterly irrelevant. The fact that the enemy goes away after sowing seeds is unimportant. The bundles into which the weeds are gathered is entirely local color. Similarly, the sleeping of the servants does not suggest negligence. This is only what workmen did after a hard day. In the same manner,

---

[13] See the standard studies by Trench, A. B. Bruce, M. Dods. See also A. Plummer, *Mark* (1914), p. 125; N. Geldenhuys, *Luke* (1950), pp. 240f.

[14] For the presence of the Kingdom in Jesus' words, see G. E. Ladd, *Jesus and the Kingdom,* pp. 160ff.

nothing is to be made of the fact that the tares are gathered first before the gathering of the wheat.

The interpretation of the parable that dominated the older Protestant scholarship sees an identification of the Kingdom with the church. The parable describes the state of things that is to exist in the Kingdom-church. When the Son of Man comes, he will gather out of his Kingdom all causes of offense and all evildoers (Mt. 13:41). This shows that the church contains both good men and evil, and that the Kingdom exists in the world as the church before the final consummation.[15] However, the parable says that the field is the world (v. 38), not the church.

The coming of the Kingdom, as predicted in the Old Testament and in Jewish apocalyptic literature, would bring about the end of the age and inaugurate the Age to Come, disrupting human society by the destruction of the unrighteous. Jesus affirms that in the midst of the present age, while society continues with its intermixture of the good and the bad, before the coming of the Son of Man and the glorious manifestation of the Kingdom of God, the powers of that future age have entered into the world to create "sons of the kingdom," men who enjoy its power and blessings. The Kingdom has come, but society is not uprooted. This is the mystery of the Kingdom.

The only real difficulty for this interpretation is the expression, "they [the angels] will gather out of his kingdom all causes of sin and all evildoers" (Mt. 13:41). This language appears to distinguish between the Kingdom of the Son and the Kingdom of the Father. Does this not plainly indicate that the wicked are already in the Kingdom (perhaps in the church) before the eschatological consummation? Granted that at first sight such an interpretation suggests itself, it is by no means the only interpretation, nor is it a compelling one. There is no adequate warrant, from either the Gospels or the rest of the New Testament, to distinguish between the Kingdom of the Son of Man and the Kingdom of God.[16] Furthermore, there are no sayings of Jesus where the Kingdom is clearly identified with the church; and such an identification ought not to be made here unless it is unavoidable.

Neither the parable nor its interpretation requires this identification. The language of Matthew 13:41 cannot be pressed to mean that the evildoers who will be gathered "out of his kingdom" have actually been in the Kingdom. It means no more than that they will be separated from the righ-

---

[15] Cf. N. B. Stonehouse, *The Witness of Matthew and Mark to Christ* (1944), p. 238. A similar view will be found in B. F. C. Atkinson in *The New Bible Commentary* (F. Davidson *et al.*, eds., 1953), p. 790; and in the studies on the parables by A. B. Bruce, R. C. Trench, S. Goebel, and H. B. Swete.

[16] O. Cullmann in *Christ and Time* (1950), p. 151, and in *The Early Church* (A. J. B. Higgins, ed., 1956), pp. 109ff., attempts to distinguish between the Kingdom of Christ and the Kingdom of God. This may be a valid theological distinction, but it cannot be exegetically supported. See Eph. 5:5; Rev. 11:15; Jn. 3:5; Col. 1:13.

teous so that they do not enter the Kingdom. This is supported by Matthew 8:12 where strangers will come from afar to enter the Kingdom of Heaven along with the patriarchs, while "the sons of the kingdom will be thrown into the outer darkness." The Greek word, "will be cast out," indicates that the Jews who by history and covenant were "sons of the kingdom" will be excluded from entering the Kingdom, not rejected after having once entered. So the statement that the evil are to be gathered "out of his kingdom" means no more than that they will be prevented from entering it.

The meaning of the parable is clear when interpreted in terms of the mystery of the Kingdom: its present but secret working in the world. The Kingdom has come into history but in such a way that society is not disrupted. The sons of the Kingdom have received God's reign and entered into its blessings. Yet they must continue to live in this age, intermingled with the wicked in a mixed society. Only at the eschatological coming of the Kingdom will the separation take place. Here is indeed the revelation of a new truth: that the Kingdom of God can actually come into the world, creating sons who enjoy its blessings without effecting the eschatological judgment. However, this separation is sure to come. The Kingdom that is present but hidden in the world will yet be manifested in glory. Then there will be an end of the mixed society. The wicked will be gathered out and the righteous will shine like the sun in the eschatological Kingdom.

THE MUSTARD SEED. The parable of the mustard seed illustrates the truth that the Kingdom, which one day will be a great tree, is already present in the world in a tiny, insignificant form. Many interpreters have seen in the parable a forecast of the growth of the church into a great institution.[17] This interpretation is based on the identification of the Kingdom and the church,[18] a view that we hold to be untenable. Other interpreters, without applying the parable to the church, find its meaning in the growth of the circle of Jesus' disciples,[19] who may be considered to be the new community.[20] However, the quick-growing mustard plant is not an apt illustration of slow, gradual growth, if that is what was intended. An oak growing from an acorn would provide a much better illustration of this truth (Amos 2:9).

The majority of modern exegetes see the emphasis of the parable in the

---

[17] Cf. Trench, Goebel, and H. B. Swete on the parables; cf. also N. Geldenhuys, *Luke,* p. 377; and B. F. C. Atkinson, *The New Bible Commentary* (F. Davidson *et al.,* eds., 1953), p. 790; H. Balmforth, *Luke* (1930), p. 227.

[18] Other interpreters who would deny that Jesus foresaw the church believe that this is in fact what the parable taught, and therefore the parable cannot be authentic. Cf. C. G. Montefiore, *The Synoptic Gospels* (1927), I, 107-8.

[19] Cf. C. J. Cadoux, *The Historic Mission of Jesus* (n.d.), pp. 113-14, 131; T. W. Manson, *The Teaching of Jesus* (1935), p. 113.

[20] R. N. Flew, *Jesus and His Church* (1943), pp. 27f.

contrast between the tiny beginning and the large end,[21] and this certainly lies at the heart of the parable. The mustard seed, while not actually the smallest seed known, was a proverbial illustration of smallness.[22] The burning question faced by Jesus' disciples was how the Kingdom of God could actually be present in such an insignificant movement as that embodied in his ministry. The Jews expected the Kingdom to be like a great tree under which the nations would find shelter. They could not understand how one could talk about the Kingdom apart from such an all-encompassing manifestation of God's rule. How could the coming glorious Kingdom have anything to do with the poor little band of Jesus' disciples? Rejected by the religious leaders, welcomed by tax collectors and sinners, Jesus looked more like a deluded dreamer than the bearer of the Kingdom of God.

Jesus' answer is, first the tiny seed, later the large tree. The smallness and relative insignificance of what is happening in his ministry does not exclude the secret presence of the very Kingdom of God.[23]

THE LEAVEN. The parable of the leaven[24] embodies the same basic truth as that of the mustard: that the Kingdom of God, which one day will rule over all the earth, has entered into the world in a form that is hardly perceptible.

This parable is of particular interest because it has been used to prove diametrically different things. Many interpreters have found the central truth in the slow but persistent process of permeation and penetration. The parable is thought to show how the Kingdom grows. On the one hand are those who find the truth that the Kingdom of God is destined to permeate all human society until all the world is transformed by a process of slow, gradual penetration and inner permeation.[25] Some of these interpreters contrast the leavening character of the Kingdom with the apocalyptic view, to the detriment of the latter.

On the other hand is the interpretation of so-called Dispensationalism, which interprets leaven as evil doctrine permeating an apostate Christian church.[26] However, leaven in Hebrew and Jewish thought was not always a symbol of evil,[27] and the concept of the Kingdom as a transforming

---

[21] Cf. W. G. Kümmel, *Promise and Fulfilment* (1957), p. 131; A. E. Barnett, *Understanding the Parables of Our Lord* (1940), pp. 55-57; B. T. D. Smith, *The Parables of the Synoptic Gospels* (1937), pp. 120-21.

[22] Cf. Mt. 17:20; Lk. 17:6.

[23] N. A. Dahl, *StTh* V (1952), pp. 147-48; Jeremias, *The Parables of Jesus,* p. 148.

[24] This parable is missing in Mark, but it appears in Lk. 13:20 alongside the parable of the mustard seed.

[25] W. O. E. Oesterley, *The Gospel Parables in the Light of Their Jewish Background* (1936), p. 78; R. Otto, *The Kingdom of God and the Son of Man* (1943), p. 125; W. Manson, *The Gospel of Luke* (1930), p. 166.

[26] *The Scofield Reference Bible* (1967), p. 1015; J. D. Pentecost, *Things to Come* (1958), p. 147.

[27] Unleavened bread was prepared at the time of the Exodus because it symbolized haste (Exod. 12:11, 39; Deut. 16:3; cf. also Gen. 18:6; 19:3); leavened bread was sacrificed at the Feast of Weeks (Lev. 23:17), elsewhere called the Feast

power by slow, gradual penetration may be an attractive idea in a world familiar with concepts of progress and evolution, but it is foreign both to Jesus' mind and to Jewish thought.

The interpretation that suits the historical setting of Jesus' ministry is that which sees the central truth to lie in the contrast between the absurdly small bit of leaven and the great mass of more than a bushel of meal.[28] It is true that emphasis is placed on the fact that the entire mass of dough is leavened, not on the small size of the leaven.[29] Here is the difference between this parable and the parable of the mustard seed. The latter teaches that the manifestation of the Kingdom, which will become like a great tree, is now like a tiny seed. The leaven teaches that the Kingdom will one day prevail so that no rival sovereignty exists. The entire mass of dough becomes leaven.

This parable gains its significance only when interpreted in the life setting of Jesus' ministry. The mighty, irresistible character of the eschatological Kingdom was understood by all Jews. The coming of the Kingdom would mean a complete change in the order of things. The present evil order of the world and of society would be utterly displaced by the Kingdom of God. The problem was that Jesus' ministry initiated no such transformation. He preached the presence of the Kingdom of God, but the world went on as before. How then could this be the Kingdom?

Jesus' reply is that when a bit of leaven is put in a mass of meal, nothing seems to happen. In fact, the leaven seems quite engulfed by the meal. Eventually something does happen, and the result is the complete transformation of the dough.[30] No emphasis is to be placed upon the way the transformation is accomplished. The idea of the Kingdom of God conquering the world by a gradual permeation and inner transformation was utterly foreign to Jewish thought. If this was Jesus' meaning, he certainly must have reiterated the truth again and again, even as he did the unheard-of truth that the Son of Man must die. The idea of gradualness is contradicted by the parables of the tares and the dragnet where the Kingdom comes by apocalyptic judgment and separation of evil rather than by its gradual transformation of the world.

The emphasis of the parable lies in the contrast between the final, complete victory of the Kingdom when the new order comes, and the present, hidden form of that Kingdom as it has now come into the world. One would never guess Jesus and his small band of disciples had anything to

---

of Harvest, and First Fruits (Exod. 23:16), because it represented the ordinary daily food that God provided for human sustenance. See O. T. Allis, *EQ* XIX (1947), 269ff. I. Abrahams (*Studies in Pharisaism and the Gospel* [First Series, 1917], pp. 51-53) shows that leaven did not always symbolize evil in rabbinic thought.

[28] J. Jeremias, *The Parables of Jesus,* p. 147; W. G. Kümmel, *Promise and Fulfilment,* pp. 131f.; A. H. McNeile, *Matthew* (1915), p. 199; A. E. Barnett, *Understanding the Parables of Our Lord,* pp. 58-60.

[29] H. Windisch, *TDNT* II, 905.

[30] Cf. N. A. Dahl, *StTh* V (1952), 148-49.

do with the future, glorious Kingdom of God. However, that which is now present in the world is indeed the Kingdom itself. This is the mystery, the new truth about the Kingdom. How or when the future Kingdom will come is no part of the parable.

THE TREASURE AND THE PEARL. We need not tarry long over the parables of the treasure and the pearl. The identity of the man or of the field, as well as the contrast between the accidental discovery of the treasure and the purposeful search of the merchant, is not part of the message of the parables but only local color. We must admit that the conduct of the man who found the treasure involved a bit of sharp practice, but this belongs to the lifelike character of the parabolic form. People did things like this. Nor can any objection be made to the fact that in both parables the treasure and the pearl are acquired by purchase.[31]

The one thought in both parables is that the Kingdom of God is of inestimable value and is to be sought above all other possessions. If it costs a man everything he has, that is a small price in return for gaining the Kingdom. Thus stated, however, it is a truism. If there is no "mystery" of the Kingdom, Jesus here said no more than devout Jews believed already. They longed for the Kingdom of God. What gives these parables their point is the fact that the Kingdom had come among men in an unexpected way, in a form that might easily be overlooked and despised. To accept the "yoke of the Kingdom" and join the circle of the Pharisees in their utter devotion to the Law gave one great prestige in the eyes of the Jews.[32] The offer to lead an insurrection against Rome to establish the Kingdom could arouse an enthusiastic response.[33] But to follow Jesus meant association with tax collectors and sinners. How could such an association have anything to do with the Kingdom of God?

These parables gain their central point from the fact that, contrary to every superficial evaluation, discipleship to Jesus means participation in the Kingdom of God. Present in the person and work of Jesus without outward display or visible glory was the Kingdom of God itself. It is therefore a treasure worth more than all other possessions, a pearl exceeding all else in value. Men should seek to gain possession of it at any cost.

THE NET. In the final parable illustrating the mystery of the Kingdom, a net is dragged through the sea catching all kinds of fish. When the catch is sorted out, the good fish are kept and the bad discarded.

The older interpretation saw in this parable a prophecy of the church. The Kingdom-church is to consist of a mixture of good and bad people

---

31 G. C. Morgan permitted this feature to determine his interpretation. This is a complete misunderstanding of the parabolic method (*The Parables of the Kingdom* [1907], p. 136).

32 Cf. Josephus, *Antiquities* XIII, 10.6.

33 See Acts 5:36-37; 21:38; Jn. 6:15; T. W. Manson, *The Servant-Messiah* (1953), p. 8.

who must be separated in the day of judgment.[34] Other interpreters, while not insisting upon the church, see in the parable an identification of the Kingdom of God with a society of people that includes the good and the bad.[35] This view has the weakness of failing to give due recognition to the historical setting of the parable in Jesus' ministry, and it involves an identification of the Kingdom with the church, for which clear exegetical support cannot be found.

This parable is similar to that of the wheat and the weeds, but it adds another element. Both parables must be understood in terms of the life setting of Jesus' ministry, that the Kingdom has now come into the world without effecting this eschatological separation and is to work in a mixed society. The parable of the net adds this fact—that even the community created by the working of the Kingdom in the world is not to be a pure community until the eschatological separation.

Historically, the parable answers the question of the strange character of Jesus' followers. He attracted tax collectors and sinners. In the popular expectation, the coming of the Kingdom would mean not only that the Messiah would "destroy the godless nations with the words of his mouth; . . . and . . . reprove sinners for the thoughts of their hearts"; he would also "gather together a holy people whom he shall lead in righteousness," "and there shall be no unrighteousness in his days in their midst, for all shall be holy" (Ps. Sol. 17:28, 36). Jesus did not gather together such a holy people. On the contrary, he said, "I came not to call the righteous, but sinners" (Mk. 2:17). The invitation to the messianic feast was rejected by those who were invited and their places taken by loiterers in the streets (Mt. 22:1-10). How could the Kingdom of God have anything to do with such a strange fellowship? Is not the function of the Kingdom by definition to destroy all sinners and to create a sinless community?

Jesus answers that the Kingdom will indeed one day create such a perfect community. But before this event an unexpected manifestation of God's Kingdom has occurred that is like a net gathering both good and bad fish. The invitation goes out to all kinds of men, and all who respond are accepted into present discipleship in the Kingdom. The perfect, holy community must await the last day.[36] While the parable has an application to the church which, as a later development of Jesus' disciples, is indeed a mixed people, its primary application is to the actual situation in Jesus' ministry.

---

[34] Cf. Trench, Goebel, and Swete on the parables. In more recent writings, a similar view appears in B. F. C. Atkinson, *The New Bible Commentary* (F. Davidson *et al.*, eds., 1953), p. 790; N. B. Stonehouse, *The Witness of Matthew and Mark to Christ,* p. 238; H. Martin, *The Parables of the Gospels* (1937), p. 79.

[35] W. O. E. Oesterley, *The Gospel Parables in the Light of Their Jewish Background,* p. 85: "Bad as well as good elements must exist in the kingdom during the period of its development." C. J. Cadoux, *The Historic Mission of Jesus,* emphasizes that here the Kingdom is clearly likened to a society (p. 114).

[36] See N. A. Dahl, *StTh* V (1952), 150-51.

THE SEED GROWING BY ITSELF. Mark records a parable omitted by the other evangelists that illustrates the supernatural character of the Kingdom of God (Mk. 4:26-29). We must be reminded that the parables are not allegories and that the details of the parables are not essential to their central message. The identity of the sower and the reaper should not constitute a problem, for the message of the parable has to do with the activity of the Kingdom and not with the identity of the sower. That a man sows seed means no more than that seed is sown. The sleeping and rising of the sower mean only that man cannot contribute to the life and growth of the seed. The element of growth has often been made the central truth in the parable, and great significance has been seen in the stages of growth: the blade, the ear, and finally the full grain. This has been taken to illustrate the analogy between the natural world and the Kingdom of God. Just as there are laws of growth resident within nature, so there are laws of spiritual growth through which the Kingdom must pass until the tiny seed of the gospel has brought forth a great harvest. The interpretation of gradual growth has been espoused by representatives of many theological positions.[37]

However, three facts oppose this interpretation. In his nonparabolic teachings, Jesus nowhere set forth the idea of gradualness and growth of the Kingdom. If this were an essential element in his teaching, he must have made it clear, since the gradual growth of God's Kingdom was an utterly novel idea to first-century Jews. Second, the concept of sowing and planting is frequently found in Christian and Jewish literature but is never used to illustrate gradualness and development.[38] Third, the metaphor of sowing and reaping is used in Christian literature to illustrate the supernatural.[39]

The clue to the meaning of the parable was discovered by the eschatological school, although we feel that the consistent eschatological interpretation must be modified to fit the total context of Jesus' message. The Kingdom is seen as the eschatological event, which is utterly independent of all human effort. J. Weiss felt the parable taught that Jesus had nothing to do with the coming of the Kingdom. He could not foresee it; only God could bring it. Man can do nothing but wait.[40] Many other interpreters have found the truth of the parable in the utter independence of the future eschatological harvest of all human activity.[41]

---

37 A. B. Bruce, *The Parabolic Teaching of Christ* (1882), pp. 117ff.; H. B. Swete, *The Parables of the Kingdom* (1920), pp. 16ff.; W. O. E. Oesterley, *The Gospel Parables,* p. 71; J. Orr, *HDB* II, 852-54; C. J. Cadoux, *The Historic Mission of Jesus,* pp. 113-14; T. W. Manson, *The Teaching of Jesus,* p. 133; G. C. Morgan, *The Parables and Metaphors of Our Lord* (1943), pp. 145ff.

38 See N. A. Dahl, *StTh* V (1952), 140-47, for references.

39 See I Cor. 15:35ff.; II Cor. 9:6; Gal. 6:7-8; I Clement 24. Clement uses the phenomenon of growth in nature as a proof of the resurrection, which is altogether supernatural.

40 J. Weiss, *Die Schriften des NT* (4th ed., 1929), I, 115f.

41 Cf. W. G. Kümmel, *Promise and Fulfilment,* pp. 128f.; B. T. D. Smith, *The Parables of the Synoptic Gospels,* pp. 129ff.; M. Dibelius, *Jesus* (1949), pp. 66-67.

This is certainly an indispensable truth about the Kingdom. However, this interpretation is as one-sided as that of Realized Eschatology, for it neglects the central and unique element in Jesus' message—the presence of the Kingdom in his own mission. It fails therefore to relate Jesus' ministry to the eschatological coming of the Kingdom except as an advance announcement. The most obvious difficulty with a strictly futuristic interpretation is that it is colorless; no Jew needed to be told that the eschatological consummation of the Kingdom was a miracle. It could be nothing but a supernatural act of God.

It is not allegorizing to insist that there is in the parable a necessary relationship between sowing and harvest. In some sense or other, the ministry of Jesus involved the "seed" of the Kingdom that would one day come in fullness of harvest. The seed was being sown; a harvest would one day come. Both are manifestations of God's Kingdom. "The present hiddenness and ambiguousness of the Kingdom of God [will] be succeeded by its glorious manifestation."[42]

Here is the central truth of the parable. Seedtime and harvest: both are the work of God. Both are essentially supernatural. The earth bears fruit of itself. The seed has resident within it powers that man does not place there and which utterly transcend anything he can do. Man can sow the seed, but the Kingdom itself is God's deed.

The supernatural character of the present Kingdom is confirmed by the words found in association with it. A number of verbs are used with the Kingdom itself as the subject. The Kingdom can draw near to men (Mt. 3:2; 4:17; Mk. 1:15; etc.); it can come (Mt. 6:10; Lk. 17:20; etc.), arrive (Mt. 12:28), appear (Lk. 19:11), be active (Mt. 11:12). God can give the Kingdom to men (Mt. 21:43; Lk. 12:32), but men do not give the Kingdom to one another. Furthermore, God can take the Kingdom away from men (Mt. 21:43), but men do not take it away from one another, although they can prevent others from entering it. Men can enter the Kingdom (Mt. 5:20; 7:21; Mk. 9:47; 10:23; etc.), but they are never said to erect it or to build it. Men can receive the Kingdom (Mk. 10:15; Lk. 18:17), inherit it (Mt. 25:34), and possess it (Mt. 5:4), but they are never to establish it. Men can reject the Kingdom, i.e., refuse to receive it (Lk. 10:11) or enter it (Mt. 23:13), but they cannot destroy it. They can look for it (Lk. 23:51), pray for its coming (Mt. 6:10), and seek it (Mt. 6:33; Lk. 12:31), but they cannot bring it. Men may be in the Kingdom (Mt. 5:19; 8:11; Lk. 13:29; etc.), but we are not told that the Kingdom grows. Men can do things for the sake of the Kingdom (Mt. 19:12; Lk. 18:29), but they are not said to act upon the Kingdom itself. Men can preach the Kingdom (Mt. 10:7; Lk. 10:9), but only God can give it to men (Lk. 12:32).

The character of the Kingdom reflected in these expressions is summed up in a saying preserved in John's Gospel: "My *basileia* is not of this world;

[42] C. E. B. Cranfield, *Mark* (1959), p. 168.

if my *basileia* were of this world, my servants would fight, that I might not be handed over to the Jews; but my kingdom is not from the world" (Jn. 18:36). The RSV is correct in translating *basileia* "kingship." The source and the character of Jesus' Kingdom are of a higher order than this world; it comes from God and not from this world. The Kingdom is the outworking of the divine will; it is the act of God himself. It is related to men and can work in and through men; but it never becomes subject to men. It remains God's Kingdom. It is significant that although men must receive the Kingdom, this individual human act of reception is not described as a coming of the Kingdom. The Kingdom does not come as men receive it. The ground of the demand that men receive the Kingdom rests in the fact that in Jesus the Kingdom has come into history. God has done a new thing. He has visited his people in Jesus' mission, bringing to them the messianic salvation. The divine act requires a human response even though it remains a divine act.

8

THE KINGDOM AND THE CHURCH

Literature:

G. Vos, *The Teaching of Jesus Concerning the Kingdom of God and the Church* (1903); K. L. Schmidt, "Ekklēsia," *TDNT* III, 501-36; K. Rengstorf, "Mathētēs," *TDNT* IV (1942), 415-61; J. W. Bowman, *The Intention of Jesus* (1943); G. Johnston, *The Church in the NT* (1943), pp. 46-58; R. N. Flew, *Jesus and His Church* (1943), pp. 17-99; A. R. George, "The Doctrine of the Church," *ET* 58 (1946-47), 312-16; G. Lindeskog, "The Kingdom of God and the Church," *This Is the Church*, ed. by A. Nygren (1950), pp. 136-47; K. E. Skydsgaard, "Kingdom of God and Church," *SJTh* 4 (1951), 383-97; O. Cullmann, *Peter: Disciple-Apostle-Martyr* (1953); S. M. Gilmour, "The Kingdom and the Church," *Int* 7 (1953), 26-33; D. H. Wallace, "An Exegesis of Matthew 16:13-20," *Foundations,* 5 (1962), 217-25; L. E. Keck, "An Exegesis of Matthew 16:13-20," *Foundations,* 5 (1962), 226-37; R. O. Zorn, *Church and Kingdom* (1962); H. Ridderbos, *The Coming of the Kingdom* (1963), pp. 334-96; R. Schnackenburg, *God's Rule and Kingdom* (1963), pp. 215-48; G. E. Ladd, *Jesus and the Kingdom* (1964), pp. 239-73; D. M. Stanley, "Kingdom to Church" in *The Apostolic Church in the NT* (1967), pp. 5-37; R. P. Meye, *Jesus and the Twelve* (1968).

One of the most difficult questions in the study of the Kingdom of God is its relationship to the church. Is the Kingdom of God in any sense of the word to be identified with the church? If not, what is the relationship? For Christians of the first three centuries, the Kingdom was altogether eschatological. An early second-century prayer says, "Remember, Lord, Thy church, to . . . gather it together in its holiness from the four winds to thy kingdom which thou hast prepared for it."[1] Augustine identified the Kingdom of God with the church,[2] an identification that continues in

[1] *Didachē* 10:5. See A. von Harnack, "Millennium," *Encyclopedia Britannica* (9th ed.), XVI, 328-29; D. H. Kromminga, *The Millennium in the Church* (1945).

[2] *City of God,* XX, 6-10.

Catholic doctrine,[3] although Schnackenburg claims that the new Catholic concept conceives of the Kingdom in *heilsgeschichtlichen* terms as the redemptive working of God through the church.[4] A measure of identification between the Kingdom and the church was perpetuated, though in a modified form, through the Reformed tradition[5] to recent times.[6] It is necessary to examine closely these two concepts to determine what relationship exists between them.

Many scholars have denied that Jesus had any idea of creating a church. Alfred Loisy has given this viewpoint classic expression: Jesus foretold the Kingdom of God, but it was the church that came.[7]

Amazingly, a view somewhat similar to this is that of Dispensationalism: Jesus offered Israel the earthly (millennial) Davidic kingdom, but when they rejected it, he introduced a new purpose: to form the church.[8] In this view, there is no continuity between Israel and the church. We must therefore examine many facets of the problem.

If Jesus' mission was, as we contend, that of inaugurating a time of fulfillment in advance of an eschatological consummation, and if in a real sense the Kingdom of God in his mission invaded history even though in an utterly unexpected form, then it follows that those who receive the proclamation of the Kingdom were viewed not only as the people who would inherit the eschatological Kingdom, but as the people of the Kingdom in the present, and therefore, in some sense of the word, a church. We must first examine Jesus' attitude toward Israel, the concept of discipleship, and the relation of Israel and Jesus' disciples to the Kingdom of God. Then, against this background, we may discuss the meaning of the logion about founding the church.

JESUS AND ISRAEL. In this examination, several facts are crucial. First, Jesus did not undertake his ministry with the evident purpose of starting a new movement either within or outside of Israel. He came as a Jew to the Jewish people. He accepted the authority of the Old Testament, conformed to temple practices, engaged in synagogue worship, and throughout his life lived as a Jew. Although he occasionally journeyed outside Jewish territory, he insisted that his mission was directed to the "lost sheep of the house of Israel" (Mt. 15:24). He directed the mission of his disciples away from the Gentiles, commanding them to preach only to Israel (Mt. 10:5-6). The reason for this is not difficult. Jesus took his stand squarely against the background of the Old Testament covenant and the promises of the prophets, and recognized Israel, to whom the covenant and the promises

---

[3] D. M. Stanley in *Theological Studies,* X (1955), 1-29.

[4] *God's Rule and Kingdom* (1963), pp. 116f.

[5] See Calvin on Mt. 13:47-50.

[6] See J. Orr, *The Christian View of God and the World* (1897), p. 358; H. B. Swete, *The Parables of the Kingdom* (1920), pp. 31, 56.

[7] A. Loisy, *The Gospel and the Church* (1908), p. 166.

[8] See above, p. 25.

had been given, as the natural "sons of the kingdom" (Mt. 8:12). The saying about the lost sheep of the house of Israel does not mean that the Gentiles were not also lost but that only Israel was the people of God, and to them therefore belonged the promise of the Kingdom. Therefore his mission was to proclaim to Israel that God was now acting to fulfill his promises and to bring Israel to its true destiny. Because Israel was the chosen people of God, the age of fulfillment was offered not to the world at large but to the sons of the covenant.

The second fact is that Israel as a whole rejected both Jesus and his message about the Kingdom. It is true that Jesus appealed to Israel to the very end, but it is most unlikely that he expected, to the end, to be accepted by the nation and to establish a kingdom of morality and righteousness that would have led the Jewish people to a moral conquest over Rome.[9] The reality of Jesus' disappointment and grief over Israel's rejection (Mt. 23:37ff.) and the prophecy of her destruction (Lk. 19:42ff.) do not demand the conclusion that Jesus failed to recognize at an early hour the reality and intransigence of her rejection.[10] While we may not be able to reconstruct the exact chronology of events or to trace all the stages in Jesus' rejection because of the character of the Gospels, we can conclude that rejection is one of the early motifs in his experience. Luke deliberately placed the rejection at Nazareth at the beginning of his Gospel (Lk. 4:16-30; cf. Mk. 6:1-6) to sound the notes of messianic fulfillment and rejection by Israel early in Jesus' ministry.[11] Mark pictures conflict and rejection from the beginning and records a saying that probably contains a veiled allusion to an expected violent end: "The days will come when the bridegroom is taken away from them" (Mk. 2:20). While the reasons for Jewish rejection of Jesus were complex, J. M. Robinson finds at the heart of the struggle between Jesus and the Jewish authorities their rejection of the Kingdom that Jesus proclaimed and of the repentance that proclamation demanded.[12] The proclamation of the Kingdom and the call to repentance characterized Jesus' mission from the start, and it is therefore both psychologically and historically sound that opposition was early incurred, which grew in intensity until Jesus' death was accomplished.

A third fact is equally important. While Israel as a whole, including both leaders and people, refused to accept Jesus' offer of the Kingdom, a substantial group did respond in faith. Discipleship to Jesus was not like discipleship to a Jewish rabbi. The rabbis bound their disciples not to themselves but to the Torah; Jesus bound his disciples to himself. The rabbis offered something outside of themselves; Jesus offered himself alone. Jesus required his disciples to surrender without reservation to his author-

---

[9] This is the thesis of R. Dunkerley, *The Hope of Jesus* (1953).

[10] A. M. Hunter, *The Works and Words of Jesus* (1950), p. 94.

[11] N. B. Stonehouse, *The Witness of Luke to Christ* (1951), pp. 70-76; N. Geldenhuys, *Luke* (1950), p. 170.

[12] *The Problem of History in Mark* (1957), p. 49. See also V. Taylor, *The Life and Ministry of Jesus* (1954), p. 89.

ity. They thereby became not only disciples but also *douloi,* slaves (Mt. 10:24f.; 24:45ff.; Lk. 12:35ff., 42ff.). This relationship had no parallel in Judaism.[13] Discipleship to Jesus involved far more than following in his retinue; it meant nothing less than complete personal commitment to him and his message. The reason for this is the presence of the Kingdom of God in Jesus' person and message. In him, men were confronted by God himself.

It follows that if Jesus proclaimed the messianic salvation, if he offered to Israel the fulfillment of her true destiny, then this destiny was actually accomplished in those who received his message. The recipients of the messianic salvation became the true Israel, representatives of the nation as a whole. While it is true that the word "Israel" is never applied to Jesus' disciples, the idea is present, if not the term. Jesus' disciples are the recipients of the messianic salvation, the people of the Kingdom, the true Israel.

THE BELIEVING REMNANT. This concept of Jesus' disciples as the true Israel can be understood against the background of the Old Testament concept of a faithful remnant. The prophets saw Israel as a whole as rebellious and disobedient and therefore destined to suffer the divine judgment. Still there remained within the faithless nation a remnant of believers who were the object of God's care. Here in the believing remnant was the true people of God.

It is true that Jesus makes no explicit use of the remnant concept. However, is not the designation of the disciples as a "little flock" (Lk. 12:32) an express reference to the Old Testament concept of Israel as the sheep of God's pasture, now embodied in Jesus' disciples (Isa. 40:11)? Does this not suggest precisely the faithful remnant? This does not mean a separate fold.[14] Israel is still ideally God's flock (Mt. 10:6; 15:24); but it is a disobedient, willful flock, "lost sheep." Jesus has come as the shepherd (Mk. 14:27; cf. Jn. 10:11) to "seek and to save the lost" (Lk. 19:10) in fulfillment of Ezekiel 34:15f., to rescue the lost sheep of Israel, to bring them into the fold of the messianic salvation. Israel as a whole was deaf to the voice of her shepherd; but those who heard and followed the shepherd constitute his fold, the little flock, the true Israel. There are direct and explicit links between the image of the flock and the covenant community of Israel.[15]

While the saying in Luke 12:32 emphasizes the eschatological aspect of the Kingdom, Jesus' disciples will inherit the Kingdom because they are

---

[13] K. H. Rengstorf, *TDNT* IV, 447.

[14] Jeremias is right in his insistence that Jesus refused to gather a separate remnant but extended the call to salvation to all Israel (*ZNTW* XLII [1949], 184-94). However, the prophets often think of a faithful remnant within the unfaithful nation, not separated from it. Campbell has pointed out that the remnant in the Old Testament is never identified with any special group or class, such as the Rechabites (J. C. Campbell, *SJTh* III [1950], 79). See Jer. 5:1-5; Amos 5:14-15; Isa. 6:13.

[15] P. S. Minear, *Images of the Church in the NT* (1961), p. 85.

now his little flock. The shepherd has found them and brought them home (Lk. 15:3-7). It is because they are already the true flock, God's people, that God will give them the eschatological Kingdom.

Jesus' call of twelve disciples to share his mission has been widely recognized as a symbolic act setting forth the continuity between his disciples and Israel. That the twelve represent Israel is shown by their eschatological role. They are to sit on twelve thrones, "judging the twelve tribes of Israel" (Mt. 19:28; Lk. 22:30). Whether this saying means that the twelve are to determine the destiny of Israel by judgment[16] or to rule over them,[17] the twelve are destined to be the head of the eschatological Israel.

Recognition that the twelve were meant to constitute the nucleus of the true Israel does not exclude the view that the number 12 also involved a claim upon the entire people as Jesus' *qahal*.[18] Twelve as a symbolic number looks both backward and forward: backward to the old Israel and forward to the eschatological Israel.[19]

The twelve are destined to be the rulers of the eschatological Israel; but they are already recipients of the blessings and powers of the eschatological Kingdom. They therefore represent not only the eschatological people of God but also those who accept the present offer of the messianic salvation. By the acted parable of choosing the twelve, Jesus taught that he was raising up a new congregation to displace the nation that was rejecting his message.[20]

MATTHEW 16:18-19. Against this background of discipleship and its relation to Israel and the Kingdom of God, the saying in Matthew 16:18f. is consistent with Jesus' total teaching. In fact, the saying expresses in explicit form a basic concept underlying Jesus' entire mission and Israel's response to it. The saying does not speak of the creation of an organization or institution, nor is it to be interpreted in terms of the distinctively Christian ***ekklēsia*** as the body and the bride of Christ, but in terms of the Old Testament concept of Israel as the people of God. The idea of "building" a people is an Old Testament idea.[21] Furthermore, *ekklēsia* is a biblical term designating Israel as the congregation or assembly of Yahweh, rendering the Hebrew word *qahal*.[22] It is not certain whether Jesus used the

---

16 See K. H. Rengstorf, *TDNT* II, 327.

17 See I Sam. 8:5; II Kings 15:5; Ps. 2:10; I Macc. 9:73; Ps. Sol. 17:28. So W. G. Kümmel, *Promise and Fulfilment* (1957), p. 47.

18 *Qahal* is the Hebrew word for Israel as the congregation of God. This significance of the twelve has been emphasized by W. G. Kümmel, *Promise and Fulfilment* (1957), p. 47.

19 See K. H. Rengstorf, *TDNT* II, 326.

20 See C. E. B. Cranfield, *Mark* (1959), p. 127; J. W. Bowman, *The Intention of Jesus* (1943), p. 214.

21 See Ruth 4:11; Jer. 1:10; 24:6; 31:4; 33:7; Ps. 28:5; 118:22; Amos 9:11.

22 Acts 7:38 speaks of Israel as the "*ekklēsia* in the wilderness," and does not refer to the church in the New Testament sense. See Deut. 5:22; Ez. 10:12; Ps. 22:22; 107:32; Joel 2:16; Mic. 2:5. See also G. Johnston, *The Doctrine of the Church in the NT* (1943), pp. 36f.

word *qahal* or *edhah,* each of which is used commonly in the Old Testament of Israel as God's people.[23] K. L. Schmidt has argued for a later term, *kenishta,* on the ground that Jesus viewed his disciples as a special synagogue embodying the true Israel.[24] However, Jesus showed no purpose of establishing a separate synagogue. Jesus could have looked upon the fellowship of his disciples as the true Israel within the disobedient nation and not as a separatist or "closed" fellowship. He did not institute a new way of worship, a new cult, or a new organization. His preaching and teaching remained within the total context of Israel's faith and practice. Jesus' announcement of his purpose to build his *ekklēsia* suggests primarily what we have already discovered in our study of discipleship, namely, that the fellowship established by Jesus stands in direct continuity with the Old Testament Israel. The distinctive element is that this *ekklēsia* is in a peculiar way the *ekklēsia* of Jesus: "My *ekklēsia.*" That is, the true Israel now finds its specific identity in its relationship to Jesus. Israel as a nation rejected the messianic salvation proclaimed by Jesus, but many accepted it. Jesus sees his disciples taking the place of Israel as the true people of God.

There is no need to discuss at length the meaning of the rock on which this new people is to be founded. In view of the Semitic usage lying behind the Greek text, we should see no play on the two Greek words, *petros* (Peter) and *petra* (rock). Jesus probably said, "You are *kepha* and on this *kepha* I will build my church." Many Protestant interpreters have reacted strongly against the Roman view of Peter as the rock in an official capacity, and have therefore interpreted the rock to be either Christ himself (Luther) or Peter's faith in Christ (Calvin).[25] However, Cullmann has argued persuasively that the rock is in fact Peter, not in an official capacity or by virtue of personal qualification, but as representative of the twelve confessing Jesus as Messiah. The rock is Peter the confessor.[26] Jesus anticipates a new stage in the experience of his disciples in which Peter will exercise a significant leadership. There is no hint in the context that this is an official leadership that Peter can pass on to his successors. Indeed, Peter the rock

---

[23] *Edhah* is usually translated in the LXX by *synagōgē;* it is not translated by *ekklēsia.* In the first four books of Moses and in Jeremiah and Ezekiel, *qahal* is also rendered in the LXX by *synagōgē.* Both *qahal* and *edhah* were displaced in the first century A.D. by *keneseth* (Aram. *kenishta*), which was also used by the local Jewish synagogue.

[24] K. L. Schmidt, *TDNT* III, 525. See also I. H. Marshall, *ET* 84 (1972-73), 359-364.

[25] See B. Ramm, *Foundations,* V (1962), 206-16. Knight contends that the rock is God himself (G. A. F. Knight in *TT* XVII [1960], 168-80).

[26] *Peter: Disciple-Apostle-Martyr* (1941), pp. 206-12; see also A. Oepke, *StTh* II (1948), 157; O. Betz, *ZNTW* XLVIII (1957), 72f.; D. H. Wallace and L. E. Keck, *Foundations,* V, 221, 230. That such an expression need carry no official authority is illustrated by an interesting analogy in a rabbinic midrash on Isa. 51:1. God was troubled because he could build nothing upon godless men. "When God looked upon Abraham who was to appear, he said, 'See I have found a rock upon which I can found and build the world.' Therefore he called Abraham a rock" (Strack and Billerbeck, *Kommentar,* I, 733).

foundation can readily become the rock of stumbling, as the next verses show.[27]

The saying about founding the church fits the total teaching of Jesus and means that he saw in the circle of those who received his message the sons of the Kingdom, the true Israel, the people of God. There is no intimation as to the form the new people is to take. The saying about discipline in the "church" (Mt. 18:17) views the disciples as a distinct fellowship analogous to the Jewish synagogue, but it throws little light on the form or organization the new fellowship is to take.[28] The church as a body separate from Judaism with its own organization and rites is a later historical development; but it is an historical manifestation of a new fellowship brought into being by Jesus as the true people of God who, having received the messianic salvation, were to take the place of the rebellious nation as the true Israel.

THE KINGDOM AND THE CHURCH. We must now examine the specific relationship between the Kingdom and the church, accepting the circle of Jesus' disciples as the incipient church if not yet the church itself.[29] The solution to this problem will depend upon one's basic definition of the Kingdom. If the dynamic concept of the Kingdom is correct, it is never to be identified with the church. The Kingdom is primarily the dynamic reign or kingly rule of God, and derivatively, the sphere in which the rule is experienced. In biblical idiom, the Kingdom is not identified with its subjects. They are the people of God's rule who enter it, live under it, and are governed by it. The church is the community of the Kingdom but never the Kingdom itself. Jesus' disciples belong to the Kingdom as the Kingdom belongs to them; but they are not the Kingdom. The Kingdom is the rule of God; the church is a society of men.[30]

THE CHURCH IS NOT THE KINGDOM. This relationship can be expounded under five points. First, the New Testament does not equate believers with the Kingdom. The first missionaries preached the Kingdom of God, not the church (Acts 8:12; 19:8; 20:25; 28:23, 31). It is impossible to substitute "church" for "kingdom" in such sayings. The only references to the people as *basileia* are Revelation 1:6 and 5:10; but the people are so designated not because they are the subjects of God's reign but because they will share Christ's reign. "They shall reign on earth" (Rev. 5:10). In these sayings, "kingdom" is synonymous with "kings," not with the people over whom God rules.

None of the sayings in the Gospels equates Jesus' disciples with the

---

27 See P. S. Minear, *Christian Hope and the Second Coming* (1954), p. 186.

28 The authenticity of this passage is frequently rejected, but "nothing justifies the view that Jesus could not have spoken the words" (F. V. Filson, *Matthew* [1960], p. 201).

29 Via speaks of them as the "embryo church." Cf. D. O. Via, *SJTh* XI (1958), 271.

30 See R. N. Flew, *Jesus and His Church* (1943), p. 13; H. Roberts, *Jesus and the Kingdom of God* (1955), pp. 84, 107.

Kingdom. Such an identification has often been seen in the parable of the tares; and indeed the statement that the Son of Man will gather all causes of sin "out of the kingdom" (Mt. 13:41) before the coming of the Kingdom of the Father (13:43) seems to suggest that the church is equated with the Kingdom of Christ.[31] However, the parable itself expressly identifies the field as the world, not as the church (Mt. 13:38). The message of the parable has nothing to do with the nature of the church but teaches that the Kingdom of God has invaded history without disrupting the present structure of society. Good and evil are to live mixed in the world until the eschatological consummation, even though the Kingdom of God has come. The language about gathering evil out of the Kingdom looks forward not backward.[32]

It is also erroneous to base an identification of the Kingdom and the church on Matthew 16:18-19. Vos presses metaphorical language too far when he insists that this identification must be made because the first part of the saying speaks of the founding of the house and the second part sees the same house complete with doors and keys. "It is plainly excluded that the house should mean one thing in the first statement and another in the second." Therefore Vos confidently affirms that the church is the Kingdom.[33]

However, it is precisely the character of metaphorical language to possess such fluidity. This passage sets forth the inseparable relationship between the church and the Kingdom, but not their identity. The many sayings about entering into the Kingdom are not equivalent to entering the church. It is confusing to say that "the church is the form of the Kingdom of God which it bears between the departure and the return of Jesus."[34] There is indeed a certain analogy between the two concepts in that both the Kingdom as the sphere of God's rule and the church are realms into which men may enter. But the Kingdom as the present sphere of God's rule is invisible, not a phenomenon of this world, whereas the church is an empirical body of men. John Bright is correct in saying that there is never the slightest hint that the visible church can either be or produce the Kingdom of God.[35]

---

[31] This identification is found in the studies on the parables by Trench, A. B. Bruce, S. Goebel, H. B. Swete. See also N. B. Stonehouse, *The Witness of Matthew and Mark to Christ,* p. 238; T. W. Manson, *The Teaching of Jesus* (1935), p. 222; S. E. Johnson, *IB* VII, 415, 418; A. E. Barnett, *Understanding the Parables of Our Lord* (1940), pp. 48-50; G. MacGregor, *Corpus Christi* (1958), p. 122.

[32] See above, Ch. 7, for the interpretation of this parable.

[33] *The Teaching of Jesus concerning the Kingdom of God and the Church* (1903), p. 150.

[34] E. Sommerlath, *ZSysTh* XVI (1939), 573. So Lindeskog, "Christ's kingdom on earth is the church" (*This Is the Church* [A. Nygren, ed., 1958], p. 144); S. M. Gilmour, "The Church [not as the institution, but as the beloved community] has been the Kingdom of God within the historical process" (*Int* VII [1953], 33).

[35] *The Kingdom of God* (1953), p. 236.

The church is the people of the Kingdom, never that Kingdom itself. Therefore it is not helpful even to say that the church is a "part of the Kingdom," or that in the eschatological consummation the church and Kingdom become synonymous.[36]

THE KINGDOM CREATES THE CHURCH. Second, the Kingdom creates the church. The dynamic rule of God, present in the mission of Jesus, challenged men to response, bringing them into a new fellowship. The presence of the Kingdom meant the fulfillment of the Old Testament messianic hope promised to Israel; but when the nation as a whole rejected the offer, those who accepted it were constituted the new people of God, the sons of the Kingdom, the true Israel, the incipient church. "The church is but the result of the coming of God's Kingdom into the world by the mission of Jesus Christ."[37]

The parable of the draw net is instructive as to the character of the church and its relation to the Kingdom. The Kingdom is an action that is likened to drawing a net through the sea. It catches in its movement not only good fish but also bad; and when the net is brought to shore, the fish must be sorted out. Such is the action of God's Kingdom among men. It is not now creating a pure fellowship; in Jesus' retinue could even be a traitor. While this parable must be interpreted in terms of Jesus' ministry, the principles deduced apply to the church. The action of God's Kingdom among men created a mixed fellowship, first in Jesus' disciples and then in the church. The eschatological coming of the Kingdom will mean judgment both for human society in general (tares) and for the church in particular (draw net). Until then, the fellowship created by the present acting of God's Kingdom will include men who are not true sons of the Kingdom. Thus the empirical church has a twofold character. It is the people of the Kingdom, and yet it is not the ideal people, for it includes some who are actually not sons of the Kingdom. Thus entrance into the Kingdom means participation in the church; but entrance into the church is not necessarily synonymous with entrance into the Kingdom.[38]

THE CHURCH WITNESSES TO THE KINGDOM. Third, it is the church's mission to witness to the Kingdom. The church cannot build the Kingdom or become the Kingdom, but the church witnesses to the Kingdom—to God's redeeming acts in Christ both past and future. This is illustrated by the commission Jesus gave to the twelve (Mt. 10) and to the seventy (Lk. 10); and it is reinforced by the proclamation of the apostles in the book of Acts.

The number of emissaries on the two preaching missions appears to have

---

36 R. O. Zorn, *Church and Kingdom* (1962), pp. 9, 83, 85ff. In spite of this confusing language, Zorn for the most part adequately distinguishes between the Kingdom and the church.

37 H. D. Wendland in *The Kingdom of God and History* (H. G. Wood, ed., 1938), p. 188.

38 R. Schnackenburg, *God's Rule and Kingdom,* p. 231.

symbolic significance. Most scholars who deny that the choice of twelve disciples-apostles was intended to represent the nucleus of the true Israel recognize in the number the symbolic significance that Jesus intended his message for the whole of Israel. Therefore, we should also recognize that seventy had a symbolic meaning. Since it was a common Jewish tradition that there were seventy nations in the world and that the Torah was first given in seventy languages to all men, the sending of seventy emissaries is an implicit claim that Jesus' message must be heard not only by Israel but by all men.[39]

The inclusion of the Gentiles as recipients of the Kingdom is taught in other sayings. When Israel's rejection of the offer of the Kingdom had become irreversible, Jesus solemnly announced that Israel would no longer be the people of God's rule but that their place would be taken by others who would prove trustworthy (Mk. 12:1-9). This saying Matthew interprets to mean, "The kingdom of God will be taken away from you and given to a nation producing the fruits of it" (Mt. 21:43). Jeremias thinks that the original meaning of this parable is the vindication of Jesus' preaching the gospel to the poor. Because the leaders of the people rejected the message, their place as recipients of the gospel must be taken by the poor who hear and respond.[40] However, in view of the fact that in Isaiah 5 the vineyard is Israel itself, it is more probable that Matthew's interpretation is correct and that the parable means that Israel will no longer be the people of God's vineyard but will be replaced by another people who will receive the message of the Kingdom.[41]

A similar idea appears in an eschatological setting in the saying about the rejection of the sons of the Kingdom—Israel—and their replacement by many Gentiles who will come from the east and the west to sit down at the messianic banquet in the eschatological Kingdom of God (Mt. 8:11-12).

How this salvation of the Gentiles is to be accomplished is indicated by a saying in the Olivet Discourse. Before the end comes, "the gospel must first be preached to all nations" (Mk. 13:10); and Matthew's version, which Jeremias thinks is the older form, makes it clear that this is the good news about the Kingdom of God (Mt. 24:14) that Jesus himself had preached (Mt. 4:23; 9:35). Recent criticism has denied the authenticity of this saying[42] or has interpreted it as an eschatological proclamation by angels by which a salvation of the Gentiles will be accomplished at the end.[43] However, Cranfield points out that the verb *kēryssein* in Mark always

[39] K. H. Rengstorf, *TDNT* II, 634.

[40] J. Jeremias, *The Parables of Jesus* (1963), p. 76. A. M. Hunter points out that this interpretation appears to be arbitrary (*Interpreting the Parables* [1960], p. 94).

[41] See F. V. Filson, *Matthew,* pp. 229f. The rabbis taught that in the past the Kingdom had been taken away from Israel because of her sins and given to the nations of the world (Strack and Billerbeck, *Kommentar,* I, 876f.).

[42] W. G. Kümmel, *Promise and Fulfilment,* pp. 85f.

[43] J. Jeremias, *Jesus' Promise to the Nations* (1958), pp. 22f.

refers to a human ministry and that it is therefore far more probable that the word in Mark 13:10 has its characteristic New Testament sense. It is part of God's eschatological purpose that before the end, all nations should have the opportunity to hear the gospel.[44]

Here we find an extension of the theology of discipleship, that it will be the mission of the church to witness to the gospel of the Kingdom in the world. Israel is no longer the witness to God's Kingdom; the church has taken her place. Therefore K. E. Skydsgaard has said that the history of the Kingdom of God has become the history of Christian missions.[45]

If Jesus' disciples are those who have received the life and fellowship of the Kingdom, and if this life is in fact an anticipation of the eschatological Kingdom, then it follows that one of the main tasks of the church is to display in this present evil age the life and fellowship of the Age to Come. The church has a dual character, belonging to two ages. It is the people of the Age to Come, but it still lives in this age, being constituted of sinful mortal men. This means that while the church in this age will never attain perfection, it must nevertheless display the life of the perfect order, the eschatological Kingdom of God.[46]

Implicit exegetical support for this view is to be found in the great emphasis Jesus placed on forgiveness and humility among his disciples. Concern over greatness, while natural in this age, is a contradiction of the life of the Kingdom (Mk. 10:35ff.). Those who have experienced the Kingdom of God are to display its life by a humble willingness to serve rather than by self-seeking.

Another evidence of the life of the Kingdom is a fellowship undisturbed by ill-will and animosity. This is why Jesus had so much to say about forgiveness, for perfect forgiveness is an evidence of love. Jesus even taught that human forgiveness and divine forgiveness are inseparable (Mt. 6:12, 14). The parable on forgiveness makes it clear that human forgiveness is conditioned by the divine forgiveness (Mt. 18:23-35). The point of this parable is that when a man claims to have received the unconditioned and unmerited forgiveness of God, which is one of the gifts of the Kingdom, and then is unwilling to forgive relatively trivial offenses against himself, he denies the reality of his very profession of divine forgiveness and by his conduct contradicts the life and character of the Kingdom. Such a man has not really experienced the forgiveness of God. It is therefore the church's duty to display in an evil age of self-seeking, pride, and animosity the life and fellowship of the Kingdom of God and of the Age to Come. This display of Kingdom life is an essential element in the witness of the church to the Kingdom of God.

---

[44] C. E. B. Cranfield, *Mark,* p. 399: "The preaching of the Gospel is an eschatological event." F. V. Filson, *Matthew,* p. 254; G. R. Beasley-Murray, *Jesus and the Future* (1954), pp. 194ff.

[45] In *SJTh* IV (1951), 390.

[46] This theme has been splendidly worked out in the article by Skydsgaard cited in the preceding footnote.

THE CHURCH IS THE INSTRUMENT OF THE KINGDOM. Fourth, the church is the instrument of the Kingdom. The disciples of Jesus not only proclaimed the good news about the presence of the Kingdom; they were also instruments of the Kingdom in that the works of the Kingdom were performed through them as through Jesus himself. As they went preaching the Kingdom, they too healed the sick and cast out demons (Mt. 10:8; Lk. 10:17). Although theirs was a delegated power, the same power of the Kingdom worked through them that worked through Jesus. Their awareness that these miracles were wrought by no power resident in themselves accounts for the fact that they never performed miracles in a competitive or boastful spirit. The report of the seventy is given with complete disinterestedness and devotion, as of men who are instruments of God.

The truth is implicit in the statement that the gates of Hades shall not prevail against the church (Mt. 16:18). This image of the gates of the realm of the dead is a familiar Semitic concept.[47] The exact meaning of this saying is not clear. It may mean that the gates of Hades, which are conceived as closing behind all the dead, will now be able to hold its victims no longer but will be forced open before the powers of the Kingdom exercised through the church. The church will be stronger than death, and will rescue men from the domination of Hades to the realm of life.[48] However, in view of the verb used, it appears that the realm of death is the aggressor, attacking the church.[49] The meaning then would be that when men have been brought into the salvation of the Kingdom of God through the mission of the church, the gates of death will be unable to prevail in their effort to swallow them up. Before the power of the Kingdom of God, working through the church, death has lost its power over men and is unable to claim final victory. There is no need to relate this to the final eschatological conflict, as Jeremias does;[50] it may be understood as an extension of the same conflict between Jesus and Satan[51] in which, as a matter of fact, Jesus' disciples had already been engaged. As instruments of the Kingdom they had seen men delivered from bondage to sickness and death (Mt. 10:8). This messianic struggle with the powers of death, which had been raging in Jesus' ministry and had been shared by his disciples, will be continued in the future, and the church will be the instrument of God's Kingdom in this struggle.

THE CHURCH: THE CUSTODIAN OF THE KINGDOM. Fifth, the church is the custodian of the Kingdom. The rabbinic concept of the Kingdom of God conceived of Israel as the custodian of the Kingdom. The Kingdom of God was the rule of God that began on earth in Abraham, and

---

[47] Isa. 38:10; Ps. 9:13; 107:18; Job 38:17; Wisd. Sol. 16:13; III Macc. 5:51; Ps. Sol. 16:2.
[48] This is the view of Cullmann (*Peter: Disciple-Apostle-Martyr,* p. 202).
[49] J. Jeremias, *TDNT* VI, 927.
[50] *Loc. cit.*
[51] P. S. Minear, *Images of the Church in the NT,* p. 50.

was committed to Israel through the Law. Since the rule of God could be experienced only through the Law, and since Israel was the custodian of the Law, Israel was in effect the custodian of the Kingdom of God. When a Gentile became a Jewish proselyte and adopted the Law, he thereby took upon himself the sovereignty of heaven, the Kingdom of God. God's rule was mediated to the Gentiles through Israel; they alone were the "sons of the kingdom."

In Jesus, the reign of God manifested itself in a new redemptive event, displaying in an unexpected way within history the powers of the eschatological Kingdom. The nation as a whole rejected the proclamation of this divine event, but those who accepted it became the true sons of the Kingdom and entered into the enjoyment of its blessings and powers. These disciples of Jesus, his *ekklēsia,* now became the custodians of the Kingdom rather than the nation Israel. The Kingdom is taken from Israel and given to others—Jesus' *ekklēsia* (Mk. 12:9). Jesus' disciples not only witness to the Kingdom and are the instruments of the Kingdom as it manifests its powers in this age; they are also its custodians.

This fact is expressed in the saying about the keys. Jesus will give to his *ekklēsia* the keys of the Kingdom of Heaven, and whatever they bind or loose on earth will be bound or loosed in heaven (Mt. 16:19). Since the idiom of binding and loosing in rabbinical usage often refers to prohibiting or permitting certain actions, this saying has frequently been interpreted to refer to administrative control over the church.[52] Background for this concept is found in Isaiah 22:22 where God entrusted to Eliakim the key to the house of David, an act that included administration of the entire house. According to this interpretation, Jesus gave Peter the authority to make decisions for conduct in the church over which he is to exercise supervision. When Peter set aside Jewish ritual practices that there might be free fellowship with the Gentiles, he exercised this administrative authority (Acts 10-11).

While this is possible, another interpretation lies nearer at hand. Jesus condemned the scribes and the Pharisees because they had taken away the key of knowledge, refusing either to enter into the Kingdom of God themselves or to permit others to enter (Lk. 11:52). The same thought appears in the first Gospel. "Woe to you, scribes and Pharisees, hypocrites! Because you shut the kingdom of heaven against men; for you neither enter yourselves nor allow those who would enter to go in" (Mt. 23:13). In biblical idiom, knowledge is more than intellectual perception. It is "a spiritual possession resting on revelation."[53] The authority entrusted to Peter is grounded upon revelation, that is, spiritual knowledge, which he shared with the twelve. The keys of the Kingdom are therefore "the spiritual insight which will enable Peter to lead others in through the door of revela-

---

[52] For literature, see O. Cullmann, *Peter: Disciple-Apostle-Martyr,* p. 204.
[53] R. Bultmann, *TDNT* I, 700.

tion through which he has passed himself."[54] The authority to bind and loose involves the admission or exclusion of men from the realm of the Kingdom of God. Christ will build his *ekklēsia* upon Peter and upon those who share the divine revelation of Jesus' messiahship. To them also is committed by virtue of this same revelation the means of permitting men to enter the realm of the blessings of the Kingdom or of excluding men from such participation.

This interpretation receives support from rabbinic usage, for binding or loosing can also refer to putting under ban or to acquitting.[55] This meaning is patent in Matthew 18:18 where a member of the congregation who is unrepentant of sin against his brother is to be excluded from the fellowship; for "whatever you bind on earth shall be bound in heaven, and whatever you loose on earth shall be loosed in heaven." The same truth is found in a Johannine saying where the resurrected Jesus performs the acted parable of breathing on his disciples, thus promising them the Holy Spirit as equipment for their future mission. Then Jesus said, "If you forgive the sins of any, they are forgiven; if you retain the sins of any, they are retained" (Jn. 20:23). This cannot be understood as the exercise of an arbitrary authority; it is the inevitable issue of witnessing to the Kingdom of God. It is furthermore an authority exercised not by Peter but by all the disciples—the church.

As a matter of fact, the disciples had already exercised this authority of binding and loosing when they visited the cities of Israel proclaiming the Kingdom of God. Wherever they and their message were accepted, peace rested upon that house; but wherever they and their message were rejected, the judgment of God was sealed to that house (Mt. 10:14, 15). They were indeed instruments of the Kingdom in effecting the forgiveness of sins; and by virtue of that very fact, they were also custodians of the Kingdom. Their ministry had the actual result either of opening the door of the Kingdom to men or of shutting it to those who spurned their message.[56]

This truth is expressed in other sayings. "He who receives you receives me, and he who receives me receives him who sent me" (Mt. 10:40; see Mk. 9:37). The dramatic picture of the judgment of the sheep and the goats tells the same story (Mt. 25:31-46). This is not to be taken as a program of the eschatological consummation but as a parabolic drama of the ultimate issues of life. Jesus is to send his disciples (his "brethren"; cf. Mt. 12:48-50) into the world as custodians of the Kingdom. The character of their mission-preaching is that pictured in Matthew 10:9-14. The hospitality they receive at the hands of their hearers is a tangible evidence of men's reaction to their message. They will arrive in some towns worn out

---

[54] R. N. Flew, *Jesus and His Church,* p. 95.

[55] Strack and Billerbeck, *Kommentar,* I, 738.

[56] See the excellent discussion in O. Cullmann, *Peter: Disciple-Apostle-Martyr,* p. 205.

and ill, hungry and thirsty, and will at times be imprisoned for preaching the gospel. Some will welcome them, receive their message, and minister to their bodily needs; others will reject both the message and the missioners. "The deeds of the righteous are not just casual acts of benevolence. They are acts by which the Mission of Jesus and His followers was helped, and helped at some cost to the doers, even at some risk."[57] To interpret this parable as teaching that men who perform acts of kindness are "Christians unawares" without reference to the mission and message of Jesus lifts the parable altogether out of its historical context. The parable sets forth the solidarity between Jesus and his disciples as he sends them forth into the world with the good news of the Kingdom.[58] The final destiny of men will be determined by the way they react to these representatives of Jesus. To receive them is to receive the Lord who sent them. While this is no official function, in a very real way the disciples of Jesus—his church—are custodians of the Kingdom. Through the proclamation of the gospel of the Kingdom in the world will be decided who will enter into the eschatological Kingdom and who will be excluded.[59]

In summary, while there is an inseparable relationship between the Kingdom and the church, they are not to be identified. The Kingdom takes its point of departure from God, the church from men. The Kingdom is God's reign and the realm in which the blessings of his reign are experienced; the church is the fellowship of those who have experienced God's reign and entered into the enjoyment of its blessings. The Kingdom creates the church, works through the church, and is proclaimed in the world by the church. There can be no Kingdom without a church—those who have acknowledged God's rule—and there can be no church without God's Kingdom; but they remain two distinguishable concepts: the rule of God and the fellowship of men.

---

[57] T. W. Manson, *The Sayings of Jesus* (1949), p. 251.

[58] *Loc. cit.* See also J. R. Michaels, "Apostolic Hardship and Righteous Gentiles," *JBL* 84 (1965), 27-37.

[59] D. O. Via, *SJTh* XI (1958), 276f.

9

THE ETHICS OF THE KINGDOM

Literature:

M. Dibelius, *The Sermon on the Mount* (1940); S. M. Gilmour, "How Relevant Is the Ethic of Jesus?" *JR* 21 (1941), 253-64; F. C. Grant, "Ethics and Eschatology in the Teaching of Jesus," *JR* 22 (1942), 359-70; L. H. Marshall, *The Challenge of NT Ethics* (1947), pp. 1-215; L. Dewar, *NT Ethics* (1949), pp. 13-98; A. N. Wilder, *Eschatology and Ethics in the Teaching of Jesus* (1950); W. Schweitzer, *Eschatology and Ethics* (1951); H. Windisch, *The Meaning of the Sermon on the Mount* (1951); A. N. Wilder, "The Sermon on the Mount," *IB* VII (1951), 155-64; A. M. Hunter, *A Pattern for Life* (1953); J. W. Bowman and R. W. Tapp, *The Gospel from the Mount* (1957); H. K. McArthur, *Understanding the Sermon on the Mount* (1961); H. Ridderbos, *The Coming of the Kingdom* (1963), pp. 285-333; J. Jeremias, *The Sermon on the Mount* (1963); G. E. Ladd, *Jesus and the Kingdom* (1964), pp. 274-300; R. Schnackenburg, *The Moral Teaching of the NT* (1965), pp. 15-167; V. Furnish, *The Love Command in the NT* (1972).

Much of Jesus' teaching was concerned with human conduct. The Beatitudes, the Golden Rule, and the parable of the Good Samaritan are among the choicest selections of the world's ethical literature. We must here attempt to understand the relationship between Jesus' ethical teaching and his preaching about the Kingdom of God. As background for our analysis, we may outline several of the more important interpretations.

SURVEY OF THE PROBLEM. Many scholars disapprove of Jesus' theology but laud his ethical teaching, finding in it an enduring significance. According to F. G. Peabody, Jesus' first demand was not for orthodox instruction or for ecstatic religious experience but for morality.[1] The Jewish scholar Klausner would like to omit the miracles and the mystical sayings, which tend to deify the Son of Man, and preserve only the moral precepts and parables, thus purifying one of the most wonderful collections of ethical teaching in the world. "If ever the day should come and this ethical

[1] F. G. Peabody, *Jesus Christ and Christian Character* (1905), p. 103.

code be stripped of its wrappings of miracles and mysticism, the Book of the Ethics of Jesus will be one of the choicest treasures of the literature of Israel for all time."[2]

The old liberal interpretation found the essential truth of the Kingdom of God in personal religious and ethical categories. Apocalyptic was the husk that encased this spiritual kernel of Jesus' religious and ethical teaching and could be cast aside without affecting the substance of his teaching. From this point of view, the ethic of Jesus was the ideal standard of conduct, which is valid for all time in all situations and carries in itself its own authentication and sanction.

Reference to this old liberal interpretation would have only archaic interest except for the fact that the same basic viewpoint is still with us. Marshall's recent analysis of Jesus' ethics gives eschatology little more place than did King's. Marshall expresses skepticism about efforts to define and classify the conceptions of the Kingdom of God in the Gospels. However, the relationship between Jesus' idea of the Kingdom and ethics is as "clear as crystal." The locus classicus is Luke 17:20-21, which teaches that the Kingdom of God is God's rule in the individual soul. Marshall appeals to Harnack for this interpretation. While he admits that Jesus often spoke of an eschatological coming of the Kingdom, this plays no role in Marshall's study; for if the Kingdom comes to society only as it is realized in the present, it follows that the consummation of the Kingdom will occur when all men have been won. "All the ethical teaching of Jesus is simply an exposition of the ethics of the Kingdom of God, of the way in which men inevitably behave when they actually come under the rule of God."[3]

C. H. Dodd's widely influential Realized Eschatology, although using eschatological language, amounts to the same kind of interpretation. The teaching of Jesus is not an ethic for those who expect the end of the world but for those who have experienced the end of this world and the coming of the Kingdom of God. Jesus' ethic is a moral idea given in absolute terms and grounded in fundamental, timeless, religious principles,[4] for the Kingdom of God is the coming of the eternal into the temporal. W. Schweitzer made no mistake in saying that it is difficult to see any difference between Dodd's view and an ethic based on the idea of the continuous creative activity of God or a belief in providence. The upshot would seem to be that ethics can in the last resort dispense with eschatology, and that all that is really needed is the Old Testament doctrine of the judgment and grace of God in history.[5]

---

[2] J. Klausner, *Jesus of Nazareth* (1925), p. 414; see also p. 381.

[3] L. H. Marshall, *The Challenge of NT Ethics* (1947), p. 31.

[4] C. H. Dodd, *History and the Gospel* (1938), p. 125; "The Ethical Teaching of Jesus" in *A Companion to the Bible* (T. W. Manson, ed., 1939), p. 378. Dodd's viewpoint is accepted by L. Dewar, *An Outline of NT Ethics* (1949), pp. 58f., 121.

[5] W. Schweitzer, *Eschatology and Ethics* (1951), p. 11. This pamphlet in the "Ecumenical Studies" is an excellent but brief survey of this problem in recent thought.

Diametrically opposed to these non-eschatological interpretations is Albert Schweitzer's "interim ethics." Albert Schweitzer held that Jesus did not teach the ethics of the future Kingdom, for the Kingdom would be supra-ethical, lying beyond distinctions of good and evil. Jesus' ethics, designed for the brief interval before the Kingdom comes, consisted primarily of repentance and moral renewal. However, the ethical movement would exert pressure on the Kingdom and compel its appearance. Since Jesus' ethics is the means of bringing the Kingdom, eschatological ethics can be transmuted into ethical eschatology and thus have permanent validity.[6]

Few scholars who have accepted the substance of Albert Schweitzer's eschatological interpretation have adopted his interim ethics. Hans Windisch[7] re-examined the Sermon on the Mount in the light of Schweitzer's view and discovered that it contained two kinds of ethical teaching standing side by side: eschatological ethics conditioned by the expectation of the coming Kingdom and wisdom ethics, which were entirely non-eschatological. Windisch insists that historical exegesis must recognize that these two types of ethics are really foreign to each other. Jesus' predominant ethics are eschatological and essentially diverse from wisdom ethics. They are new legislation, i.e., rules of admittance to the eschatological Kingdom; therefore they are to be understood literally and fulfilled completely. Their radical character is not conditioned by the imminence of the Kingdom but by the absolute will of God. It is irrelevant to ask whether or not these ethical demands are practical, for the will of God is not governed by practical considerations. Jesus considered men capable of fulfilling his demands; and their salvation in the coming Kingdom depended on obedience. The religion of the Sermon on the Mount is predominantly a religion of works. However, this eschatological ethic is an extreme, heroic, abnormal ethic that Jesus himself was unable to fulfill.

Other scholars, such as Martin Dibelius, who believe Jesus proclaimed an eschatological Kingdom, interpret his ethics as the expression of the pure, unconditioned will of God, without compromise of any sort, which God lays upon men at all times and for all time. It is incapable of complete fulfillment in an evil world and will therefore attain full validity only in the eschatological Kingdom of God.[8]

A. N. Wilder's study on *Eschatology and Ethics in the Teaching of Jesus* is one of the most important recent analyses of this problem. In our sketch of Wilder's interpretation, we noted that he appears to admit the importance of eschatology. Jesus cast his ethics in the form of entrance requirements into the coming eschatological Kingdom, and the sanctions of reward or punishment are patent. However, Wilder believes that apocalyptic by its

---

[6] A. Schweitzer, *The Mystery of the Kingdom of God* (1913), pp. 94-115.

[7] *The Meaning of the Sermon on the Mount* (1951).

[8] M. Dibelius, *The Sermon on the Mount* (1940), pp. 51f.; see also *Jesus* (1949), p. 115; P. Ramsey, *Basic Christian Ethics* (1952), p. 44; E. F. Scott, *The Ethical Teaching of Jesus* (1924), pp. 44-47.

very nature is mythical in character. It is an imaginative way of describing the ineffable. Jesus looked forward to a great historical crisis which he described in poetical apocalyptic language that is not intended to be taken literally. Therefore the eschatological sanction of Jesus' ethics is formal and secondary. In addition to the apocalyptic Kingdom with its eschatological sanction, Jesus taught that a new situation had arisen with the presence of John the Baptist and himself; and the ethics of this new situation were determined not by eschatology but by the nature and character of God. The relation between the future eschatological Kingdom and the present time of salvation is only a formal one.[9]

Rudolf Bultmann accepts Consistent Eschatology but finds the meaning of Jesus' message not in the imminence of the Kingdom but in his overwhelming sense of the nearness of God. Bultmann views Jesus' ethics as setting forth the conditions for entering the coming Kingdom. These conditions are not, however, rules and regulations to be obeyed in order that one may merit entrance into the coming Kingdom. The content of Jesus' ethics is a simple demand. Because the Kingdom is at hand, because God is near, one thing is demanded: decision in the final eschatological hour.[10] In this way, Bultmann translates Jesus' ethics into the existential demand for decision. Jesus was not a teacher of ethics, either personal or social. He did not teach absolute principles or lay down rules of conduct. He demanded only one thing: decision.

Dispensationalism with its theory of the postponed Davidic kingdom interprets the ethic of the Sermon on the Mount as a new legalism that has nothing to do with the gospel of grace but only with the Davidic form of the Kingdom. This sermon has a moral application to the Christian but its literal and primary application is to the future earthly kingdom and not to Christian life. It is the constitution of the righteous government of the earth for the millennial era. "It tells us not how to be acceptable to God, but it does reveal those who will be pleasing to God in the kingdom. . . ." "The Sermon on the Mount is legal in its character; it is the law of Moses raised to its highest power."[11] "All the kingdom promises to the individual are based on human merit. . . . It is a covenant of works only and the emphatic word is do. . . . As the individual forgives so will he be forgiven."[12] "As a rule of life, it is addressed to the Jews before the cross and to the Jew in the coming Kingdom, and is therefore not now in effect."[13] "How far removed is a mere man-wrought righteousness which exceeds the righteousness of the scribes and Pharisees from the 'gift of righteousness' bestowed on those who receive 'abundance of grace.' Yet many embrace a system demanding supermerit requirements and seem not

---

9 A. N. Wilder, *Eschatology and Ethics in the Teaching of Jesus* (1950).
10 R. Bultmann, *Jesus and the Word* (1934), pp. 72ff.
11 C. Feinberg, *Premillennialism or Amillennialism?* (1954), p. 90.
12 L. S. Chafer, *Systematic Theology* (1947), IV, 211f.
13 *Ibid.*, V, 97.

to recognize that the priceless things pertaining to both a perfect standing and eternal security in Christ are omitted."[14]

Recent dispensational writings have been more cautious in the form of expression and have tried to combine the Law of the earthly kingdom—the Sermon on the Mount—with grace. "The Sermon on the Mount expresses the legal demands of the kingdom which only grace can enable men to fulfill."[15] This, however, is to misunderstand the Kingdom of God and the Sermon on the Mount.

This survey makes it obvious that Jesus' ethical teaching and his view of the Kingdom must be studied together. We would contend that Jesus' ethics can be best interpreted in terms of the dynamic concept of God's rule, which has already manifested itself in his person but will come to consummation only in the eschatological hour.[16]

JESUS AND THE LAW. Jesus stood in a relationship to the Law of Moses that is somewhat analogous to his relationship to Israel as the people of God. He offered to Israel the fulfillment of the promised messianic salvation; but when they rejected it, he found in his own disciples the true people of God in whom was fulfilled the Old Testament hope. There are also elements of both continuity and discontinuity in Jesus' attitude toward the Law of Moses. He regarded the Old Testament as the inspired Word of God and the Law as the divinely given rule of life. He himself obeyed the injunctions of the Law (Mt. 17:27; 23:23; Mk. 14:12) and never criticized the Old Testament per se as not being the Word of God. In fact, his mission accomplishes the fulfillment of the true intent of the Law (Mt. 5:17).[17] The Old Testament therefore is of permanent validity (Mt. 5:17-18).

This note of fulfillment means that a new era has been inaugurated that requires a new definition of the role of the Law. The Law and the prophets are until John; after John comes the time of the messianic salvation (Mt. 11:13=Lk. 16:16). In this new order, a new relationship has been established between man and God. No longer is this relationship to be mediated through the Law but through the person of Jesus himself and the Kingdom of God breaking in through him.[18] Jesus viewed the entire Old Testament

---

[14] *Ibid.*, p. 112. For a thorough discussion and critique, see G. E. Ladd, *Crucial Questions About the Kingdom of God* (1952), pp. 104ff., and the literature there cited.

[15] See especially A. J. McClain, *The Greatness of the Kingdom* (1959), and *The New Scofield Reference Bible* (1967), p. 987.

[16] See S. M. Gilmour in *JR* XXI (1941), 253-64, for a similar argument. See also A. M. Hunter, *A Pattern for Life* (1953), pp. 106-7.

[17] The word translated "fulfill" can mean to "establish, confirm, cause to stand" and need mean only that Jesus asserted the permanence of the Law and his obedience to it (see B. H. Branscomb, *Jesus and the Law of Moses* [1930], pp. 226-28). However, in terms of Jesus' total message, "fulfill" probably has the meaning of bringing to full intent and expression. "His own coming is the fulfillment of the law" (H. Kleinknecht and W. Gutbrod, *TDNT* IV, 1062).

[18] H. Kleinknecht and W. Gutbrod, *TDNT* IV, 1060.

movement as divinely directed and as having arrived at its goal in himself. His messianic mission and the presence of the Kingdom are the fulfillment of the Law and the prophets.

Therefore Jesus assumed an authority equal to that of the Old Testament. The character of his preaching stands in sharp contrast to the rabbinic method, which relied upon the authority of earlier rabbis. His preaching does not even follow the prophetic formulation, "Thus saith the Lord." Rather, his message is grounded in his own authority and is repeatedly introduced by the words, "I say unto you." His frequently repeated "Amen," by which he introduced so many sayings, is to be understood in this light, for it has the force of the Old Testament expression, "Thus saith the Lord."[19]

On the authority of his own word, Jesus rejected the scribal interpretations of the Law, which were considered part of the Law itself. This includes the scribal teachings regarding the Sabbath (Mk. 2:23-28; 3:1-6; Lk. 13:10-21; 14:1-24), fasting (Mk. 2:18-22), ceremonial purity and washings (Mt. 15:1-30; Mk. 7:1-23; Lk. 11:37-54), and distinctions between "righteous" and "sinners" (Mk. 2:15-17; Lk. 15:1-32). Furthermore, he reinterpreted the role of the Law in the new era of the messianic salvation. When he declared that a man could not be defiled by food (Mk. 7:15), he thereby declared all food clean, as Mark explains (7:19), and in principle annulled the entire tradition of ceremonial observance. On his own authority alone, Jesus set aside the principle of ceremonial purity embodied in much of the Mosaic legislation. This is a corollary of the fact that the righteousness of the Kingdom is to be no longer mediated by the Law but by a new redemptive act of God, foreseen in the prophets, but now in process of being realized in the event of his own mission.[20]

THE ETHICS OF THE REIGN OF GOD. We must now consider the question of the positive relationship between Jesus' ethical teaching and his message about the Kingdom of God. One of the most important contributions of Windisch's book[21] is his distinction between historical and theological exegesis. Historical exegesis must interpret the Sermon on the Mount strictly in terms of Old Testament and Jewish categories and regard the Kingdom as the "holy habitation of the messianic salvation, etc.," i.e., the Age to Come. This is Consistent Eschatology; and in this light, Jesus' ethics are rules to determine who will enter the eschatological Kingdom. This historical interpretation has little relevance for the modern man, for he is no longer looking for an apocalyptic Kingdom; and Jesus' eschatological ethics are really impractical and unfulfillable. Therefore the modern man must resort to the theological exegesis that "will make grateful use of

19 J. Jeremias, *NT Theology*, I (1971), 36.

20 The sayings about a new garment and new wineskins indicate that the blessings of the messianic age, now present, cannot be contained in the old forms of Judaism (Mk. 2:21-22).

21 H. Windisch, *The Meaning of the Sermon on the Mount.*

the important discovery of historical exegesis that in the Talmud the word that Jesus must have used (*malkuth*) almost always means the Lordship of God, the rule that is established wherever men undertake to fulfill God's law."[22]

Windisch's use of this distinction appears to the present writer arbitrary, obscuring the fundamental meaning of the Kingdom of God. If historical exegesis has discovered that *malkuth* in rabbinic thought means the Lordship of God, and if rabbinic thought is an important fact in the historical milieu of Jesus, is it not possible that this was historically the fundamental meaning of the term in Jesus' teaching?[23] Windisch admits that the imminence of the eschatological Kingdom is not the central sanction; it is the fact that God will rule.[24] In the light of these facts, we would contend that Jesus' proclamation about the Kingdom of God historically considered meant the rule of God. Furthermore, the two types of ethics can be understood against this background, for the so-called wisdom ethics are ethics of God's present rule. Windisch admits that the Sermon on the Mount is for disciples, "for those already converted, for the children of God within the covenant of Israel. . . ."[25] Yet when Windisch adds, "or the Christian community," he has said far more than the text suggests. Granted that the Gospels are the product of the Christian community, the Sermon presupposes nothing about the new birth or the indwelling of the Holy Spirit or the new life in Christ, but only about the Kingdom of God, which may be understood as the reign of God both future and present. It is true, as Jeremias has pointed out,[26] that the Sermon presupposes something: the proclamation of the Kingdom of God. The Sermon is not Law but gospel. God's gift precedes his demand. It is God's reign present in the mission of Jesus that provides the inner motivation of which Windisch speaks.[27] The God whom Jesus proclaimed is the God who has visited men in the person and mission of Jesus to bring them the messianic salvation of forgiveness and fellowship. It is this fact which binds together the wisdom and eschatological ethics. It is those who have experienced the present rule of God who will enter into the eschatological consummation. The "different soteriology" that Windisch detects in the Beatitudes is not really different; it is in fact the most distinctive feature about Jesus' mission and message. "Understood apart from the fact that God is now establishing his realm here on earth, the Sermon on the Mount would be excessive idealism or pathological, self-destructive fanaticism."[28]

---

[22] *Ibid.*, pp. 199f., 62, 28f.
[23] See G. E. Ladd, *JBL* LXXXI (1962), 230-38.
[24] H. Windisch, *The Meaning of the Sermon on the Mount*, p. 29.
[25] *Ibid.*, p. 111.
[26] *The Sermon on the Mount* (1963), pp. 23, 30.
[27] See p. 282, n. 25. Dibelius, like Windisch, denies that the Kingdom of God is a present power; but when he says that the message of the Kingdom "lays hold on [one's] entire being and changes him" (*Jesus* [1949], p. 115), he is in effect admitting the presence of the Kingdom as the transforming power of God.
[28] O. Piper, "Kerygma and Discipleship," *Princeton Seminary Bulletin*, LVI (1962), 16.

A second important recent study comes to very different conclusions from Windisch's. Wilder, like Windisch, finds both eschatologically sanctioned ethics and non-eschatological ethics of the present time of salvation whose sanction is the pure will of God. Wilder differs from Windisch in insisting that the primary sanction is the will of God, while the eschatological sanction is merely formal and secondary. As we have seen, this led some critics to conclude that Wilder has attempted to eliminate the significance of the eschatological sanction altogether. We agree with Wilder that apocalyptic imagery is not meant to be taken with wooden literalness, but is employed to describe an ineffable future.[29] This is also true of nonapocalyptic statements about the future. Jesus said that in the resurrection redeemed existence will differ from the present order to such a degree that sex will no longer function as it now does, but that "the sons of that age" will be like the angels, having no need for procreation (Mk. 12:25=Lk. 20:35). Who can imagine in terms of known human experience what life will be like without the sex motivation? Who can picture a society that is not built around the home and the husband-wife, parent-child relationships? Such an order is indeed ineffable.

The recognition of the symbolic character of eschatological language does not require the conclusion that the eschatological sanction is really secondary and only formal, for symbolic language can be used to designate a real, if ineffable, future. Perhaps one might say that the form of the eschatological sanction, such as the lake of fire or outer darkness, on the one hand, and the messianic banquet, on the other, is formal and secondary; but it does not follow that the eschatological sanction itself is secondary. The heart of the eschatological sanction is the fact that at the end men will stand face to face with God and will experience either his judgment or his salvation; and this is no formal sanction but an essential one, standing at the heart of biblical religion. Wilder has not clearly established that Jesus used apocalyptic language only as symbolic imagery of an historical, this-worldly crisis that he saw lying in the future. Wilder admits that beyond the historical crisis, Jesus saw an eschatological event. We have concluded that those critics who feel that Wilder is attempting to eliminate the eschatological dimension altogether have not correctly interpreted him, for he expressly denies that he wishes to rule out entirely the place of the eschatological sanction. Therefore, although apocalyptic language is symbolic language used to describe an ineffable future, it is nevertheless a real future that will be God's future. If then, as Wilder correctly says, the primary sanction of Jesus' ethics is the present will of God made dynamically relevant to men because of the new situation created by Jesus' mission, which may be characterized as the time of salvation,[30] the eschatological sanction

[29] A. N. Wilder, *Eschatology and Ethics in the Teaching of Jesus,* pp. 26, 60. For the author's view of apocalyptic language, see *Jesus and the Kingdom* (1964), pp. 45ff., 58ff.

[30] *Ibid.,* pp. 145ff.

is also to be taken as a primary sanction, because the eschatological consummation is nothing less than the ultimate, complete manifestation of the reign and the will of God that has been disclosed in the present.

The ethics of Jesus, then, are Kingdom ethics, the ethics of the reign of God. It is impossible to detach them from the total context of Jesus' message and mission. They are relevant only for those who have experienced the reign of God. It is true that most of Jesus' ethical maxims can be paralleled in Jewish teachings; but no collection of Jewish ethics makes the impact upon the reader that Jesus' ethics do. To read a passage from the Mishnah is a different experience from reading the Sermon on the Mount. The unique element in Jesus' teaching is that in his person the Kingdom of God has invaded human history, and men are not only placed under the ethical demand of the reign of God, but by virtue of this very experience of God's reign are also enabled to realize a new measure of righteousness.

ABSOLUTE ETHICS. If Jesus' ethics are in fact the ethics of the reign of God, it follows that they must be absolute ethics. Dibelius is right; Jesus taught the pure, unconditioned will of God without compromise of any sort, which God lays upon men at all times and for all time.[31] Such conduct is actually attainable only in the Age to Come when all evil has been banished; but it is quite clear from the Sermon on the Mount that Jesus expected his disciples to practice his teachings in this present age. Otherwise the sayings about the light of the world and the salt of the earth are meaningless (Mt. 5:13-14). Jesus' ethics embody the standard of righteousness that a holy God must demand of men in any age.

It is this fact which has raised the difficult question of the practicality of Jesus' ethics. Viewed from one point of view, they are impractical and quite unattainable. If the Sermon on the Mount is legislation to determine admission into the future Kingdom, then all men are excluded, as Windisch recognizes. We might add, even Jesus himself is excluded; for Windisch admits that Jesus did not fulfill his own heroic ethic. His castigation of the Pharisees does not sound like an expression of love (Mt. 23); and before Annas he did not turn the other cheek (Jn. 18:22f.).[32] Jesus taught that anger is sin and leads to condemnation. Lust is sin, and whoever looks upon a woman to lust is guilty of sin. Jesus required absolute honesty, an honesty so absolute that Yes and No are as good as an oath. Jesus required perfect love, a love as perfect as God's love for men. If Jesus demanded only legalistic obedience to his teaching, then he left men hanging over the precipice of despair with no word of salvation. However, the Sermon is not law. It portrays the ideal of the man in whose life the reign of God is absolutely realized. This righteousness, as Dibelius has said, can be perfectly experienced only in the eschatological Kingdom of God. It can nevertheless to a real degree be attained in the present age,

[31] See above, note 7.
[32] H. Windisch, *The Meaning of the Sermon on the Mount*, pp. 103-4.

insofar as the reign of God is actually experienced. An important question is whether the perfect experience of God's rule in this age is a necessary prerequisite to enter the eschatological Kingdom, and this question cannot be answered apart from Jesus' teaching about grace.

There is an analogy between the manifestation of the Kingdom of God itself and the attainment of the righteousness of the Kingdom. The Kingdom has come in Jesus in fulfillment of the messianic salvation within the old age, but the consummation awaits the Age to Come. The Kingdom is actually present but in a new and unexpected way. It has entered history without transforming history. It has come into human society without purifying society. By analogy, the righteousness of the reign of God can be actually and substantially experienced even in the present age; but the perfect righteousness of the Kingdom, like the Kingdom itself, awaits the eschatological consummation. Even as the Kingdom has invaded the evil age to bring to men in advance a partial but real experience of the blessings of the eschatological Kingdom, so is the righteousness of the Kingdom attainable, in part if not in perfection, in the present order. Ethics, like the Kingdom itself, stand in the tension between present realization and future eschatological perfection.

ETHICS OF THE INNER LIFE. The ethics of the Kingdom place a new emphasis upon the righteousness of the heart. A righteousness that exceeds that of the scribes and the Pharisees is necessary for admission into the Kingdom of Heaven (Mt. 5:20). The illustrations of this principle contrast with the Old Testament as it was interpreted in current rabbinic teaching. The primary emphasis is on the inner character that underlies outward conduct. The Law condemned murder; Jesus condemned anger as sin (Mt. 5:21-26). It is difficult to understand how this can be interpreted legalistically. Legislation has to do with conduct that can be controlled; anger belongs not to the sphere of outward conduct but to that of inner attitude and character. The Law condemned adultery; Jesus condemned lustful appetite. Lust cannot be controlled by laws. The regulations about retaliation are radical illustrations of an attitude of the will; for a person could actually turn the other cheek in legal obedience to an external standard and yet be raging with anger or inwardly poisoned with a longing for revenge. Love for one's enemies is deeper than mere kindliness in outward relationships. It involves one of the deepest mysteries of human personality and character that a man can deeply and earnestly desire the best welfare of one who would seek his hurt. This and this alone is love. It is character; it is the gift of God's reign.

T. W. Manson has insisted that the difference between Jesus' ethics and those of the rabbis was not the difference between the inner springs of action and outward acts.[33] It is of course true that Judaism did not altogether neglect the inner motivation. The ethical teaching of the Testaments of the Twelve Patriarchs is a moving demand for an inner righteousness.

[33] *Ethics and the Gospel* (1960), pp. 54, 63.

"Love ye one another from the heart; and if a man sin against thee, speak peaceably to him, and in thy soul hold not guile, and if he repent and confess, forgive him. But if he deny it, do not get into a passion with him . . ." (Gad 6:3). "He that hath a pure mind in love looketh not after a woman with a view to fornication; for he hath no defilement in his heart, because the Spirit of God resteth upon him" (Benjamin 8:2).

However, this is not typical. The most casual reading of the Mishnah makes it clear that the focus of rabbinic ethics was upon outward obedience to the letter of the Law. In contrast, Jesus demanded a perfect inner righteousness. Wilder summarizes Jesus' teaching as demanding "no anger, no desire to retaliate, no hatred, that hearts must be wholly pure."[34] Anger, desire, hatred belong to the sphere of the inner man and the intention that motivates his deeds. The primary demand of Jesus is for righteous character.

This demand appears elsewhere in Jesus' teachings. A good man out of the good treasure of his heart produces good, and the evil man out of his evil treasure produces evil. Conduct is a manifestation of character (Lk. 6:45). Good or evil fruit is the manifestation of the inner character of the tree (Mt. 7:17). In the judgment, men will render account for every careless word they utter (Mt. 12:36); for in the careless word when one is not on guard, the true character of the heart and disposition is manifested. Final acquittal and condemnation will rest not on one's formal conduct but on conduct that evidences the true nature of one's inner being.

Thus the essential righteousness of the Kingdom, since it is a righteousness of the heart, is actually attainable, qualitatively if not quantitatively. In its fullness it awaits the coming of the eschatological Kingdom; but in its essence it can be realized here and now, in this age.

THE ATTAINMENT OF RIGHTEOUSNESS. How is the righteousness of the Kingdom to be attained? While Windisch insists that Jesus' ethics are legalistic, i.e., a righteousness determined by obedience to commandments, he also admits that Jesus presupposed an inner renewal that would enable men to fulfill his teachings. This inner renewal is either assumed to have been already experienced by the covenant people of God, or Jesus believed that his own teaching would implant God's commands in the hearts of his hearers. "The faith in the Kingdom that is thus kindled by Jesus' proclamation is therefore also the particular attitude that releases the willingness and the power to obey these new Kingdom commandments." "Power becomes available to the person who believes in the Kingdom."[35] "Jesus, having demonstrated the interrelation of being a child of God and of having a loving disposition toward one's persecutors, is convinced that he has actually planted this disposition in the hearts of his pious hearers."[36] The problem is that Windisch does not explain how this new disposition and

[34] A. N. Wilder, "The Sermon on the Mount," *IB* VII, 161, 163.
[35] H. Windisch, *The Meaning of the Sermon on the Mount,* pp. 113, 115; cf. also pp. 102, 73.
[36] *Ibid.,* p. 120.

energizing of the will is accomplished. This problem is unavoidable for the adherents of Consistent Eschatology; but it is no problem if the Kingdom of God is not only the future eschatological realm of salvation, but also the present redeeming action of God. The future Kingdom has invaded the present order to bring to men the blessings of the Age to Come. Men need no longer wait for the eschatological consummation to experience the Kingdom of God; in the person and mission of Jesus it has become present reality. The righteousness of the Kingdom therefore can be experienced only by the man who has submitted to the reign of God that has been manifested in Jesus, and who has therefore experienced the powers of God's Kingdom. When a man has been restored to fellowship with God, he becomes God's son and the recipient of a new power, that of the Kingdom of God. It is by the power of God's reign that the righteousness of the Kingdom is to be attained. Gutbrod summarizes this new situation by saying that Jesus looked upon the Law no longer as something to be fulfilled by man in an effort to win God's verdict of vindication. On the contrary, a new status as a child of God is presupposed, which comes into existence through companionship with Jesus and has its being in the forgiveness thus bestowed.[37]

The righteousness of the Kingdom is therefore both attainable and unattainable. It can be attained, but not in its full measure. S. M. Gilmour has expressed this idea vividly from the later Christian perspective: "In so far as the Christian is part of the church . . . the ethics of Jesus is a practicable ethic. In so far as he is part of the world, it is relevant but impracticable."[38]

This interpretation is supported by the fact that the most basic demand Jesus laid upon men if they would be his disciples was for a radical, unqualified decision.[39] A man must make a decision so radical that it involves turning his back upon all other relationships. It may involve forsaking one's home (Lk. 9:58). The demand of the Kingdom must take supremacy over the normal human obligations (Lk. 9:60). It may even involve the rupture of the closest family relationships (Lk. 9:61). In fact, when loyalty to the Kingdom conflicts with other loyalties, even though they involve life's most cherished relationships, the secondary loyalties must give way. Discipleship will mean sometimes that a man is set against his father, the daughter against her mother, the daughter-in-law against her mother-in-law; and a man's foes will be those of his own household. He who loves father or mother more than he loves Jesus is not worthy of the Kingdom (Mt. 10:34-39). The affection one sustains for his loved ones is described as hate (Lk. 14:26) compared to his love for the Kingdom of God.

Any tie or human affection that stands in the way of one's decision for

---

[37] H. Kleinknecht and W. Gutbrod, *TDNT* IV, 1064f.

[38] *JR* XXI (1941), 263.

[39] To this extent Bultmann is right in saying that God is the Demander (*der Fordernde*) who requires absolute decision.

the Kingdom of God and for Jesus must be broken. This is why Jesus commanded the rich young ruler to dispose of his possessions and then to become a disciple. Jesus put his finger on the particular object of this man's affection; it must be renounced before discipleship could be realized. A man must be ready to renounce every affection when he renders a decision for the Kingdom (Lk. 14:33). The most radical form of this renunciation includes a man's very life; unless he hates his own life he cannot be a disciple (Lk. 14:26). Obviously, this does not mean that every disciple must die; he must, however, be ready to do so. He no longer lives for himself but for the Kingdom of God. What happens to him is unimportant, for the fate of the Kingdom is all-important. This is the meaning of the words, "If any man would come after me, let him deny himself and take up his cross and follow me" (Mt. 16:24). This does not mean self-denial, that is, denying oneself some of life's enjoyments and pleasures. Self-denial can have a selfish end. By practicing self-denial men have sought their selfish advantage. Denial of self is the opposite; it means the renunciation of one's own will that the Kingdom of God may become the all-important concern of life. Taking up one's cross does not mean assuming burdens. The cross is not a burden but an instrument of death. The taking of the cross means the death of self, of personal ambition and self-centered purpose. In the place of selfish attainment, however altruistic and noble, one is to desire alone the rule of God.

Man's destiny rests upon this decision. When one has made this radical decision to deny and mortify himself, when he has thereby forfeited his life, he has the promise of the Son of Man that in the day of the parousia he will be rewarded for what he has done. In the person of Jesus, men are confronted here and now by the Kingdom of God; and he who decides for Jesus and the Kingdom will enter into the future Kingdom; but whoever denies Jesus and his Kingdom will be rejected (Mt. 10:32, 33). Those who experience the Kingdom of God and its righteousness in this age will enter into the eschatological Kingdom in the Age to Come.

A corollary of the demand for decision is the demand to love God with all one's being (Mk. 12:28ff.; Mt. 22:40); Jesus demands love with an exclusiveness which means that all other commands lead up to it and all righteousness finds in it its norm.[40] Love is a matter of will and action. Love for God means "to base one's whole being in God, to cling to him with unreserved confidence, to leave with him all care or final responsibility."[41] Love for God excludes love of mammon and love of self. Love of prestige and personal status is incompatible with the love of God (Lk. 11:43).

Love for God must express itself in love for neighbor. Judaism also taught love for neighbor, but such love does not for the most part extend

---

[40] E. Stauffer, "Agapaō," *TDNT* I, 44.
[41] *Ibid.*, p. 45.

beyond the borders of the people of God.[42] The command to love one's neighbor in Leviticus 19:18 applies unequivocally toward members of the covenant of Yahweh and not self-evidently toward all men.[43] Striking in this connection is the ideal of the Qumran community to "love all the sons of light"—the members of the community—and to "hate all the sons of darkness"—all who were outside the community (IQS 1:9-10). Jesus redefines the meaning of love for neighbor: it means love for any man in need (Lk. 10:29ff.), and particularly one's enemies (Mt. 5:44). This is a new demand of the new age Jesus has inaugurated.[44] Jesus himself said that the law of love subsumes all the ethical teaching of the Old Testament (Mt. 22:40). This law of love is original with Jesus, and is the summation of all his ethical teaching.

REWARDS AND GRACE. Many sayings in Jesus' teachings suggest that the blessings of the Kingdom are a reward. Contemporary Jewish thought made much of the doctrine of merit and reward, and at first sight this seems to be true also of Jesus' teachings. There will be a reward for persecution (Mt. 5:12), for practicing love toward one's enemies (Mt. 5:46), for the giving of alms when done in the right spirit (Mt. 6:4), for fasting (Mt. 6:18). The relation between God and man is that of employer or master to his laborers or slaves (Mt. 20:1-16; 24:45-51; 25:14-30). Reward seems sometimes to be posited as a strict equivalent for something done (Mt. 5:7; 10:32, 41f.; 25:29), or a compensation for loss or self-sacrifice (Mt. 10:39; Lk. 14:8-11). Rewards are sometimes promised according to the measure of success with which a duty is performed (Mt. 5:19; 18:1-4; Mk. 9:41; Lk. 19:17, 19); and sometimes punishment is similarly graduated (Mt. 10:15; 11:22, 24; Lk. 12:47f.). In such sayings Jesus' teachings seem close to the ordinary Jewish concept of merit in which reward was payment quantitatively conceived.

There are, however, other sayings that place the teaching about rewards in an entirely different light. While Jesus appeals to reward, he never uses the ethic of merit. Faithfulness must never be exercised with a view to reward; the reward itself is utterly of grace. Precisely those parables which speak of reward make it clear that all reward is after all a matter of grace.[45] When a man has exercised the largest measure of faithfulness, he still deserves nothing, for he has done no more than his duty (Lk. 17:7-10). The same reward is accorded to all who have been faithful regardless of the outcome of their labor (Mt. 25:21, 23). The reward is the Kingdom of Heaven itself (Mt. 5:3, 10), which is given to those for whom it has been prepared (Mt. 20:23; 25:34). Even the opportunities for service are themselves a divine gift (Mt. 25:14f.). Reward

---

[42] *Ibid.*, p. 43.
[43] J. Fichtner, "Plēsion," *TDNT* VI, 315.
[44] E. Stauffer, *TDNT* I, 46.
[45] C. A. A. Scott, *NT Ethics* (1943), pp. 53, 54. See A. N. Wilder, *Eschatology and Ethics in the Teaching of Jesus*, pp. 107-15.

therefore becomes free, unmerited grace and is pictured as out of all proportion to the service rendered (Mt. 19:29; 24:47; 25:21, 23; Lk. 7:48; 12:37). While men are to seek the Kingdom, it is nevertheless God's gift (Lk. 12:31, 32). It is God's free act of vindication that acquits a man, not the faithfulness of his religious conduct (Lk. 18:9-14).

This free gift of grace is illustrated by the healing of the blind, the lame, the lepers, the deaf, the raising of the dead, and the preaching of the good news to the poor (Mt. 11:5). The parable of the laborers in the vineyard is designed to show that the divine standard of reward is utterly different from human standards of payment; it is a matter of sheer grace (Mt. 20:1-16). The laborers who put in the full day received a denarius, which was a usual day's wages; this was what they deserved. Others who were sent into the field at the eleventh hour and worked only one hour received the same wages as those who had borne the heat and burden of the day. This is God's way: to bestow upon those who do not deserve it on the basis of grace the gift of the blessings of the Kingdom of God. Man's reckoning is: a day's work, a day's pay; God's reckoning is: an hour's work, a day's pay. The former is merit and reward; the latter is grace.[46]

In view of these teachings, we can hardly conclude that the Kingdom in its eschatological form is a reward bestowed in return for obedience to Jesus' teachings. It is the gift of God's grace. But the Kingdom is not only a future gift; it is also a present gift to those who will renounce all else and throw themselves unreservedly upon the grace of God. To them both the Kingdom and its righteousness are included in God's gracious gift.

---

[46] The fact that the one-hour workers had worked for one hour and therefore deserved something, if not a full day's pay, is one of the colorful details of the parabolic form and cannot be pressed.

10

THE MESSIAH

Literature:

K. Lake and F. J. Foakes-Jackson, *The Beginnings of Christianity,* I (1920), 345-418; V. Taylor, *The Names of Jesus* (1953); J. Klausner, *The Messianic Idea in Israel* (1955); S. Mowinckel, *He That Cometh* (1956), pp. 3-186, 261-345; O. Cullmann, *The Christology of the NT* (1959), pp. 109-36; G. Bornkamm, "The Messianic Question," *Jesus of Nazareth* (1960), pp. 169-78; W. C. van Unnik, "Jesus the Christ," *NTS* 8 (1962), 101-16; S. E. Johnson, "Christ," *IDB* A-D (1962), pp. 563-71; V. H. Neufeld, *The Earliest Christian Confessions* (1963); R. H. Fuller, *The Foundations of NT Christology* (1965), pp. 23-30, 109-14; F. Hahn *The Titles of Jesus in Christology* (1965), pp. 136-60; M. de Jonge, "The Use of the Word 'Anointed' in the Time of Jesus," *NT* 8 (1966), 132-48; R. N. Longenecker, *The Christology of Early Jewish Christianity* (1970), pp. 63-81.

The title and concept of Messiah (*Christos* = *Mashiah* = anointed) is the most important of all the christological concepts historically if not theologically, because it became the central way of designating the Christian understanding of Jesus. This is proven by the fact that *Christos,* which is properly a title designating "the anointed one," early became a proper name. Jesus became known not only as Jesus the Christ or Messiah (Acts 3:20), but as Jesus Christ or Christ Jesus. Only occasionally does Paul speak of Jesus; he almost always uses the compound name; and he more often speaks of "Christ" than he does of "Jesus." Although we cannot be sure, it seems that *Christos* became a proper name when the gospel of Jesus as the Messiah first moved into the Gentile world that did not understand the Jewish background of anointing and for whom therefore "the anointed one" was a meaningless term. This is suggested by the fact that disciples were first called "Christians" (*Christianoi*) in Antioch (Acts 11:26); and this word designates partisans of a certain group.[1]

[1] See *Herodianoi* (Mk. 3:6). See H. J. Cadbury in *Beginnings of Christianity,* ed. by F. J. Foakes-Jackson and K. Lake (1933), V, 130. Neufeld believes that the earliest Christian confession is not "Jesus is Lord" but "Jesus is the Christ." V. H. Neufeld, *The Earliest Christian Confessions* (1963).

The historical question arises, Why did the early Christians designate Jesus as the Messiah when the role he filled was so different from current Jewish expectations? Does the title, "the Christ," go back to Jesus himself? Was he recognized in the days of his flesh as the Messiah? To answer these questions, we must survey both the Old Testament messianic hope and contemporary Jewish messianic expectations, and then study the messianic question in the Synoptic Gospels.

MESSIAH IN THE OLD TESTAMENT

Literature:

See particularly S. Mowinckel, *He That Cometh* (1956), pp. 3-186; J. Klausner, *The Messianic Idea in Israel* (1955), pp. 7-243.

In the Old Testament economy, various persons were anointed with oil and thereby set apart to fulfill some divinely ordained office in the theocracy. Thus priests were anointed (Lev. 4:3; 6:22), kings were anointed (I Sam. 24:10; II Sam. 19:21; 23:1; Lam. 4:20), and possibly prophets (I Kings 19:16). This anointing indicated divine appointment to the theocratic office concerned and therefore indicated that by virtue of the unction the anointed persons belonged to a special circle of the servants of God and that their persons were sacred and inviolable (I Chron. 16:22). The person anointed was conceived as participating in the holiness of his office (I Sam. 24:6; 26:9; II Sam. 1:14).[2] Sometimes God speaks of certain persons as "his anointed" because in the mind of God they were set apart to carry out the divine purpose even though they were not actually anointed with the consecrating oil. Thus Cyrus the Persian is called "his [the Lord's] anointed" (Isa. 45:1), the patriarchs are called "my anointed" (Ps. 105:15), and Israel is also called God's anointed (Hab. 3:13).

It is frequently supposed that the Old Testament is replete with the messianic title "the Messiah." This, however, is contrary to the facts. In fact, the simple term "the Messiah" does not occur in the Old Testament at all. The word always has a qualifying genitive or suffix such as "the messiah of Jehovah," "my messiah." Some scholars insist that nowhere in the Old Testament is messiah applied to an eschatological king.[3] This conclusion is, however, debatable. In Psalm 2:2, the title seems to refer to a messianic king.[4] This is the most outstanding messianic use of the word in the Old Testament. The coming king is both God's son and the anointed one who will rule in behalf of God and over all the earth. Daniel 9:26 is probably also messianic: it speaks of the coming of "an anointed one." Conservative critics have seen this as a prophecy of Christ.[5]

---

[2] G. Dalman, *The Words of Jesus* (1909), p. 295.

[3] *Ibid.*, p. 289.

[4] G. Vos, *The Pauline Eschatology* (1954), pp. 105-6. For further study of this problem in the Psalms see Vos, "The Eschatology of the Psalter" in the *Pauline Eschatology* (1952), pp. 321-65.

[5] E. J. Young, *The Prophecy of Daniel* (1949), pp. 206-7.

Others see it as a reference to Onias III, who was high priest at the time of the Maccabean uprising, or to some other unknown leader in Maccabean times.

The earliest use of "messiah" in a messianic context is that in the song of Hannah (I Sam. 2:10) when she prays, "The Lord will judge the ends of the earth; he will give strength to his king, and exalt the power of his anointed." This prophecy looks beyond its immediate fulfillment in the house of David and Solomon to its eschatological fulfillment in the greater messianic King, the Son of David. In most of the prophecies looking forward to the final Davidic King, "messiah" is not applied to him. There are, however, a number of important prophecies that look forward to the rule of a Davidic king. The prophecy in II Samuel 7:12ff. promises that David's kingdom will last forever. When history seemed to deny the fulfillment of this prophecy, its fulfillment was expected in a greater Son of David in a day of eschatological fulfillment.[6]

The most notable Old Testament messianic prophecies, which set the tone for later Judaism, were Isaiah 9 and 11. Although he is not called "messiah," he is a king of David's line who will be supernaturally endowed to "smite the earth with the rod of his mouth, and with the breath of his lips he shall slay the wicked" (Isa. 11:4). He will purge the earth of wickedness, gather faithful Israel together, and reign forever from the throne of David over a transformed earth.[7]

Zechariah pictures the king as one who has secured victory and won peace for the sons of Jerusalem. He will ride into Jerusalem in triumph and victory upon an ass, and will banish war, bring peace to the nations, and rule over all the earth (Zech. 9:9-10). The fact that he rides upon an ass instead of a horse or chariot (Jer. 22:4) suggests that he has won the victory and returns to Jerusalem in peace.

THE MESSIANIC IDEA IN JUDAISM. The word "messiah" does not occur with great frequency in intertestamental literature. The Psalms of Solomon were produced by an unknown author who moved in the circle of the Pharisees shortly after Pompey brought Palestine under the rule of Rome in 63 B.C. This devout Jew prays for the coming of God's Kingdom (17:4) through the promised king, the Son of David (17:5, 23). This king is to be "the anointed of the Lord" (17:6), who when he arises will smite the earth with the word of his mouth, will purge the earth from sin, will crush the heathen nations and deliver Jerusalem, and after gathering the tribes of Israel will reign as king forever. Here is a prayer for fulfillment of the Old Testament prophecies of the Davidic king who should rise from among the people to deliver Israel from her enemies, to bring in the Kingdom of God, and to rule over it as God's Anointed King. The desired Kingdom is earthly and political in form although a strongly religious note is

---

[6] See Ps. 89:3f.; Jer. 30:8f.; Ezek. 37:21ff.

[7] The idea of a Davidic messianic king appears in Ps. 89:3f.; Jer. 30:8f.; Ezek. 37:21ff.; Amos 9:11. See the surveys by Mowinckel and Klausner.

sounded. This Davidic king will be endowed with supernatural gifts, for his weapons will not be those of mere physical violence and military armament, but "with a rod of iron he shall break in pieces all their substance, he shall destroy the godless nations with the word of his mouth" (17:26, 27).

The Qumran community looked for two anointed ones: an anointed priest (of Aaron) and an anointed king (of Israel).[8] The priestly messiah takes precedence over the kingly messiah because the Qumran sectarians were of priestly extraction and exalted their office. However, the Davidic messiah plays an important role in their expectations. "A monarch will not be wanting to the tribe of Judah when Israel rules, and a descendant seated on the throne will not be wanting to David. For the commander's staff is the Covenant of kingship, and the feet are the thousands of Israel. Until the Messiah of Righteousness comes, the Branch of David; for to him and to his seed has been given the covenant of the kingship of his people for everlasting generations."[9]

The Similitudes of Enoch have a different concept: a pre-existent, heavenly, supernatural Son of Man, kept in the presence of God until the time comes, and then establishing the Kingdom of God on earth. This is obviously a midrash on the "one like a son of man" in Daniel 7:13. This heavenly Son of Man is quite different from the earthly Davidic king, and it has been customary for scholars to use the term "messiah" only for the Davidic king. However, in two places (En. 48:10; 52:4) the Son of Man is called Messiah.

The Messiah appears in two first-century-A.D. apocalypses. In IV Ezra, "My son the Messiah" is "revealed" and reigns over a temporary messianic kingdom of four hundred years' duration. Then he dies, together with all other men; and after that is inaugurated the world to come (IV Ez. 7:28, 29). In another passage the Messiah is one "whom the Most High has kept until the end of days, who will arise from the posterity of David. . . . He will set them (the wicked) before his judgment seat, and when he has reproved them he will destroy them. But he will deliver in mercy the remnant of my people" (IV Ez. 12:32-34). In the Apocalypse of Baruch, the principate of the Messiah is revealed that he may reign in a temporary messianic kingdom (Apoc. Bar. 29:3; 30:1). He will destroy the "last leader of that time" and reign (Apoc. Bar. 40:1-3). He will judge the nations in terms of their treatment of Israel, and will reign in a kingdom of peace (Apoc. Bar. 72:1ff.). While these two apocalypses are themselves post-Christian, they undoubtedly preserve views current in the days of Jesus.

In rabbinic literature, no rabbi before A.D. 70 can be cited as using *mashiah* in the absolute sense. The index to the Mishnah lists messiah

---

[8] For reference see R. N. Longenecker, *Christology*, pp. 65f.

[9] 4Q Patriarchal Blessings. See A. Dupont-Sommer, *The Essene Writings from Qumran* (1961), pp. 314f. See also IQSb 5:20 (*ibid.*, p. 112) where the "Prince of the Congregation" will rule with equity, devastate the earth by his scepter, and slay the ungodly with the breath of his mouth.

only twice.[10] However, in the rabbinic literature as a whole the Davidic kingly messiah becomes the central figure in the messianic hope, while the Son of Man drops out of usage.[11]

THE MESSIANIC EXPECTATION IN THE GOSPELS. Many studies of the Jewish messianic hope omit one of the most important sources: the Gospels themselves. When one reads them to find the hope entertained by the Jewish people, he finds a hope similar to that reflected in the Psalms of Solomon. It is quite clear that the people expected a messiah to appear (Jn. 1:20, 41; 4:29; 7:31; Lk. 3:15). He was to be a son of David (Mt. 21:9; 22:42), and while he would be born in Bethlehem (Jn. 7:40-42; Mt. 2:5), there was a tradition that he would suddenly appear among the people from an obscure origin (Jn. 7:26-27).[12] When the Messiah appeared, he would remain forever (Jn. 12:34).

The most important element in this expectation is that the messiah would be the Davidic king. The wise men from the East came seeking the one who was born king of the Jews. The scribes understood the significance of the question of the wise men about such a king and directed them to Bethlehem where the promised ruler would be born. Herod the Great understood this prophecy in terms of political power, for he feared for his own throne. He could brook no rival and therefore sought to destroy Jesus (Mt. 2:1-18). That Jesus' ministry appeared to involve a messianic element with political implications is apparent from the fear of the Pharisees and the priests that his popularity would stir up a movement of such a character that the Romans would interpret it as rebellion and would intervene to crush both the movement and the Jewish nation (Jn. 11:47-48). A mighty leader who would overthrow Rome is precisely what the people desired of their messiah. At the zenith of his popularity, when Jesus had manifested the divine power resident within him in the multiplication of the loaves and the fish to feed five thousand people, a spontaneous move resulted in which crowds attempted to take Jesus by force and to make him their king (Jn. 6:15), in the hope that he might be persuaded to employ his remarkable powers to overthrow the pagan yoke and deliver God's people from their hated bondage and thus inaugurate the Kingdom of God. The significance of this hope that Jesus would be such a political messianic deliverer can be appreciated when one recalls the series of messianic revolts that characterize these times.[13] Had it been Jesus' purpose to offer to the Jews such an earthly, political Davidic kingdom, they would have accepted it on the spot and have been willing to follow him to death if need be to see the inauguration of such a kingdom. However, when Jesus refused this and indicated that his mission was of an entirely

---

[10] H. Danby, *The Mishnah* (1933), pp. 3, 396.

[11] J. Klausner, *The Messianic Hope in Israel* (1955), pp. 458-69.

[12] Cf. E. Schürer, *The Jewish People* (1890), II, 2, pp. 163-64; P. Volz, *Die Eschatologie der jüdischen Gemeinde* (1934), p. 208.

[13] Cf. W. F. Farmer, *Maccabees, Zealots, and Josephus* (1956).

different character and that his Kingdom was to be a spiritual Kingdom in which men were to eat his flesh and drink his blood, the crowds turned against him and his popularity waned (Jn. 6:66). They wanted a king to deliver them from Rome, not a saviour to redeem them from their sins.

When brought to trial before Pilate, Jesus was accused of claiming to be king, messiah (Lk. 23:2). Pilate must have understood the meaning of "the anointed," but Jesus looked like anything but a threat to the Roman rule. When he referred to Jesus as "the so-called Christ" (Mt. 27:17, 22), he was probably speaking in sarcasm. Jesus was certainly not a messianic king.[14] On the cross, the priests and scribes mockingly called Jesus the Christ, the King of Israel (Mk. 15:32).

If then, as appears to be the case, "messiah" suggested to the minds of the people a kingly son of David who would be anointed by God to bring to Israel political deliverance from the yoke of the heathen, and to establish the earthly kingdom, it is at once evident that it would be necessary for Jesus to employ the term only with the greatest reserve. Had Jesus publicly proclaimed himself to be the Messiah, that proclamation would have been received by the people as a rallying call to rebellion against Rome. In this case the fear of the Pharisees and priests would certainly have been fulfilled at once (Jn. 11:47-48). The messiahship that Jesus came to exercise was of a very different character from that which the term suggested to the popular mind. In the epistles of Paul, the messianic concept has come to have very different connotations of a soteriological sort; and if Jesus' ministry actually lay in such a direction and was not to involve at this time any form of political manifestation, we can understand why he did not make extensive use of a term that suggested to the popular mind something very different from what Jesus intended. Against this background we can understand why the word became generally used of Jesus only after his resurrection when his messianic mission was finally understood and the messianic category so completely reinterpreted that the term underwent a complete transformation (Jn. 20:31).

JESUS AND THE MESSIAH. The word *Christos* with very few exceptions appears in all four Gospels as a title and not as a proper name. In four places[15] the word is used as a proper name in editorial passages where it is entirely legitimate. Pilate apparently used the word in sarcasm.[16] In several other places, the word occurs without the definite article, but it seems to have been used, nevertheless, as a title and not as a proper name.[17] According to our Greek text in Mark 9:41, *Christos* appears on the lips of Jesus as a proper name; but there is the real possibility of a text that has been corrupted in transmission, and that Mark originally wrote, "be-

---

14 A. H. McNeile, *Matthew* (1915), p. 411.
15 Mt. 1:1; Mk. 1:1; Lk. 2:11; Jn. 1:17.
16 Mt. 27:17, 22.
17 Mt. 26:68; Lk. 2:11; 23:2; Jn. 1:41.

cause you are mine."[18] Nowhere do the disciples address Jesus as Messiah. In all other references, the word is used as a title of the Messiah.

These data at once suggest a strong element of historical control over the gospel tradition in the Christian community. If the tradition had really been as radically colored by the faith of the Christian community as many form critics allege, we would expect to find the word Christ as a proper name in the gospel tradition, for the word was widely used as a proper name in the Hellenistic church when the Gospels were written. That the Christian church preserved the messianic terminology in its correct historical form without blending into it its own christological terminology suggests that the tradition is historically sound.

There are two passages that must receive close attention: Peter's confession at Caesarea Philippi and Jesus' trial before the Sanhedrin. Mark records that in the midst of his ministry, Jesus confronted his disciples with the question of his identity: "Who do men say that I am?" (Mk. 8:27).[19] Peter answered, "You are the Messiah" (Mk. 8:29). Jesus then charged them that they tell no one about him. From that time Jesus began to teach the disciples that he must suffer and die. When Peter rebuked him for such an idea, Jesus in turn rebuked Peter, calling him Satan (Mk. 8:33).

Matthew enlarges the incident. Peter's answer is, "You are the Christ, the Son of the living God" (Mt. 18:16). Matthew then adds a brief section from his special source that records the words about the building of his church on the rock, Peter, and Jesus' answer to Peter's confession: "Blessed are you, Simon Bar-Jona! For flesh and blood has not revealed this to you, but my Father who is in heaven" (Mt. 16:17).

What Peter meant by his confession of Jesus' messiahship is disputed. Some critics believe that by "messiah," Peter had in mind the contemporary Jewish hope of a divinely anointed, supernaturally endowed Davidic king who would destroy the contemporary evil political power structures and gather Israel into God's Kingdom. A radical form criticism reduces the Markan narrative to Peter's confession and Jesus' flat rejection of messiahship as a diabolical temptation. Jesus calls Peter Satan not because Peter rejected the idea of a suffering Messiah but because he entertained the idea of messiahship at all.[20] A similar solution understands the Matthean form of Peter's confession and Jesus' beatitude given to Peter as an event that occurred in a different historical context (see Jn. 6:69) but which is wrongly conflated by the Evangelist with the Caesarea Philippi incident. In this view, Jesus also rejects Peter's confession of messiahship as a complete misunderstanding of Jesus' mission that embodied a satanic temptation that Jesus rejects and for which he rebukes Peter.[21]

However, it is a serious question whether Peter meant by "the anointed

---

18 See the commentaries by V. Taylor and C. E. B. Cranfield, *in loc.*
19 Mt. 16:13 interprets, "Who do men say that the Son of man is?"
20 R. H. Fuller, *The Foundations of NT Christology*, p. 109.
21 O. Cullmann, *Christology*, pp. 122, 280f.

one" the kingly conqueror of the Psalms of Solomon. The request of James and John to have positions of honor in the Kingdom reflects the apocalyptic Kingdom of the Son of Man rather than the victorious kingdom of the Davidic conqueror (Mk. 10:37). Furthermore, there was nothing in Jesus' conduct that could have suggested that he was to be a conquering king. The disciples must have heard Jesus' answer to the question of John the Baptist in which Jesus affirmed that he was indeed the fulfillment of the Old Testament messianic hope, but in a way that could give men offense (Mt. 11:2-6). Peter had heard Jesus' message about the Kingdom of God and seen his miracles of exorcism and healing. It is easier, therefore, to conclude that by Messiah, Peter means the one who is to fulfill the Old Testament messianic hope, *even though it is not in terms of a conquering king.* Peter does not yet understand what Jesus' messiahship means, but he has caught a glimmering of it. Matthew makes this explicit by interpreting his confession of messiahship as referring to one who is the Son of God. It is clear, too, that this must have been Mark's understanding of Jesus' messiahship, for Mark has a Son of God Christology (Mk. 1:1). The blessing Jesus pronounced on Peter because this truth had been *revealed* to him (Mt. 16:17) must have to do with sonship to God more than messiahship. An understanding of Jesus' divine sonship would indeed require divine revelation as messiahship would not.

A second passage is Jesus' hearing before the Sanhedrin, who sought some legal ground for putting Jesus to death. A series of witnesses gave conflicting testimony and are therefore called false witnesses (Mk. 14:56). Finally, the High Priest addressed to him the direct question, "Are you the Christ, the Son of the Blessed?"[22] (Mk. 14:61). It is not altogether clear what the Priest meant by "Son of God." Since this was not a popular messianic title,[23] it is probable that the High Priest had heard rumors that Jesus had made some such claim.[24] According to Mark's account, Jesus answered with an unqualified affirmative, "I am" (Mk. 14:62), but immediately defines the nature of this messiahship; it is of the heavenly Son of Man sort, not that of messianic king.

Matthew has a variant form of Jesus' answer: "You have said so" (Mt. 26:64). A well-attested alternate text for Mark has the same reading as Matthew. If Jesus did not answer with an unqualified affirmative, the variant form of the answer is no denial. "The reply is affirmative, but it registers a difference of interpretation,"[25] a difference that Jesus expounds by the words about the heavenly Son of Man, and on the basis of which he was at once condemned to death on the ground of blasphemy. There is no

---

[22] "The Blessed" is a typical Jewish synonym for God, akin to "heaven" (Lk. 15:18).

[23] See below, Ch. 12.

[24] C. E. B. Cranfield, *Mark,* p. 443. This supports our interpretation of Mt. 16:16 above.

[25] V. Taylor, *Mark,* p. 568. See also C. E. B. Cranfield, *Mark,* p. 444.

evidence that a claim to be Messiah was blasphemous.[26] It was Jesus' claim that he would be seated at the right hand of God that led to his condemnation by the Sanhedrin; however, this would be of no concern to a Roman governor, and he was accused to Pilate of claiming to be a "messiah" (Lk. 23:2). Pilate asked him if he was the King of the Jews (Mk. 15:2), and Jesus answered in words similar to his answer to the Sanhedrin, "You have said so." This was neither a bold denial nor a flat affirmation; but it was obvious to Pilate that Jesus was innocent of sedition. Yet Pilate yielded to pressure from the Jewish leaders, and Jesus was executed under the formal accusation of sedition, of claiming to be a kingly pretender in defiance of Rome (Mk. 15:26).

We summarize this survey with the conclusion that Jesus made no overt claim to be Messiah, yet he did not reject messiahship when it was attributed to him; and before the Sanhedrin, when directly accused of claiming messiahship, he assented, but gave his own definition to the term. He was the heavenly Messiah of the Son of Man sort.

It is probable that in his last entrance into Jerusalem, riding upon an ass, Jesus intended by this symbolic act to fulfill the prophecy of Zechariah 9:9 of a peaceful king. The enthusiastic welcome of the crowd and their cry, "Blessed be the kingdom of our father David that is coming" (Mk. 11:10), make it clear that Jesus' words and deeds had roused the messianic hopes of the people to fever pitch. However, when a few days later Jesus was presented to the crowds by Pilate, beaten, bound, and bloody, he looked like anything but a victor over the enemies of Israel. Their complete reversal of judgment about Jesus and their readiness to see him crucified (Mk. 15:13) are psychologically sound against the background of Jewish messianic hopes.

THE SON OF DAVID. The Old Testament looked forward to a king who would be of Davidic descent (Jer. 23:5; 33:15). The Lord's anointed in the Psalms of Solomon is the Son of David (Ps. Sol. 17:23). In post-Christian Judaism, "Son of David" occurs frequently as a title of the Messiah.[27] On several occasions, Jesus was recognized as the Son of David, according to Matthew's account.[28] This title appears only once in Mark (10:47), for it would have less meaning to a Gentile audience than to Jewish readers. That Jesus was known to be of Davidic descent is clear from Romans 1:3. Jesus was "descended from David according to the flesh."

One passage is of particular interest. Jesus took the offensive against the Jewish leaders with the question, "How can the scribes say that the Messiah is the son of David? David himself, inspired by the Holy Spirit, declared, 'The Lord said to my Lord, Sit at my right hand, till I put thy enemies under thy feet.' David himself calls him Lord; so how is he his

[26] Strack and Billerbeck, *Kommentar,* I, 1017.
[27] G. Dalman, *The Words of Jesus,* p. 317.
[28] Mt. 9:27; 12:23; 15:22; 20:30.

son?" (Mk. 12:35-37). Some scholars interpret this to be a complete rejection of Davidic sonship. This is unlikely, for the Davidic descent of the Messiah is never denied in first-century Christian writings. Others interpret it to mean that Davidic sonship is of no value in Jesus' messianic mission.[29] A better interpretation is that Jesus is accusing the scribal experts of an inadequate understanding of the Messiah. He is indeed David's Son; but this is not enough. David himself wrote, "The Lord [God] said to my Lord [the messianic King], Sit at my right hand." There is, of course, no rational answer to the question, How can the Messiah be David's Son if he is also David's Lord, at least from scribal presuppositions. Here Jesus touches on the true messianic secret. "It appears but does not state the claim, that Jesus is supernatural in dignity and origin and that his Sonship is no mere matter of human descent."[30]

This is the clue to Jesus' use of messiah. He was the Messiah, but not the warlike conqueror of contemporary Jewish hopes. He avoided the title because of its nationalistic implications to the Jews; on occasion he accepted the title, but he reinterpreted it, particularly by his use of the term "Son of Man."

Historically, there is every reason to accept the accuracy of the gospel tradition. Jesus started a movement that led many people to believe that he was the "messiah."[31] He claimed to be the one who was fulfilling the messianic promises of the Old Testament (Lk. 4:21; Mt. 11:4-5), through whom the Kingdom of God is present in the world (Lk. 11:20=Mt. 12:28).[32] The Sanhedrin queried him as to whether he was the Messiah, and turned him over to Pilate with the accusation of claiming to be a messianic king. For this reason he was crucified. So important was the category of messiahship that *Christos* was converted into a proper name. The memory of the church clearly viewed him as the Messiah.

The most natural explanation for these facts is that Jesus in some way acted like the Messiah; yet a Messiah very different from contemporary Jewish hopes. It is difficult to believe that Jesus filled a role of which he was unconscious. He must have known himself to be the Messiah.

---

[29] O. Cullmann, *Christology*, p. 132.
[30] V. Taylor, *Mark*, p. 493.
[31] Bornkamm calls it a "movement of broken messianic hopes." *Jesus of Nazareth*, p. 172.
[32] See W. C. van Unnik, "Jesus the Christ," *NTS* 8 (1962), 101-16.

11

THE SON OF MAN

Literature:

There is an enormous literature on the Son of Man. For surveys of recent study, see C. C. McCown, "Jesus, Son of Man: A Survey of Recent Discussion," *JR* 28 (1948), 1-12; A. J. B. Higgins, "Son of Man—*Forschung* since 'The Teaching of Jesus,'" *NT Essays,* ed. by A. J. B. Higgins (1959), pp. 119-35; P. C. Hodgson, "The Son of Man Problem and the Problem of Historical Knowledge," *JR* 41 (1961), 91-108; M. Black, "The Son of Man in Recent Research and Debate," *BJRL* 45 (1962-63), 305-18; I. H. Marshall, "The Synoptic Son of Man Sayings in Recent Discussion," *NTS* 12 (1966), 327-51; R. Marlow, "The Son of Man in Recent Journal Literature," *CBQ* 28 (1966), 20-30; M. Black, "The Son of Man Passion Sayings in the Gospel Tradition," *ZNTW* 60 (1968), 1-8; A. J. B. Higgins, "Is the Son of Man Problem Insoluble?" *Neotestamentica et Semitica,* ed. by E. E. Ellis and M. Wilcox (1969), pp. 70-87; J. N. Birdsall, "Who Is This Son of Man?" *EQ* 42 (1970), 7-17; I. H. Marshall, "The Son of Man in Contemporary Debate," *EQ* 42 (1970), 67-87.

For recent study, see G. Vos, *The Self-Disclosure of Jesus* (1926, 1954), pp. 227-54; T. W. Manson, *The Teaching of Jesus* (1945), pp. 210-33; V. Taylor, "The Son of Man Sayings Relating to the Parousia," *ET* 58 (1946-47), 12-15; W. Manson, *Jesus the Messiah* (1946), pp. 158-68, 237-49; M. Black, "The 'Son of Man' in the Teaching of Jesus," *ET* 60 (1948-49), 32-36; H. E. W. Turner, *Jesus Master and Lord* (1953), pp. 196-212; V. Taylor, *The Names of Jesus* (1953), pp. 25-35; S. Mowinckel, *He That Cometh* (1956), pp. 346-450; O. Cullmann, *The Christology of the NT* (1959), pp. 137-92; C. E. B. Cranfield, *Mark* (1959), pp. 272-77; E. Schweizer, "The Son of Man," *JBL* 79 (1960), 119-29; E. Schweizer, *Lordship and Discipleship* (1960), pp. 32-41; E. Schweizer, "The Son of Man Again," *NTS* 9 (1963), 256-61; A. J. B. Higgins, *Jesus and the Son of Man* (1964); H. M. Teeple, "The Origin of the Son of Man Christology," *JBL* 84 (1965), 213-50; H. E. Tödt, *The Son of Man in the Synoptic Tradition* (1965); M. D. Hooker, *The Son of Man in Mark* (1967); N. Perrin, *Rediscovering the Teaching of Jesus* (1967), pp. 164-99; F. H. Borsch, *The Son of Man in Myth and History* (1967); R. Maddox, "The Function of the Son of Man According to the Synoptic Gospels," *NTS* 15 (1968), 45-74; F. Hahn, *The Titles of Jesus in Christology* (1969), pp. 15-67; R. N. Longenecker, "Displacement of Son of Man," *The Christology of Early Jewish Christianity* (1970), pp. 82-92; J. Jeremias, *NT Theology,* I (1971), 257-75; C. Colpe, *TDNT* VIII, 400-77; R. Leivestad, "Exit the Apocalyptic Son of Man," *NTS* 18 (1972), 243-67; R. G. Hammerton-Kelly, *Pre-existence, Wisdom, and the Son of Man* (1973).

Theologically, one of the most important messianic designations in the Synoptic Gospels is the Son of Man. Three facts are of superlative importance. In the gospel tradition the Son of Man was Jesus' favorite way of designating himself; in fact, it is the only title he freely used. Second, the title is never used by anyone else to designate Jesus.[1] Third, there is no evidence in Acts or the epistles that the early church called Jesus the Son of Man. The only appearance of the title outside the Gospels is the vision of Stephen (Acts 7:56). The Gospels place it on the lips of Jesus over sixty-five times. It is a striking thing that the title never became a messianic designation for Jesus in the early church.

The church fathers understood the phrase to refer primarily to the humanity of the incarnate Son of God. Jesus was the God-man, the Son of God and Son of Man. Many of the older discussions and commentaries assume this theological meaning of the phrase and interpret it to refer primarily to Jesus' humanity and his identity with men.[2] This interpretation is in error because it neglects the historical background and significance of the expression.

One objection to the gospel portrait is that Jesus could never have applied this title to himself because the title does not exist in Aramaic—Jesus' mother tongue—and for linguistic reasons is an impossible term. It is true that the Greek expression, *ho huios tou anthrōpou,* is intolerable Greek and is a literal translation of the Aramaic *bar enasha.* This idiom could mean nothing more than "man." This is clear from the Old Testament. "God is not a man, that he should lie, or a son of man, that he should repent" (Num. 23:19). "O Lord, what is man that thou dost regard him, or the son of man that thou dost think of him?" (Ps. 144:3). This argument has been carefully examined by Dalman, who has concluded that while it was not a common title, it could be used as a messianic designation in the elevated diction of poetry and prophecy.[3]

It is indeed strange, if the linguistic argument holds any weight, that the expression is never used elsewhere in the Gospels as a periphrasis for man, an argument that is especially forceful in view of the fact that the plural, the sons of men, does occur in Mark 3:28. Dalman's conclusion that the

---

1 Jn. 12:34 is not a true exception, for here the crowd is only echoing the words of Jesus.

2 Cf. W. Hoyt, *The Teaching of Jesus Concerning His Own Person* (1909), pp. 87-121; B. F. Westcott in *The Bible Commentary: The NT*, II, 33-35; A. Plummer, *The Gospel According to Saint John* (1882), pp. 88-89.

3 See G. Dalman, *The Words of Jesus* (1909), pp. 234-41.

Son of Man could be a messianic title has been widely accepted in contemporary biblical scholarship.[4]

A further objection has been raised that Son of Man on the lips of Jesus is nothing but a substitute for the first person pronoun and therefore means no more than "I."[5] A few places occur that suggest such a usage (cf. Mt. 5:11 with Lk. 6:22); but again Dalman has pointed out that it was not a general custom among the Jews to speak of one's self in the third person, and if Jesus had done so, the term he employed for that purpose was so uncommon as to require a special explanation.[6]

The way in which a common expression can become a technical title may be illustrated in modern times by the German "Der Führer." The word means simply the leader, guide, conductor, director; but as applied to Hitler, it becomes the technical designation of the head of the German Reich.

Several questions must be discussed in connection with the title "Son of Man." What connotations did it have for Jesus' contemporaries? This is a very important consideration, for it should be obvious that Jesus would not employ a designation without regard to the significance and overtones of meaning it conveyed for his hearers. Second, how did Jesus use the title? And finally, what content did he pour into the expression? What meaning did he seek to convey?

THE BACKGROUND OF THE SON OF MAN. We have already seen that "son of man" is not an uncommon idiom in the Old Testament simply designating man. This usage has frequently been appealed to, to explain some of the gospel idioms. The expression occurs in the book of Ezekiel as the particular name by which God addresses the prophet.[7] Some interpreters have found the background for Jesus' usage in Ezekiel.[8] However, this quite fails to explain the eschatological use of Son of Man in the Gospels.

The probable Old Testament background is the vision of Daniel, where he sees four fierce beasts arise successively out of the sea. These symbolize four successive world empires. Afterwards "I saw . . . and behold, with the clouds of heaven there came one like a son of man, and he came to the Ancient of Days and was presented before him. And to him was given dominion and glory and kingdom, that all peoples, nations, and languages should serve him; his dominion is an everlasting dominion, which shall not pass away, and his kingdom one that shall not be destroyed" (Dan. 7:13-14). In the following verses, which interpret this vision, the one like a son of man is not mentioned. In his place are "the saints of the Most

---

[4] Cf. the references in J. W. Bowman, *The Intention of Jesus* (1943), pp. 122-25. See J. Jeremias, *NT Theology* (1971), I, 260-62.

[5] See R. Leivestad, *NTS* 18 (1972), 243-67.

[6] G. Dalman, *The Words of Jesus,* pp. 249-50.

[7] Ezek. 2:1, 3, 6, 8; 3:1, 34, etc. The expression occurs some ninety times.

[8] W. A. Curtis, *Jesus Christ the Teacher* (1943), pp. 135-43; G. S. Duncan, *Jesus, Son of Man* (1947), pp. 145f.; A. Richardson, *Theology of the NT* (1958), pp. 20f., 128ff.; E. M. Sidebottom, *The Christ of the Fourth Gospel* (1961), pp. 73-78.

High" (Dan. 7:22), who are first oppressed and afflicted by the fourth beast, but who receive an everlasting kingdom and rule over all the earth (Dan. 7:21-27).

One thing is clear. In Daniel the idiom "son of man" is less than a messianic title. It is a form resembling a man in contrast to the four beasts who have already appeared in the visions. Beyond this, interpretations differ[9] particularly at three points: Is the one like a son of man to be understood as an individual person, or is he only a symbol representing the saints of the Most High? Does the one like a son of man come to earth, or is his "coming" only to the presence of God? Is the one like a son of man only a heavenly figure or does he combine suffering with vindication? That the one like a son of man is identified with and represents the saints is clear; but this does not negate the possibility that he is also an individual personage.[10] While the text does not affirm that the manlike figure comes to earth, it seems to be clearly implied. He does indeed come into the presence of God with clouds, but when the kingdom is given to the saints to reign over all the dominions on earth, we may assume that this happens because the manlike figure who has received the kingdom in heaven brings it to the saints on earth.

While many scholars feel that the Danielic figure combines suffering and vindication because the saints are first oppressed and later vindicated,[11] this is not at all clear; for the saints suffer on earth while the son of man receives the kingdom in heaven, and then presumably brings it to the afflicted saints on earth.[12] We conclude that the Danielic son of man is a heavenly messianic eschatological figure who brings the kingdom to the afflicted saints on earth.

In the Similitudes of Enoch, the Son of Man has become a messianic title of a pre-existent heavenly figure who descends to earth to sit upon the throne of judgment to destroy the wicked of the earth, to deliver the righteous, and to reign in a kingdom of glory when the righteous will be clothed with garments of glory and of life and enter into a blessed fellowship with the Son of Man forever.[13]

It is not altogether clear what use can be made of this heavenly Son of Man for New Testament backgrounds. Enoch obviously consists of five

---

[9] See M. Black, "The 'Son of Man' in the Old Biblical Literature," *ET* 60 (1948-49), 11-15; T. W. Manson, "The Son of Man in Daniel, Enoch, and the Gospels," *BJRL* 32 (1950), 171-93; S. Mowinckel, *He That Cometh* (1956), pp. 346ff.; O. Cullmann, *Christology,* pp. 137ff.

[10] I. H. Marshall in *EQ* 42 (1970), 72; F. F. Bruce, *NT Development of OT Themes* (1968), p. 26. Mowinckel (*He That Cometh,* pp. 352f.) thinks that an individual concept lies behind Dan. 7.

[11] See C. F. D. Moule, *The Phenomenon of the NT* (1967), pp. 34f., 87ff.; F. F. Bruce, *NT Development of OT Themes,* p. 29; M. Hooker, *The Son of Man,* pp. 27ff.

[12] The question of the origin of the concept in Daniel need not concern us. See the writings of Mowinckel, Cullmann, and Borsch.

[13] See En. 46:48; 62:6-16; 69:26-29.

parts, and fragments of four parts have been found among the Qumran writings, but no fragments of the Similitudes have been found. This has led many scholars to the conclusion that the Similitudes cannot be pre-Christian and cannot be used for interpreting the New Testament concept of the Son of Man.[14] While this is persuasive, it seems impossible to accept the Similitudes as a Jewish Christian writing, for it lacks entirely all Christian features.[15] Therefore we must conclude that while the date of the Similitudes is later than the rest of Enoch, it is a Jewish writing that reflects how certain Jewish circles interpreted the Danielic son of man in New Testament times. There is, however, no evidence that Jesus knew the Similitudes. At best, we can use it only to understand contemporary Jewish thinking in which the Son of Man has become a messianic title for a pre-existent heavenly being who comes to earth with the glorious Kingdom of God.[16]

SON OF MAN IN THE SYNOPTIC GOSPELS. The use of Son of Man in the Synoptics falls into three distinct categories: the Son of Man on earth serving; the Son of Man in suffering and death; the Son of Man in eschatological glory.

A. THE EARTHLY SON OF MAN

Mk. 2:10 = Mt. 9:6 = Lk. 5:24. Authority to forgive sins.
Mk. 2:27 = Mt. 12:8 = Lk. 6:5. Lord of the sabbath.
Mt. 11:19 = Lk. 7:34. The Son of Man has come eating and drinking.
Mt. 8:20 = Lk. 9:58. The Son of Man has nowhere to lay his head.
Mt. 12:32 = Lk. 12:10. A word against the Son of Man will be forgiven.
[Mt. 16:13] (Mk. 8:28 omits). Who do men say that the Son of Man is?
Mt. 13:37. The Son of Man sows the good seed.
[Lk. 6:22] (Mt. 5:11 omits). Persecution on account of the Son of Man.
Lk. 19:10. The Son of Man came to seek and save the lost.
Lk. 22:48. Judas, would you betray the Son of Man with a kiss?

B. THE SUFFERING SON OF MAN

Mk. 8:31 = Lk. 9:22 (Mt. 16:21 omits).	The Son of Man must suffer.
Mk. 9:12 = Mt. 17:12.	The Son of Man will suffer.

14 See J. T. Milik, *Ten Years of Discovery in the Wilderness of Judea* (1959), pp. 33f.; F. M. Cross, Jr., *The Ancient Library of Qumran* (1957), pp. 150f.; R. N. Longenecker, *Christology*, pp. 83f.

15 See J. Jeremias, *NT Theology*, I, 269.

16 There are many debated questions about Enoch that we cannot here discuss. See M. Black, "The Son of Man in the Old Biblical Literature," *ET* 60 (1948-49), 11-15; *idem*, "The Eschatology of the Similitudes of Enoch," *JTS* 3 (1952), 1-10; T. W. Manson, "The Son of Man in Daniel, Enoch and the Gospels," *BJRL* 32 (1950), 171-93; S. Mowinckel, *He That Cometh*, pp. 358ff.; R. H. Fuller, *NT Christology*, pp. 34-41. The Son of Man concept also appears in IV Ez. 13:3, 26, 37-38.

Mk. 9:9=Mt. 17:9.	The Son of Man risen from the dead.
Mk. 9:31=Mt. 17:22=Lk. 9:44.	The Son of Man delivered into the hands of men.
Mk. 10:33=Mt. 20:18=Lk. 18:31.	The Son of Man delivered to chief priests, condemned to death, rises again.
Mk. 10:45=Mt. 20:28.	The Son of Man came to serve and give his life.
Mk. 14:21=Mt. 26:24=Lk. 22:22.	The Son of Man goes as written but woe to the betrayer.
Mk. 14:41=Mt. 26:45.	The Son of Man is betrayed to sinners.
Mt. 12:40=Lk. 11:30.	Son of Man will be three days in the earth.

C. THE APOCALYPTIC SON OF MAN

Mk. 8:38=Mt. 16:27=Lk. 9:26.	When he comes in the glory of his Father with the holy angels.
Mk. 14:26=Mt. 24:30=Lk. 21:27.	They will see the Son of Man coming with clouds and great glory.
Mk. 14:62=Mt. 26:64=Lk. 22:69.	You will see the Son of Man sitting at the right hand of power, and coming with the clouds of heaven.
Lk. 12:40=Mt. 24:44.	The Son of Man is coming at an hour you do not expect.
Lk. 17:24=Mt. 24:27.	As the lightning flashes across the sky, so will be the Son of Man in his day.
Lk. 17:26=Mt. 24:37.	As in the days of Noah, so in the days of the Son of Man.
Mt. 10:23 [This may not be apocalyptic].	You will not have gone through all the towns of Israel before the Son of Man comes.
Mt. 13:41.	The Son of Man will send his angels.
[Mt. 16:28] (Mk. 9:1).	Some will not taste death before they see the Son of Man coming in his Kingdom.
Mt. 19:28.	The Son of Man shall sit on his his glorious throne.

Mt. 24:30.	The powers of the heavens will be shaken. Then will appear the sign of the Son of Man. . . .
[Mt. 24:39] (Lk. 17:27 omits).	So will be the coming of the Son of Man.
Mt. 25:31.	When the Son of Man comes in his glory.
Lk. 12:8 (Mt. 10:32 omits).	Everyone who acknowledges me before men, the Son of Man will acknowledge before the angels of God.
Lk. 17:22.	You will desire to see one of the days of the Son of Man.
Lk. 17:30.	So will it be on the day when the Son of Man is revealed.
Lk. 18:8.	When the Son of Man comes, will he find faith on earth?
Lk. 21:36.	Praying that you may have strength to escape all these things . . . and to stand before the Son of Man.

The references that are bracketed are probably editorial. Mark reports sayings of all three types; Q reports only one possible saying about suffering; Matthew's source and Luke's source report sayings about the earthly Son of Man and the apocalyptic Son of Man. There is a fairly wide distribution in all sources of the Gospels.

The question of whether these sayings go back to the times of Jesus or have been incorporated into the gospel tradition at various stages of its history is answered in different ways. Five major types of interpretation may be listed.[17] (1) The "conservative" wing of scholarship, represented by Vos, Turner, Mowinckel, Cranfield, Taylor, Cullmann, Maddox, and Marshall accept all three types, if not all the particular sayings, as coming from Jesus and representing his own mind. (2) The position of A. Schweitzer, now supported by J. Jeremias, that only the eschatological sayings are authentic, and that Jesus expected to be the heavenly Son of Man at the imminent end of the age. (3) The view of Bultmann, followed by Bornkamm, Tödt, Hahn, and Higgins, that only the apocalyptic sayings are authentic, but Jesus was not referring to himself as the future Son of Man but to another apocalyptic figure who would judge men at the end of the age on the basis of their relationship to Jesus (Lk. 12:8). (4) Recently, a few radical scholars have rejected the authenticity of all the sayings and attributed them to the Christian community. See Teeple and Perrin. (5) A

[17] See I. H. Marshall in *EQ* 42 (1970), 68. Marshall's conclusions are here modified and enlarged.

few scholars, primarily E. Schweizer, argue for the authenticity of the sayings about the earthly Jesus, but are skeptical about the present form of the other two groups. Schweizer does accept the authenticity of a few apocalyptic sayings, but interprets them in terms of exaltation. Jesus expected God to exalt him out of his sufferings and humiliation and to witness for or against those who appear before the throne of God in the last judgment. M. Black has expressed approval of Schweizer's view.[18]

Dogmatic considerations influence the judgment of scholars in their evaluation of the Son of Man sayings. It is clear that a given scholar's understanding of the nature of history will help determine what he decides could have been true about Jesus. "The decisive issue at stake in the Son of Man problem is not the authenticity of one group of sayings against the others, but the question of the nature of history."[19] Modern scholarship recognizes that the gospel portrait of Jesus is that of a man with a transcendent self-consciousness, who, the early church believed, had claimed that he would be the eschatological Son of Man in the day of judgment. However, "history" is the story of men, not of divine men. History has no room for the category of incarnate deity. Therefore, the portrait of Jesus in the Gospels *must* be a community product—the creation of Christian faith.

A somewhat different approach to the same question is seen in those scholars who are sure that Jesus could not have claimed to be the eschatological Son of Man, for this is a claim that no sane man or good man could make.[20] Furthermore, the use of the title Son of Man for his earthly ministry involves an explicit claim that few scholars have noted; it involves the claim to be a pre-existent heavenly kind of messiah who has unexpectedly appeared as a man among men. Teeple has recognized this significance of Son of Man: "If Jesus believed that *he already in his present career was the Son of Man,* he would have to take equally improbable steps in his thinking. He would have to believe that he himself had existed in heaven as the Son of Man from the beginning of time, had descended to earth, would ascend to heaven again and would return to earth again."[21] The very statement that such a belief on the part of Jesus is "improbable" reflects presuppositions about what could and could not be true in history.

Another factor influencing scholarly judgment is the insistence upon a formal consistency. If one set of sayings is authentic, this *ipso facto* excludes the authenticity of another group. "If the Son of Man can only mean the supraterrestrial transcendent Messiah . . . then we cannot ex-

---

[18] M. Black in *BJRL* 45 (1963), 305-18.

[19] P. Hodgson, "The Son of Man and the Problem of Historical Knowledge," *JR* 41 (1961), 103.

[20] See F. C. Grant, *The Gospel of the Kingdom* (1940), p. 63; J. Knox, *The Death of Christ* (1959), pp. 52-77; A. J. B. Higgins, *Jesus and the Son of Man* (1964), pp. 19, 199. Bultmann calls it "fantastic." *The History of the Gospel Tradition* (1963), p. 137.

[21] H. M. Teeple, "The Origin of the Son of Man Christology," *JBL* 84 (1965), 221. See also p. 250. Cullmann recognizes that Jesus' use of Son of Man implies incarnation. *Christology,* p. 162.

plain how Jesus already in the present could claim for himself the predicate and rights of the Son of Man."[22] That the ideas of an apocalyptic and an earthly Son of Man are not necessarily mutually exclusive is proven by the fact that these two concepts are brought together in the Gospels. There is therefore no *a priori* reason why they might not have been brought together in the mind of Jesus.[23] The idea that the Son of Man might be an eschatological figure other than Jesus—the prevailing view in German theology—is exceedingly difficult because there is no scrap of evidence that Jesus expected one greater than himself to come, but there is much evidence to the contrary.[24]

We maintain that the one solid critical position is the fact that in all our New Testament sources, Jesus and Jesus alone used the term Son of Man to designate himself. Form critics emphasize the criterion of dissimilarity; i.e., only those sayings can be surely reckoned authentic which have no parallel either in Judaism or in the early church.[25] If this principle is applied to the Son of Man sayings, the idea that the Son of Man would appear on earth in humiliation to suffer and die has no parallel in Judaism or in the early church. The church often spoke of the sufferings of the Christ or of Jesus Christ, but never of the Son of Man. The fact that the Son of Man appears only in Jesus' own words, "seems to prove conclusively that the title Son of Man must have been truly and incontestably Jesus' own designation of himself."[26] This is bedrock, although the majority of critics, including Bornkamm, fail to recognize the force of it. If Jesus did speak of himself as the Son of Man in his earthly activity, then the only compelling argument against the authenticity of the eschatological sayings is their alleged incompatibility with the earthly sayings.[27] Furthermore, it fits the criterion of dissimilarity to apply the idea of an eschatological Son of Man to one already on earth in humiliation.[28] There is, therefore, good critical reason for an open-minded inductive approach to accept all three classes of sayings as authentic.

THE EARTHLY SON OF MAN. There is a pattern that can be detected in Mark's Gospel.[29] Caesarea Philippi and Peter's recognition of Jesus' mes-

---

22 W. Bousset, *Kyrios Christos* (1913, 1970), p. 40.

23 I. H. Marshall in *NTS* 12 (1966), 338.

24 *Loc. cit.* See also C. E. B. Cranfield, *Mark,* p. 274.

25 Perrin makes much of this principle. See *Rediscovering the Teaching of Jesus* (1967), p. 39.

26 G. Bornkamm, *Jesus of Nazareth* (1960), p. 176. Bornkamm does not, however, accept this conclusion.

27 I. H. Marshall, *NTS* 12, 343.

28 For the problem around En. 71, where Enoch may be identified with the heavenly Son of Man, see S. Mowinckel, *He That Cometh,* pp. 437ff.

29 Form criticism assumes that all connectives of time and place indicating historical sequence are editorial and not historical. There is clearly some truth in this; many pericopes are strung together without clear connectives (see G. E. Ladd, *The NT and Criticism* [1967], ch. VI). However, the tradition about Jesus preserved by the church consisted not only of many detached pericopes;

siahship marks a turning point in Jesus' self-disclosure to his disciples. Before Caesarea Philippi, he had spoken of himself only as the earthly Son of Man. After Caesarea Philippi, two new notes are introduced: the Son of Man must suffer and die, but afterward he would come as the eschatological Son of Man to judge and to rule in the eschatological Kingdom of God.

Mark records two uses of the title early in Jesus' ministry. When criticized for forgiving the sins of the paralytic, Jesus said, ". . . the Son of man has authority on earth to forgive sins" (Mk. 2:10). The expression in this saying has often been interpreted as a synonym for man and not as a messianic title, but in the context this is hardly possible. It must remain the prerogative of God rather than men to forgive sins. Indeed, Jesus was here accused of blasphemy since God alone could forgive sins (v. 7). Jesus as Son of Man here claims the authority to forgive sins. Furthermore, the expression "on earth" cannot be overlooked. A contrast between heaven and earth is involved, but the contrast may not be between the divine prerogative exercised in heaven as against Jesus' authority on earth.[30] The contrast may suggest rather two spheres of Jesus' authority. As the heavenly Son of Man he possesses this authority; now he has brought that authority to earth and is exercising it among men.[31]

Jesus contrasted his own conduct with that of John the Baptist. John came as an ascetic; Jesus, on the other hand, as the Son of Man came as a normal human being, eating and drinking (Mt. 11:19=Lk. 7:34).

Again, Jesus was condemned by the Pharisees for failing to observe the traditions of the scribes with reference to sabbath keeping. Defending his conduct, Jesus said, "The sabbath was made for man, not man for the Sabbath; so the Son of man is Lord even of the sabbath" (Mk. 2:27, 28). Whatever this saying involves, it cannot suggest that mankind as such is sovereign over the sabbath and therefore every man can make his own regulations for sabbath keeping. Jesus claims authority as the Son of Man to interpret the scribal regulations concerning the sabbath. The principle here employed is that the sabbath is not an end in itself but was made for man. In this context, the title Son of Man involves certain implications with reference to Jesus' human nature. Jesus' messianic office involves participation in human nature; and whatever concerns man as such therefore falls under the authority of the Son of Man. It is quite impossible that Jesus could have considered that man as such was sovereign over the sabbath. It is further significant that Jesus said that the Son of Man is Lord *even* of the sabbath. The authority that the Son of Man possesses is manifested at this particular point, even to the extent of reaching to the sabbath.

In speaking of the blasphemy against the Holy Spirit, Jesus associated

---

it included a memory of the basic outline of Jesus' career. See C. H. Dodd, "The Framework of the Gospel Narratives" in *NT Studies* (1953), pp. 1-11.

30 V. Taylor, *Mark*, p. 198.

31 See Maddox' appealing interpretation that in the mission of Jesus the eschatological judgment has already begun. *NTS* 15 (1968), 57.

himself with the power that was at work in his person. One may speak against the Son of Man and be forgiven; but when a man is so spiritually blind that he cannot distinguish between the Spirit of God and satanic power and therefore attributes the power at work in Jesus to the devil, he has reached a state of obduracy that can never be forgiven (Mt. 12:31-32). Jesus did not mean here to contrast his own work as the Son of Man with that of the Holy Spirit; he describes rather two stages in the progressive darkening of men's hearts. They might speak a word against Jesus, the Son of Man, and yet be forgiven. Jesus recognized that his messianic role was such that it was easy for people to take offense at him (Mt. 11:6). But when a man goes beyond the point of speaking against Jesus to that of asserting that Jesus' messianic power is of satanic origin, he is beyond salvation.

Another saying that is very difficult to place chronologically is best understood in terms of messianic dignity. To a scribe who would follow him Jesus replied, "Foxes have holes, and birds of the air have nests; but the Son of man has nowhere to lay his head" (Mt. 8:20; Lk. 9:58). This saying is quite colorless if Son of Man is only a synonym for "I"; but when the heavenly connotations in the title are recognized, this saying is filled with significance. "I who possess the messianic dignity of the Son of Man am subjected to a life of humiliation that is not in keeping with the dignity of the Son of Man."

The consciousness of messianic mission is reflected in the saying, "The Son of man came to seek and to save the lost" (Lk. 19:10).[32]

All of these earthly sayings would be perplexing to Jesus' Jewish hearers. Whether or not the Similitudes of Enoch represent current Jewish thought, they did know Daniel's vision of one like a son of man, and if Jesus used this title to designate himself in his earthly ministry, it embodies an implicit claim to be a heavenly, pre-existent, manlike being. In this context, the use of the title embodied an amazing claim, amounting to a claim to deity.[33] It was at the same time an unheard-of thing that the Son of Man should appear on earth as a man among men. How Jesus could be the heavenly Son of Man in humility and lowliness, and at the same time the heavenly, pre-existent Man was the essence of the messianic secret.

THE SUFFERING SON OF MAN. Once the disciples have become convinced that Jesus was in some real sense the Messiah who was fulfilling the prophetic hope of Israel, Jesus began to sound a new note: "The Son of man must suffer many things, and be rejected by the elders and the chief priests and the scribes, and be killed, and after three days rise again" (Mk. 8:32). It was for this idea that the Son of Man must die that Peter rebuked him; the idea of a dying Son of Man or Messiah was incredible and a contradiction in terms.

---

[32] J. Schneider, *TDNT* II, 668.

[33] See A. W. Argyle, "The Evidence for the Belief That Our Lord Himself Claimed to Be Divine," *ET* 61 (1949-50), 231.

This raises another question about contemporary Jewish expectations: Had any conflation occurred between the concepts of the messianic Son of Man and the Suffering Servant of Isaiah 53? It is clear that Judaism sometimes interpreted this great prophecy messianically. It is of little relevance to us what Isaiah 53 meant in its own historical context; we are only concerned about the way the Jews understood it. Jeremias has argued that the idea of a suffering Messiah can be traced back to pre-Christian times.[34] However, when in Judaism the Messiah suffers it is not in an atoning death but in conflict with his enemies.[35] It is true that the Son of Man in Enoch shares certain characteristics with the Servant of Isaiah 53,[36] but the important characteristic—that of vicarious suffering—is completely lacking in Enoch.[37] Therefore we must agree with those scholars who cannot find any conflation of the Messiah and Suffering Servant in pre-Christian Judaism.[38]

After the initial announcement, Mark records that Jesus told his disciples repeatedly that he must be delivered up into the hands of men and be put to death. Jesus spoke of his death in terms of the Son of Man, not Messiah; but this only intensified the problem for the disciples. If the Messiah is a Davidic king who destroys his enemies with the breath of his mouth, the Son of Man is a heavenly, supernatural being. How could such a one possibly die?

The most vivid statement about his death is found in Mark 10:45, which states that it is his messianic mission as the Son of Man to die for men. "The Son of man also came not to be served but to serve, and to give his life as a ransom for many" (Mk. 10:45). "Here we hear the central theme of the *ebed yahweh* hymns, and this is a clear allusion to Isa. 53:6. . . . Jesus consciously united in his person the two central concepts of the Jewish faith, *barnasha* and *ebed yahweh*."[39] The idea of ransom (*lutron*) alludes to the offering for sin in Isaiah 53:10, and the phrase "for many" looks like an echo of the repeated "many" in Isaiah 53:11f.[40] This has been the widely accepted "conservative" view of Jesus' use of Son of Man. He took over a term that appears in Daniel but which was not widely used

---

[34] J. Jeremias and W. Zimmerli, *TDNT* V, 654-717; also published as *The Servant of God* (1957). F. F. Bruce believes that the servant of Isaiah 53 is also the Davidic king, on the basis of Isaiah 55:3, but he fails to show the relationship between suffering and reigning. See *NT Development of OT Themes*, ch. VII.

[35] S. Mowinckel, *He That Cometh*, pp. 327f.

[36] See W. Manson, *Jesus the Messiah* (1946), pp. 233-36.

[37] See M. Black, "Servant of the Lord and Son of Man," *SJTh* 6 (1953), 19f.

[38] See H. H. Rowley, "The Suffering Servant and the Davidic Messiah," *The Servant of the Lord* (1952), pp. 63-93; O. Cullmann, *Christology*, pp. 52-60; R. H. Fuller, *NT Christology*, pp. 43-46.

[39] O. Cullmann, *Christology*, p. 65. Fuller says, "It should be taken as firmly established that Isa. 53 is constitutive for Mark 10:45b and 14:24" (*NT Christology*, p. 153), but he attributes it to the early church and not to Jesus.

[40] C. E. B. Cranfield, *Mark*, p. 342. This is denied by M. Hooker, *Jesus and the Servant* (1959).

in contemporary Jewish hopes, but radically reinterpreted it. The Son of Man is not only a heavenly, pre-existent being; he appears in weakness and humility as a man among men to fulfill a destiny of suffering and death. In other words, Jesus poured the content of the Suffering Servant into the Son of Man concept.[41]

THE APOCALYPTIC SON OF MAN. At the same time that Jesus announced his suffering, he announced his coming in glory. After Caesarea Philippi, predictions of his glorious coming as the Son of Man occur with relative frequency. This idea would be familiar enough to his hearers, for they knew the prophecy of Daniel. But the idea that the heavenly Son of Man should first live as a man among men and submit to suffering and death was an utterly novel idea.

Perhaps the most vivid of the apocalyptic sayings is one already discussed—Jesus' answer to the question of the High Priest as to whether he was the Messiah, the Son of God. Whether Jesus answered, "I am" (Mk. 14:62), or "You say that I am" (Mt. 26:64), the result is the same.[42] He immediately defines what he means by his claim to messiahship: "You will see the Son of man sitting at the right hand of power, and coming with the clouds of heaven." Jesus is the Messiah, but a heavenly Son of Man kind of Messiah, not an earthly Davidic king. Jesus said, in effect, to his accusers that the day would come when the situation would be reversed. Now he was standing before their tribunal being tried. The day would come when they—his judges—would stand before his tribunal, and he, the heavenly Son of Man, would fill the role of eschatological judge.

Ever since Glasson's study on *The Second Advent,* many scholars have accepted his suggestion that Jesus in his answer to the priest speaks not of a coming to earth but only of an exaltation and a coming to the presence of God.[43] However, it is difficult to avoid the argument about the order of the words. The coming follows the sitting.[44] The saying combines exaltation (sitting) and parousia (coming.)[45]

CONCLUSION. We may conclude, then, that by the use of the term Son of Man, interpreted in the light of its historical and religious background, Jesus laid claim both to messianic dignity and to a messianic role. In fact, the claim involved implicitly more than mere messianic dignity, for it carried overtones of essential supernatural character and origin.[46] He did not call himself the Messiah, because his mission was utterly different from that connoted to the popular mind by this messianic term. He called him-

---

41 M. Black, "Servant of the Lord and Son of Man," *SJTh* 6, 1-11.

42 See p. 142.

43 T. F. Glasson, *The Second Advent* (1963), pp. 54-62.

44 C. E. Cranfield, *Mark,* p. 144.

45 R. H. Fuller, *NT Christology*, p. 145. Fuller, however, takes it as a secondary saying.

46 "In using this self-designation, Jesus implied his own pre-existence." R. G. Hamerton-Kelly, *Pre-existence, Wisdom, and the Son of Man* (1973), p. 100.

self the Son of Man because this title made an exalted claim and yet at the same time permitted Jesus to fill the term with new meaning. This he did by coupling the role of the Son of Man with that of the Suffering Servant. Once the disciples were convinced that Jesus was indeed the Messiah, although a Messiah of a novel sort, he instructed them in the larger aspects of the destiny of the Son of Man. He was first to suffer and die, and then he would come in glory as Daniel 7 prophesied to inaugurate the Kingdom of God with power and glory. By the term Son of Man, Jesus laid claim to heavenly dignity and probably to pre-existence itself and claimed to be the one who would one day inaugurate the glorious Kingdom. But in order to accomplish this, the Son of Man must become the Suffering Servant and submit to death.

Jesus' teachings about the Son of Man and the Kingdom of God are closely analogous in certain aspects of their structure. We have seen that the Kingdom of God is the perfect realization of the glorious reign of God that will be experienced only with the inauguration of the Age to Come. In advance of the manifestation of the Kingdom in glory, however, this same Kingdom of God, his kingly reign, has manifested itself among men in an unexpected form. The Kingdom is to work secretly among men. While the evil age continues, the Kingdom of God has begun to work quietly in a form almost unnoticed by the world. Its presence can be recognized only by those who have spiritual perception to see it. This is the mystery of the Kingdom: the divine secret that in the ministry of Jesus has for the first time been disclosed to men. The future apocalyptic, glorious Kingdom has come secretly to work among men in advance of its open manifestation.[47]

So it is with the Son of Man. Jesus will be the heavenly, glorious Son of Man coming with the clouds to judge men and to bring the glorious Kingdom. However, in advance of this apocalyptic manifestation as the Son of Man, Jesus is the Son of Man living among men incognito, whose ministry is not to reign in glory but in humiliation to suffer and to die for men. The future, heavenly Son of Man is already present among men but in a form they hardly expected. There is indeed a messianic secret even as there is a mystery of the Kingdom of God.

By designating himself the Son of Man, Jesus claimed to be the Messiah; but by the way in which he used the term, he indicated that his messiahship was of a very different order from that which was popularly expected. The "Son of Man" permitted him to lay claim to messianic dignity but to interpret that messianic office in his own way. It was a claim, therefore, that would not be readily recognized by the people who possessed an erroneous concept of the Messiah, but which nevertheless was designed to alert those who were spiritually responsive to the actual presence of the Messiah, although in an unforeseen messianic role.

---

[47] See T. W. Manson, "Realized Eschatology and the Messianic Secret" in *Studies in the Gospels,* ed. by D. E. Nineham (1955), pp. 209-21.

12

THE SON OF GOD

Literature:

G. Dalman, *The Words of Jesus* (1909), pp. 268-88; G. Vos, *The Self-Disclosure of Jesus* (1926, 1954), pp. 141-70; E. Huntress, " 'Son of God' in Jewish Writings Prior to the Christian Era," *JBL* 14 (1935), 117-23; T. W. Manson, *The Teaching of Jesus* (1935), pp. 89-115; A. W. Argyle, "The Evidence for the Belief That Our Lord Himself Claimed to Be Divine," *ET* 61 (1949-50), 228-32; R. Bultmann, *Theology of the NT* (1951), pp. 121-33; V. Taylor, *The Names of Jesus* (1953), pp. 52-65; H. E. W. Turner, *Jesus, Master and Lord* (1953), pp. 213-35; O. Cullmann, *The Christology of the NT* (1959), pp. 270-89; W. D. Davies, " 'Knowledge' in the Dead Sea Scrolls and Matthew 11:25-30" in *Christian Origins and Judaism* (1962), pp. 97-118; A. M. Hunter, "Crux Criticorum—Matt. xi:25-30—A Re-appraisal," *NTS* 8 (1962), 241-48; A. J. B. Higgins, "The OT and Some Aspects of NT Christology" in *Promise and Fulfilment,* ed. by F. F. Bruce (1963), pp. 128-41; R. H. Fuller, *The Foundations of NT Christology* (1965); J. Jeremias, *The Central Message of the NT* (1965), pp. 9-30; I. H. Marshall, "The Divine Sonship of Jesus," *Int* 21 (1967), 87-103; F. Hahn, *The Titles of Jesus in Christology* (1969), pp. 279ff.; R. N. Longenecker, *The Christology of Early Jewish Christianity* (1970), pp. 93-99.

INTRODUCTION. The most important messianic phrase in the study of the self-disclosure of Jesus is the Son of God. In the history of theological thought, this expression connotes the essential deity of Jesus Christ. He is the Son of God, that is, God the Son, the second person of the triune Godhead. However, as we approach the study of this expression in the Synoptic Gospels, we ought not to conclude without careful study that the expression conveys such lofty connotations, for it is a matter of historical fact that this expression was used in the religious literature of Judaism and in the Old Testament with different meanings from that which we customarily recognize. Therefore we must survey the history and the use of this expression in its several meanings and then come to the Gospels to attempt to determine how high a concept is conveyed by the use of the term.

MEANING OF "SON OF GOD." Vos has pointed out that "son of God" can be used in at least four different ways.[1] A creature of God may be called the son of God in a *nativistic* sense because he owes his existence to the immediate creative activity of God. Adam is called the son of God in approximately the same sense that Seth was the son of Adam (Lk. 3:38). This would appear to be, in part, the meaning of Exodus 4:22 where God speaks of Israel as his son, his firstborn. "Have we not all one father? Has not one God created us?" (Mal. 2:10). It is probably in this sense that Jesus is to be called son of God in Luke 1:35, because his birth was due to an immediate creative act of the Holy Spirit in the body of Mary.[2]

This is not a distinctive Jewish conception; Plato speaking of God says, "Now to discover the Maker and Father of this Universe were a task indeed; and having discovered Him, to declare Him unto all men were a thing impossible."[3] A similar theology is found in Paul's speech at Athens, where he draws upon Stoic idiom to illustrate Christian truth: "For we are indeed his offspring" (Acts 17:28). Here is a theology of the universal Fatherhood of God; and it follows that all men, being the creatures of the one God, are brothers. However, this is a theology of creation, not of redemption. In this theology man's sonship to God is a universal truth that belongs to all men by nature, and since men are intrinsically the children of God, this fact should be determinative of their attitude toward God and of their relationship to one another. We must try to determine to what extent this theology of common creaturehood entered into Jesus' teaching.

Second, the expression son of God can be used to describe the relationship men may sustain to God as the peculiar objects of his loving care. This is the *moral-religious* use and may be applied both to men and to the nation Israel. This is the deeper meaning of Exodus 4:22. Israel is not only a nation brought into being by the activity of God, but also God's firstborn, the special object of his fatherly love. Israel is God's elect people. Repeatedly throughout the Old Testament, the relationship that Israel sustains to God is described in terms of sonship.[4] In the New Testament, this concept is filled with deeper significance as Christians are described in terms of sonship to God, whether by birth (Jn. 3:3; 1:12) or by adoption (Rom. 8:14, 19; Gal. 3:26; 4:5). We have already considered this dimension of sonship in the discussion of the Fatherhood of God.[5]

A third meaning is *messianic;* the Davidic king is designated the son of God (II Sam. 7:14). This usage involves no necessary implication as to

---

[1] See G. Vos, *The Self-Disclosure of Jesus* (1954), pp. 141f.

[2] *Ibid.,* p. 183. No discussion of the theology of the virgin birth has been included in this book because the Gospels make no explicit theological use of it. For its place in *Heilsgeschichte,* see O. A. Piper, "The Virgin Birth," *Int* 18 (1964), 131-48.

[3] *Timaeus* 28C (Loeb ed.).

[4] See, for instance, Deut. 14:1; Jer. 3:19, 20; Hos. 11:1; cf. also IV Ez. 7:58; Ps. Sol. 18:4.

[5] See pp. 84ff.

the divine nature of the messianic personage; it has reference to the official position of messiahship.

A fourth meaning is the *theological*. In the New Testament revelation and later in Christian theology, "Son of God" came to have a higher significance; Jesus is the Son of God because he is God and partakes of the divine nature. The purpose of the Gospel of John is to demonstrate that Jesus is both the Christ and the Son of God, and it is clear from the prologue of John that Jesus as the Son of God, the Logos, was personally preexistent, was himself God, and became incarnate for the purpose of revealing God to men. This is what Paul means when he says that God sent his own Son in the likeness of sinful flesh to do for men what the Law could not do (Rom. 8:3; see also Gal. 4:4). In describing the high-priestly ministry of our Lord, the author of Hebrews speaks of him as Jesus, the Son of God; and by placing the two titles side by side, he suggests the two natures of our Lord (Heb. 4:14).

Our primary question is whether Jesus is the Son of God merely in the religious sense; or is he the messianic Son of God; or does the theological concept that he is Son of God in the sense of sharing God's nature as John and Paul conceive it go back to Jesus himself? We have already seen that Jesus in some way set himself apart from his disciples in their relationship to God. In some sense, God is the Father of Jesus in a way that he could not be to Jesus' disciples.[6] What this involves can be determined by a closer survey of "Son of God."

MESSIANIC SON OF GOD IN JUDAISM. The idea of the messianic Son of God goes back to the promise to David with reference to his descendants who should succeed him on the throne of Israel, and it looks beyond the immediate descendants of David to that greater descendant who should be the messianic Son of God in the fullest sense of the word. Of David's son, God said, "I will be his father, and he shall be my son" (II Sam. 7:14). This promise is enlarged in Psalm 89 where God said of David, "And I will make him the firstborn, the highest of the kings of the earth. . . . I will establish his line forever and his throne as the days of the heavens" (vv. 27, 29). David's posterity is included in his person, and the high promise, never fully realized in any of his successors, points forward to the greater son of David who should become the Prince of the kings of the earth.[7] The messianic significance of this phrase is most clearly seen in Psalm 2 where the coming ruler is called the anointed of the Lord, the king, and God's Son: "You are my son, today I have begotten you" (Ps. 2:7). The anointed King by virtue of his office is here called God's Son.

It is of considerable importance that while there is an Old Testament background for messianic sonship, the expression Son of God never became a familiar messianic designation. It appears in only one passage before

[6] See p. 86.
[7] A. F. Kirkpatrick, *The Book of Psalms* (1900), II-III, 538.

the first century. In the fifth book of Enoch, God says, "For I and my Son will be united with them forever" (En. 105:2). However, this chapter does not appear in the Greek Enoch fragment.[8] "Son of God" appears as a messianic title in a first-century-A.D. apocalypse, IV Ezra. Here in several places the supernatural Messiah is called "My Son."[9] G. H. Box has demonstrated that this usage rests squarely upon the messianic interpretation of Psalm 2.[10] However, most scholars agree that the term underlying the extant versions of this writing was the Servant rather than the Son.[11] A kindred writing, the Apocalypse of Baruch, speaks of "my Servant Messiah" (Apoc. Bar. 70:9). Contemporary scholarship agrees with Dalman that Son of God was not a common messianic designation in New Testament times,[12] although some think it was possible.[13]

One reference has been found in Qumran, where the Davidic Messiah is referred to in the words of II Samuel 7:14.[14] This has led Fuller to the conclusion that "Son of God" was first coming into use as a messianic title in pre-Christian Judaism.[15] Therefore we must be open to the possibility that "Son of God" in the Gospels is a term designating Jesus as the Messiah.

THE DIVINE MAN. Another possible background for "Son of God" is the Greek idea of divine men. In oriental religions, all kings were thought to be begotten of gods. In Hellenism, there were men supposed to possess divine power and the ability to work miracles; they were called *theioi andres*—divine men. Bultmann has supposed that this Hellenistic concept of the divine man lies behind the "Son of God" in the Gospels. "They picture Jesus as the Son of God who reveals his divine power and authority through miracles."[16]

SON OF GOD IN THE GOSPELS. Mark makes it obvious at the outset that his understanding of Christ is that of the Son of God (Mk. 1:1), and Matthew understands Peter's confession of Jesus as Messiah in the sense of being Son of God (Mt. 16:16). We must examine the Gospels to discover what this means.

One thing at once strikes us: in the Synoptics Jesus never uses the full title to designate himself; but he frequently refers to himself as the Son. This leads at once to the conclusion that whatever it means, "Son of God" was not a title by which Jesus designated himself. This is all the

---

8 See C. Bonner, *The Last Chapters of Enoch in Greek* (1937).

9 IV Ez. 7:28-29; 13:32, 37, 52; 14:9.

10 G. H. Box, *The Ezra Apocalypse* (1912), p. lvi.

11 O. Cullmann, *Christology*, p. 274.

12 G. Dalman, *The Words of Jesus* (1909), p. 272; W. Bousset, *Kyrios Christos* (1970), pp. 92-93.

13 R. Bultmann, *Theology*, I, 50.

14 4Q Florilegium 10-14. See A. Dupont-Sommer, *The Essene Writings from Qumran* (1961), p. 313.

15 R. H. Fuller, *NT Christology*, p. 32.

16 R. Bultmann, *Theology*, I, 130.

more striking in view of the fact that in the epistles,[17] Son of God is a favorite designation for Jesus.

Jesus is called the Son of God by the heavenly voice at his baptism (Mk. 1:11) and at the transfiguration (Mk. 9:7). The temptations assault Jesus on the assumption that he is the Son of God (Mt. 3:11=Lk. 4:41). Demons recognize him as the Son of God (Mk. 5:7). The High Priest challenges him with the question of whether he is the Son of the Blessed (Mk. 14:61). Matthew adds "Son of God" in several places where Mark does not have it;[18] and it is clear that the traditions embodied in Mark and Q represent Jesus as being acknowledged as the Son of God by both men, demons and God. Places where Matthew adds the phrase do not change but only accentuate this tradition.

It is obvious that in these passages, Son of God is not the equivalent of Messiah. The Messiah is a Son of David, divinely anointed to establish the Kingdom of God in power. Jesus is hailed as the Son of God because of his power over the spirit world (Mk. 3:11; 5:7). The taunt to Jesus on the cross that he should save himself if he was the Son of God indicates that he claimed to stand in a special relationship to God so that he had supernatural power. This verse, if it is not a secondary Matthean addition (Mark and Luke lack the verse), reflects a situation in which the people believed that Jesus claimed to be not only Messiah but also the Son of God.

These verses could be interpreted to mean that Jesus was viewed as a typical Hellenistic divine man or wonder-worker. But there is one bit of evidence that makes this impossible. The temptations during the forty days challenged Jesus to fill precisely this role and convince the people that he was the Son of God by performing miracles; to satisfy his hunger by changing stones to bread; to amaze the crowds by leaping down from the wing of the temple unharmed; and to assert a political mastery over the world (Mt. 4:1-11=Lk. 4:1-13). Jesus firmly rejected this role of the Son of God. As we shall see, at the baptism Jesus was called as the Son of God to fulfill the mission of the Servant of the Lord. The temptations suggested that he forsake that role and pursue his path by miraculous means. Jesus' rebuff of Satan meant in effect that he would not forsake the role of the Servant of God. "Jesus is the Son of God not as a miracle-worker, but in the obedient fulfillment of his task—precisely his task of suffering."[19]

We can determine the content of Son of God by examining several passages where Jesus is called, or calls himself, the Son.

THE BAPTISM. At the beginning of his ministry, Jesus was acclaimed by a voice from heaven to be the Son of God and the chosen Messiah: "Thou art my beloved Son; with thee I am well pleased" (Mk. 1:11). In what sense is Jesus here designated God's Son? Some would interpret it in terms

---

[17] Seven times in Romans, six times in Hebrews, sixteen times in I John.
[18] Mt. 14:33; 16:16; 27:40; 27:43.
[19] O. Cullmann, *Christology*, p. 277.

of the filial love toward God that dawned on Jesus at his baptism.[20] Others interpret this in terms of an adoptionist Christology. At his baptism Jesus was appointed to be the Messiah, the Son of God, and was installed in that office.[21] This has been a very influential interpretation, identifying sonship and messiahship. Jesus became God's Son because he was chosen at his baptism to be the Messiah.

However, if this declaration means inauguration into messianic office expressed in terms of sonship, we would expect different language. The verse is an allusion to Psalm 2:7, which reads, "You are my son, today I have begotten you." These words would be much more suitable to designate installation into the messianic office of sonship.[22] However, instead of quoting Psalm 2:7 in its entirety, the voice conflates the first half of the verse with the words from Isaiah 42:1, "Behold my servant, whom I uphold, my chosen, in whom my soul delights." The Greek word translated in Mark 1:11, "I am well pleased," might be rendered, "On whom my good pleasure has settled," involving the idea of choice. "What is meant is God's decree of election, namely, the election of the Son, which includes His mission and His appointment to the kingly office of Messiah. As *huios ho agapētos* Jesus is the Recipient of this elective good pleasure."[23]

Furthermore, the Greek word *agapētos,* translated "beloved," is sometimes a synonym for *monogenēs:* "only."[24] The heavenly voice may therefore be rendered, "This is my only Son; him have I chosen." Sonship and messianic status are not synonymous. Rather sonship is the prior ground and the basis of Jesus' election to fulfill his messianic office. The reference to Isaiah 42:1 also includes a hint of the fact that the messianic office is to be carried out in terms of the servant of the Lord.[25] The voice from heaven confirms the already existing filial consciousness that was at the heart of the temptation experience (Mt. 4:3, 6) and on the basis of this filial relationship confirms Jesus' dedication to his messianic mission in terms of the servant.[26] "This is my only Son" describes the permanent status of Jesus. He does not *become* the Son; he *is* the Son. Sonship is antecedent to messiahship, and not synonymous with it: "Messiahship is not . . . the primary category here, nor is the 'Son of God' to be explained in terms of messiahship. The voice is . . . a confirmation of His already existing filial consciousness."[27]

THE TEMPTATION of Jesus is to be understood against this back-

---

20 Cf. W. Manson, *Luke* (1930), p. 32.
21 Cf. B. H. Branscomb, *Mark* (1937), pp. 16ff.
22 The Western text of Luke 3:22 has these very words.
23 G. Schrenk in *TDNT* II, 740. It should be noted that the words in Mk. 1:11 are an allusion, not a direct quotation, of Ps. 2:7; the word order differs.
24 In Gen. 22:2; 12:16; Amos 8:10; Jer. 6:26, *agapētos* appears in the Septuagint for the Hebrew *yachid,* "only."
25 V. Taylor, *Mark,* p. 162.
26 C. E. B. Cranfield, *Mark,* p. 55.
27 C. E. B. Cranfield, "A Study of St. Mark 1:9-11," *SJTh* 8 (1955), 62.

ground. Satan did not challenge Jesus with the words, "If you are the Messiah," but "If you are the Son of God." Satan recognized that Jesus, as the Son of God, could call upon angelic aid to assure personal safety. The temptations have to do indeed with Jesus' messianic office, but with the messianic office that is grounded in his sonship.

That sonship involves a supernatural element is further supported by the recognition of Jesus by the demons. Mark records that at the very outset of his ministry, a demon-possessed man in the synagogue at Capernaum saw Jesus, recognized him, and cried out, "What have you to do with us, Jesus of Nazareth? Have you come to destroy us? I know who you are, the Holy One of God" (Mk. 1:24). Recognition by the demons was immediate and direct. It was not grounded upon observation and interpretation of Jesus' words or deeds; it was not acquired, inferential knowledge; it was rather intuitive recognition of a supernatural kind. A comparison of this incident with Paul's experience with the demon-possessed girl in Acts 16 gives support to this interpretation. The expression, "the Holy One of God," is not a known messianic title nor a common primitive Christian designation of Jesus. Its background is the designation in the Old Testament of God as the Holy One.[28] The demoniac recognized in Jesus the presence of a supernatural person.[29]

MATTHEW 11:25-27. The most important passage for the study of Synoptic Christology is a Q passage in Matthew 11:25-27=Luke 10:21-22. Dibelius admits that this pericope is penetrated by a "mythological," i.e., supernatural idea.[30] It has been widely held, especially in German theology, that this was a late product of Hellenistic Christianity.[31] However, Jeremias has established that its Semitic character demands a Jewish milieu,[32] and "if we reject it, it must be on the grounds of our general attitude to the person of Jesus, not on the ground that its form or language is 'hellenistic' in any intelligible sense."[33]

Referring to the kingly activity of God that is at work in his own person in the world, Jesus said, "I thank thee, Father, Lord of heaven and earth, that thou hast hidden these things from the wise and understanding and revealed them to babes." The meaning of Jesus' ministry can be understood only by divine revelation. The presence and the power of the Kingdom of God among men were not universally acknowledged. John the Baptist had announced that the Kingdom of God was at hand, and Jesus had manifested the power of the Kingdom in his messianic ministry. While some recognized that prophecy about the coming Kingdom was being fulfilled,

---

[28] Cf. Isa. 40:25; 57:15.
[29] Cf. also the meeting with demons in Lk. 4:41; Mk. 3:11; 5:7.
[30] M. Dibelius, *From Tradition to Gospel* (1935), p. 279.
[31] W. Bousset, *Kyrios Christos,* pp. 84ff.
[32] J. Jeremias, *The Prayers of Jesus* (1967), pp. 45ff.
[33] W. L. Knox, *Some Hellenistic Elements in Primitive Christianity* (1944), p. 7. See also A. M. Hunter, "Crux Criticorum," *NTS* 8 (1962), 241-48.

"this generation" as a whole was blind, calling John a demoniac and Jesus a glutton and drunkard, and sometimes, demon-possessed (Mt. 12:24). Correct understanding of the person and mission of Jesus could be acquired only by revelation from the Father who is sovereign Lord of heaven and earth and who manifests his sovereignty by hiding these things from the wise and understanding but revealing them to babes.

In the process of revelation, the Son fills an indispensable role. "All things have been delivered to me by my Father; and no one knows the Son except the Father, and no one knows the Father except the Son and anyone to whom the Son chooses to reveal him" (11:27). "All things" refers to "these things" in verse 25, namely, to the entire content of the divine revelation.[34] God, the Lord of heaven and earth, has imparted to the Son the exercise of authority in revelation; it involves the act of entrusting the truth to Christ for communication to others. The ground of this impartation is Jesus' sonship; it is because God is his Father (v. 25) that God has thus commissioned his Son. Because Jesus is the Son of God, he is able to receive all things from his Father that he may reveal them to others. The messianic mission of revelation thus rests upon the antecedent sonship.

What is involved in this relationship is made clear in verse 27: "No one knows the Son except the Father, and no one knows the Father except the Son." Something more is involved in this knowledge of God than a mere filial consciousness. *Jesus knows the Father in the same way that the Father knows the Son.* There exists between the Father and the Son an exclusive and mutual knowledge. God possesses a direct and immediate knowledge of the Son because he is the Father. It is very clear that this knowledge possessed by the Father is not an acquired knowledge based on experience, but a direct, intuitive and immediate knowledge. It is grounded in the fact that God is the Father of Jesus. In the same sense Jesus knows the Father. His knowledge of the Father is thus direct, intuitive and immediate, and is grounded upon the fact that he is the Son. Thus both the Father-Son relationship and the mutual knowledge between the Father and Son are truly unique and stand apart from all human relationships and human knowledge. Christ as the Son possesses the same innate, exclusive knowledge of God that God as the Father possesses of him.

Because Jesus is the Son and possesses this unique knowledge, God has granted to him the messianic mission of imparting to men a mediated knowledge of God. Man may enter into a knowledge of God only through revelation by the Son. As the Father exercises an absolute sovereignty in revealing the Son, so the Son exercises an equally absolute sovereignty in revealing the Father; he reveals him to whom he chooses. This derived knowledge of God, which may be imparted to men by revelation, is similar but not identical with the knowledge that Jesus has of the Father. The Son's knowledge of the Father is the same direct, intuitive knowledge that

---

[34] See J. Jeremias, *The Prayers of Jesus,* p. 49.

the Father possesses of the Son. It is therefore on the level of divine knowledge. The knowledge that men may gain of the Father is a mediated knowledge imparted by revelation through the Son. The knowledge of the Father that Jesus possesses is thus quite unique; and his sonship, standing on the same level, is equally unique. It is a derived knowledge of God that is imparted to men, even as the sonship that men experience through Jesus the Son is a relationship mediated through the Son.

It is clear from this passage that sonship and messiahship are not the same; sonship precedes messiahship and is in fact the ground for the messianic mission. Furthermore, sonship involves something more than a filial consciousness; it involves a unique and exclusive relationship between God and Jesus.

THE IGNORANCE OF THE SON. Jesus refers to himself as the Son of God in his word about the time of his parousia. "But of that day or that hour no one knows, not even the angels in heaven, nor the Son, but only the Father" (Mk. 13:32). The force of this saying is found in the fact that such things ought to be known to angels and to the Son as well as to the Father. The point is that Jesus classes himself with the Father and the angels—all partaking normally of supernatural knowledge. At this point, contrary to expectations, the Son is ignorant.[35]

THE WICKED HUSBANDMAN. In the parable of the wicked husbandman (Mk. 12:1-12), sonship is again differentiated from messiahship and provides the antecedent ground of the messianic mission. After the visit of the several servants had proven fruitless, the landowner sent his son to receive the inheritance. It is because he was the son that the owner expects this last mission to be successful, and his sonship is quite independent of and anterior to his mission. It is because he is the son that he becomes the heir of the vineyard and is sent to enter into his inheritance.

THE DEBATE WITH THE PHARISEES. In the debate with the Pharisees during his last week, Jesus asked them the question, "How can the scribes say that the Christ is the son of David?" Jesus did not deny the truthfulness of their claim. The Davidic descent of the Messiah was so widely accepted that it could not be denied (Rom. 1:3), and there is no evidence that Jesus resented being called the Son of David. Jesus corrected the current evaluation of the Messiah by pointing out that he must be more than David's Son, since David calls him Lord. "The Lord said to my Lord, Sit at my right hand, till I put thy enemies under thy feet" (Ps. 110:1). Then Jesus pressed the question: "David himself calls him Lord; so how is he his son?" (Mk. 12:37). The point is that the Pharisees' concept of Messiah was not wrong; it was inadequate. The Messiah must be not only the Son of David; he must also be the Son of God, and as the

---

[35] For the authenticity of this saying, see I. H. Marshall, "The Divine Sonship of Jesus," *Int* 21 (1967), 95.

Son of God he is David's Lord. As the Son of God, he is to sit at God's right hand to exercise a universal sovereignty. David's Son was to rule the world; God's Son was to rule the world to come. Jesus suggests that, according to the Psalm here quoted, the Messiah must be a supernatural being who will be seated at God's right hand. These words may even involve a reference to Jesus' pre-existence.[36] The Messiah is at the same time an earthly man of Davidic descent and the coming world Judge—David's Lord and Judge.

BEFORE THE SANHEDRIN. A similar claim to sonship of an exalted order is found on the occasion of Jesus' trial before the Sanhedrin. Various charges were laid against Jesus, to which he did not reply. Finally the High Priest put him under oath (Mt. 26:63) and asked him the direct question, "Are you the Christ, the Son of the Blessed?" (Mk. 14:61). Some scholars insist that it is inconceivable that a high priest should have asked such a question,[37] but if the High Priest had heard reports that Jesus had claimed to be the Son of God and was seeking a ground to condemn him, there is nothing incredible about the question. It is not clear whether on the lips of the High Priest the expression "the Son of the Blessed," or "the Son of God" involved anything more than a designation of the messianic office and is synonymous to "the Christ"; but in view of the fact that the expression is not a familiar title for the Messiah, we may suspect that there is more involved in the question. At least Jesus' reply removed a measure of this ambiguity. He said, "I am; and you will see the Son of man sitting at the right hand of Power, and coming with the clouds of heaven" (Mk. 14:62). Immediately the Sanhedrin agreed in condemning him to death, and that on the ground of blasphemy. It is important to note that the claim to messiahship of itself was no ground in the Jewish law for condemnation. The assertion of mere messianic rank could not of itself have led to the death sentence. Such a claim would never have been construed as blasphemy.[38] Jesus' claim then involved far more than messiahship; it involved messiahship of an exalted Son of Man kind. Jesus in effect said this: Now I am standing before your court and being judged; but the day will come when this circumstance will be reversed and when you will see the one whom you are now judging sitting as the Son of Man to judge the world. He whom you are now condemning will henceforth be your Judge. Thus Jesus claimed the prerogative of final judgment, a function that belonged to God alone, and it is because of this claim to future exaltation and to the exercise of the prerogatives of God himself that he was condemned to death on the ground of blasphemy.

CONCLUSION. We conclude that Jesus thought of himself as the Son of God in a unique way, that he was set apart from all other men in that he

---

[36] J. Schniewind, *Das Evangelium nach Matthäus* (1949), p. 163.
[37] Cf. J. Klausner, *Jesus of Nazareth* (1925), p. 342.
[38] Cf. G. Dalman, *The Words of Jesus*, p. 313.

shared a oneness with God impossible to ordinary men. There are other evidences;[39] we have limited our discussion to the use of the term Son of God. There is a close connection between Son of Man and Son of God. Marshall has suggested that Jesus used the title Son of Man "to give cautious expression to his own unique relationship with God as his Son and agent of salvation. The title Messiah was both inadequate . . . and misleading . . . while that of Son was only too clear in its implications. But the title of Son of man had distinct merits. It was admirably fitted to express Jesus' conception of his own person, since it referred to a person closely linked with God and of heavenly origin. . . . 'Son of Man' was thus a perfect vehicle for expressing the divine self-consciousness of Jesus while at the same time preserving the secrecy of his self-revelation from those who had blinded their eyes and closed their ears."[40] In the early church "Son of God" could be used without restraint to indicate the supreme place occupied by Jesus.

THE MESSIANIC SECRET. Before we leave this chapter, we must consider briefly the theory of "the messianic secret." There is another important line of evidence appearing in the Gospels concerning the question of Jesus' messiahship that goes along with Jesus' reticence in the use of the title. On a number of occasions when Jesus had performed some miracle that would gain for him great public attention, he warned the persons healed to keep the matter quiet and to avoid publicity. A cleansed leper is sternly charged to say nothing to anyone (Mk. 1:43f.). Demons who recognized Jesus were forbidden to speak and make him known (Mk. 1:34; 3:11f.). When Jesus raised Jairus' daughter, he forbade the parents to make the events known (Mk. 5:43). A deaf and dumb demoniac after being healed was charged to tell his deliverance to no one (Mk. 7:36). After Peter's confession of Jesus' messiahship, Jesus commanded the disciples not to disclose this fact until after the resurrection (Mk. 8:30; 9:9).

These commands to secrecy provided the basis for an elaborate theory called the messianic secret.[41] Wrede suggested that all of these commands to secrecy are not historical but are editorial additions by the Evangelist. The early church—so theorizes Wrede—was faced with a contradictory situation. It possessed a completely nonmessianic tradition about the life of Jesus. Jesus never claimed to be the Messiah, and he was never recognized as such in his earthly ministry. However, the early church had come to believe that he was the Messiah—Messiah of a supernatural kind—be-

---

39 A. W. Argyle, "The Evidence for the Belief That Our Lord Himself Claimed to Be Divine," *ET* 61 (1949-50), 228-32.

40 I. H. Marshall, "Synoptic Son of Man Sayings," *NTS* 12 (1966), 350f.

41 See W. Wrede, *The Messianic Secret* (1901; Eng. 1973), and A. Schweitzer, *The Quest of the Historical Jesus* (1911), pp. 336f.

cause of the resurrection. Here was a contradiction! The church believed in Jesus as a supernatural Messiah, but its tradition about Jesus was nonmessianic.

To resolve this contradiction and to explain how the Messiah could have left a nonmessianic tradition, there arose the theory of the messianic secret. Jesus was in fact the Messiah, but this was not recognized until after the resurrection (Mk. 9:9 is the key verse). Throughout his ministry Jesus kept it a secret. Therefore the tradition of Jesus' life was a nonmessianic tradition. Jesus was known to be the Messiah only after his resurrection. The Gospel of Mark conflates the two traditions—Christian belief in Jesus as the Messiah with a tradition in which Jesus did not claim to be the Messiah—by the device of the messianic secret.

This is a clever theory, but utterly lacking in evidence. There is no historical trace whatsoever that a nonmessianic tradition ever existed.[42] Every detectable strand of gospel tradition is thoroughly messianic. The existence of a nonmessianic tradition is a critical hypothesis without historical foundation. It has been accepted almost as a fact of "critical orthodoxy" in Germany, but many scholars remain completely unconvinced. T. W. Manson called the "Wredestrasse" the "road to nowhere."[43] There is no compelling reason not to accept the messianic secret as an historical fact that was an important element in the mission of Jesus.[44] The secret of messiahship is closely analogous to the secret about the Kingdom of God.

The Gospels reveal two strands of evidence. They clearly represent Jesus as possessing a messianic consciousness, of accepting the designation Messiah when it was applied to him, of pronouncing a beatitude upon the disciples when they began to apprehend the character of his messiahship, and of flatly affirming his messiahship when challenged by the Sanhedrin. On the other hand, Jesus did not widely and publicly proclaim his messiahship, and he frequently enjoined secrecy upon those who recognized it.

This tension may be adequately solved by the recognition that Jesus knew himself to be the Messiah but not the sort of Messiah popularly expected. His mission was to bring the Kingdom of God but not the sort of

---

[42] This is the thesis of the exciting book by E. Hoskyns and N. Davey, *The Riddle of the NT* (1947).

[43] T. W. Manson, "Present-day Research in the Life of Jesus" in *The Background of the NT and Its Eschatology*, ed. by W. D. Davies and D. Daube (1956), p. 216. Perrin has replied that "the Wredestrasse becomes the Hauptstrasse" (*JR* 46 [1966], 296-300), but he can do so only by a myopic view that regards advanced German criticism as the only scholarship worthy of serious consideration!

[44] See V. Taylor, *Mark,* pp. 122-24; C. E. B. Cranfield, *Mark,* pp. 78-79; G. H. Boobyer, "The Secrecy Motif in St. Mark's Gospel," *NTS* 6 (1960), 225-35; J. C. O'Neill, "The Silence of Jesus," *NTS* 15 (1969), 153-67; R. P. Meye, *Jesus and the Twelve* (1968), pp. 125-36; R. N. Longenecker, *The Christology of Early Jewish Christianity* (1970), pp. 71-73; R. N. Longenecker, "The Messianic Secret," *EQ* 51 (1969), 207-15; and especially J. D. G. Dunn, "The Messianic Secret in Mark," *Tyndale Bulletin*, 21 (1970), 92-117.

kingdom the people wanted. He was indeed recognized as the King of Israel (Mt. 2:2; Lk. 1:32; Jn. 1:50), but his Kingdom was a spiritual Kingdom and his messianic mission was a spiritual mission. In the future he will be the glorious King (Mt. 25:34), and his Kingdom will then be manifested in great power (Mt. 13:41-43; Lk. 22:29-30). But meanwhile, his messiahship involved not a throne but a cross, not glory but humility, not reigning but dying. His present role is that of the Suffering Servant; only in the future will he be the glorious messianic King. The messianic concept, as entertained by the people, must undergo a radical transformation. Jesus could not therefore make free usage of the word Messiah, for it connoted to the people a kind of messiahship that it was not his purpose now to fulfill. Yet, since he actually was the Messiah, he could not in honesty deny the application of the term when it was attributed to him. For he was the Messiah; but he must suffer before he should enter his glory (Lk. 24:26).

The messianic consciousness of Jesus must be distinguished from the messianic revelation. The Gospels unquestionably portray Jesus as possessing a messianic consciousness. His infrequent public affirmations of this fact and his emphasis upon secrecy must be understood against the setting of the popular expectations of the Messiah and Jesus' self-revelation of a radically different messianic function. His messianic self-revelation therefore involves the re-education of his disciples to a new interpretation of the messianic mission as it was actually embodied in his person.

LORD. In the early church, one of the most honorific titles for Jesus was "Lord." It was the primary confession of faith in Jesus (Rom. 10:9), and it carried connotations of deity. As Lord, Jesus, resurrected and exalted, was seated at God's right hand (Acts 2:36, 33), where he would reign until all creation recognized his Lordship (Phil. 2:9-11). If the tradition of the Jesus of history has been as radically transformed by Christian faith as the form critics say, we would expect this title to find its way into the tradition about Jesus.

This, however, is not what we find. The word does indeed frequently occur, but not with high christological connotations. The word is frequently used in the vocative as a form of polite address (Mt. 18:26; 15:27; Lk. 7:6; 9:57, etc.) where it has the force of the English "Sir" or "Milord." Its Hebrew equivalent is "Rabbi"—the term by which pupils addressed their master.[45] Luke uses the term many times in a deliberate anachronism, equal to, "He, whom we now know to be the Lord" (Lk. 7:13, 19; 10:1, 39, 41, etc.).[46] There are several sayings where the word is used as a designation of high honor, but with less than the Christology of the early church (Lk. 5:8; Mt. 7:21).[47] Jesus used the word to designate his own dignity in Mark 2:28; 11:3; and 12:37. The last passage, in which Jesus

---

[45] V. Taylor, *The Names of Jesus* (1953), p. 41.
[46] *Ibid.*, p. 42.
[47] See G. Vos, *The Self-Disclosure of Jesus*, pp. 119f.; O. Cullmann, *Christology*, pp. 204f.

points to Psalm 110:1 where the Messiah is called *Kyrios,* is very important. Taylor thinks that this probably is one of the factors that led the early Christians to think of Jesus as *Kyrios.*[48]

The use of the title in the Fourth Gospel is impressive. In the first nineteen chapters, *Kyrios* appears only three times (4:1; 6:23; 11:2), aside from those places where the vocative is a form of respectful address. However, in the last two chapters there are fifteen appearances of the term. "It is clear that the Evangelist feels it appropriate to speak of 'the Lord' in these contexts, but does not feel at liberty to use the title in connection with the earlier ministry."[49] Taylor rightly concludes that it is highly improbable that this title was in use in the lifetime of Jesus. It is as the risen and ascended Lord that he is *Kyrios*.

---

[48] V. Taylor, *The Names of Jesus,* p. 42.
[49] *Ibid.,* p. 43.

13

THE MESSIANIC PROBLEM:
The Jesus of History and the Historical Jesus

Literature:

A. Schweitzer, *The Quest of the Historical Jesus* (1911, 1969); T. W. Manson, "The Life of Jesus: Some Tendencies in Present-Day Research," *The Background of the NT and Its Eschatology,* ed. by W. D. Davies and D. Daube (1956), pp. 211-21; C. F. D. Moule, "The Intention of the Evangelists," *NT Essays,* ed. by A. J. B. Higgins (1959), pp. 165-79; J. M. Robinson, *A New Quest of the Historical Jesus* (1959); G. Bornkamm, *Jesus of Nazareth* (1960); R. Bultmann, *Existence and Faith,* ed. by S. M. Ogden (1960); B. Reicke, "Incarnation and Exaltation," *Int* 16 (1962), 156-68; C. E. Braaten and R. A. Harrisville, *Kerygma and History* (1962); R. H. Fuller, *The NT in Current Study* (1962); H. Zahrnt, *The Historical Jesus* (1963); M. Kähler, *The So-called Historical Jesus and the Historic Biblical Christ,* ed. by C. E. Braaten (1964); H. Anderson, *Jesus and Christian Origins* (1964); J. Jeremias, *The Problem of the Historical Jesus* (1964); C. E. Braaten and R. A. Harrisville, *The Historical Jesus and the Kerygmatic Christ* (1964); A. Hanson, ed., *Vindications. Essays on the Historical Basis of Christianity* (1966); G. E. Ladd, "History and Theology in Biblical Exegesis," *Int* 20 (1966), 54-64; G. E. Ladd, "The Problem of History in Contemporary NT Interpretation," *StEv V* (1968), 88-100; C. C. Anderson, *Critical Quests of Jesus* (1969); H. K. McArthur, *In Search of the Historical Jesus* (1969); G. E. Ladd, "A Search for Perspective," *Int* 25 (1971), 41-62.

THE PROBLEM. In the preceding chapters we have studied the portrait of Jesus as found in the Synoptic Gospels. At various points in the study we have found objective grounds in the gospel data for believing that this is fundamentally an accurate portrayal; e.g., that the portrait basically corresponds to the facts of the history of Jesus. We must deal at somewhat greater length with this question, for many scholars today would discount the portrait we have drawn with the objection that it represents the faith of the church, not the actual history about Jesus. Such scholars insist that we must go behind the Jesus of the Gospels, who is essentially one with the Christ of faith, to recover the historical Jesus, i.e., a Jesus uncolored by faith.

The problem must be frankly faced. The Gospels portray a man who was conscious that in him dwelt transcendence. He was the Messiah in whom God's kingly reign had come to men; but he wasn't the nationalistic, political Messiah corresponding to the contemporary Jewish hopes. He was the anointed of the Lord to fulfill the messianic promises of the Old Testament, but their fulfillment was occurring in the spiritual realm, not in the socio-political realm. He was also the Son of Man—a heavenly, pre-existent, divine being now appearing on earth in humility to suffer and die but who is destined to be exalted to heaven and to come in glory to judge the world and to inaugurate the Kingdom of God in the transformed order of the Age to Come. In the earthly stage of his mission, however, he is the Suffering Servant who is to give his life a ransom for many, pouring out his blood in a sacrificial, atoning death. Furthermore, Jesus not only claims to be the heavenly Son of Man; he also reflects a consciousness of enjoying a unique relationship with God. His designation of himself as the Son includes elements that go beyond the messianic and point to a unique sense of oneness with God, i.e., a divine self-consciousness.

The issue must be honestly faced. The essential issue is that of transcendence. Jesus is pictured as a transcendent being who is conscious of this dimension of transcendence. It is because he knows himself to be uniquely the Son of God that he brings directly to men the immediate presence of God.[1]

Why has the historical accuracy of the gospel portrait of Jesus been so widely rejected in modern critical study? Have the Gospels been proven untrustworthy? Has new archeological and historical evidence come to light that has undermined their reliability in reporting history?

The problem is the modern understanding of the nature of history. The rejection of the gospel portrait does not arise from an objective, open-minded, inductive study of the Gospels, but from philosophical presuppositions about the nature of history and the nature of the Gospels. History, it is claimed, is exclusively the study of man and his experiences. The Gospels, on the other hand, are witnesses to faith in God and what this faith believed that God had done in Jesus. Since God is not an historical character but a transcendent being, history cannot deal with the claim of faith that God was actually revealing himself in Jesus of Nazareth. Therefore historical study of the Gospels must lay aside this postulate of faith and re-create the story of Jesus of Nazareth in purely "historical," i.e., nonsupernatural terms.

THE NATURE OF THE GOSPELS. At the outset, it must be freely

---

[1] Bornkamm accepts this immediate presence of God in the words and deeds of Jesus as belonging to the historical Jesus (*Jesus of Nazareth* [1960], p. 58). He would reject our conclusions about Jesus' use of the messianic titles.

admitted that the Gospels were written by men of faith who belonged to the believing community. They are not "neutral, objective" historical reports, if by neutral and objective we mean an attitude of detached indifference. They are *gospels*—good news of what God has done in Jesus.[2] An unbeliever could not have written a *gospel*. He could report Jesus' words and deeds, but he would do so in a context of doubt and skepticism that would view Jesus either as a charlatan or one deranged. The question is: Does the fact that the Evangelists were committed, believing men require them to distort and misrepresent the facts of history? Many studies about Jesus place faith and history in antithetical categories. Whatever in the Gospels corresponds to Christian faith cannot be historically trustworthy. This, however, is a false assumption. Exactly the opposite may be true; only faith could really appreciate and adequately report what happened in the Jesus of history. Most historians today admit that all good history is *interpreted* history. History that is not interpreted is not real history; it is only a dry, meaningless chronicle of people, places, events, and dates. History always tries to understand the *meaning* of the events it reports; and the fact that a man has a viewpoint does not mean that he is a poor historian and distorts facts to support his interpretation.

Again, it is obvious that the Gospels are not historical and biographical in the strict modern sense of the word. The Evangelists clearly exercised a certain measure of freedom in reporting both the words and deeds of Jesus that violates the technical norms of modern history writing. Matthew and Luke feel free to rearrange Markan material, and to report Jesus' words with some variation from their Markan source,[3] in a way that a modern historian would not do. Also, there can be little doubt that the Evangelists often wrote as they did to meet the current life and needs of the church.

Furthermore, it is also obvious that the gospel tradition existed for some years in oral form before it was reduced to writing, and it is highly probable that during the oral state the traditions assumed more or less stylized forms and were to some degree modified in transmission.[4]

FORM CRITICISM AND THE GOSPELS. The radical form critics have treated the gospel tradition as an uncontrollable, free-floating tradition that passed through a series of stages from the historical Jesus to orthodox Christology. The "criterion of dissimilarity" has become almost a sacred tenet of "orthodox" criticism. Only those sayings of Jesus can be accepted as authentic which cannot be paralleled in either Judaism or the early church. Wherever parallels are found, the saying in question may have been produced by Jewish or Christian influences.

This norm violates the rights of historical probability. It is incredible that Jesus as a Jew would not have made use of ideas current in Judaism that in turn rested squarely upon the Old Testament. It is incredible that

---

[2] See G. E. Ladd, *The NT and Criticism* (1967), pp. 153ff.

[3] *Ibid.*, pp. 109-40.

[4] *Ibid.*, pp. 141-69. See F. F. Bruce, *Tradition: Old and New* (1970), pp. 39ff.

Jesus would have interpreted the Old Testament at complete variance with the scribes. It is incredible that the early church, looking back to Jesus and remembering his words, would not have made use of his teachings in their interpretations of him.[5]

Nevertheless, such form critics ignore the norm of historical probability and seek to create the history of the gospel tradition by postulating several stages in its development: from the historical Jesus to the primitive Jewish church, the Hellenistic Jewish church, the Hellenistic Gentile church.[6] However, these several alleged stages do not clearly emerge from our historical sources; they are created only by a critical hypothetical reconstruction of the materials preserved in the Gospels. They rest on a general historical presupposition in which form-critical investigations are carried out in terms of a *religionsgeschichtliche* interpretation of primitive Christianity.[7] This is not inductive historical criticism but a methodology based on a set of presuppositions as to how history must have unfolded. The "radical negative results [of many form critics] are due more to their presuppositions than to the data with which they deal."[8]

Over against this approach is the fact that the gospel tradition throughout its entire life was under the control of eyewitnesses who had seen and heard Jesus (see I Cor. 15:6). The Gospels assumed written form in about a generation after Jesus' death when eyewitnesses were still in the church. The controlling influence of eyewitnesses is altogether ignored by the form critics. In the famous words of Vincent Taylor, "If the Form Critics are right, the disciples must have been translated to heaven immediately after the resurrection."[9]

Form critics ignore another fact: while the early church did indeed preserve the words and deeds of Jesus to meet her own immediate needs, one of the most urgent of these needs was the question: Who was Jesus? What did he say and do? In our view, there can be little question that the intention of the Evangelists was to set down in writing the church's living memory of Jesus' person, words, and deeds.[10]

---

[5] W. G. Kümmel rejects the criterion of dissimilarity and casts the burden of proof on those who reject sayings as unauthentic. See *JR* 49 (1969), 60.

[6] See Bultmann's *Theology* and F. Hahn's and R. H. Fuller's works on Christology. Bultmann omits the Hellenistic-Jewish phase.

[7] R. Bultmann, *Existence and Faith,* ed. by S. M. Ogden (1960), pp. 52-53.

[8] F. V. Filson, *A NT History* (1964), p. 78. See also the penetrating critique of form criticism by R. P. C. Hanson in *Vindications,* ed. by A. Hanson (1966), pp. 28-73.

[9] V. Taylor, *The Formation of the Gospel Tradition* (1936), p. 41. The importance of eyewitness control over the tradition is recognized by C. H. Dodd, *About the Gospels* (1950), pp. 13f.; F. V. Filson, *A NT History,* p. 78; O. Cullmann, *Salvation in History* (1967), pp. 90, 98 *et passim;* B. M. Metzger, *The NT* (1965), p. 87; C. F. D. Moule, *The Phenomenon of the NT* (1967), p. 79.

[10] See C. F. D. Moule, "The Intention of the Evangelists" in *NT Essays,* ed. by A. J. B. Higgins (1959), pp. 165-79; A. R. C. Leaney in *Vindications,* ed. by A. Hanson (1966), p. 114.

HISTORICITY. As a matter of fact, the Gospels contain many evidences that the tradition was not completely recast by the faith of the primitive community but embodies a sound historical sense. We have noted in our study of the messianic terminology that the Gospels reflect the *Sitz im Leben Jesu* rather than the *Sitz im Leben der Urkirche*. Although the early church attributed messiahship to him so freely that "Christ" soon became a proper name, this fact was not read back into the Gospels. Jesus avoided the title Messiah, and "Christ" as a proper name appears anachronistically on only a very few occasions. Jesus' favorite designation for himself was "the Son of Man," but this was never picked up by the early church as a messianic designation. While the early church regarded Jesus as the Son of God, the Gospels do not attribute this title to him, but only the rather veiled term, the Son. While one of the earliest confessions of the church is that Jesus is Lord, and while Luke uses this freely as a deliberate anachronism, it is seldom used of Jesus in the theological sense. Jesus was called the Servant (*pais*) in the early church (Acts 3:13, 26; 4:25, 30), but this usage is not read back into the gospel tradition.

Other evidences strengthen the view that the gospel tradition is historically sound and not the creation of early Christian theology. While the redemptive meaning of the death of Christ was a central theological tenet in the early church, the Gospels have little to say about the meaning of Jesus' death. The Lord's Prayer in both Matthew and Luke contains no word that is explicitly Christian. The Sermon on the Mount has never a word about the grace of God.[11] Other evidences indicate that the remembered teachings of Jesus and the needs of the church were not fused as form criticism suggests. One of the most pressing issues in the early church was the validity of the Gentile mission and the terms under which Gentiles might enter the church; no support for either side of this problem is read back into the teaching of Jesus.[12] Jesus concentrated his mission on Israel; the early church did not.[13]

Enough has been said to suggest that the church possessed a sound memory in reporting the words and deeds of Christ. They do not intend to give anything like a modern biography, and they obviously exercise considerable freedom in reporting many details; they are painting a portrait of Jesus. They knew the difference between the pre-resurrection Jesus and the glorified Christ,[14] and they were interested in telling the story of Jesus not only because his words and deeds met many of the needs in the church but for its own sake.[15]

THE HISTORICAL JESUS. The problem of the historicity of the gospel

---

11 See for these illustrations and others like them, C. F. D. Moule in *NT Essays*, pp. 172f.

12 A. R. C. Leaney, *Vindications*, p. 125.

13 C. F. D. Moule, *The Phenomenon of the NT*, p. 66.

14 C. F. D. Moule in *NT Essays*, p. 173.

15 H. Riesenfeld, *The Gospel Tradition and Its Beginnings* (1957).

portrait of Jesus has been raised largely because of the modern concept of history and the historical Jesus. From the christological controversies in the early centuries, the integrity of the gospel portrait was seldom seriously questioned; but the use of modern "critical" biblical study has challenged its historicity. The rise of deism in England and the Enlightenment (*Aufklärung*) in Germany made an impact on biblical scholarship that persists to this day. The same secularistic methodology employed in the humanities was applied to biblical interpretation. This movement was motivated in part by antisupernaturalistic presuppositions. Albert Schweitzer, an excellent spokesman for the new point of view, attributes to Greek theology the creation of a "new supernatural-historical Gospel." The Christ of Chalcedonian formulation clouded the historical Jesus. "This dogma had first to be shattered before men could once more go out in quest of the historical Jesus, before they could even grasp the thought of His existence."[16] In this idiom, the "historical Jesus" is a technical phrase, designating a hypothetical Jesus who could be interpreted exclusively in human, ordinary historical categories. The gospel portrait of Jesus is that of a divine man; the "historical Jesus" could not be divine, for history has no room for the category of deity. The "historical Jesus" is a hypothesis reconstucted from the Gospels by the use of the historical-critical method on the basis of naturalistic presuppositions. Such a Jesus must by definition be altogether and only human—a Jesus without transcendence. "If we want to speak of the historical Jesus we must accustom ourselves at first to disregard the christological dogmas of the Gospels."[17] Robinson has clearly recognized this fact. He acknowledges that the "historical Jesus" is not simply identical with "Jesus" or "Jesus of Nazareth" but is a technical term designating "what can be known of Jesus of Nazareth by means of the scientific methods of the historian. . . . The clear implication is that 'Jesus of Nazareth as he actually was' may be considerably different from the 'historical Jesus.' "[18] It is Bultmann's merit to have made his methodology crystal clear. "The historical method includes the presupposition that history is a unity in the sense of a closed continuum of effects in which individual events are connected by the succession of cause and effect."[19] The "historical Jesus" is a pure hypothesis, a cipher so far as the Gospels are concerned.[20] An "historical Jesus" has not been found who stands the tests of scholarship. Old Liberalism thought it had discovered an ethical prophet. Schweitzer discovered an apocalyptic Jesus, who he himself admits is not a help but an offense to modern man. Bultmann became skeptical of ever reconstructing the historical Jesus. The post-Bultmannians, illustrated

---

[16] A. Schweitzer, *The Quest of the Historical Jesus* (1911), p. 3.

[17] E. Fuchs, *Studies of the Historical Jesus* (1964), p. 56.

[18] J. M. Robinson, *A New Quest of the Historical Jesus* (1959), pp. 26, 31.

[19] R. Bultmann, *Existence and Faith,* p. 291.

[20] B. Reicke in *Int* 16 (1962), 163.

by Bornkamm and Robinson,[21] have found an existential Jesus who achieved authentic existence. But now the post-Bultmannians seem to have lost their zest for the new quest and are turning to other interests.[22] The futility of the quest illustrates Piper's judgment that "there is no satisfactory method by which the Gospel records can be brought into agreement with the modern idealistic or positivistic views of history."[23]

This failure of the historical-critical method to discover an historical Jesus who was big enough to account for the rise of the Christian faith and the gospel portrait long ago led M. Kähler to postulate a difference between the *historische* Jesus and the *geschichtliche* Christ. The *historische* Jesus is the creation of the historical-critical method—a *Holzweg,* a road that leads nowhere. The Jesus who lived in history is the *geschichtliche,* biblical Christ who is portrayed in the Gospels. Kähler believed in the principle of causality; he insisted that only the Christ pictured in the Gospels, in whom dwelt the supernatural (*übergeschichtlich*), is big enough to account for the rise of the Christian faith.[24] "Whoever tries to account for the beginnings of Christianity by some purely historical, nontranscendental event, runs up against the difficulty that there seems to be no such event of sufficient magnitude or of a kind such as to fulfill the need."[25] The rejection of the biblical portrait of Jesus in favor of a hypothetical historical Jesus, and the effort to trace the stages between the two, is not the result of open-minded inductive study of our sources, but of philosophical presuppositions about the nature of history. There is good reason to accept the gospel portrait as basically sound.

HISTORY AND FAITH. Our conclusions raise the question of the relationship between history and faith. Does historical and critical study prove the transcendence of Jesus? How can faith really be faith if it is established by historical and critical findings? Bultmann is the outstanding advocate of the position that faith must be faith in the Word of God alone. If faith rests upon historical verification, it is no longer authentic faith but is reduced to good works—of the historian.

However, it has not been our purpose to verify faith by critical findings. Our purpose has been to try to discover the historical situation in which Jesus taught and lived, for it is the first task of biblical theology to be a descriptive discipline.[26] It is difficult to agree with Jeremias that the final result of critical study of the historical Jesus is "always the same: we find

---

[21] G. Bornkamm, *Jesus of Nazareth;* J. M. Robinson, *A New Quest of the Historical Jesus.*

[22] G. E. Ladd, "The Search for Perspective," *Int* 25 (1971), 45.

[23] O. A. Piper, "Christology and History," *TT* 19 (1962), 333.

[24] For a discussion of Kähler, see G. E. Ladd in *Int* 25, 52-55. It is important to note that Bultmann *et al.* use these two terms differently from Kähler. See *ibid.,* p. 54.

[25] C. F. D. Moule, *The Phenomenon of the NT,* p. 77.

[26] G. E. Ladd in *Int* 25, 48.

ourselves confronted with God himself."[27] History does not necessarily lead to God. A rationalistic orthodoxy could give intellectual assent to the findings of the present study and not be confronted by God. Theology and history are intellectual pursuits; faith is commitment of the whole man. The historian might possibly conclude that Jesus claimed to be the incarnate Son of Man, the unique Son of God, and yet laugh at his claims. History is studded with men possessed of a Messiah complex. Faith is a second step to historical research and is not necessarily demanded by it.

While history does not prove the validity of my faith, history is essential to true faith—at least to the man who is concerned about history. Most people come to faith in response to the proclaimed Word of God without critically testing the historicity of the events that Word proclaims. But when one has believed the Word and then becomes aware of history, if he is compelled to conclude that the alleged events are unhistorical, it is difficult to see how faith can sustain itself. In this sense we agree with Moule: "Neither is *blind* faith real faith. For belief it is necessary to see—at least something. The decision to accept Jesus as Lord cannot be made without historical evidence—yes, historical—about Jesus. If it were a decision without any historical evidence it would not be about Jesus (a historical person) but only about an ideology or an ideal."[28]

If the construct "the historical Jesus" is the product of philosophical presuppositions about the nature of history, is not the construct "the biblical Christ" the product of faith? The answer is No. The biblical portrait of Christ is the product of the apostolic biblical witness. My faith does not create that construct but my faith that the nature of God and history has room for such a Jesus as the Gospels picture makes it possible for me to accept the biblical witness. For the man aware of history, history must provide an adequate foundation for faith. But in the last analysis, faith comes by hearing, and hearing by the Word of God (Rom. 10:17).

---

[27] J. Jeremias, *The Problem of the Historical Jesus* (1964), p. 21.
[28] C. F. D. Moule, *The Phenomenon of the NT*, pp. 78f.

14

THE MESSIANIC MISSION

Literature:

V. Taylor, *Jesus and His Sacrifice* (1937), pp. 79-217; F. Büchsel, "Lutron," *TDNT* IV, 341-49; V. Taylor, *The Atonement in NT Teaching* (1945), pp. 13-16; J. Denney, *The Death of Christ* (1950), pp. 17-40; O. Cullmann, "Death of Christ," *IDB* A-D, pp. 804-8; R. Schnackenburg, *God's Rule and Kingdom* (1963), pp. 182ff.; H. Ridderbos, *The Coming of the Kingdom* (1963), pp. 397-443; J. Jeremias, "The Sacrificial Death," *The Central Message of the NT* (1965), pp. 40-50; L. Morris, *The Cross in the NT* (1965), pp. 13-143; J. Jeremias, "The Passion," *NT Theology* (1971), pp. 276-99; J. Jeremias, "This Is My Body," *ET* 83 (1971-72), 196-203.

The messianic mission of Jesus had as its objective the preparation of men for the future Kingdom of God. Jesus constantly looked forward to the coming of the eschatological Kingdom when the final judgment would effect a separation of men, the righteous entering into the life and blessings of the Kingdom, and the wicked into the doom of punishment. This future destiny was dependent upon present decision, for the powers of the future eschatological Kingdom of God were present in Jesus, confronting men in his person, and demanding of them decision for or against God's rule. Men encountered the powers of the future eschatological Kingdom in the person of the messianic King. As men rendered a decision for the King, which meant a decision for the future Kingdom, they experienced the forgiveness of their sins. As men repented and turned from their sins to submit themselves to the reign of God, they were able to realize in the present the blessings of the Kingdom in reality, though in part. They were delivered from the bondage of Satan's kingdom and from slavery to sin, and experienced an inner righteousness that is entirely the gracious work of God. It was the messianic mission of Jesus to bring the history of God's redemptive purpose to a great crisis. By his presence on earth and by his mission, he brought into history such a manifestation of the powers of the Kingdom of God that its future, glorious consummation was guaranteed. This centrality of the person and work of Christ in the history of redemption is the key to the entire Bible. The whole New Testament bears explicit testimony to this fact, and the Old Testament cannot be properly understood apart from it.[1] The messianic mission of Jesus, as reflected in the Gospels, bears the same witness. Because of this crisis in the person and mission of Christ, the future Kingdom is not only guaranteed, but men may already experience the powers of the future Kingdom and the reality of its soteriological blessings.

The early church viewed Jesus' death as one of the most essential events in the accomplishing of his mission. This is proved by the earliest confessional statement—that of I Corinthians 15:1-3, which includes the words, "Christ died for our sins in accordance with the scriptures."

THE EVENT OF THE CRUCIFIXION. Historically, the death of Jesus was a tragedy of a man caught between the forces of power politics. Jesus had incurred the deadly hostility of the scribes and Pharisees by rejecting their interpretation of the Law and thus undercutting the whole foundation of scribal Judaism. He incurred the fear and hostility of the noble and priestly classes by his triumphal entry into Jerusalem and by challenging their authority by cleansing the temple. There can be little question of the Sanhedrin's sincerity in seeking Jesus' death. As a religious teacher, he was a threat to Pharisaic religion, and his popularity with the people made him politically dangerous. John reports an historically credible reaction of the Sanhedrin: "What are we to do? For this man performs many signs. If we let him go on thus, everyone will believe in him, and the Romans will come and destroy both our holy place and our nation" (Jn. 11:47-48). When the Sanhedrin condemned Jesus for blasphemy for claiming to be the heavenly Son of Man who would be enthroned at the right hand of God (Mk. 14:64), they were acting according to their understanding of the Old Testament. Their sin consisted in hardness of heart that blinded them to the meaning of the new revelatory and redemptive event occurring in Jesus before their very eyes. Pilate must share the blame for the actual execution of Jesus. He recognized that Jesus was a harmless man and not a dangerous revolutionary, yet he yielded to pressure from the Sanhedrin and crucified Jesus as a seditious zealot.

Our concern is with the theology of Jesus' death. Did he foresee his death? What meaning did he see in it?

PREDICTIONS OF THE PASSION. The Gospels represent Jesus as clearly predicting his passion. The gospel record makes Peter's confession of Jesus' messiahship at Caesarea Philippi a turning point in his ministry. After Caesarea Philippi a new note entered Jesus' teaching, "He began to teach them that the Son of man must suffer many things, and be rejected by the elders and the chief priests and the scribes, and be killed, and after three days rise again" (Mk. 8:31). This instruction about his impending

---

[1] O. Cullmann, *Christ and Time* (1950), pp. 81-93, 121-49.

death became an important element in the teaching of the subsequent days (Mk. 9:12, 31; 10:33; Mt. 17:12; 20:18, 19; Lk. 17:25).

How is this new note to be explained? An older criticism interpreted Caesarea Philippi as marking off two phases in our Lord's ministry: the first phase was one of success and happiness; the second, one of disappointment and failure. In the first part of his ministry, Jesus' message was widely accepted and he was confident of success.[2] However, hostility arose among the scribes and Pharisees, and it soon became evident to Jesus that his death was inevitable. Caesarea Philippi marks the turning point in Jesus' interpretation of his own ministry. However, this interpretation is not popular today. "The Gospels seem more likely to be historically correct when they report that success and failure, popularity and enmity, had been part and parcel of Jesus' life from the start."[3]

It is popular to question the historicity of these passion sayings on the ground that they are such a detailed prediction of what happened that they must be a *vaticinium ex eventu*—a product of the early church in the light of Jesus' death and resurrection. While it is probable that the form of these sayings has been molded by the church in the preservation of the tradition, two facts are impressive. The idea of a suffering Son of Man is limited to the words of Jesus. We have seen that there is no clear evidence that Judaism had merged the Old Testament concepts of Son of Man and Suffering Servant; and the early church did not apply to Jesus the title Son of Man.[4] If we apply the criterion of dissimilarity, we ought to conclude that the nucleus of these sayings stems from Jesus. Furthermore, unless Jesus had some interpretation for his own death, it is difficult to explain how the theology of atonement arose in the early church. Long ago, Schweitzer criticized Wrede's nonmessianic theory on the grounds that resurrection would never constitute Jesus as Messiah in the mind of the church,[5] and the validity of this criticism still stands.[6] No more could belief in Jesus' resurrection have caused the church to attribute atoning value to his death. The source of a theology of Jesus' death must go back to Jesus himself.

JESUS' EXPECTATION OF DEATH. The importance of his death in the accomplishment of his mission does not rest on these few predictions. In fact, the death of Jesus is one of the main themes of the Gospels. This is obvious from the space the Evangelists devote to the story of his death. The Gospel of Mark has often been described as a passion story with a long introduction. Indeed, one of the best explanations for the writing of the Gospel was to explain to Gentile readers how it could have happened

---

2 R. Dunkerley, *The Hope of Jesus* (1953), interprets Jesus' eschatology upon this basic premise.
3 G. Bornkamm, *Jesus of Nazareth* (1960), p. 153.
4 See above, Ch. 11.
5 A. Schweitzer, *The Quest of the Historical Jesus* (1911), p. 343.
6 O. Betz, *What Do We Know About Jesus?* (1968), p. 86.

that if Jesus was the Son of God, he could have come to such an ignominious death as execution on a Roman cross.

The question of Jesus' death is inseparable from the question of the Servant of the Lord. We have maintained that Jesus understood his mission in terms of the Son of Man who fulfills the mission of the Suffering Servant,[7] who deliberately identified himself with men in their suffering and death. When John was reluctant to baptize Jesus, he insisted, saying, "Thus it is fitting for us to fulfil all righteousness" (Mt. 3:15). These words are best understood to mean identification with the people. In baptism, Jesus united himself with those who were undergoing John's baptism, even though he had no confession of sin. The righteousness he would fulfill is probably that of Isaiah 53:11: "By this knowledge shall the righteous one, my servant, make many to be accounted righteous; and he shall bear their iniquities."[8] Jesus began his ministry by numbering himself with sinners.

We have seen[9] that the voice from heaven at Jesus' baptism combined allusions to Psalm 2:7 and Isaiah 42:1, and constituted a call to the mission of God's Servant. Because he was the Son of God, God had chosen him to fill the role of the obedient Servant. This allusion to the servant passage in Isaiah indicates that Jesus realized from the very beginning that his messianic mission was to be carried out in terms of the Suffering Servant of the Lord rather than in terms of the ruling Davidic king.

Numerous sayings in the Gospels reflect Jesus' consciousness that a violent fate awaited him. When asked why he did not teach his disciples to fast, Jesus replied that the wedding guests cannot fast while the bridegroom is with them. However, "the days will come, when the bridegroom is taken away from them, and then they will fast in that day" (Mk. 2:20). The concept of the bridegroom is admittedly a messianic one,[10] and the taking away of the bridegroom cannot be interpreted in terms of ordinary human experience. It indicates, on the contrary, that Jesus expected some unusual fate to befall him that would bring grief to his disciples. A tragic event will take place that will disrupt the festivities usually associated with the joy of the bridegroom and his fellows. This can be nothing other than his death.

On one occasion James and John came to Jesus with a request for places of honor in his coming Kingdom. Jesus answered, "You do not know what you are asking. Are you able to drink the cup that I drink or to be baptized with the baptism with which I am baptized?" (Mk. 10:38). The cup is clearly the cup of suffering and death;[11] but in the light of the meta-

---

[7] See Ch. 11.

[8] L. Morris, *The Cross in the NT* (1965), p. 41.

[9] Cf. above, Ch. 12.

[10] The metaphor of the bridegroom is never applied to Messiah in late Judaism; but this is the obvious meaning in Mk. 2:20. See J. Jeremias, *TDNT* IV, 1102ff.

[11] W. G. Kümmel, *Die Theologie des NT* (1969), p. 77.

phor of the cup in the Old Testament, Jesus is apparently thinking of the cup of God's wrath against sin.[12]

The same idea of being overwhelmed in death appears in a saying in Luke 12:50: "I have a baptism to be baptized with; and how I am constrained until it is accomplished!" Such a saying indicates not only that Jesus is conscious that death awaits him; it suggests more than this—that somehow his death is the goal of his mission.

At the last supper Jesus told his disciples, "You will all fall away; for it is written, 'I will strike the shepherd, and the sheep will be scattered' " (Mk. 14:27). This is a citation from Zechariah 13:7. The prophet sees not only the smiting of the shepherd and the scattering of the flock; he also sees the purification of a surviving remnant who become God's people in the time of salvation. Zechariah does not suggest how his cleansing is to be accomplished. However, a hint is given in the context. On the day of lament for the one "whom they have pierced" (Zech. 12:10), a fountain shall be opened for the house of David to cleanse them from sin and uncleanness (Zech. 13:1). This leads to the thought of a representative death for the flock.[13] This passage illustrates the way the thought of Jesus' death absorbed his mind and led him to ponder the meaning of the Old Testament prophecies.[14]

These several passages suggest that Jesus is conscious not only that he is the Son of God and the one by whom God brings his Kingdom to men; his very mission includes suffering and death. In the predictions of his death and in the several passages we have considered, there is little by way of explanation as to the reason for his death or its theological meaning. It is seen somehow simply as an essential element in his mission.

THE MEANING OF THE CROSS. There are two places where Jesus explains something of the meaning of his death: the important saying in Mark 10:45, and at the last supper. After the request of James and John for places of honor and Jesus' answer about the cup and the baptism that await him, Mark adds the saying, "The Son of Man also came not to be served but to serve, and to give his life as a ransom for many." This saying has often been attributed to Pauline influence in the later formation of the gospel tradition,[15] but there is no good reason for rejecting its authenticity. "Anyone who regards the nucleus of the eucharistic words as genuine will have no hesitation in deriving the substance of this *logion* from Jesus."[16]

All three Gospels, and Paul in addition, record words of Jesus instituting the last supper with his disciples. Here we meet an amazing variation

---

[12] C. E. B. Cranfield, *Mark* (1959), p. 337. Cranfield lists many Old Testament references.

[13] J. Jeremias, *NT Theology,* I (1971), 297.

[14] V. Taylor, *Jesus and His Sacrifice* (1937), p. 147.

[15] W. Parsons, *The Religion of the NT* (1939), pp. 129f.

[16] J. Jeremias, *NT Theology,* I, 294. See also F. Büchsel, *TDNT* IV, 342.

in the reported words of Jesus—amazing because we would think that Jesus' words instituting the one repeated Christian ritual would be remembered with precision. Matthew (26:28) follows Mark (14:24): "This is my blood of the covenant which is poured out for many."[17] Matthew alone adds the words, "for the forgiveness of sins." Again, Matthew follows Mark in the saying that Jesus will not drink again of the fruit of the vine until he drinks it "new in the kingdom of God" (Mk. 14:25). Paul adds a word of explanation with an eschatological reference: "As often as . . . you drink the cup, you proclaim the Lord's death until he comes" (I Cor. 11:26).

It is notable that these are the only two sayings (Mk. 10:45 and the last supper) that speak of the meaning of Jesus' death. The realization that death is an essential element in his messianic mission is found throughout his ministry, as we have seen. However, most of the passion passages include no *theology* of the passion. If the gospel tradition had been as completely recast in terms of early Christian faith as form criticism supposes, we would expect to find a far more explicit theological interpretation read into the passion sayings. As the tradition stands, only on a few occasions did Jesus speak of the meaning of his death. From these passages the following conclusions can be drawn.

JESUS' DEATH IS MESSIANIC. This is deduced partly from the evidence cited that Jesus regarded his death as an essential element in his total ministry, and partly from the language of his predictions of his sufferings: "The Son of man *must* suffer many things" (Mk. 8:31). Jeremias argues that this cannot represent the actual words of Jesus, because there is nothing in the Semitic languages to correspond to the Greek *dei* ("it is necessary").[18] That this is not a compelling argument is proven by the occurrence of *dei* several times in the Septuagint, particularly in the translation of Daniel 2:28: "But there is a God in heaven revealing mysteries, who has made clear to the king Nebuchadnezzar the things which must (*dei*) happen in the last of the days." This may not be an *exact* translation of the Aramaic. There is therefore good reason to conclude that Mark's *dei* may represent the meaning of Jesus' words.

Some would interpret this necessity as belonging to the outward sphere and urge that Jesus recognized that the movement of events was such that it became apparent that his death was inevitable. He would therefore cooperate with the inevitable and transform an outward necessity into an experience possessing religious value. This interpretation, however, does not suit the evidence, for when Peter rebuked Jesus for announcing his impending death, Jesus in turn rebuked Peter with the words, "Get behind me, Satan! Because you do not understand the things of God but the things of men" (Mk. 8:33). Peter was thinking on a purely human

---

[17] Lk. 22:20 has the same words in a famous Lukan "non-interpolation." See E. E. Ellis, *Luke* (1966), pp. 253-54.

[18] J. Jeremias, *NT Theology,* I, 277.

level; he was unable to rise to God's level of thought at this point. Jesus' death was not an event that was merely the result of human forces; it was part of the divine purpose of things—it was God's affair. This interpretation is supported by the otherwise unnecessarily sharp rebuke of Peter in which he is labeled the mouthpiece of Satan. This suggests that it would be Satan's purpose to deter Jesus from death; or at least that Satan's purpose would be served by turning aside from the path that leads to death. His death therefore is one of the deepest elements in his messianic mission and is in fact God's purpose for him.

This interpretation is further supported by the language of Mark 10:45: "The Son of man came to give his life." The giving of his life is the objective for which Jesus came; the consummation and the purpose of his messianic mission are embodied in the laying down of his life. His death will not be merely the result of external forces coming to an unfortunate and tragic climax; it is rather the realization of the very purpose of his mission, the highest manifestation of his entire life of service to God and man.[19]

That Jesus' death is an essential part in his messianic mission is made more explicit in John than in the Synoptics. John makes it clear that Jesus' death is not merely an event in history; it is also a deliberate redemptive act of Jesus: he is the good shepherd who laid down his life (*psychē*) for his sheep (Jn. 10:11, 15, 17). If it were not within his messianic mission, no one could take his life away from him. His death is a deliberate act of laying down his life; this is a charge he has received from his Father (Jn. 10:18).

JESUS' DEATH IS ATONING. The redemptive significance of Jesus' death is seen in the ransom saying of Mark 10:45. A complex of ideas is involved in this saying that the Son of Man will give his life (*psychē*) for many. The first is that the life (*psychē*) of a man can be lost or forfeited. "For what does it profit a man, to gain the whole world and forfeit his life?" When a man's life has been lost, there is no possible way of buying it back. No price will prove sufficient to redeem it. The entire world does not possess sufficient value to ransom a life when it has become forfeited. Viewing the lives of the many as forfeited, Jesus would give his life to redeem them.

The second concept is that of ransom. "The idea of ransom (*lutron*) was a common one in the Hellenistic world and involved the price which was paid to redeem a slave from servitude"[20] or to ransom prisoners of war or to gain release from a bond. The Jewish view is the same as the general view of antiquity. "Ransom money . . . is . . . an equivalent for forfeited life."[21] The word also has the wider meaning of substitutionary offering,

---

[19] It has been argued that the cause of Jesus' death was nothing external but was a deliberate act of his will. See J. Wilkinson, *ET* 83 (1971-72), 104-7.

[20] A. Deissmann, *Light from the Ancient East* (1910), pp. 331ff.

[21] F. Büchsel, *TDNT* IV, 341.

atonement offering, that *asham* has in Isaiah 53:10.[22] The goal of Jesus' mission is to give his life as a ransom price that those whose lives were lost might be regained. We need not recoil from this concept of ransom because of the use made of it by the early Greek fathers, who interpreted the ransom as the price paid to the devil so that men might be redeemed from his control. Origen taught that God offered the soul of Christ to the devil in exchange for the souls of men, and Satan after accepting the bargain found that he was unable to hold Christ after he had him in his possession. Through the divine stratagem, the devil lost his domination over both men and Christ. The cross was sometimes interpreted as the bait by which God hooked the devil, or the mousetrap baited with Christ's blood by which the devil was trapped.[23] There is no hint either in this word of our Lord or in the later teaching of Paul that Christ's life was paid to the devil. Jesus did nevertheless view his own death as the price by which the forfeited lives of men might be reclaimed; but he does not explain how this is to come about. We must look to Isaiah 53 for the background of this concept: there the servant of the Lord pours out his soul unto death, is numbered with the transgressors, and bears the sin of many (v. 12).[24]

JESUS' DEATH IS SUBSTITUTIONARY. Jesus' death is not only redeeming; the atonement is accomplished by substitution. A substitutionary element must be recognized both in the general concept involved and in the particular language employed.[25] The preposition in Mark 10:45 is *anti,* which means specifically "in the stead of." The many whose lives have been forfeited will be redeemed because Jesus gives his life in their place. What is involved in this element of substitution is not explained in this passage, nor could we expect a satisfying explanation before the event had taken place. As we have seen, the very fact of the messianic death was a stumbling block to the disciples. How little, then, should we expect to find an articulated doctrine of atonement. Nevertheless the basic elements are indeed present, including the element of substitution. This factor is admitted by such modern writers as Vincent Taylor. "Undoubtedly, it contains a substitutionary idea, since something is done for the many which they cannot do for themselves."[26]

JESUS' DEATH IS SACRIFICIAL. The death of Christ is not only redeeming by way of substitution; it is also a sacrificial death. The description of the suffering servant in Isaiah 53, which, as we have seen, lies behind our Lord's interpretation of his own death, envisages God's servant as mak-

---

[22] J. Jeremias, *NT Theology,* I, 293.
[23] Cf. H. H. Rowley, *The Unity of the Bible* (1953), pp. 126f., for references.
[24] Cf. V. Taylor, *Jesus and His Sacrifice,* p. 102.
[25] Cf. F. Büchsel, "Lutron," *TDNT IV,* 343.
[26] V. Taylor, *Jesus and His Sacrifice,* p. 104. Taylor prefers the term "representative" rather than substitutionary; and while he is compelled to recognize the substitutionary element in this saying of our Lord, it is clear that he is unwilling to admit the implications of this fact. Cf. pp. 282f.

ing his soul an offering for sin (Isa. 53:10).[27] The sacrificial element is present in the words of our Lord connected with the last supper. Not only is his body to be broken; giving to his disciples the cup, he said, "This is my blood of the covenant which is poured out for many" (Mk. 14:24). Matthew's account adds the words, "for the forgiveness of sins" (Mt. 26:28). The form in I Corinthians 11:25 differs slightly. "This cup is the covenant in my blood." Background for this teaching about the covenant, which certainly can be nothing but a new covenant, is found in the covenant of Sinai and that of forgiveness. When Moses received the Law from the hand of God, he took the blood of burnt offerings and peace offerings and threw half of it against the altar. After reading to the people the covenant and securing from them the promise of obedience, he threw the other half of the blood upon the people, saying, "Behold the blood of the covenant which the Lord has made with you in accordance with all these words" (Exod. 24:8). This covenant is connected with *sacrifice,* but there is no mention of the forgiveness of sins.

The *second covenant* is specifically a covenant of *forgiveness.* God promised through the prophet Jeremiah a new covenant when he would write his Law within the hearts of his people and would enter into a new intimacy of relationship with them in which he would forgive their iniquity and remember their sin no more (Jer. 31:34). In the symbolism of the cup, Jesus in effect asserts the fulfillment of this new covenant, whose objective is the forgiveness of sins. Furthermore, this new covenant is associated with his broken body and his blood poured out for many. This terminology involves the fundamental question of the significance of shed blood. Some scholars recognize formally at least the sacrificial element and yet insist that the primary significance of the shedding of blood is the releasing of life, which is thus made available for the participation of men.[28] Elsewhere Taylor explicitly denies that the biblical allusions to blood are synonyms for death. The blood of Christ rather signifies "the life of Christ, freely surrendered and offered for men."[29] By the blood of the covenant, Jesus meant that "his life, surrendered to God and accepted by him, is offered to, and made available to men. Of this life the wine is a symbol; but, since it is given to them to drink, it is more than a symbol. It is a means of blessing, an opportunity for appropriation. It is not transformed into blood, but is a vehicle of the life released for many in the shedding of blood."[30] This concept of the shedding of blood as symbolizing life that is poured out and made available to men was defended by Bishop Westcott[31] and has found a warm reception among many English scholars. How-

27 Cf. H. H. Rowley, *The Unity of the Bible,* p. 129, where the death of the servant as a sacrifice is fully recognized. See also the parallels cited by Jeremias, *NT Theology,* I, 286-87.

28 V. Taylor, *Jesus and His Sacrifice,* pp. 125, 124, 138.

29 *The Atonement in NT Teaching* (1945), p. 63.

30 V. Taylor, *Jesus and His Sacrifice,* p. 138.

31 B. F. Westcott, *The Epistles of St. John* (1883), pp. 34-37.

ever attractive this interpretation may seem to be, the biblical concept of shed blood is *not* that of life released: it is of life poured out in death, especially in the form of sacrificial death. Shed blood is not life released for others, it is life surrendered in death. The blood of Christ is a synonym for the death of Christ, for the shedding of blood involves the destruction of the seat of life. The blood of Christ is "only a more vivid expression for the death of Christ in its redemptive significance."[32] Jesus' blood shed for many refers to his sacrificial death by which the many shall profit. That his disciples are to drink the cup does not symbolize a participation in his life but rather a share in the redemptive blessings that were wrought by the sacrificial death of Christ.

JESUS' DEATH IS ESCHATOLOGICAL. The death of Christ has an eschatological significance, for he said, "Truly, I say to you, I shall not drink again of the fruit of the vine until the day when I drink it new in the kingdom of God" (Mk. 14:25). The death of Christ creates a new fellowship that will be fully realized only in the eschatological Kingdom of God. This eschatological orientation may also be seen in Paul's comment, "For as often as you eat this bread and drink the cup, you proclaim the Lord's death until he comes" (I Cor. 11:26).

The objection that this teaching about a redemptive sacrificial death can hardly be an authentic part of our Lord's teaching because it is not consonant with the body of his teaching about the nature of God cannot be successfully sustained, either from the exegesis of specific passages or from his teaching about the character of God as a whole. It has often been insisted that the central theme in our Lord's teaching about God and the forgiveness of sins is that God out of his fatherly disposition toward men forgives them their sins freely without any need of sacrifice or atonement. The parable of the prodigal son has often been cited as an illustration of this free, unmediated forgiveness of God. The father forgave the prodigal when he returned home without sacrifice or shedding of blood. This, however, is a dangerous argument, for in the parable of the prodigal, there is no mediator of any sort; and if on the ground of this parable we are to eliminate atonement, we must also eliminate the mediation of any savior whatsoever. The parable of the prodigal is designed to teach one truth, namely, the character of God's love toward sinners. No theology of forgiveness can be erected on a single parable.

We have already seen that Jesus' teaching about the nature and character of God involves the recognition that God is both love and vindictive righteousness. In other words, God is *holy* love. Since God is love, he provides forgiveness for the sins of men; and since he is holy love, he provides that forgiveness through the medium of the sacrificial, atoning death of Christ. While Vincent Taylor has not adequately recognized all that is involved in the death of Christ, he has expressed himself effectively when he says,

---

[32] Cf. A. M. Stibbs, *The Meaning of the Word "Blood" in Scripture* (1947), p. 8 and 9, and the literature there cited.

"The idea that no act of requital is due to a holy God, or is needed by men, is a modern notion which it would be a libel to attribute to the ancient world; and to say that Jesus cannot have spoken of his death in this way is to modernize his figure and his thought."[33]

THE EXPERIENCE OF THE CROSS. Two details of Jesus' passion suggest a far deeper meaning in his dying than physical death, fearful as it was. All three Synoptics relate Jesus' agonizing prayer in Gethsemane that his Father would remove "this cup" from him (Mk. 14:36). Luke adds that he was in such anguish of spirit that "his sweat became like great drops of blood falling down upon the ground" (Lk. 22:44).

Cullmann contrasts the deaths of Socrates and Jesus, pointing out that Socrates died impassively and heroically, while Jesus cried out in real fear of death.[34] Cullmann recognizes that death meant to Jesus to be separated from God, surrendered to the hands of the enemy; but this seems to be the meaning of death for all men. "It is alien to the spirit of Jesus that He should ask for the cup to be taken away if it is no more than one of personal suffering and dying,"[35] especially in light of subsequent Christian martyrdoms when men gladly suffered the same form of death out of love for Jesus. Something deeper must be seen in the cup than simply physical death. In the Old Testament, the cup is a metaphor for punishment and divine retribution for sin.[36] In his identification with sinful men, he is the object of the holy wrath of God against sin, and in Gethsemane as the hour of the passion approaches the full horror of that wrath is disclosed.[37] Even though he has known that his death was at the heart of his messianic mission, and even though he has set himself to fulfill this mission, the awfulness of the cup of God's wrath against sin is so bitter that he cannot but cry out for deliverance—"if it were possible" (Mk. 14:35). Yet he submits himself in full surrender to accomplish his mission.[38]

The second event is the cry of dereliction on the cross: "My God, my God, why hast thou forsaken me?" (Mk. 15:34). This is indeed a quotation from Psalm 22:1, and certainly means, at least, that Jesus is one with suffering humanity.[39] More satisfactory is the view that Jesus experienced a feeling of utter abandonment by his Father.[40] Still, it is possible that "the burden of the world's sin, his complete self-identification with sinners, involved not merely a felt, but a real abandonment by his Father."[41]

---

33 V. Taylor, *Jesus and His Sacrifice,* p. 105.
34 O. Cullmann, *Immortality or Resurrection?* (1958), pp. 19ff.
35 V. Taylor, *Mark* (1952), p. 554.
36 *Loc. cit.*
37 C. E. B. Cranfield, *Mark,* p. 433.
38 See V. Taylor, *Jesus and His Sacrifice,* p. 152; L. Morris, *The Cross in the NT,* pp. 46-48.
39 S. E. Johnson, *Mark* (1960), p. 256.
40 V. Taylor, *Jesus and His Sacrifice,* pp. 160f.
41 C. E. B. Cranfield, *Mark,* p. 458; see L. Morris, *The Cross in the NT,* pp. 48f.; D. H. C. Read, "The Cry of Dereliction," *ET* 68 (1956-57), 260-62.

JESUS' DEATH A VICTORY. A few sayings in John bring out another aspect of the meaning of Jesus' death. We have seen that at the heart of Jesus' mission was a spiritual struggle with the powers of evil. In Jesus' person and mission the Kingdom of God was conquering the kingdom of Satan. John indicates that this struggle extends to the cross. The hour of death meant that "the ruler of this world" tries to engulf Jesus. His betrayal by Judas is described as an act motivated by the devil (6:70; 13:2, 27). Yet the death of Jesus means that the ruler of this world is "cast out" (Jn. 12:31; see also 16:11). Somehow, in a way the Evangelist does not try to describe, the death of Jesus is both an act of Satan and an act in which Jesus wins the victory over Satan.[42]

[42] See L. Morris, *The Cross in the NT*, pp. 170f.

15

ESCHATOLOGY

Literature:

T. W. Manson, "The Final Consummation," *The Teaching of Jesus* (1935), pp. 244-84; V. Taylor, "The Apocalyptic Discourse of Mark 13," *ET* 60 (1948-49), 94-98; A. N. Wilder, *Eschatology and Ethics in the Teaching of Jesus* (1950); G. R. Beasley-Murray, "A Century of Eschatological Discussion," ET (1952-53), 312-16; C. K. Barrett, "NT Eschatology," *SJTh* 6 (1953), 136-55, 225-43; C. E. B. Cranfield, "Mark 13," *SJTh* 6 (1953), 189-96, 287-303; 7 (1954), 284-303; G. R. Beasley-Murray, *Jesus and the Future* (1954); O. Cullmann, "The Return of Christ" in *The Early Church,* ed. by A. J. B. Higgins (1956), pp. 141-62; W. G. Kümmel, *Promise and Fulfilment* (1957); G. R. Beasley-Murray, *A Commentary on Mark Thirteen* (1957); J. A. T. Robinson, *Jesus and His Coming* (1957); F. F. Bruce, "Eschatology," *London Quarterly and Holborn Review,* 27 (1958), 99-103; H. P. Owen, "The Parousia in the Synoptic Gospels," *SJTh* 12 (1959), 171-92; T. F. Glasson, *The Second Advent* (1963[3]); W. G. Kümmel, "Futuristic and Realized Eschatology in the Earliest Stages of Christianity," *JR* 43 (1963), 303-14; I. H. Marshall, *Eschatology and the Parables* (1963); H. Ridderbos, *The Coming of the Kingdom* (1963), pp. 444-539; G. E. Ladd, *Jesus and the Kingdom* (1964), pp. 303-26; A. L. Moore, *The Parousia in the NT* (1966); R. H. Hiers, *The Kingdom of God in the Synoptic Tradition* (1970).

The subject of eschatology is the most difficult problem in the Synoptics. It is attended by a host of difficult, complex questions that we can do little more than mention in this chapter, and state conclusions without argument.

INDIVIDUAL ESCHATOLOGY: THE INTERMEDIATE STATE. Jesus had little to say about the destiny of the individual apart from his place in the eschatological Kingdom of God. The entire New Testament distinguishes clearly between Hades, the intermediate state, and Gehenna (hell), the place of final punishment. Hades is the Greek equivalent of the Old Testament Sheol. In the Old Testament, human existence does not end with death. Rather, man continues to exist in the nether world. The Old Testament does not speak of man's soul or spirit descending to Sheol; men continue to exist as "shades" (*rephaim*). The *rephaim* are "weak shadowy continuations of the living who have now lost their vitality and strength." They are "not extinct souls but their life has little substance."[1] Sheol, where the shades are gathered, is pictured as a place beneath (Ps. 86:13; Prov. 15:24; Ezek. 26:20), a region of darkness (Job 10:22), a land of silence (Ps. 88:12; 94:17; 115:17). Here the dead, who are gathered in tribes (Ezek. 32:17-32), receive the dying (Isa. 14:9, 10). Sheol is not so much a place as the state of the dead. It is not non-existence, but it is not life, for life can be enjoyed only in the presence of God (Ps. 16:10, 11). Sheol is the Old Testament manner of asserting that death does not terminate human existence.

There are a few intimations in the Old Testament that death will not be able to destroy the fellowship that God's people have enjoyed with him. Since God is the living God and the Lord of all, he will not abandon his people to Sheol, but will enable them in some undefined way to enjoy continued communion with him (Ps. 16:9-11; 49:15; 73:24; Job 19:25-26).[2] These passages do not have a clear teaching of a blessed intermediate state, but they embody the germ of such a teaching. The psalmists cannot conceive that communion with God can ever be broken, even by death.

In the Old Testament, Sheol is not a place of punishment. The fate of the righteous and unrighteous is the same. In Judaism there emerges a distinct doctrine of Sheol as a place of blessedness for the righteous but a place of suffering for the unrighteous (En. 22-23; IV Ez. 7:75-98).

Jesus has almost nothing to say about Hades. The word occurs a few times (Mt. 11:23 = Lk. 10:15; Mt. 16:18) as a well-known concept. In one parable Jesus draws upon contemporary ideas about Hades to set forth the danger men face if they refuse to hear the word of God. The parable of the rich man and Lazarus (Lk. 16:19-31) has often been taken as a didactic passage to teach explicitly the state of the dead. This, however, is very difficult, for if this is a didactic passage, it teaches something contrary to the rest of Jesus' teaching, namely, that wealth merits Hades and poverty itself is rewarded in Paradise.[3] This parable is no commentary on contemporary social life, nor does it intend to give teaching about the afterlife. It is really not a parable about the rich man and Lazarus, but about the five brothers. Jesus used contemporary folk-material to set forth the single truth that if men do not hear the word of God, a miracle such as a resurrection would not convince them.[4]

In a single saying, Jesus sheds a ray of light on the fate of the righteous.

---

[1] R. F. Schnell, *IDB* R-Z, p. 35.

[2] See R. Martin-Achard, *From Death to Life* (1960), pp. 146-81.

[3] J. Jeremias, *The Parables of Jesus* (1963), p. 184.

[4] *Ibid.*, pp. 186f.

To the dying thief who expressed faith in Jesus, he promised, "Today you will be with me in Paradise" (Lk. 23:43). Here is a clear affirmation that the soul or spirit of the dying man would be with Jesus in the presence of God. "Paradise," meaning park or garden, is used in the LXX of the garden of Eden (Ezek. 28:13; 31:8) and is sometimes used of the messianic age when the conditions of Eden will be restored (Ezek. 36:35; Isa. 51:3). The word is also used in intertestamental literature of the messianic age of blessedness (Test. Lev. 18:10f.; Test. Dan. 5:12; IV Ez. 7:36; 8:52; Apoc. Bar. 51:11). There also developed in this literature the idea that the blessed dead were at rest in a garden of God (En. 60:7, 23; 61:12). The word appears only three times in the New Testament—in the passage in Luke, in II Corinthians 12:3, and in Revelation 2:7—where it simply designates the dwelling place of God. We must conclude that Jesus gives no information about the state of the wicked dead, and only affirms that the righteous dead are with God.

RESURRECTION. It is clear that individual destiny is seen in terms of bodily resurrection. On several occasions Jesus raised dead people to life. These are not isolated miracles but signs of the messianic age.[5] It is obvious that Jesus shared the prevailing Jewish view of the resurrection. In the Old Testament there is a hint of resurrection in Isaiah 26:19, and a positive affirmation in Daniel 12:2. While there was no orthodox eschatology in Judaism and a great variety of views are to be found in the literature, resurrection became a standard belief of the Jews,[6] with the exception of the Sadducees, who denied the idea of resurrection. This provides background for their insincere question about the woman who had seven husbands (Mk. 12:18-23). Jesus replied that the life of the resurrection will be a different kind of life: it is undying and therefore will no longer need the natural functions of male and female. It is important to note that Jesus does not say that men will *become* angels—only that they will be *like* angels in that they no longer die (Mk. 12:25). Luke adds that the resurrection introduces men to the life of the future age, i.e., the Kingdom of God. One other casual reference to resurrection occurs in Luke 14:14: "You will be repaid at the resurrection of the just."[7]

HELL. The New Testament word for the place of final punishment is *Gehenna,* which derives from the Hebrew *ge hinnom. Ge hinnom* was a valley south of Jerusalem where sacrifices were offered to Moloch in the days of Ahaz and Manasseh (II Kings 16:3; 21:6). The threats of judgment uttered over this sinister valley in Jeremiah 7:32; 19:6 are the reason why the Valley of Hinnom came to be equated with the hell of the last judgment in apocalyptic literature.[8] In the Synoptics, Gehenna is a place

---

[5] A. Oepke, *TDNT* I, 370.
[6] *Loc. cit.*
[7] See Oepke's interesting comment on this verse in *ibid.,* p. 371.
[8] J. Jeremias, *TDNT* I, 657.

of eternal torment in unquenchable fire (Mk. 9:43, 48). While only the bodies of men are in the grave, the whole man can be cast into hell (Mt. 10:28). It is pictured as a fiery abyss (Mk. 9:43), as a furnace of fire (Mt. 13:42, 50), as an eternal fire prepared for the devil and his angels (Mt. 25:41). Vivid pictures of the punishments to be endured in hell, which are frequently met in apocalyptic writings, are quite lacking in the Gospels.

On the other hand, final punishment is pictured as outer darkness (Mt. 8:12; 22:13; 25:30). This suggests that both fire and darkness are metaphors used to represent the indescribable. "I never knew you; depart from me, you evildoers" (Mt. 7:23); "Truly, I say to you, I do not know you" (Mt. 25:12). Exclusion from the presence of God and the enjoyment of his blessings—this is the essence of hell.

JESUS' VIEW OF THE FUTURE: THE SOURCES. Most of the eschatology of Jesus as reported by the Synoptics has to do with the events attending the coming of the eschatological Kingdom of God. Eschatological ideas and hints are found scattered throughout his teaching. The Gospels report two eschatological discourses: a passage in Luke (17:22-37) in response to a question from the Pharisees about the time of the coming of the Kingdom, and the Olivet Discourse (Mk. 13; Mt. 24; Lk. 21). Matthew adds considerable eschatological material, some of it paralleled in Luke (Mt. 24:27-51), and three eschatological parables (Mt. 25) that are found only in the first Gospel.

Two facts make it obvious that even the Olivet Discourse does not report a single entire sermon of Jesus. This is not to say that Jesus did not give an eschatological discourse on Olivet; quite certainly he did. However, the three reports of this sermon, in their present form, are clearly the result of the editorial work of the Evangelists drawing upon available traditions.[9] This is proven by the fact that Mark 13:9b-12 is not reproduced in Matthew 24 but is found in Matthew 10:17-21 in the missionary discourse to the twelve. Again, the brief pericope in Matthew 24:26-28 appears to be a bit of Q material, and appears also in Luke 17:23-24.

A second fact makes the problem even more difficult. According to Mark 13:4, the disciples asked Jesus a twofold question: When will the temple be destroyed (Mk. 13:1-2), and what will be the sign "when these things are all to be accomplished"? There can be little doubt but that the disciples thought of the destruction of the temple as one of the events accompanying the end of the age and the coming of the eschatological Kingdom of God. Matthew interprets the disciples' question to involve these two

---

[9] We need not be detained by the famous "Little Apocalypse" theory of T. Colani (1864) that the Olivet Discourse of Mark 13 is not a trustworthy report of Jesus' words but is a brief apocalypse reflecting Jewish messianic ideas that Mark embodied in his Gospel. This has been exhaustively studied by G. R. Beasley-Murray, *Jesus and the Future* (1954), but the theory in one form or another persists. See E. Schweizer, *Mark* (1970), p. 263.

events: "When will this be [i.e., the destruction of the temple], and what will be the sign of your coming and of the close of the age?" (Mt. 24:3). The question is: Did Jesus, like the disciples, expect the destruction of the temple and the end of the age both to occur in the near future?

The problem is compounded by the fact that these two events seem to be inextricably interwoven in the three reports, although the eschatological stands out most clearly in Matthew and the historical in Luke. All three Gospels relate the coming of the Son of Man in the clouds with power and great glory (Mk. 13:26 and par.), to gather his people into the eschatological Kingdom (Mk. 13:27; omitted by Luke). It is reasonably certain that the "great tribulation" (Mk. 13:19 and par.) refers to the "time of messianic woes" that finds its roots in the Old Testament (Jer. 30:7; Dan. 12:1). The identity of the "desolating sacrilege" (Mk. 13:14) is more difficult. The word translated "sacrilege" (*bdelugma*) is used in the Old Testament of everything connected with idolatry. The phrase is used in Daniel 11:31 of the profanation of the altar by the representative of Antiochus Epiphanes in 167 B.C.[10] The phrase is also used in Daniel 12:11, where it is more likely that it refers to the eschatological antichrist.[11] The phrase in the Olivet Discourse has usually been understood to be a reference to antichrist.[12]

Beasley-Murray has made a strong case for understanding the phrase to refer to the profanation of the sacred precincts by the Roman armies bearing their heathen insignia.[13] In any case, some of the admonitions fit the historical situation better than the eschatological. The warning to flee to the mountains, to haste, the hope that the tribulation occur not in winter when the wadis are flooded with water, can be related to an historical situation but only with difficulty to a worldwide tribulation waged by an eschatological antichrist.

The greatest difficulty is found in the fact that if the "desolating sacrilege" in Mark and Matthew is primarily eschatological, in Luke it has become "Jerusalem surrounded by armies" (Lk. 21:20).

This striking difference between Mark, Matthew, and Luke has been solved in several ways. Many conservative interpreters would follow Luke's account and interpret Matthew and Mark in the light of Luke. The great tribulation and the desolating sacrilege are to be understood historically to refer to the siege of Jerusalem and the destruction of the temple by Titus in A.D. 66-70.[14] The difficulty with this view is that the parousia will take place "*immediately* after the tribulation of those days" (Mt. 24:29). It

---

[10] The phrase is used of this sacrilegious act in I Macc. 1:54.

[11] See E. J. Young, *Daniel* (1949), pp. 255ff.

[12] See W. Foerster, *TDNT* I, 600.

[13] G. R. Beasley-Murray, *A Commentary on Mark Thirteen* (1957), pp. 56-57.

[14] Cf. J. A. Broadus, *Matthew* [*American Commentary*] (1880), pp. 485f.; A. Plummer, *Matthew* (1909), pp. 332-34; G. Vos, "Eschatology of the NT," *ISBE* II, 983.

places the tribulation and the abomination of desolation eschatologically in the events of the last days.

Another solution to the problem is that Mark and Matthew record accurately what Jesus taught while Luke gives us his interpretation in the light of later history. Jesus' teaching was primarily eschatological; but when the destruction of Jerusalem occurred, Luke, writing after the event, interpreted the teachings of Jesus to refer to the historical event.[15] However, it is by no means certain that Luke's Gospel was written after A.D. 70; an earlier date is far more likely, in the late fifties or early sixties.[16]

Again, some interpreters have suggested that the Gospels record two different discourses spoken at different times; and while the two prophetic addresses are similar in structure, one deals with the immediate historical future, the other with the eschatological consummation.[17] However, the structure of the discourse in the three Gospels is so similar that this is most unlikely.

There is another solution. We have noted that the discourse was spoken by Jesus to answer a twofold question: When will the temple be destroyed, and what will be the sign of Jesus' parousia and the end of the age (Mk. 13:4; Mt. 24:3)? We have also seen that Mark's account embodies both historical and eschatological references. We must conclude that in spite of the exhaustive work of the form critics, we cannot recover the history of the tradition and re-create the *ipsissima verba* of Jesus. However, from the totality of his teaching one thing is clear: Jesus spoke both of the fall of Jerusalem and of his own eschatological parousia. Cranfield has suggested that in Jesus' own view the historical and the eschatological are mingled, and that the final eschatological event is seen through the "transparency" of the immediate historical.[18] The present author has applied this thesis to the Old Testament prophets and found this foreshortened view of the future to be one of the essential elements in the prophetic perspective. In Amos, the Day of the Lord is both an historical (Amos 5:18-20) and an eschatological event (Amos 7:4; 8:8-9; 9:5). Isaiah describes the historical day of visitation on Babylon as though it was the eschatological Day of the Lord (Isa. 13). Zephaniah describes the Day of the Lord (Zeph. 1:7, 14) as an historical disaster at the hands of an unnamed foe (Zeph. 1:10-12, 16-17; 2:5-15); but he also describes it in terms of a worldwide catastrophe in which all creatures are swept off the face of the earth (Zeph. 1:2-3) so that nothing remains (Zeph. 1:18).[19] This way of viewing the future expresses the view that "in the crises of history the eschatological is foreshadowed. The divine judgments in history are, so to speak, rehearsals of the last judgment and the successive incarnations

---

15 Cf. T. Zahn, *Introduction to the NT* (1909), III, 157-59.
16 Cf. F. F. Bruce, *The Acts of the Apostles* (1951), pp. 13-14.
17 G. Campbell Morgan, *Luke* (1931), p. 236.
18 C. E. B. Cranfield, "St. Mark 13," *SJTh* 6 (1953), 297-300.
19 See G. E. Ladd, *Jesus and the Kingdom* (1964), pp. 60-66.

of antichrist are foreshadowings of the last supreme concentration of the rebelliousness of the devil before the End."[20]

JESUS' VIEW OF THE FUTURE: HISTORICAL. The Gospels report Jesus as anticipating certain events to happen in the historical future. We have already seen that Jesus anticipated a divine judgment to fall upon Israel because of her spiritual obtuseness. This judgment would be both historical and eschatological.[21] Judgment will fall upon Jerusalem and its inhabitants (Lk. 13:34f.=Mt. 23:37-39; Lk. 19:41-44; 23:27-31). The temple is to be destroyed and razed to the ground (Mk. 13:1-2). Judgment will fall upon this evil generation (Mt. 11:16-19; Lk. 13:1-5). The Kingdom of God will be taken away from Israel and given to another people. In the parable of the faithless tenants, Jesus taught that because Israel has rejected the prophets and even God's own Son, God will visit her in judgment to "destroy the tenants, and give the vineyard to others" (Mk. 12:9). The interpretation of this parable is vigorously debated. Many critics think that in its present form it is an allegory created by the church.[22] Jeremias insists that since the parable in its present form has allegorical details, it cannot be authentic. The original parable must have had a single point: it vindicates Jesus' ministry to the poor. The leaders have rejected Jesus' preaching of the Kingdom while the poor have accepted it.[23] However, Hunter remarks that this is "a choice example of how doctrinaire theory can lead a fine exegete astray."[24] Furthermore, the parable is not pure allegory.[25] The details are necessary elements of the story. The substance of the parable is found in an unquestioned Q saying in Luke 11:49-51=Matthew 23:34-35, where Jesus speaks of the murder of the prophets and God's judgment on the present generation. The parable of the wicked tenants adds only the fact that the Son is also to be killed, and the Kingdom given to "others." Mark's account does not identify who the "others" are. However, the parable clearly affirms that because Israel as represented by her religious leaders has rejected God's offer of the Kingdom, God has rejected the nation Israel, whose place as God's people is to be taken by "others"; and if, as we have argued above,[26] Jesus regarded his disciples as the remnant of the true Israel because they have accepted God's offer of the Kingdom, the "others" must be the circle of Jesus' disciples. Matthew only makes this more explicit by adding the words, "the kingdom of God will be taken away from you and given to a nation producing the fruits of it" (Mt. 21:43).[27]

---

[20] C. E. B. Cranfield in *SJTh* 6, 300.

[21] See above, p. 89.

[22] E. Schweizer, *Mark* (1970), p. 239.

[23] J. Jeremias, *The Parables of Jesus,* p. 76.

[24] A. M. Hunter, *Interpreting the Parables* (1960), p. 95.

[25] V. Taylor, *Mark,* p. 474. See also C. E. B. Cranfield, *Mark,* p. 366.

[26] See Ch. 8.

[27] The dispensational interpretation is that "nation" means "generation"; the Kingdom is taken from the Jews of Jesus' generation but will be given to a future

Jesus foresees a period of time in which his disciples will carry out a mission of preaching the Kingdom beyond the confines of Palestine. Matthew 10 follows Mark 6 (see also Lk. 9:1-6) in relating a preaching mission of the twelve that was to be limited to "the lost sheep of the house of Israel" (Mt. 10:6). They are expressly charged not to go to the Gentiles. However, Matthew inserts a passage found in Mark's Olivet Discourse (Mk. 13:9-13) that anticipates a mission among the Gentiles. Jesus' emissaries will be delivered to councils, dragged before governors and kings for his sake (Mt. 10:17=Mk. 13:9=Lk. 21:12). It is in this context that Mark has the saying, "And the gospel must first be preached to all nations" (Mk. 13:10). Matthew includes an expansion of this verse in his account of the Olivet Discourse: "This gospel of the kingdom will be preached throughout the whole world, as a testimony to all nations; and then the end will come" (Mt. 24:14). This need not be interpreted as a prophecy of the present worldwide mission of the church; but it definitely announces a worldwide mission of Jesus' disciples.

In his mission discourse, Matthew has a different interest. He includes a difficult saying: "Truly, I say to you, you will not have gone through all the towns of Israel, before the Son of man comes" (Mt. 10:23). This verse was used by Schweitzer to mean that Jesus expected the mission of the twelve to create a great movement of repentance among Israel so that the eschatological Kingdom would come before they had finished their mission.[28] This interpretation does not reckon with the composite character of the chapter. This pericope clearly looks beyond the immediate mission of the twelve to their future mission in the world. The present verse says no more than that the mission of Jesus' disciples to Israel will last until the coming of the Son of Man. It indicates that in spite of her blindness, God has not given up Israel. The new people of God are to have a concern for Israel until the end comes.

There are other hints in the Gospels that Jesus sees not only a mission to the Gentiles but also the final salvation of Israel. When Jesus wept over Jerusalem because of the impending divine judgment, he added, "For I tell you, you will not see me again, until you say, 'Blessed be he who comes in the name of the Lord' " (Mt. 23:39). This is a saying that anticipates the repentance of Israel so that when he comes at the end of history to carry out God's judgment and final redemption,[29] a repentant Israel will welcome him.

A similar idea is implicit in a saying included by Luke in his version of the Olivet Discourse. After telling of the destruction of Jerusalem and the scattering of the people, Luke adds the words, "Jerusalem will be trodden down by the Gentiles, until the times of the Gentiles are fulfilled" (Lk.

---

generation of Jews who will believe. See J. D. Pentecost, *Things to Come* (1958), p. 465. This, however, is a forced interpretation.

28 A. Schweitzer, *The Quest of the Historical Jesus* (1911), pp. 358-60.

29 F. V. Filson, *Matthew* (1960), p. 249.

21:24). Here Jesus clearly anticipates a time between the fall of Jerusalem and the parousia that he names "the times of the Gentiles."[30] Furthermore, it is possible that this saying implies a future repossession of Jerusalem by Israel when the "times of the Gentiles" are ended.[31]

The sayings we have just considered make it clear that Jesus has an indeterminate historical perspective in which he sees the historical judgment of Israel, the destruction of the temple, the scattering of the Jewish people, a mission of his disciples both to the Gentiles and also to Israel, and probably the final repentance of Israel. This is supported by the Olivet Discourse in Mark 13. The first section of the Discourse contains two parts: the signs of the end (Mk. 13:5-23) and the events of the end (Mk. 13:24-27). The signs of the end include false messiahs, woes, persecution, world-wide evangelization, the desolating sacrilege, and the great tribulation. The disciples had asked, "What will be the sign when these things all are to be accomplished?" (Mk. 13:4). Matthew understands this to mean "the sign of your coming" (Mt. 24:3). Jewish apocalyptic was fond of relating the signs that would presage the imminence of the end. The author of IV Ezra writes: "Concerning the signs: . . . the sun shall suddenly shine forth at night and the moon during the day. Blood shall drip from wood, and the stone shall utter its voice. . . . The sea of Sodom shall cast up fish . . . and fire shall often break out, and the wild beasts shall roam beyond their haunts, and menstruous women shall bring forth monsters, and salt waters shall be found in the sweet, and all friends shall conquer one another; then shall reason hide itself, and wisdom shall withdraw into its chamber" (IV Ez. 5:1ff.).[32] The motif of the apocalypses is that the evil that has dominated the age will become so intense at the end that complete chaos will reign, both in human social relationships and in the national order. When evil has become so intense that it is practically unendurable, then God will intervene and bring in his Kingdom.[33] However, this is not the motif of the Olivet Discourse. The troubles Jesus describes are not really signs of the approaching end. In fact, he expressly said that when these "signs" appear, "the end is not yet" (Mk. 13:7). Far from being signs by which the coming of the end can be calculated, these are signs that *the end is delayed.* Cranfield suggests that the topic of the entire first part of the Discourse is "the End is not yet."[34] Perhaps the most important verse in the Discourse is the saying, "This is but the beginning of the sufferings" (Mk. 13:8). The word used (*ōdines*) means "woes" and is used in the Old Testament of the pains of birth (Isa. 26:17). The Old Testament speaks of the birth of a nation through a period of woes (Isa. 66:8; Jer. 22:23; Hos. 13:13; Mic. 4:9f.) and from these verses there

[30] G. R. Beasley-Murray, *Jesus and the Future,* p. 128.
[31] E. E. Ellis, *Luke* (1966), p. 245.
[32] For other references, see G. E. Ladd, *Jesus and the Kingdom,* p. 323.
[33] It is interesting to note that a similar motif is found in dispensational theology in its interpretation of the course of the age.
[34] C. E. B. Cranfield, *Mark,* p. 394.

arose in Judaism the idea that the messianic Kingdom must emerge from a period of suffering that was called the messianic woes or "the birth pangs of the Messiah."[35] This does not mean the woes that the Messiah must suffer, but the woes out of which the messianic age is to be born.[36] Explicit reference to these messianic woes is made in Mark 13:19-20: "For in those days there will be such tribulation as has not been from the beginning of the creation . . . until now. And if the Lord had not shortened the days, no human being would be saved." This is a direct allusion to the time of trouble in Daniel 12:1. The wars and persecutions that characterize the time of the delayed end will only be the beginnings of the woes that immediately precede the end.

The motif in the Olivet Discourse is different from that of the apocalypses. It is the contrast between the character of the age and the Kingdom of God, and the conflict between the two. God has not abandoned the age to the powers of evil. "The gospel must first be preached to all nations" (Mk. 13:10). But the gospel is not to conquer the world and subdue all nations to itself. Hatred, conflict, and war will continue to characterize the age until the coming of the Son of Man. Not only that, but the age is hostile to the gospel and will persecute its emissaries.

Here is a somber note running throughout the teachings of Jesus. More than once he said that to be a disciple, a man must be willing to take up his cross (Mk. 8:34 and par.; Mt. 10:38 = Lk. 14:27). The saying in Matthew 10:38 is in the setting of the disciples' mission in the world. They are not to expect a uniformly cordial response. They will be flogged and condemned and put to death; governors and kings will oppose them (Mt. 10:17-21). Suffering, persecution, and martyrdom must be the expectation of Jesus' disciples. The saying that he that endures "to the end" (*eis telos,* Mt. 10:22; Mk. 13:13) may well mean "to the point of death." A cross is not a burden; it is an instrument of death. To take up one's cross means to be willing to go as Jesus went to a martyr's death. The nexus between suffering and participation in the community of the Son of Man is not accidental but rooted in the very being of that community. It came into existence through obedience to the call of the rejected Messiah and by virtue of his sacrificial death. "The rebellion of the world against God expressed itself in the murder of the Son of God; the community that stands by him must needs be the object of the same hostility."[37] From the perspective of the conflict between the world and the Kingdom of God, the loss of life is not the real issue. Luke's account reads, "some of you they will put to death; . . . But not a hair of your head will perish. By your endurance you will gain your lives" (Lk. 21:16-19).

Seen from this perspective, the final fearful persecution of the messianic woes of "the great tribulation" (Mt. 24:21) is in character with the rela-

---

[35] See J. Klausner, *The Messianic Idea in Israel* (1955), pp. 440-50.
[36] See H. L. Strack and P. Billerbeck, *Kommentar zum NT* (1922), I, 950.
[37] G. R. Beasley-Murray, *A Commentary on Mark Thirteen,* p. 51.

tionship of the church to the world throughout the age. Jesus agrees with the apocalyptists that evil will mark the course of the age; the Kingdom of God will abolish evil only in the Age to Come. *But God has not abandoned the age to evil.* The Son of God has brought the life and power of the Kingdom of God into history. It is entrusted to Jesus' disciples to be proclaimed in all the world. But their mission will not be an unalloyed success. They will indeed take the gospel into all the world but will do so only in the context of the same struggle with the powers of evil in the age that sent Jesus to his death. At the end the hatred of the world for God's gospel will find expression in a last convulsive persecution that will decimate the church. This will be new only in its intensity. But in the end God's Kingdom will come and vindicate his people.[38]

THE COMING OF THE KINGDOM. The end of the age and the coming of the Kingdom are briefly described in Mark 13:24. First, Jesus speaks of a cosmic catastrophe: the darkening of the sun and of the moon, the falling of the stars, and the shaking of the powers of the heavens. This is poetic language and must be understood against its Old Testament background. The present author has made a thorough study of this language and has concluded that it is poetic and not meant to be taken with strict literalness, yet at the same time it is meant to describe actual cosmic events.[39] We agree with Beasley-Murray: "Poetic expression is not to be confused with allegorism. . . . When God steps forth for salvation, the universe pales before him."[40] This language does not mean necessarily the complete break-up of the universe; we know from similar language elsewhere that it designates the judgment of God upon a fallen world that has shared the fate of man's sin, that out of the ruins of judgment a new world may be born.[41]

In the Olivet Discourse, the coming of the Kingdom of God is described altogether in terms of the coming of the Son of Man. He will be seen "coming in clouds with great power and glory" (Mk. 13:26). This language is based directly upon Daniel 7:13 where one like a Son of Man comes with the clouds of heaven to the Ancient of Days to receive an everlasting kingdom. The same truth is expressed in the Lukan passage: "For as the lightning flashes and lights up the sky from one side to the other, so will the Son of man be in his day" (Lk. 17:24). Several recent scholars have tried to empty this language of any futuristic eschatological significance. C. H. Dodd interpreted such apocalyptic language as symbolic of the inbreaking of the eternal order in which there is no before or after. "The

---

38 For the entire question of signs of the end, see G. R. Beasley-Murray, *Jesus and the Future*, pp. 172-82.

39 See G. E. Ladd, *Jesus and the Kingdom,* pp. 41-71.

40 G. R. Beasley-Murray, *A Commentary on Mark Thirteen,* pp. 87-88.

41 See Rev. 6:12-14; 21:1-4.

Day of the Son of Man stands for the timeless fact."[42] T. F. Glasson[43] argues that the parousia hope was no part of Jesus' teaching but arose in the church in the middle of the first century, while J. A. T. Robinson[44] interprets the parousia sayings in terms of the vindication of Jesus in his Father's presence. Background for this is sought in the argument that in Daniel 7:13 the one like a Son of Man comes to the Father, not to earth; and it pictures vindication by God, not a "second advent" to earth. However, in Daniel 7, while the Son of Man comes first to the Father to receive his kingdom, this kingdom is then given to the saints on earth, and this clearly implies that their representative, the Son of Man, brings it to them. "It is distinctly stated in Dan. 7:22 that the ancient of Days *came,* i.e., to earth, for the purpose of judgment and deliverance."[45]

It is impossible to render a visual image of this event, but the idea is clear. Jesus has already been exalted to heaven; the clouds of his parousia unveil his hitherto hidden glory, which is the glory of God, the Shekinah; he is seen to be the eternal Son of God, sharing in the majesty and power of God.[46] The underlying theology is that the coming of the Kingdom of God in its eschatological consummation is altogether an act of God. The history of this age will be one of conflict, war, hatred, and persecution; only an act of God in the parousia of Christ can establish his Kingdom.[47]

It is of great interest that the Olivet Discourse says almost nothing about the nature of the Kingdom. We have noted the diversity with which the prophets describe the messianic Kingdom. Sometimes Jewish apocalyptic described the Kingdom in very earthly terms, sometimes in more transcendental terms.[48] Sometimes Judaism combined the two, picturing first a temporal earthly kingdom,[49] then an eternal Kingdom. Later Judaism spoke of this temporal kingdom as "the days of the Messiah" in contrast to the eternal Age to Come.[50] The Revelation of John anticipates a temporal kingdom of a thousand years (Rev. 20:1-5). American evangelicalism has placed an unwarranted emphasis on this doctrine of a millennium. However, the Synoptic Gospels give no hint as to the nature of the Kingdom Jesus expected. One thing is clear; he is not concerned to teach a temporal earthly kingdom before the eternal order in the Age to Come. If he shared such an expectation, a temporal kingdom was not important in his thinking. The reason for this is clear. As Kümmel has put it, Jesus was interested in

---

[42] C. H. Dodd, *The Parables of the Kingdom* (1936), p. 108. Dodd now admits to a future consummation of the Kingdom "beyond history." See *The Founder of Christianity* (1970), pp. 115-16.

[43] *The Second Advent* (1963).

[44] *Jesus and His Coming* (1957).

[45] G. R. Beasley-Murray, *A Commentary on Mark 13,* p. 91.

[46] *Ibid.,* p. 89.

[47] See F. F. Bruce, "Eschatology," *London Quarterly and Holborn Review,* 27 (1958), 103.

[48] See above, Ch. 4.

[49] See IV Ez. 7:28; Apoc. Bar. 29:3ff.

[50] See J. Klausner, *The Messianic Idea in Israel,* pp. 408-19.

holding out an eschatological promise, not to give apocalyptic instruction.[51] The preaching of Jesus was directed to impress men with the importance of recognizing the present sovereignty of God in order that they might live in the Age to Come.[52]

The fact is that when Jesus speaks of the consummation, he always uses symbols.[53] God is King, and on the right hand of his throne sits the Son of Man (Mk. 14:62), who is accompanied by his twelve disciples in a new world (Mt. 19:28), and who is surrounded by the holy angels (Mk. 8:38). As the Good Shepherd, he feeds the purified flock (Mk. 14:28; Mt. 25:32f.). Judgment of the living and dead has taken place (Mt. 12:41f.) and the final separation has been completed (Mt. 13:30, 48). Satan and his angels have been thrown into eternal fire (Mt. 25:41); death is banished (Lk. 20:36). The pure in heart see God (Mt. 5:8); they receive a new name (Mt. 5:9), and have entered into immortality (Mk. 12:25) or eternal life (Mk. 9:43), and live unto God (Lk. 20:38). God recompenses the righteous (Lk. 14:14) with blessed rewards (Mt. 5:12); the treasure laid up in heaven is distributed (Mt. 6:20). The harvest is gathered in (Mt. 13:30), the marriage is celebrated (Mk. 2:19), Gentiles pour in to enjoy the feast with the patriarchs (Mt. 8:11) at the table of the Son of Man (Lk. 22:29). With them he drinks the wine of the Kingdom of God (Mk. 14:25), and the communion between God and man, broken by sin, is restored.

The one emphasis in the Olivet Discourse is the gathering of his elect from the four corners of the earth (Mk. 13:27). This is represented as being accomplished by the angels. Again, we cannot visualize this event. This appears to be the same event described by Paul as "the rapture" of the saints, when the dead in Christ are raised from their graves and the living saints shall be caught up (*rapiemur*) in the air to meet the returning Christ (I Thess. 4:17). Although the Olivet Discourse says nothing about it, we must assume that the resurrection of the dead occurs at this time.[54]

JUDGMENT. Jesus, as reported by Matthew, often spoke of judgment. To the Sanhedrin he claimed to be the eschatological judge (Mk. 15:62), and he often made casual reference to a day of judgment (Mt. 10:15; 11:22, 24; 12:36, 41, 43; 23:33) and to a final separation of men (Mt. 13:41, 49). Apart from the parable of the judgment, he says little about it. It is impossible to construct an eschatological scheme from Jesus' teaching. He is concerned with the certainty of the future and the *bearing of the future on the present,* not with apocalyptic schemata.

The only extended passage that deals with the judgment is the parable of the sheep and goats in Matthew 25:31-46. The Son of Man will sit on

---

[51] W. G. Kümmel, *Promise and Fulfilment* (1957), p. 88.
[52] F. J. Foakes-Jackson and K. Lake, *The Beginnings of Christianity* (1920), I, 282.
[53] J. Jeremias, *The Parables of Jesus,* p. 221.
[54] G. R. Beasley-Murray, *Mark Thirteen,* p. 90.

the throne of his glory to judge the nations. The basis of judgment will be the way the nations have treated Jesus' "brethren" (Mt. 25:40). This is not didactic eschatology but a dramatic parable. It has been interpreted in two utterly diverse ways. A prominent interpretation is that many men will be saved by their good deeds. Those who, out of human compassion, feed the hungry, clothe the naked, visit the sick and imprisoned are "Christians unawares." Jesus' "brethren" are all men in need. Men who in love minister to the needs of suffering people are manifesting the love of Christ; and even though they have never heard of Christ, they will inherit eternal life in the day of judgment as a reward for their good deeds.

A radically different interpretation is that of Dispensationalism. Jesus' "brethren" are a Jewish remnant who will go among the nations during the great tribulation proclaiming the "gospel of the kingdom." In earlier dispensationalist literature, the purpose of the judgment was to determine which nations entered the millennial kingdom and which were excluded, dependent upon their treatment of the converted Jewish remnant. More recent literature holds the same basic interpretation but admits that the issue of the judgment is final salvation or condemnation, as Matthew 25:46 makes clear.[55]

The clue to the meaning of the parable is Jesus' "brethren," and we have clear evidence as to its meaning. Jesus himself said that his brothers are those who do the will of the Father—Jesus' disciples (Mt. 12:50). Jesus used a parabolic incident of the nightly separation of sheep and goats to tell his disciples that they have a mission to the nations of the world. The destiny of men will be determined by the way they treat Jesus' representatives—his brethren. They are to go as itinerant preachers, finding lodging and food from those who receive them (Mt. 10:8-11). However, they will meet persecution and imprisonment (Mt. 10:17-18). Those who receive these preachers and treat them well in reality receive Christ. "He who receives you receives me" (Mt. 10:40). Those who reject these preachers and treat them ill do so because they are rejecting their message, and in doing so reject Christ. Judgment awaits them (Mt. 10:14-15). The destiny of the nations will be determined by the way they respond to Jesus' representatives.[56] This is not a program of eschatology but a practical parable of human destiny.

THE TIME OF THE KINGDOM. The most difficult problem in Jesus' view of the future is his expectation of the time of the coming of the Kingdom. The difficulty resides in the fact that the Synoptics record three different types of sayings about the future.

IMMINENCE. Three sayings have been interpreted to mean that Jesus expected the eschatological Kingdom to come in the immediate future. When he sent out the twelve on their preaching mission in Galilee, his instructions

---

[55] See J. D. Pentecost, *Things to Come,* p. 420.
[56] For this interpretation see T. W. Manson, *The Sayings of Jesus* (1949), p. 251.

included the saying, "You will not have gone through all the towns of Israel, before the Son of man comes" (Mt. 10:23). We have seen that Schweitzer interpreted this to mean that Jesus expected the Kingdom to come before the twelve had completed their mission in Galilee, i.e., within a few days. We have already examined this verse and found that it looks into an indeterminate future when the disciples will pursue their mission both among the Gentiles and to Israel.[57]

A second saying is found just before the transfiguration. After Peter's confession of Jesus' messiahship, Jesus began to instruct the disciples in the fact of his messianic death and his parousia. Although he is now to be humiliated in suffering and death, the way men relate to him here and now will determine their future destiny (Mt. 9:38). Then Jesus said, "There are some standing here who will not taste death before they see the Kingdom of God come with power" (Mk. 9:1). Matthew renders the saying, "before they see the Son of man coming in his kingdom" (Mt. 16:28). Luke has simply, "before they see the kingdom of God" (Lk. 9:27). This is immediately followed by the account of the transfiguration.

A third saying is found in the Olivet Discourse. Mark, followed by both Matthew and Luke, records, "Truly, I say unto you, this generation will not pass away before all these things take place" (Mk. 13:30, par.). On the surface of it, the last two sayings appear to be a bald affirmation that the eschatological Kingdom would come within a generation—some thirty years or so—when some of the disciples would still be alive.

DELAY. These sayings are balanced by other sayings that emphasize delay rather than imminence. We have already seen[58] that in the Olivet Discourse Jesus had taught that troubled times would come with wars and rumors of wars; and pretenders would arise claiming to be the Messiah; "but the end is not yet" (Mk. 13:7). In fact, the gospel must first be preached to all nations (Mk. 13:10). Luke records a parable about a nobleman who went into a *far* country to get a kingdom and then return because the people "supposed that the kingdom of God was to appear immediately" (Lk. 19:11). A note of delay is heard in the saying, "The days are coming when you will desire to see one of the days of the Son of man, and you will not see it" (Lk. 17:22). The disciples will find themselves in difficult situations where they will desire the deliverance of Christ's return, but they will not see it.

Delay is sounded in the parable of the importunate widow (Lk. 18:1-8). Those who believe in God are to remain steadfast in supplication for divine vindication, even though it seems to be delayed. The parables Matthew attaches to the Olivet Discourse sound the note of delay. When the bridegroom delayed, the wedding guests went to sleep (Mt. 25:5). A wealthy man entrusted various sums of money to his servants, and did not return to settle accounts with them until after a long time (Mt. 25:19).

---

[57] See above, p. 200.
[58] See above, p. 201.

UNCERTAINTY. The strongest note is one of uncertainty as to the time of the coming of the Kingdom. Jesus flatly affirmed that he did not know when the Kingdom would come (Mk. 13:32). "Take heed, watch; for you do not know when the time will come" (Mk. 13:33). "Watch therefore—for you do not know when the master of the house will come. . . , lest he come suddenly and find you asleep. And what I say to you I say to all: Watch" (Mk. 13:36).

Matthew adds some Q material emphasizing the indefiniteness of the time and the need to watch. In the days of Noah, the flood came suddenly and swept away wicked men. "Watch therefore, for you do not know on what day your Lord is coming" (Mt. 24:42). If the householder knew when the thief would break into his house, he would be awake. "Therefore, you also must be ready; for the Son of man is coming at an hour you do not expect" (Mt. 24:44=Lk. 12:40). The wicked servant who utilizes the master's delay as an occasion for mistreating his fellow servants will be surprised. "The master of that servant will come in a day when he does not expect him and at an hour he does not know" (Mt. 24:30=Lk. 12:46). The parables of Matthew 25 of the delayed bridegroom and the delayed nobleman were told to emphasize the theme: "Watch therefore, for you know neither the day nor the hour" (Mt. 25:13).

The word translated "watch" in these several verses does not mean "to look for" but "to be awake." It does not denote an intellectual attitude but a moral quality of spiritual readiness for the Lord's return. "You must also be ready" (Lk. 12:40). The uncertainty as to the time of the parousia means that men must be spiritually awake and ready to meet the Lord whenever he comes.

THE PROBLEM. These three kinds of sayings appear to be flatly contradictory to each other, and many commentators see them as mutually exclusive. The prevailing tendency is to accept the sayings about the imminence of the Kingdom as authentic on the grounds that the church never would have invented sayings that were not fulfilled. In fact, in much of Continental scholarship imminence is understood to be the most central emphasis in Jesus' teaching about the eschatological Kingdom. When the parousia did not occur, the church had to adjust to the delay of the parousia; and this is taken as one of the determinative facts in the development of Christian doctrine.[59] The sayings about the delay of the parousia are understood to be church formulations, not words of Jesus.

Others try to reconcile the differing statements by the position that Jesus affirmed that the Kingdom would come soon—within the present generation—but only God knows the *exact* day and hour.[60] Others frankly admit that Jesus was mistaken in his expectation of the *imminent* coming of the Kingdom; but this was inevitably one of the human factors involved in the

---

[59] See M. Werner, *The Formation of Christian Dogma* (1957).
[60] V. Taylor, "The Apocalyptic Discourse of Mark 13," *ET* 60 (1948-49), 97.

incarnation—the sharing of human perspective about the future.[61] Cullmann admits that Jesus was in error in his expectation of the time of the end, but this mistake does not affect the basic structure of his teaching about the Kingdom, which is the tension between the already and the not yet. Jesus was not mistaken about the real futurity of the Kingdom, although he was mistaken about the time of the Kingdom. Indeed, the fundamental meaning of the nearness of the Kingdom is not chronological but is the certainty that the future determines the present.[62] Kümmel interprets the emphasis on the *imminence* of the Kingdom to mean that men are confronted "with the end of history as it advances towards the goal set by God."[63] A. N. Wilder interprets the eschatological language as mythological in that it represents the unknown future. The future lay beyond Jesus' knowledge but he used apocalyptic concepts to express his confidence that the final outcome would be decided by the power of God.[64]

EXEGETICAL CONSIDERATIONS. It is not altogether certain that the two sayings in Mark 9:1 and 13:30 refer to the parousia or advent of Christ. Many scholars understand the word about the Kingdom of God coming in power (Mk. 9:1, par.) to be a reference to the transfiguration, which was itself a kind of preview of the parousia.[65] F. F. Bruce sees the fulfillment of Mark 9:1 in Pentecost. "The outpouring of the Spirit and the coming of the kingdom of God are two different ways of viewing the ministry of Jesus; both are manifested in partial measure before his death, but only after his death . . . will the kingdom come with power, will the Spirit be poured out in fulness."[66]

In the interpretation of Mark 13:30, the exegetical question is the antecedent of "all these things" (*tauta panta*). In the preceding verse, Jesus has said, "When you see these things (*tauta*) taking place, you know that he is near, at the very gates" (Mk. 13:29). *Tauta* cannot include the parousia itself. It would be obviously pointless to say, "When you see the Son of man coming, you know that he is near." The word *tauta* in verse 29 must refer to the signs of the end outlined in verses 5 to 23; and *tauta* in verse 29 appears to be the antecedent of the *tauta panta* that are to take place in this generation. What Jesus appears to be saying is that the signs that presage the end are not to be confined to a remote future; his hearers would themselves experience them.[67]

Other scholars have interpreted "this generation" (*genea*) to mean the

---

61 H. P. Owen, "The Parousia in the Synoptic Gospels," *SJTh* 12 (1959), 171-92.

62 O. Cullmann, "The Return of Christ" in *The Early Church,* ed. by A. J. B. Higgins (1957), p. 153.

63 W. G. Kümmel, *Promise and Fulfilment,* p. 152.

64 A. N. Wilder, *Eschatology and Ethics in the Teaching of Jesus* (1951), pp. 50f.

65 C. E. B. Cranfield, *Mark,* pp. 286-88; A. L. Moore, *The Parousia in the NT* (1966), pp. 125-31, 175-77.

66 F. F. Bruce, *NT History* (1969), p. 197.

67 See C. E. B. Cranfield, *Mark,* p. 409; "St. Mark 13," *SJTh* 7, 291.

Jewish people, or this kind of people, namely, unbelievers.[68] Another possibility has been pointed out by Ellis.[69] In the Qumran commentary on Habakkuk, the last generation is said to last long and to exceed everything spoken by the prophets (1QP Hab. 7:2, 7). The last generation is that in which the Qumranians lived, and designated the final period before the end, however long. However, Cranfield's solution seems to be the most probable one.

THE MEANING OF IMMINENCE. We conclude that it is not proven that Jesus flatly affirmed in error that the eschatological Kingdom would shortly come. He does teach that a great manifestation of God's Kingdom would be seen by some of his disciples, and that the signs that point to the coming of the Kingdom would be seen by his own generation. Other sayings point to a delay of the Kingdom to an indeterminate future. The predominating emphasis is upon the uncertainty of the time, in the light of which men must always be ready. This is the characteristic perspective of the Old Testament prophets. The Day of the Lord is near (Isa. 56:1; Zeph. 1:14; Joel 3:14; Obad. 15); yet the prophets have a future perspective. They are able to hold the present and the future together in an unresolved tension. "The tension between imminence and delay in the expectation of the end is characteristic of the entire biblical eschatology."[70] "One word can sound as though the end was near, another as though it only beckoned from a distance."[71] This may not be the thought pattern of the modern scientifically trained mind, and the dissection of the prophetic perspective by a severe analytic criticism may serve only to destroy it. A proper historical methodology must try to understand ancient thought patterns in terms of themselves, rather than forcing them into modern analytical categories. The overall impression of the Synoptics is clear. They leave the reader in a situation where he cannot date the time of the end; he cannot say that it will surely come tomorrow, or next week, or next year; neither can he say that it will not come for a long time. The keynote is: "Watch therefore, for you know neither the day nor the hour."

---

[68] For references, see C. E. B. Cranfield, *SJTh* 7, 290-91.
[69] E. E. Ellis, *Luke,* p. 246.
[70] A. Oepke, *StTh* 2 (1949-50), 145.
[71] M. Meinertz, *Theologie des NT* (1950), I, 58.

PART 2

THE FOURTH GOSPEL

16

THE CRITICAL PROBLEM

For an extensive bibliography see E. Malatesta, *St. John's Gospel, 1920-1965* (1967).

Surveys of Interpretation:

J. H. Scammon, "Studies in the Fourth Gospel, 1931-1940," *ATR* 23 (1941), 103-17; A. M. Hunter, *Interpreting the NT, 1900-1950* (1951), pp. 78-92; P. F. Barackman, "The Gospel According to John," *Int* VI (1952), 63-78; W. F. Howard, *The Fourth Gospel in Recent Criticism and Interpretation,* rev. by C. K. Barrett (1955); W. Grossouw, "Three Books on the Fourth Gospel," *NT* 1 (1956), 35-46; D. M. Stanley, "The Johannine Literature," *ThSt* 17 (1956), 516-31; C. L. Mitton, "The Provenance of the Fourth Gospel," *ET* 71 (1959-60), 337-40; R. H. Fuller, *The NT in Current Study* (1962), pp. 101-32; A. M. Hunter, "Recent Trends in Johannine Studies," *Teaching and Preaching the NT* (1963), pp. 59-73; J. W. Montgomery, "The Fourth Gospel Yesterday and Today," *Con Theol Monthly,* 34 (1963), 197-222; S. Neill, *The Interpretation of the NT 1861-1961* (1964), pp. 313-24; H. S. Songer, "The Gospel of John in Recent Research," *Rev and Exp* 62 (1965), 417-28; B. Lindars, "New Books on John," *Theology,* 72 (1969), 153-58; A. M. Ward, "The Fourth Gospel in Recent Study," *ET* 81 (1969-70), 68-72; R. E. Brown, "The Kerygma of the Gospel According to St. John," *NT Issues,* ed. by R. Batey (1970), 210-25.

The Critical Problem:

In addition to the standard introductions to the New Testament, see C. K. Barrett, *The Gospel According to St. John* (1955), pp. 3-119; W. F. Albright, "Recent Discoveries in Palestine and the Gospel of John," *The Background of the NT and Its Eschatology,* ed. by W. D. Davies and D. Daube (1956), pp. 153-71; G. D. Kilpatrick, "The Religious Background of the Fourth Gospel," *Studies in the Fourth Gospel,* ed. by F. L. Cross (1957), pp. 34-66; C. L. Mitton, "The Provenance of the Fourth Gospel," *ET* 71 (1959-60), 337-40; A. J. B. Higgins, *The Historicity of the Fourth Gospel* (1960); H. M. Teeple, "Qumran and the Origin of the Fourth Gospel," *NT* 4 (1960), 6-25; O. Cullmann, "A New

Approach to the Interpretation of the Fourth Gospel," *ET* 71 (1959-60), 8-12, 39-43; C. K. Barrett, "The Theological Vocabulary of the Fourth Gospel and of the Gospel of Truth," *Current Issues in NT Interpretation,* ed. by W. Klassen and G. F. Snyder (1962), pp. 210-23; J. Munck, "The NT and Gnosticism," *ibid.,* pp. 224-38; J. A. T. Robinson, "The New Look on the Fourth Gospel," *Twelve NT Studies* (1962), pp. 94-106; R. E. Brown, "The Gospel of Thomas and St. John's Gospel," *NTS* 9 (1962-63), 155-77; J. P. Martin, "History and Eschatology in the Lazarus Narrative, Jn. 11:1-44," *SJTh* 17 (1964), 332-43; R. E. Brown, *The Gospel According to John* (1966), I, xxi-cxxxvii; R. E. Brown, *NT Essays* (1968), pp. 77-271; A. M. Hunter, *According to John. The New Look at the Fourth Gospel* (1968); J. L. Martyn, *History and Theology in the Fourth Gospel* (1968); J. Marsh, *The Gospel of St. John* (1968), pp. 17-81; R. Schnackenburg, *The Gospel According to St. John* (1968), I, 11-217; L. Morris, *Studies in the Fourth Gospel* (1969); E. Haenchen. "History and Interpretation in the Johannine Passion Narrative," *Int* 24 (1970), 198-219; G. W. MacRae, "The Fourth Gospel and *Religionsgeschichte,*" *CBQ* 32 (1970), 13-24; R. Schnackenburg, "On the Origin of the Fourth Gospel," *Jesus and Man's Hope* (1970).

Theology of John:

In addition to the standard New Testament theologies, see the following: E. F. Scott, *The Fourth Gospel, Its Purpose and Theology* (1906); J. H. Bernard, *The Gospel According to St. John* (1929), I, cxii-clxxxvi; W. F. Howard, *Christianity According to St. John* (1946); E. K. Lee, *The Religious Thought of St. John* (1950); W. F. Howard, "The Gospel According to St. John," *IB* VIII (1952), 442-45; W. H. Rigg, *The Fourth Gospel and Its Message for Today* (1952); C. H. Dodd, *The Interpretation of the Fourth Gospel* (1953); E. Schweizer, "Orthodox Proclamation," *Int* 8 (1954), 387-403; C. K. Barrett, *The Gospel According to St. John* (1955), pp. 56-82; F. L. Cross, ed., *Studies in the Fourth Gospel* (1957); A. Corell, *Consummatum Est* (1958); J. E. Davey, *The Jesus of St. John* (1958); T. C. Smith, *Jesus in the Gospel of John* (1959); E. M. Sidebottom, *The Christ of the Fourth Gospel* (1961); J. N. Sanders, "John: Teaching," *IDB* E-J (1962), pp. 938-44; E. R. Achtemeier, "Jesus Christ, the Light of the World. The Biblical Understanding of Light and Darkness," *Int* 17 (1963), 439-49; T. F. Glasson, *Moses in the Fourth Gospel* (1963); F. C. Grant, "Theology of John," *Hastings Dictionary of the Bible* (1963), pp. 519-23; T. W. Manson, *On Paul and John* (1963); R. Schnackenburg, "The Theology of St. John," *NT Theology Today* (1963); J. Crehan, *The Theology of St. John* (1965); W. Grossouw, *Revelation and Redemption: An Introduction to the Theology of St. John* (1965); R. E. Brown, "Crucial Questions in John's Theology," *The Gospel According to St. John* (1966), I, cv-cxxviii; W. D. Davies, "The Fourth Gospel," *Invitation to the NT* (1966), pp. 373-518; F. V. Filson, "The Gospel of Life. A Study in the Gospel of John," *Current Issues in NT Interpretation,* ed. by W. Klassen and G. F. Snyder (1968), pp. 111-23; E. Käsemann, *The Testament of Jesus According to John 17* (1968); R. Schnackenburg, "Theological and Topical Interests," *The Gospel According to St. John* (1968), I, 153-72; B. Vawter, "Johannine Theology," *The Jerome Biblical Commentary* (1968), pp. 828-38; J. M. Boice, *Wit-*

ness and Revelation in the Gospel of John (1970); J. L. Price, "The Search for the Theology of the Fourth Evangelist" in *NT Issues,* ed. by R. Batey (1970), pp. 226-41; B. Lindars, *Behind the Fourth Gospel* (1971), pp. 61-79.

In the chapters dealing with the mission and teaching of Jesus, we have made use primarily of the Synoptic Gospels, with only occasional reference to the Fourth Gospel. An uncritical approach might study the teachings of Jesus synthetically in all four Gospels; but critical biblical theology must study the theology of the Fourth Gospel by itself. The reason for this is patent. The Fourth Gospel is so different from the Synoptics that the question must be honestly faced whether it reports accurately the teachings of Jesus or whether Christian faith has so modified the tradition that history is swallowed up in theological interpretation.

The differences between John and the Synoptics must not be glossed over. These differences in theology are corollaries to differences in matters of introduction. There is a difference in the locale of Jesus' ministry. In the Synoptics, with the exception of the last week, Jesus' ministry is largely devoted to Galilee; while in John his ministry centers around several visits to Jerusalem. There is a difference in time. The Synoptics mention only one passover and seem to report the events of only a year or two; but in John there are at least three passovers (2:13; 6:4; 13:1), possibly four (5:1). The Fourth Gospel lacks important materials found in the Synoptics: Jesus' birth, baptism, transfiguration, exorcism of demons, agony in Gethsemane, the last supper, the Olivet Discourse.

A very important difference, closely related to the question of theology, is that of literary usage. The most distinctive literary form in the Synoptics is the parable; and there are also many short, vivid sayings, easily remembered, and short incidents coupled with a teaching utterance. In John the style of Jesus' teaching is that of long discourses. Parables have been largely displaced by discourses, and short pithy sayings are lacking.

The style of the Greek is also different. The simple paratactic style of the Fourth Gospel is found both in the Gospel and the epistles of John. The solution that lies closest to hand is that the teachings of Jesus are expressed in Johannine idiom. This is an easier conclusion than to think that John's style was assimilated to Jesus' style, and that John wrote his epistle in the idiom he learned from Jesus.

If this is the correct solution, and if we must conclude that the Fourth Gospel is couched in Johannine idiom, this important question follows: To what extent is the theology of the Fourth Gospel that of John rather than that of Jesus? To what extent has the teaching of Jesus been so assimilated in John's mind that what we have is a Johannine interpretation rather than an accurate representation of Jesus' own teaching?

That this is no academic problem may be seen from the fact that some of the most prominent themes in the Synoptics are lacking in John; and most characteristic emphases in John are not obvious in the Synoptics.

John has nothing to say about repentance; neither the verb nor the noun appears in the Fourth Gospel. The Kingdom of God, which was central in the Synoptics, has almost altogether disappeared from Jesus' teachings (see John 3:3, 5; 18:36). Its place is taken by the concept of eternal life as Jesus' central message. However, while eternal life does appear a few times in the Synoptics, it is always as a future eschatological blessing (Mk. 9:43, 45 and par.; Mt. 7:14; 25:46); whereas in John the main emphasis is upon eternal life as a present realized blessing (Jn. 3:36 *passim*).

On the other hand, most distinctive Johannine emphases are lacking in the Synoptics. Perhaps the most distinctive Johannine idiom is the *ego eimi* saying: "I am the bread of life" (Jn. 6:35), "the light of the world" (Jn. 8:12), "the door" (Jn. 10:7), "the good shepherd" (Jn. 10:11), "the resurrection and the life" (Jn. 11:25), "the way, the truth, and the life" (Jn. 14:6), "the true vine" (Jn. 15:1). All of these are reflections of an absolute consciousness: "before Abraham was, I am" (Jn. 8:58).

Not only are there differences in specific theological emphases, but the entire structure of the Fourth Gospel appears to be different from that of the Synoptics. In the Synoptics the basic structure of Jesus' teaching is that of Jewish apocalyptic with its expectation of the eschatological act of God to bring history to its end and establish the Kingdom of God in the Age to Come. The dualism is a temporal dualism of the two ages, with its constant contrast between the present and the future (Mk. 10:15; Mt. 7:21).

The structure of John's thought, at first glance, seems to move in a different world. Gone is the idiom of this age and the Age to Come. Missing is the Olivet Discourse with its eschatological expectation of the end of the age and the coming of the Son of Man in glory to establish the Kingdom of God. This temporal-eschatological dualism seems to be replaced by a different kind of dualism. Instead of the tension between the present and the future is the tension between the above and the below, heaven and earth, the sphere of God and the world. This is most vividly expressed in the statement, "You are from below, I am from above; you are of this world, I am not of this world" (Jn. 8:23; see Jn. 3:12, 13, 31; 6:33, 62). The expression "the world" (*kosmos*), which appears only a few times in the Synoptics, is one of John's favorite words and designates the realm of men and human affairs set in contrast to the world above and the realm of God. When Jesus said that his kingship was not of this world (Jn. 18:36), he meant that his authority was not derived from the lower world of human governments but from the world of God.

Another striking element in the Johannine dualism is the contrast between light and darkness. One of the themes sounded in the first words of the Gospel is the conflict between light and darkness. "The light shines in the darkness, and the darkness has not overcome it" (1:5). The world is the realm of darkness, but God is light (I Jn. 1:5), and Jesus came to bring light into the darkness (3:19; 12:46; 8:12). Here is the one source of true light; every man who finds light must find it in Christ (1:9).[1] This light is still shining and the darkness has not been able to quench it (1:5). The antithesis of light and darkness is a further aspect of the Johannine dualism of above versus below, heaven versus the world, and appears to substitute a present "vertical" dualism for the Synoptic temporal-eschatological dualism.

The basic vocabulary of Jesus as reported by John is different from the Synoptics. In addition to such words as eternal life, light and darkness, many words appear frequently in John that are used sparingly in the Synoptics; both the verb to love and the noun love; truth, true, and genuine (*alēthinos*); to know; to work; world; to judge; to abide; to send; to witness; and especially to believe in (*eis*). Furthermore, many common Synoptic words are lacking in John: righteous; power or miracle (*dunamis*); to feel mercy or pity; to call; to repent; parable; to pray.[2]

These striking differences between John and the Synoptics led many scholars of a generation or more ago to interpret the Gospel as a second-century product of the Hellenistic world in which the message of Jesus about the Kingdom of God had been transmuted into a Hellenistic religion of salvation. "For many years the prevailing critical opinion was that John was 'the gospel of the Hellenists'; it was written by a Greek thinker for Greeks; it marks a decisive point in the hellenization of the Christian faith."[3]

From this point of view, the Gospel is far removed from Jesus. It is interested in eternal truth, not objective fact; in theology, not history. Its miracles are only symbols of spiritual realities; its sayings are allegories.[4] Since then the discovery of three papyri containing all or part of John dating back to the early second century exclude such views.[5] However, the search has continued to find the religious *Sitz im Leben* that might explain the language and theology of the Fourth Gospel.[6] It cannot be denied that some of the characteristic terminology of John is very similar to the idiom of the Hermetica—a collection of religious writings produced in Egypt probably in the second and third centuries. These writings have much to say about light and life, the word, and salvation by knowledge, as well

---

1 "Every man" is potential, not actual. See W. F. Howard in *IB* VIII, 470. However, the verb may mean "to shed light upon," i.e., to show whether one is good or evil. The light is judicial as well as illuminating.

2 See the table in C. K. Barrett, *John,* pp. 5-6.

3 C. K. Barrett, *John,* p. 3. A good illustration of this is E. F. Scott, *The Fourth Gospel: Its Purpose and Its Theology* (1906). Recently, E. Käsemann has defended the thesis that John's Christology is a naïve docetism at variance with the mainstream of Christian theology. See *The Testament of Jesus* (1968).

4 See B. W. Bacon, *The Gospel of the Hellenists* (1933).

5 See J. L. Price, *Interpreting the NT* (1961), p. 546.

6 For surveys of such recent efforts, see W. F. Howard, *The Fourth Gospel in Recent Criticism* (1955); C. H. Dodd, *The Fourth Gospel* (1953), pp. 3-130; R. E. Brown, *John,* I, lii-lxv; W. G. Kümmel, *Introduction to the NT* (1966), pp. 154-61; R. Schnackenburg, *John,* I, 119-52.

as regeneration or new birth. C. H. Dodd feels that the Hermetica porvide a valuable background for understanding John.[7] However, many of the most distinctive *theological* terms in the Hermetica, such as *gnōsis,*[8] *mystērion, athanasia, demiourgos, nous,* are lacking in John, and the Johannine idiom in general shares far more with the LXX than it does with the Hermetica.[9]

Bultmann has sponsored a critical view that has been accepted by many of his disciples, that from the Mandean literature dating from the seventh and eighth centuries A.D. can be reconstructed a movement going back to pre-Christian times that represented a syncretism between popular Hellenistic philosophy and Eastern mysticism issuing in a kind of "proto-gnostic" religion. This pre-Christian "gnosis" finally gave rise to full-fledged gnosticism in the second and third centuries A.D., reflected in such church fathers as Irenaeus. Whereas the prevailing critical view had been that second-century gnosticism was a distinctly Christian heresy, this new view assumed that it was only the crystallization of a movement that in its essentials antedated Christianity and which greatly influenced Johannine theology. The essentials of this gnostic theology consist of a cosmological dualism in which the material world is evil. The souls of men, which belong to the heavenly realm of light and life, have fallen into the material world of darkness and death. God sent a heavenly redeemer to men to enlighten them by giving them knowledge (*gnōsis*) of their true nature, thus enabling them at death to escape their involvement in the material world and return to their true heavenly home. Heaven is man's natural home; the world is a prison. Salvation comes from knowledge imparted by the descending and ascending heavenly redeemer.[10]

A vigorous debate has been carried on by scholars as to whether this gnostic theology antedated Christianity and influenced the theology of the pre-existent, incarnate, and ascending Christ. It must be emphasized that while this gnostic theology can be found in second-century-A.D. gnosticism as a Christian aberration, the theory that it was a pre-Christian syncretistic movement that helped mold Christian, especially Johannine, Christology is a critical reconstruction based upon post-Christian texts. While tendencies toward gnostic thinking can be found in Judaism and Hellenism, the figure of a heavenly redeemer cannot be found in any pre-Christian documents.[11]

---

[7] C. H. Dodd, *The Fourth Gospel,* pp. 10-53 *et passim.* Similarities between John and the Hermetica have been conveniently set forth in W. D. Davies, *Invitation to the NT* (1966), pp. 398-408.

[8] Only the verb occurs in John.

[9] See G. D. Kilpatrick, "The Religious Background of the Fourth Gospel" in *Studies in the Fourth Gospel,* ed. by F. L. Cross (1957), pp. 36-44.

[10] See R. Bultmann, *Primitive Christianity in Its Contemporary Setting* (1956), pp. 163ff. See also H. Jonas, *The Gnostic Religion* (1958).

[11] See R. McL. Wilson, *The Gnostic Problem* (1958); *Gnosis and the NT* (1968); J. Munck, "The NT and Gnosticism" in *Current Issues in NT Interpretation,* ed. by W. Klassen (1962), pp. 224-38. For the question of a pre-Christian gnostic movement, see the essays by G. Quispel, R. McL. Wilson and H. Jonas, "Gnos-

The discovery of a gnostic library in 1947 at Nag Hammadi in Egypt consisting of thirteen manuscripts containing forty-nine different documents has given us for the first time a large collection of primary sources for Egyptian gnosticism.[12] While Robinson expresses the hope that this literature may provide documentation that bridges the gulf between pre-Christian Jewish literature and Christian gnosticism,[13] one of our greatest authorities in Hellenistic religion expressed the conviction that the new texts from Nag Hammadi "vindicate completely the traditional view of Gnosticism as Christian heresy with roots in speculative thought."[14] Nock also reminds us that the Hermetica have no personal redeemer figure.

Another archaeological discovery has revolutionized the search for the setting of the theology of the Fourth Gospel. Beginning with an accidental discovery in 1947 of several ancient scrolls at Khirbet Qumran near the head of the Dead Sea, the remains of the library of a separatist monastic group whom most scholars identify either as the Essenes or the forerunners of the Essenes have been found.[15] Such amazing parallels of language and thought exist between John and the Qumran writings that many scholars have felt there must be some meaningful connection between the two. Possibly John the Baptist had been a Qumranian during his years in the wilderness.[16]

Even if direct dependence cannot be established between John and the Qumran writings, the similarities have proven that the idiom and thought patterns of the Fourth Gospel could have arisen in Palestine in the mid-first century A.D.—a position few critical scholars of a generation ago would have dared to support. This has led to "The New Look on the Fourth Gospel,"[17] which has revolutionized Johannine criticism. Many

---

ticism and the NT" in *The Bible in Modern Scholarship,* ed. by J. P. Hyatt (1965), pp. 252-93.

12 For a brief survey, see W. C. van Unnik, *Newly Discovered Gnostic Writings* (1960); for a detailed study, see J. Doresse, *The Secret Books of the Egyptian Gnostics* (1958); for a more recent report, see J. M. Robinson, "The Coptic Gnostic Library Today," *NTS* 14 (1968), 356-401.

13 J. M. Robinson in *NTS* 14, 380. A heavenly redeemer appears in the Coptic "Apocalypse of Adam," but it is not yet clear that this represents a pre-Christian tradition. See G. W. MacRae, "The Coptic Gnostic Apocalypse of Adam" in *Heythrop Journal,* 6 (1965), 27-35; K. Rudolph in *TLZ* 90 (1965), 361-62.

14 A. D. Nock, "Gnosticism," *HTR* 57 (1964), 276.

15 For this community and the significance of its literature, see K. Stendahl, ed., *The Scrolls and the NT* (1958); F. M. Cross, Jr., *The Ancient Library of Qumran and Modern Biblical Studies* (1957); J. T. Milik, *Ten Years of Discovery in the Wilderness of Judaea* (1959). For a good translation of the Qumran texts, see A. Dupont-Sommer, *The Essene Writings from Qumran* (1961).

16 Cf. R. E. Brown, "The Qumran Scrolls and the Johannine Gospel and Epistles" in *NT Essays* (1968), pp. 138-73. For other possible connections, see W. G. Kümmel, *Introduction to the NT,* pp. 156-58. L. Morris (*Studies in the Fourth Gospel* [1969], p. 353) admits the necessity of recognizing an indirect if not a direct relationship.

17 J. A. T. Robinson, *Twelve NT Studies* (1962), pp. 94-106; see also A. M. Hunter, *According to John. The New Look at the Fourth Gospel* (1968).

contemporary scholars now recognize a solid Johannine tradition independent of the Synoptics, stemming from Palestine and dating from A.D. 30 to 66,[18] and attribute to the Fourth Gospel a degree of historical worth hardly dreamed of a generation ago except by the most conservative scholars.

When all this has been said, the problem of the difference between the Synoptic Jesus and the Johannine Jesus remains. The problem is compounded by the fact that the idiom and theology of the Gospel are very much the same as the First Epistle of John. We must face the alternative that the Fourth Gospel is the end product of a tradition that John remembered, proclaimed, and pondered, until he became completely absorbed in this tradition and expressed it in his own words and ideas. If, however, the idiom and thought came from John more than from Jesus, we are faced with the problem that the author of the Gospel was a greater creative genius than Jesus.[19]

Another solution is that John deliberately recast and interpreted the words of Jesus to fit his own contemporary situation, sensing behind his work the authority of Jesus himself, now glorified and risen from the dead, continuing to instruct his people through the Spirit (Jn. 14:26; 16:12).[20]

Another solution is that Jesus was too great a teacher to be limited to a single style and idiom of teaching. Possibly he used a vivid, picturesque, parabolic style with the crowds in Galilee and a more profound, extended form of discourse with the more educated people of Jerusalem and with his own disciples.[21] A difficulty here is the discourse on the bread of life in John 6, delivered in Galilee after the feeding of the five thousand, which is couched in thoroughly "Johannine" idiom. However, John 6:59 affirms that Jesus uttered this discourse in the synagogue in Capernaum rather than as a popular address to the crowds, and a recent study has shown the ideas in this discourse to be thoroughly consistent with Jewish conceptions of the passover.[22] It is possible that in the last days Jesus in fact used a different style that opened up the deeper truths of his person and mission to his disciples, and John deliberately cast the entire Gospel

---

[18] See C. H. Dodd, *Historical Tradition in the Fourth Gospel* (1963). Dodd does not, however, appeal to the Qumran writings to support his conclusions.

[19] D. Guthrie, *NT Introduction* (1965), I, 268.

[20] See G. W. Barker *et al., The NT Speaks* (1969), p. 395. This view is defended in detail by the Catholic scholar, F. Mussner, *The Historical Jesus in the Gospel of St. John* (1967).

[21] D. Guthrie, *NT Introduction,* pp. 266ff. See also H. Riesenfeld, *The Gospel Tradition and Its Beginnings* (1957), p. 28. R. E. Brown (*John,* I, lxiv) recognizes that Jesus probably used more than one style of expression, and A. J. B. Higgins acknowledges that Jesus probably used "Johannine" phraseology and ideas. See A. J. B. Higgins, "The Words of Jesus According to St. John," *BJRL* 49 (1966-67), 384.

[22] B. Gärtner, *John 6 and the Jewish Passover* (1959). R. E. Brown thinks there is a core of authentic tradition in John 6 (*John,* I, xlix).

in this idiom. This is a problem for which a final solution may never be found. We may, however, quote the forceful words of W. F. Albright:

> There is no fundamental difference in teaching between John and the Synoptics; the contrast between them lies in the concentration of tradition along certain aspects of Christ's teachings, particularly those which seem to have resembled the teaching of the Essenes most closely.
>
> There is absolutely nothing to show that any of Jesus' teachings have been distorted or falsified, or that a vital new element has been added to them. That the needs of the early Church influenced the selection of items for inclusion in the Gospel we may readily admit, but there is no reason to suppose that the needs of that Church were responsible for any inventions or innovations of theological significance.
>
> One of the strangest assumptions of critical New Testament scholars and theologians is that the mind of Jesus was so limited that any apparent contrast between John and the Synoptics must be due to differences between early Christian theologians. Every great thinker and personality is going to be interpreted differently by different friends and hearers, who will select what seems most congenial or useful out of what they have seen and heard.[23]

This does not mean that we may gloss over the differences between John and the Synoptics, especially in the divergent theological emphases. It is difficult to avoid the conclusion that John reflects a larger measure of theological interpretation than do the Synoptics. However, the day is long past when we may think of the Synoptics as "bare" history. They were written by men who had become convinced by the resurrection that Jesus was the Messiah and the Son of God (Mk. 1:1) and wrote "good news" in the light of that faith. The Synoptic Gospels are theology as well as history.[24] John does no more than make even more explicit what was always implicit in the Synoptics and at times became explicit (Mt. 11:25-30). "The difference between them is not that John is theological and the others are not but that all are theological in different ways."[25] Interpreted history may represent more truly the facts of a situation than a mere chronicle of events. If John is a theological interpretation, it is an interpretation of events that John is convinced happened in history. It is obviously not the intent of the Synoptic Gospels to give a report of the *ipsissima verba* of Jesus nor a biography of the events of his life. They are portraits of Jesus and summaries of his teaching. Matthew and Luke feel themselves free to rearrange the material in Mark and to report Jesus' teaching with considerable freedom.[26] If John used more freedom than Matthew and Luke, it is because he wished to give a more profound and ultimately more real

---

[23] W. F. Albright, "Recent Discoveries in Palestine and The Gospel of John" in *The Background of the NT and Its Eschatology*, ed. by W. D. Davies and D. Daube (1956), pp. 170-71.

[24] See G. E. Ladd, *The NT and Criticism* (1967), pp. 153ff.

[25] A. M. Ward in *ET* 81 (1969/70), 69.

[26] See G. E. Ladd, *The NT and Criticism*, ch. 5.

portrait of Jesus. The historical, "objective" tradition is so interwoven with Johannine interpretation that it is impossible to separate them.[27]

The fact that John writes a profound theological interpretation does not account for the particular form and idiom of the Gospel. The similarities between John and Qumran prove at the minimum that the idiom and ideas of the Fourth Gospel could have taken rise in Palestine in the early first century A.D. It does not fully answer the problem why the Fourth Gospel took its distinctive shape. The thesis that the Gospel must be understood as a product of Hellenistic philosophical or gnostic thought has little to commend it.[28] However, the similarities between John and popular Hellenistic thought can hardly be accidental, in spite of the similarities to Qumran. The best solution seems to be that John was written, as patristic tradition suggests, late in the first century to refute a gnostic tendency in the church. A clue may be found in the First Epistle, probably coming from the same circle as the Gospel: the denial that Jesus had come in the flesh (I Jn. 4:2). False teachers had risen in the church who embodied the spirit of antichrist (I Jn. 2:18-19) and denied the true messiahship of Jesus. If the Gospel, like the First Epistle,[29] was written to refute an incipient gnosticism, the reason for its particular idiom and message becomes clear. John makes use of words and ideas familiar in gnostic circles to refute these very gnostic tendencies. The base of this idiom goes back to Palestine, and undoubtedly to Jesus himself. But John chose to formulate his entire Gospel in language that probably was used by our Lord only in intimate dialogue with his disciples or in theological argument with learned scribes in order to bring out the full meaning of the eternal Word that became flesh (Jn. 1:14) in the historical event of Jesus Christ.[30]

In any case, our task in studying the theology of the Fourth Gospel is not only to set forth positively the Johannine thought but to attempt to discover to what degree it is similar or dissimilar to that of the Synoptics. Did John expound a radically reinterpreted theology, or does his Gospel embody the same essential theology but with different emphases? This is our twofold task.

---

[27] See R. Schnackenburg, "The Origin of the Fourth Gospel" in *Jesus and Man's Hope* (1970), p. 226.

[28] See A. M. Ward's critique of Käsemann in *ET* 81 (1969-70), 72.

[29] See F. V. Filson, "First John: Purpose and Message," *Int* 23 (1969), 268ff.

[30] An excellent illustration of how John writes with "bifocal historical vision," i.e., recording events of the past but adapting them to his own day, is found in J. P. Martin's essay, "History and Eschatology in the Lazarus Narrative," *SJTh* 17 (1964), 332-43.

There are many different theories as to the purpose of John's Gospel. For a summary see W. G. Kümmel, *Introduction to the NT,* pp. 161-65; R. E. Brown, *John,* I, lxvii-lxxix.

17

THE JOHANNINE DUALISM

Literature:

There is very little literature in English that discusses the complex problem of the Johannine dualism against the background of Judaism and Hellenistic philosophy. Even the German works are inadequate. O. Böcher, *Der johanneische Dualismus im Zusammenhang des nachbiblischen Judentums* (1965), finds the background for Johannine dualism in the Old Testament, not in later Jewish writings; and he does not consider Hellenistic dualism. See "Dualism: Greek, Iranian, Jewish," *HERE* (1912), V, 107-16; R. Bultmann, "Johannine Dualism," *Theology* (1955), II, 15-32; R. Marcus in *Biblical Research,* I (1957), 34; M. Rist, "Dualism," *IDB* A-D (1962), p. 873; G. E. Ladd, *Jesus and the Kingdom* (1964), pp. 83-89; R. E. Brown, "The 'Vertical' and the 'Horizontal' View of God's Salvific Action," *John* (1966), pp. cxvf.; R. E. Brown, "The Qumran Scrolls and the Johannine Gospels and Epistles" in *NT Essays* (1968), pp. 138-73; J. H. Charlesworth, "A Critical Comparison of the Dualism in 1QS iii, 13—iv, 26 and the 'Dualism' contained in the Fourth Gospel," *NTS* 15 (1969), 389-418.

THE TWO WORLDS. The most difficult problem in the Johannine theology is its apparently different dualism from that of the Synoptics. The dualism in the Synoptic Gospels is primarily horizontal: a contrast between two ages—this age and the Age to Come. The dualism of John is primarily vertical: a contrast between two worlds—the world above and the world below. "You are from below, I am from above; you are of this world, I am not of this world" (John 8:23). The Synoptics contrast this age with the Age to Come, and we know from the Pauline use that "this world" can be an equivalent of "this age" in an eschatological dualism.[1] But in John, "this world" almost always stands in contrast with the world above. "This world" is viewed as evil with the devil as its ruler (16:11). Jesus has come to be the light of this world (11:9). The authority of his mission does not come from "this world" but from the world above—from

---

[1] See I Cor. 1:20; 2:6-8; 3:19 where the two terms are used interchangeably.

God (18:36). When his mission is completed, he must depart from "this world" (13:1).

The same dualism is obvious in the language of Jesus descending from heaven to earth and ascending again to heaven. "No one has ascended into heaven but he who descended from heaven" (3:13). Jesus has come down from heaven to fulfill a mission that he received from God (6:38). He has come down from heaven as the "living bread." If any man eat of this bread, he shall never die but have eternal life (6:33, 41, 50, 51, 58). When his mission is fulfilled, he must ascend to heaven whence he had come (6:62). After the resurrection, when Mary would cling to him, he told her not to hold him, for he had not yet ascended to the Father. She was instead to go to the disciples and say to them, "I am ascending to my Father and your Father, to my God and your God" (20:17).

DARKNESS AND LIGHT. The world below is the realm of darkness, but the world above is the world of light. Christ has come into the realm of darkness to bring the light. Light and darkness are seen as two principles in conflict with each other. "The light shines in the darkness, and the darkness has not overcome it" (1:5). Jesus is himself the light (8:12) and has come that men may not remain in darkness but may have the light of life and be enabled to walk in the light so that they may not stumble (8:12; 9:5; 11:9; 12:35, 46). Those who receive the light become sons of light (12:36). However, in spite of the fact that the light has come into the world, men loved darkness rather than light and refused to come to the light because their deeds were evil. Whoever "does the truth" comes to the light that his true nature may be disclosed (3:19-20). In John the crowning evil is hatred of the light—unbelief in Jesus.

FLESH AND SPIRIT. Another contrast in this dualism, although of more limited usage, is that between flesh and Spirit. Flesh belongs to the realm below; Spirit to the realm above. The flesh is not sinful, as in Paul, but represents the weakness and impotence of the lower realm. Ordinary human life is "born . . . of the will of the flesh" (1:13), i.e., by natural human procreation. The flesh is not sinful, for "the Word became flesh and dwelt among us" (1:14). Flesh is synonymous with humanity—mankind. However, the flesh is limited to the lower realm; it cannot reach up to the life of the world above. "That which is born of the flesh is flesh" (3:6); men must be born from above.[2] Being born from above is further described as being born of the Spirit. Man in and of himself is weak and mortal; only by an inner work of God's Spirit can he either understand or experience the blessings of the heavenly realm (3:12). Eternal life is the gift of God's Spirit; in the light of eternity, the flesh is of no avail. It cannot enable a man to attain to life eternal (6:63).

[2] In view of the contrast between the worlds above and below, *anōthen* can here best be translated "from above" rather than "again" (RSV). See R. E. Brown, *John,* I, 128; R. Schnackenburg, *John,* I, 373.

A different dimension is interjected into the Johannine dualism in the saying about worship. "God is spirit, and those who worship him must worship in spirit and truth" (4:24). "Worship in spirit" does not mean worship in the human spirit in contrast to worship by the use of external forms and rites; it means worship that is empowered by the Spirit of God.[3] The contrast here is not so much between the world above and the world below as between worship in the former time and worship in the new era inaugurated by Jesus. The contrast is between worship in Spirit and truth as compared with worship in Jerusalem or Gerizim.[4] Here is an "eschatological replacement of temporal institutions like the Temple." The "Spirit raises men above the earthly level, the level of flesh, and enables them to worship God properly."[5] Here we meet for the first time the joining of the vertical with the horizontal. Because Jesus has come into the world from above, he has instituted a new order of things.

KOSMOS. In carrying out our study of Johannine theology, it is important to understand his use of the word "world," *kosmos.* This term is used in several distinct ways. Sometimes paralleling the Synoptic usage, *kosmos,* as in Greek philosophical idiom, can designate both the entire created order (Jn. 17:5, 24)[6] and the earth in particular (Jn. 11:9; 16:21; 21:25).[7] The earth is frequently referred to as the dwelling place of men in language that is paralleled in Jewish idiom: coming into the world (6:14; 9:39; 11:27; 18:37), being in the world (9:5a), departing out of the world (13:1; 16:28b). While some of these sayings acquire theological significance because of the context in which they are used, the idiom itself is familiar Jewish terminology. To come into the world means merely to be born; to be in the world is to exist; and to depart from the world is to die.[8]

There is no trace of the idea that there is anything evil about the world. "All things were made through him, and without him was not anything made that was made" (1:3). There is no element of cosmological dualism or of world denial in John. The created world continues to be God's world.

By metonymy, *kosmos* can designate not only the world but also those who inhabit the world: mankind (12:19; 18:20; 7:4; 14:22). A study of these verses shows that *kosmos* is not specifically intended to designate all the men who inhabit the earth, but simply mankind in general. "The world has gone after him" (12:19) means that Jesus has secured a large response. That Jesus has spoken openly to the world (18:20) means that he has engaged in a public ministry. This is a use John shares with Hellenis-

3 See R. E. Brown, *John,* I, 180; R. Schnackenburg, *John,* I, 439.
4 R. E. Brown, *John,* I, 180.
5 *Loc. cit.*
6 See Mt. 13:35; 24:21; 25:34; Lk. 11:50.
7 See Mk. 14:9; Lk. 12:30; Mt. 4:8; 13:48.
8 H. Sasse, *TDNT* III, 888; see also I Jn. 4:1, 17; II Jn. 7; Heb. 10:5; I Tim. 1:15.

tic and LXX Greek that was not usual in classical Greek. It is found also in the Synoptics in Matthew 5:14 and 18:7.

The most interesting use of *kosmos* for mankind is found in the sayings where the world—mankind—is the object of God's love and salvation. God loves the world (3:16) and sent his Son to save the world (3:17c; 12:47). Jesus is the Savior of the world (4:42); he came to take away the sin of the world (1:29) and to give life to the world (6:33). Like the first group of references, these sayings carry no distinctively universalistic emphasis but merely designate mankind at large as the object of God's love and saving action.[9]

KOSMOS: MAN AT ENMITY WITH GOD. Thus far the Johannine use of *kosmos* is paralleled in the Synoptics. However, John has a distinctive use of *kosmos* that is lacking in the Synoptics. Men are viewed not simply as the inhabitants of the earth and the objects of God's love and redeeming acts, but in contrast to God, as sinful, rebellious, and alienated from God, as fallen humanity. The *kosmos* is characterized by wickedness (7:7), and does not know God (17:25) nor his emissary, Christ (1:10). This is not so because there is something intrinsically evil about the world. When John says that "the *kosmos* was made through him" (1:10), the context suggests that *kosmos* here is mankind and not simply the universe or earth. What makes the *kosmos* evil is not something intrinsic to it, but the fact that it has turned away from its creator and has become enslaved to evil powers. The alienation of the world from God is shown in its hatred for God's emissary (7:7; 15:18), who came to save it. The evil power that has enslaved the world in its rebellion to God is three times referred to as the ruler of this world (12:31; 14:30; 16:11; see I Jn. 5:19). The world stands in sharp contrast with Jesus' disciples. They formerly belonged to the world, but have been chosen out of the world to belong to Christ (17:6), even though they are to continue to live in the world (13:1; 17:11, 15). They no longer share the same character as the world because they belong to Jesus Christ, having received his word (17:14). Even as Jesus' purpose is to live in accordance with his Father's will rather than to live for purely human goals and he is therefore not of the world although in the world, so can it be said of his disciples, who have changed their affections from merely human goals to God, that they are not of the world (15:19; 17:14). The coming of Jesus has in effect created a division among men even though they continue to live together. God has chosen men out of the world (15:19) that they should form a new fellowship centering

[9] In passing, we may note that a variation of this usage appears in the epistles of John and the Synoptics but not in the Fourth Gospel. *Kosmos* can designate not only mankind as such but the whole pattern of human activities and interests. If a man gains "the whole world" (Mk. 8:36), i.e., fulfills all human ambitions and goals on a merely human level, but loses himself, he has ultimately gained nothing. This is what John means by loving the world (I Jn. 2:15f.), i.e., finding the object and goal of one's affection and striving purely on the human level.

around Jesus (17:15). Since the world hated Jesus, it will also hate the followers of Jesus (15:18; 17:14).

The disciples' reaction is not to be one of withdrawal from the world, but of living in the world, motivated by the love of God rather than the love of the world.[10] The disciples are to carry out a mission in the world that is nothing less than a continuation of Jesus' mission (17:18). As Jesus had devoted himself to fulfilling his Father's will in the world and carrying out his redemptive purpose,[11] so his followers are not to find their security and satisfaction on the human level as does the world, but in devotion to the redemptive purpose of God (17:17, 19). They are to keep themselves from the evil (17:15) of the world by centering their affection on God.

This separation of mankind into the people of God and the world is not, therefore, an absolute division. Men may be transferred from the world to God's people by hearing and responding to the mission and message of Jesus (17:6; 3:16). Thus the disciples are to perpetuate Jesus' ministry in the world that men may know the gospel and be saved (20:31) out of the world. The world cannot receive the Spirit (14:17) or it would cease to be the world; but many in the world will accept the witness of Jesus' disciples (17:21), and will believe on him without ever having seen him (20:39).

SATAN. In the Fourth Gospel, as in the Synoptics, the world is seen to be in the grip of an evil supernatural power called the devil (8:44; 13:2) and Satan (13:27). He is described in language very similar to that of Paul as the "ruler of this world" (12:31; 14:30; 16:11).[12] The Synoptics speak of him as the "prince" (*archōn*—ruler) of demons (Mt. 12:24). John does not speak of his rule over demons, but, like Paul, says "the whole *kosmos* is ruled by this *archōn*."[13] It is his purpose to frustrate the work of God. When Judas was on the point of betraying Jesus, "Satan entered into him" (13:27). The Jews claimed that they were the children of Abraham and for that very reason were heirs of the blessings promised to Abraham. Jesus replied that their hatred for him proved that they were not children of Abraham, indeed, they were the children of the devil, for the devil was a murderer from the beginning and has nothing to do with the truth because there is no truth in him (8:39ff.). Jesus came to bring men the truth (1:17); but the devil is a liar and the father of lies.

Although John, unlike the Synoptics, does not relate Jesus' struggle with demons, it is clear that his mission involves the same conflict with supernatural powers.[14] As the ruler of this world, Satan tries to overcome Jesus (14:30), but is powerless to do so. On the contrary, Jesus is to emerge

---

[10] This is made explicit in I Jn. 2:15f.
[11] See the meaning of "truth" in Ch. 19.
[12] In II Cor. 4:4, Paul speaks of Satan as "the god of this age."
[13] G. Delling in *TDNT* I, 489.
[14] *Loc. cit.*

victorious over his enemy. In his cross Jesus effects a victory over Satan so that he can be said to be "cast out" (12:31). In other words, this victory can be described as the judgment of the ruler of this world (16:11). John does not speculate about the origin of Satan or his nature. He is simply pictured as an evil supernatural power who is master of this world but who is overcome by Jesus in his cross.

Many modern scholars cannot accept the idea of such a supernatural power, especially Jesus' words about the Jews being children of the devil. "It is simply inconceivable that Jesus of Nazareth ever said these words."[15] They are held to reflect not the teachings of Jesus but a vigorous anti-Semitic polemic by the author of the Gospel. However, it must be admitted that the words are in character with the total teaching of the Fourth Gospel. "(The Jews) cannot claim divine parentage, for their deeds deny it. Their attitude to him in resisting the truth which he revealed to them from the Father, and in resolving to put him to death was quite consistent with the character of their father, the Devil, who rebelled against God whose kingdom is truth, and who was a man-slayer from the beginning. He is essentially false, and his native tongue is falsehood. His envy and malice brought disobedience and death to the human race. His children cannot welcome the revelation which comes from the only true God, and they are bent on compassing the destruction of the Son whom the Father has sent to bring light and liberty to the world of men."[16]

SIN. In the Synoptics *hamartia* was employed of acts of sin, manifestations of sin. In John there is a greater emphasis placed upon the principle of sin. The Holy Spirit is to convict the world *of sin* (not sins) (16:8). Sin is a principle that in this instance manifests itself in unbelief in Christ. Everyone who lives in the practice of sin is in bondage—he is a slave of sin (8:34). "Human sin is servitude to demonic power and therefore complete separation from God."[17] Unless men believe that Jesus is the Christ, they will die in their sins (8:24).

Sin is darkness; and the character of the sinful world is darkness. But God has not abandoned the world. The light is shining in the darkness, i.e., through the Logos God has pierced the darkness with the light of supernatural revelation; and black as the darkness is, it has failed to quench the light (1:5). Jesus refers to his mission in similar terms. He tells men that the light is to be with them a little longer and they must walk while they have the light, lest, by refusing the light, the darkness engulf them (*katalambanō*). The man who refuses the light stumbles blindly in darkness, not knowing where he is going. Only by believing in the light can men become sons of the light (12:35).

SIN IS UNBELIEF. Unbelief in Christ is a further manifestation of

---

[15] See F. C. Grant, *An Introduction to NT Thought* (1950), p. 94.
[16] W. F. Howard, *Christianity According to St. John* (1946), p. 89.
[17] W. Grundmann, *TDNT* I, 306.

a basic hatred for God. Jesus' presence among men brought their hatred for God to a crisis so that it became clearly manifest as hatred for Christ (3:19-21). If a man renders this decision against Christ, he will die in his sins (8:24). In this context is probably to be understood the saying in I John 5:16f. about the sin that is unto death, i.e., the sin of inflexible unbelief that of itself condemns a man to everlasting separation from God. For this reason, belief in Christ (*pisteuō eis*) receives strong emphasis. In the Synoptics the phrase is found only once (Mt. 18:6). In John the phrase is found thirteen times in Jesus' words and twenty-one times in John's interpretation. Unbelief is of the essence of sin (16:9). Unless men believe, they will perish (3:16), and the wrath of God rests upon them (3:36).

DEATH. John does not say much about death except as a fact of human existence in the world. He offers no speculations either about the origin of Satan, of sin, or of death. Apart from the life brought by Christ, the human race is given up to death, and it is responsible for this because it is sinful. Death is the characteristic of this world; but life has come into this world from above that all men may escape death and enter into eternal life (5:24).

ESCHATOLOGICAL DUALISM. Thus far we have traced the dualism of John in its vertical dimension. The world below is the realm of darkness, of satanic power, of sin, and of death. The world above is the world of the Spirit, of light, and life. In Jesus' mission light and life have invaded the darkness to deliver men from darkness, sin, and death, to give them the life of the Spirit.

This, however, is not the whole story. The fact is that there appears in John a tension between vertical and horizontal eschatology. John not only is conscious of the invasion of the world above into the world below. It is an invasion into *history*. Bultmann interprets Johannine dualism as a gnostic, cosmological dualism that has been translated into a dualism of decision,[18] and Dodd interprets it in terms of platonic dualism, in which "things and events in this world derive what reality they possess from the eternal ideas they embody."[19] It is therefore important to determine whether John has a sense of redemptive history.

Cullmann has defended the thesis that the Johannine theology must be viewed in the context of redemptive history.[20] While some of the Johannine idiom does indeed occur in gnostic thought, and while it is probably true that John deliberately used this terminology to interpret the gospel to people with gnostic leanings, we no longer need to feel that the Johannine idiom is derived from gnostic thought. This idiom is also found in Palestinian thought, in particular the Qumran writings. Equally important is the fact

[18] R. Bultmann, *Theology* (1955), II, 21.
[19] C. H. Dodd, *The Interpretation of the Fourth Gospel* (1953), p. 143.
[20] O. Cullmann, *Salvation in History* (1967), pp. 268-91.

that John places the coming of the Logos in the midst of history. To be sure, John does not use the Old Testament to the same degree that the Synoptics do to show that Jesus is the fulfillment of the Old Testament expectation, but on numerous occasions he does quote prophecy to show that it is fulfilled in the events of Jesus' life. John was the voice preparing the way of the Lord, as Isaiah said (1:23). Jesus' sovereignty over the temple fulfills the word of Psalm 69:9. That Jesus has inaugurated a new day when all men may have a more immediate knowledge of God than in the old order fulfills the prophets, probably Isaiah 54:13 (6:45). The final entry into Jerusalem is the visitation of Israel's king, as foretold in Psalm 118:25 and Zechariah 9:9 (12:13-15). Jesus' rejection by Israel is foreseen in Isaiah 53:1 and 6:10 (12:38-40). An anticipation of Jesus' betrayal is seen in Psalm 41:10 (13:18). Even the events of his death fulfill Psalm 22:19; 34:20, and Zechariah 12:10 (19:24, 36-37). However, more impressive than specific quotations is the general tone of the Gospel and its attitude toward the Old Testament as a whole. "It was not (in general) his method to bolster up the several items of Christian doctrine and history with supports drawn from this or that part of the Old Testament; instead the whole body of the Old Testament formed a background or framework, upon which the new revelation rested."[21] Supporting this is the fact that the whole historical setting of much of the Gospel is the Jewish feasts in Jerusalem.[22]

John is very conscious that Jesus has inaugurated a new era that provides the reality anticipated in the Old Testament order. He sounds this as one of his major chords in the prologue. The Law was given through Moses; grace and truth (the equivalent of the Old Testament *hesed* and *emeth*) came through Jesus Christ (1:17). In the rather frequent references to Moses (11 times) and the debate over the meaning of descent from Abraham (8:33-58), Jesus asserts that he has come to offer the true freedom that the Jews thought they had in Abraham (8:33, 36). He even affirms that "Abraham rejoiced that he was to see my day; he saw it and was glad" (8:56). However we exegete this verse, it is an affirmation that Jesus has fulfilled Abraham's hope, which he found in the promises of God.

That Jesus is the fulfillment of the Old Testament messianic hope is seen in the fact that the same terms are used of him as in the Synoptics: Messiah, King of Israel, Son of Man, and Son of God,[23] even though the terms may be used somewhat differently. It is not unimportant that Jesus never represents himself as the Logos of God. This is John's own distinctive witness to Jesus.

There can be little doubt but that many of the events related by John have a symbolical significance that places Jesus' ministry in the stream

---

[21] C. K. Barrett, "The OT in the Fourth Gospel," *JTS* 48 (1947), 168.
[22] See R. Morgan, "Fulfillment in the Fourth Gospel," *Int* 11 (1957), 155-65.
[23] See Ch. 18.

of redemptive history. The first miracle—the changing of water at the wedding in Cana—is a sign (2:11). A wedding is a symbol of the messianic days (Isa. 54:4-8; 62:4-5), and both a wedding and a banquet appear in the Synoptics as symbols of the messianic era (Mt. 8:11; 22:1-14; Lk. 22:16-18). Revelation pictures the messianic consummation in terms of a wedding (Rev. 19:9). In our Gospel, the wedding at Cana symbolizes the presence of the messianic salvation; wine symbolizes the joy of the messianic feast (see Mk. 2:19); the six stone jars used for Jewish rites of purification symbolize the Old Testament era that is now ending; and Mary's statement, "they have no wine," becomes a pregnant reflection on the barrenness of Jewish purification, much in the vein of Mark 7:1-24.[24]

John deliberately places the cleansing of the temple at the very beginning of his Gospel, much as Luke places Jesus' rejection at Nazareth at the beginning of Jesus' ministry[25] as another sign (2:23). John interprets this to represent the Messiah's lordship over the temple. It will be destroyed and replaced by all that is represented in Jesus' resurrection (2:19-20). The idea that the temple worship, both in Jerusalem and in Samaria, is to be displaced by worship inspired by the Spirit is overtly asserted in 4:20-24.

Two of John's favorite words are truth (*alētheia*) and true (*alēthinos*). When John speaks of what is true or genuine,[26] he usually contrasts the revelation in Christ not only as heavenly blessings in contrast to earthly, but as blessings of the new age in contrast to what has gone before. "The true light" (1:9) contrasts indeed with the darkness of earth; but the contrast is not with the false lights of pagan religions but with the partial and imperfect light that preceded him. John was in a sense a light (5:35), but Jesus was the full light. The "true bread" (6:32) is that which satisfies spiritual hunger; but it is not contrasted with daily food but with the manna provided by God through Moses that could only sustain bodily life. Christ is the true vine (15:1) because he provides the source of real life for those who abide in him in contrast to membership in Israel as the vine of the former dispensation (Jer. 2:21; Ezek. 15:1-8; Ps. 8:8-16).

The centrality of Jesus in salvation history is further emphasized by the "hour" of which we hear so much in John (2:4; 8:20; 12:23, etc.). It is the hour of Jesus' passion, death, resurrection and ascension as the culminating hour in the long history of God's dealings with men.[27] The same emphasis is found in the repeated use of "now" (*nun*). "The hour is coming and now is" (4:23; 5:25). "Now" the mission of Jesus will come to its climax, which will mean victory over the devil and the world (12:31), his own glorification in death (17:5), and his return to the Father (16:5; 17:13). The climax of redemptive history is also an anticipation of the

---

24 R. E. Brown, *John,* I, 105.
25 See Lk. 4:16ff. In Mark this occurs well along in Jesus' ministry. See Mk. 6:1-6.
26 See pp. 267ff.
27 R. E. Brown, *John,* I, cxvi.

eschatological consummation. "Already in this *nun* of the Fourth Gospel . . . there is awareness of being in transition, of being almost completely absorbed into the realization that in the Now of Christ the end, the consummation is present. But the Johannine *nun* . . . is not unique. It is simply an enhanced form of the general view of primitive Christianity."[28]

John also looks into the future. Although John has no explicit doctrine of the church,[29] he foresees a mission for Jesus' disciples. It is his mission "to gather into one the children of God who are scattered abroad" (11:52). This clearly reflects the Gentile mission, as does the saying that as the Good Shepherd he must bring "other sheep that are not of this fold" (10:16).

As we shall see, John has the elements of a realistic, futuristic eschatology. While eternal life in John is usually a present life of "realized eschatology," it is sometimes future and eschatological (3:36; 5:39).[30] One saying reflects the eschatological dualism of the two ages, even if the distinctive idiom is not used, more clearly than the parallel saying in the Synoptics: "He who hates his life in this world will keep it for life eternal" (12:25). Life is the life of the Age to Come, and in this saying, "this world" is synonymous to the "this age" of the Synoptics.[31]

We conclude that "the Johannine view of salvation is both vertical and horizontal. The vertical expresses the uniqueness of the divine intervention in Jesus; the horizontal aspect establishes a relationship between this intervention and salvation history."[32] The question remains whether this is a truly biblical way of thinking which is not inconsistent with the Synoptics, or whether it represents a blending of the Hebrew and the Hellenistic approaches to salvation that in effect distorts the gospel.

GREEK DUALISM. The dualism of John must be discussed against the background of Greek dualism including gnosticism and the newly discovered Jewish dualism as represented by the Qumran literature. As noted above,[33] some scholars, of whom Bultmann is the most outstanding, using the *religionsgeschichte* method, feel that gnosticism is not primarily the result of a synthesis of Greek dualism with the gospel but is the final product of a syncretistic Eastern religious movement whose beginnings antedate Christianity. However, until pre-Christian Jewish or Eastern sources are found that clearly reflect this dualism,[34] it is safer to conclude that "Gnosti-

---

[28] G. Stählin, *TDNT* IV, 1119.

[29] See below, pp. 281ff.

[30] See Ch. 22.

[31] See Mk. 8:35 and par. See C. K. Barrett, *John,* p. 353.

[32] R. E. Brown, *John*, I, cxvi.

[33] See p. 218.

[34] Some scholars see in the Qumran literature a definite link between Judaism and gnosticism. See B. Reicke, "Traces of Gnosticism in the Dead Sea Scrolls?" *NTS* 1 (1954), 137-40.

cism . . . was in reality only the development of a deeply rooted Greek tendency of thought."[35]

That dualism was deeply rooted in Greek philosophical and religious thought is proven by a survey of such diverse writers as the philosopher Plato, the litterateur Plutarch, and the Jew Philo.[36] It is by no means insignificant that the Jew Philo, who accepted the Old Testament as the divine revelation, interpreted it in terms of a thoroughgoing philosophical dualism. In this view, there are two realms of existence—the phenomenal and the noumenal: the changing, transitory, visible world and the invisible, eternal realm of God. Ultimate reality belongs only to the higher world. Man, like the universe, is a duality: body and soul. The body belongs to the phenomenal world, the soul to the noumenal. The visible world, including man's body, is not considered evil in itself, but it is a burden and hindrance to the soul. The famous idiom describing the relation between the two is *sōma-sēma:* the body is the tomb or prison house of the soul.[37] The wise man is he who succeeds in mastering his bodily passions and allowing his *nous* (mind) to reign over his lower desires. "Salvation" is for those who master their passions; and at death their souls will be liberated from their earthly, bodily bondage and set free to enjoy a blessed immortality. Salvation is a human attainment—by knowledge. Plato taught that human reason can apprehend the true nature of the world and of man's own being, and thus master the body. Philo also taught that liberation from earthly bondage was by knowledge of God and the world; but while Plato achieved this knowledge by dialectical reasoning, Philo substituted prophecy, revelation in the Law of Moses.

The most important early sources for gnosticism are the Hermetic writings, which reflect a synthesis of Platonism with other philosophies. We have already noted that striking similarities exist between John and the Hermetica.[38]

God is called mind, light and life. The first tractate, *Poimandres,* starts with a vision of infinite light, which is God. Over against the primal light stands a chaotic ocean of darkness. A holy word (*logos*), the Son of God, comes forth from the light and separates the higher elements from the lower. From the lower elements, earth and water, the cosmos is formed—the lower elements of nature being left without reason so that they were mere matter. Man was made in the likeness of *nous,* who is light and life, but falling in love with the creation, fell and became mingled with the nature

---

[35] W. Barclay, "John 1:1-14," *ET* 70 (1958-59), 115.

[36] See G. E. Ladd, *The Pattern of NT Truth* (1968), pp. 13-31 where this dualism is expounded with considerable reference to the primary sources.

[37] *Ibid.*, pp. 17, 28.

[38] See above, p. 217. See W. D. Davies, *Invitation to the NT* (1966), pp. 398-408; C. H. Dodd, *The Interpretation of the Fourth Gospel*, pp. 10-53; C. H. Dodd, *The Bible and the Greeks* (1935), pp. 99-248, for a detailed discussion of two of the most important tractates. For the text of the first tractate, *Poimandres,* in English, see H. Jonas, *The Gnostic Religion* (1958), pp. 148-53.

that was devoid of reason. This man is twofold: mortal through his body, immortal in his essential being. Salvation can be achieved after death when man, by stages, strips off the elements of his sensuous nature and, by attaining *gnōsis,* becomes deified. Here the divine realm is light and life, the lower realm is chaotic darkness.

In fully developed gnosticism matter is *ipso facto* evil, and man can be saved only by receiving the *gnōsis* imparted by a descending and ascending redeemer.

QUMRAN DUALISM. The Qumran writings embody a very different dualism. A good representative passage containing all the essential elements of this dualism is the Scroll of the Rule (1QS) 3:13-4:26.[39] There are two spirits that war with each other—the Spirit of Truth and the Spirit of Perversity, and the angel of destruction will vent the wrath of The Spirit of Truth comes from a fountain of light, the Spirit of Perversity from a fountain of darkness. Each of these two spirits rules over a part of humanity, which is divided sharply into two camps—the sons of light and truth and the sons of perversity. However, both spirits wage their warfare also in the hearts of men—a concept paralleled in rabbinic thought that every man has two tendencies in him—the good tendency (*yetzer hatob*) and the evil tendency (*yetzer hara*).[40] The Spirit of Truth is dominant when men—like the Qumranians—devote themselves in strict obedience to the Law as the Teacher of Righteousness had interpreted it. All others are ruled by the Spirit of Perversity. The conflict is not only limited to the hearts of men, but has a cosmic dimension. This is evident in that the conflict between the two spirits will be resolved only in an eschatological conflagration. In the day of judgment God will banish the Spirit of Perversity, and the angels of destruction will vent the wrath of God both on the evil Spirit and upon all who walk in this Spirit. Another scroll (The Scroll of the War Rule) describes the eschatological battle in detail (1QM). The Gospel and the passage from Qumran under discussion share certain linguistic formulae: the spirit of truth, the holy spirit, sons of light, eternal life, the light of life, to walk in darkness, the wrath of God, blind eyes, fullness of grace, the works of God.[41]

COMPARISON WITH JOHN. What use can be made of Hellenistic and Jewish dualism in interpreting the Johannine dualism? In spite of the weightiness of Bultmann's scholarship, it is difficult to think that John is influenced by gnostic dualism. On the contrary, John seems to oppose a gnostic type of dualism. When John emphasizes that "the Word became flesh and dwelt among us" (1:14), he is deliberately opposing gnostic ideas that placed a gulf between the spiritual and the material worlds. Further-

[39] See A. Dupont-Sommer, *The Essene Writings from Qumran* (1961), pp. 77-82.
[40] See G. F. Moore, *Judaism* (1927), I, 479ff.; W. D. Davies, *Paul and Rabbinic Judaism* (1958), pp. 20ff.
[41] See J. H. Charlesworth, "A Critical Comparison of . . . Dualism," *NTS* 15 (1969), 414-15.

more, although John "plays down" eschatology, salvation for him does not mean the flight of the soul from the world and history as for the gnostics but a living fellowship with God in the world and in history, which will ultimately be consummated in the resurrection. The discovery of the Qumran dualism has robbed the similarities between John and the Hermetica of their force. "The scrolls showed that the dualism of the Fourth Gospel has nothing to do with Gnosis but is, rather, Palestinian in origin."[42] Jeremias goes on to point out that the Johannine dualism is like the Essene in that it is monotheistic, ethical, and eschatological, expecting the victory of the light.

However, there are striking differences between the Johannine and the Qumranian dualism. In Qumran the conflict is between two spirits, both of whom were created by God; in John the conflict is between the world and its ruler, and the incarnate Jesus. While there is admittedly a verbal similarity between light and darkness, and sons of light and sons of perversity (darkness), in John these do not represent two spirits ruling over two distinct classes of men; but the incarnate Logos is the light, and *all men are in darkness* but are invited to come to the light. Furthermore, the coming of light into the darkness of the world is a piece of realized eschatology, utterly different from anything in Qumran theology. Again, the theology of sin is very different. In Qumran the sons of light are those who dedicate themselves to keep the Law of Moses as interpreted by the Teacher of Righteousness, who separate themselves from the world (sons of perversity). In John the sons of light are those who believe in Jesus and thereby receive eternal life. For Qumran darkness is disobedience to the Law; for John darkness is rejection of Jesus. These differences lead to the conclusion that any influence of Qumran on John is in the area of idiom and terminology and not in fundamental theology.

At one point a similarity exists between Qumran and John that is important in understanding the Johannine dualism. Qumran has both an ethical dualism—light versus darkness—and an eschatological dualism that looks forward to the final eschatological triumph of the light. The Qumran scrolls—no more than John—make use of the dualistic language of the two ages. But it is clear that the Qumranians looked for a day of judgment—of divine visitation upon the powers of darkness—when the wicked would be destroyed in a great eschatological battle, when rewards and punishments would be meted out. Some scholars think the Qumranians looked for a bodily resurrection;[43] and fragments that appear to describe a new Jerusalem suggest that the Qumranians expected the creation of a new world.[44]

The blending of a vertical and a horizontal dualism is evident in Jewish apocalyptic writings. I Enoch contains many revelations of secrets hidden

---

42 J. Jeremias, *The Central Message of the NT* (1965), p. 83.
43 K. Schubert, *The Dead Sea Community* (1939), p. 108.
44 H. Ringgren, *The Faith of Qumran* (1963), pp. 164-65.

in heaven in the presence of God; but its main concern is with the eschatological consummation in the day of divine visitation. The apocalypses of Ezra and Baruch know of a heavenly Jerusalem that was revealed to Adam and to Moses, and, together with Paradise, will be revealed after the final judgment.[45]

The same twofold dualism characterizes the biblical writings. While the the basic structure of the Synoptic Gospels is an eschatological dualism—the message of an eschatological Kingdom that has broken into history in Jesus—they reflect also a vertical dualism. Heaven is conceived of as the dwelling place of God to which Jesus' disciples become dynamically related. Those who know the blessedness of God's reign and suffer for it have great reward in heaven (Mt. 5:12). Jesus urges men to lay up treasure in heaven (Mt. 6:20). If the rich young ruler would shake off his love for earthly things and follow Jesus, he would have treasure in heaven (Mt. 19:21). The most vivid illustration is the New Testament apocalypse where John is caught up in vision into heaven to witness the denouement of God's redemptive plan for history. While he sees the souls of the martyrs under the heavenly altar (Rev. 6:9ff.), the consummation means nothing less than the descent of the heavenly Jerusalem to earth (Rev. 21:2). The basic structure of the biblical literature is that there is a God in heaven who visits men in history and will finally visit them to transform a fallen order and dwell among men on a redeemed earth. It is utterly different from Greek dualism, which finds salvation in the flight of the soul from history into the heavenly world.[46] John's dualism is biblical, for its message is the proclamation of the divine visitation of men in history in the person of the incarnate Jesus; and the final goal is resurrection, judgment, and life in the Age to Come. If the emphasis is different in John than in the Synoptics, the fundamental theology is not. The Synoptics proclaim salvation in the eschatological Kingdom of God that has broken into history in Jesus' person and mission. John proclaims a present salvation in the person and mission of Jesus that will have an eschatological consummation.

[45] See G. H. Box, *The Ezra Apocalypse* (1912), p 198.
[46] See G. E. Ladd, *The Pattern of NT Truth.*

18

CHRISTOLOGY

Literature:

A. E. J. Rawlinson, "The Incarnation of the Word," *The NT Doctrine of the Christ* (1926), pp. 199-228; J. E. Davey, *The Jesus of St. John* (1958), pp. 81-89; C. M. Laymon, *Christ in the NT* (1958), pp. 151-78; V. Taylor, *The Person of Christ in NT Teaching* (1958), pp. 99-123; O. Cullmann, *The Christology of the NT* (1959); T. C. Smith, *Jesus in the Gospel of John* (1959), pp. 57-74; E. M. Sidebottom, *The Christ of the Fourth Gospel* (1961), pp. 26-68.

The Evangelist himself declares the purpose of his writing: "These are written that you may believe that Jesus is the Christ, the Son of God, and that believing you may have life in his name" (20:31). A textual variant is important in trying to determine the audience to whom John addresses his Gospel. The present tense (*pisteuēte*) has the support of the first hand of Sinaiticus, Vaticanus, and probably the Bodmer papyrus (66), while the aorist (*pisteusēte*) is supported by a corrector of Sinaiticus, Alexandrinus, and the majority of other manuscripts. If the present tense is adopted, John's purpose is to confirm Christians in their faith in Jesus as the Messiah and Son of God in the face of deviating interpretations that were arising in the church. A proper understanding of Christ is, then, John's main objective. Christology is central to the book, for eternal life is dependent upon a correct relationship to Christ.

THE LOGOS

Literature:

J. H. Bernard, *John* (1929), I, cxxxvii-cxlvii; G. Kittel, "Legō," *TDNT* (1942, 1967), IV, 84-91, 128-36; W. F. Howard, *Christianity According to St. John* (1946), pp. 34-56; E. K. Lee, *The Religious Thought of St. John* (1950), pp. 74-108; A. W. Argyle, "Philo and the Fourth Gospel," *ET* 63 (1951-52), 385-86; V. Taylor, *The Names of Jesus* (1953), pp. 161-66; R. McL. Wilson, "Philo and the Fourth Gospel," *ET* 65 (1953-54), 47-49; W. Barclay, "John 1:1-14," *ET* 70 (1958), 78-82, 114-17; A. Corell, *Consummatum Est* (1958), pp. 113-18; T. E. Pollard, "Cosmology and the Prologue of the Fourth Gospel," *Vig Chr* 12 (1958), 147-53; J. A. T. Robinson, "The Relation of the Prologue to the Gospel of St. John," *NTS* 9 (1962-63), 120-29; T. W. Manson, "The Johannine Logos Doctrine" in *Paul and John* (1963), pp. 136-60; J. Jeremias, "The Revealing Word" in *The Central Message of the NT* (1965), pp. 71-90; W. D. Davies, "The Word Became Flesh," *Invitation to the NT* (1966), pp. 421-31; R. E. Brown, *John* (1966), I, 519-24; M. McNamara, "*Logos* of the Fourth Gospel and *Memra* of the Palestinian Targum (Ex. 12:42)," *ET* 79 (1968), 115-17.

John strikes the christological note in his introduction, designating Jesus the "Logos." "In the beginning was the Logos, and the Logos was with God, and the Logos was God. . . . And the Logos became flesh and dwelt among us" (1:1, 14). We cannot enter the debate as to whether the theology of the prologue about the Logos (1:1-18) dominates the entire Gospel[1] or whether it was composed after the body of the Gospel as a sort of prefixed appendage.[2] Even if it is the remains of a Christian hymn to Christ, as many scholars think, it strikes a note that would appeal to both Jews and Greeks.

Scholars have often attempted to find the source of John's concept of the Logos in Hellenistic thought. The present tendency is to interpret the term against its Old Testament background. T. W. Manson may have overstated the case when he wrote, "It is, I think, indisputable that the roots of the doctrine are in the Old Testament and that its main stem is the *d*ᵉ*bar Yahweh,* the creative and revealing Word of God, by which the heavens and earth were made and the prophets inspired."[3] The question of the possible background of the term is an historical question. We must be primarily concerned with the question of what John means by calling Jesus the Logos and what it would mean to his readers.

It is of some significance that Jesus is not represented as referring to himself as the Logos, although he says many things that are consistent with Logos theology. The Logos terminology is found only in the Johannine literature: John 1:1ff.; I John 1:1; Revelation 19:13. It seems that John deliberately seized upon a term widely known in both the Hellenistic and the Jewish worlds in the interests of setting forth the significance of Christ.

The idea of Logos goes back to the philosopher Heraclitus (sixth century B.C.). He taught that all things were in a state of flux, that nothing ever remains the same. However, order and pattern can be perceived amidst the eternal ebb and flow of things in the Logos—the eternal principle of order in the universe. It is the Logos behind everlasting change that makes the world a cosmos, and an ordered whole.

The Logos was one of the most important elements in Stoic theology.

---

[1] B. Vawter, *The Jerome Biblical Commentary* (1968), p. 832.

[2] J. A. T. Robinson, "The Relation of the Prologue to the Gospel of St. John," *NTS* 9 (1962-63), 120-29.

[3] T. W. Manson, *Studies in the Gospels and Epistles* (1962), p. 118.

The Stoics used the idea of the Logos to provide the basis for a rational moral life. Faced with the usual Greek dualism of God and the world, they employed the concept of Logos as a unitary idea to solve the problem of duality. The entire universe was conceived as forming a single living whole that was permeated in all its parts by a primitive power conceived as never-resting, all-pervading fire or fiery vapor. The precise character of this essential fire is not clear; writers differ in their understanding of it. It was a diffused, tenuous kind of fiery air, possessing the property of thought. This very refined substance was thought to be immanent in all the world and to appear in living beings as the soul. It is a divine world-power, containing within itself the conditions and processes of all things, and is called Logos or God. As a productive power, the divine Logos was called the *spermatikos logos,* the Seminal Logos or generative principle of the world. This vital energy both pervades the universe and unfolds itself into innumerable *logoi spermatikoi* or formative forces that energize the manifold phenomena of nature and life. This Logos, by pervading all things, provides the rational order of the universe and supplies the standard for conduct and for the proper ordering of life for the rational man. The rational man is the one who lives in accordance with nature, and thereby finds an all-determining law of conduct.

Philo, an Alexandrian Jew (*ca.* 20 B.C.-A.D. 42), attempted the formidable task of wedding the Jewish religion with Hellenistic philosophy. He preserved the Jewish attitude toward the Old Testament as the inspired Word of God; but by his extreme allegorical interpretation he found philosophical concepts in the Old Testament Scriptures. He held the Greek view of a God utterly transcendent and separated from the world; and he employed the concept of Logos to provide a means of mediation between the transcendent God and the creation. God himself is absolute and outside the material universe. He comprehends all things and yet is himself uncomprehended. He is outside of time and space and is in his being unknowable. The only name by which God can be designated in himself is pure being, *to on,* being himself without attributes. Since God himself cannot be the immediate creator of the world, Philo conceives of intermediate forces or "ideas," which are manifestations of the divine activity. Manifested thus as creative power, directing and sustaining the universe, God is called Logos (Reason). Philo does not present any consistent concept of the Logos and its relationship to God. The Logos is conceived as inward, i.e., as the universal plan of things in the mind of God; and as outward, i.e., the plan made objective in the world. The Logos is both the original pattern of the world and the power that fashions it. It is at once the chief of the series of forces or ideas emanating from God, and the totality of them. In brief, the Logos concept is employed by Philo in diverse applications to provide a concept of a mediator between the transcendent God and the universe, an immanent power active in creation and revelation.

The Logos played a role also in the Hermetic literature. In the account of creation, *Poimandres* at first beheld a boundless light, and after a while a downward-moving darkness, appalling and hateful. The darkness then changed into a humid nature. From out of the light came a holy Logos as a creative and formative power, separating the lower from the higher element. The Logos invades the ocean of chaos, bringing it to order. The Hermetic logos is the active expression of the mind of God.

The word of God was an important concept to the Jew; creation came into being and was preserved by the word of God (Gen. 1:3, "and God said"; see Ps. 33:6, 9; 47:15-18); and the word of God is the bearer of salvation and new life (Ps. 107:20; Isa. 4:8; Ezek. 37:4-5). In the Old Testament, the word is not merely an utterance; it is a semi-hypostatized existence so that it can go forth and accomplish the divine purpose (Isa. 55:10-11). The word of God uttered at creation, expressed through the mouth of the prophets (cf. Jer. 1:4, 11; 2:1) and in the Law (Ps. 119:38, 41, 105), has a number of functions that may very well be compared with those attributed to the Logos in John.

The concept of personified wisdom also provides Jewish background for the Logos concept. In Proverbs 8:22-31, wisdom is semi-hypostatized. Wisdom was the first of all created things and at the creation of the world, "I was beside him, like a master workman" (Prov. 8:30). Wisdom came forth from God to dwell in Israel to make them God's people (Sir. 24:8). The most developed concept of wisdom is found in the Wisdom of Solomon 7:22-9:18. She is the fashioner of all things, she penetrates all spirits, her pureness pervades all things, she is a pure emanation of the glory of the Almighty, the reflection of eternal light. She can do all things, renew all things, and by passing into holy souls make friends of God and prophets. She orders all things well, is the fashioner of all that exists, and initiates men into the knowledge of God and brings them into immortality. In such passages, wisdom is a poetic personification of the power of God at work in all the world. Many striking similarities can be drawn between the Logos and wisdom.[4] However, wisdom is never called the word of God, even though she came forth from the mouth of the Most High (Sir. 24:3), and wisdom is placed in parallelism to the word in the Wisdom of Solomon (9:1-2).[5]

Some scholars still insist that the Johannine Logos can be understood only in the light of the Hellenistic usage. "The opening sentences, then, of the Prologue are clearly intelligible only when we admit that *Logos,* though it carries with it the associations of the Old Testament Word of the Lord, has also a meaning similar to that which it bears in Stoicism as modified by Philo, and parallel to the idea of Wisdom in other Jewish writers. It is the rational principle in the universe, its meaning, plan or purpose, conceived as a divine hypostasis in which the eternal God is revealed and

---

[4] See C. H. Dodd, *Interpretation,* pp. 274-75.
[5] For further discussion, see R. E. Brown, *John,* I, 522-23.

active."[6] However, in spite of certain similarities, neither the idea of Logos nor wisdom approaches the truth John sets forth by his Logos doctrine: the *personal* pre-existence and the *incarnation* of the Logos. The Philonic Logos is sometimes hypostatized and personified, but it is never personalized. Neither is Jewish wisdom. Philo's Logos concept is employed in the interests of a dualistic cosmology that removes God from immediate contact with creation, whereas John uses the Logos concept to bring God in Christ directly into his creation. What is "foreign to both is the idea that revelatory action, this speech of God to the world, happens finally and definitely in the historical framework of an earthly human life."[7]

The important question is the theological use John makes of the Logos, and this can be paralleled neither in Hellenistic philosophy nor in Jewish thought. The first and most important meaning is the pre-existence of Jesus, who is the Logos. "In the beginning" points behind creation, for the Logos was the agent of creation. This phrase is certainly a deliberate allusion to Genesis 1:1: "In the beginning God created the heavens and the earth." "The beginning" in John 1:1 goes behind Genesis 1:1. At the very beginning of the eternity past existed the Word.

The pre-existence of Jesus is reflected elsewhere in Jesus' own reported teaching. "Before Abraham was, I am" (8:58). This amazing affirmation is an allusion to the Old Testament usage. God revealed himself to Moses as "I am who I am" (Exod. 3:14). "See now that I, even I, am he, and there is no God beside me" (Deut. 32:39). Pre-existence is also predicated in Jesus' last prayer: "Father, glorify thou me with the glory which I had with thee before the world was made" (17:5; cf. 6:62). The idea of pre-existence was no invention of the Evangelist. Paul expresses it clearly in his great incarnation hymn (Phil. 2:6; cf. Col. 1:15ff.) and alludes to it in earlier correspondence (I Cor. 8:6; II Cor. 8:9). It is impossible to say with certainty when and how the church became conscious of pre-existence. The comparative religions school insists that the early church interpreted Jesus in terms of the myth of the descending and ascending savior. However, pre-existence was a Jewish idea. In Enoch, the Son of Man is clearly a pre-existent, heavenly (if not divine) being who comes to earth to establish the reign of God (En. 39:7-8; 48:6; 62:7). Jesus' very use of the term Son of Man involved an implicit claim to pre-existence. The Johannine Jesus only affirms more explicitly what is implicit in the Synoptics.[8] However, the idea of pre-existence could be understood and come to full expression only after Jesus' resurrection and ascension; and from the evidence in Paul's letters, this happened early in the life of the church.

---

6 C. H. Dodd, *Interpretation,* p. 280. See J. E. Davey, *The Jesus of St. John* (1958), pp. 81ff. For Johannine and Philonic similarities, see C. H. Dodd, *Interpretation,* p. 276. See further A. W. Argyle, "Philo and the Fourth Gospel," *ET* 63 (1951-52), 385-86, and the response by R. McL. Wilson, "Philo and the Fourth Gospel," *ET* 65 (1953-54), 47-49.

7 O. Cullmann, *Christology,* p. 258.

8 See on pre-existence the Excursus in R. Schnackenburg, *John,* I, 494-506.

Second, John uses the Logos idea to assert the deity of Jesus.[9] The Logos was with (*pros*) God, and the Word was God (*theos ēn ho logos*). The Greek words express two ideas: the Word was deity, but the Word was not fully identical with deity. The definite article is used only with *logos.* If John had used the definite article also with *theos,* he would have said that all that God is, the Logos is: an exclusive identity. As it is, he says that all the Word is, God is; but he implies that God is more than the Word.

Third, John asserts that the Logos was the agent of creation. He is not the ultimate source of creation, but the agent through whom God, the ultimate source, created the world. This same theology is expressed in Paul's words: that all things come from (*ek*) God through (*dia*) Christ (I Cor. 8:6; see also Col. 1:16).

Fourth, there is the amazing assertion that "the Word became flesh" (1:14). Such an affirmation would amaze and refute all Hellenistic philosophical and gnostic dualisms that separated God from his world. Even Philo, with his Jewish background of a creating God, conceives of God as utterly transcendent. God gave birth to an original world of ideas; but the Logos, here a second derived deity, begotten by God in eternity, fashions the visible world.[10] John wishes to emphasize that it was God himself in the Word who entered human history, not as a phantom, but as a real man of flesh. The word translated "to dwell" (*eskenōsen*), or "to tabernacle," is a biblical metaphor for God's presence. This statement "implies that God himself was present in the flesh, in abasement."[11]

The fifth meaning of Logos is that he has come in the flesh as revealer. He comes to reveal to men life (1:4), light (1:4-5), grace (1:14), truth (1:14), glory (1:14), even God himself. "No one has ever seen God; the only Son, who is in the bosom of the Father, he has made him known" (1:18). While John may not make further use of the Logos idiom beyond the prologue, it is clear that the Logos theology pervades the entire Gospel.

MESSIAH

Literature:

E. K. Lee, *The Religious Thought of St. John* (1950), pp. 152-56; C. H. Dodd, *Interpretation* (1953), pp. 228ff.; W. A. Meeks, *The Prophet King* (1967).

We have seen that in contemporary Jewish thought the Messiah (Christ) was conceived of as an anointed, divinely endowed Son of David who would shatter the hated pagan rule and deliver God's people. It is a striking fact, in view of the degree to which the Fourth Gospel embodies theological interpretation, that it does not also embody later Christian usage. Everywhere in John, with two exceptions (1:17; 17:3), Christ is used as a title,

---

[9] We employ the name "Jesus" instead of "Christ" because this is John's own practice.

[10] See the references in *TDNT* III, 76-77.

[11] J. Jeremias, *The Central Message of the NT* (1965), p. 83.

not a proper name; and the first of these two exceptions is a legitimate anachronism. At this point the Gospel soundly reflects its Jewish setting. The Gospel was written, not that men might believe in Jesus Christ, but that they might believe that Jesus is the Christ. Jesus was his name, not Jesus Christ. Christ became a proper name only when the gospel moved into the Hellenistic world (Acts 11:26). John scarcely reflects this fact.

The Gospel sounds the christological note at the very beginning: one of the first disciples, Andrew, tells Peter that he has found the Messiah (1:41).[12] The next day Nathaniel confesses Jesus to be "the Son of God; . . . the King of Israel" (1:49). The Gospel accurately reflects the political situation of the time. "King of Israel" does not mean a militant revolutionary as the Jews understood it. In fact, after one of Jesus' most notable miracles, the people tried to take him by force and make him King (6:15), but he refused them. The last entry into Jerusalem is described in terms of the coming of Israel's King (12:13, 15). That Jesus was accused of political sedition before Pilate is reflected in the latter's question, "Are you the King of the Jews?" (18:33). Jesus replied that his kingly authority did not come from this world and could not be promoted by worldly means of force of arms (18:36). Jesus was later mocked as King of the Jews (19:3) and executed with the title "King of the Jews" on his cross (19:19).

It is obvious that his messianic kingship is not on the political but on the spiritual level. In the same way, the title "Christos" is not of itself adequate to designate the person and the mission of Jesus. He is not only the Messiah; he is the Messiah who is also the Son of God (20:31; 1:49; 11:27). He is the Messiah in the sense that he fulfills the Old Testament hope of a coming deliverer (1:45). The Messiah was expected to remain hidden until he would suddenly appear on the scene (7:27),[13] but Jesus was a well-known figure. When Jesus talked of his imminent death, the Jews answered him by saying: "We have heard from the law that the Christ remains forever" (12:34). By citing these words, John is not referring to any specific prophecies but to the way the Jews interpreted the Old Testament (see Isa. 9:6). It was a contradiction in terms that the Messiah should die, for it would be his mission to reign in God's eternal Kingdom.

Although the idea of Jesus as the messianic King is not central in Johannine thought, the casual references in his Gospel[14] reflect an historical situation[15] that Jesus did and said things that made some people think he

---

[12] The fact that the Evangelist must interpret the meaning of "Messiah" (which means Christ) clearly suggests that John is writing in part at least for Gentiles who are not familiar with Jewish terms.

[13] See references in C. K. Barrett, *John*, p. 266.

[14] See also 1:20; 3:28; 4:29; 7:31, 41, 42; 9:22; 10:24.

[15] "The emphasis on the importance of this issue [messiahship] chains the Fourth Gospel irrevocably to history." E. M. Sidebottom, *The Christ of the Fourth Gospel* (1961), p. 70.

was the Messiah, and yet he did not conform to the expected pattern. It is difficult to believe that this reflects the situation of the Evangelist's own day unless he was writing primarily for a Jewish audience. The normative confession of Jesus in the Gentile world was not that Jesus was the Christ but Lord (Rom. 10:9). The situation in John's own day is better reflected in the epistles of John, where Christ is usually a proper name.[16] However, the Christ and the Son of God are not interchangeable and are not quite synonymous.[17]

THE SON OF MAN

Literature:

J. H. Bernard, *John,* I (1929), cxxii-cxxxiii; C. H. Dodd, *Interpretation* (1953), pp. 241-49; E. M. Sidebottom, "The Son of Man as Man in the Fourth Gospel," *ET* 68 (1957), 231-35, 280-83; E. M. Sidebottom, "The Ascent and Descent of the Son of Man in the Gospel of John," *ATR* 39 (1957), 115-22; O. Cullmann, *Christology* (1959), pp. 184-87; E. M. Sidebottom, *The Christ of the Fourth Gospel* (1961), pp. 69-136; A. J. B. Higgins, *Jesus and the Son of Man* (1964), pp. 153-84; F. H. Borsch, *The Son of Man in Myth and History* (1967), pp. 257-313; E. D. Freed, "The Son of Man in the Fourth Gospel," *JBL* 86 (1967), 402-9; R. Schnackenburg, *John,* I (1968), 529-42; S. S. Smalley, "The Johannine Son of Man Sayings," *NTS* 15 (1969), 278-301.

As in the Synoptics, the phrase "Son of Man" is an expression used only by Jesus of himself; it is never applied to him by his disciples or by the people. There is reflected even more clearly the perplexity as to its meaning when applied to a man among men. Jesus asked the man born blind if he believed in the Son of Man; and the man replied, "And who is he, sir, that I may believe in him?" (9:35). When Jesus referred to the death of the Son of Man (12:23), the Jews asked, "We have heard from the law that the Christ remains forever. How can you say that the Son of man must be lifted up? Who is this Son of man?" (12:34). This may reflect ignorance of the meaning of the phrase "Son of Man" and be understood as evidence that the expression has no messianic connotations; but it may equally well indicate confusion on the part of the Jews when the expression is applied to a man among men. The fact that in John, as in the Synoptics, the title is used only by Jesus of himself seems to reflect an historical reminiscence that Jesus did use the title as distinct from the other titles given him by his disciples after his resurrection.[18] The Son of Man was a heavenly, supernatural being who should come to earth with apocalyptic glory; how could he be among men that one should believe on him? How could he die? Such ideas about the Son of Man were indeed unheard of.

We have seen that in the Synoptics, the Son of Man sayings divide

---

[16] I Jn. 2:22 and 5:1 are the two exceptions where the Jewish idiom is preserved.

[17] M. de Jonge, "The Use of the Word *Christos* in the Johannine Epistles" in *Studies in John* (1970), p. 74.

[18] R. E. Brown, *John,* I, 91.

themselves into three groups: the Son of Man ministering on earth, the Son of Man in humiliation and death, and the Son of Man coming in apocalyptic glory to judge men and inaugurate the Kingdom of God. The Johannine sayings do not fall into this classification; John is making use of an independent tradition. There are several sayings that refer to the Son of Man in his passion, but the idiom is different from the Synoptics. John speaks of Jesus' being lifted up from the earth, and sees therein Jesus' glorification. As the serpent was lifted up in the wilderness, so must the Son of Man be lifted up that he may impart eternal life to those who believe in him (3:14-15; see 8:28). His uplifting in his death would be the means of drawing all men unto himself (12:32). This uplifting is also his glorification (12:23; 13:31). His death will not be a mere human tragedy but will be the means by which he will re-enter the glory from which he had come. "Now, Father, glorify thou me in thy own presence with the glory which I had with thee before the world was" (17:5). It seems that the crowds understood that being lifted up meant death, for they replied that this did not fit their expectation that the Messiah would remain forever (12:34).

A reflection of his suffering is seen in another saying about the bread of life. Jesus asserts that he is the bread of life that came down from heaven (6:33-35), that as the Son of Man he gives the food that endures to eternal life (6:27), that men must eat the flesh and drink the blood of the Son of Man to experience this life (6:53), that the bread that he will give them is his flesh (6:51). "These passages show conclusively that a reference to the death of Jesus is intended—he will give his flesh in death—and suggest a sacrificial meaning."[19]

These sayings, which to some extent are analogous to the Synoptic sayings about the suffering and death of the Son of Man, provide background for the most distinctive element in the Johannine usage. As the Son of Man, Jesus is the one who descended from heaven and who ascends into heaven (3:13). This idea in turn provides the clue for the interpretation of the most difficult Son of Man saying in John: "You will see heaven opened and the angels of God ascending and descending upon the Son of man" (1:51). Some scholars interpret this saying in terms of the eschatological coming of the Son of Man, parallel to Jesus' promise before the Sanhedrin (Mk. 14:62) that they would see the Son of Man coming with the clouds of heaven.[20] Black thinks this saying pictures the heavens opened and the angels from above and beneath converging on the Son of Man, the central figure.[21] However, this saying clearly embodies an allusion to Jacob's vision of a ladder reaching to heaven, and a more natural interpretation in the context of Johannine thought is that Jesus as the Son of

---

19 C. K. Barrett, *John*, p. 246.

20 See J. H. Bernard, *John*, I, 68.

21 M. Black, *An Aramaic Approach to the Gospels and Acts* (1954[2]). This suggestion is omitted from the latest edition of his book. See also C. Colpe in *TDNT* VIII, 469.

Man has come to establish communication between heaven and earth. This is a bit of "realized eschatology." The disciples will experience ("see") in all Jesus' work the union with God that is his and his alone. Thus the Son of Man is the "gate of heaven," the place of the presence of God's grace on earth, the tent of God among men.[22]

Another bit of realized eschatology is that God has committed to Jesus as the Son of Man all authority to execute judgment (5:27). This saying occurs in a passage that exhibits a tension between futuristic (5:28-29) and realized (5:25) eschatology. In both cases, Jesus as the Son of Man is judge. Jesus has come into the world to execute judgment (9:38), and all who refuse to believe in him stand already under judgment (3:18). This does not, however, militate against the reality of a future eschatological judgment. There awaits a resurrection of judgment (6:29).

The difference between the Synoptic and Johannine uses of Son of Man does not require us to conclude that the Evangelist or the early church radically transformed the true historical tradition. John does indeed play down the eschatological sayings by omitting them and emphasizes one aspect that is implicit in the Synoptic sayings: the pre-existence and incarnation of the Son of Man. John probably emphasizes the reality of Jesus' flesh in the Son of Man sayings (6:51) to counter docetic tendencies. There is certainly no need to look to a Hellenistic background for the descent-ascent motif; this is at home on Jewish soil.[23] It is probable that John draws upon a Son of Man tradition that is independent of the Synoptic tradition,[24] that supplements but does not contradict the Synoptic tradition.[25]

THE SON OF GOD

Literature:

W. F. Lofthouse, "Fatherhood and Sonship in the Fourth Gospel," *ET* 43 (1931-32), 442-48; W. F. Lofthouse, *The Father and the Son* (1934); W. F. Howard, *Christianity According to St. John* (1946), pp. 65-71; E. K. Lee, *The Religious Thought of St. John* (1950), pp. 59-73; C. H. Dodd, *Interpretation* (1953), pp. 250-62; G. Schrenk, "Patēr," *TDNT* V (1954, 1967), 996-1003; J. E. Davey, *The Jesus of St. John* (1958); V. Taylor, *The Person of Christ* (1958), pp. 99-107; O. Cullmann, *Christology* (1959), pp. 298-303; E. M. Sidebottom, *The Christ of the Fourth Gospel* (1961), pp. 149-65; T. W. Manson, *On Paul and John* (1963), pp. 128-35; T. E. Pollard, *Johannine Christology and the Early Church* (1970), pp. 3-22.

One of the most distinct differences between the Synoptics and John is the different role Jesus' sonship to God plays. In the Synoptic tradition,

---

[22] R. Schnackenburg, *John,* I, 321; J. Schneider, *TDNT* I, 521.

[23] See R. N. Longenecker, *The Christology of Early Jewish Christianity* (1970), pp. 58-62; E. M. Sidebottom, *The Christ of the Fourth Gospel* (1961), pp. 122ff.

[24] S. E. Johnson, *IDB* R-Z, p. 416.

[25] See S. S. Smalley, "The Johannine Son of Man Sayings," *NTS* 15 (1969), 278-301.

Jesus is reticent to speak of his sonship and God's Fatherhood. *Patēr* is used by Jesus of God in Mark four times, Q eight or nine, Matthew some twenty-three times. In the Synoptics this form of speech is confined to the latter half of his ministry, and is used by Jesus only when speaking to his disciples. However, Jesus speaks of God as Father 106 times in John, and the usage is not restricted to any period of his ministry or to any group of hearers.[26] He speaks of "my Father" twenty-four times in John, eighteen in Matthew, six in Mark, three in Luke. It is obvious that Jesus' sonship is the central christological idea in John, and that he writes his Gospel to make explicit what was implicit in the Synoptics. The Gospel is written that men may believe that Jesus is the Messiah, but more than Messiah; he is the Son of God (20:31).

John sounds this note in his prologue: "we have beheld his glory, glory as of the only Son from the Father" (1:14). Furthermore, John has the Baptist confessing that Jesus is the Son of God at the very outset of his ministry (1:34; cf. also 1:49), while the Synoptics represent the disciples as grasping this truth only in the midst of the ministry (Mk. 8:29).[27] In any case, John sets forth Jesus as the only, the unique Son of God. It is not altogether clear how much meaning John intends to express by the adjective "only" (*monogenēs*). He uses it also in 3:16 and 18; and in 1:18, according to the best textual reading, John refers to Jesus as the only God.[28] If, as the RSV punctuates the text, the quoted words of Jesus end at verse 15, the term "only Son" is not attributed to Jesus himself. It is possible that John intends the term to include the idea that Jesus was begotten by God, for I John 5:18 says: "He who was born [begotten] of God keeps him."[29] However, the word translated "begotten" comes from *genos,* meaning kind or sort, not from *gennaō,* to beget. At the least, John means to say that Jesus is the only one of his class. Others may become sons of God,[30] but Jesus' sonship stands apart from that of all other sons.[31] This is supported by the fact that Jesus never speaks of God as "our Father" in such a way as to place himself on the same relationship to God as his disciples. On the contrary, he sets his sonship apart when he says to Mary, "I am ascending to my Father and your Father, to my God and your God" (20:17).

---

26 See T. W. Manson, *On Paul and John* (1963), pp. 128-31.

27 See above, p. 141, for the meaning of Peter's confession. Howton argues that John's confession is authentic but that the Baptist meant less by "Son of God" than the Evangelist expounds throughout his Gospel. See J. Howton, "Son of God in the Fourth Gospel," *NTS* 10 (1963-64), 227-37.

28 The RSV translates it "the only Son," but all three critical Greek New Testaments read "the only God."

29 See F. Büchsel, *TDNT* IV, 741.

30 Jn. 1:12; 11:52. John uses *teknon,* not *huios.* Except for 12:36, *huios* is not used to describe men in their relation to God.

31 For *monogenēs,* see R. Schnackenburg, *John,* I, 270-72; D. Moody, "God's Only Son," *JBL* 72 (1953), 213-19; T. C. de Kruijf, "The Glory of the Only Son," *Studies in John* (1970), pp. 88-96.

The relationship between the Father and the Son is interwoven throughout the entire fabric of the Gospel. This is reflected above all else in Jesus' claim to have been sent by the Father. Frequently God is spoken of simply as the one who sent Jesus. His whole ministry and activity is dominated by a consciousness that he has been divinely commissioned.[32]

The Son is the special object of the divine love. "For the Father loves the Son, and shows him all that he himself is doing" (5:20). "For this reason the Father loves me, because I lay down my life, that I may take it again" (10:17). Jesus' whole mission is carried out in the love of the Father. In turn, Jesus shares this love with his disciples (15:9).

Because he is sent by God, his works are divine works—the works of God himself. When Jesus said, "My Father is working still, and I am working" (5:17), the Jews understood him to be making himself equal with God (5:18). Jesus added, "Whatever he [the Father] does, that the Son does likewise" (5:19). Jesus' works came from the Father (10:32); indeed, it is the Father dwelling in Jesus who does the works (14:10).

Not only the works but also the words of Jesus are the words of God. Jesus declares to the world what he has heard from the Father (8:26); he speaks only what the Father has taught him (8:28). The truth that he utters he has heard from God (8:40). Jesus' word is not his own but the word of the Father who sent him (14:24).

As the Son, Jesus claims to possess an exclusive knowledge of the Father. No one has seen the Father except him who is from God; he has seen the Father (6:47). As the Father knows the Son, so the Son knows the Father (10:15). Here, as in Matthew 11:27, the knowledge the Son has of the Father is the same direct, unmediated knowledge the Father has of the Son. The knowledge the Son has of the Father stands in contrast to the ignorance of other men (17:25).

Because the Father loves the Son and has sent him into the world to fulfill the divine will, he has given all things into the Son's hand (3:35). Therefore Jesus the Son claims equal honor with God from men (5:23). Jesus has the right to demand this because he and the Father are one (10:30). This oneness seems to be more than oneness of purpose and intent; in some way, incomprehensible to men, the Father is in the Son and the Son in the Father (10:38; see also 14:10, 11).

THE MISSION OF THE SON. As the Son of God, Jesus has a divinely appointed mission to fulfill. The most frequently reiterated element in this mission is to mediate life to men. The Son has the same power to confer life as the Father (5:21). As the Father has life in himself, so he has granted the Son to have life in himself (5:26). Therefore, faith in Jesus as the Son of God issues in the possession of eternal life (3:35; 6:40, 47; 10:10). Jesus can even say, "I am the resurrection and the life" (11:25).

---

[32] See 3:17; 4:34; 5:36, 38; 6:29, 44, 57; 7:29; 8:16, 26, 42; 10:36; 11:42; 12:49; 14:24; 15:21.

He has power over all flesh to give eternal life to whom the Father wills (17:2).

This eternal life is no static matter, for Jesus mediates not only eternal life but the person of God himself. John strikes this note in his prelude, "No one has ever seen God; the only Son, who is in the bosom of the Father [at the time John is writing his Gospel], he has made him known" (1:18). Jesus himself repeats this. He accuses the Jews, even though they have the Old Testament, that they have never heard God's voice or seen him (5:37; cf. 8:19). Jesus claims to be the way, the truth, and the life, and that no one can come to God except through his own person (14:6-7).

He not only gives eternal life to all who believe; he executes judgment upon those who reject him; and as judge, he stands in the place of God himself. "The Father judges no one, but he has given all judgment to the Son, that all may honor the Son as they honor the Father" (5:22-23).

Jesus' mission of salvation involves his death. The gift of eternal life is mediated through his death. This is expressed in a brief parable that is not unlike the Synoptic parables: "Unless a grain of wheat falls into the earth and dies, it remains alone; but if it dies, it bears much fruit" (12:24). The immediate context of this saying is Jesus' "glorification" (12:23), i.e., his death. This thought is again expressed in verse 32: "and I, when I am lifted up from the earth, will draw all men to myself." This cannot mean universal salvation, for John frequently indicates that many, particularly the "Jews," are rejecting Jesus' claim and stand under his judgment. It does indicate that salvation is universal in its scope.

Jesus is fully conscious that the goal of his mission is his death. The emphasis on the lifting up of the Son of Man, on his exaltation, and on Jesus' consciousness that his earthly career was focused on a fateful "hour" (2:4; 12:23, 27; 13:1; 17:1)[33] together with explicit statements show that death was an essential and climactic part of his mission. "The good shepherd lays down his life for his sheep. . . . I lay down my life for the sheep" (10:11, 15). His death was not a mere event in human history; it was an event over which Jesus had full control; it was a deliberate act. "No one takes it [my life] from me, but I lay it down of my own accord. I have power to lay it down, and I have power to take it again; this charge I have received from my Father" (10:18).[34]

John strikes the note of redemptive suffering at the very outset of his Gospel. The Baptist pointed to Jesus with the words "Behold, the Lamb of God, who takes away the sin of the world" (1:29; see also 1:36). This passage has given modern exegetes much trouble. Some think that the lamb is the symbol of the conquering Messiah, the leader of the flock of God's

[33] See also 7:30; 8:20 where the idea occurs in editorial comments.

[34] See W. D. Chamberlain, "The Need of Man. The Atonement in the Fourth Gospel," *Int* 10 (1956), 157-66; G. Styler, "The Place of the Passion in the Johannine Theology," *ATR* 29 (1947), 232-51.

people. In the Revelation, the "Lion of the tribe of Judah" is *a lamb* with seven horns, denoting fullness of power (Rev. 6:5-6).[35] Others think that the symbol of the lamb points to the suffering servant of Isaiah 53 on the grounds that the Aramaic word *talya* can be rendered either by "lamb" or by "boy, servant."[36] Others think that the saying deliberately blends the symbolism of the lamb slain at the passover, and the servant who, "like a sheep that before its shearers is dumb, so he opened not his mouth" (Isa. 53:7).[37] In any case, John thinks of Jesus as the Lamb, not as the conquering Messiah but as the atoning Savior. He "takes away the sin of the world." The natural meaning of the verb (*airō*) is to "remove, take away, blot out," not to take upon oneself. What John understood by this saying is undoubtedly illustrated in the First Epistle: "You know that he appeared to take away [*airē*] sins" (I Jn. 3:5); and John understands "take away" in the sense of expiation (I Jn. 2:2; 4:10; cf. 1:10). The Lamb of God is he who atones by the shedding of his blood.[38]

THE DIVINE SON. As the Son of God, Jesus is more than a chosen, dedicated man; he partakes of deity. John attests to his deity in his first sentence, "The Word was God" (1:1), and again, according to the best-attested reading, he refers to Jesus as "the only God, who is in the bosom of the Father" (1:18).[39] Jesus' consciousness of deity is expressed both in sayings about his unity with the Father, already considered, but especially in the "I am" sayings. These appear in two forms: "I am" with a predicate, and in an absolute form. "I am the bread of life" (6:20); "I am the light of the world" (8:12); "I am the door of the sheep" (10:7); "I am the good shepherd" (10:10); "I am the resurrection and the life" (11:25); "I am the way, the truth, and the life" (14:6); "I am the true vine" (15:1). In addition to such sayings are several where Jesus designates himself simply by the words, "I am" (*egō eimi;* cf. 4:26; 6:20; 8:24, 28; 13:19; 18:5, 6, 8). This is a phrase almost impossible to translate literally; in most contexts, the simple "I am" is not meaningful in English. But in John 8:58, the RSV translates "Before Abraham was, I am." The language is much stronger in Greek than in English. "Before Abraham was born (*genesthai*), I am (*egō eimi*). "This is the only passage in the New Testament where we have the contrast between *einai* and *genesthai*."[40] The Jews picked up stones to throw at him because of this seemingly blasphemous statement, but he escaped them. In John's Gospel, the hos-

---

[35] See also Test. Joseph 19:8 where a lamb is the symbol of the Messiah who conquers all the other hostile animals. This is supported by C. H. Dodd, *Interpretation,* pp. 232ff.

[36] J. Jeremias, *TDNT* I, 339-40.

[37] On the whole subject, see R. Schnackenburg, *John,* I, 298-301; S. Virgulin, "Recent Discussion of the Title 'Lamb of God,'" *Scripture,* 13 (1961), 74-80; C. K. Barrett, "The Lamb of God," *NTS* 1 (1954-55), 210-18.

[38] See J. Jeremias, *TDNT* I, 185-86.

[39] All three critical Greek texts have this as the preferred reading.

[40] E. Stauffer, *TDNT* II, 399.

tility and opposition of the Jews was incurred because the implicit claims of Jesus' language made him equal with God (5:18)—indeed, of claiming to be God (10:33). Jesus in no way refuted these charges.

Background for these "I am" sayings, especially those used absolutely, is not to be found in the Hellenistic world[41] but in the Old Testament. God revealed himself to Moses as "I am who I am" (Exod. 3:14), and in Isaiah, God is to be known as "I am" (Isa. 41:4; 43:10; 46:4, etc.).[42] Stauffer has argued that this expression is "the most authentic, the most audacious, and the most profound affirmation of Jesus of who he was."[43] By this idiom Jesus lifted himself far above all contemporary messianic hopes and claimed that in his life the historical epiphany of God was taking place. "God himself had become man, more human than any other man in the wide expanse of history."[44] Most scholars think that Stauffer defends an extreme position, but it seems beyond question that in the use of the absolute *egō eimi,* Jesus is in some real sense identifying himself with the God of the Old Testament. In the Johannine narrative, this comes to full expression after the resurrection in the confession of Thomas, "My Lord and my God" (20:28).

However, this identification is not complete, for Jesus constantly distinguishes between himself and the Father. The Son has been sent by the Father; he obeys the Father's commandments (15:10); he can do nothing of his own accord (5:19-20); his words are the Father's words (14:10, 24; 17:8); the Father is greater than the Son (14:28). Davey has worked out this dependence motif in detail.[45]

"Thus more explicitly and more emphatically than the other New Testament writers does St. John declare the divinity of Jesus Christ as eternal Son of God and at the same time the distinction between the Son and the Father."[46]

THE HUMANITY OF JESUS. Not only is Jesus as the Son utterly dependent on the Father; he is also portrayed in thoroughly human terms. He is pictured as a normal man enjoying usual family relations. He attends a wedding with his mother and brothers, apparently within the circle of friends or relatives. He stays for a time in the family circle at Capernaum (2:12). He is thirsty and tired on the journey through Samaria (4:6-7). His brethren undertake to lecture him about his conduct (7:3-8). On the cross he displays a deep filial concern for the care of his mother (19:25-26). He experienced the human emotion of sorrow at the bereave-

[41] See P. B. Harner, *The "I Am" of the Fourth Gospel* (1970), p. 29; R. E. Brown, *John,* I, 535.

[42] See P. B. Harner, *The "I Am" of the Fourth Gospel,* pp. 6ff.

[43] E. Stauffer, *Jesus and His Story* (1960), p. 174. The phrase has parallels in the Synoptics in Mk. 6:50; 14:62. See E. Stauffer, *Jesus and His Story,* pp. 183ff. See also E. Stauffer, *TDNT* II, 343-53.

[44] E. Stauffer, *Jesus and His Story,* p. 195.

[45] J. E. Davey, *The Jesus of St. John.* See the summary on p. 78 with references.

[46] T. E. Pollard, *Johannine Christology* (1970), p. 18.

ment of close friends and wept at the grave of Lazarus (11:33, 35). He was troubled in soul at the thought of death (12:27). He even shows a momentary indecision as to whether he should pray to be delivered from his hour. In 8:40 he actually calls himself a man. His sufferings on the cross are focused in the cry, "I thirst" (19:28).[47]

The words of Pilate, "Here is the man!" (19:5), are not easy to interpret with any certainty. Jesus was beaten and bloody from the scourging, his head torn by jagged thorns; he was arrayed in a purple robe in the mock regalia of royalty. Pilate's words may have been meant as a rough jest[48] or as an exclamation of pity and contempt.[49] All this illustrates one of the main themes of John: the Word became flesh.

Some scholars have questioned the reality of the humanity of the Johannine Jesus, arguing that he was only man in appearance, not in reality. His tears for Mary and Martha are said to be not tears of human emotion but the tears of divine love.[50] This is contradicted by 11:5: "Now Jesus loved Martha and her sister and Lazarus." This is certainly not the love of God for the world but the love of a human personality for special friends. The same denial of Jesus' real humanity has been recently stated by Käsemann: "In what sense is he flesh . . . who at the well of Samaria is tired and desires a drink, yet has no need of drink and has food different from that which his disciples seek?"[51] This says far more than the text says. "The woman left her water jar" (4:28), and it is natural to suppose that Jesus refreshed himself from the water she had drawn from the well. It is no more likely that John understands Jesus' words, "I have food to eat of which you do not know" (v. 33), to mean that Jesus no longer needed physical food than to understand Jesus' words to the woman that whoever drinks of the water he has to give will never thirst because he will have an inner spring of water (v. 14) to mean that spiritual water will satisfy physical thirst. The entire incident is an acted parable to point out the primacy of spiritual things. The Synoptic Jesus said that it would profit nothing to gain the whole world but forfeit one's life (Mk. 8:36).

We may conclude that John portrays Jesus in a twofold light without reflection or speculation. He is equal to God; he is indeed God in the flesh; yet he is fully human. John provides some of the most important biblical materials for the later doctrine of the dual nature of Jesus, but John is not interested in such speculations. He reports a sound memory of the impact Jesus made without indulging in speculative questions.

It is no longer possible to hold that the Synoptics present a human, "historical" Jesus while John presents a radically reinterpreted, "deified" picture of Jesus. It is a commonplace that the Synoptics portray Jesus as the

[47] See E. K. Lee, *The Religious Thought of St. John* (1950), p. 139.
[48] W. F. Howard in *IB* VIII, 771.
[49] C. K. Barrett, *John,* p. 450. See especially G. Sevenster, "The Humanity of Jesus" in *Studies in John* (1970), pp. 185ff.
[50] G. M. Davis, Jr., "The Humanity of Jesus in John," *JBL* 70 (1951), 109.
[51] E. Käsemann, *The Testament of Jesus* (1968), p. 9.

Son of God, essentially no less than does John. Rather than offering an eccentric picture, John "enables us precisely to see the Synoptic Christ in depth."[52]

[52] J. A. T. Robinson, "The Place of the Fourth Gospel" in *The Roads Converge,* ed. by P. Gardner-Smith (1963), p. 68.

19

ETERNAL LIFE

Literature:

R. Bultmann *et al.*, "Zaō," *TDNT* II (1935, 1964), 832-72; D. B. Lyons, *The Concept of Eternal Life in the Gospel to St. John* (1938); E. K. Lee, *The Religious Thought of St. John* (1950), pp. 191-219; W. Turner, "Believing and Everlasting Life," *ET* 64 (1952-53), 50-52; C. H. Dodd, *The Interpretation of the Fourth Gospel* (1953), pp. 144-53; U. E. Simon, "Eternal Life in the Fourth Gospel," *Studies in the Fourth Gospel*, ed. by F. L. Cross (1957), pp. 97-110; F. V. Filson, "The Gospel of Life" in *Current Issues in NT Interpretation*, ed. by W. Klassen and G. F. Snyder (1962), pp. 111-23; O. A. Piper, "Life," *IDB* K-Q (1962), pp. 124-30; T. W. Manson, *On Paul and John* (1963), pp. 111ff.; D. Hill, *Greek Words and Hebrew Meanings* (1967), pp. 163-201; R. W. Thomas, "The Meaning of the Terms 'Life' and 'Death' in the Fourth Gospel and in Paul," *SJTh* 21 (1968), 199-212.

The expressed purpose for the writing of the Fourth Gospel is that its readers may know the way to eternal life through faith in Jesus the Messiah (Jn. 20:31). The purpose of Jesus' coming into the world was that men might enjoy this life (10:10). Eternal life is the central theme of Jesus' teaching according to John; but according to the Synoptic Gospels, it is the proclamation of the Kingdom of God. Furthermore, the primary emphasis in John is upon eternal life as a present experience—an emphasis that is quite lacking both in the Synoptic Gospels and in Judaism. This has led some critics to conclude that the Johannine concept of life has nothing to do with Old Testament teaching but rests upon the assumptions of Greek philosophy.[1] C. H. Dodd thinks that the concept of eternal life has platonic overtones of a life that is timeless.[2] John's platonic view stands in contrast to the Jewish view of eternal life, which Dodd also finds in John. If this is true, the heart of the Johannine theology represents a substantial Hellenizing of the Gospel.

---

[1] E. F. Scott, *The Fourth Gospel* (1906), p. 253.

[2] C. H. Dodd, *Interpretation*, p. 150.

THE LINGUISTIC DATA. *Zōē* occurs thirty-six times in John, the infinitive *zēn* sixteen times, the compound verb *zōopoiein* three times. The words *zōē aiōnios* occur seventeen times with no apparent difference of meaning from the simple *zōē*. The adjective *aiōnios* does not of itself carry a qualitative significance, designating a life that is different in kind from human life. The primary meaning of the word itself is temporal. It is used of fire (Mt. 18:8; 25:41, 46), punishment (Mk. 3:29), sin (Mk. 3:29), and places of abode (Lk. 16:9); and these uses designate unending duration.

THE JEWISH BACKGROUND. The exact phrase occurs in the LXX only at Daniel 12:2, where it translates *hayye olam*, "the life of the age," designating the life of the future age after the resurrection of the dead. The basic meaning of "life" in the Old Testament is not immortality or life after death, but complete well-being in earthly existence. However, this well-being is viewed not as an end in itself, but as God's gift. To enjoy life means to enjoy the fullness of God's blessings and gifts, which include length of days (Ps. 91:16), family blessings (Eccl. 9:9), prosperity (Deut. 28:1ff.), security (Deut. 8:1), and especially fellowship with God (Ps. 16:11; 36:9; Deut. 8:3; Jer. 2:13). Therefore the good gifts of God, which constitute life, must be enjoyed in relationship with God (Deut. 30:15-20). Eventually, this feeling that life meant fellowship with God and the enjoyment of the divine presence and blessings led to the conviction that even death could not destroy this relationship but that, somehow, the living God would enable his people to transcend death (Ps. 16:9-11; 49:15; 73:24). This conviction, dimly seen at first, led to the conviction of the resurrection of the body and life in the Age to Come (Isa. 26:19; Dan. 12:1-2).[3]

In intertestamental Judaism, the conviction that death is not the end of human existence led to the idea of Sheol as an intermediate state where the dead await resurrection (En. 22). Sometimes Sheol becomes the place of final doom and destruction for the wicked while only the righteous experience the resurrection.[4] "Eternal life" is the term sometimes used of the life of the resurrection (Ps. Sol. 3:16; En. 37:4; 40:9; 58:3; Test. Asher 5:2).[5] Sometimes the simple word "life" can also be used instead of "eternal life" (Ps. Sol. 14:7; II Macc. 7:9-14; IV Ez. 7:137), as can the verb "to live" (IV Ez. 14:22).

When the dualism of "this age" and "the Age to Come" emerged in Jewish idiom, the rabbis frequently spoke of "the life of the Age to Come."[6]

[3] See G. von Rad, *TDNT* II, 848; R. Martin-Achard, *From Death to Life* (1906).

[4] See references in T. H. Gaster, "Resurrection," *IDB* R-Z, p. 41.

[5] II Macc. 7:36 speaks of "everflowing" life. In En. 10:10, "eternal life" is a long but not everlasting life; see En. 5:9; 25:6. It is possible that "eternal life" means a blessed immortality instead of resurrection in IV Macc. 15:3. See 18:23.

[6] See G. Dalman, *The Words of Jesus* (1909), p. 158; D. Hill, *Greek Words and Hebrew Meanings* (1967), pp. 180-83; R. Bultmann, *TDNT* II, 856-57.

The idiom of the two ages is found in IV Ezra quite frequently, but not the idiom "eternal life." The Age to Come will bring the blessing of immortality (IV Ez. 7:12-13; 8:54). The Apocalypse of Baruch speaks of inheriting the coming age (Apoc. Bar. 44:13, 15). Eternal life in Judaism, as in Daniel 12:2, is primarily the life of the Age to Come, the life of the resurrection.[7]

LIFE IN GNOSTICISM. The Hermetic writings (*ca.* second and third centuries A.D.) represent an early type of gnostic religious thought in which life plays an important role. Life belongs to God. In the first tractate, *Poimandres,* God is called mind (*nous*), who is light and life (Corp. Herm. I.9, 12). God first created the primal man in his own likeness, but man fell in love with the created world and mixed with it. Thus man is twofold: mortal by reason of his body, but immortal by reason of the essential man (I.15). Thus man became ignorant of his true being and subject to death (I.20); involvement in the material world means ignorance, which leads to death. If man can dispel his ignorance and learn his true being, by this *gnōsis* he will return to Life and Light (I.21). *Gnōsis* is achieved by asceticism and by loathing the bodily senses. At death the man who has gotten *gnōsis* ascends by stages through the heavenly spheres, giving up different bodily passions at each stage until he enters into God—he becomes one with God (*theothēnai*) (I.24-26).

LIFE IN THE SYNOPTICS. The Synoptic Gospels also speak of eternal life; but here, as in Judaism, it is the life of the Age to Come. When the rich young ruler asked how to inherit eternal life (Mk. 10:17), he was thinking of the life of the resurrection, and Jesus answered him in the same terms. This eternal life is the life of the Kingdom of God (10:23), which will be inherited in the Age to Come (10:30; see also Mt. 25:46). The coming of the Son of Man will effect a separation of men: the wicked will go into eternal punishment and the righteous into eternal life (Mt. 25:46). In several other places in the Synoptics, the simple "life" is used of this eschatological blessing (Mt. 7:14; Mk. 9:43, 45). In the Synoptics, the idiom "life" and "eternal life" in its redemptive significance is always a future eschatological blessing (Lk. 10:25).

ETERNAL LIFE IN JOHN: ESCHATOLOGICAL. In the Fourth Gospel, life still retains its eschatological character. The usual Jewish attitude is reflected in the Jewish expectation of finding eternal life in the Scriptures (Jn. 5:39). It was a commonplace in rabbinic teachings that the study of the Torah would lead to "life in the Age to Come."[8] When Jesus said that "whoever does not obey the Son shall not see life" (3:36), he was

---

[7] In a few places, the "Age to Come" is conceived of as already existing in heaven (En. 71:15) into which the righteous enter at death. See D. Hill, *Greek Words and Hebrew Meanings,* p. 182.

[8] "Who has gained for himself words of Torah has gained for himself the life of the world to come." Pirke Aboth 2:8.

referring to man's ultimate destiny. This eschatological character of life is most vividly seen in John 12:25: "He who loves his life loses it, and he who hates his life in this world will keep it for eternal life." The Johannine form of the saying more clearly sets forth the antithetical structure of the two ages than the sayings in the Synoptic Gospels where the similar thought occurs (Mk. 8:35; Mt. 10:39; 16:25; Lk. 9:24; 17:33). "The Fourth Evangelist alone has given it a form which obviously alludes to the Jewish antithesis of the two ages: he who hates his soul in the *olam haze* will keep it in the *olam haba;* and consequently will possess *hayye haolam haba.*"[9] The one who drinks of the living water will find it to be a source of life in the Age to Come (4:14). There is also a food that Christ can give which will produce eternal life (6:27). This eternal life is to be experienced at the last day when the righteous will be brought forth "to the resurrection of life" (5:29). This saying is very close to Daniel 12:2. "Eternal life" is the life of the Age to Come. Dodd admits that these sayings represent life as an eschatological blessing.[10]

ETERNAL LIFE: PRESENT. While eternal life is eschatological, the central emphasis of the Fourth Gospel is not to show men the way of life in the Age to Come but to bring to them a present experience of this future life. Here is a teaching that is not found in any explicit form in the Synoptics, that the life of the Age to Come is already imparted to the believer. The purpose of Jesus' mission was to bring men a present experience of the future life (10:10). He came down from heaven to give life to the world (6:33), to satisfy the world's spiritual hunger and thirst (6:35). This life is not a quickening of any innate powers resident in man; it is the impartation of a new life, mediated through Christ; and those who do not "eat his flesh and drink his blood" cannot share life (6:35). This life is mediated both through Jesus' person and his words. His very words are life (6:63) because his words come from the Father who has given him commandment what to say, and God's commandment is eternal life (12:49-50).

This life is not only mediated through Jesus and his word; it is resident in his very person (5:26). He is the living bread who gives life (6:51ff.) and the living water (4:10, 14). God is the ultimate source of life; but the Father has granted the Son to have life in himself (5:26). Therefore Jesus could say, "I am the life" (11:25; 14:6).

That this life which is resident in Jesus is nothing less than the life of the Age to Come is illustrated by the frequent connection between the present reception of life and its future enjoyment. Drinking of the living water that Jesus gives means that one will have within him a fountain of life that will issue in eschatological eternal life (4:14). The one who partakes of the

---

[9] C. H. Dodd, *Interpretation*, p. 146.

[10] *Ibid.*, pp. 146ff. Bultmann insists that they are not eschatological in the Jewish sense at all but merely meant to designate the moments of decision when one is confronted by the word. *TDNT* II, 870.

life in Jesus will live forever (6:51). Those who receive eternal life will never perish (10:28).

The future dimension of eternal life includes the resurrection of the body; and those to whom Jesus has given eternal life, he will raise up in the last day (6:40, 54). Jesus is both life and resurrection. The one who believes in him may die physically; but he will live again at the last day. Since he already has this life through faith in Jesus, he will never die (11:25-26).

These two dimensions of life—present and future—are inseparably associated in Jesus' discourse about his relationship to the Father. Since God is the source of life, it is he alone who can raise the dead, but he has entrusted this prerogative to his Son (5:21). This mission of raising the dead is fulfilled in two stages. The hour has already come when the dead hear the voice of the Son of God and come to life (5:25). That this refers to "spiritual" resurrection, i.e., the present experience of eternal life, is proven by the words, "The hour is coming and *now* is." This event of rising into life is taking place in Jesus' ministry because the Father "has granted the Son also to have life in himself" (5:26). However, this present experience of life is not all that life means; "the hour is coming when all who are *in the tombs* [i.e., the physically dead] will hear his voice and come forth . . . to the resurrection of life, and . . . to the resurrection of judgment" (5:28, 29).

In the sayings about eternal life as an eschatological blessing, John is in agreement with the Synoptic Gospels. In his emphasis upon life as a present spiritual reality, John goes beyond the Synoptics with a different emphasis. Dodd finds the solution to the central emphasis in John in a platonizing of the more primitive eschatological mode of thought. Eternal life is to be understood in the platonic sense in that "it is a life not measured by months and years, a life which has properly speaking neither past nor future, but is lived in God's eternal to-day."[11] This, however, is to misunderstand John, for eternal life undeniably has a future. John weds present and future in an indissoluble bond. The one who believes in Jesus may die physically but he will experience the life of the resurrection, and whoever has life spiritually now and believes in Jesus shall live forever (11:25-26). Because the believer has eternal life now, he will be raised up in the last day (6:40). Dodd does not show the relationship between the eschatological sayings about life and the timeless, platonized sayings. This interpretation juxtaposes two diverse concepts of life—one Greek and one Jewish-Christian—without establishing an inner bond of essential relationship.

Much more satisfactory is Piper's analysis that John's message of life is rooted in the Old Testament idea that God is life. He has imparted his life to men through the incarnation of the eternal "word of life." The eschatological resurrection is not extraneous to the center of John's thought but is the

[11] C. H. Dodd, *Interpretation*, p. 150.

full manifestation of life in believers.[12] This can be illustrated by the analogy between the Johannine teaching of life and the Synoptic teaching of the Kingdom of God. It is noteworthy that in John eternal life is first mentioned after the only references in the Gospel to the Kingdom of God (3:15). Both in the Synoptics and in John, eternal life is the life of the eschatological Age to Come. In the Synoptics this life is also the life of the Kingdom of God, which belongs to the Age to Come. However, the unique element in Jesus' preaching of the Kingdom in the Synoptics is that the eschatological Kingdom has invaded this age. The Kingdom has come (Mt. 12:28), while the Age to Come remains future. In the same way John sees that the life that belongs to the Age to Come has come to men in the old age. "In this, *zōē aiōnios* in John resembles the kingdom of God in the synoptic gospels. That which is properly a future blessing becomes a present fact in virtue of the future in Christ."[13] Therefore while the idiom is different, and we are not to identify the Kingdom of God and eternal life, the underlying theological structure is the same, though expressed in different categories. If eternal life is indeed the life of the eschatological Kingdom of God, and if the Kingdom is present, it follows that we might expect the Kingdom to bring to men a foretaste of the life of the future age.

There is clearly little similarity between the Johannine idea of eternal life and the Hermetic-gnostic concept. For John, life is to be found in the concrete historical figure of Jesus; life is received by faith; and possession of eternal life assures the believer of participation in the eschatological resurrection. In the Hermetica, while life belongs to God, it can be attained by man after death through the ascetic control and suppression of the bodily appetites. This *gnōsis* appears to be within the reach of all men, for the author of *Poimandres* concludes on an evangelistic note when he calls upon men who have given themselves up to drunkenness and ignorance of God to awake to soberness, cease to be sodden with strong drink and lulled in sleep devoid of reason, and thus learn the beauty of piety and of the knowledge of God. He sees men as those who have given themselves up to death when they have the power to partake of immortality. He summons them to rid themselves of darkness, to lay hold of Light and so partake of immortality and forsake corruption (Corp. Herm. I.27-29).

THE NATURE OF ETERNAL LIFE: KNOWLEDGE OF GOD

Literature:

M. E. Lyman, *Knowledge of God in Johannine Thought* (1925); R. Bultmann, "Ginōskō," *TDNT* I (1949, 1963), 389-719; C. H. Dodd, *The Interpretation of the Fourth Gospel* (1953), pp. 151-69; O. A. Piper, "Knowledge," *IDB* K-Q (1962), pp. 43-48; J. Gaffney, "Believing and Knowing in the Fourth Gospel," *ThSt* 26 (1965), 215-41.

A final question will further illuminate the inner bond between eternal

[12] O. Piper, "Life," *IDB* K-Q, pp. 128-29.
[13] C. K. Barrett, *John*, p. 179.

life as future and present. One statement explains the essential nature of eternal life: knowledge of God mediated through Jesus Christ (17:3). Barrett regards this as "a definition of eternal life,"[14] and both Dodd and Piper understand it as stating the nature of eternal life.[15] This raises the further question as to the nature of knowledge. Do we not find here a clear instance of gnostic influence, of salvation by knowledge? Dodd thinks so. He asserts, "In the Hermetic as in the Johannine writings, knowledge of God conferring eternal life, is for those who have passed by rebirth from the realm of *sōma* or *sarx* into the realm of *nous* or *pneuma.*"[16] Such a bold statement demands that we look at the Greek idea of knowledge, compare it with the Hebrew, and analyze John's thought against this dual background.

KNOWLEDGE IN GREEK THOUGHT.[17] Knowledge is used in two different ways in the Greek background. In philosophical thought knowledge meant the contemplation of its object to ascertain its essential qualities. The mind by reason can grasp the permanent essence of that which it beholds. Knowledge is the apprehension of ultimate reality.

Knowledge in gnostic thought, as represented by the Hermetic writings, is not rational thought. It is rather direct apprehension of God by the mind (*nous*), not by hard thinking but by direct intuition and inner illumination. Bultmann emphasizes that such knowledge in the Hermetica is not a natural capacity but is divine illumination—a gift of God.[18] This is true. God, who is *nous, comes* to men who are devout and gives to them the saving knowledge (Corp. Herm. I.22). God wishes to be known by man (Corp. Herm. I.31, X.15). It is clear that the Hermetica are gnostic in that they constantly emphasize the necessity of *gnōsis* as the way of salvation.[19] *Gnōsis* leads to the vision of God—in fact, to oneness with God—to deification (Corp. Herm. I.26; IV.7 [Nock]; XII.1). This *gnōsis* is a kind of ecstatic mystical vision, not rational thought. The first tractate, *Poimandres,* describes the experience of the author. He fell into an unusual sleep that restrained his bodily senses and had a vision in which he came to understand the true nature of the universe and of his own self (I.30). This enabled him to attain true *gnōsis* (I.27, 32), the divine breath of the truth (I.30).[20] God can be seen by the heart and mind alone (VII.2). In the tractate on regeneration, the experience of deification is described: "Having

[14] C. K. Barrett, *John,* p. 419: "Knowledge of God and Christ confers, or rather is, eternal life."

[15] "Such life for men consists in the knowledge of God." C. H. Dodd, *Interpretation,* p. 151. See O. Piper, "Life," *IDB* K-Q, p. 128.

[16] C. H. Dodd, *Interpretation,* p. 49.

[17] See R. Bultmann, *TDNT* I, 689ff.; C. H. Dodd, *Interpretation,* pp. 151ff.

[18] R. Bultmann, *TDNT* I, 694ff.

[19] "Now piety is the knowledge of God; and he who has come to know God is filled with all things good; his thoughts are divine" (Corp. Herm. IX.4; cf. X.15).

[20] The text translated in W. Scott's *Hermetica* (1924-36) must be corrected by the critical text in A. D. Nock and A. J. Festugière, *Hermes Trismegistus* (1960).

been brought into rest by God, O Father, I behold not with the sight of the eyes but with the spiritual energy from the Powers. I am in heaven, on earth, in the water, in the air; I am in the animals, in the plants; I am in the womb, I am before the womb (birth); I am after birth, everywhere" (XIII.11). This one who has been born again "will be God, the Son of God, the all in all, composed of all the Powers" (XIII.2). "Seeing in myself a vision not formed of matter, produced by the mercy of God, I have passed forth from myself to enter into an immortal body and I am no more what I was but I have been born again in mind" (XIII.3). Such a man who has attained knowledge and thereby become one with God will after death pass through the spheres to a blessed immortality.

This beatific vision which brings knowledge is within the reach of all men if they will control, subdue, extinguish their bodily appetites. "If you do not first hate your body, my son, you cannot love yourself; but if you love yourself, you will have mind, and having mind, you will partake of knowledge also. . . . It is not possible, my son, to attach yourself both to things mortal and to things divine. For as there are two sorts of things, the corporeal and the incorporeal . . . and that these two categories partake of the mortal and the divine, one is faced with the choice of one or the other, if he wishes to choose; for it is not possible to take at one time the one and the other" (IV.6).

The content of this knowledge is self-knowledge in the sense that man recognizes his true nature and his true place in the universe. "God the Father is Light and Life; man was born of him. If then you learn that you yourself have come from Life and Light, you will depart again to life" (I.21). This means that the man who has knowledge knows why and by whom he was created—not for bodily pleasures but for Mind (IV.4-5). He who knows his true nature will scorn his body and thus will be able to ascend to God after death.

KNOWLEDGE IN THE OLD TESTAMENT. Knowledge is very different in the Old Testament. It connotes experience rather than contemplation or ecstasy. "The ox knows its owner, and the ass its master's crib, but Israel does not know, my people does not understand" (Isa. 1:3). The intelligent beasts recognize their owner and obediently take their place at the feeding trough; so should Israel recognize her master and give to him similar obedience. Knowledge (*yada*) involves relationship, fellowship, concern. "The Lord knows the way of the righteous" (Ps. 1:6). His knowledge of Israel means his election of Israel to be his people (Amos 3:2; Jer. 1:5; Hos. 5:3). Those whom God does not know are those excluded from his family (Ps. 138:6).

Man's knowledge of God means response, obedience, fellowship, a relationship that is more conspicuous in the Old Testament by its absence than by its presence (Judg. 2:10; Jer. 10:5; Isa. 45:4, 5, 20; Hos. 5:4). That such knowledge is possible is seen from such passages as Isaiah 26:13 (LXX); Psalm 36:10 (LXX 35:10); 87:4 (LXX 86:4); but such verses are exceptional. Prophets were indeed held to know God (I Sam. 3:7), but in no place does a prophet declare that he knows God; and the prophets rarely affirm that Israel knows God. Rather, the knowledge of God is the goal of man (Jer. 9:24). In the great majority of sayings, the knowledge of God is the object of exhortation, aspiration, or promise (I Chron. 28:9).

This knowledge of God is the goal of the Kingdom of God and will be fulfilled in the eschatological consummation. Jeremiah looks forward to a new covenant when God will write his Law upon the heart, and the fellowship involved in the covenant is realized. "And no longer shall each man teach his neighbor and each his brother, saying, 'Know the Lord,' for they shall all know me, from the least of them to the greatest, says the Lord; for I will forgive their iniquity, and I will remember their sin no more" (Jer. 31:34). The same truth is brought out in the Greek rendering of Hosea 6:2-3: "In the third day, we shall arise and we shall live before him, and we shall know. We shall press on to know the Lord." To know the Lord is to live before him, to have eternal life.

KNOWLEDGE IN JOHN. While there are indeed formal similarities between the Johannine idiom of the knowledge of God and the Hermetica,[21] the content is utterly different. In John knowledge is experiential relationship. An intimate, mutual relationship exists between the Father and the Son; Jesus in turn knows his disciples, and they know him; and in knowing him, they also know God. "I know my own and my own know me, as the Father knows me and I know the Father" (10:14-15). The thing that sets apart Jesus' disciples from the world is the fact that they know him while the world does not (17:25). Because of the intimate knowledge between the Father and the Son, he is able to mediate to his disciples the knowledge of God (14:7).

The importance of Jesus' mission of bringing men to the knowledge of God is seen in the repeated affirmation that the world, in contrast to his disciples, does not know him (1:10; 8:55; 16:3; 17:25). However, Jesus' mission is to be extended through his disciples, who are to demonstrate such mutual love that the world may come to know who Jesus is (17:23).

Knowledge of Jesus includes knowledge of the meaning of his mission. He is the one sent by God (17:8, 25); he is the "I am" who comes to speak the word of God (8:28); he and the Father mutually indwell each other (10:38), yet the Son is completely dependent on the Father (17:7).

It should be obvious that the knowledge of God of which John speaks is of a different order from the Hermetic knowledge. It is essentially a personal relationship. The knowledge of God in John is mediated through the flesh—through the Word that became flesh. *Pneuma* in John is not equivalent to *nous* but is the Holy Spirit of God present in the person of Jesus. Knowledge of God is mediated by faith, not by suppression of the bodily senses. Men are not in ignorance of God because they give themselves up

---

[21] See C. H. Dodd, *Interpretation,* pp. 50-51.

to bodily pleasures but because they reject Jesus. Furthermore, knowledge of God does not lead to the merging of the self with God but to a life of love and obedience. So while John uses Hellenistic language, "he does so in order to present in an apologetic way what is a typically Hebrew concept of knowledge."[22] Indeed, this knowledge of God may be seen as the eschatological blessing promised in the Old Testament. If eternal life is the life of the Age to Come that has been brought to men by Jesus, then we need not be surprised to find it explained in terms of the knowledge of God, which is from the Old Testament perspective an eschatological blessing. If the presence of eternal life is realized eschatology, so is the knowledge of God. The intimate fellowship with God promised as a blessing in the eschatological Kingdom of God has been brought to men by Jesus.

THE VISION OF GOD. This knowledge of God further is associated with the vision of God. "If you had known me, you would have known my Father also; henceforth you know him and *have seen him*" (14:7). Judaism held that the vision of God was impossible in this life; it was a blessing reserved for the hour of death or for the Age to Come.[23] In John, since the blessings of the Age to Come have already come to men, the vision of God can be realized. This is, however, a mediated experience. It remains true that "no one has ever seen God; the only Son, who is in the bosom of the Father, he has made him known" (1:18). But because Christ has come into the world, the one who has seen him has seen the Father (14:9); the one beholding him beholds the one who sent him (12:45). For this reason, great emphasis is placed in this Gospel upon seeing and beholding Christ (1:14; 6:36, 40; 9:37; 14:19; 16:16-17).

It is obvious that this "vision of God" differs utterly from the mysticism of the Hermetica. John's vision of God is neither ecstatic nor mystical; it is personal confrontation and recognition, mediated by Jesus.

KNOWLEDGE OF THE TRUTH

Literature:

C. H. Dodd, *The Bible and the Greeks* (1935), pp. 65-75; E. Hoskyns and N. Davey, *The Riddle of the NT* (1947), pp. 26-34; R. Bultmann, "Alētheia," *TDNT* I (1949, 1963), 232-57; E. T. Ramsdell, "The OT Understanding of Truth," *JR* 31 (1951), 264-73; C. H. Dodd, *The Interpretation of the Fourth Gospel* (1953), pp. 170-78; O. Piper, "Truth," *IDB* R-Z (1962), pp. 713-17; S. Aalen, "Truth, A Key Word in St. John's Gospel," *Studia Evangelica,* ed. by F. L. Cross (1964), II, 3-24; L. J. Kuyper, "Grace and Truth: An OT Description of God and Its Use in the Fourth Gospel," *Int* 18 (1964), 3-19.

If eternal life can be defined in terms of knowledge of God, it is paralleled by the knowledge of the truth. "You will know the truth, and the truth will make you free" (8:32). Clearly, in John there is a close relationship

---

[22] O. Piper, "Knowledge," *IDB* K-Q, p. 45.
[23] H. L. Strack and P. Billerbeck, *Kommentar,* I, 207ff.

between life and truth. Jesus is the way, the truth, and the life (14:6). He is the true light (1:9) who is at the same time the life of men (1:4). He gives knowledge of the *true* God (17:3), which means life for men. He is the true bread (6:32) who has come from heaven to give life to men (6:33).

The saying about knowing the truth (8:32) is a saying where Dodd finds "truth" standing for the realm of pure and eternal reality, having almost entirely shed the Hebraic associations that lie behind it in the LXX.[24] This knowledge of the truth is a characteristic Greek conception, and that such knowledge brings freedom is also congenial to Greek thought.

There can be little doubt that a Greek, reading the saying as it stands, would understand it in terms of Hellenistic thought as Dodd interprets it. "Truth" in Greek designates reality as over against falsehood or mere appearance and unreality, and this saying would suggest to the Greek mind that freedom is to be found through intellectual apprehension of reality. This appears to be very different from the Hebrew concept of "truth" (*emeth*), which is "steadfastness," "trustworthiness," or "firmness, fidelity" (*emunah*). Dodd points out that *alētheia* is primarily an intellectual category while *emeth* is a moral category,[25] and he has made a fascinating study of the shifts in meaning from the Hebrew *emeth* to the septuagintal *alētheia,* where the "faithfulness" of God becomes the abstract "truth" in God.[26]

However, it is a too easy solution of a very involved problem to make such a simple contrast between Hebrew "faithfulness" and Greek "abstract truth" and to interpret John in terms of the latter. While the Johannine concept of "truth" is undoubtedly colored by the Greek concept of reality, its fundamental meaning is to be found against the Hebrew background. Support for this thesis requires a brief survey of the Old Testament concept of *emeth.*

TRUTH IN THE OLD TESTAMENT. When used of men and things, *emeth* designates their trustworthiness and reliability. A man who acts with *emeth* is one whose conduct can be trusted because he recognizes the ties of family or friendship and acts loyally (Gen. 24:49; 42:16; 47:29; Josh. 2:14). A "truthful" witness (a witness of *emeth*) is one whose word can be trusted because it corresponds to the facts (Prov. 14:25). In such uses, *emeth* is close to the Greek *alētheia,* "reality." Deeds or words or reports or judgments are *emeth*—reliable—because they correspond to the facts (Deut. 13:14; 22:20; I Kings 10:6; 22:16; Prov. 12:19; Zech. 8:16). "Seed of *emeth*" (Jer. 2:21) is seed whose quality can be trusted. A "peace of *emeth*" is a trustworthy peace, one that endures (Jer. 14:13). "Justice of *emeth*" is justice that can be trusted, genuine justice (Ezek. 18:8).

Emeth finds its most distinctive use in the Old Testament in describing

---

24 C. H. Dodd, *Interpretation,* pp. 159, 176.
25 *Ibid.,* p. 173.
26 C. H. Dodd, *The Bible and the Greeks,* pp. 67-75.

God, or rather, in describing the character of God's acts. *Emeth* does not describe primarily God in himself, but the character of God's acts in dealing with his people. God can be trusted; he is not arbitrary or capricious. Therefore his people can rely upon him to deal with them with *emeth*—faithfully. *Emeth* is often coupled with *chesed,* which designates God's loyalty in fulfilling his promises and his covenant.[27] God manifested his *chesed* and *emeth* by leading Abraham's servant to find a wife for Isaac (Gen. 24:27). He manifested his *chesed* and *emeth* to Jacob by causing him to prosper in the house of Laban (Gen. 32:10). His *chesed* and *emeth* were most notably displayed in giving the covenant at Sinai (Exod. 34:6) and provide the basis of all of God's dealings with his people.[28] God also shows his *emeth* by punishing the wicked (Ps. 54:5); he is acting "in character." The God of *emeth* (II Chron. 15:3; Jer. 10:10) is not the God who is guardian of some abstract entity called "truth" or one who belongs to the realm of eternal truth as over against the realm of appearance; he is the God who can be trusted, who is able to act, and whose care for his people is sure. To be sure, this leads to the concept of the true God in contrast to false or unreal gods; but he is the true God because he is able to act, because he can visit the earth in both blessing and judgment, and because his acts are trustworthy and reliable. God's people are so to glorify God that his *chesed* and *emeth* will be evident, and the Gentiles will have no occasion to ask in derision, "Where is their God?" (Ps. 115:1-2).

God's *emeth* is also eschatological. The future salvation of restored Israel will mean the disclosure of God's *emeth* promised to Jacob, and the *chesed* promised to Abraham (Mic. 7:18-20). God will dwell among his people and "will be their God in *emeth* and in righteousness" (Zech. 8:8). This perfecting of fellowship between God and his people will be the final disclosure of his *emeth.*

In return for his acts of *emeth,* God seeks a response from men in *emeth.* Men who fear God are called men of *emeth* (Exod. 18:21; Neh. 7:2), i.e., men who faithfully respond to God's *emeth.* God always acts with *emeth,* but man often responds with wickedness (Neh. 9:33). Men are called upon to serve God with *emeth* (Josh. 24:14; I Sam. 12:24), to walk in *emeth* (I Kings 2:4; II Chron. 31:20; Ps. 26:3; 86:11; Isa. 38:3). *Emeth* becomes essentially *the revealed will of God.*

This provides background to understand statements where "truth" or *emeth* stands alone. Hezekiah's desire to see "peace and *emeth*" in his days (II Kings 20:19) refers not merely to "security" (RSV), but to a security that results from the faithfulness of God, who preserves his people. The failure of *emeth* is a situation in which men are not living in accordance with the revealed will of God (Isa. 59:15; Dan. 8:12). When "*chesed* and

---

[27] *Chesed* is often translated "tender mercies" in the KJV but is much more accurately rendered "steadfast love" in the RSV.

[28] See II Sam. 2:6; Ps. 25:10; 40:10, 11; 57:3; 61:7; 86:15; 89:14; 108:4; 111:7-8; 117:2; 146:6.

emeth meet" and "*emeth* springs up from the ground" (Ps. 85:10-11), God manifests his salvation, filling the land with glory and giving his people what is good (Ps. 85:9, 12). When Jerusalem becomes a city of truth (Zech. 8:3), it will be the place where God's will is disclosed and his people ever respond to it, and therefore enjoy God's salvation.

Truth and the knowledge of God are related concepts. The disobedience of Israel means that "There is no *emeth* or *chesed,* and no knowledge of God in the land" (Hos. 4:1). However, the future salvation of Israel is described in the words "I will betroth you to me in righteousness and in justice, in *chesed,* and in mercy. I will betroth you to me in truth [*emunah,* a cognate word] and you shall *know* the Lord" (Hos. 2:20).

TRUTH IN JOHN. "It is obvious that to John *alētheia* is the OT *emeth.*"[29] This is clear in the first two uses of the word at the beginning of the book: "The Word became flesh and dwelt among us, full of grace and truth" (1:14); "For the law was given through Moses, grace and truth came through Jesus Christ" (1:18). "Grace" and "truth" stand for the Old Testament *chesed* and *emeth* and place the Johannine interpretation of the incarnate Christ squarely in the stream of Old Testament redemptive history. It is notable that this is the one place in the New Testament where the equivalents of the Old Testament *chesed* and *emeth* appear together. The covenant love (*chesed*) and steadfastness (*emeth*) that God had displayed through the history of Israel have now come to fullness in the incarnation. In fact, this fulfillment of God's redemptive acts in history is now such that it stands in contrast to all that God has done before; for the full understanding of God's grace and truth, which could never be attained in terms of the Mosaic Law, is now embodied in Christ.

These two sayings indicate that all of the previous manifestations of God's *chesed* and *emeth* in fact pointed toward God's deed in Christ. That the contrast between the Law and Christ is not meant to be absolute is shown by such sayings as 5:39, where the Old Testament is not an end in itself but a witness to the truth (5:33) that is in Christ (see also 5:46; 1:45). The point of comparison between the Law and Christ is suggested by the words in 1:16: "and from his fullness have we all received, grace upon grace." "It is as the inexhaustible gift of God that the Gospel is contrasted with the Law."[30]

Therefore when Christ said, "I am the truth" (14:6), he means that he is the full revelation and embodiment of the redemptive purpose of God. The coming of Christ is the disclosure of the faithfulness of God to his own character, of his continuing purpose to make his saving will known. His entire mission was to bear witness to this saving truth (18:37). In this context, the "truth" is closely allied with Jesus' kingship (*basileia*). He is a king; but to Pilate, Jesus said that the source of his redemptive rule was not from the world, and was not to be established by physical force.

[29] O. Piper, "Truth," *IDB* R-Z, p. 716.
[30] E. K. Lee, *The Religious Thought of St. John* (1950), p. 120.

Now we can understand the saying that initiated this study of "truth." "To know the truth" (8:32) means to come to know God's saving purpose as it is embodied in Christ; and the freedom promised is freedom from sin (8:34), which could not be accomplished under the old covenant but only by the Son (8:36).

This redemptive understanding of the truth is further illustrated by the adjective *alēthinos*. The Greek word carries the sense of something that is genuine and not counterfeit. The word was used on numerous occasions in the LXX to translate *emeth* to mean "trustworthy," "reliable."[31] Zechariah 8:3 is very interesting. When God returns to Zion to dwell in the midst of his people, Jerusalem shall be called *polis hē alēthinē*. Such a saying would be difficult for a Greek unfamiliar with Semitic idiom, and the Greek hardly conveys the meaning of the Hebrew text, that Jerusalem will be a city where men have responded to God's revelation of himself and loyally walk in his precepts.

The Johannine use of *alēthinos* does carry something of the Greek meaning of "real," but it is the real because it is the full revelation of God's truth. "The true light" (1:9) stands not so much in contrast to false and unreal lights of pagan religions as to the partial light that preceded him. John was in a sense a light (5:35), but Christ was the full light. The "true bread" (6:32) is that which satisfies spiritual hunger in contrast to the manna that only sustained bodily life. Christ is the true vine (15:1) because he provides the source of real life for those who abide in him in contrast to membership in Israel as the vine in the former dispensation (Jer. 2:21; Exod. 15:1-8; Ps. 80:8-16). The true worshippers (4:33) who are to be created by the new revelation in Christ are contrasted with the Jews who think they must worship in Jerusalem and the Samaritans who worship in Gerizim. This does not mean that their worship was false or unreal; but after the truth has come to men in the person of Jesus, men must now worship in this truth. Henceforth, such alone are true worshippers, i.e., worshippers whose response is determined by God's revelation of truth. This Hebrew idea expressed in Greek language readily shades off into the idea of real worshippers in contrast to those whose worship is unreal; but the center of emphasis is not the reality or unreality of worship but the revelation of truth that brings worship to its full reality.

God is the "true God" (17:3) not so much because he stands in contrast with false or unreal gods, but because he is the God who in the mission of Christ is acting consistent with his own being, with the relationship that exists between the Creator and a sinful world,[32] and with his own redemptive purpose. Thus there is a frequent reiteration of the fact that God is true (3:33; 7:28; 8:26; cf. I Jn. 5:20).

God's truth is not only embodied in Christ but is also manifested in his

---

31 See, e.g., Exod. 34:6; II Sam. 7:28; I Kings 10:6; 12:24; Ps. 18:10; 85:15; Prov. 12:19; Jer. 2:21; Dan. 10:1 (Th.); Zech. 8:3.

32 O. Piper, "Truth," *IDB* R-Z, p. 716.

word, for he speaks truth (8:40, 45) and came to bear witness to the truth (18:37). This truth is not simply the disclosure of what God is, but is the manifestation of God's saving presence in the world. Therefore all that Jesus does and offers is true (7:18; 8:16), i.e., in accordance with his nature and with God's plan.[33] This redeeming purpose is God's word (17:6, 14) and is itself the truth (17:17), which is one with the person of Jesus himself (1:1).

This manifestation of God's truth extends beyond the earthly mission of Jesus. After his departure from his disciples, Jesus will send another Helper (*paraklētos*), the Holy Spirit, who is called the "Spirit of truth" (14:17; 15:26; 16:13; cf. I Jn. 4:6; 5:7), because his mission also has to do with the outworking of God's redemptive purpose in the world. His mission will be that of bearing witness to Christ who is the truth (15:26), i.e., to direct the attention of men to what God has done in Jesus. He will lead the disciples into all truth (16:13). In its Johannine setting, this does not indicate so much an intellectual apprehension of theological truths as a full personal apprehension of the saving presence of God that has come to men in Jesus. The "many things" Jesus has not yet been able to disclose to the disciples (16:12) involve the further explication of the meaning of his person and saving works. The work of the Spirit is Christ-centered ("He will glorify me") by giving a larger understanding of what pertains to Christ (16:14). This mission of the Spirit is also described in the words, "he will declare to you the things that are to come" (16:13). This ought not to be understood primarily in terms of predictions of future events but in terms of the future consummation of God's redemptive plan in Christ. If the incarnation means the end term of a long series of redemptive acts in which God has disclosed his *emeth,* there remains yet in the future the consummation of the redemptive work accomplished in Christ. This is also the explication of the truth; and it is the work of the Spirit to lead Jesus' disciples into this truth.

The manifestation of the truth demands a response from men. "He who does the truth comes to the light" (3:21; cf. I Jn. 1:6). This is a thoroughly Hebraic phrase, which in the Old Testament meant to act in a trustworthy manner in terms of the bonds of family relationship and friendship (Gen. 24:49; 47:29; Neh. 9:33). In John, to do the truth means to respond to God's revelation of his truth in Christ in the right way. It is "rightness of speech, of motive, and of action, based upon the historical revelation of God."[34] Another way of describing this response is to receive Christ's word, for "every one who is of the truth hears my voice" (18:37; cf. 10:3; 16:27). This is identical with receiving Christ himself (1:11-12), of being born again (3:3). This means to be indwelt by the Spirit of truth (14:17), and by the truth itself (II Jn. 2). All of this is but commentary on the saying that initiated this study, "You will know the truth, and the truth

---

[33] *Loc. cit.*

[34] E. Hoskyns and N. Davey, *The Riddle of the NT* (1947), p. 29.

will make you free" (8:32). The organ of reception is not the mind but the whole man. The Greek concepts of "mind" and "reason" play no part in the Fourth Gospel.[35]

As Jesus has come to bear witness to the truth, he commits to his disciples the same task after his departure (17:18). Jesus had "sanctified himself," i.e., dedicated himself to his mission (17:19); and as Jesus sends his disciples into an alien world to continue his witness, he prays that they too may be "sanctified in truth" (17:17, 19). This means that the disciples, too, are to be dedicated to the truth. As Jesus completely committed himself to the task of accomplishing the redemptive purpose of the true God, so his disciples are to be committed unreservedly to the task of making God's truth, his word, known in the world.

Truth in John does not designate a platonic realm of pure, eternal reality; it is a soteriological concept, designating what God has done in Jesus. Nowhere does John speak of truth existing in heaven and coming into the world. It finds its reality in what God has done in Jesus for man's salvation.[36] Eternal life, knowledge of God, knowledge of the truth—all are redemptive concepts designating the fulfillment of God's redemptive plan in Jesus.

---

[35] S. Aalen, "Truth," *StEv* II (1964), 9.
[36] *Ibid.,* p. 23.

20

THE CHRISTIAN LIFE

FAITH

Literature:

W. H. P. Hatch, *The Idea of Faith in Christian Literature* (1925), pp. 37-46; W. F. Howard, *Christianity According to St. John* (1946), pp. 151-74; E. K. Lee, *The Religious Thought of St. John* (1950), pp. 220-37; C. H. Dodd, *Interpretation* (1953), pp. 179-86; G. L. Phillips, "Faith and Vision in the Fourth Gospel," *Studies in the Fourth Gospel,* ed. by F. L. Cross (1957), pp. 83-96; A. Corell, *Consummatum Est* (1958), pp. 128-39; R. Bultmann, "Pisteuō," *TDNT* VI (1959, 1968), 174-228; E. C. Blackman, "Faith," *IDB* E-J (1962), pp. 222-34; R. E. Brown, "Pisteuein; ginōskein," *John* (1968), I, 512-15; R. Schnackenburg, *John* (1968), I, 558-75; B. Vawter, "The Role of Faith," *The Jerome Biblical Commentary* (1968), p. 835.

The one demand Jesus makes of men to receive his gift of eternal life is faith, belief. This becomes explicit in John in a way that is not evident in the Synoptics. Faith does indeed play an important role in the Synoptics, but in terminology at least, faith is primarily in God, the presence and the power of whose kingly reign Jesus proclaimed. The Synoptics often speak of having faith or believing without a specific object. Faith is particularly associated with Jesus' miracles of healing. To the man with the sick daughter, Jesus said, "Do not fear, only believe" (Mk. 5:36). Again, "All things are possible to him who believes" (Mk. 9:23). In one place, the object of faith is stated: "Have faith in God" (Mk. 11:22). Such faith means complete confidence in God's power and goodness, and in his willingness to bless men who trust him.

However, there are places where faith is clearly directed toward Christ. Matthew 18:6 speaks of the "little ones" who believe in Jesus.[1] That Jesus sought faith in himself as Messiah is reflected in the mocking words of the scribes and priests: "Let the Christ, the King of Israel, come down now

[1] *Pisteuō eis.* The textual support for the parallel verse in Mk. 9:42 is divided, but support for this reading is so strong that the RSV includes the words "in me."

from the cross, that we may see and believe" (Mk. 15:32). This is also reflected in Jesus' demand to be confessed before men (Mt. 10:32 = Lk. 12:8; cf. Mk. 8:38). The destiny of men in the day of the coming of the Son of Man will be determined by their relationship to Jesus. These few sayings only reflect what is everywhere implicit in the Synoptics, that Jesus required faith in himself.[2]

What is implicit in the Synoptics is made explicit in John. *Pisteuō* occurs ten times in Mark, eleven times in Matthew, nine times in Luke. *Pisteuō* occurs by itself thirty times in John, eighteen times with the dative, thirteen times with *hoti,* thirty-six times with *eis,* once with *en* (3:15), and once with the neuter accusative (11:26b). Clearly faith plays a role in salvation in the Fourth Gospel that is entirely lacking in the Synoptics. The verb *pisteuō*[3] occurs in a variety of forms. It can be used, as in classical Greek, with the dative, to mean simply to believe that something or someone is true, to trust him (4:21, 50). It can also be used in this sense with the accusative.

This simple sense of believing and accepting the truthfulness of the witnesses to the person and mission of Jesus is basic to the Johannine idea of faith. Men are called upon to believe the witness of the Scriptures (2:22), Moses (5:46) and his writings (5:47), and beyond this to believe the words (2:22; 4:50; 5:47b) and works (10:38) of Jesus, which in turn means believing Jesus himself (5:38, 46b; 6:30; 8:31, 45, 46; 10:37, 38a). To believe Jesus and his word means to believe God (5:24).

Such faith means acceptance of Jesus' messianic mission. This is made clear by the use of *pisteuō hoti.* The content of faith is that Jesus is the Holy One of God (6:69); that he is the Christ, the Son of God (11:27); that God has sent him (11:42; 17:8, 21); that Jesus is one with the Father (14:10-11); that he has come from the Father (16:27, 30); and that Jesus is the "I am" (8:24; 13:19). Such faith in Jesus' person is the way to eternal life, and is the reason why the Gospel was written (20:31).

That such faith involves more than a correct theology is seen in the distinctive Johannine idiom, *pisteuō eis.* This is a unique Christian idiom that has no parallels in secular Greek or in the LXX,[4] and may have been patterned after the Semitic idiom, *he^{e}min be.*[5] However, since the LXX does

---

2 R. Schnackenburg, *The Moral Teaching of the NT* (1965), p. 35.

3 The noun *pistis,* which is common elsewhere in the New Testament, is never used in the Fourth Gospel, and appears in the First Epistle only at I Jn. 5:4. The best solution for John's avoidance of the noun in favor of the verb is that he wished to avoid the possibility that faith would be understood merely as correct theology. See Jude 3; II Pet. 1:1.

4 C. H. Dodd, *Interpretation,* p. 183; R. Bultmann, *TDNT* IV, 203. The idiom is found in Acts (10:43; 14:23; 19:4), in Paul (Rom. 10:14; Gal. 2:16; Phil. 1:29), in I Pet. (1:8), and in I Jn. (5:10, 13). It occurs once in the Synoptics: Mt. 18:6=Mk. 9:42.

5 C. H. Dodd, *Interpretation,* p. 183. The LXX does not use *eis* but *pisteuō* with the dative. The translation of this idiom in the KJV, which varies between "to believe in" and "to believe on," is confusing.

not render the Hebrew preposition by *eis* but uses the simple dative, it is more likely that the idiom *pisteuō eis* is a distinctive Christian creation[6] designed to express the personal relationship of commitment between the believer and Jesus. This is supported by the parallelism between the idiom of belief and baptism. One must believe on (*eis*) Christ or on the name of Christ (1:12; 2:23; 3:18) and be baptized into Christ (Rom. 6:3; Gal. 3:27) or *into* the name of Christ (I Cor. 1:13; Mt. 28:19; Acts 8:16). As baptism into Christ represents union with Christ in death and newness of life (Rom. 6:4-5), so faith in (*eis*) Christ means personal identification with him. It is obviously far more than intellectual assent to certain facts, although this is included, or to creedal correctness, although it includes affirmations about Christ. It means the response of the whole man to the revelation that has been given in Christ. It involves much more than trust in Jesus or confidence in him; it is an acceptance of Jesus and of what he claims to be and a dedication of one's life to him. "The commitment is not emotional but involves a willingness to respond to God's demands as they are presented in and by Jesus."[7]

That faith means complete commitment and personal union between the believer and Christ is evident from other terms that are equivalent to faith. To believe means to receive him (1:12; 5:43; 13:20), to receive the testimony (3:11), to receive Jesus' words (12:48; 17:8).

It is further supported by the fact that faith and vision are associated together. "This is the will of my Father, that every one who sees the Son and believes in him should have eternal life" (6:40). Obviously "seeing the Son" is something more than ocular vision. Jesus was physically visible to all who came near him. "Seeing the Son" means to recognize him as the Son. Many people saw Jesus but did not believe (6:36). No one has ever seen God (1:18); but Jesus has brought the vision of God to men. "He who has seen me has seen the Father" (14:9).

FAITH AND SIGNS

Literature:

A. Richardson, *The Miracle Stories of the Gospels* (1941), pp. 114-22; A. Richardson, "Signs in the NT," *IDB* R-Z (1962), pp. 346-47; R. H. Fuller, *Interpreting the Miracles* (1963), pp. 88-109; P. Riga, "The Use of '*Sēmeion*' in St. John's Gospel," *Int* 17 (1963), 402-24; K. H. Rengstorf, "Sēmeion," *TDNT* VII (1964, 1971), 243-57; R. E. Brown, "Signs and Works," *John* (1966), I, 525-32; R. E. Brown, "The Gospel Miracles," *NT Essays* (1968), pp. 218-45.

Two characteristic Johannine words related to believing are "signs" (*sēmeia*) and "works" (*erga*). Both words are used with reference to miracles. This idiom is different from the Synoptic Gospels where Jesus' miracles are usually called "acts of power" (*dunameis*)—a word that does

---

[6] A. Oepke, *TDNT* II, 432.
[7] R. E. Brown, *John*, I, 513.

not occur in John. The Synoptics sometimes refer to Jesus' miracles as "works" (Mt. 11:2; Lk. 24:19), and they use the word *sēmeion* for miracles (Mt. 12:38-39; 16:1-4; Lk. 23:8). However, miracles have a different role in the Synoptics than in John.[8] In the Synoptics *dunameis* are acts of power manifesting the inbreaking of the reign of God into history. The miracles of Jesus are not external proofs of his claims, but more fundamentally acts by which he establishes God's reign and defeats the reign of Satan.[9] In John miracles are mighty works that authenticate the person and mission of Jesus and demonstrate the miracle-working presence of God in his words and deeds. In the Synoptics exorcism of demons is the most notable evidence of the presence of God's kingly rule (Mt. 12:28). In John there are no exorcisms, and John does not connect miracles with the destruction of the power of Satan, even though this motif is present (Jn. 12:31).

The "works" of Jesus are his deeds, primarily his miraculous deeds (5:20; 9:3). Although the word *erga* is not used clearly with reference to nonmiraculous works, it is likely that such nonmiraculous deeds are included, because *erga* is used of good or bad deeds of the Jews that show them to be either sons of Abraham or sons of the devil (8:39, 41). In such a passage, *erga* designates the basic quality of one's life manifested by his conduct. So Jesus' deeds reflect the fact that the Father is present in them (10:32). They are in fact the works of God himself (10:37-38), for God is present and active in Jesus (14:10). These works bear witness to the fact that Jesus is the one sent by God (5:36; 10:25). Such works should lead those who witness them to faith in Jesus (10:38; 14:11).

That *erga* designates all Jesus' activity and not merely his miracles is suggested by the fact that the singular, *ergon,* can be used with reference to the entire life mission of Jesus. His real food is to accomplish the work of God (4:34). At the end, he is conscious of having accomplished his work (17:4).

Some of the works of Jesus are designated signs (*sēmeia*) and refer clearly to his miraculous deeds. A "sign" is a mighty work wrought by Jesus that represents the revelatory and redemptive event happening in him. John records far fewer miracles than do the Synoptics—seven in fact: the changing of the water into wine at Cana (2:1-11), the healing of the ruler's son (4:46-54), the healing at the pool of Bethesda (5:2-9), the multiplication of the loaves (6:4-13), the walking on the water (6:16-21), the cure of a blind man (9:1-7), and the raising of Lazarus (11:1-44). Most of these are designated by the word *sēmeion* (2:11; 4:54; 6:2, 14, 26; 9:16; 11:47; 12:18). That this is a deliberate selection from many miracles is clear from the fact that John asserts that Jesus did many other signs (20:30; 2:23; 11:47; 12:37). The theological significance of these signs is given in John's own words: "These [signs] are written that you

---

[8] R. N. Flew, *The Miracle-Stories of the Gospels* (1941), p. 114.
[9] R. E. Brown, *John,* I, 525.

may believe that Jesus is the Christ, the Son of God" (20:31). Signs, like works, witness to the presence and power of God in the person of Jesus (3:2). There can be no question but that the Evangelist believed the signs really happened in history; but they are not ends in themselves. Their meaning is in the revealing of the redemptive action of God in Jesus that they represent. The turning of water into wine at Cana symbolizes the sterility of Judaism (the empty water pots) and the new wine of the messianic era (Mk. 2:22; Joel 2:24; Amos 9:13; Zech. 10:7). The feeding of the five thousand represents the messianic banquet to which the Old Testament frequently refers, and which has parallels in the Synoptics.[10] John sees the actual multiplying of the loaves as a symbol of the bread of life that alone can satisfy the deepest human hunger. The raising of Lazarus only illustrates the fact that the eternal life that is present in Jesus is, in fact, the life of the eschatological resurrection realized on the spiritual level in history (11:25). These miracles as a whole are the kind of miracles expected by the Jews with the dawn of the messianic age.[11] This is analogous to Jesus' answer in the Synoptics to the question of John's disciples. In his works the prophecies of the messianic Kingdom were being fulfilled (Mt. 11:2ff.).[12]

The question of the relationship of the signs to faith is not easy, because the data seem to look in two different directions. Sometimes signs are designed to lead to faith in Jesus (2:23; 6:14; 7:31; 10:42). On the other hand, there were those who beheld the signs and did not believe (6:27; 11:47; 12:37). Furthermore, on occasion Jesus rebukes the Jews because they will not believe unless they see signs (4:48; 6:30). The answer must be found in a sort of tension between signs and faith. It requires faith to recognize the true meaning of the signs and their witness to Jesus; to those who had no faith, the signs are merely meaningless prodigies. To those who are responsive, the signs are the means of confirming and deepening faith. It is clear that Jesus' signs were not designed to compel faith.[13] On the other hand, the works of Jesus are sufficient testimony to those able to see what is happening in his mission. Jesus' works will serve as a means of condemnation and confirming blind men in their sinfulness. "If I had not done among them the works which no one else did, they would not have sin; but now they have seen and hated both me and my Father" (15:24).

This leads to the conclusion that John does not use his idiom about believing in a uniform way but recognizes levels of faith. While the signs evoke no faith at all in some people, in others they evoke a superficial kind of faith that recognizes in Jesus a man sent by God but falls short

---

[10] G. E. Ladd, *Jesus and the Kingdom* (1964), p. 204; J. Jeremias, *The Parables of Jesus* (1963), pp. 117f. See Isa. 25:6.

[11] See K. H. Rengstorf, *TDNT* VII, 246.

[12] See G. E. Ladd, *Jesus and the Kingdom,* p. 154.

[13] See R. E. Brown, *John,* I, 412; K. H. Rengstorf, *TDNT* VII, 251. In this John agrees with the Synoptics (Mt. 4:5-7), where Jesus flatly refuses to do mighty deeds that would awe the beholder into faith.

of the total commitment of full-fledged faith. The signs Jesus did in Jerusalem at the passover led many to "believe in his name" (2:23), but Jesus "did not trust himself to them, because he knew all men . . . he himself knew what was in man" (2:24-25). Nicodemus recognized Jesus as a man sent from God because of his signs (3:2); but this was not enough. Nicodemus needed to be born from above. After the healing of the sick man, many "followed" Jesus because of his signs (6:2). After the multiplication of the loaves, many confessed that he was the prophet who was to come into the world (6:14). However, while such a statement reflects a measure of faith, it is inadequate; for after Jesus explained that the reality behind the loaves pointed not to a victorious messianic King (6:15) but to a broken human body (6:51), "many of his disciples drew back and no longer went about with him" (6:66). The Gospel seems to indicate that a certain acceptance of signs is not real belief. It is not sufficient to be impressed by the miracles as wonders wrought by the power of God; they must also be seen as a revelation of who Jesus is, and his oneness with the Father.[14]

This is supported by the fact that Jesus reserves his warmest commendation for those who will have no signs whatsoever but still believe (20:29). Such faith without signs will not be mere credibility but a believing response to the disciples' word of witness, both spoken (17:20) and written (20:31). Faith is always the human response to witness, whether it be the witness of John the Baptist (1:7, 15, 34), of Jesus' words (3:11; 8:14, 18), of Jesus' works (5:36; 10:25), of the Scriptures (5:39), of other people (4:39), of the Paraclete (15:26), or of the disciples (15:27, 19:35).

GLORY. The signs that witness to Jesus also reveal the divine *doxa*—the glory of God. This is a term that has its roots in the Old Testament. The basic meaning of *doxa* is "praise," "honor," and it appears in John with this usage, referring to the praise and honor of men that Jesus despised (5:41; 7:18). The only *doxa* that is worthwhile is that given to God (7:18; 12:43). However, *doxa* was the translation of the Hebrew *kabodh,* which referred to visible manifestations of the presence and power of God. God himself is invisible, but he made his presence known by visible acts of glory (Exod. 16:10; 24:16; I Kings 8:11). God's glory is also an eschatological concept. In the Day of the Lord, the glory of the Lord will be manifested and will fill the earth (Isa. 60:1-3; 66:18; Ezek. 39:21; 43:1).

In the New Testament, glory is primarily an eschatological concept, referring to the visible manifestation of God at the end of the age to establish his Kingdom (Mk. 8:38; 10:37; 13:36). This glory will be shared by believers (Rom. 8:18; Col. 3:4). In John *doxa* has eschatological connotations, but not in the same sense as the rest of the New Testament. The death-resurrection-ascension of Jesus is his glorification (7:39; 12:16, 23;

[14] R. E. Brown, *John,* I, 531.

13:31). In his last prayer, Jesus prays to be glorified "in thy own presence with the glory which I had with thee before the world was made" (17:5). Jesus came from the glory of God's presence and will return to it after his death. One day his disciples will share this glory (17:24). This refers to the future consummation when Jesus' followers will behold his unveiled glory within the Godhead.[15] However, in John, unlike the Synoptics, the glory of God is manifested in Jesus' ministry. The Synoptics do indeed relate the story of the transfiguration, when Jesus' glory was made visible (Mk. 9:2-8, par.)—a story lacking in John. But John differs from the Synoptics in making the entire ministry of Jesus a manifestation of glory. This is another key Johannine idea. "The Word became flesh . . . and we beheld his glory" (1:14). After the first miracle in Cana, John explains that in the miraculous production of wine, Jesus manifested his glory, "and his disciples believed in him" (2:11). His death on the cross was his most notable act of glorifying God (21:19). This glory, manifest in Jesus, was obviously a veiled glory.[16] It could only be seen by the eyes of faith. "If you would believe you would see the glory of God" (11:40). Yet it led to faith; "and his disciples believed on him" (2:11). It is obvious that the miracle at Cana and the crucifixion were no glorious acts to many observers. There is no hint that the servants at Cana who filled the large jars with water and drew out wine saw his glory in this act; only *his disciples* believed on him. The crucifixion was no act of glory *at the time* even to the disciples. John emphasizes how difficult it was for Thomas to believe that Jesus was risen (20:25). For him the cross meant only the cruel and ignominious death of his master. God's glory was manifested in humiliation and suffering, visible only to the eye of faith. It is obvious that when John speaks of Jesus manifesting his glory, he is speaking from the post-resurrection point of view. It is the understanding of Jesus' life from the point of view of his exaltation.[17]

FAITH AND KNOWLEDGE. There is obviously a close connection between faith and knowledge in the Fourth Gospel, for they are directed toward the same objects. The two ideas are sometimes held in close association. Jesus' disciples "know in truth that I came from thee; and they have believed that thou didst send me" (17:8). Jesus prays for the unity of his disciples so that the world may believe (17:21) and know (17:23) that he is the one sent by God. However, the two concepts are not strictly synonymous. Jesus is said to know the Father but never to believe or have faith in the Father. Two verses suggest that knowledge is the assurance to which faith leads. "We have believed, and come to know,[18] that you are

---

[15] C. K. Barrett, *John,* p. 429.

[16] Riga likens the Johannine signs to the Synoptic parables, which both reveal and conceal the truth. P. Riga, "The Use of *Sēmeion* in St. John's Gospel," *Int* 17 (1963), 402-24.

[17] G. Kittel, *TDNT* II, 249.

[18] Perfect tense: *egnōkamen.*

the Holy One of God" (6:69). Knowledge for Jesus is an innate possession; but for men it is the result of discipleship. "If you continue in my word you are truly my disciples, and you will know the truth, and the truth will make you free" (8:31-32). The fact that knowledge sometimes precedes faith (16:30; 18:8) makes it impossible to differentiate faith and knowledge as the initial and the final stages of Christian experience. It certainly rules out the possibility of two levels of Christians: beginners who are believers, and advanced believers who are knowers. It is apparent that "knowledge can never take us beyond faith or leave faith behind. As all knowledge begins with faith, so it abides in faith. Similarly, all faith is to become knowledge. If all knowledge can only be a knowledge of faith, faith comes to itself in knowledge. Knowledge is thus a constitutive element in genuine faith."[19]

PREDESTINATION. Some sayings in John seem to reflect a high view of predestination—that only those chosen by God are able to come to faith. Jesus' disciples constitute a flock who have been given him by his Father. "All that the Father gives me will come to me; and him who comes to me I will not cast out" (6:37). "No one can come to me unless the Father who sent me draws him" (6:44; see 6:65). "You did not choose me, but I chose you and appointed you that you should go and bear much fruit" (15:16). It is only men who are "of God" who hear his voice with faith (8:47; 18:37).

Side by side with such sayings are other sayings in which unbelief is due to human moral failure. Men's attachment to evil prevents them from coming to the light (3:19). They seek their own glory and not the glory from God (5:44). Their actions prove them to be children of the devil (8:44). They are blind because they willfully refuse to see (9:39-41).

John makes no effort to reconcile systematically these sayings about divine predestination and moral responsibility. He sees no contradiction that faith is the free decision of man's will and at the same time the gift of God's grace. This makes it clear that the decision of faith is not a human meritorious achievement like the Jewish works of the Law, but simply the fitting answer, made possible by the grace of God, to the revelation given by Jesus.[20]

ABIDING. If faith is the way of entrance into life, abiding is the one demand for continuing in the faith. This idiom of abiding is usually called mysticism, but it is difficult to define. There is a mutual abiding of the believer in Christ (16:56; 14:20, 21; 15:5; 17:21) and Christ in the believer (6:56; 14:20, 23; 15:5; 17:23, 26). This is analogous to the Son abiding in the Father (10:38; 14:10, 11, 20, 21; 17:21) and the Father abiding in the Son (10:38; 14:10, 11, 21; 17:21, 23).[21] Once it is said that be-

---

[19] R. Bultmann, *TDNT* VI, 227.

[20] R. Schnackenburg, *John*, I, 575.

[21] Sometimes the verb *menō* is used, sometimes only the preposition *en;* but the idea is the same.

lievers are in both the Father and the Son (17:21); and once it is said that both the Father and the Son will come to make their abode in believers (14:23).

This "Johannine mysticism" is very different from the mysticism of Hellenistic religions as represented by the Hermetica where the worshipper becomes one with God in the sense of being deified.[22] In John there is no merging of personalities or loss of human identity. There is no evidence that the Johannine mysticism involves ecstasy. Rather, it is mysticism of personal and ethical fellowship involving the will rather than the emotions.[23] The idea is somewhat similar to the Pauline idiom of being in Christ, and Christ being in the believer;[24] but the Pauline idiom is eschatological while the Johannine idiom involves more of the idea of personal fellowship. Some more specific idea of what John means may be found in other uses of the verb *menō*. To abide in Jesus means to abide in his word (8:31), not to abide in darkness (12:46), to abide in the light (I Jn. 2:10), to abide in the doctrine (II Jn. 9), to abide in his love (15:9-10), to keep his commandments (I Jn. 3:24), to love one another (I Jn. 4:16). For Jesus to abide in his disciples means that his word abides in them (5:38), that God's love abides in them (I Jn. 3:17), that the truth abides in them (II Jn. 2).[25] By way of contrast, unbelievers abide in darkness (12:46) and in death (I Jn. 3:14). Abiding in Christ means to maintain unbroken fellowship with him.

THE JOHANNINE ETHICS

Literature:

J. Moffatt, *Love in the NT* (1929), pp. 253-308; L. Dewar, *An Outline of NT Ethics* (1949), pp. 183-200; S. Cave, *The Christian Way* (1949), pp. 90-93; E. K. Lee, "Theology and Ethics," *The Religious Thought of St. John* (1950), pp. 238-59; R. N. Flew, *Jesus and His Way* (1963), pp. 149-77; R. Schnackenburg, *The Moral Teaching of the NT* (1965), pp. 307-46.

John's description of the Christian life is very different from that in the Synoptics, especially Matthew, who is greatly concerned about the righteousness of the Kingdom of God (Mt. 5:20) and expounds it at length in the Sermon on the Mount. John, like the Synoptics, is concerned about Christian conduct, but he expresses it in very different terms. Followers of Jesus are to do the truth (3:21). This is an entirely un-Greek expression, but it has an Old Testament background (Isa. 26:10, LXX; see Tobit 4:6; 13:6) and the idiom appears frequently in the Qumran writings.[26] In John, "truth" takes on its coloration from the fact that Jesus is

[22] See above, pp. 260f.

[23] A. Oepke, *TDNT* II, 543.

[24] See pp. 379ff.

[25] The references from the epistles indicate how the Evangelist understands the idea of abiding.

[26] For references, see R. Schnackenburg, *John,* I, 407f.

the embodiment of God's redemptive purpose,[27] and to do the truth means to live in the light of the revelation brought by Christ. That Jesus inaugurated a new era that supersedes that of the Mosaic Law is clear from 1:17. Jesus is the one to whom the Law and the prophets point (1:45; 5:39). In place of the Law as a guide for conduct are the words of Jesus (8:51; 12:47; 15:7), which are, in fact, the words of God himself (17:8). The disciples of Jesus must hear these words, receive them, and keep them. Jesus also speaks of his commandments, which his disciples must keep (14:15, 21; 15:10). Furthermore, the belief in Jesus that leads to eternal life is obedience to him (3:36). Such a life can also be described as doing the will of God (7:17). Such sayings have led one student of ethics to the conclusion that John regards Jesus as a second lawgiver, having plenary authority "in faith and morals," and that Jesus' words constitute a second Law, given by a second Moses.[28] Closer examination, however, makes it clear that all that John means by Jesus' words and commands is focused in a single word: love. "This is my commandment, that you love one another as I have loved you" (15:12). "A new commandment I give to you, that you love one another; even as I have loved you, that you also love one another" (13:34). It is not too much to say that Jesus' whole ethic in John is summed up in love.

The command to love is not itself new. The Mosaic Law commands, "You shall love your neighbor as yourself" (Lev. 19:18). However, the scope of this command in the Old Testament is limited in its context, and "applies unequivocally towards members of the covenant of Yahweh and not self-evidently towards all men."[29] Fraternal love played an important part in Judaism.[30] The Manual of Discipline, discovered at Qumran, commands to love all the "sons of light" and hate all the "sons of darkness."[31] In the Synoptic Gospels Jesus sounds a new note. He summarizes the entire content of the demands of the Law by the command, "You shall love the Lord your God with all your being," and "You shall love your neighbor as yourself" (Mk. 12:30-31). However, he redefines who the neighbor is in the parable of the Good Samaritan. The neighbor is not a member of the covenant family, but any man who is in need of loving help (Lk. 10:30ff.). Jesus carries his teaching even further by saying, "You have heard that it was said, 'You shall love your neighbor and hate your enemy.' But I say to you, Love your enemies and pray for those who persecute you" (Mt. 5:43-44). He adds that it is natural to love one's friends; even the Gentiles do this. But those who would be children of the heavenly Father must love even their enemies.

---

27 See above, pp. 266ff.

28 L. Dewar, *NT Ethics* (1949), pp. 189f.

29 J. Fichtner, *TDNT* VI, 315.

30 I. Abrahams, *Studies in Pharisaism and the Gospels* (First Series, 1917), pp. 150-67.

31 1QS 1:9-10. The sons of light are members of the sectarian fellowship; all others are the sons of darkness.

Against this background, what can be *new* about the command of the Johannine Jesus to love one another (13:34)? The answer is found in the words, "As I have loved you." Christian love has its example in Jesus' love, which is in turn a reflection of God's love. "God is love" (I Jn. 4:8), and this love manifests itself in the giving of his Son up to death (3:16). "There is little in profane Greek, or in the LXX, to illuminate the meaning of this *agapaō* in the New Testament."[32] "Having loved his own who were in the world, he loved them to the end" (13:1). The phrase, *eis telos,* can well mean "to the uttermost"—to the point of death. The revelation of God's love for men and the depth of Jesus' love for his disciples are found in the cross. This is the meaning of the "new" commandment of love: that a man lay down his life for his friends (15:13).

This love is illustrated by Jesus' washing the disciples' feet. This task was the customary duty of a menial slave; it was so despised that it was not required of Jewish slaves. Jesus expressed his love for his own by humbling himself to perform the most menial task. This was no act of self-disparagement; he was in full and positive possession of his faculties. He knew "that the Father had given all things into his hands, and that he had come from God and was going to God" (13:3). Indeed, the act of foot-washing was itself the expression of his full consciousness of divine mission. Christian love means following Jesus' example. "You call me Teacher and Lord; and you are right, for I am. If I then, your Lord and Teacher, have washed your feet, you ought to wash one another's feet" (13:14). This parallels Jesus' words in the Synoptics, "Whoever would be great among you must be your servant, and whoever would be first among you must be slave of all" (Mk. 10:43-44). Love means utterly selfless service—the willingness to fill the most humble and menial tasks of service to one's fellows.

John's understanding of the centrality of love is evident in his First Epistle. "By this we know love, that he laid down his life for us; and we ought to lay down our lives for the brethren" (I Jn. 3:16). "We know that we have passed out of death into life, because we love the brethren. He who does not love remains in death" (I Jn. 3:14). "This is his commandment, that we should believe in the name of his Son Jesus Christ, and love one another, just as he has commanded us" (I Jn. 4:7). "If we love one another, God abides in us and his love is perfected in us" (I Jn. 4:12). This verse suggests that the "Johannine mysticism" is a mysticism of love.

It has often been pointed out that John differs from the Synoptics in that he does not command love for one's enemies as do the Synoptics, but only for one's brethren or "friends" (15:13). Sometimes this is compared with the Qumran teaching where love is explicitly limited to the community.[33] But this fact is counterbalanced by statements that God loved the world (3:16); that Christ came to take away the sin of the world (1:29); that

---

[32] C. K. Barrett, *John,* p. 180.

[33] F. M. Cross, *The Ancient Library of Qumran* (1957), p. 156.

it is God's good pleasure to save the world (3:17); that Christ came to give life to the world (6:33).[34]

THE CHURCH

Literature:

R. N. Flew, *Jesus and His Church* (1943), pp. 172-80; J. Cadier, "The Unity of the Church," *Int* 11 (1957), 166-76; A. Corell, *Consummatum Est* (1958); T. E. Pollard, "'That All May Be One'—and the Unity of the Church in the Gospel and Epistle of St. John," *NT Essays*, ed. by A. J. B. Higgins (1959), pp. 230-45; E. Schweizer, *Church Order in the NT* (1961), pp. 117-24; D. O. Via, "Darkness, Christ and the Church in the Fourth Gospel," *SJTh* 14 (1961), 172-93; N. A. Dahl, "The Johannine Church and History" in *Current Issues in NT Interpretation*, ed. by W. Klassen and G. F. Snyder (1962), pp. 124-42; R. Schnackenburg, *The Church in the NT* (1965), pp. 105-13; R. E. Brown, "Ecclesiology," *John* (1966), I, cv-cx; S. Pancaro, "People of God in St. John's Gospel?" *NTS* 16 (1970), 114-29.

There are clearly no explicit references to the church that parallel the saying in Matthew 16:18. However, it is clear that Jesus as he is pictured by John looks forward to the formation of a new people of God. The term "Israel" occurs a few times and always with the feeling of Israel as the people of God. Jesus is the King of Israel (1:50); Nicodemus was the teacher of Israel (3:10). As in the Synoptics, Jesus is hailed as the King of Israel when he enters Jerusalem (12:13). On the other hand, the term "the Jews" (*hoi Ioudaioi*) has become a pejorative word for those who rejected Jesus. The term occurs many times in John to indicate those in Israel who were blind and refused to believe. However, we must remember that those who did follow him were Jews, and the term "disciples" (*mathētai*) occurs as often as it does in Matthew. The disciples may be regarded as a new fellowship representing an embryonic church.[35]

While we agree with Moule that the theology of the Fourth Gospel is primarily concerned with the message of salvation for the individual,[36] we are not to conclude that John views the individual as standing in isolation from other believers. The particular Johannine emphasis is the unity of the church. This is clear from the parabolic discourse about the shepherd and his flock (Jn. 10:1-18). The thought of Yahweh as the Shepherd and Israel as the sheep is a common one in the Old Testament (Ps. 23:1; 28:9; 77:20; 78:52; 80:1; 94:7; 100:3; Isa. 40:11; Jer. 23:1; Ezek. 34:11). Here Jesus is forming a new flock, to which he himself is the door. Anyone who does not enter the sheepfold by the door but climbs in by another way,

---

[34] On the entire question, see V. P. Furnish, *The Love Command in the NT* (1972), pp. 146-48. He concludes that the restrictive nature of the love command is patent but need not exclude love for neighbors and enemies.

[35] See D. O. Via, "Darkness, Christ and the Church in the Fourth Gospel," *SJTh* 14 (1961), 172-93.

[36] C. F. D. Moule, "The Individualism of the Fourth Gospel," *NT* 5 (1962), 171-90.

"that man is a thief and a robber" (10:1). That this is a parabolic discourse is clear from the fact that Jesus is both the door to the fold (10:7) and the good shepherd (10:14) at the same time. The thieves and robbers must be Jews who claimed the ability to lead men into the true people of God apart from Christ. The reference may be to messianic pretenders, who tried to bring God's Kingdom without regard to the person of Jesus,[37] or it could refer to the scribes and priests who claimed to be the spiritual leaders of God's people. The statement, "all who came before me are thieves and robbers" (10:8), cannot refer to the Old Testament saints, for such men as Abraham and Moses are recognized in John as divinely appointed leaders. In any case, Jesus is forming a new flock in contrast to the old Israel. This new people is to be made up of both Jews and Gentiles. This is reflected in the statement, "I have other sheep, that are not of this fold; I must bring them also, and they will heed my voice. So there shall be one flock, one shepherd" (10:16). The easiest way to understand this is that "this fold" is the fellowship of Jesus' Jewish disciples, while the "other sheep" represent Gentiles who must be included in the one flock. The flock must be one, because it finds its unity in the one shepherd.

That Gentiles are to be included in Jesus' disciples is hinted at when Greeks came to Philip asking to see Jesus (12:21). Jesus at first seems to rebuff them by turning to the theme of his approaching decease. But his answer is not really a rebuff; it is an implied assertion that the only Jesus who can be the object of Gentile devotion is the crucified and glorified one. "Jesus now has no further place in Judaism, which has rejected for itself its place in the purpose of God."[38]

Another verse that envisages the future people of God is the word of Caiaphas, who unwittingly uttered a prophecy: "You do not understand that it is expedient for you that one man should die for the people, and that the whole nation should not perish" (11:50). The precise meaning of "people" and "nation" is not easy to determine.[39] John goes on to say that "Jesus should die for the nation, and not for the nation only, but to gather into one the children of God who are scattered abroad" (11:52). The scattered "children of God" must refer to Gentiles who are destined by faith to be brought into the people of God.[40] Pancaro[41] thinks that the "people of God" refer to the Christian community; but this is not important for the overall meaning of the text. The passage again emphasizes the unity of the new people of God.

A final passage that alludes to the people whom Jesus brings into being is the parabolic discourse of the vine and the branches (15:1-6). This

---

[37] See K. H. Rengstorf, "Lēstēs," *TDNT* IV, 261.
[38] C. K. Barrett, *John,* p. 350.
[39] See S. Pancaro, "'People of God' in St. John's Gospel?" *NTS* 16 (1970), 114-29.
[40] J. A. T. Robinson (*Twelve NT Studies* [1962], p. 120) thinks that they are Jews of the dispersion.
[41] *NTS* 16, 130-48.

metaphor reflects the Old Testament idiom of Israel as the vineyard of Yahweh (Jer. 2:21; Ezek. 15:1-2; 19:10-14; Ps. 80:9-16). In place of apostate Israel, Jesus is the true and the new vine, and he and the branches, which exist in union with him, constitute the new people of God. The branches of the new vine have their true existence only as they abide in Christ.[42] The fruit is love—the supreme evidence of the Christian life in John.[43] The metaphor of the vine and the branches is analogous to the Pauline doctrine of the body and its members, where Christ is both the head of the body (Eph. 1:22) and yet is identified with the body itself (I Cor. 12:12).

In his last prayer, Jesus looks forward to those who are to believe through the word of his immediate disciples (17:20). The burden of his prayer is for their unity: "That they may be one; even as thou, Father, art in me, and I in thee, that they also may be in us, so that the world may believe that thou hast sent me" (17:21). These words have often been cited in support of organic church unity that finds oneness in external visible structures. However, such is not the primary intention of the passage. The unity of believers is analogous to the unity of the Son with the Father, and the unity of believers with both the Father and Son. It would be possible to have a single visible church and yet have its life rent by internal strife and divisions. This unity is far deeper than organizational structure. Even as the Father and the Son are one while remaining separate persons, so the unity of the church must allow for outward distinctions. Unity is not uniformity.[44] However, the unity for which Christ prayed cannot be altogether relegated to an invisible, spiritual realm; it is to be so visible that it will be a witness to the world of Jesus' divine origin. This means at least that the unity of the church means cordial, free fellowship and intercourse between diverse churches. The bond that binds all believers together—the person of Christ—is greater and stronger than the so-called denominational distinctives that separate them organically. But when denominational distinctives become barriers to Christian fellowship and mutual love, they fracture the unity for which Christ prayed.

THE SACRAMENTS

Literature:

J. C. Lambert, *The Sacraments in the NT* (1903), pp. 64-72, 393-407; W. F. Flemington, *The NT Doctrine of Baptism* (1953), pp. 85-96; O. Cullmann, *Early Christian Worship* (1953); C. K. Barrett, "Sacraments," *John* (1955), pp. 69-71; S. S. Smalley, "Liturgy and Sacrament in the Fourth Gospel," *EQ* 29 (1957), 161-70; A. Corell, *Consummatum Est* (1958); G. R. Beasley-Murray, *Baptism in the NT* (1962), pp. 216-32;

---

[42] The expression, "every branch *in me* which bears no fruit, he takes away" should cause no trouble by seeming to present a contradiction, for this is a *parabolic* discourse in which the details cannot be pressed. See the parable of the soils, where many seeds sprout and take root, but finally die (Mt. 13:3-8).

[43] See above, pp. 279ff.

[44] See T. E. Pollard, "That They May All Be One," *ET* 70 (1958-59), p. 150.

O. S. Brooks, "The Johannine Eucharist," *JBL* 82 (1963), 293-300; G. H. C. MacGregor, "The Eucharist in the Fourth Gospel," *NTS* 9 (1963), 111-19; V. Ruland, "Sign and Sacrament. John's Bread of Life Discourse," *Int* 18 (1964), 450-62; J. K. Howard, "Passover and Eucharist in the Fourth Gospel," *SJTh* 20 (1967), 329-37; R. E. Brown, "The Eucharist and Baptism in John" in *NT Essays* (1968), pp. 77-152; J. D. G. Dunn, *Baptism in the Holy Spirit* (1970), pp. 183-94.

The question of the sacraments in John is one about which no unanimity of opinion is to be found among contemporary interpreters. Catholic scholars have been inclined to interpret John in a sacramental way. Cullmann, among Protestants, takes a "high view" of the Johannine attitude toward the sacraments.[45] He argues that one of the main purposes of the Gospel is to relate the worship of the church of the Evangelist's day to the historical Jesus, especially in baptism and the Eucharist. He finds that sacramental allusions belong to the very warp and woof of the Gospel. He sees baptism in the healing of the man at the pool of Bethzatha (5:1ff.), in the washing of the eyes of the man born blind (9:7), in Jesus' act of washing his disciples' feet (13:1ff.), in the blood and water that flowed from Jesus' pierced side (19:34). This, however, seems quite far-fetched and requires strained exegesis.[46] If there is sacramentalism in John, it is found in the word about birth "of water and the Spirit" (3:5), and the eating of Jesus' flesh and drinking his blood (6:54).

A contemporary Baptist scholar understands the word about birth of water and of the Spirit in sacramental terms. "Water" designates baptism as "the occasion when the Spirit gives to faith the regeneration that qualifies for the Kingdom."[47] The new life of the Spirit is bestowed in baptism. This author does indeed think that Jesus was actually referring to John's baptism of repentance and telling the proud teachers of Israel that they must humbly submit to the baptism of repentance and, furthermore, to be born from above. Water and the Spirit are parallel to repentance and faith. It is entirely possible that this was Jesus' meaning. The Evangelist mentions that Jesus and his disciples baptized (3:22-4:1), apparently in a continuation of John's baptism of repentance in view of the coming of the Kingdom of God. If this was Jesus' meaning, it is easy to see how the later church interpreted these words in terms of Christian baptism.[48] However, it is equally possible that birth of water is no reference to baptism at all. Water and Spirit are linked with a single preposition and both seem to refer to the life from above. Water is coordinate, not contrasted with the Spirit. Elsewhere John uses water as a symbol of the life-giving operation of the Spirit (4:14; 7:38). If both the water and the Spirit belong to the heavenly things (3:12)—the things above (*anōthen*) that are wholly outside the

[45] O. Cullmann, *Early Christian Worship* (1953).

[46] See the criticisms by S. Smalley, *EQ* 29 (1957), 159-70, and in G. R. Beasley-Murray, *Baptism in the NT* (1962), pp. 216-26.

[47] G. R. Beasley-Murray, *Baptism in the NT*, p. 231.

[48] See J. Marsh, *Saint John* (1968), p. 178.

realm of earthly things and outside the grasp of man (3:4), water can hardly refer to the water of baptism. Furthermore, it seems impossible to interpret the water as the place where the Spirit is given, for the birth from above is birth from the Spirit, who, like the wind, "blows where it wills" (3:8), and cannot be pinned down to a precise time and mode. In the Old Testament water is a symbol of God's activity in quickening men to life (Isa. 55:1-3; Jer. 2:13; 17:13; Zech. 14:8; Ezek. 47:9) and is often linked with the eschatological re-creation and renewal to be effected by the gift of the Spirit (Isa. 32:15-17; 44:3-5; Ezek. 36:25-27; 39:29; Joel 2:28). The reference to water, then, far from being a literal reference to the sacrament of baptism, is a symbol of the spiritual cleansing effected by the Spirit. Rather than expressing a sacramental view of baptism, John "seems to be challenging any sacramentalism which he assumes on the part of his readers."[49]

The same line of thought applies to the words about eating Jesus' flesh and drinking his blood (6:54). The great majority of modern commentators understand this as an obvious reference to the bread and wine of the Eucharist.[50] However, precisely the opposite can be argued. Eating and drinking in this context do not refer to a literal act but to a spiritual feeding upon Christ. Eating his flesh and drinking his blood is a symbolic way of describing feeding upon the bread that came down from heaven. The fathers ate manna in the wilderness and died (6:31, 49); Jesus is the bread that came down from heaven, which a man may eat and live forever. Rather than representing a sacramental view, John contrasts literal eating with spiritual eating.[51] We conclude that John is not a sacramentalist, not only because of his silence about baptism and the Eucharist but also because of his correction of literalistic sacramentalism and because of his emphasis that the sacramental elements are essentially symbols. By his insistence on focusing attention on the life-giving activity of the Spirit, he is seeking to counter magical-sacramental views that were exerting a dangerous influence on many Christians.[52]

---

49 J. D. G. Dunn, *Baptism in the Holy Spirit* (1970), p. 190. Dunn's whole discussion of this question is of outstanding value.

50 "This unmistakably points to the Eucharist." C. K. Barrett, *John*, p. 247.

51 See J. D. G. Dunn, *Baptism in the Holy Spirit*, p. 189.

52 *Ibid.*, p. 194; see also W. F. Howard, *Christianity According to St. John* (1946), pp. 149-50.

21

THE HOLY SPIRIT

Literature:

H. B. Swete, *The Holy Spirit in the NT* (1910), pp. 129-68; W. Bousset, *Kyrios Christos* (1913, 1970), pp. 211-44; H. Windisch, *The Spirit-paraclete in the Fourth Gospel* (1927, 1968); N. H. Snaith, "The Meaning of the Paraclete," *ET* 57 (1945-60), 47-50; C. K. Barrett, "The Holy Spirit in the Fourth Gospel," *JTS* 1 (1950), 1-15; T. Preiss, "Justification in Johannine Thought," *Life in Christ* (1952), pp. 9-31; C. H. Dodd, *The Interpretation of the Fourth Gospel* (1953), pp. 213-27; J. G. Davies, "The Primary Meaning of Paraklētos," *JTS* 4 (1953), 35-38; W. F. Howard, *Christianity According to St. John* (1953), pp. 299-314; J. Behm, "Paraklētos," *TDNT* V (1954, 1967), 800-14; E. Schweizer, "Pneuma," *TDNT* VI (1959, 1968), 435-44; D. Hill, *Greek Words and Hebrew Meanings* (1967), pp. 285-93; R. E. Brown, "The Paraclete in the Fourth Gospel," *NTS* 13 (1967), 113-32; D. Moody, *Spirit of the Living God* (1968), pp. 150-81; R. E. Brown, "The 'Paraclete' in the Light of Modern Research," *StEv* IV (1968), 158-65; G. Johnston, "The Spirit-Paraclete in the Gospel of John," *Perspective* 9 (1968), 29-38; G. Johnston, *The Spirit-Paraclete in the Gospel of John* (1970).

One of the most striking differences between the Synoptics and the Fourth Gospel is the place the latter gives to the Holy Spirit, especially in the upper room discourse with its unique teaching about the Paraclete. To appreciate the difference, we need to survey briefly the teaching about the Holy Spirit in the Old Testament and in the Synoptics; and because of the problem of the Hellenistic background of John, we must look briefly at the idea of spirit in Hellenistic religion.

PNEUMA IN HELLENISTIC RELIGION.[1] There is, of course, great variety in Hellenistic religion; we are concerned primarily with the possible gnostic background for Johannine thought. The Greeks usually thought of the most essential element of man's being as *psychē,* not *pneuma.* In Greek dualism, *psychē* stands in contrast to the body as the noumenal

[1] See H. Kleinknecht, *TDNT* VI, 334-59; E. Schweizer, *TDNT* VI, 389-96.

world stands in contrast to the phenomenal world.[2] However, sometimes *pneuma* takes on the meaning and function of *psychē*.[3] In Stoicism, *pneuma* was a universal power or substance—a fine invisible fiery gaseous substance that interpenetrated all the visible world. "The constitutive factor of *pneuma* in the Greek world is always its subtle and powerful corporeality."[4] In scientific and philosophical thought *pneuma* as a physical or physiological term remains essentially materialistic and vitalistic. In gnostic thought, power was conceived of as a substance, and *pneuma* included the concept of the stuff of life (*Lebenssubstanz*).[5] God is spiritual. At creation a spiritual substance united with matter; but it yearns for release. Redemption means the reassembling of all the sparks of *pneuma*. The Redeemer descends to gather the remnants of spirit and with them reascends. The somatic and psychic elements are left behind but the spiritual element is committed to God. Thus the redeemed becomes pure spirit by liberation from the fetters of the body.[6]

PNEUMA IN THE OLD TESTAMENT.[7] The *ruach Yahweh* in the Old Testament is not a separate, distinct entity; it is God's power—the personal activity in God's will achieving a moral and religious object. God's *ruach* is the source of all that is alive, of all physical life. The Spirit of God is the active principle that proceeds from God and gives life to the physical world (Gen. 2:7). It is also the source of religious concerns, raising up charismatic leaders, whether judges, prophets, or kings. "The *ruach yahweh* is a term for the historical creative action of the one God which, though it defies logical analysis, is always God's action."[8]

PNEUMA IN THE SYNOPTICS. Both Matthew (1:18) and Luke (1:35) attribute the birth of Jesus to the creative power of the Holy Spirit. All three Gospels relate the preaching of the Baptist that it would be the mission of the coming one to baptize with the Holy Spirit (Mk. 1:8).[9] All of the Gospels relate the baptism of Jesus and the descent of the Holy Spirit like a dove. All three Gospels relate that the Spirit led him into the wilderness for forty days. Matthew says that Jesus' power over evil spirits was given him by the Holy Spirit (Mt. 12:28); the other two Gospels imply it by preserving the saying about the blasphemy against the Holy Spirit. Although in different contexts, both Matthew (12:18) and Luke (4:18) point to the fulfillment of the prophecy that the Messiah

---

2 This is worked out in detail in Plato, Plutarch and Philo in G. E. Ladd, *The Pattern of NT Truth* (1968), pp. 13-31.

3 *TDNT* VI, 336.

4 *Ibid.*, p. 357. See also C. H. Dodd, *Interpretation*, pp. 213-20. Dodd also brings out the ambivalence in the Hermetic writings because of their mixture of platonic and stoic thought.

5 E. Schweizer, *TDNT* VI, 390.

6 *Ibid.*, p. 394.

7 See W. Bieder, *TDNT* VI, 359-75.

8 *Ibid.*, p. 367.

9 Matthew (3:11) and Luke (3:16) add "with fire"; this is lacking in Mark.

would be endowed with the Spirit. Luke quotes a promise that the Father will give the Spirit to Jesus' disciples (Lk. 11:13).[10] Both Matthew (10:20) and Luke (12:12) preserve an important saying that when Jesus' disciples face formal persecution, they are not to worry about what to say, for "the Holy Spirit will teach you in that very hour what you ought to say" (Lk. 12:12). Mark has the substance of this saying in the Olivet Discourse (Mk. 13:11).

In summary, the Synoptics agree that Jesus was endowed by the Spirit to fulfill his messianic mission, that his mission would include a general endowment of the Spirit, and that his disciples would be enabled by the Spirit to meet whatever difficulties they might encounter.[11] Our concern is only to compare and contrast the teaching of the Synoptics and of John.

THE HOLY SPIRIT IN JOHN. The picture in John is quite different, although not contradictory. The Evangelist like the Synoptics relates the descent of the Spirit upon Jesus (Jn. 1:32-34), although John places a different emphasis on it; it is a sign to the Baptist. However, in view of a later saying, it is important to John that Jesus was filled with the Spirit at his baptism. "For it is not by measure that he [God] gives [to the Son] the Spirit" (3:34). Certainly Barrett is right: "Jesus has the Spirit in order that he may confer it; and it is the gift of the Spirit which pre-eminently distinguishes the new dispensation from the old."[12] There is surely some significance in the fact that John does not picture Jesus as performing his miraculous signs by the power of the Spirit, as in the Synoptics he conquered demonic powers. It rings true to the historicity of John that, in the light of John's full understanding of Jesus' sonship and deity, he relates the descent of the Spirit. Why should the incarnate Son of God need the Spirit to fulfill his messianic mission? The answer must lie in John's conviction of the full humanity of Jesus.

The saying quoted above, "For it is not by measure that he gives the Spirit" (3:34), is difficult to exegete because neither the subject nor the object of the verb "gives" is stated. However, this verse may be understood in the light of the next saying. "The Father loves the Son, and has given all things into his hand" (3:35). This suggests that it is the Father who gives the Son a full measure of the Spirit. This is the one saying in John that implies that it was by the power of the Spirit that Jesus carried out his ministry—a note that is prominent in the Synoptics.

---

[10] Mt. 7:11 has "good things" instead of "the Holy Spirit." Probably Luke is secondary.

[11] This survey ignores many critical questions. C. K. Barrett holds that Jesus said little about the Holy Spirit because he did not foresee the interval lying between his resurrection and his parousia (C. K. Barrett, *The Holy Spirit and the Gospel Tradition* [1947]). He placed his emphasis upon the two great acts of *Heilsgeschichte,* not on the interval lying between them. "The Holy Spirit and the Gospel Tradition," *ET* 67 (1955-56), 142-45.

[12] C. K. Barrett, *John,* p. 148.

That John conceives of Jesus as carrying out his mission in the power of the Spirit is proven by the fact that after his resurrection he imparts to the disciples the Holy Spirit to equip them for their ministry, which will involve the forgiveness of men's sins. "He breathed on them, and said to them, 'Receive the Holy Spirit. If you forgive the sins of any, they are forgiven; if you retain the sins of any, they are retained' " (20:22-23). However this verse be interpreted, it means at the least that Jesus was bestowing on his disciples the same Spirit that had descended on him at his baptism and had filled him during his ministry. He endows them with the Spirit because he is sending his disciples into the world to continue the mission for which he was sent (20:21).

This passage raises difficulties in the light of the coming of the Spirit at Pentecost, which may be solved in one of three ways. Either John did not know about Pentecost and substitutes this story so that it becomes in effect the Johannine Pentecost; or there were actually two gifts of the Spirit; or Jesus' breathing on the disciples was an acted parable promissory and anticipatory to the actual coming of the Spirit at Pentecost. It is difficult to think that any Christian writing in Ephesus in the first century did not know about Pentecost. It is equally difficult to believe there were actually two impartations of the Spirit. The Spirit could not be given until Jesus' ascension (7:39), and if Jesus actually gave his disciples the Spirit, we must assume two ascensions (see 20:17). Furthermore, there is no evidence that the disciples entered into their Christian mission until after Pentecost. There is no substantial objection to taking the Johannine incident as an acted parable that was actually fulfilled at Pentecost.

The gift of the Holy Spirit and the subsequent blessing to men is reflected in another saying, "He who believes on me, as the scripture has said, 'Out of his heart shall flow rivers of living water' " (7:38). This is quoted as a saying of Jesus. John adds this commentary: "Now this he said about the Spirit, which those who believed in him were to receive; for as yet the Spirit had not been given, because Jesus was not yet glorified" (7:39). Jesus was the source of living water. Those who drink this water would never thirst again (4:14). However, Jesus was going back to the Father and men would no longer be able to hear his word. Instead of his personal presence his disciples would continue his ministry, and the Holy Spirit would be given them so that their words and deeds would no longer be merely human acts but channels of divine grace. They would in effect themselves become sources of life for those who heard their word and believed it. However, this new ministry cannot begin until the Holy Spirit is given to men; and this cannot be in the divine economy until after Jesus' death and glorification. The Spirit will come to take Jesus' place and to enable the disciples to do what they could not do in and of themselves, namely, bring men to faith and to eternal life.

The same idea is reflected in a Paraclete saying: "He dwells with you, and will be in you" (14:17).[13] Ever since the disciples came in contact with their Master, this Spirit of truth, or reality, has dwelt with them in the Lord, and now, owing to the Lord's departure, will be in them.[14] The Spirit had been, of course, with the Old Testament saints, and in some real sense had been in them (Ps. 51:10-11). However, the Old Testament speaks more often of the Spirit coming upon men than being within them. The Old Testament looks forward to the messianic salvation when a new dimension of the Spirit will be given God's people (Joel 2:28; Ezek. 36:26-27). Since Jesus was filled with the Spirit, his presence meant that the Spirit had been with the disciples in a new way. However, Jesus promises them that they, too, are yet to be indwelt by the same Spirit. The eschatological promise is to be fulfilled, and a new dimension of the inwardness of the Spirit experienced.

The saying about birth by the Spirit is another instance where John integrates the doctrine of the Spirit into his vertical dualism of the world of God above and the world of men below. This is clear in the affirmation, "Unless a man is born from above, he cannot see the kingdom of God." *Anōthen* can be rendered either "again" (RSV) or "from above." In view of the vertical structure of John's thought, "from above," i.e., from God, fits the context better than "again."[15] This birth from above is the same as birth by water and the Spirit.[16] The idea is, of course, that man does not possess life, that this life is a gift of God that can only be realized by an inner work of the Holy Spirit constituting the believer a child of God. The idea of the new birth is no different from the Pauline idea of being baptized into Christ and so entering into newness of life (Rom. 6:4). The metaphor is different—new birth, union with Christ—but the theology is the same. In Pauline thought, men become children of God by adoption rather than by new birth (Rom. 8:15-16).

John combines the vertical and the temporal by his reference to the Kingdom of God. Only those who are born from above can experience or enter the Kingdom. There is no reason to identify the Kingdom of God with the realm above; the language for the realm of God is heaven (Jn. 1:52; 3:13). "The reference to the Kingdom of God reflects the Synoptic view of two ages and the coming age of glory. When the glory of the Kingdom is revealed, then those born from above will enter it."[17]

However, there is also a note of "realized eschatology" here. In the

---

[13] There are textual difficulties with this verse that we cannot discuss. We follow the RSV.

[14] R. H. Lightfoot, *St. John's Gospel* (1956), p. 270.

[15] See F. Büchsel, *TDNT* I, 378.

[16] If water is a reference to baptism, there is no need to think of baptismal regeneration. In the early church profession of faith in Christ and baptism were practically simultaneous events. Baptism in water, along with confession of Christ, was the outward sign of faith. Cleansing with water has an Old Testament background—Ezek. 36:25-27.

[17] See D. Moody, *Spirit of the Living God* (1968), p. 153.

Old Testament God is regarded as the Father of the nation Israel (Hos. 11:1; Isa. 63:16). However, in the day of salvation, God's people will be called "sons of the living God" (Hos. 1:10). This expectation persisted in the post-exilic period (Wis. Sol. 5:5; Ps. Sol. 17:30); and in a few places the righteous man is regarded as a son of God in the present life (Sir. 4:10; 23:1, 4; Wis. Sol. 2:13, 16, 18). The word in John's Gospel is essentially eschatological, i.e., it indicates that in some real sense the new age of salvation is present.

Dodd interprets John's doctrine of the Spirit in terms of Greek dualism. It is only birth by the Spirit that "makes possible for man the *anabasis*" or ascension.[18] However, this view founders on the fact that John never speaks of an *anabasis* for men, only for Jesus. It is rather surprising that Dodd does not interpret John 14:2-3 in terms of an *anabasis* of believers upon their death to ascend to the Father's house in heaven. However, he does not do so. He admits that this is the language of traditional eschatology and that Jesus' words, "I come again," can refer to his parousia.[19] Dodd does see realized eschatology and a transformation of traditional eschatology in these words. He treats the death and resurrection of Jesus as eschatological events, and the "return" of Jesus is his return in the Spirit after his death. We must conclude that John does not here represent Greek dualism but the basic biblical concept of God's coming to meet man in his historical existence.

The understanding of the Spirit in terms of the vertical structure is again evident in the discourse about the bread of life. After the feeding of the five thousand, Jesus used the broken loaves as a parable of the bread of life, which is his flesh, given for the life of the world (6:51). He is the bread of life that came down from heaven (6:58); but the word about his flesh suggests the necessity of his sacrificial death.[20] One must eat his flesh and drink his blood to have eternal life (6:53-54). Whether or not this is an oblique reference to the Eucharist, it means that the believer must derive eternal life only from the person of Christ, given for men in sacrificial death. The saying, "It is the Spirit that gives life, the flesh is of no avail" (6:63)[21] is easy to misinterpret, especially as the RSV renders it. The passage taken out of context could reflect a sort of Greek dualism of a realm of spirit over against a realm of flesh, with connotations that the realm of flesh is evil. This would mean that spiritual realities are to be sought in complete detachment from the fleshly realm. This, however, cannot be John's thought. "The Word became flesh." Flesh in this saying stands for the realm of human existence uninformed by the Holy Spirit. As a matter of fact, it is basic to Johannine theology that flesh becomes a vehicle of the Spirit. The point here is that Jesus' death as a hu-

---

[18] C. H. Dodd, *Interpretation*, p. 226; see also p. 224.
[19] *Ibid.*, p. 395; see also pp. 393, 405.
[20] C. K. Barrett, *John*, p. 246.
[21] The RSV renders "Spirit" with a small s. This, however, can be misleading. See R. E. Brown, *John*, I, 295; Barrett, *John*, p. 251.

man being and a mere historical event has no saving power. It is only when his death is interpreted and apprehended by the Holy Spirit that it becomes a saving event. This is the meaning of the next statement: "The words that I have spoken to you are Spirit and life" (6:63). However, some do not believe (6:64); they have not responded to the Spirit's illumination. To them Jesus was an imposter and blasphemer who falsely claimed to be Messiah and Son of God.

The contrast between the realm above and that below is the contrast between the realm of the Holy Spirit and the realm of human existence. But the Holy Spirit has entered into human existence in the person of Jesus and made his flesh the way of salvation. The same contrast has already appeared in the saying about the new birth: "That which is born of the flesh is flesh, and that which is born of the Spirit is spirit" (3:6). The flesh is not evil; it is simply incapable in itself of reaching up to the world of God and grasping divine realities. This can be accomplished only by the descent of the Spirit into the sphere of flesh, of human history.

The perspective of realized eschatology is evident in the saying to the woman at Samaria: "The hour is coming, and now is, when the true worshipers will worship the Father in spirit and in truth" (4:23). Again, "spirit" refers to the Holy Spirit and not to inner "spiritual" worship as opposed to outward forms.[22] This is evident from the context: "God is spirit." Because God is spirit, he cannot be limited to any one place, be it Jerusalem or Gerizim. Because the Holy Spirit is to come into the world, men may worship God anywhere if they are motivated by the Holy Spirit. Only those born of the Spirit can worship God in the way he desires to be worshipped.

Worship in truth to the Greek ear would mean worship in reality as over against the unreality of empty forms. This, however, is not the Johannine meaning. "Truth" has basically the Old Testament idea of God's faithfulfulness to himself, and therefore it refers to what God is doing in the coming of Jesus. Truth came through Jesus Christ (1:17), i.e., the full disclosure of God's redemptive purpose for men. This is so exclusively embodied in Jesus that he himself is the truth (14:5). Worship in truth, therefore, is synonymous with worship in the Spirit. It means worship mediated through the person of Jesus, and inspired by the Holy Spirit. Form and place of worship are irrelevant.

All of these sayings about the Spirit reflect a twofold dualism. The Spirit comes from above—from God—but the Spirit comes to inaugurate a new age of redemptive history in contrast to the old age of the Law. John does not consciously reflect on this twofold dualism, but it clearly underlies the structure of his teaching about the Spirit.

THE PARACLETE. A group of five unique sayings are found in the upper

[22] See R. E. Brown, *John,* I, 167; R. Schnackenburg, *John,* I, 436; C. K. Barrett, *John,* p. 199.

room discourse (14-16), having to do with the coming of the Holy Spirit, who is called the Paraclete.[23]

The essential meaning of *paraklētos* is vigorously debated. Some derive the Greek word and find its meaning in the verb *parakaleō*,[24] while others deny this possibility.[25] The translation of the AV, "comforter," goes back to Wycliffe's early English translation (fourteenth century) when the word, coming from the Latin *confortare*, meant to make strong or to fortify. Few contemporary scholars find much of the idea of comfort in the paraclete sayings.[26] The Greek word has an unambiguous meaning, "advocate," in the forensic sense, and is applied in this sense in I John 2:1 to Jesus, who is the advocate before the Father in heaven for his disciples on earth. These are the only places in the New Testament where the word occurs. The paraclete in the Gospel does indeed exercise a forensic ministry in convincing the world, but it is the work of a prosecuting advocate (16:8) rather than a defending advocate. The linguistic problem is found in the fact that the Johannine paraclete is primarily a teacher to instruct and lead the disciples rather than an advocate to defend them.

The linguistic solution may be found in the Hebrew word *m^{e}lits*. It is used in Job 33:23 with the meaning "mediator." The idea of mediator, although not the word *m^{e}lits*, is found in Job 16:19 and 19:25, with the meaning of vindicator. In these two places the Targum of Job uses the loan word *p^{e}rakleta*. The Hebrew word *m^{e}lits* appears also in the Qumran writings with the meaning of interpreter of knowledge or teacher,[27] and in another place as mediator.[28] Clearly *m^{e}lits* combines the idea of mediator and teacher. Since the loan word *p^{e}rakleta* appears in the Targum, it is quite possible, if not almost certain, to have had wide currency in Greek Judaism as well as in Palestinian Judaism during the first century A.D. and later.[29] Furthermore, the ideas of advocacy and instruction are combined in mediating angels in intertestamental literature,[30] and in the Testament of Judah 20:1 the "spirit of truth" in man "testifieth all things and accuseth

---

23 We cannot deal with such critical questions as whether the Paraclete sayings are part of the original Gospel or are interpolated with the Gospel. See the writings of H. Windisch and G. Johnston for this problem. Our interest must be limited largely to the theology of the Gospel as it stands. Certainly in the Gospel, the Holy Spirit, the Spirit of truth, and the Paraclete are one and the same.

24 N. Snaith, "The Meaning of the Paraclete," *ET* 57 (1945-46), 47-50; C. K. Barrett, *John*, p. 385.

25 J. Behm, "Paraklētos," *TDNT* V, 804.

26 But see J. G. Davies, "The Primary Meaning of Paraklētos," *JTS* 4 (1953), 35-38.

27 1QH 2:13.

28 1QH 6:13. See the note on this word in M. Mansoor, *The Thanksgiving Hymns* (1961), p. 143.

29 G. Johnston, *The Spirit-Paraclete* (1970), p. 99. For a survey of the entire problem, see D. E. Holwerda, *The Holy Spirit and Eschatology* (1959), pp. 26-37.

30 For references see J. Behm, "Paraklētos," *TDNT* V, 810.

all."[31] There is therefore a background in Jewish thought for combining the roles of advocacy and instruction that somewhat parallels the dual usage of *paraklētos* in John.

THE NATURE OF THE PARACLETE. Jesus spoke of the Spirit's coming as "another (*allon*) Paraclete" (14:16). This implies that Jesus has already been a paraclete with his disciples, and that the Spirit will come to take his place and continue his ministry with the disciples. This fact is strikingly evident in the similarity of language used of the Spirit and of Jesus. The Paraclete will *come;* so also has Jesus come into the world (5:43; 16:28; 18:37). The Paraclete comes forth from the Father; so also did Jesus come forth (16:27-28) from the Father. The Father will *give* the Paraclete at Jesus' request; so also the Father gave the Son (3:16). The Father will *send* the Paraclete; so also Jesus was sent by the Father (3:17). The Paraclete will be sent *in Jesus' name;* so also Jesus came in the Father's name (5:43). "In many ways the Paraclete is to Jesus as Jesus is to the Father."[32]

If the Paraclete is the Spirit of Truth, Jesus is the Truth (14:6). If the Paraclete is the Holy Spirit, Jesus is the Holy One of God (6:69). "As 'another Paraclete,' the Paraclete is, as it were, another Jesus."[33] Jesus has been with the disciples but a short time; the Paraclete will come to be with them forever (14:16).

It is probable that Jesus' promise, "I will not leave you desolate, I will come to you" (14:18), means that he will come to them in the Spirit.[34] This means that Jesus' work will not be broken off at his death and glorification; nor is the fellowship his disciples have known to be broken off upon his departure from them. He will continue both his work and his fellowship with his disciples in the person of the Spirit. "You heard me say to you, 'I go away, and I will come to you.' If you loved me, you would have rejoiced, because I go to the Father" (14:28). That there is a coming of Jesus in the coming of the Spirit in no way detracts from the fact of his parousia or "second coming" at the end of the age.

Some commentators go so far as to identify the glorified Christ and the Spirit.[35] However, while there is indeed an identity of function, John maintains a distinction: the Spirit is not Jesus; the Spirit is *another* Para-

---

[31] See R. H. Charles, *Testaments of the Twelve Patriarchs* (1908), p. 90. The "spirit of truth" is not the Spirit of God but a spirit of good counterbalanced by a "spirit of deceit" who acts upon man. The two spirits are found in the Qumran theology.

[32] R. E. Brown, "The Paraclete," *NTS* 13 (1967), 126.

[33] *Ibid.*, p. 128.

[34] E. Schweizer, "Pneuma," *TDNT* VI, 443. Others think this is a promise of reunion after the resurrection (C. K. Barrett, *John*, p. 387). The promise that "you will see me" (v. 19) does not militate against this interpretation, for the same verb can be used for seeing death (8:51) and for seeing God himself (12:54).

[35] See G. B. Stevens, *The Theology of the NT* (1899), pp. 214-15; E. F. Scott, *The Fourth Gospel* (1906), p. 343.

clete. If John reflected upon it he would probably say that Christ was present in the Spirit.

Indeed, the idiom John employs suggests that the Paraclete is a separate personality, more than the divine power in Old Testament thought. The word for spirit, *pneuma,* is grammatically neuter, and we would expect pronouns and adjectives, following the rules of grammatical agreement, to be in the neuter gender (so 14:17, 26; 15:26). Such correct agreement bears no witness either for or against the personality of the Holy Spirit. But where pronouns that have *pneuma* for their immediate antecedent are found in the masculine, we can only conclude that the personality of the Spirit is meant to be suggested. "But the *paraclete,* the Holy Spirit, which (*ho*) the Father will send in my name, he (*ekeinos*) will teach you all things" (14:26). The same language is found in 15:26: ". . . the Spirit of truth which (*ho*) proceeds from the Father, he (*ekeinos*) will bear witness to me." The language is even more vivid in 16:13: "When the Spirit of truth comes, he (*ekeinos*) will guide you into all truth." Here the neuter *pneuma* stands in direct connection with the pronoun, but the masculine form rather than the "normal" neuter is employed. From this evidence we must conclude that the Spirit is viewed as a personality.[36]

THE MISSION OF THE SPIRIT TO THE DISCIPLES. The Holy Spirit will come to indwell Jesus' disciples. There is unquestionably an inner work of the Spirit of God in the Old Testament in the hearts of God's people. However, it is clear that under the new covenant, the work of the Spirit would involve a new inwardness. The Spirit will do a work within the hearts of the redeemed that will go far beyond anything previously experienced. "He who believes in me, as the scripture has said, 'Out of his heart shall flow rivers of living water.' Now this he said about the Spirit, which those who believed in him were to receive; for as yet the Spirit had not been given, because Jesus was not yet glorified" (7:38-39). Because of this new work within the hearts of men, they would be able to impart streams of life-giving power to others.

This new inwardness is contrasted with the work of the Spirit in the former dispensation. The most notable work of the Spirit in the Old Testament was an "official ministry," i.e., the Spirit endowed certain people because they filled particular offices in the theocracy and the man in the office required the energy of the Spirit for his official work. The symbol of this official impartation of the Spirit was the anointing with oil. The Spirit empowered the judges (Judg. 3:10; 6:34; 11:29; 13:25; 14:6), endowed those who built the tabernacle with wisdom and skill (Exod. 31:2-4; 35:31) and those who built Solomon's temple (I Kings 7:14; II Chron. 2:14). This official empowering of the Spirit is not associated with moral and ethical qualifications, for sometimes the Spirit endowed a man with supernatural gifts who was not a good man. Balaam, the evil prophet (II

---

[36] C. K. Barrett, *John,* p. 402: "The Spirit is thought of in personal terms."

Pet. 2:15; Rev. 2:14), was actually the mouthpiece of the Spirit of God (Num. 24:2).

Because the Spirit endowed men to fulfill certain official functions in the theocracy, when a man became unusable the Spirit might leave him. Thus the Spirit departed from Saul (I Sam. 16:14) when he became useless to God. The Spirit of God left Samson when he violated his vow (Judg. 14:6 and 16:20). We should probably understand David's prayer that God should not take the Spirit away from him against this background (Ps. 51:11). David was praying that he should not be cast aside as had Samson and Saul as an instrument of the Spirit of God.

The new work of the Spirit is to involve a permanent indwelling within God's people. "I will pray the Father, and he will give you another Counselor, to be with you forever, even the Spirit of truth, whom the world cannot receive, because it neither sees him nor knows him; you know him, for he dwells with you, and will be in you" (14:16-17). There is to be a new indwelling power that shall be the privilege of all God's people, not only of the official leaders.

The Spirit will glorify Christ. His ministry is to call attention to the one whom he represents, to reveal to men the things of Christ (16:14). His purpose is to bear witness to Christ, who will be no longer bodily in the world (15:26).

He is the Spirit of truth (14:17; 16:13), and as such, he will bear witness to the truth and will lead men into the larger revelation of redemptive truth. Jesus promised that the Spirit would lead his disciples into all the truth (16:13), i.e., into the full revelation of the mind of God in redemption. Jesus had spoken with divine authority. He had claimed the same authority for his teachings as that enjoyed by the Law. However, there is a larger revelation yet to be given, and the Spirit is to bring the disciples that complete revelation of the truth. Jesus was conscious that his instruction was incomplete, because the disciples were not able to receive all that he could impart to them. Before the resurrection the disciples never did understand that it was in the purpose of God that the Son of Man should die. But after the death and resurrection of the Messiah, the Spirit would interpret the meaning of these things to the disciples (16:12-13). He will show them "things to come" (16:13). This phrase probably refers not only to prophetic events of the end time, but to the events that were yet future in the experience of the disciples: the formation of the church and the deposit of truth that was to be given through the apostles and prophets. We have here *in nuce* the full revelation contained in the Acts, epistles, and Revelation. This ministry of the Spirit will include both recalling what Jesus had taught them and leading into new areas of divine truth (14:25-26).

The Spirit will empower believers. At first sight it is amazing that Jesus said that the disciples would be better off after he had left them (16:7). But men are able to do greater exploits for God when the Holy Spirit has come and indwelt them than they could do with Jesus' bodily presence in their midst; for the coming of the Spirit meant the infusion of a new divine power. In this light we are to understand the saying that Jesus' disciples are to perform greater works than he did, *"because I go to the Father"* (14:12). These greater works are surely in the spiritual realm and not in the physical realm. No man can perform a physical work greater than raising the dead to life as Jesus did with Lazarus, even when he had been dead for four days. The "greater works" consist of the transformation of lives wrought by the Holy Spirit as a result of the preaching of the gospel. Included in this is the ministry that results in the forgiveness of sins (John 20:22). Jesus, anticipating Pentecost, promised his disciples the impartation of the Divine Spirit by which they should engage in the ministry of preaching the gospel. Those who accepted their message would experience the forgiveness of sins; but those who rejected them would find their sins retained. Only as the representative of Christ is endowed with the Spirit of God can he successfully engage in this ministry of turning men from their sins. It is noteworthy that John attributes nothing of the ecstatic or marvelous to the coming of the Spirit. His primary function is to exalt Jesus and interpret his work of salvation.

THE MISSION OF THE SPIRIT TO THE WORLD. If the primary function of the Spirit to believers is that of teacher and interpreter, he is to the world an accuser. "And when he comes, he will convince the world of sin and of righteousness and of judgment; of sin, because they do not believe in me; of righteousness, because I go to the Father, and you will see me no more; of judgment, because the ruler of this world is judged" (16:8-11). Jesus here is describing how the Holy Spirit will work through the ministry of his disciples in the world as they proclaim the truth as it is in Jesus. Of themselves, their word is only a human word; but empowered by the Spirit, it will have convicting power. It will convict the world of sin, because the greatest sin is that of the unbelief that sent Jesus to his cross. The world puts its confidence in human good works; but the Spirit will convict them of the greatest of all sins. He will convict men that Jesus was indeed the righteous one, as God is righteous (17:25). Although he was condemned by the Jews as a blasphemer and crucified by Pilate ostensibly on the grounds of political sedition, his resurrection and ascension will vindicate his claim to be the Holy One of God (6:69). "The return to the Father is God's imprimatur upon the righteousness manifested in the life and death of His Son."[37] The world will also be convicted when it is confronted by the proclamation of the meaning of the cross and resurrection that God is not passing over evil, that sin is not to have the last word. The death of Christ in fact meant the defeat of the prince of this world,[38] and carried with it the assurance that there will be a day of judgment when not only the prince of this world but the world itself will be judged.

[37] E. Hoskyns and F. N. Davey, *The Fourth Gospel* (1942), II, 573.
[38] See the parallel idea in the Synoptics in Lk. 10:18.

22

ESCHATOLOGY

Literature:

R. H. Charles, *A Critical History of the Doctrine of a Future Life* (1913²), pp. 420-31; W. G. Kümmel, *Die Eschatologie der Evangelien* (1936), pp. 21-32; C. H. Dodd, *The Apostolic Preaching and Its Developments* (1936), pp. 155-89; W. F. Howard, *Christianity According to St. John* (1946), pp. 106-28; G. R. Beasley-Murray, "The Eschatology of the Fourth Gospel," *EQ* 18 (1946), 97-108; C. K. Barrett, "The Place of Eschatology in the Fourth Gospel," *ET* 59 (1947-48), 302-5; R. Bultmann, *Theology of the NT,* II (1955), 3-94; E. Stauffer, "Agnostos Christos," *The Background of the NT and Its Eschatology,* ed. by W. D. Davies and D. Daube (1956), pp. 281-99; J. A. T. Robinson, *Jesus and His Coming* (1957), pp. 162-80; A. Corell, *Consummatum Est* (1958); D. E. Holwerda, *The Holy Spirit and Eschatology in the Gospel of John* (1959); R. Summers, "The Johannine View of the Future Life," *Rev and Exp* 58 (1961), 331-47; L. van Hartingsveld, *Die Eschatologie des Johannes-Evangeliums* (1962); C. F. D. Moule, "The Individualism of the Fourth Gospel," *NT* 5 (1962), 171-90; R. E. Brown, "Eschatology," *John,* I (1966), cxv-cxxi; C. F. D. Moule, "A Neglected Factor in the Interpretation of Johannine Eschatology," *Studies in John* (Sevenster Festschrift, 1970), pp. 155-60.

THE CRITICAL PROBLEM. The question of the eschatological teaching of the Fourth Gospel brings the entire Johannine problem into sharp focus. The most superficial comparison of the Synoptics and John leaves one with the impression that the Johannine Jesus is little interested in eschatology. The central theme of the Synoptic Jesus is the eschatological Kingdom of God that has broken into history in Jesus' person. Eternal life belongs to the eschatological Kingdom. In John the Kingdom of God is mentioned only twice (3:3, 5); instead, the central message of Jesus is eternal life, which he offers men in the present. John quite completely lacks the apocalyptic vision of the parousia of the Son of Man with the clouds of heaven. Instead of the Olivet Discourse with its outline of the events of the end time, John seems to have substituted the upper room discourse (13-16) with the coming of the Spirit taking the place of the parousia of Christ.

This has led many scholars to the conclusion that John has either radically transformed the Synoptic apocalyptic tradition into a Christ-mysticism, or else preserves a very different tradition in which the apocalyptic elements were lacking.

Long ago that great student of apocalyptic, R. H. Charles, in his sketch of the Johannine eschatology, attributed to John an expectation of a real parousia of Jesus in 14:2-3. This passage cannot be interpreted of Jesus' coming to receive his disciples at death, because of the saying in 21:22: "If I will that he tarry till I come, what is that to thee? Follow thou me." "According to the New Testament, death translates believers to Christ . . . , but nowhere is He said to come and fetch them."[1] However, he insists that the words about bodily resurrection in 5:28-29 are in direct contradiction to the present spiritual resurrection in 5:25-27. "It would be hard to find a more unspiritual description of the resurrection in the whole literature of the first century A.D."[2] For this reason, the words in 5:28-29 must be excised to restore unity of thought to the passage. Not only so, but the sayings about "the last day" (6:39, 40, 44, 54; 12:48) must be regarded as interpolations and excised. John views resurrection life as following immediately on death; but its perfect consummation cannot be attained till the final consummation of all things when the present world will pass away (I Jn. 2:17) and Christ will take his own to heaven—a state rather than a locality.[3] Charles utterly fails to show why there must be a consummation if the believer achieves resurrection life at death. It would seem that at best John retained elements from traditional eschatology that are quite incongruous with John's true view.

C. H. Dodd's view of the history of New Testament eschatology has had wide influence in England. He believes that Jesus' message was the proclamation of the inbreaking of the eternal into the temporal world. Jesus thought of a single complex event consisting of his death, resurrection, ascension, and parousia in which the Kingdom of God broke into history. Jesus indeed used apocalyptic language to describe this event, but it was only a symbolic way of describing the otherness—the transcendental character of the Kingdom of God. When the parousia did not occur, it was separated from the rest of the Christ-event and reinterpreted in terms of Jewish apocalyptic (II Thess. 2; Mk. 13). John represents the end term in New Testament eschatology by refining away "the crudely eschatological elements in the kerygma."[4] The eschatological outlook does indeed survive in the anticipation of a day of resurrection; but this means that "after the death of the body, . . . the dead (will be raised) to renewed existence in a world beyond."[5] However, John so completely sublimates eschatology

---

[1] R. H. Charles, *Future Life,* p. 421.
[2] *Ibid.,* p. 429.
[3] *Ibid.,* p. 430.
[4] C. H. Dodd, *The Apostolic Preaching,* p. 155.
[5] C. H. Dodd, *Interpretation,* p. 364.

into mysticism (i.e., the indwelling of Christ) in terms of platonic dualism, which conceives of an eternal order of being of which the phenomenal order of history is the shadow and symbol, that eternal life is "no longer a hope for the last day."[6] In Johannine thought, "all that the church hoped for in the second coming of Christ is already given in its present experience of Christ through the Spirit."[7] Thus the Fourth Gospel, which in time is farthest removed from Jesus, is in its central meaning closest to him.[8]

Bultmann reinterprets eschatology along existential lines. He calls the coming of the Redeemer an "eschatological event," "the turning-point of the ages," from such verses as 3:19; 9:39. But he believes that John completely forsakes any scheme of redemptive history with its attendant eschatology for a gnostic dualism that is expressed in mythological terms. However, John's mythological ideas of a pre-existent divine being who became incarnate in history are not presented in literal seriousness. John has transmuted the eschatological dualism into a dualism of decision, in which he uses symbolic pictures to indicate that the believer feels himself searched and known by God and that his own existence is exposed by the encounter with the revealer. The words about coming (14:3, 18, 28) and the eschatological language "in that day" (14:20; 16:23, 26) and "the hour is coming" (16:25) do not mean an external event but an internal one: "The victory which Jesus wins when faith arises in man by the overcoming of the offense that Jesus is to him."[9] However, there is an eschatological refrain recurring in the Gospel—"on the last day" (6:39, 40, 44, 54; 12:48)—and a clear saying about bodily resurrection (5:28-29) that is in "direct contradiction" to the present resurrection in 5:25. Bultmann solves the problem by holding that these eschatological fragments are redactional interpolations to make the existential eschatology of John conform to the traditional futuristic eschatology.[10]

J. A. T. Robinson thinks that the Johannine nonapocalyptic eschatology is closer to the teaching of Jesus than the Synoptics. He does not follow Dodd in thinking that John is a deliberate corrective of the apocalyptic eschatology of the Synoptics. Rather, he represents an early tradition connected with southern Palestine, independent of the Synoptic Gospels. The Synoptic tradition has suffered a radical influence by apocalyptic. John represents a tradition that has not been influenced in this way.[11] The eschatology of John looks forward to a single day involving the death,

[6] C. H. Dodd, *Apostolic Preaching,* p. 170.
[7] *Ibid.,* p. 174.
[8] *Ibid.,* p. 181. E. Stauffer is another scholar who thinks John is closer to Jesus than the Synoptics, which have been profoundly influenced by apocalyptic ideas.
[9] R. Bultmann, *Theology,* II, 57.
[10] *Ibid.,* p. 39. For other places where Bultmann excises these alleged interpolations to make them fit his own understanding of John, see pp. 9, 36, 37, 54, 58, 59. He even suggests that the vivid eschatological sayings in I Jn. 2:28; 3:2 may be cases of addition by an ecclesiastical editor.
[11] J. A. T. Robinson, *Jesus and His Coming* (1957), pp. 163-64.

resurrection, and exaltation of Jesus. The sayings about a future coming of Jesus do not refer to a "coming *again*" but merely to his coming. Here are to be found the real foundations in the words of Jesus about his coming. But this coming is no second eschatological event but the consummation and fruition of that which is being brought to fulfillment: the coming of Jesus in the Paraclete. The resurrection inaugurates the parousia.[12] Apocalyptic thought later separated these two events and reinterpreted the parousia in terms of Jewish apocalyptic.

Such views of a completely realized eschatology have not persuaded all scholars. They have seen the difference between John and the Synoptics as one of emphasis, and have held that John indeed shares the essentials of primitive Christian eschatology. Kümmel answered Bultmann's interpretation of the eschatology of the Fourth Gospel with an essay in which he argued that a futuristic eschatology is essential to the structure of the Johannine thought. John does not purpose to supplement the Synoptics but to set forth their true meaning. The glory of God was present in Jesus but was recognized only by a few who had faith. The hiddenness of both the Christ and of salvation must come to an end, and therefore the full disclosure of salvation and the final overcoming of death must await in the future. Jesus came from eternity as the one sent by God in the present. Such a person with a past and a present must also have a future. Therefore the hope of the parousia and an eschatological consummation is an essential element in Johannine thought. John does not express this hope in apocalyptic terms, for his concern is primarily the destiny of the individual, not the destiny of the cosmos.[13]

One of the best surveys of Johannine eschatology is that of W. F. Howard.[14] He argues that there is no conflict between Johannine eschatology and mysticism, and appeals to the line of thought argued by Kümmel,[15] that the veiled revelation of God's glory in the historical Jesus demands a real future fulfillment.

C. K. Barrett represents the point of view of many British scholars when he says that "it has been impossible since the publication of Dr. Howard's Dale lectures to deny the presence of both a mystical and an eschatological element."[16] He insists that Bultmann's removal of obvious eschatological elements from the gospel is only by "the use of quite uncritical scissors."[17]

C. F. D. Moule has published two articles in which he insists that the eschatology of John is much more "normal" than is usually recognized. He

---

[12] *Ibid.*, pp. 175-77.

[13] W. G. Kümmel, *Die Eschatologie der Evangelien* (1936), pp. 26-28.

[14] W. F. Howard, *Christianity According to St. John* (1946), pp. 106-28.

[15] See above. Howard gives a translation of a paragraph from Kümmel's essay.

[16] C. K. Barrett, "The Place of Eschatology in the Fourth Gospel," *ET* 59 (1947-48), 302. See also his commentary, *John* (1955), pp. 56-58.

[17] *Loc. cit.* This drastic procedure of Bultmann led one reviewer to designate him "our twentieth-century Marcion." See *ET* 67 (1955-56), 98.

develops the theme touched on by Kümmel, namely, that John differs from the Synoptics in his emphasis on "realized" instead of futuristic eschatology because he is interested in the future of the individual rather than with the people of God as a whole. "The only 'realized eschatology' in the Fourth Gospel is on the individual level; and such a type of 'realized eschatology,' far from *replacing* a futuristic eschatology, need be only its correlative."[18]

THE ESCHATOLOGICAL STRUCTURE. In an earlier chapter we defended at length the thesis that underlying the structure of Johannine thought is a twofold dualism: a vertical dualism of above and below, and a horizontal dualism of present and future. The horizontal (eschatological) is not as obvious in John as it is in the Synoptics. Jesus' discussion with the rich young ruler, which is reported by all three Synoptics, makes it clear that eternal life is the life of the Kingdom of God, and the Kingdom of God belongs to the Age to Come (Mk. 10:17-30). The idiom of this age—the Age to Come occurs only infrequently, but it clearly forms the substructure of the Synoptic proclamation of the Kingdom of God.

While the primary emphasis of John is on the vertical dualism of above-below, the Gospel does not lose sight of the eschatological dualism. This is reflected, as noted above,[19] in one particular saying: "He who loves his life loses it, and he who hates his life in this world will keep it for eternal life" (12:25). This same saying is recorded in the Synoptics (Mk. 8:35 par.) but without the phrase "in this world." We have noted that sometimes the idioms "this world" and "this age" are interchangeable.[20] Such is the case here. Dodd admits that "the Fourth Evangelist alone has given it a form which obviously alludes to the Jewish antithesis of the two ages: he who hates his soul *beolam hazzeh* will keep it *leolam habba,* and consequently will possess *hayye haolam habba.*"[21] It simply is not true, then, to say that "a spiritual, cosmic, eternal order takes the place, in his thought, of the old-fashioned eschatology with its time sequence of the two ages."[22] In the face of such clear data, one is faced with two alternatives: either to hold that such a saying is a vestigial remnant left over from "traditional" eschatology which does not fit John's basic structure—indeed, which flatly contradicts it; or else to take it seriously and recognize in John an eschatological as well as a vertical dualism. We have argued in an earlier chapter that these two do not conflict with each other.[23]

This viewpoint is supported by the use of the word "eternal" (*aiōnios*),

---

[18] C. F. D. Moule, "The Individualism of the Fourth Gospel," *NT* 5 (1962), 174.

[19] See p. 232.

[20] See above, p. 223.

[21] C. H. Dodd, *Interpretation,* p. 146.

[22] F. C. Grant, *Introduction to NT Thought* (1950), pp. 156-57.

[23] See Ch. 17.

which characterizes life. The very word involves an eschatological expectation.[24] It is primarily the "life of the age to come."[25]

The eschatological dualism again is seen in the fact that Satan is regarded as "the ruler of this world" (12:31). This is parallel to the Pauline expression "the god of this age" (II Cor. 4:4). Here *kosmos houtos* is used instead of the more common *aiōn houtos*.[26]

There is no reason to reject the eschatological meaning of the Kingdom of God. "Unless one is born from above, he cannot see the Kingdom of God. . . . Unless one is born of water and the Spirit, he cannot enter the Kingdom of God" (3:3, 5). This is the Johannine equivalent of a Synoptic saying: "Whoever does not receive the Kingdom of God like a child shall not enter it" (Mk. 10:15). In this saying the Kingdom of God is a present reality to be received now that qualifies one to enter the Kingdom of God in the future. Present and future are inseparably bound together. There is no reason not to understand the Johannine saying in the same way. The Kingdom of God is an eschatological blessing. Furthermore, the Synoptics regard those who have received the Kingdom as sons of God (Mt. 5:9, 45).

In summary, we would recall that the Synoptics have a vertical dualism as well as an eschatological dualism. Heaven is the realm above where God's children may treasure up rewards (Mt. 5:12; 6:1, 20). If the Synoptics recognize a vertical dualism but emphasize the eschatological, John recognizes the eschatological but emphasizes the vertical.

THE COMING OF CHRIST. We have recognized that the Johannine idea of the "coming" of Jesus is far more complex than in the Synoptics. Jesus speaks of his departure and return after his resurrection. "A little while, and you will see me no more; again a little while, and you will see me" (16:16). While Jesus does not use the language of coming and going, the idea is present.

Again, we have concluded that Jesus speaks of a coming again in the coming of the Paraclete (14:18). Some scholars have taken this promise to refer to the parousia;[27] but it is easier to understand this to refer to Jesus' coming in the Spirit.[28]

Another saying does indeed refer to Jesus' parousia. "When I go and prepare a place for you, I will come again and will take you to myself, that where I am you may be also" (14:3). Many interpreters insist that

---

[24] See H. Sasse, "Aiōnios," *TDNT* I, 209.

[25] C. K. Barrett, *John*, p. 353; W. F. Howard, *Christianity According to St. John*, p. 109.

[26] H. Sasse, "Kosmos," *TDNT* III, 885.

[27] See G. R. Beasley-Murray, "The Eschatology of the Fourth Gospel," *EQ* 18 (1946), 99; W. F. Howard, *Christianity According to St. John*, pp. 109-10; L. van Hartingsveld, *Die Eschatologie* (1962), pp. 116-17. Howard has apparently changed his mind and now regards this saying to refer to the Easter appearance. W. F. Howard, "John," *IB* VIII, 709.

[28] See above, pp. 294f.

this is the same coming of Jesus in the Spirit as that mentioned in 14:28. However, it cannot be established that John intended to substitute the Paraclete for the parousia.[29] A popular interpretation is that Jesus comes for the believer at death to receive him to himself in heaven. However, the idea of Jesus coming at death does not occur in the New Testament. The nearest to it is Stephen's vision of the Son of Man standing to receive him (Acts 7:56), but this is not represented as a coming. Dodd admits that "here we have the closest approach to the traditional language of the church's eschatology."[30] Dodd likens this saying to Paul's words in I Thessalonians 4:13-18, which represented the current belief about the departure and return of Christ and his disciples' reunion with him—a belief that is echoed in 14:3. Robinson also recognizes that this saying is the equivalent of I Thessalonians 4:14-17, expressed in nonapocalyptic terms.[31] He goes further to suggest that the saying about the coming of Jesus in John 14:3 may be the "word of the Lord," to which Paul appeals in I Thessalonians 4:15.[32]

This view is supported by Jesus' word to Peter with reference to the beloved disciple, "If it is my will that he remain until I come, what is that to you?" (21:22). This is clearly a reference to the eschatological coming of Jesus, for the word went out that this disciple would not die (v. 23). But between the first and second comings of Jesus lies the coming of the Paraclete.[33] Furthermore, the parousia of Jesus is expressed in more traditional language in I John 3:2. Dodd avoids the force of the language of I John by holding that it was written by a different author.

Again, it is difficult to believe that John conceived of the redemptive event as comprising a single complex event consisting of death, resurrection, ascension, and (spiritual) parousia, as scholars like Dodd and Robinson maintain. John places distinct emphasis upon the ascension as an event separate from the resurrection. The resurrected Jesus bade Mary that she need not cling to him, for he is still with her and not yet withdrawn from her sight (20:17).[34] "But if it be once allowed that the Gospel recognizes an *ascension* (in the 'Lucan' manner), it is not going beyond the evidence to say that this also implies a *return*."[35] We conclude that Jesus' word about coming in the Paraclete and his eschatological coming reflect the tension between realized and futuristic eschatology.

RESURRECTION. The teaching of the resurrection in the Fourth Gospel involves both a future objective eschatological event and a present spiritual reality. We find a reiterated emphasis upon the bodily resurrection at

---

29 C. F. D. Moule, "Individualism," *NT* 5, 179; C. K. Barrett in *ET* 59, 304.
30 C. H. Dodd, *Interpretation*, p. 404.
31 J. A. T. Robinson, *Jesus and His Coming* (1957), p. 178.
32 *Ibid.*, p. 25.
33 T. Schneider, "Erchomai," *TDNT* II, 673.
34 C. F. D. Moule, "Individualism," *NT* 5, 175.
35 *Ibid.*, p. 181.

the last day when the dead shall be raised in the fullness of eternal life; but we also find that the life that pertains to the resurrection has reached back into the present age and has become available to men in the spiritual realm. This present anticipatory enjoyment of the resurrection is due to the fact of Christ in whom is resurrection and life. Faced with the death of Lazarus, Jesus said, "I am the resurrection and the life; he who believes in me, though he die, yet shall he live, and whoever lives and believes in me shall never die" (11:25-26). Resurrection life both future and present resides in Christ; whoever believes in him, though he shall die physically, shall live again; and whoever enjoys the blessing of present spiritual life through faith in him shall one day enter upon an immortal existence.

The reality of the resurrection life in the present is vividly expressed in 5:25: "The hour is coming, *and now is,* when the dead will hear the voice of the Son of God, and those who hear will live. For as the Father has life in himself, so he has granted the Son also to have life in himself" (Jn. 5:25, 26). In some sense the hour that is coming is already present and men spiritually dead may come to life by responding to the voice of the Son of God. This teaching of the present enjoyment of a future eschatological reality is another illustration of the basic eschatological structure that occurs throughout the entire New Testament in which this age and the Age to Come have so overlapped that men living still in the present evil age may enter into actual enjoyment of the powers and blessings of the Age to Come.

The full recognition of the significance of this fact does not permit us, however, to agree with Dodd when he says that the resurrection of Lazarus illustrates that eternal life through Christ is a present possession "and no longer a hope for the last day."[36] The resurrection according to the Fourth Gospel is both a matter of subjective enjoyment here and now and an objective reality in the eschatological consummation.

This anticipation of future bodily resurrection appears in numerous places. "And this is the will of him who sent me, that I should lose nothing of all that he has given me, but raise it up at the last day. For this is the will of my Father, that everyone who sees the Son and believes in him should have eternal life; and I will raise him up at the last day" (6:39). "No one can come to me unless the Father who sent me draws him; and I will raise him up at the last day" (6:44). "He who eats my flesh and drinks my blood has eternal life, and I will raise him up at the last day" (6:54).

This eschatological resurrection is portrayed most vividly in the same passage where Jesus has spoken of resurrection as a present spiritual reality. After asserting that the hour has come when those who hear the voice of the Son of God enter into life, he says, "Do not marvel at this; for the hour is coming when all who are in the tombs will hear his voice and will come forth, those who have done good, to the resurrection of life,

[36] C. H. Dodd, *The Apostolic Preaching*, p. 170.

and those who have done evil, to the resurrection of judgment" (5:28, 29). Here it is clearly affirmed that those who enjoy the present reality of life, who have been raised out of death into spiritual life, will in the future be raised out of the grave in a bodily resurrection. The clue to this is the omission of the phrase "and now is," which locates the resurrection of the preceding passage in the present; and the addition of the words "in the tombs," which gives the passage an unavoidable reference to bodily resurrection. The significance of these words, however, has been set aside by various techniques. Many critics insist that these cannot be authentic words of the author of the Fourth Gospel since they are so utterly unlike John's teaching; we must therefore recognize a later interpolation by which a foreign element has been interjected into the spiritual eschatology of the Fourth Gospel. Others would give both passages a spiritual reference; but the words "in the tombs" make that impossible. Still others suggest that this passage involves an awkward combination of two eschatologies: the eschatology of the evangelist himself and the popular realistic eschatology that the author was unable altogether to neglect in spite of the fact that it disagreed with his own. His inclusion of sayings like this resulted in the combination of two unassimilated eschatologies, one spiritual and the other realistic.[37] However, there is no conflict between them; there is only the tension between realized and futuristic eschatology.

The only interpretation that does justice to these words is that which recognizes that there will be a life in the Age to Come that is different from life in this age. In this expectation, the eschatology found in the Fourth Gospel agrees closely with that of the Synoptics and the rest of the New Testament. Life is to be experienced in two stages: life in the present in the spiritual realm and life in the future in the resurrection of the body. Eternal life may be enjoyed here and now by those who respond to the word of Christ, and the same power that assures eternal life to believers during their earthly existence will after the death of the body raise the dead to renewed existence in a world beyond.

The importance of resurrection in John's thought is reflected in his emphasis upon Jesus' resurrection as a real bodily resurrection. Mary apparently was able to cling to him (20:17) as though not to let him get away. John emphasizes the fact that Jesus' resurrection body bore the scars of crucifixion (20:25-27). Clearly bodily resurrection played an important role in John's thought.

THE JUDGMENT. As eternal life and the resurrection involve both present and future, so is judgment conceived of both as a future separation at the last day and also as a present spiritual separation between men based upon their relationship to Christ. Future eschatological judgment is affirmed in 12:48: "He who rejects me and does not receive my sayings has a judge; the word that I have spoken will be his judge on the last day."

---

[37] H. H. Guy, *The NT Doctrine of the Last Things* (1948), pp. 165-66.

This is eschatological language that looks forward to a final day when men will be judged. In this instance the standard of judgment will be the words of Jesus. The same thought is found at the conclusion of the Sermon on the Mount where Jesus refers to a day of judgment (Mt. 7:22) when men will be turned away because they have rendered only lip service but have not been obedient to the teachings of Jesus. The thought of separation between the good and the evil also occurs in the saying about the resurrection when those who have done good will come forth to the resurrection of life, and those who have done evil to the resurrection of judgment (Jn. 5:28, 29). The righteous will be raised up to enjoy the fullness of eternal life; but the wicked will experience resurrection in order to be judged for their evil deeds.

This future judgment has reached back into the present in the person of Christ; and the future eschatological judgment will essentially be the execution of the sentence of condemnation that has in effect been determined on the basis of men's response to the person of Christ here and now. "He who believes in him is not condemned; he who does not believe is condemned already because he has not believed in the name of the only Son of God. And this is the judgment, that light has come into the world, and men loved darkness rather than light, because their deeds were evil" (3:18, 19). The future condemnation is determined already because men have refused to believe in Christ. While the Synoptic Gospels do not emphasize the element of belief in the person of Jesus, we do nevertheless find the same thought that the future fate of men rests upon their present reaction to the person and mission of Jesus. Everyone who acknowledges Jesus Christ before men will be acknowledged before his Father in heaven; but whoever denies him before men will be denied before his Father in heaven (Mt. 10:32, 33; see also Mk. 8:38; Lk. 12:8, 9). We have discovered in our study of the Synoptic Gospels that the Kingdom became present in the world in the person of Christ, and in his person men were confronted by the Kingdom of God and a decision for the Kingdom was required. As men responded affirmatively in faith to the Kingdom that was present in the person of Christ, they were made ready to enter the future Kingdom in its eschatological coming. This is essentially the thought expressed here in somewhat different terms in the Fourth Gospel. The one who believes in Jesus has in a sense passed beyond judgment; it is as though he were already on the other side of judgment, having passed from death into life (Jn. 5:24).

This recognition of judgment as a present spiritual reality by no means permits us to evacuate the eschatological judgment of its content. It is not correct to say that "the eschatological idea of judgment has received a conclusive reinterpretation,"[38] or that this spiritual judgment is in fact the "last judgment" of which prophecy and apocalypse spoke. Future eschatological judgment is not converted into present spiritual judgment. The

---

[38] C. H. Dodd, *The Apostolic Preaching*, p. 171.

future judgment remains. Rather we have again an instance of the basic eschatological structure of New Testament theology in which the two ages are no longer exclusively divided by the parousia but have through the incarnation so overlapped that the eschatological experiences associated with the Age to Come have reached back into the present age and have taken place in the essence of their spiritual reality. Thus judgment, like the resurrection, is still a future eschatological experience; but it is also a present spiritual reality as men respond favorably or unfavorably, in faith or in unbelief, to the person and ministry of Jesus. For such who believe, judgment has in effect taken place and they have been acquitted and found righteous. For those who disbelieve, their doom is sealed, their judgment is certain, and the reason is that they have been faced with the light but have rejected it. Therefore the final judgment will in reality be the execution of the decree of judgment that already has been passed. The "eschatological judgment 'at the last day' is . . . a final manifestation of the judgment which is taking place here and now according to the nature of the human response to the divine call and demand given in Jesus Christ."[39]

[39] W. F. Howard, "John," *IB* VIII, 444.

PART 3

THE PRIMITIVE CHURCH

23

THE THEOLOGY OF ACTS: THE CRITICAL PROBLEM

The book of Acts purports to give an outline of the history of the church from its earliest days in Jerusalem to the arrival of its greatest hero—Paul—in the chief city of the Roman empire. The book gives a picture of the life and preaching of the primitive Jerusalem community and traces the movement of the gospel from Jerusalem via Samaria and Antioch to Asia Minor, Greece, and finally Italy. Acts reports a number of sermons by Peter, Stephen, and Paul that provide the data for the faith of the early church. Since these speeches, particularly those of Peter, are ostensibly the primary source for the beliefs of the Jerusalem church, the critical question must be faced as to whether these chapters with their report of apostolic speeches are historically trustworthy.

At the turn of the century, the writings of two scholars—W. M. Ramsay in England and Adolf Harnack in Germany—exercised great influence for the view that Luke, the companion of Paul, wrote Acts in the 60's, and that he was a competent and reliable historian. Ramsay based his conclusions on geographical and archeological studies,[1] Harnack on literary criticism of Acts.

The most massive work ever to appear on Acts was *The Beginnings of Christianity,* edited by F. J. Foakes-Jackson and K. Lake (1920-33). H. J. Cadbury wrote, "From Thucydides downwards, speeches reported by the historians are confessedly pure imagination. . . . If they have any nucleus of fact behind them, it would be the nearest outline in the hypomnemata."[2] Hans Windisch argued against the Lukan authorship because the writer had no proper knowledge of Paul's career or theology.[3]

The modern period in Germany was introduced by Martin Dibelius, who

---

[1] His books today retain their value, although they are often ignored in the study of Acts. See *The Church in the Roman Empire* (1893); *The Bearing of Recent Discovery on the Trustworthiness of the NT* (1915); *St. Paul the Traveller and Roman Citizen* (1895).

[2] *Beginnings,* II, 13.

[3] *Ibid.,* II, 298-348.

applied the method of form criticism to Acts.[4] He allowed that Luke was the author and that he could be called an historian, but his interest was not in the history reported by Acts so much as in the life and theology of the church at the end of the first century when Acts was written.

Dibelius initiated an approach to Acts that has been followed by many of the German scholars. Vielhauer wrote an essay defending the view that the theology of Acts is more that of "early catholicism," i.e., of second-century Christianity, than primitive Jewish Christianity.[5] Hans Conzelmann wrote a widely influential book that argued that Luke-Acts[6] has completely abandoned the primitive Christian apocalyptic expectation and has substituted for it a theology of *Heilsgeschichte* that embodies an extended historical perspective. This means that Luke is no longer an historian but a theologian; indeed, a theologian of the sub-apostolic age, standing at the threshold of early catholicism. In a subsequent essay Conzelmann defended the view that there never was an "apostolic age." This is a later idea created by the church at the turn of the century to authenticate its own tradition.[7] This point of view was reinforced by the weighty commentary in the famous Meyer series by Haenchen. He admits that Luke had some historical sources, but his primary interest was not in history but in edifying the church.[8]

If Acts is primarily a theological work reflecting the life and thought of the church around A.D. 90, it can hardly be considered a source book for the history of primitive Christianity. One would think from some surveys of recent study that this "advanced" German criticism alone had anything significant to say about the historicity of Acts.[9] This is a very one-sided view.[10] The fact of the matter is that many scholars still consider Luke to have been the companion of Paul and a competent historian who drew both upon personal experience[11] and personal investigation. In the introduction to the Gospel, which also serves for the Acts, he claims to

---

[4] M. Dibelius, *Studies in the Acts of the Apostles* (1956; the first of his essays was published in Germany in 1923).

[5] See P. Vielhauer, "On the 'Paulinism' of Acts," *Studies in Luke-Acts,* ed. by L. E. Keck and J. L. Martyn (1966; German ed. 1950).

[6] *The Theology of Saint Luke* (1960; German ed. 1953). See the critique by I. H. Marshall in *ET* 80 (1968-69), 4-8.

[7] H. Conzelmann, "The First Christian Century," *The Bible in Modern Scholarship,* ed. by J. P. Hyatt (1965), pp. 217-26.

[8] E. Haenchen, *Die Apostelgeschichte* (1956; Eng. tr. 1971). See his essay, "The Book of Acts as Source Material for the History of Early Christianity" in *Studies in Luke-Acts,* pp. 258-78. For a further survey of the situation in Germany, see J. Rohde, *Rediscovering the Teaching of the Evangelists* (1968), pp. 153-239.

[9] See R. H. Fuller, *The NT in Current Study* (1962), pp. 86-100. This is somewhat less evident in C. K. Barrett, *Luke the Historian in Recent Study* (1969).

[10] See for a more balanced survey W. W. Gasque, "A Study of the History of the Criticism of the Acts of the Apostles," unpublished Ph.D. thesis at the University of Manchester (1969); to be published in 1973-74.

[11] The "we" sections.

have gained his information from "those who from the beginning were eyewitnesses and ministers of the word" (Lk. 1:2), and that he had personally investigated the matters about which he was to write.[12]

Cadbury thinks that by the use of this word Luke means to say that he has participated in the events he is to relate.[13] However, the usual meaning of the word in this context is "to follow or investigate something." If Luke was with Paul during his Caesarean imprisonment (Acts 21:18; 24:27; 27:1), he had ample opportunity to meet and talk with people who had both known Jesus and been participants in the life of the earliest church.[14] Furthermore, it is altogether probable that the early church was interested not only in the tradition about Jesus but also in the tradition about the apostles and its own early leaders.[15] Although Cadbury's judgment about the role of historical imagination in Hellenistic historians in the writing of speeches has been widely accepted, it has also been protested. Thucydides expressly says he was present on some occasions and used the reports of other men who were present. In any case, he intended to adhere "as closely as possible to the general sense of what was actually spoken."[16] Thucydides was not alone in seeking to be historically accurate in reporting the speeches of his *dramatis personae*.[17] While a basic pattern can be detected in the speeches in Acts, there is also considerable variety,[18] which lends them historical verisimilitude.[19] This judgment is reinforced by the persistent question of the Semitisms in the first half of Acts, which only with difficulty can be attributed to Luke's skill in imitating septuagintal Greek but which betray an Aramaic tradition.[20] Added to this is the fact that in the early speeches in Acts, "Luke seems to have been able to give us an extraordinarily accurate picture of the undeveloped theology of the earliest Christians."[21] Furthermore, in those areas where Luke's writing can be checked against knowledge drawn from secular

---

12 *Parēkolouthēkoti* (Lk. 1:3).

13 *Beginnings,* II, 502.

14 See B. Reicke, *Glaube und Leben der Urgemeinde* (1957), pp. 6-7; see also F. F. Bruce, *Commentary on the Book of Acts* (1954), p. 19.

15 See J. Munck, *The Acts of the Apostles* (1967), pp. xxxix-xliv; A. J. B. Higgins, "The Preface to Luke and the Kerygma in Acts" in *Apostolic History and the Gospel,* ed. by W. W. Gasque and R. P. Martin (1970), pp. 86-87.

16 See T. F. Glasson, "The Speeches in Acts and Thucydides," *ET* 76 (1964-65), 165.

17 See A. W. Mosley, "Historical Reporting in the Ancient World," *NTS* 12 (1965), 10-26.

18 See C. H. Dodd, *The Apostolic Preaching* (1936), pp. 1-74.

19 See F. F. Bruce, *The Speeches in Acts* (1943); H. N. Ridderbos, *The Speeches of Peter in the Acts of the Apostles* (1961); M. H. Scharlemann, *Stephen: A Singular Saint* (1968); B. Gärtner, *The Areopagus Speech* (1955).

20 See M. Black, "The Semitic Element in the NT," *ET* 77 (1965-66), 20-23; R. H. Martin, "Syntactical Evidence of Aramaic Sources in Acts I-XV," *NTS* 11 (1964), 38-59; D. F. Payne, "Semitisms in the Book of Acts," *Apostolic History and the Gospel,* pp. 134-50.

21 F. J. Foakes-Jackson, *The Acts of the Apostles* (1931), p. xvi.

sources, he is, as Ramsay argued, amazingly accurate. This line of study has recently been revived by a classical scholar, who concludes, "For Acts the confirmation of historicity is overwhelming."[22] It therefore should not be surprising that many good critical scholars believe that Luke has given us a trustworthy picture of the life and thought of the Jerusalem church.[23]

One can appreciate the judgment of Williams: "Some modern essays which seek to drive a wedge between the apostles and their converts or to deprecate Luke's phrase 'eye-witnesses and ministers of the word' (Luke 1:2) read like studies in historical improbability."[24]

We conclude, then, that we may use the early chapters of Acts as a reliable source for the theology of the Jerusalem church. This does not require us to believe that the sermons Luke reports are verbatim accounts; they are altogether too short for that. Nor need we demur at the judgment that Luke is the author of these speeches in their present form. We may, however, accept the conclusion that they are brief but accurate summaries of the earliest preaching of the apostles. It is also clear that Luke is not a critical historian in the modern sense of the word. He is highly selective of the events he relates; he introduces important facts without explanation (11:30); his characters appear and disappear from the scene in a frustrating way (12:17).[25] However, all real historical writing must involve selection and interpretation, and Luke selects from the sources of information available to him, both written and oral, what to him are the most important events in tracing the extension of the church from a small Jewish community in Jerusalem to a Gentile congregation in the capital city of the Roman empire.

---

[22] A. N. Sherwin-White, *Roman Society and Roman Law in the NT* (1963), p. 189.

[23] See C. S. C. Williams, *The Acts of the Apostles* (1958), p. 11; F. V. Filson, *A NT History* (1965), p. 161; see also *Three Crucial Decades* (1963); J. Munck, *The Acts of the Apostles,* pp. xxxix-xlv; L. Goppelt, *Apostolic and Post-Apostolic Times* (1970), p. 36; W. F. Albright in J. Munck, *Acts,* p. 263; I. H. Marshall, *Luke, Historian and Theologian* (1970), pp. 67ff. Metzger even suggests that the Jerusalem church may have had written archives that Luke could have consulted (B. Metzger, *The NT* [1965], p. 173).

[24] C. S. C. Williams, "Luke-Acts in Recent Study," *ET* 73 (1961-62), 135.

[25] See G. E. Ladd, *The Young Church* (1964), pp. 9-21.

24

RESURRECTION

Literature:

There are several older books that still possess great value, including J. Orr, *The Resurrection of Jesus* (n.d.); W. Milligan, *The Resurrection of Our Lord* (1883); W. J. Sparrow-Simpson, *The Resurrection and Modern Thought* (1911).

Recent Literature:

A. M. Ramsay, *The Resurrection of Christ* (1946); W. Künneth, *The Theology of the Resurrection* (1965; Ger. 1951); G. W. Stählin, "On the Third Day," *Int* 10 (1956), 282-99; R. R. Niebuhr, *Resurrection and Historical Reason* (1957); R. H. Fuller, "The Resurrection of Jesus Christ," *Biblical Research,* 4 (1960), 8-24; J. A. T. Robinson, "The Resurrection in the NT," *IDB* 4 (1962), 43-53; M. C. Tenney, *The Reality of the Resurrection* (1963); W. Pannenberg, *Jesus—God and Man* (1968; Ger. 1964), pp. 54-114; L. Goppelt *et al., The Easter Message Today* (1964); G. E. Ladd, "The Resurrection of Christ," *Christian Faith and Modern Theology,* ed. by C. F. H. Henry (1964), pp. 261-84; D. P. Fuller, *Easter Faith and History* (1965); H. Anderson, "The Easter Witness of the Evangelists," *The NT in Historical and Contemporary Perspective,* ed. by H. Anderson and W. Barclay (1965), pp. 35-55; W. Lillie, "The Empty Tomb and the Resurrection," *Historicity and Chronology in the NT* (1965), pp. 117-34; D. P. Fuller, "The Resurrection of Jesus and the Historical Method," *JBR* 34 (1966), 18-24; N. Clark, *Interpreting the Resurrection* (1967); S. H. Hooke, *The Resurrection of Christ* (1967); C. F. D. Moule, ed., *The Significance of the Message of the Resurrection for Faith in Jesus Christ* (1968); C. F. Evans, *Resurrection and the NT* (1970); W. Marxsen, *The Resurrection of Jesus of Nazareth* (1970).

THE IMPORTANCE OF THE RESURRECTION. Jesus' disciples had held steadfastly to the hope of the early establishment of the Kingdom of God. They had argued over who would have the highest status in the Kingdom (Mt. 18:1), and the mother of two of the disciples had tried to influence Jesus and give her sons places of preference in the coming Kingdom (Mk. 10:37=Mt. 20:21). The post-Easter question of the disciples, "Lord, will you at this time restore the kingdom to Israel?" (Acts

1:6), shows that their thinking continued to be dominated by the hope of an earthly theocratic kingdom. Undoubtedly these disciples were among the most vocal of those who hailed Jesus' entry into Jerusalem with the cry, "Blessed be the kingdom of our father David that is coming" (Mk. 11:10).

Jesus' death had shattered all these hopes. When Jesus was seized by the temple soldiers, his disciples forsook him and fled for safety lest they too be taken prisoners (Mk. 14:50). The conduct of the disciples after his death is not recorded. Luke tells us that Jesus' acquaintances watched the crucifixion at a distance (Lk. 23:49). However, they did not closely identify themselves with him in the hour of his suffering. A stranger—one Simon of Cyrene (Lk. 23:26)—was pressed into service to help Jesus by carrying his cross when he stumbled under its weight. Apparently only one of the disciples was actually present at the hour of his death (Jn. 19:26). None of the disciples seemingly had the courage to ask his body for burial. This tender ministration was undertaken by a member of the Sanhedrin whose position gave him nothing to fear, either from his colleagues or from Pilate (Mk. 15:43). Evidently the disciples did not dare show their faces lest they should suffer the fate of their master. Furthermore, it was not the disciples who came to the tomb and discovered it empty, but the women who came to care for Jesus' body. The disciples were apparently somewhere in hiding out of fear (Jn. 20:19). The death of Jesus meant the death of their hopes. The coming of the Kingdom was a dead dream, incarcerated in the tomb along with the body of Jesus (Lk. 24:21). Although Jesus had foretold his death, so strange was the idea of a dying Messiah, and so utterly alien was the idea that a cross could play any role in the mission of the Messiah, that the crucifixion of Jesus could mean only the complete disillusionment of his followers. This is what Paul means by the words, "Christ crucified [is] a stumbling block to Jews" (I Cor. 1:23). By definition Messiah was to be a reigning king, not a crucified criminal.

In a few days, however, all this was changed. These disillusioned Galileans began to proclaim a new message in Jerusalem. They asserted that Jesus was indeed the Messiah (Acts 2:36), that his death had been in the will and plan of God even though it was humanly an inexcusable murder (Acts 2:23). They asserted boldly that the one whom the Jews had murdered was the author of life (Acts 3:15), and that through this crucified Jesus, God not only offered to them repentance and the forgiveness of sins, but would also bring to fulfillment all he had promised in the Old Testament prophets (Acts 3:21).

What was the cause of this radical transformation both in the conduct of the disciples and in their attitude toward Jesus? The answer of the New Testament is that Jesus was raised from the dead. While the outpouring of the Holy Spirit on the day of Pentecost is pictured as the event that gave birth to the church as a self-conscious fellowship, the transformation of Jesus' disciples from a terrified, hopeless, disappointed band to the bold preachers of Jesus as Messiah and the agent of salvation was caused by his resurrection from the dead.

In fact, the resurrection stands as the heart of the early Christian message. The first recorded Christian sermon was a proclamation of the fact and significance of the resurrection (Acts 2:14-36). Peter said almost nothing about the life and earthly career of Jesus (Acts 2:22). He made no appeal to the character and personality of Jesus as one who was worthy of devotion and discipleship. He did not recall Jesus' high ethical teachings nor try to demonstrate his superiority to the many rabbinic teachers among the Jews. He made only passing reference to the mighty deeds that had marked Jesus' ministry as evidence that God's blessings had rested on him (Acts 2:22). The all-important thing was the fact that Jesus who had been executed as a criminal had been raised from the dead (Acts 2:24-32). It is not on the basis of Jesus' incomparable life or excellent teachings or awe-inspiring works that Peter made his appeal, but simply because God had raised him from the dead and exalted him to his own right hand in heaven. On the ground of this fact, Peter calls upon Israel to repent, to receive the forgiveness of sins, and to be baptized in the name of Jesus Christ (Acts 2:38).

The primary function of the apostles in the earliest Christian fellowship was not to rule or govern, but to bear witness to the resurrection of Jesus (Acts 4:33). This is shown by the qualifications for the successor of Judas; he must "become with us a witness to his resurrection" (Acts 1:22). Throughout the sermons in the first chapters of Acts, the resurrection continues to be a central theme (3:14, 15). It was because God had raised up Jesus that the apostles were able to do mighty works (4:10), and to offer to Israel the gift of salvation (4:12). It was the persistent witness to the resurrection that caused the first official opposition from the religious leaders against this new sect (4:1-2; see also 5:31-32).

In short, the earliest Christianity did not consist of a new doctrine about God nor of a new hope of immortality nor even of new theological insights about the nature of salvation. It consisted of the recital of a great event, of a mighty act of God: the raising of Christ from the dead. Any new theological emphases are the inevitable meanings of this redemptive act of God in raising the crucified Jesus from the dead.

THE FACT OF THE RESURRECTION. For the modern student of biblical history and theology, difficult questions cluster around the New Testament witness to the resurrection of Christ. The fact of the resurrection, as it is portrayed in the Bible, is impossible for many modern men to accept; however, the resurrection only serves to focus attention most intensely upon the character of the entire course of redemptive history. Paul wrote in I Corinthians 15:14 that if Christ is not risen from the dead our faith is futile. This seems like a bold statement. Is it not faith in the living God that is fundamental to life? Can faith in the living God be disturbed by the reality or the unreality of a single event? Did not the author to the

Hebrews lay down faith in God as the basic principle underlying all else when he wrote, "For whoever would draw near to God must believe that he exists and that he rewards those who seek him" (Heb. 11:6)? Ought we not to say that it is faith in the living God that vindicates our confidence in the resurrection of Christ?

This is persuasive, but it is contradicted by the course of Paul's thought. If Christ is not risen, faith is a futile thing. The reason for this is not obscure. The God who is worshipped in the Christian faith is not the product of that faith nor the creation of theologians or philosophers. He is not a God who has been invented or discovered by men. He is the God who has taken the initiative in speaking to men, in revealing himself in a series of redemptive events reaching back to the deliverance of Israel from Egypt, and beyond. God did not make himself known through a system of teaching nor a theology nor a book, but through a series of events recorded in the Bible. The coming of Jesus of Nazareth was the climax of this series of redemptive events; and his resurrection is the event that validates all that came before. If Christ is not risen from the dead, the long course of God's redemptive acts to save his people ends in a dead-end street, in a tomb. If the resurrection of Christ is not reality, then we have no assurance that God is the *living* God, for death has the last word. Faith is futile because the object of that faith has not vindicated himself as the Lord of life. Christian faith is then incarcerated in the tomb along with the final and highest self-revelation of God in Christ—if Christ is indeed dead.

Our understanding of the resurrection of Christ is a question far larger than the resurrection itself; it involves the entire nature of the Christian faith, the nature of God and of God's redemptive work. The Bible represents God as a living God who is creator and sustainer of all life and existence, who can neither be identified with his creation pantheistically nor separated from it deistically. He stands above creation and history, and yet is continually active in it. As the living God, he is able to act in ways that transcend ordinary human experience and knowledge.

Many modern thinkers cannot accept this concept of God. They assume that the world must always and everywhere be subject to inflexible "laws of nature." There is no room for God to act in his world in ways that deviate from his usual ways of acting. Thus a prominent modern theologian flatly rejects the possibility that the resurrection of Jesus means the restoration to life of a dead body, for such an action "is inextricably involved in a nature miracle. Such a notion he [the modern man] finds intolerable, for he can see God at work only in the life of the spirit (which is for him the only real life) and in the transformation of his personality. But quite apart from the incredibility of such a miracle, he cannot see how an event like this could be the act of God, or how it could affect his own life." Therefore, "an historical fact which involves a resurrection from the dead is utterly inconceivable."[1]

Such an attitude prejudices the case in advance and makes a decision before the evidence is heard. Bultmann assumes that the place where God acts is in human existence and not in history. He rejects the biblical witness as to the nature of redeeming events, which sees God's self-revealing activity not only in the lives of men but also in objective events. In other words, the definition of Christianity that is formulated from such presuppositions is bound to be other than the Bible's witness to God's redeeming acts.

The witness of the New Testament is that an objective act took place in a garden outside of Jerusalem in which the crucified and entombed Jesus emerged from the grave into a new order of life. As we deal with the objective fact of the resurrection, it is not our intention to *prove* the fact of the resurrection and thereby compel faith. We recognize that faith cannot be compelled by a recital of "historical" or objective facts but only by the working of the Holy Spirit upon the human heart. But the Holy Spirit used the witness of the disciples to the reality of the resurrection of Christ, and we must here bear witness to the facts of the New Testament record.

There are several facts that are attested by the Gospels. First, Jesus was dead. Few serious scholars will question this. Second, the hopes of the disciples were also dead. Jesus had preached the coming of the Kingdom of God; and his disciples followed him in the vibrant expectation that they would witness its coming (Lk. 19:11) and see the redemption of Israel (Lk. 24:21). Even though Jesus had on at least several occasions warned them of his impending death and tried to prepare them for it (Mk. 8:31), they never really understood what he was saying. It is important to recall that first-century Jews did not understand the suffering servant of Isaiah 53 to apply to the Messiah. By definition the Messiah was to reign in his Kingdom, not suffer and die; and when Jesus surrendered himself helplessly into the hands of his enemies, when he suffered execution as a common criminal, their hope was broken. For them it was the end of Jesus and his preaching and the end of their hopes.

A third fact is this: the disciples' discouragement and frustration was suddenly and abruptly transformed into confidence and certainty. Suddenly they were certain Jesus was no longer dead. Something happened that convinced them that Jesus was alive. They were sure they had seen him again, heard his voice, recognized his person.

A fourth fact is the empty tomb. This is witnessed to by all the Gospels, and it is presupposed in Paul's creedal statement in I Corinthians 15:1-3. There would be no point in emphasizing the burial of Jesus or

[1] R. Bultmann, *Kerygma and Myth* (H. W. Bartsch, ed., 1961), I, 8, 39; "The event of the Resurrection has nothing to do with the resuscitation of a corpse." N. Clark, *Interpreting the Resurrection* (1967), pp. 97f.

the fact that his resurrection took place *on the third day* unless the resurrection meant emptying the tomb. Many scholars maintain that the reports of the empty tomb are late legendary accretions designed to support Christian belief in the resurrection; but many scholars today feel compelled to accept the historicity of the empty tomb.[2]

A fifth historical fact is the resurrection faith. Few will deny today that it is a solid fact of history that the disciples believed that Jesus was raised from the grave. Those scholars who are unable to believe in an actual resurrection of Jesus admit that the disciples believed it. They believed that their teacher and master, who was dead and buried, was alive again. They were confident that they saw him once again, heard his voice, listened to his teachings, recognized his features. They believed that his presence was not a "spiritual," i.e., nonmaterial, "ghostly" thing, but an objective bodily reality. *This was the faith that created the church.* That which brought the church into being and gave it a message was not the hope of the persistence of life beyond the grave, a confidence in God's supremacy over death, a conviction of the immortality of the human spirit. It was belief in an *event* in time and space: Jesus of Nazareth was risen from the dead. Belief in the resurrection of Jesus is an unavoidable historical fact; without it there would have been no church.

But we must go further to the final and crucial fact. *Something happened to create in the disciples belief in Jesus' resurrection.* Here is the crucial issue. It was not the disciples' faith that created the stories of the resurrection; it was an event lying behind these stories that created their faith.

They had lost faith. They were "foolish men, and slow of heart to believe all that the prophets [had] spoken" (Lk. 24:25). The fact of the resurrection and faith in the resurrection are inseparable but not identical. The fact created the faith.

Here is the heart of the problem for twentieth-century man: What is this *fact* of the resurrection? What happened to produce the disciples' faith? The problem is structured by the modern understanding of history and historical events. The ancient world faced no such problem, for men believed that the gods could come down upon the earth to converse with men and produce all sorts of unusual phenomena. The modern world has left these views behind and interprets history in terms of continuity and analogy. Historical experience is an unbroken nexus of cause and effect. All historical events must have rational, historical causes.

Since the rise of this historical method, criticism has attempted to explain on historical grounds the rise of the resurrection faith and the resurrection narratives. Here is our central problem: the "historicity" of the resurrection.

It is of course an historical fact that death is the end of personal histori-

---

[2] R. H. Fuller in *Biblical Research,* IV, 12; W. Pannenberg, *Jesus—God and Man* (1968), pp. 100-6; L. Goppelt, *Apostolic and Post-Apostolic Times* (1970), p. 16; J. A. T. Robinson in *IDB* 4, 45-46; W. Lillie in *Historicity and Chronology* (1965), pp. 130, 134.

cal existence. When a man dies, he leaves forever this earthly scene. His body returns to dust. What may happen to his spirit or soul is not an historical question but a theological or metaphysical one. Therefore it is an accepted historical fact that the resurrection cannot mean the "resuscitation of a corpse." Many religions have stories of such restorations to life, but the historian treats them as legendary. The form of the stories of Jesus' return to life must be understood in terms analogous to similar stories in other religions.

The question remains for historical criticism: What *did* happen? What "historical" event created the resurrection faith and produced the stories of the resurrection appearance and of the empty grave?

Historical criticism has offered numerous solutions to this problem. One of the earliest historical explanations of the resurrection faith was that the disciples stole Jesus' body and concealed it, and then began to proclaim that he was not dead but had returned to life. This theory founds the resurrection message on a deliberate fraud. The Christian gospel of life and salvation rests on a lie. Such a view hardly requires refutation.

Another theory is that Jesus really was not dead but only swooned from weakness and loss of blood. The coolness of the tomb and the fragrance of the aromatic spices together with the hours of rest revived him. Returning to consciousness, he emerged from the tomb, appeared to his disciples, and led them to believe that he was risen from the dead.[3]

Another more modern attempt explains that the resurrection stories began with Mary. She lost her way in the garden and coming to the wrong tomb found it empty. Then through her tear-flooded eyes, beholding the form of the gardener, she leaped to the conclusion that it was Jesus, risen from the dead.

Such stories refute themselves. The only plausible "historical" explanation is that the disciples had real experiences, but their experiences were subjective and not objective. In human experience, imagination is just as *real* as objective reality; it merely belongs to a different order of reality. This theory holds that the disciples experienced *real* visions that they interpreted to mean that Jesus was alive and victorious over death. To be sure, the gospel stories are couched in terms of physical and objective contacts with Jesus, but by definition such stories cannot be historical. The reality behind them was a series of real subjective experiences, visions, or hallucinations in which the disciples were sure they experienced the living Jesus.

This theory, however, leads to another problem: What caused the subjective experiences? What produced the visions? Visions are psychological facts; they are reality. But visions do not occur arbitrarily. The experience of visions requires certain preconditions on the part of the subjects concerned; and these preconditions were totally lacking in the disciples of

[3] A modern variant of this view is found in H. Schonfield, *The Passover Plot* (1965).

Jesus. To picture the disciples after Jesus' death as nourishing fond memories of Jesus, of longing to see him again, of expectancy that he could not really die, is contrary to the evidence of the Gospels. To portray the disciples as so infused with hope because of the impact Jesus had made upon them that their faith leaped over the barrier of death and posited Jesus as their living, risen Lord requires a radical rewriting of the gospel tradition. It may not be flattering to the disciples' faith to say that it could come into being only as the result of an experience with some objective reality; but this is the testimony of the Gospels. Does faith require some kind of objectivity to sustain it? Is faith its own support? In the case of the disciples, NO! Faith did not produce the visions, and visions did not produce faith. There is no adequate explanation to account for the rise of the resurrection faith except this: that Jesus rose from the dead.

Many scholars have been oblivious to the difficulties involved in the "vision" theory. Bultmann, as an historian, can only account for the resurrection faith on the ground of the personal intimacy the disciples had enjoyed with Jesus during his earthly life. This personal impact of Jesus led the disciples to experience subjective visions.[4] A classic statement of this position is that of Johannes Weiss, who wrote that "the appearances were not external phenomena but were merely the goals of an inner struggle in which faith won the victory over doubt . . . the appearances were not the basis of their faith, though so it seemed to them, so much as its product and result." A faith that could be awakened only by objective appearances "would not possess very much in the way of moral or religious value."[5] However flattering such a view may be to the disciples' faith, it requires a radical rewriting of the New Testament data.

However, the problem simply cannot be so easily solved. This is clearly recognized by one of Bultmann's most able and influential disciples, Günther Bornkamm. He admits that the despair and discouragement of the disciples do not allow for a subjective explanation of the resurrection event in the inner nature of the disciples. He furthermore concedes the point for which we are contending: namely, that "the appearances of the risen Christ and the word of his witnesses have in the first place given rise to this faith."[6] This seems to be an unavoidable conclusion. The question remains: What was the nature of these appearances?

THE NATURE OF THE RESURRECTION. The admission of the priority and objectivity of the resurrection event does not settle all the problems. We have yet to deal with the most important question: What is the nature of the resurrection? Since the resurrection is the event that gave rise to the church, the nature of the resurrection is one of the most important questions we can ask.

---

[4] R. Bultmann, *Kerygma and Myth,* I, 42.
[5] J. Weiss, *The History of Primitive Christianity* (1959), I, 30.
[6] G. Bornkamm, *Jesus of Nazareth* (1960), p. 183.

Bultmann interprets the resurrection in existential terms. He accepts the criticism that the resurrection means that Jesus is risen in the kerygma, i.e., in the proclamation of the gospel, that the kerygma is itself an eschatological event, and that Jesus therefore is actively present to meet the hearer in the kerygma. All speculations over the nature of the resurrection, all accounts of an empty grave and the like, are irrelevant to this resurrection fact.[7]

Since Bornkamm admits that the vision theory is not adequate to explain the rise of the resurrection faith, we might expect a more satisfying answer from him. He says that the Easter faith is "that God himself had intervened with his almighty hand in the wicked and rebellious life of the world, and had wrested this Jesus of Nazareth from the power of sin and death which had risen against him, and set him up as the Lord of the world."[8] However, this language appears to mean something far less than some form of a bodily resurrection, for he goes on at once to explain, "An event in this time and this world, and yet at the same time an event which puts an end and a limit to this time and this world."[9] Such language again appears to interpret the resurrection in existential terms; but it must be remembered that to an existentialist, the experience of "authentic existence" or, in Christian terminology, saving faith, involves objectivity and not mere subjectivity.[10]

Bultmann says that the resuscitation of a corpse is incredible. Even if this should be a valid objection, it carries no weight, for the New Testament does not picture the resurrection of Jesus in terms of the resuscitation of a corpse, but as *the emergence within time and space of a new order of life.*

Certain elements in first-century Judaism believed in the resurrection of the physical body, i.e., in the return to life of the same body that died. This is illustrated by the story of the Jewish elder called Razis in the days of the Seleucid persecution. Rather than fall into the hands of the hated Greeks, Razis took a sword and disembowelled himself. Then "standing on a steep rock . . . he tore out his bowels, taking both his hands to them, and flung them at the crowds. So he died, calling on Him who is lord of life and spirit to restore them to him again" (II Macc. 14:46).

Such a story does not describe the nature of Jesus' resurrection. Jesus' resurrection is not the restoration to physical life of a dead body; it is the emergence of a new order of life.[11] It is the embodiment in time and space

---

[7] R. Bultmann in *The Historical Jesus and the Kerygmatic Christ,* ed. by C. E. Braaten and R. A. Harrisville (1964), p. 42.

[8] G. Bornkamm, *Jesus of Nazareth,* pp. 183ff.

[9] *Loc. cit.*

[10] R. Bultmann, *Kerygma and Myth,* I, 199ff.

[11] Some Jewish apocalypses describe the resurrection in terms of putting on garments of glory (En. 62:16). Pannenberg thinks Paul derived his idea of a "spiritual body" from this apocalyptic background. See *Jesus—God and Man,* pp. 79-80.

of eternal life. It is the beginning of the eschatological resurrection. This is clear from Paul's argument in I Corinthians 15.

The eschatological character of the resurrection of Jesus is not explicitly affirmed in the Gospels or in the Acts, but it is clearly implied at two points. The first is the nature of the apostolic preaching of the resurrection. We are told in Acts 4:1 that the opposition of the Sadducees was aroused because the disciples were "proclaiming in Jesus the resurrection from the dead." This statement is very striking. Wherein lies its significance? The Pharisees believed and taught resurrection from the dead. It was the custom for Jewish rabbis or theologians to sit in the vast courts of the temple surrounded by groups of disciples. Undoubtedly if one had wandered through the temple area looking for this new sect of Jesus and stopped long enough to listen to several rabbis instructing their followers, he would sooner or later have heard the resurrection of the dead mentioned. Why then should the Sadducees be exercised over a similar teaching by these followers of Jesus?

The answer can only be that the proclamation of Jesus' resurrection by his disciples gave the doctrine both new proportions and new significance. The rabbis taught resurrection as a matter of theoretical theology; and various rabbis debated questions as to the time and subjects of the resurrection. With the Christian message it was different. Here was no abstract theory or cold theology; here was the proclamation of a contemporary fact that, if true, challenged all Judaism to recognize that a new redemptive act of God had occurred in their midst to which they could not assume a neutral or indifferent attitude. Furthermore, the wording of the statement indicates that the disciples were not merely proclaiming an event they had witnessed—the resurrection of a crucified teacher; they were proclaiming "in Jesus the resurrection from the dead." The resurrection of Jesus carried with it implications of incalculable significance. No longer was the resurrection of the dead a debated theological hope for the future; it was a fact of the present that placed the entire matter in a new perspective so that it could be neither ignored nor merely tolerated.

The eschatological nature of Jesus' resurrection is further attested by the nature of his resurrection body as it is reported in the Gospels. Jesus' resurrection was clearly a *bodily* resurrection; yet it was a body that possessed new and higher powers than had his physical body before his death.

The Gospels go to great lengths to attest that the resurrection of Jesus was indeed a bodily resurrection. Here lies the significance of the empty tomb. The factuality of the empty tomb is rejected by many biblical critics, who claim that it is a later apologetic story designed to support belief in the resurrection. However, this objection overlooks the important fact that the Gospels do not make apologetic use of the empty tomb to prove the reality of the resurrection. The empty tomb by itself was a puzzling fact that needed explanation. Mark records that the first reaction of the women to the empty tomb (as well as to the message of the angels) was of fear and astonishment. Luke tells of two disciples who knew of the empty tomb but did not believe the resurrection until they were confronted by the risen Jesus (Lk. 24:22ff.). John relates that Mary could only conclude from the empty tomb that Jesus' body had been removed (Jn. 20:2). It was not the empty tomb that aroused belief in John, but the appearance of the grave clothes (Jn. 20:6-8). Apart from the appearances of Jesus, the empty tomb was an enigma. The empty tomb, therefore, is not a witness to the fact of the resurrection so much as it is a witness to the nature of the resurrection; it was a resurrection of Jesus' body.

The bodily character of his resurrection is attested in other ways. His body made an impression on the physical senses: of feeling (Mt. 28:9; Jn. 20:17, 27), of vision, of audition (Jn. 20:16; it is probable that Mary recognized Jesus by the tone of his voice when he pronounced her name). Other elements are included that seem to suggest that Jesus' body was nothing more than a physical body. He said, "A spirit has not flesh and bones as you see me have" (Lk. 24:39). However, from the context it seems evident that this is not meant to be a "scientific" analysis of the composition of his body but is intended only to prove that he had a real body and was not a disembodied spirit. Paul also insists on the bodily nature of the resurrection. We ought therefore not to place too much stress on the words "flesh and bones" in Luke 24:39, assuming that they designate a body exactly like the physical body.

Again, the resurrected Jesus was capable of eating. He ate a piece of fish in the presence of his disciples (Lk. 24:42-43), but again, the words "before them" (v. 43) make it clear that this was done as a sign that his resurrection was bodily.

However, Jesus' resurrection body possessed new and wonderful powers that set it apart from the natural and physical body. It possessed capacities never before experienced on earth. It had the amazing power to appear and disappear at will. On two occasions, John records that Jesus suddenly appeared to his disciples, "the doors being shut" (Jn. 20:19, 26). This can only mean that Jesus did not enter through an open door. *Although* the doors were shut, "Jesus came and stood among them" (v. 26). At Emmaus, after breaking bread with two disciples Jesus suddenly vanished out of their sight (Lk. 24:31). When they returned to Jerusalem and related their experience, suddenly Jesus stood among them. He came with such suddenness that they were startled and frightened and supposed that it was a spirit (Lk. 24:36-37). The resurrected body of Jesus possessed new and amazing powers. It seemed to belong to a different order of reality.

Furthermore, a close study of the text nowhere suggests that the stone of the tomb was rolled away from the tomb to let Jesus out. The earthquake and rolling back of the stone are recorded by Matthew (28:2) as a sign of a wonderful event, not as the event itself. There can be only one conclusion: the body of Jesus was gone before the stone was rolled away. It did not need to be removed for him to escape the tomb; he had already escaped it. The removal of the stone was for the disciples, not for Jesus.

These two sets of items point to a twofold conclusion: the resurrection of Jesus was a bodily resurrection; but his resurrection body possessed strange powers that transcended physical limitations. It could interact with the natural order, but it at the same time transcended this order. C. K. Barrett is correct in speaking of "the mysterious power of the risen Jesus, who was at once sufficiently corporeal to show his wounds and sufficiently immaterial to pass through closed doors."[12] This is indeed the same twofold witness of Paul. Jesus' resurrection belongs to a new and higher order: the order of the Age to Come, of eternal life.

This witness of the Gospels is reinforced by Paul's discussion of the resurrection in I Corinthians 15. While Paul is here concerned with the eschatological resurrection of saints at the parousia, this eschatological resurrection is inseparable from the resurrection of Jesus because he describes these two resurrections as two parts of a single event. The resurrection of Jesus is the first fruits of the eschatological resurrection (I Cor. 15:20). All who are in Christ stand in solidarity with him as all men in Adam stand in solidarity with Adam. All in Adam share Adam's death, so all who are in Christ will share Christ's life. "But each in his own order: Christ the first fruits, then at his coming those who belong to Christ" (I Cor. 15:23).

The resurrection of Christ and the resurrection of those who belong to Christ constitute two parts of a single entity, two acts in a single drama, two stages of a single process. The temporal relationship is unimportant. It matters not how long an interval of time intervenes between these two stages of the resurrection. This does not affect the logical relationship or, it would be better to say, the theological relationship. Jesus' resurrection is the "first fruits" of the eschatological resurrection at the end of the age. First fruits were common in Palestinian agriculture. They were the first grain of the harvest, indicating that the harvest itself was ripe and ready to be gathered in. The first fruits were not the harvest itself, yet they were more than a pledge and promise of the harvest. They were the actual beginning of the harvest. The act of reaping had already begun: the grain was being cut.

Jesus' resurrection is not an isolated event that gives to men the warm confidence and hope of a future resurrection; it is the beginning of the eschatological resurrection itself. If we may use crude terms to try to describe sublime realities, we might say that a piece of the eschatological resurrection has been split off and planted in the midst of history. The first act of the drama of the Last Day has taken place before the Day of the Lord.

The resurrection of Jesus is not simply an event in history. It ought not to be described simply as a supernatural event—a miracle, as though God had interfered with the "laws of nature." The resurrection of Jesus means

[12] C. K. Barrett, *John* (1955), p. 472.

nothing less than the appearance upon the scene of the historical of something that belongs to the eternal order! Supernatural? Yes, but not in the usual sense of the word. It is not the "disturbance" of the normal course of events; it is the manifestation of something utterly new. Eternal life has appeared in the midst of mortality.[13]

It is the eschatological nature of Jesus' resurrection that gives the modern historian so much trouble. According to the witness of the New Testament, the resurrection has no historical cause; it is an act of God, and the historian as such cannot talk about God. It is without analogy, being utterly unique, and this places it outside ordinary historical experience. It is the emergence of eternal life in the midst of mortality, and the historian knows nothing about eternal life or the Age to Come. Yet it occurred as an objective event in the midst of history even though it transcends all ordinary human categories. This is why the modern historian often interprets the resurrection in some other way than bodily resurrection. Yet he must account for the resurrection faith and the rise of the church; and to anyone who believes in the existence of a living, omnipotent God, the "hypothesis" that Jesus was raised bodily from the grave is the only adequate explanation for the "historical" facts.

Marxsen makes much of the fact that none of the disciples experienced the resurrection: no one saw him rise.[14] The resurrection of Jesus is an inference drawn from the appearances. This must be admitted. But we must also insist that it is an absolutely necessary inference that is compelled by the evidences. Marxsen is surely wrong when he says that all the evangelists wanted to show by their stories of the resurrection was that the activity of Jesus goes on,[15] and when he reduces the several narratives so as to arrive at a single point: Peter's having believed.[16] The meaning of the resurrection stories is that Jesus is continuing his activity—because he is alive in person; and that the disciples, including Peter, believed—because they had personally met the risen Lord in bodily form.

Thus we conclude that the resurrection of Jesus is an eschatological event that occurred in history and gave rise to the Christian church. It sounds a note that provides the clue for understanding the character and message of the primitive church. The church was brought into being by an eschatological event; it is itself an eschatological community with an eschatological message. In some real sense, the events that belong to the end of the age and the eschatological consummation have invaded history.

---

[13] See G. W. Stählin, "On the Third Day," *Int* 10 (1956), 282-99.

[14] W. Marxsen, *The Resurrection of Jesus of Nazareth* (1970).

[15] *Ibid.*, p. 77.

[16] *Ibid.*, p. 96.

25

THE ESCHATOLOGICAL KERYGMA

Literature:

A. E. J. Rawlinson, "The Christology of the Jewish-Christian Church," *The NT Doctrine of Christ* (1926), pp. 27-52; C. H. Dodd, *The Apostolic Preaching and Its Developments* (1936), pp. 1-74; D. M. Stanley, "The Theme of the Servant of Yahweh in Primitive Christian Soteriology," *CBQ* 16 (1954), 385-93; G. B. Caird, "The Gospel," *The Apostolic Age* (1955), pp. 36-56; D. M. Stanley, "The Concept of Salvation in Primitive Christian Preaching," *CBQ* 18 (1956), 231-54; H. J. Cadbury, "Acts and Eschatology," *The Background of the NT and Its Eschatology,* ed. by W. D. Davies and D. Daube (1956), pp. 300-21; J. A. T. Robinson, "The Most Primitive Christology of All?" *JTS* 7 (1956), 177-89; O. Cullmann, *Christology of the NT* (1959); B. Reicke, "The Risen Lord and His Church," *Int* 13 (1959), 157-69; W. C. van Unnik, "The 'Book of Acts.' The Confirmation of the Gospel," *NT* 4 (1960), 26-59; B. Lindars, *NT Apologetic* (1961), pp. 32-50; S. S. Smalley, "The Christology of Acts," *ET* 73 (1961-62), 358-62; C. F. D. Moule, "The Christology of Acts," *Studies in Luke-Acts,* ed. by L. E. Keck and J. L. Martyn (1966), pp. 159-85; R. P. C. Hanson, "Doctrine in Acts," *The Acts* (1967), pp. 39-46; G. E. Ladd, "The Christology of Acts," *Foundations* 11 (1968), 27-41; J. H. Hayes, "The Resurrection as Enthronement and the Earliest Church Christology," *Int* 22 (1968), 333-45; R. N. Longenecker, *The Christology of Early Jewish Christianity* (1970); J. D. G. Dunn, *Baptism in the Holy Spirit* (1970).

The most primitive interpretation of the meaning of Jesus is found in the book of Acts with its account of the preaching of the early church. The Gospels end with stories of Jesus' resurrection and brief statements about his ascension. Mark has a broken ending; Matthew records a commission from the risen Jesus to his disciples to carry the gospel into all the world. Luke alone relates the sequel to the resurrection: a small group of 120 Jewish disciples, convinced that their crucified master was indeed risen from the dead, began to proclaim his messiahship and to call upon the rest of Israel to repent and turn in faith to the one they had crucified. At first this small band constituted what must have appeared to be nothing but a sect within Judaism. Luke tells the story of how this new fellowship (the church) came to break with Judaism and to be extended throughout the Mediterranean world. The most important instrument in this extension of the church was the converted rabbi Paul; and we have enough of his writings to be able to structure his interpretation of the meaning of Christ. Here we must analyze the earlier chapters of the book of Acts to understand the earliest interpretation of Jesus and the early church's understanding of itself. This is to be found primarily in the speeches of Acts.[1]

THE TIME OF SALVATION. C. H. Dodd, in a book that has had far-reaching influence,[2] summarized the primitive preaching under the following topics:

First, the age of fulfillment has dawned. "This is what was spoken by the prophet Joel" (Acts 2:16). "But what God foretold by the mouth of all the prophets . . . he thus fulfilled" (Acts 3:18). "And all the prophets who have spoken, from Samuel and those who came afterwards, also proclaimed these days" (Acts 3:24). The apostles declared that the messianic age has dawned.

Second, this has taken place through the ministry, death, and resurrection of Jesus, of which a brief account is given, with proof from the Scriptures that all took place "according to the definite plan and foreknowledge of God" (Acts 2:23).

Third, by virtue of the resurrection, Jesus has been exalted at the right hand of God as messianic head of the new Israel (Acts 2:33-36; 3:13).

Fourth, the Holy Spirit in the church is the sign of Christ's present power and glory. "Being therefore exalted at the right hand of God, and having received from the Father the promise of the Holy Spirit, he has poured out this which you see and hear" (Acts 2:33).

Fifth, the messianic age will shortly reach its consummation in the return of Christ. "That he may send the Christ appointed for you, Jesus, whom heaven must receive until the time for establishing all that God spoke by the mouth of his holy prophets from of old" (Acts 3:21).

Finally, the kerygma always closes with an appeal for repentance, the offer of forgiveness and of the Holy Spirit, and the promise of salvation, that is, of the life of the Age to Come to those who enter the elect community. "Repent, and be baptized every one of you in the name of Jesus Christ for the forgiveness of your sins; and you shall receive the gift of the Holy Spirit. For the promise is to you and to your children and to all that are far off, every one whom the Lord our God calls to him" (Acts 2:38-39).

These several points merit detailed study, although not necessarily in the order listed by Dodd.

THE HISTORICAL JESUS. The primitive kerygma had its focal point in the death and exaltation of Jesus. Modern criticism makes a sharp dis-

[1] For the trustworthiness of these speeches, see Ch. 23.

[2] *The Apostolic Preaching* (1936), pp. 38-45.

tinction between the historical Jesus and the exalted Christ, often regarding the latter as mythological and therefore unhistorical. This was not, however, the way the early church viewed the matter. Their kerygma proclaimed the fate of a real man, Jesus of Nazareth (Acts 2:22). This title is used five times in the early chapters of Acts, and appears elsewhere only in the Gospels. Furthermore, he is often referred to by the simple name Jesus, without further qualification. On the day of Pentecost, Peter spoke of one whom both he and his audience had known from personal observation and experience. His life and deeds were still fresh in their memory (2:22f.). The apostles were witnesses to his mighty deeds all over the land of Israel (10:38-39). The most vivid impression was that of a man mightily empowered by God.

While the kerygma is concerned with an actual historical figure, the life and words and deeds of Jesus do not provide the content of the kerygma. They provide only background for what happened to him in his death, resurrection, and exaltation. However, it is important to note that the full humanity and historicity of Jesus are everywhere assumed.

JESUS' SUFFERINGS. If the kerygma is concerned more with Jesus' death than with his life, a natural question follows: What meaning of his death, i.e., what view of the atonement did the early church proclaim? The answer to this question reflects the primitive character of this theology, for it is impossible to formulate any doctrine of atonement from the sermons in Acts. The fact of Jesus' death is all-important and is emphasized again and again. However, some idea of atonement is implicit in the statements that the death of Jesus was not merely a tragic event but occurred within the will and redeeming purpose of God. Although Jesus was killed by lawless men, his death happened according to the definite plan and foreknowledge of God (2:23). Herod and Pilate together with the Gentiles and Jews could do with Jesus only what "thy hand and thy plan had predestined to take place" (4:28).

A most significant development is found in reference to the fact that Jesus' sufferings had fulfilled "what God foretold by the mouth of all the prophets that his Messiah [Christ] should suffer" (3:18). His sufferings and death are part of his messianic mission. Why did the primitive church attribute sufferings to messiahship? The Old Testament does not do so; the suffering servant of Isaiah 53 is not identified as the Messiah. Pre-Christian Judaism did not expect a suffering and dying Messiah. Jesus did not teach that he must suffer as the Messiah but as the Son of Man (Mk. 8:31). Messiah designated the Davidic king who is to reign, not die. Yet the early church believed that his death was part of his messianic mission.

A clue to this is found in the use of a title for Jesus in the early chapters of Acts that appears nowhere else in the New Testament: the Servant (*pais*). Jesus suffered the hostility and violence of the rulers both as the Lord's Anointed and as God's holy Servant (4:26-27). Although his

Servant was put to death, God glorified him (3:13-14), raising him from the dead (3:26). It is in the name of this holy Servant, Jesus, that God is showing his power. Philip also saw in the humiliation of the *ebed Yahweh* of Isaiah 53:7-8[3] a prophecy of the sufferings of Jesus.[4] Jesus is the *ebed Yahweh,* the *pais theou* who will accomplish a redemptive mission of suffering. The early church saw in these sufferings the fulfillment of the role of Messiah. The distinct conflation of the roles of Servant and Messiah is thus effected; Jesus as Messiah fulfills the role of the suffering servant.

The best explanation for this conflation of messianic functions is that it goes back to Jesus himself. "Jesus Himself [had] accepted and fulfilled His Messianic mission in terms of the prophecy of the suffering servant, and the apostles' interpretation followed His own."[5] Indeed, Luke tells us that the risen Lord explicitly instructed the disciples that it was the mission of the Messiah first to suffer and then to enter into his glory (Lk. 24:26).

The primitive character of the Christology of Acts is illustrated by the fact that *Christos* had not yet become a proper name. In fourteen places "the Christ" is clearly a title (2:31, 36; 3:18, 20, etc.). The primitive kerygma proclaimed that Jesus was the Messiah (5:43; 8:5; 9:22). In eleven places "Christ" is joined to "Jesus" not so much as a proper name but as a formal construction. Peter told the Jews to be baptized in the name of Jesus the Christ (2:38; see also 3:6; 4:10; 8:12).[6]

It will also be as Messiah that Jesus will return to bring the Kingdom to its eschatological consummation. "Repent therefore, and turn again, that your sins may be blotted out, that times of refreshing may come from the presence of the Lord, and that he may send the Christ appointed for you, Jesus, whom heaven must receive until the time for establishing all that God spoke by the mouth of his holy prophets from of old" (3:19-21). Jesus has suffered as Messiah, he is now exalted as Messiah, he must yet come as Messiah to bring the eschatological consummation.

J. A. T. Robinson has argued that this Christology of the eschatological Christ is contradictory to the exaltation Christology and is, in fact, the earliest Christology of the early church.[7] The exaltation Christology represents a later stage in the evolution of Christology.[8] However, this flies

---

3 See Isa. 42:1; 49:1-3; 50:4-10; 52:13.

4 O. Cullmann, *Christology of the NT* (1959), pp. 73ff. See also R. N. Longenecker, *The Christology of Early Jewish Christianity* (1970), pp. 104ff.

5 F. F. Bruce, *The Book of Acts* (1954), p. 90.

6 See A. Harnack, *The Date of Acts* (1911), pp. 104ff., followed by V. Taylor, *The Names of Jesus* (1953), p. 21; H. J. Cadbury, *Beginnings of Christianity* (1933), IV, 358.

7 J. A. T. Robinson, "The Most Primitive Christology of All?" *Twelve NT Studies* (1962), pp. 139-53.

8 R. Bultmann, *Theology of the NT* (1951), I, 49, has a similar understanding of the earliest Christology. The early Jerusalem church identified the exalted Jesus with the heavenly Son of Man and awaited his return in glory. The idea of his

in the face of the text and "makes Luke appear incredibly naive in placing two distinct and differing christologies side by side."[9]

THE BEGINNING OF THE RESURRECTION. We have seen in the preceding chapter that the resurrection of Jesus was something far more than the restoration of a dead body to physical life; it was itself an eschatological event. The resurrection of the dead belongs to the end of the age and will usher in the righteous dead unto the eternal life of the Age to Come. The resurrection stands at the dividing point between the ages.

The resurrection of Jesus was a completely unexpected event. It means nothing less than that an event belonging to the Age to Come has occurred in history. This again means that the transition from this age to the Age to Come will not occur in a single apocalyptic event at the end of history, but in two events, the first of which has happened in the midst of history. Thus the resurrection of Jesus has indeed ushered in a new age—the messianic age—while the Age to Come remains future. While the resurrection of the dead remains an event at the last day, in the resurrection of Christ this eschatological event has already begun to be unfolded. The "halfway" point is passed. The early church found itself living in a tension between realization and expectation—between "already" and "not yet." The age of fulfillment has come; the day of consummation stands yet in the future.

THE KINGDOM OF GOD. The central theme of Jesus' preaching was the Kingdom of God. While this theme is not represented as one of the central themes of the early apostolic preaching, it is not altogether absent. Luke records that in the days after Jesus' resurrection, he continued to teach them about the Kingdom of God (1:3). We are undoubtedly to understand this to mean that he was instructing them in the relationship between his proclamation of the Kingdom of God and his death and resurrection. The need for this is seen in the fact that the disciples still retained nationalistic, theocratic ideas about the Kingdom; for they ask Jesus, "Will you at this time restore the kingdom to Israel?" (1:6). Earlier, two of Jesus' disciples had asked him to grant them the positions of primary authority in the restored Israelitic order for which they longed (Mk. 10:35ff.). Now Jesus has told them that the promise of the gift of the Holy Spirit, which in the Old Testament belonged to the new age, was about to be fulfilled, and they naturally assumed that the Old Testament promises of Israel's conversion and restoration in the Kingdom were about to be fulfilled.

Jesus did not answer with a flat denial that the Kingdom had nothing to do with Israel. Rather, he said that it was not given to them to understand the full program of God. "It is not for you to know the times or seasons which the Father has fixed by his own authority" (1:7). Paul later de-

---

present messianic Lordship is a later development. See also F. Hahn, *The Titles of Jesus* (1969), p. 162.

[9] R. N. Longenecker, *The Christology of Early Jewish Christianity*, p. 78. See also the critique of G. E. Ladd in *Foundations*, XI (1968), 37-38.

voted three chapters to the present rejection and the future salvation of Israel (Rom. 9-11), but Jesus told the disciples that they were not to be concerned about prophetic programs, but were instead to be witnesses of him in all the world. "The question in v. 6 appears to have been the last flicker of their former burning expectation of an imminent political theocracy with themselves as its chief executives."[10]

However, it is clear that the disciples still looked for an eschatological fulfillment of the Old Testament promises. In his second sermon, Peter said that "heaven must receive [Christ] until the time for establishing all that God spoke by the mouth of the prophets from of old" (Acts 3:21). In God's own time, he will send "the Messiah, Jesus," to accomplish this fulfillment (Acts 3:20). The noun for establishing in Acts 3:21 (*apokatastasis*) is from the same root as the verb "restore" in Acts 1:6 (*apokathistanai*). Jesus' answer to the disciples "does not repudiate the expectation as such (of the coming of God's Kingdom), but simply deprives it of political significance and refers it to the pneumatic sphere."[11] The promise in Acts 3:20 of the restoration of all things refers not primarily to Israel but to the restoration of divine order in the new messianic creation.[12]

When the early disciples refer to the Kingdom of God in Acts it is not clear whether the reference is to the eschatological order or not. Sometimes the "Kingdom of God" has, in effect, become almost a synonym for the gospel. Philip went to Samaria preaching good news about the Kingdom of God (8:12). However, this is coupled with "the name of Jesus Christ." In Ephesus, Paul for three months argued and pleaded about the Kingdom of God (19:8), and he summarized his Ephesian ministry by the words "preaching the kingdom" (20:24). In Rome, he testified to the Jewish leaders who came to him of the Kingdom of God, but this means "trying to convince them about Jesus both from the law of Moses and from the prophets" (28:23). Luke summarized Paul's ministry in Rome by saying that he devoted two years to "preaching the kingdom of God and teaching about the Lord Jesus Christ" (28:31). We may assume that such passages mean that the apostles proclaimed in summary form what had been the burden of Jesus' message. The one remaining reference may be distinctly eschatological: "Through many tribulations we must enter the kingdom of God" (14:22). It is of great interest that Luke summarizes the content of Paul's preaching to the Gentiles by the utterly non-Hellenistic phrase "the Kingdom of God."

THE ASCENSION

Literature:

H. Sasse, "The Exalted," *Mysterium Christi,* ed. by C. K. A. Bell and A. Deissmann (1930), pp. 115-20; A. M. Ramsay, "What Was the Ascension?" *SNTS,* Bulletin II (1951), 43-50; A. W. Argyle, "The Ascen-

---

[10] F. F. Bruce, *The Book of Acts,* p. 38.
[11] A. Oepke in *TDNT* I, 389.
[12] *Ibid.,* p. 392.

sion," *ET* 66 (1954-55), 240-42; C. F. D. Moule, "The Ascension," *ET* 68 (1956-57), 205-9; J. G. Davies, *He Ascended Into Heaven* (1958), pp. 27-68; P. A. van Stempvoort, "The Interpretation of the Ascension in Luke and Acts," *NTS* 5 (1958), 30-42; B. M. Metzger, "The Ascension of Jesus Christ," *Historical and Literary Studies* (1968), pp. 77-87.

The most notable use of Messiah in connection with Jesus is in his ascension (Acts 2:36). Luke says that forty days after his resurrection, he told the disciples to wait in Jerusalem for the coming of the Holy Spirit; and then, "as they were looking on, he was lifted up, and a cloud took him out of their sight" (Acts 1:9). This story of the ascension of Jesus to heaven involves many difficulties. It suggests in the first place that the early Christians conceived of a three-decker world with heaven as a literal place above the atmosphere. However, if heaven, understood as the dwelling place of God, is a realm of existence other than and different from the physical universe, there is no other way Jesus could have signalled his departure into that other world than by a visible ascension as Luke describes it. It is doubtful that Luke was thinking in cosmological terms. He was describing the cessation of the resurrection appearances of Jesus—"an acted declaration of finality."[13] The cloud was probably not a cloud of vapor but the cloud of glory signalizing the divine presence. At his transfiguration Jesus had entered the cloud of the divine presence but did not remain there. At the ascension he enters it again and remains with the Father.[14]

The meaning of the ascension raises another, different question. Some scholars urge that the bodily nature of Jesus' resurrection demands the ascension, for it would be inappropriate for Jesus to remain permanently on earth;[15] others that the ascension is the taking of his redeemed humanity into heaven.[16] However, such views, as easy as they first seem, are not without difficulty. The relationship between the resurrection and the ascension is not a simple one. The resurrection, as we have seen, was not a return to earthly existence; it was an eschatological event, the first fruits of the eschatological resurrection. The resurrection of Jesus was the emergence of eternal life in the midst of mortality. As Paul later wrote, Jesus has "brought life and immortality to light through the gospel" (II Tim. 1:10). There is good reason to believe that the glorification and exaltation of Jesus occurred at the time of resurrection. The exaltation is one of the central themes of Peter's first sermon, and it is held in close association with the resurrection. "This Jesus God raised up. . . . Being therefore exalted at the right hand of God" (Acts 2:32, 33).

---

[13] C. F. D. Moule, "The Ascension," *ET* 68 (1956-57), 208.

[14] J. G. Davies, *He Ascended Into Heaven* (1958), pp. 63-64. Van Stempvoort thinks it was a cloud caused by eschatology. See *NTS* 5 (1958), 38.

[15] B. Metzger, "The Ascension of Jesus Christ," *Historical and Literary Studies* (1968), p. 84.

[16] C. F. D. Moule, "The Ascension," *ET* 68, 209. See also A. W. Argyle, "The Ascension," *ET* 66 (1954-55), 240.

This exaltation theme, which appears in this earliest reported sermon, recurs frequently in the New Testament. The christological hymn in Philippians 2 is probably pre-Pauline in form and substance.[17] The humiliation and death of Jesus is followed by his exaltation, with no explicit mention either of resurrection or ascension. This same conjunction of ideas appears in Acts 5:30-31: "The God of our fathers raised Jesus whom you killed by hanging him on a tree. God exalted him at his right hand as Leader and Savior." In such passages, the resurrection and the exaltation can be understood as a single event. This theme of Jesus' exaltation at the right hand of God is a prominent one throughout the New Testament.[18]

It is possible, therefore, that the resurrection of Jesus was itself his glorification and exaltation. Paul was speaking of the resurrection of Jesus when he said, "The first man Adam became a living being, the last Adam became a life-giving spirit" (I Cor. 15:45). This corresponds to the appearance of the resurrected, glorified Jesus to Paul on the Damascus Road. He appeared in radiance and glory (Acts 9:3). However, this was more than a vision. While it had the nature of a "revelation"—a disclosure from the world of God to Paul on earth (Gal. 1:16)—Paul classes his vision of Jesus with the appearances to the other disciples (I Cor. 15:8), although he recognizes something irregular in his experience; he is like one "untimely born." Still, Paul never confuses his seeing of Jesus with other visions, apparently of an ecstatic nature, that he experienced (II Cor. 12:1ff.). If this analysis is correct, then the appearances of Jesus to the disciples in normal bodily form were condescensions of the glorified Christ to convince them that he was really alive again. We must admit to profound mystery here, for the resurrection is "intrinsically 'incomprehensible' because it is an event of the other-worldly 'history' in the realm of heavenly reality. But in the appearances of the resurrected Jesus the heavenly reality was, for a definite period of time, visible and comprehensible in this world."[19] If this analysis is correct, the basic meaning of the ascension is to convince the disciples that the appearances of the resurrected Jesus are now at an end. He has returned to the Father to abide. A passing reference in John's Gospel supports this interpretation. When Mary first saw the risen Jesus in the garden, she apparently attempted to embrace him; but he said, "Do not hold me, for I have not yet ascended to the Father" (Jn. 20:17).[20] Jesus is merely reassuring her that he is to be with her and the other disciples for a brief period before he leaves them to return to the Father.

THE MESSIANIC KING. The exaltation of Jesus to the right hand of God means nothing less than his enthronement as messianic King. Peter

---

17 See A. M. Hunter, *Paul and His Predecessors* (1961²), pp. 40-44, 122-23.

18 See A. M. Ramsay, "What Was the Ascension?" in *Historicity and Chronology in the NT* (1965), pp. 137-39.

19 G. Stählin, "On the Third Day," *Int* 10 (1956), 299.

20 The AV translation "touch me not" obscures the meaning of the text. See C. F. D. Moule in *NT* 5 (1962), 175; C. K. Barrett, *John* (1955), p. 480.

concludes his first sermon with the affirmation, "God has made him both Lord and Christ, this Jesus whom you crucified" (2:36). Taken out of context, this saying could mean that Jesus *became* Messiah at his exaltation and represents an "adoptionist" Christology.[21] However, the context makes it clear that Jesus was the Messiah in his earthly ministry, and the immediate context makes it clear that Peter means to say that Jesus has entered in upon a new stage of his messianic mission. He has now been enthroned as messianic King.

Peter recalls that David had received a promise from God that one of his descendants would be set upon his throne (2:30). This promise appears explicitly in Psalm 132:11; but it is also implicit in such prophecies as II Samuel 7:13, 16; Isaiah 9:7; 11:1-9; Jeremiah 33:17, 21. Because David foresaw that his Greater Son should sit upon his throne, he foretold also the resurrection of the Messiah. This event has now been fulfilled; the Messiah has been both raised from the dead and exalted at the right hand of God (2:33),[22] so as to sit enthroned at God's right hand. To prove this messianic enthronement, Peter quotes from Psalm 110:1, where the Lord (Yahweh) tells David's Lord that he is to sit at God's right hand until his enemies are conquered (2:34-35). In its Old Testament context, this psalm envisages an enthronement of David's Lord upon the throne of the Lord in Jerusalem. This is proven by Psalm 110:2, where the messianic King sends forth his scepter from Jerusalem (Zion), ruling over his foes. That the throne of the Lord's anointed king could be called the throne of the Lord is proven by I Chronicles 29:23.

In other words, the new redemptive events in the course of *Heilsgeschichte* have compelled Peter to reinterpret the Old Testament. Because of the resurrection and ascension of Jesus, Peter transfers the messianic Davidic throne from Jerusalem to God's right hand in heaven. Jesus has now been enthroned as the Davidic Messiah on the throne of David, and is awaiting the final consummation of his messianic reign. This is one of the meanings included in Peter's final summary proclamation, that God has made the crucified Jesus both Lord and Christ. Jesus has entered upon a new function of his total messianic mission. In the days of his flesh he had been anointed (4:27; 10:38), and it was as the Messiah that he had suffered (3:18). But in his exaltation Jesus becomes the Messiah in a new sense: he has begun his messianic reign as the Davidic king.

This involves a rather radical reinterpretation of the Old Testament prophecies, but no more so than the entire reinterpretation of God's redemptive plan by the early church. In fact, it is an essential part of this reinterpretation demanded by the events of redemptive history. If the first

---

[21] Weiss, *The History of Primitive Christianity* (1937), I, 118f. J. A. T. Robinson agrees, but goes even further, finding in Acts 3:20 an even more primitive Christology, namely, that Jesus will only be Messiah at his return from heaven. See J. A. T. Robinson, *Twelve NT Studies,* pp. 139ff.

[22] The passage can be rendered either "by the right hand" or "to the right hand" of God.

stage of the eschatological resurrection has taken place, then the messianic age has begun and the messianic blessings have been given because the Messiah has already begun his reign.

However, here, as in the other eschatological features of the kerygma, there remains something for the future. Jesus is enthroned as the Messiah, but his reign is not complete. He must reign until his enemies are made a stool for his feet (2:35). The consummation of his victory still stands in the future. He is reigning; but his enemies are not yet subdued. This is why Peter later spoke about a future coming of the Messiah to accomplish the establishment of all that God had promised. Jesus is the Messiah; he is reigning; the messianic age with its blessings is present. But he is waiting a future victory; the consummation of his reign awaits his future coming. Fulfillment-consummation: such is the tension in the eschatological kerygma.

THE SON OF MAN. According to the Gospels, Jesus' favorite self-designation was the Son of Man. It is a striking fact that this term quite falls into disuse in the Acts. It is as the Messiah, not the Son of Man, that Jesus will return to bring times of refreshing for his people and accomplish the restoration of all things spoken by the prophets (3:19-21). Jesus is designated the Son of Man only by Stephen, who, at the moment of death, sees "the heavens opened, and the Son of man standing at the right hand of God" (7:56). The significance of Jesus' posture in standing rather than in being seated seems to be that he is standing as a witness in vindication of his oppressed disciple.[23] Many critics have propounded the theory that the Son of Man was not a self-designation of Jesus, but that he used it to designate an eschatological figure, not himself, who would come in glory to inaugurate the eschatological Kingdom of God.[24] The primitive church, believing that Jesus was raised from the dead and exalted to heaven, remembered his teaching about an eschatological Son of Man and *identified the exalted Jesus with the eschatological Son of Man.* Thus the most primitive Christology is a Son-of-Man Christology. The early church awaited the coming of Jesus as the Son of Man.[25] This conclusion is based not upon inductive exegesis of the texts but upon the application of the comparative religions approach to the New Testament, namely, that the Christology of the Jerusalem church must be formulated in terms of Jewish expectations. A question such scholars cannot answer is this: "Why should the church have been so careful to insert the title Son of man into the words of Jesus alone when (as the Bultmannians assert) it really represented their Christology and not his?"[26] There is no evidence in the entire New Testament, aside from the presuppositions of an extreme form criticism, that the early church called Jesus the Son of Man.

---

23 C. F. D. Moule, "From Defendant to Judge," *SNTS,* Bulletin III (1952), p. 47.
24 See p. 151.
25 R. Bultmann, *Theology,* I, 33f.; F. Hahn, *The Titles of Jesus in Christology,* pp. 32f.; R. H. Fuller, *The Foundations of NT Christology* (1965), pp. 143ff.
26 R. N. Longenecker, *Christology,* p. 89.

As to why this title was dropped when it was Jesus' favorite self-designation we can only speculate. The best guess is that it did not seem an appropriate title for Jesus during the period between his earthly ministry and his parousia. The Gospels put the title on Jesus' lips to designate his humiliation and suffering, and his coming in glory. Therefore, from the perspective of the early church, "Half its content was already a thing of the past, and half was yet in the future. It was naturally assumed that the Church was in a *Zwischenzeit,* between the going and the return; and what relevance has the term Son of man to that? Far more relevant is the title Lord."[27]

JESUS AS LORD. The exaltation of Jesus means that he is Lord (*kyrios*) as well as Messiah. "God has made him both Lord and Christ" (2:36). This term is used of Jesus in a number of places in the Gospels. It is almost never used by Matthew and Mark in narrative passages, and only three times by John (Jn. 4:1; 6:23; 11:2), but some fifteen times by Luke in what appears to be a deliberate anachronism. Jesus is the one whom we now know to be the Lord (Lk. 7:13; 10:1; 11:39, etc.). *Kyrios* is used rather frequently in the Gospels in direct address to Jesus. Taylor thinks that *Kyrie* in the vocative form is only an expression of courtesy, like the English "Milord," and carries no christological significance.[28] However, in some passages the term seems to bear a greater significance, involving a high honor in the thought of the speaker, although less than the distinctively Christian connotation. This conclusion rests on the fact that *Kyrie* does not appear indiscriminately in the speech of all sorts of persons but is usually restricted (though not in Luke) to Jesus' disciples or to those appealing for supernatural help.[29]

The clue to the history of the word is found in John's Gospel, where the word is used of Jesus in the narrative portions of the first nineteen chapters only three times, but in the resurrection stories of the last two chapters it is used nine times. The Evangelist feels free to speak of Jesus as Lord after his resurrection but does not feel the designation is appropriate in the earlier ministry. This suggests that the title belongs primarily to Jesus as the Risen and Ascended One.[30]

In the primitive kerygma, Jesus has become Lord. The title is used in the narrative of Acts at least twenty times; and it appears frequently in the combination "the Lord Jesus," "the Lord Jesus Christ," "our Lord Jesus Christ." Whatever the date of Acts, this use of the title probably represents the earliest preaching with fidelity, and it is significant that the great majority of the passages are found in the first half of the book.[31]

---

[27] C. F. D. Moule, "The Influence of Circumstances on the Use of Christological Terms," *JTS* 10 (1959), 257.

[28] V. Taylor, *The Names of Jesus,* p. 41.

[29] See Mt. 8:21; 26:22; Lk. 5:8; G. Vos, *The Self-Disclosure of Jesus* (1954), pp. 129ff.

[30] V. Taylor, *The Names of Jesus,* p. 43.

[31] *Ibid.,* p. 44.

The impressive fact is that in Acts, *kyrios* is used simultaneously for God and for the exalted Jesus. The word appears in several quotations from the Septuagint for God (2:20, 21, 25, 34; 3:22; 4:26). In 3:19, *kyrios* is clearly used for God (2:39; 4:29; cf. 4:24; 7:31 and 33). This usage goes back to the Septuagint where *kyrios* is the translation not only of *Adonai* but the ineffable covenant name *Yahweh.* It is therefore amazing to find the term used at the same time of both Jesus and God. Not only is Jesus,[32] like God, *kyrios;* the term is used of both God and the exalted Jesus in practically interchangeable contexts. Peter on the day of Pentecost cites language from Joel that speaks of the Day of the Lord (Yahweh) and of calling on the name of the Lord for salvation (2:20-21); and this means calling on the name of Jesus of Nazareth (4:10, 12). Jesus has been made Lord while God continues to be the Lord (2:36, 39). Jesus, as Lord, has entered upon the exercise of certain divine functions. He has poured out the Spirit (2:33); he has become the object of faith (2:21; 3:16); he gives repentance and forgiveness (5:31); he is the Holy One (3:14); the author of life (3:15); the recipient of prayer (4:29); he will be the judge of the world (10:42); and he stands at the right hand of God to receive the spirit of the first martyr (7:55, 59).

For the full significance of the *kyrios* designation, we must turn to the Pauline epistles, which reinforce and interpret the facts presented in Acts. *The heart of the early Christian confession is the Lordship of Christ.* This fact is sadly obscured by the language of the Authorized Version. Salvation comes not by confessing the Lord Jesus but by confessing Jesus as Lord (Rom. 10:9). This confession of the Lordship of Jesus can only be made by the enabling of the Holy Spirit (I Cor. 12:3). The heart of the apostolic kerygma is the proclamation of the Lordship of Jesus (II Cor. 4:5). Christians are those who have received Christ Jesus as Lord (Col. 2:6). All of this is but acceptance and personal appropriation of what God has done in exalting Jesus. God has raised him above every other authority and power, has exalted him above every other so-called lord (I Cor. 8:5-6), and has bestowed upon him the superlative name *Kyrios,* before which every knee must finally bow in obedience and submission (Phil. 2:9-11). Jesus *is* the Lord, exalted over every hostile power, beneath whose feet every such power must finally be subdued (I Cor. 15:24ff.). The Christian confession of the Lordship of Jesus means the recognition of what God has done in exalting Jesus, and personal submission to and acceptance of his Lordship.

All of this is implicit in the most primitive kerygma of Jesus as Lord, because at his exaltation Jesus was made both Messiah and Lord (Acts 2:36). He has become the one by whom God will bring under control every rebellious power in the world. This is seen in Peter's citation from Psalm 110:1: "The Lord [Yahweh] said to my Lord [Messiah], Sit at my right hand, till I make thy enemies a stool for thy feet" (Acts 2:34). This reign

---

[32] See 1:6, 21, 24; 4:33; 5:14; 7:59, 60; 8:16.

of Jesus as the exalted, enthroned *Kyrios* stood at the heart of the primitive kerygma.

That this high Christology goes back to the primitive church has been denied by many modern scholars, particularly by W. Bousset, and more recently by R. Bultmann, who follows Bousset.[33] Bultmann holds that the primitive church did not think of Jesus as *Kyrios* but only as eschatological Messiah or heavenly Son of Man. Jesus had been exalted to heaven and would shortly return as the eschatological Son of Man to fulfill the Jewish hopes of the eschatological Kingdom of God. Bultmann denies that the primitive church had any sense of "realized" eschatology. The messianic era stood altogether in the future and would be inaugurated by the coming of Jesus as the Son of Man. The church was an eschatological congregation, not because it had experienced the blessings of the messianic age but because it was the people designated for the future eschatological age. The primitive church was thoroughly Jewish in its eschatology, modifying this hope only by the confidence that the exalted Jesus would be the returning Son of Man.

Only when the gospel moved out from Jewish soil to a Gentile milieu did Jesus begin to be thought of as Lord. The religious background for this term is not the Greek translation of the Old Testament where *Kyrios* is a name for God, but the Hellenistic cults that flourished in Egypt, Asia Minor, and especially Syria. Such religious societies gathered in the name of various lords (I Cor. 8:5f.) to perform certain cultic acts by which the worshipper could achieve union with the deity of the cult and thus attain immortality. Bousset and Bultmann argued that the early church did not think of Jesus as Lord until the gospel came to Antioch (Acts 11:19ff.) and there arose a church in which the Jewish idea of an apocalyptic Son of Man coming to inaugurate an eschatological kingdom was foreign. Jesus was reinterpreted by this Hellenistic church as a cult deity who works supernaturally in the worship of the church as a cultic body. In Antioch the disciples were for the first time called Christians (Acts 11:26), and Jesus was for the first time called Lord. He had been converted from the Jewish eschatological Messiah into a Hellenistic cult deity. Only after Jesus had come to be known as Lord as a result of syncretistic influences were Christians able to interpret him in terms of the LXX *Kyrios*.[34]

The "Achilles heel" to this theory of evolving Christology is a prayer of Paul's, "If any man love not the Lord Jesus Christ, let him be Anathema Maran-atha" (I Cor. 16:22, AV). The King James Version transliterates the Greek into meaningless English. *Anathema* is a Greek word

---

[33] See W. Bousset, *Kyrios Christos* (1921, 1970), pp. 121ff.; R. Bultmann, *Theology*, I, 51-52, 124-28. For a criticism of Bousset see J. G. Machen, *The Origin of Paul's Religion* (1921), ch. 8; A. E. J. Rawlinson, *The NT Doctrine of Christ* (1926), pp. 231-37; see also R. N. Longenecker, *Christology*, pp. 120ff., for the entire problem.

[34] For a similar but independent interpretation see F. C. Grant, *Introduction to NT Thought* (1950), pp. 133-34.

meaning "cursed." *Maranatha* is the transliteration of an Aramaic expression that may be rendered *maran atha,* "(The) Lord has come," or *marana tha,* "Our Lord, come." *Mar* is the Aramaic word for Lord. This was a liturgical expression, invoking both the presence of the Lord at the Lord's Supper, and his return to establish his Kingdom. Here it is a prayer for the return of Jesus as Lord to establish his Kingdom.[35] That Paul should use an Aramaic expression in a letter to a Greek-speaking church that knew no Aramaic proves that the use of *mar* (*Kyrios*) for Jesus goes back to the primitive Aramaic church and was not a product of the Hellenistic community. This liturgical expression, stemming from the primitive community, had become so widely used that the Corinthians needed neither translation nor explanation of its meaning. Jesus was *Kyrios* to the Greek churches as he had been *Mar* to the Jerusalem Aramaic Christians. Therefore we may conclude that Acts 2:36 correctly describes the primitive Christian attitude toward Jesus as *Kyrios.* By his exaltation, Jesus stood so close to God that he exercised many of the divine prerogatives. The early church worshipped God; it also worshipped Jesus as the exalted *Kyrios.* Here in the earliest Christology of the primitive church are the beginnings of trinitarian theology, although they are not reflected upon. Implicit in the recognition of the Lordship of Jesus is the acknowledgment of his essential divinity.[36]

The origin of this usage can best be explained as deriving from Jesus himself. In his last debates with the scribes, Jesus had suggested that the Messiah was to be more than David's son; he was to be David's Lord. Jesus implied that he himself was this divine Lord.[37] Taylor is right in suggesting that the early Christian understanding of Jesus as exalted Lord ultimately derives from Jesus himself.[38]

---

35 See *Didachē* 10:6; Rev. 22:20. Bultmann's explanation that the prayer is addressed to God and not to Christ is utterly inadequate.

36 V. Taylor, *The Names of Jesus,* p. 51.

37 See above, p. 167.

38 V. Taylor, *The Names of Jesus,* pp. 50-51.

26

THE CHURCH

Literature:

G. Johnston, "The Primitive Community," *The Doctrine of the Church in the NT* (1943), pp. 59-66; W. L. Knox, "The Theology of Acts," *The Acts of the Apostles* (1948), pp. 69-99; J. E. L. Dulton, "The Holy Spirit, Baptism, and the Laying On of Hands in Acts," *ET* 66 (1954-55), 236-40; G. B. Caird, "The Spirit," *The Apostolic Age* (1955), pp. 57-72; B. Reicke, "The Constitution of the Primitive Church in the Light of Jewish Documents" in *The Scrolls and the NT,* ed. by K. Stendahl (1958), pp. 143-56; E. Schweizer, "Pneuma. Luke and Acts," *TDNT* VI (1959, 1968), 404-15; E. Schweizer, "The Primitive Church in Jerusalem," *Church Order in the NT* (1961), pp. 34-50; G. Johnston, "The Constitution of the Church in the NT" in *Peake's Commentary on the Bible,* ed. by M. Black and H. H. Rowley (1962), pp. 724-27; F. V. Filson, *A NT History* (1965), pp. 153-74; R. Schnackenburg, "The Primitive Church's View of Itself," *The Church in the NT* (1965), pp. 56-61; C. S. Mann, "The Organization and Institutions of the Jerusalem Church in Acts" in J. Munck, *The Acts of the Apostles* (1967), pp. 276-84; C. S. Mann, "Pentecost in Acts" in J. Munck, *The Acts of the Apostles* (1967), pp. 271-75; J. Munck, "Primitive Jewish Christianity," *The Acts of the Apostles* (1967), pp. lxii-lxx; L. Goppelt, *Apostolic and Post-Apostolic Times* (1970), pp. 8-60; J. D. G. Dunn, *Baptism in the Holy Spirit* (1970); J. K. Pratt, "The Holy Spirit and Baptism," *ET* 82 (1970-71), 266-71.

THE BEGINNING OF THE CHURCH: PENTECOST. Jesus looked upon his disciples as the nucleus of Israel who accepted his proclamation of the Kingdom of God and who, therefore, formed the true people of God, the spiritual Israel. He indicated his purpose to bring into being his *ekklēsia* who would recognize his messiahship and be the people of the Kingdom and at the same time the instrument of the Kingdom in the world. However, Jesus and his disciples did not form a separate synagogue, nor start a separate movement, nor in spite of constant conflict with the Jewish leaders break with either the temple or synagogue in any outward way. His disciples formed an open fellowship within Israel whose only external distinguishing mark was their discipleship to Jesus.

After Jesus' death and resurrection this small group of disciples, now numbering 120, for several weeks apparently did nothing but wait on God for divine direction. During a period of forty days, Jesus appeared to them from time to time, continuing to instruct them in the same theme that had been his central message—the Kingdom of God (Acts 1:3). They still believed that this meant the restoration of the Jewish theocracy (1:6), but Jesus indicated that God had a different purpose for the present. The promise made by John the Baptist that the coming Messiah would fulfill Joel's prophecy of baptizing God's people with the Holy Spirit would shortly take place.

On the day of Pentecost, a marvelous thing happened: Jesus' disciples experienced a divine visitation that was accompanied by certain visible and audible manifestations, which convinced them that God had poured out his Holy Spirit upon them.

The prophets had foreseen a day when God would pour out his Spirit upon all his people, not only upon the appointed leaders—kings, priests, and prophets. This gift would result in a revival of prophecy and revelation (Joel 2:28-29). As the prophecy stands in Joel, this gift of the Spirit is an eschatological event belonging to the day when God finally redeems his people Israel, and gathers them into his Kingdom. It is therefore associated with the Day of the Lord, which will be both a day of judgment and of salvation (Joel 2:30-32).

In the same vein, although with a different emphasis, Ezekiel looks forward to the day of the messianic salvation when God will restore his people, cleanse them from their sins, and give them a new heart by placing his Spirit within them, thus enabling them to be God's people (Ezek. 36:22ff.).

Intertestamental literature was conscious of the loss of the Spirit. In the apocryphal and pseudepigraphical writings there is an awareness that the period of prophetic inspiration is over. Prophecy is defunct. Prophetic inspiration departed from Israel with the last prophets. In rabbinic literature it is expressly stated that the Holy Spirit departed from Israel after the last prophets. It is even accepted that the Spirit was no longer present in the second temple. There was no longer any inspired revelation.[1] The sectarians of Qumran believed that God had given his Spirit to some of the members of the community;[2] but this did not convey fresh revelations but the ability rightly to interpret the Old Testament.

John the Baptist had appeared as a prophet speaking directly the word of God. Jesus in turn received the Holy Spirit at his baptism. In Nazareth he claimed to be endowed with the Spirit (Lk. 4:18), and he claimed that it was by the power of the Spirit that he did his mighty works of power (Mt. 12:28). The presence of the prophetic Spirit in John and the power of the Holy Spirit in Jesus presaged something new: the coming

---

[1] E. Sjöberg, *TDNT* VI, 385.
[2] References in F. F. Bruce, *NT History* (1969), p. 197.

of the messianic age.[3] John promised that Jesus should be the one to effect the baptism of the Spirit (Mk. 1:8).

When the little band of 120 believers experienced the pentecostal gift of the Holy Spirit, Peter interpreted it by saying, "This is what was spoken by the prophet Joel" (Acts 2:16). The promise given to Israel to be fulfilled at the Day of the Lord, said Peter, has now been fulfilled, not to the nation, but to a group of men who believed in the messiahship of Jesus. Furthermore, Peter adds an expression that gives the event pointed eschatological significance. He substitutes for Joel's "after this" the words, "and in the last days" (Acts 2:17). In the prophets, "the last days" was an expression designating the time of the Kingdom of God, the messianic era. In the last days God's rule is to be established in all the earth; all nations will worship the God of Israel; and peace will prevail among all men (Isa. 2:2-4). It is the time when Israel will be saved under the blessed rule of David their king (Hos. 3:5). Peter reinterprets Joel by asserting that the outpouring of the Spirit also belongs to the last days. By so doing he also reinterprets the meaning of the last days themselves; he separates the last days from the Day of the Lord and places them in history. *The last days have come.* The last days are the days of the Spirit who has now been given. In some real sense of the word, the messianic era has come, the eschatological salvation is present. Yet the Day of the Lord remains a future event at the end of the age, which has not yet come.[4] However, the eschaton does not remain "intact in the future."[5] Peter's preaching requires a radical modification of the eschatological structure. The Day of the Lord remains an object of hope, but the "last days" of the messianic salvation have been realized. Therefore it is also incorrect to insist, as does C. H. Dodd, that the early church believed that the eschaton had come. The eschaton designates "all that the prophets meant by the Day of the Lord."[6] Dodd correctly emphasizes the element of messianic fulfillment in the primitive kerygma; but he goes too far in saying that the early church looked for the coming of Christ only to finish what he had already begun, not to introduce a new order of things. This interpretation misses the significance of Peter's reinterpretation of the last days and their separation from the Day of the Lord, and places the emphasis altogether upon fulfillment rather than upon the tension between the fulfillment of the last days and the consummation at the Day of the Lord. The time of fulfillment has come; but the Day of the Lord remains an eschatological event in the indeterminate future.

The coming of the Spirit manifested itself in several ways evident to the physical senses. A mighty rushing sound filled the upper room where the

[3] See J. E. Yates, *The Spirit and the Kingdom* (1963); J. D. G. Dunn, *Baptism in the Holy Spirit* (1970), pp. 23-37.

[4] See H. C. Cadbury, "Acts and Eschatology," *The Background of the NT and Its Eschatology*, ed. by W. D. Davies (1956), pp. 300-31.

[5] *Ibid.*, p. 321.

[6] C. H. Dodd, *The Apostolic Preaching* (1936), p. 214.

disciples were gathered. They saw some kind of appearance that looked like a flame of fire, splitting up into separate tongues and resting upon each of them. They felt themselves filled with a wonderful sense of the presence of God, so much so that they broke forth into spontaneous praise to God. The language in which they spoke was neither Aramaic nor Greek, but an unknown language that gave the impression to some of their hearers that they were intoxicated (2:13). Apparently these tongues possessed an ecstatic dimension that sounded to some quite unintelligible. However, many others heard intelligible speech. These Palestinian Jews seemed to have the capacity to speak many different languages. Diaspora Jews who lived in various countries surrounding the Mediterranean Sea, who had made a pilgrimage to Jerusalem to celebrate the Feast of Weeks, heard these Aramaic-speaking Jews praising God in the indigenous dialects of their native lands.

Peter explained that this marvelous power to speak in other tongues (*glossolalia*) was the outward sign of the fulfillment of Joel's prophecy that God would pour out his Holy Spirit on all his people. In Joel this promise was associated with the Day of the Lord; Peter asserts that this event has now occurred in history. It results from the fact that God had exalted the crucified Jesus, had enthroned him at his right hand, thus inaugurating his messianic reign; and the outpouring of the Holy Spirit upon his people was nothing less than the blessing of the messianic age. This outpouring of the Spirit is also called the baptism of the Spirit (1:5) and the "gift of the Holy Spirit" (2:38).[7]

The meaning of the baptism of the Spirit can be discovered from a study of the several uses of the term. The 120 disciples were baptized with the Spirit at Pentecost, and at the same time they were filled with the Spirit (2:2). These two terms—baptism and filling—do not appear to be strictly synonymous, for Acts relates that there were recurrences of the filling with the Spirit,[8] but never is it said that believers were baptized with the Spirit a second time. The pentecostal gift of the baptism of the Spirit is promised to all who will repent and be baptized in water (2:38). Whenever baptism with the Spirit is mentioned after Pentecost, it is never an experience of believers who have already been baptized once with the Spirit but only of new groups of people who are brought to faith in Christ.

When Philip took the gospel to Samaria, we are told that the Samaritans believed and were baptized; but they did not at once receive the Holy Spirit, "but they had only been baptized in the name of the Lord Jesus" (8:12, 16), i.e., they were not at once baptized with the Holy Spirit. Only after Peter and John had come down from Jerusalem and prayed, laying their hands on these new believers, was the gift of the Holy Spirit given.

---

7 "The gift of the Spirit" is not to be confused with the gifts of the Spirit of I Corinthians 12-14. The Spirit is himself the gift; and he bestows various gifts or spiritual faculties upon the church. For a more detailed study of the ecclesiology of Acts, see G. E. Ladd, *The Young Church* (1964).

8 Acts 2:4; 4:8; cf. 9:17 and 13:9.

Now they were not only baptized in the name of the Lord Jesus but also with the Holy Spirit.

The baptism with the Spirit is explicitly mentioned at the conversion of Cornelius and his family. The gift of the Spirit, which was given even as Peter was preaching (10:44f.), is identified as the baptism with the Spirit (11:16); but it did not require the laying on of hands.[9]

These two instances are not a repetition of the pentecostal experience but its extension beyond the circle of Jewish believers, first to the Samaritans and then to the Gentiles. We may say that there is a Jewish Pentecost, a Samaritan Pentecost, and a Gentile Pentecost.[10] A final allusion to the pentecostal experience occurred in Ephesus where Paul found a small group of disciples who had never heard of the pentecostal gift of the Spirit (19:2). They had only been baptized "into John's baptism," i.e., they knew of John's preaching about Jesus as the Messiah and had been baptized into repentance for the remission of sins in anticipation of the coming Kingdom. They had not heard of Jesus' death and resurrection, and of the coming of the Holy Spirit. Perhaps they were converts of Apollos who knew only the baptism of John until he met Priscilla and Aquila (18:25-26). When they were baptized in the name of the Lord Jesus, Paul laid his hands on them, and they too were baptized with the Spirit and spoke in tongues and prophesied (19:6).

This survey of incidents reported by Luke of the coming of the Spirit raises the question: What is the role, if any, of the laying on of hands in the gift of the Holy Spirit? Some Christians pick out the experience at Samaria where the gift of the Spirit was subsequent to faith and resulted only from the imposition of hands and have defended the theology that the baptism of the Spirit is a "second work of grace" after saving faith, by which the believer is empowered either for holy living or effective ministry. It is obvious that there is no single pattern in Acts. The question is: Which is the normative pattern, Samaria or Cornelius? If Samaria is normative, then a strong case can be made for the view that the baptism of the Spirit is an experience subsequent to saving faith.

However, Samaria seems to be the exception. With both the household of Cornelius and Paul, the Spirit was given at the time of believing; and the disciples of John in Ephesus received the Spirit when they were baptized in the name of Jesus. The conversion of the Samaritans was the first movement of the gospel beyond Jerusalem. The first Christians did not at first realize that it was their mission to preach the gospel in all the world. They remained in Jerusalem, and the worldwide mission did not even begin until persecution drove the Hellenists out of the capital city. However, there was cordial dislike between Jews and Samaritans: "Jews have no dealings with Samaritans" (Jn. 4:9). Therefore, "some special evidence may have been necessary to assure these Samaritans, so accus-

[9] See G. W. H. Lampe in *Peake's Commentary,* ed. by M. Black and H. H. Rowley (1962), p. 897.

[10] *Loc. cit.*

tomed to being despised as outsiders by the people of Jerusalem, that they were fully incorporated into the new community of the people of God."[11] And even more than this, Peter and John as leaders of the Jewish church needed the experience that God was moving toward the Gentile world, for they clearly did not yet have this vision. Peter regarded himself as a good Jew and intended to remain a good Jew (Acts 10:14), in spite of the fact that he was a Christian.[12] We may conclude that the normal pattern is that the baptism of the Spirit occurs at the moment of saving faith, which in New Testament times was practically simultaneous with water baptism, incorporating believers into the church.

The theological significance of the baptism with the Spirit is nowhere expounded in Acts, and there is only one statement in the entire New Testament that states its meaning. Although this is found in Paul, the several extensions of Pentecost related in Acts can be understood in the light of this statement, "For by one Spirit we were all baptized into one body—Jews or Greeks, slaves or free—and were all made to drink of one Spirit" (I Cor. 12:13). The baptism with the Spirit is the act of the Holy Spirit joining together into a spiritual unity people of diverse racial extractions and diverse social backgrounds so that they form the body of Christ—the *ekklēsia*. Strictly speaking the *ekklēsia* was born at Pentecost when the Holy Spirit was poured out upon the small circle of Jewish disciples of Jesus, constituting them the nucleus of Christ's body. The disciples before Pentecost should be considered only the embryo church.[13] The *ekklēsia* is not to be viewed simply as a human fellowship, bound together by a common religious belief and experience. It is this, but it is more than this: it is the creation of God through the Holy Spirit. Therefore there is and can be properly only one *ekklēsia*. The fact of the oneness of the *ekklēsia* is the theological meaning of the several extensions of Pentecost in Acts. The Spirit came first to the Jewish believers, then to the Samaritan believers, then to Gentiles, and finally to a little group of disciples of John the Baptist. These four comings of the Spirit mark the four strategic steps in the extension of the *ekklēsia* and teach that there is but one *ekklēsia* into which all converts, whether Jews, Samaritans, Gentiles, or followers of John, are baptized by the same Spirit.

The baptism with the Spirit is not identical with the filling of the Spirit. The former is a once-and-for-all event occurring when one believes in Christ.[14] It is the act of the Spirit constituting individual believers members of the body of Christ. It is therefore impossible to be a believer and not to be in the *ekklēsia*, for when one believes, he is baptized with all other believers into the body of Christ. The baptism with the Spirit can only

---

[11] F. F. Bruce, *The Book of Acts* (1954), p. 182.

[12] Dunn believes the Spirit was not given because the Samaritans had as yet an inadequate faith. See his excellent summary of the entire problem in *Baptism in the Holy Spirit*, pp. 55-68.

[13] See D. O. Via, *SJTh* 11 (1958), 270.

[14] See F. F. Bruce, *The Book of Acts*, p. 56.

happen to individual believers, but it is primarily a social, ecclesiological fact. The filling with the Spirit is primarily an individual experience that can be repeated, and has to do with Christian devotion (Eph. 5:19ff.) and ministry (Acts 4:8; 13:9). The New Testament nowhere commands believers to be baptized with the Spirit as it does to be filled with the Spirit (Eph. 5:19), for the baptism is a fact that occurs at initial faith.

The oneness of the *ekklēsia* is illustrated by the two phenomena on the day of Pentecost. The appearance of something like tongues of fire dividing and resting on each one (2:3) suggests unity and diversity. These firelike tongues are not to be understood as the fulfillment of John's promise that the Messiah will baptize with the Holy Spirit and with fire, for the baptism with fire is the eschatological baptism of judgment, as the context in the Gospels proves. The chaff is to be burned with unquenchable fire (Mt. 3:12). Furthermore, the pentecostal phenomenon was not tongues of fire, but tongues *like* fire, and is no doubt designed to suggest a wonderful theophany, somewhat analogous to Moses' experience at the burning bush.

The phenomenon of glossolalia also suggests the oneness of the *ekklēsia* and its universal scope. This phenomenon at Pentecost differed from its later appearance in the churches, as we know from Paul's discussion of spiritual gifts in I Corinthians 12 and 14. In Corinth, and apparently in usual Christian experience, glossolalia was an ecstatic form of utterance that brought a great sense of spiritual exaltation to the speaker but which was unintelligible to the hearers. It could be made intelligible only if another person present was also gifted by the same Spirit to interpret the unknown tongue into the *lingua franca.* At Pentecost there was no need for an interpreter. Although it is not clear whether the miracle was one of speaking or hearing, it is easiest to conclude that the disciples spoke in unknown tongues and the Holy Spirit translated them into the diverse languages spoken by the hearers. Such a miracle was not necessary merely to provide a means of communication, for Koine Greek would be understood by all, as Peter's sermon shows.[15] The pentecostal tongues have a symbolic significance, and suggest that this new event in redemptive history is designed for the whole world and would unite men of diverse tongues in a new unity of the *ekklēsia.*

THE LIFE OF THE PRIMITIVE CHURCH. The pentecostal experience did not lead the first Christians to break with Judaism and to form a separate and distinct community. On the contrary, this new fellowship appeared outwardly to be nothing but a new Jewish synagogue, which recognized Jesus as the Messiah. They continued the Jewish worship of God in the temple (2:46); and doubtless "the prayers" included the regularly stated Jewish prayers. That the first Christians did not break with Jewish practices is attested by the attitude of the populace (2:47; 5:13).

---

[15] See Acts 22:2, where a similar crowd in Jerusalem expects Paul to address them in Greek and is surprised that he can use the Aramaic dialect.

Such statements could not be made had the disciples of Jesus rejected the Jewish religion and worship in favor of the new Christian way. Their Christian faith was simply added to their old Jewish religion. This is supported by the fact that sometime later Peter claims still to be living as a consistent Jew, observing the legal distinctions about clean and unclean foods (10:14).

However, certain distinctive Christian elements are evident, the first of which is "the apostles' teaching" or *didachē*. This included the meaning of the life, death, and exaltation of Jesus, his enthronement as messianic King and Lord inaugurating the messianic age of blessing, and the future eschatological consummation. As Bruce points out, it is the core of that which later took written shape in the New Testament Scriptures.[16] These redemptive events constituted the *ekklēsia* an eschatological community that was destined to experience the eschatological consummation because it had already experienced the eschatological blessings of the messianic age.

The worship of the primitive church is marked by great simplicity. In addition to worship in the temple are gatherings in Christian homes (2:46; 5:42) for the breaking of bread and taking of food. The wording suggests the same twofold meal observed later in the Pauline churches: a common fellowship meal or *agapē* with which is associated the Lord's Supper (I Cor. 11:20 and 34). Common meals had played a large role in Jesus' ministry (Mt. 9:10-11; 11:19; Lk. 15:1-2; Acts 1:4) and continued to be an important factor in the religious experience of the early church. Private homes provided the meeting places for the distinctive Christian acts of worship. At Pentecost a large number of Jews embraced the Christian faith (2:41; see also 4:4; 5:14), and there is no evidence that so large a group could assemble in a single place. The pattern is rather that of many smaller "house-churches"—separate congregations, analogous to Jewish synagogues.[17] This is also the pattern of the Pauline churches, for we frequently read of the church in somebody's house.[18] We do not know how large the upper room was where the 120 gathered before Pentecost (1:13), and although it is clear that the church had a central meeting place (12:12), it is difficult to imagine a place large enough to contain the entire body of believers.

BAPTISM. The *ekklēsia* welcomed into its fellowship all who accepted the proclamation of Jesus as Messiah, repented, and received water baptism. The practice of water baptism was carried over from the days of Jesus, but given a new significance. John had baptized in anticipation of the coming of the Kingdom, and the Fourth Gospel tells us that Jesus' disciples continued this practice (Jn. 3:22; 4:1-2). Now that Jesus is

---

[16] F. F. Bruce, *The Book of Acts,* p. 79.

[17] Only ten men were required to form such a synagogue. E. Schürer, *A History of the Jewish People* (1890), II, 2, 73.

[18] See Rom. 16:5; I Cor. 16:19; Col. 4:15; Phlm. 2. See also F. V. Filson in *JBL* 58 (1939), 105-12.

recognized as the resurrected and exalted Lord, baptism becomes the outward sign of admission to the Christian fellowship, and believers are baptized "in the name of Jesus Christ" (2:38). No significant interval of time elapsed between believing in Christ and baptism. This is evident from the day of Pentecost (2:41), the baptism of the Samaritans (8:12), the baptism of the Ethiopian eunuch (8:36-37), Cornelius (10:47-48), Saul (9:18), Lydia (16:14-15), etc.[19]

The question of the baptism of infants cannot be settled on the basis of exegetical data in Acts but only on theological grounds.[20] The promise in Acts 2:39 need not mean that children are to be baptized; the promise may mean no more than that the gospel is a blessing not only for the present generation but to their descendants as well—not only to people in Jerusalem but also to those of distant lands—and is analogous to "your sons and daughters" in 2:17.[21] The "children" are limited by the following phrase, "every one whom the Lord our God calls to him." The references to the baptism of households (11:14; 16:15, 31; 18:8) may refer to the "wife, children, servants and relatives living in the house,"[22] but they may equally well designate only those of mature age who confessed their faith in Christ.[23] It is difficult to believe that such passages mean that the faith of the head of the household sufficed for his children any more than it did for his relatives and slaves.

CHRISTIAN FELLOWSHIP. One of the most striking elements in the life of the primitive churches was its sense of fellowship. "They devoted themselves to the apostles' teaching and fellowship" (2:42). The several statements that the early Christians were "together" (2:44, 47) designate the quality of their fellowship as much as their common assemblage. The early Christians were conscious of being bound together because they were together bound to Christ. They were an eschatological people not only because they were called to inherit the eschatological Kingdom but because they had already experienced the blessings of the messianic era. In a sense, their fellowship was a foretaste of the fellowship of the eschatological Kingdom, displayed in history in the midst of Judaism. It was inconceivable that a believer should be such in isolation. To be a believer

---

19 Many scholars have argued that water baptism was the necessary agency for receiving the Spirit. This is refuted by J. D. G. Dunn, *Baptism in the Holy Spirit.*

20 See K. Barth, *The Teaching of the Church Regarding Baptism* (1948); O. Cullmann, *Baptism in the NT* (1951); J. Murray, *Christian Baptism* (1952); P. C. Marcel, *The Biblical Doctrine of Infant Baptism* (1953); W. F. Flemington, *The NT Doctrine of Baptism* (1953), pp. 37-57; J. Schneider, *Baptism and the Church in the NT* (1957); J. Jeremias, *Infant Baptism in the First Four Centuries* (1962); K. Aland, *Did the Early Church Baptize Infants?* (1962); J. Jeremias, *The Origins of Infant Baptism* (1963); G. R. Beasley-Murray, *Baptism in the NT* (1962), pp. 93-126.

21 G. R. Beasley-Murray, *Baptism in the NT,* p. 342. See Acts 13:33.

22 O. Michel, "Oikos," *TDNT* V, 130.

23 G. R. Beasley-Murray, *Baptism in the NT,* pp. 312-20.

meant to share with other believers the life of the coming age, to be a believer in fellowship, to be in the *ekklēsia.*

This sense of fellowship expressed itself in the Jerusalem community in a distinctive way. The community was apparently characterized by many poor people, especially widows, who had no family and therefore no source of support. The sense of sharing the blessings of the messianic age led to an actual sharing of possessions. No man considered his property to be his own, but to be used for the good of all. Therefore, many believers sold their lands and properties and made the proceeds available for the support of the indigent (2:44-45). That this was strictly a voluntary matter is shown by the incident of Ananias and Sapphira. Peter reminds Ananias that he was not obliged to sell his property, and once sold, the property was still his to dispose of as he desired (5:4). The sin in this instance consisted in pretending to give everything when a part of the proceeds was deliberately kept back. Apparently the money thus contributed was used to provide daily rations for the poor, who otherwise would have nothing (6:2). This "Christian communism," as it has often been called, ought not to be considered a social experiment that failed but an expression of the deep bond of Christian fellowship in the primitive community. This same sense of fellowship ought to assume other forms of expression in different historical situations.

THE ORGANIZATION OF THE EKKLĒSIA. In examining the organization of the *ekklēsia,* we must trace the emergence of church leaders beyond the most primitive period. The earliest *ekklēsia* consisted of a free fellowship of Jewish believers who had in no way broken with Judaism, who continued in Jewish religious practices and worship. They believed that Jesus was the Messiah and had inaugurated the messianic era, and they gathered together in homes and (apparently) in the upper room for common meals and the celebration of the Lord's Supper, for praise and worship, and to listen to the apostles' teaching. Their only leaders were the apostles, whose authority was apparently spiritual but not legal. There was no organization and no appointed leaders. The *ekklēsia* was not what it is today: an organized institution. It was a small, open fellowship of Jews within Judaism. Of the twelve, three—Peter, James and John—filled a role of prominence as leaders over the other nine (Acts 1:13).

Aside from the apostles, the first formal leadership was chosen when an internal problem arose within the church. Greek-speaking Jews who had returned to live in Jerusalem from the Diaspora began to complain because the widows of the native Hebrew-speaking Jews seemed to be favored in the daily distribution of food. Apparently the distribution of food had been under the direct superintendence of the apostles, and the task had become so unwieldy that they were laid open to the accusation of partiality (6:1-2). To solve the problem, the twelve called a meeting of the church and had seven men chosen to superintend this ministration. Possibly this is the source of the later office of Deacon. Paul's instructions for qualifications for this position suggest financial responsibility (I Tim. 3:8-13; see Phil. 1:1). One of these "deacons," Stephen, proved to be a man very gifted in the ministry of the Word (6:8ff.); but for the most part, the ministry of teaching and preaching remained the province of the apostles.

Very shortly, a group of elders appear as leaders of the Jerusalem church (11:30). We are not told when or how or why they were chosen; we can only use our historical imagination to reconstruct what probably happened. Both Jewish communities and synagogues were ruled by a group of elders;[24] and since the primitive church externally was little different from a Jewish synagogue, we may assume that when the apostles began to engage in preaching outside of Jerusalem, elders were chosen to take their place and to rule over the Jerusalem church. If so, we must think of a college of elders, not of a single elder over each congregation. At the time of the Jerusalem council, the elders shared with the apostles the role of leadership (15:2, 22; 16:4). When Paul established churches in Asia, he appointed elders in the churches he had founded (14:23). However, both at the election of the seven (6:2) and at the Jerusalem council (15:12, 22), the voice of the entire congregation entered into the decision. It is obvious that there is no uniform pattern of government in Acts. The form of leadership was an historical development in which the apostles, elders, and the congregation shared.

The word "elder" is the translation of *presbyteros,* from which we also derive the word "presbyter." These leaders were called not only elders but bishops (*episkopoi*), a term designating their function of overseeing the church. That these are two designations of the same office is shown by the fact that the elders whom Paul called together at Miletus from Ephesus are also called bishops (20:17, 28).[25] Furthermore, the two terms are used interchangeably in Paul's directions to Titus for administering the church in Crete (Tit. 1:5, 7).

The churches at large were bound together by no ties of organization or appointed officials, but stood under the spiritual authority of the apostles. The apostles were originally appointed by Jesus when he chose twelve to be with him and to share his ministry (Mk. 3:14ff.). The significance of the number 12 rests in the fact they were designed to represent the new Israel, the church. The calling of twelve is a symbolic act, designating them the nucleus of the new Israel Jesus is founding (Mt. 16:18). When Peter confessed faith in Jesus' messiahship and was designated the rock on which the church was to be founded, it was not as a private individual but as the spokesman and representative of the twelve in his apostolic capacity.[26] When Judas defected, the gap thus created was filled by the election of Matthias (Acts 1:15ff.). Thereafter, the circle of apostles was

---

[24] E. Schürer, *A History of the Jewish People,* II, 2, pp. 59ff.

[25] The RSV translates *episkopoi* by the word "guardians," doubtless because the term is considered not yet to be a technical term designating an office.

[26] O. Cullmann, *Peter* (1953), pp. 207ff.

closed so far as human appointment was concerned. However, the Holy Spirit could raise up new apostles, whose apostolic function was recognized by the churches as resting on their charismatic (i.e., Spirit-imparted) gifts and not on human authorization. In addition to the twelve, Barnabas and Paul are recognized as apostles (Acts 14:14), as are James, the Lord's brother (Gal. 1:19), Andronicus and Junias (Rom. 16:7).

The apostles were a circle of men raised up by God to provide the foundation for the church (Eph. 2:20; see also Rev. 21:14) and to be the vehicles of the divine revelation (Eph. 3:5) of the meaning of the person and redemptive work of Christ. Therefore they spoke with an authority that derived from God himself, with which no modern leaders in the church can speak. The apostles were custodians of the teaching of the early church (Acts 2:42), and the New Testament writings may be understood as the end product of the apostolic witness to the meaning of the redemptive event in Christ. Once the church was successfully founded, and the apostolic word of interpretation of the meaning of Christ deposited in written form, no further need existed for the continuation of the apostolic office.

Coupled with apostles were prophets (Eph. 2:20; 3:5), who were men endowed by the Holy Spirit sometimes to prophesy future events (Acts 11:28; 21:10) but more often to speak words of revelation for the edification of the church (I Cor. 14:6, 29-30). The gifts of both apostleship and prophecy were given by the Holy Spirit (I Cor. 14:4, 28; Eph. 4:11), and were not offices to which men could be elected by the church. The authority of both was spiritual and not appointive or official or legal. The apostles exercised an authority in ruling the churches that apparently was not exercised by the prophets. The authority of the latter was largely in the area of teaching.

Although the churches were bound together by no ecclesiastical ties or formal authority, they had a profound sense of oneness. This can be illustrated by the use of the word *ekklēsia* in Acts. The word is often used of local congregations (Acts 11:26; 13:1; 14:23), which apparently met in single houses (8:3). The plural is therefore used to designate all the churches (15:41; 16:5). The singular can also be used to designate all the believers in a given city (5:11; 8:1); and it can even designate the church at large—"So the church throughout all Judea and Galilee and Samaria had peace and was built up" (9:31). The only attribute used of the church in Acts appears in the expression, "the church of God" (20:28), and here it is used of the Ephesian church as the representative of the total church.

These uses of *ekklēsia* suggest that *the* church is not merely the total number of all local churches or the totality of all believers; rather, the local congregation is the church in local expression. The church in Ephesus is *the* church of God, not merely a part of the church of God. This is a reflection of the fact that all churches felt they belonged to one another because they jointly belonged to Christ. There could be but one church; and this one church of God expressed itself locally in the fellowship of believers. However, this unity was not something formally imposed or outwardly sustained; it was a reflection in concrete experience of the true nature of the one church.

THE CHURCH AND ISRAEL. Acts outlines the steps by which the church gradually broke with the synagogue and became an independent movement. In fact, one of the central motifs in Acts is the explanation of how a small fellowship of Jews in Jerusalem, to all intents and purposes hardly distinguishable from their Jewish milieu, became a Gentile fellowship in the capital city of the empire, completely freed from all Jewish practices.[27]

The first evidence of a breach with Judaism occurs as a result of the ministry of Stephen. The seven who were chosen to superintend the distribution of food all have Greek names; and we may surmise that they are therefore Greek-speaking Jews who were reared in the Diaspora and who had somewhat more liberal leanings than Palestinian Jews. In any case, Stephen was accused of speaking against the temple and the Law of Moses (Acts 6:13), which apparently means that Jews who became Christians need no longer observe temple worship or keep the Old Testament Law. In his defense Stephen does not try to prove the falsity of these charges. His sermon is a record of God's dealings with Israel outside the land and without a temple. He concludes by insisting that God is not limited to the temple (7:47), and by charging that the possession of the temple did not assure the Jews of correct religion (7:51-53). We may infer that Stephen was the first to realize indeed that temple worship and observance of the Law were no longer necessary for Jewish Christians.

The next step was taken when Peter, in response to divine leading that transcended his Jewish convictions, joined in Christian table fellowship with Gentiles in Caesarea. When Peter returned to Jerusalem, he was accused not simply of taking the gospel to Gentiles, but of eating with them (Acts 11:2), i.e., of violating the Jewish Law. The "circumcision party" who brought these charges were Jewish Christians who refused to recognize any divergence between Judaism and Christianity. For them Christianity was the fulfillment of Judaism, not its successor. At this point Peter successfully defended his break with Jewish practices by relating God's obvious acceptance of the Gentiles.

The problem came to a new head after Paul's first missionary journey when he successfully established churches in the Gentile world that were completely free from Jewish legal observances. Christian brethren came down from Jerusalem to Antioch, the new center of the Gentile Christian movement, and insisted that all Christians must embrace the Law of Moses, i.e., become Jews, to be saved (15:1-2). This led to a council in Jerusalem to decide the role of the Jewish Law in the Christian community. The conservative party, insisting on the permanence of the Law, was led by

[27] See A. C. Winn, "Elusive Mystery," *Int* 13 (1959), 144-56.

converts from the Pharisees (15:5), while Paul represented the liberal party, which held that the Law was not binding on Gentile Christians. The conference was brought to a decision by the speech of James, the brother of Jesus, who had become the spiritual head of the Jerusalem church. He recalled Peter's experience at Caesarea when the Gentiles were obviously brought into the family of faith. Then he said, "With this the words of the prophets agree, as it is written, 'After this I will return and will rebuild the dwelling of David . . . that the rest of men may seek the Lord, and all the Gentiles who are called by my name'" (15:15-17). James cites the prophecy of Amos 9:11-12 to prove that Peter's experience with Cornelius was a fulfillment of God's purpose to visit the Gentiles and take out of them a people for his name. It therefore follows that the "rebuilding of the dwelling of David," which had resulted in the Gentile mission, must refer to the exaltation and enthronement of Christ upon the (heavenly) throne of David and the establishment of the church as the true people of God, the new Israel. Since God had brought Gentiles to faith without the Law, there was no need to insist that the Gentiles become Jews to be saved. Therefore the council decided that the Gentiles need not carry the burden of the Law. They were requested, however, in the interests of Christian charity, to abstain from certain practices that were particularly odious to the Jews, who were to be found in every important city in the Mediterranean world (15:21), namely, from eating food that had idolatrous associations, from meat of strangled animals from which the blood had not been properly drained, from mixing blood with their drink, and from immorality.[28] This council apparently freed the Gentiles from obligation to keep the Law and in effect set aside Jewish practices in all Christian congregations where there were Gentiles, although Jewish Christians might continue to observe the Law as Jews.[29]

The narrative of the first fifteen chapters of Acts shows how a Gentile church arose, free from the Law. The last thirteen chapters tell how a final breach developed between the church and the synagogue. Wherever Paul went with the gospel, he first preached in Jewish synagogues. Almost invariably he was opposed by the Jewish leaders and by the majority of the synagogue, but found a warm reception primarily among the Gentiles who worshipped in the synagogues. This motif illustrates Jewish rejection of the gospel and Gentile acceptance. After three successful missionary journeys, on which Paul repeatedly met Jewish opposition and Gentile

---

[28] The last requirement may seem strange, but we must remember that five miles from Antioch was Daphne, which contained a temple sacred to Apollo and Diana where sacred prostitution was practiced as an element of religious worship. Gentile converts coming from such a background needed special emphasis upon basic morality.

[29] Paul circumcised Timothy because he was half Jewish (Acts 16:3), and continued to observe certain Jewish practices on particular occasions (Acts 18:18; 21:26). However, he did this as a Jew, not as a Christian. For him the Law was now a matter of indifference, a thing of the world (Gal. 6:14-15) to which he had been crucified.

favor, including the protection of the Gentile rulers in the face of Jewish hostility, Paul paid a final visit to Jerusalem. There must be some unexplained reason for Luke to devote five and a half chapters to the story of this final visit. No new churches were established, no theological or ecclesiastical problems solved. No positive gains come from this visit. The purpose in this long recital is to illustrate in detail how Judaism rejected the gospel. On Paul's three missions in Asia and Europe, the Jews had rejected his message but the Gentiles had received it. This experience in local cities is now repeated in Paul's experience in the capital cities of Judaism and of the Gentile world. Jerusalem would have killed Paul had not the representatives of Rome protected him. Both the populace at large and the Sanhedrin in particular rejected Paul and his message. The Holy City and official Jewry had no room for the Christian faith. The Jews thus disqualified themselves as the true people of God.

This Jewish rejection is both confirmed and contrasted by Paul's reception in Rome. He first called together the Jewish leaders and presented the claims of the Kingdom of God, only to be rejected. Then he turned to the Gentiles; and Acts closes with the sober announcement of God's judgment on Israel and the assertion: "Be it known therefore unto you that the salvation of God is sent unto the Gentiles, and that they will hear it" (28:28). Thus the church, which began as a Jewish sect in Jerusalem, became a Gentile fellowship in Rome, completely freed from Jewish associations.

PART 4

PAUL

27

PAUL: INTRODUCTION

Literature: Surveys of Interpretation:

A. Schweitzer, *Paul and His Interpreters* (1912); A. M. Hunter, *Interpreting the NT 1900-1950* (1951), pp. 61-77; E. E. Ellis, *Paul and His Recent Interpreters* (1961); R. H. Fuller, *The NT in Current Study* (1968), pp. 54-69.

Literature: Theology of Paul:

G. B. Stevens, *The Pauline Theology* (1892); A. B. Bruce, *St. Paul's Conception of Christianity* (1896); H. A. A. Kennedy, *St. Paul and the Mystery Religions* (1913); C. H. Dodd, *The Meaning of Paul for Today* (1920); J. G. Machen, *The Origin of Paul's Religion* (1921); W. L. Knox, *St. Paul and the Church of Jerusalem* (1952); C. A. A. Scott, *Christianity According to St. Paul* (1927); A. Schweitzer, *The Mysticism of Paul the Apostle* (1931); J. S. Stewart, *A Man in Christ* (1935); J. Weiss, *The History of Primitive Christianity* (1937; Harper Torchbooks 1959), Book III; W. L. Knox, *St. Paul and the Church of the Gentiles* (1939); A. M. Hunter, *Paul and His Predecessors* (1940; rev. ed. 1961); J. Klausner, *From Jesus to Paul* (1944); W. D. Davies, *Paul and Rabbinic Judaism* (1948; 2nd ed. 1955); F. Prat, *The Theology of Saint Paul* (1952, 2 vols., Catholic); M. Dibelius and W. G. Kümmel, *Paul* (1953); A. M. Hunter, *Interpreting Paul's Gospel* (1954); O. Moe, *The Apostle Paul, His Message and Doctrine* (1954); H. N. Ridderbos, *Paul and Jesus* (1958); J. Munck, *Paul and the Salvation of Mankind* (1959); W. Baird, *Paul's Message and Mission* (1960); A. Wikenhauser, *Pauline Mysticism* (1960); H. J. Schoeps, *Paul* (1961); F. F. Bruce, "The Epistles of Paul," *Peake's Commentary on the Bible*, ed. by M. Black and H. H. Rowley (1962), pp. 927-39; A. C. Purdy, "Paul the Apostle," *IDB* K-Q (1962), 690-704; R. N. Longenecker, *Paul, Apostle of Liberty* (1964); D. E. H. Whiteley, *The Theology of St. Paul* (1964); M. Bouttier, *Christianity According to Paul* (1966); G. Wagner, *Pauline Baptism and the Pagan Mysteries* (1967); J. A. Fitzmyer, "Pauline Theology," *The Jerome Biblical Commentary* (1968), pp. 800-27; G. Bornkamm, *Early Christian Experience* (1969); P. Minear, *The Obedience of Faith* (1970); G. Bornkamm, *Paul* (1971), pp. 109-240; E. Käsemann, *Perspectives on Paul* (1971); J. G. Gibbs, *Creation and Redemption* (1971).

The greatest mind in the New Testament to interpret the meaning of the person and work of Jesus is the converted Pharisee, Paul. The historian is concerned to analyze the influences that molded Paul's thought in its historical context if he is to understand the mind of Paul. This historical task is unusually difficult because Paul was a man of three worlds: Jewish, Hellenistic, and Christian. Although born in the Hellenistic city of Tarsus of Cilicia, he was reared in a Jewish home according to strict Jewish customs (Phil. 3:5) and was proud of his Jewish heritage (Rom. 9:3; 11:1). He claims to have lived as a Pharisee in faultless obedience to the Law (Phil. 3:6; II Cor. 11:22), and to have been outstanding beyond many of his contemporaries in zeal for the oral traditions of the pharisaic circles (Gal. 1:14).

Paul's own words support his reported words in Acts, when, speaking to the Jews in Jerusalem, he claims to have been "brought up in this city at the feet of Gamaliel, educated according to the strict manner of the law of our fathers" (Acts 22:3). The verb *anatethrammenos* may well mean "reared from infancy," and may express the claim that while he was born in Tarsus, his family moved to Jerusalem while he was still a child, and his entire schooling was in Jerusalem.[1] At the least, the verse claims that Paul was trained in Jerusalem in the school of the famous rabbi, Gamaliel. It is not clear that he was ordained as a rabbi, but there are many indications in his letters that Paul thinks and argues like a Jewish rabbi.[2]

Paul was also at home in the Greek world, and found his mission in extending the church throughout the Graeco-Roman world, and in interpreting the gospel in a form that was compatible with Hellenistic culture. If he spent his boyhood in Tarsus, he would have become familiar with wandering cynic-stoic popular philosophers who could be heard on the street corners of Tarsus. Whether or not he was personally acquainted with the mystery religions, he would have handled the coins that represented the burning of the god Sandan and thus would be familiar with the widespread ideas of a dying and rising god.[3] There is no evidence that Paul had any real acquaintance with Greek philosophy and literature, and it is highly unlikely that strict Pharisees would have sent their son to study in a pagan school. However, Paul was adept in the Greek tongue, and his literary metaphors reflect the city life rather than a rural background.[4] There are, indeed, elements in Paul's thought that can have come only from his Greek environment. His style is often similar to that of the stoic

---

[1] W. C. van Unnik, *Tarsus or Jerusalem?* (1962). Van Unnik thinks that Paul acquired his knowledge of Greek thought and religion in his adult years. However, does the fact that Paul went to Tarsus after his conversion (Acts 9:30; 11:25) suggest that Paul was at home in that city?

[2] E. E. Ellis, *Paul's Use of the OT* (1957), pp. 39ff.; J. Bonsirven, *Exégèse Rabbinique et Exégèse Paulinienne* (1939).

[3] See L. Goppelt, *The Apostolic and Post-Apostolic Times* (1970), p. 71; W. M. Ramsay, *The Cities of St. Paul* (1948), p. 149.

[4] For Paul's skill in Greek, see J. Weiss, *Primitive Christianity* (1937), I, 399ff. For city background, see T. R. Glover, *Paul of Tarsus* (1925), pp. 8ff.

diatribe; and he used such words as conscience (*syneidēsis,* Rom. 2:15), nature (*physis,* Rom. 2:14), the unfitting (*mē kathēkonta,* Rom. 1:28), content (*autarkēs,* Phil. 4:11), which belong distinctly to the Greek world of thought. However, the use of Greek terms does not imply the borrowing of Greek religious ideas. Such words as mystery (*mystērion*) and perfect (*teleios*) belong to the world of the mystery religions; but Paul uses them in a decidedly different way.[5]

It is difficult to assess to what extent Paul's diverse background influenced his thought. Certainly, his conversion did not empty his mind of all his previous religious ideas and replace them with a complete, ready-made theology. His insistence that he had been set apart before he was born to serve God (Gal. 1:15) must include the truth that his experiences as a child and young man were preparing him to fulfill his divinely ordained task. Therefore, we must interpret Paul's ideas against a very diverse background if we are to understand the historical influences that molded Paul to be the first Christian theologian.

While we believe that Paul's conversion can be explained in no other way than by an actual confrontation with the risen Jesus,[6] it does not necessarily follow that Paul received his whole theology at Damascus,[7] nor that we can limit the origins of Paul's thought to the Old Testament and the teaching of Jesus.[8] Rather, it seems that Paul was prepared as a Jewish theologian to think through, under the guidance of the Holy Spirit, the implications of the fact that the crucified Jesus of Nazareth was indeed the Messiah, the resurrected and ascended Son of God. This led him to many conclusions radically different from those he had held as a Jew, among the most notable of which is his new—and quite un-Jewish—interpretation of the role of the Law.[9]

Paul's rabbinic background has been richly exploited by W. D. Davies, who expounds in great detail[10] similarities between Paul and rabbinic thought. However, in view of the fact that the rabbinic literature is considerably later than Paul, and that we have Paul's thought only as a Christian, firm conclusions in details are difficult even though the overall impression may be sound.

---

5 See H. A. A. Kennedy, *St. Paul and the Mystery Religions* (1913), pp. 123-35. Philo borrows the language of the mystery religions in the interests of his Jewish faith but speaks scornfully of the mysteries themselves as a refuge for thieves and prostitutes and forbids the followers of Moses from joining them. See H. A. Wolfson, *Philo* (1948), I, 37-40.

6 See below, p. 367.

7 See J. Bonsirven, *Theology of the NT* (1963), pp. 211f.

8 See F. Prat, *The Theology of St. Paul* (1927), II, 43.

9 See below, Ch. 35.

10 *Paul and Rabbinic Judaism* (1955²). See also C. A. A. Scott, *Christianity According to St. Paul* (1927), "They [Hellenistic influences] belong to the surface rather than to the core of his thought and teaching" (p. 10); H. St. J. Thackeray, *The Relation of St. Paul to Contemporary Jewish Thought* (1900); D. E. H. Whiteley, *The Theology of St. Paul* (1964).

Other scholars have rejected Paul's alleged rabbinic background, largely because his "pessimistic" view of the Law is quite unrabbinic. They have sought to explain his ideas against a diaspora rather than Palestinian Jewish background,[11] under the assumption that diaspora Judaism held a more legalistic attitude toward the Law, a more pessimistic evaluation of human nature, a more gloomy view of the world; and that the man reflected in Paul's letters could not have been a Palestinian rabbi.

Another extreme interpretation separates Jewish apocalypticism from other religious movements in Palestine and sees Paul not as a Pharisee but as a thoroughgoing apocalyptist.[12] While Schweitzer has made it impossible to ignore the importance of eschatology, his interpretation suffers from an unsound analysis of the nature of first-century Judaism. We now know that we can no longer isolate distinct types of Jewish thought, such as rabbinic (pharisaic), apocalyptic, and diaspora Judaism. While different emphases are to be found (Philo and the Mishnah clearly represent different worlds of thought), recent scholarship has recognized that apocalyptic and pharisaic circles shared similar attitudes toward the Law and toward eschatology,[13] and that Palestinian Judaism had been deeply influenced by Hellenistic thought and culture.[14]

A generation ago, the "comparative religions" school in Germany interpreted Paul against the background of the Hellenistic mystery religions, arguing that Paul changed primitive Jewish Christianity into a full-blown mystery cult with a dying and rising god and thoroughly sacramental rites of baptism and the sacred meal.[15] Others thought that Christianity became Hellenized when it was established on Gentile soil so that Jesus was no longer regarded as the Jewish Messiah but interpreted in terms of the Gentile cultic Lord (*Kyrios*).[16] Although Deissmann recognized Paul's Jewish heritage, he interpreted the heart of his Christian faith in terms of Hellenistic mysticism in which the glorified Christ was understood to be a light ethereal substance that, like air, could infill the believer and in which the believer had his existence.[17]

Still others interpreted Paul in terms of the Hellenistic dualism of flesh versus spirit,[18] or recognized the influence of an alleged pre-Christian

---

[11] See C. G. Montefiore, *Judaism and St. Paul* (1914); J. Klausner, *From Jesus to Paul* (1944); S. Sandmel, *A Jewish Understanding of the NT* (1956), pp. 37-51; H. J. Schoeps, *Paul* (1961).

[12] A. Schweitzer, *The Mysticism of Paul the Apostle* (1931).

[13] W. D. Davies, "Apocalyptic and Pharisaism" in *Christian Origins and Judaism* (1962), pp. 19-30.

[14] W. D. Davies, *Paul,* pp. 1-16. W. L. Knox thinks that Paul could have acquired all the Greek he knew in Jerusalem at the feet of Gamaliel. See *Some Hellenistic Elements in Primitive Christianity* (1944), p. 31.

[15] R. Reitzenstein, *Die Hellenistischen Mysterienreligionen* (1910).

[16] See W. Bousset, *Kyrios Christos* (1921, 1970). This view is perpetuated by R. Bultmann (*Theology,* I, 121-32).

[17] A. Deissmann, *Paul* (1926), pp. 137-49.

[18] O. Pfleiderer, *Paulinism* (1877).

oriental gnostic movement with its concept of the heavenly origin of the soul-self and redemption through a pre-existent divine man.[19] However, no pre-Christian documents have yet been found that contain the expectation of a descending heavenly redeemer, and it is probable that the gnostic redeemer is a "radical interpretation of the Christian Jesus in terms of current [gnostic] belief."[20] Furthermore, the literature of the Qumran community has disclosed in Palestinian Judaism a sect that combined a strict Jewish attitude toward the Law with a type of "proto-gnostic" thought with a distinct ethical dualism and a strong emphasis upon "knowledge" in salvation.[21] One of the most pressing questions in contemporary biblical interpretation is that of the nature of pre-Christian Judaism and the history of the gnostic movement as background for understanding the New Testament.[22]

In view of the fact that Paul himself claims to have had a rabbinic theological education before he became a Christian, the correct approach would appear to be to accept this claim at face value and to interpret Pauline thought against a Jewish background, but to keep in mind at the crucial points the possibility of Hellenistic or gnostic influences.

PAUL AS A JEW. This assumption of a Jewish background is borne out by Paul's underlying theological assumptions. He was an uncompromising monotheist (Gal. 3:20; Rom. 3:30) and sternly rejected pagan religion (Col. 2:8), worship (I Cor. 10:14, 21), and immorality (Rom. 1:26ff.). He regards the Old Testament as the Holy Scripture (Rom. 1:2; 4:3), the inspired Word of God (II Tim. 3:16).[23] Paul's method of interpreting the Old Testament places him in the tradition of rabbinic Judaism.[24]

As a Jewish rabbi, Paul unquestionably shared the Jewish belief in the centrality of the Law. Even as a Christian, he asserts that the Law is spiritual (Rom. 7:14), holy and just and good (Rom. 7:12); and he never questions the divine origin and authority of the Law. The Law to a Pharisee meant both the written Law of Moses and the oral "traditions

19 R. Bultmann, *Theology,* I, 164-83.

20 R. McL. Wilson, *The Gnostic Problem* (1958), p. 225.

21 For literature see W. D. Davies, "Paul and Judaism" in *The Bible in Modern Scholarship,* ed. by J. P. Hyatt (1965), p. 181.

22 See the three essays on gnosticism by G. Quispel, R. McL. Wilson, and H. Jonas in *ibid.,* pp. 252-93. For surveys on the interpretation of Paul, see J. Munck, "Pauline Research Since Schweitzer," *ibid.,* pp. 166-77; A. Schweitzer, *Paul and His Interpreters* (1912); R. Bultmann, "Neueste Paulusforschung," *ThR* 6 (1934), pp. 229-46; 8 (1936), 1-22; A. M. Hunter, "St. Paul in the Twentieth Century" in *Interpreting the NT 1900-1950* (1951), pp. 61-77; R. H. Fuller, *The NT in Current Study* (1962), pp. 54-69; E. E. Ellis, *Paul and His Recent Interpreters* (1961); W. D. Stacey, *The Pauline View of Man* (1956), pp. 40-55; D. W. Riddle, "Reassessing the Religious Importance of Paul" in *The Study of the Bible Today and Tomorrow,* ed. by H. R. Willoughby (1947), pp. 314-28; R. Schnackenburg, *NT Theology* (1963), pp. 71-89; B. Rigaux, *The Letters of St. Paul* (n.d.), pp. 3-39.

23 See E. E. Ellis, *Paul's Use of the OT,* pp. 20ff.

24 *Ibid.,* pp. 39ff.

of the fathers" (Gal. 1:14). Judaism had lost the sense of God's self-revelation in historical events and his speaking through the living voice of prophecy. The Jewish doctrine of revelation centered all knowledge of God and his will in the Law. The Holy Spirit had departed from Israel with the last of the prophets,[25] but no further word from God was needed; everything was contained in the Law. Jewish theory traced the oral tradition back to Moses as well as the written Law.[26] In the Torah, revelation was final and complete. Progressive revelation was unnecessary and impossible.[27] God was no longer acting in historical events; one mighty act of God remained in the future when God would manifest his kingly power to destroy his enemies, redeem Israel, and establish his reign effectively in all the world.

We can clearly determine from Paul's writings as a Christian that Saul the Jew shared the Jewish hope of the coming of the Messiah in one form or another to destroy his enemies, redeem Israel, and establish the Kingdom of God; for this hope, which comes from the Old Testament prophets, remains the basic structure of Paul's thought as a Christian. Paul's letters reflect the idiom that was emerging in both apocalyptic and rabbinic literature of the two ages: *olam hazzeh* and *olam habbah*.[28] The complete idiom is found only in Ephesians 1:21, where the two successive ages designate the sweep of the endless future. However, Paul frequently speaks of "this age" as the time of evil and death. The wisdom of this age is incapable of bringing men to God (I Cor. 2:6; 1:20) and must be abandoned as a way of salvation (I Cor. 3:18). The men who occupy places of power in this age are as blind to the truth of God as the wise men; in their spiritual blindness they crucified the Lord of glory (I Cor. 2:8).[29] The "age of this world" (Eph. 2:2), i.e., the age identified with the world in its fallen condition, is characterized by a life of self-gratification rather than obedience to the will of God—a state Paul describes as deadness in trespasses and sins. This age, in its rebellion against the living God and its blindness to God's redeeming work in Christ, is described as subservient to Satan, "the god of this age" (II Cor. 4:4).

This age will come to its end with the Day of the Lord (I Thess. 5:2; II Thess. 2:2), which for Paul is also the Day of the Lord Jesus Christ (I Cor. 1:8; II Cor. 1:14; Phil. 1:6), when the parousia or coming of Christ will take place (I Thess. 2:19; II Thess. 2:1; I Cor. 15:23) to end "this present evil age" (Gal. 1:4). Apart from Ephesians 1:21, Paul does not speak of the future era as "the Age to Come," but he does frequently speak of the eschatological Kingdom of God (I Cor. 6:9; 15:50; Gal. 5:21;

---

[25] See G. F. Moore, *Judaism,* I, 237.

[26] *Ibid.,* p. 254.

[27] *Ibid.,* pp. 239, 276.

[28] We have seen that this was the basic pattern of Jesus' teaching. See p. 68.

[29] We are unable to follow many exegetes in interpreting *hoi archontes tou aiōnos toutou* as angelic powers standing behind earthly political powers, who really put Jesus to death. See pp. 435f.

Eph. 5:5; I Thess. 2:12; II Tim. 4:1, 18). What this means for Paul is expressed clearly in I Corinthians 15:23-26. It means the complete destruction of every power hostile to the will of God, the last of which is death. Christ must "reign as king" (*basileuein,* v. 25) until this redemptive goal is achieved. In this basic eschatological structure of the two ages divided by the Day of the Lord, when God will deliver his fallen creation from all the ravages of evil and sin (Rom. 8:21), Paul agrees with the Old Testament perspective as developed in apocalyptic Judaism, and found also in the Gospels.

As a Jewish rabbi, zealous for the Law, Saul was equally zealous to root out this new religious movement which exalted the memory of Jesus of Nazareth. The book of Acts places Paul in Jerusalem in some way participating in the death of Stephen (Acts 8:1); and Paul's own words assert that he was driven by a zealous purpose to crush the movement represented by Stephen (Gal. 1:13; I Cor. 15:9; Phil. 3:6). This persecuting zeal cannot be separated from his zeal for the Law. The latter was the ground of the former. For the Pharisees, the Law was everything. The ministry of Jesus had been a challenge of everything the Pharisees stood for. He had broken the Law, associated freely with men who did not observe the scribal elaboration of the Law, and claimed divine authority for challenging the foundation of Jewish religion. This new fellowship of Jesus' disciples was made up of men, like Jesus himself, untaught in the scribal traditions, who ignored the pharisaic definition of righteousness (Acts 4:13). Stephen's "defense" was in effect a repudiation of the Law, for it argued that the Law had never produced a people yielded and obedient to God (Acts 7:35ff.). These men claimed that Jesus was indeed the Messiah and they were the people of the Messiah. Both of these claims must obviously, on Jewish premises, be false.

Execution by the hated enemies of God's people was an outright contradiction of messiahship. The Messiah will "have the heathen nations to serve him under his yoke; . . . and he shall purge Jerusalem, making it holy as of old" (Ps. Sol. 17:32). "And he shall gather together a holy people, whom he shall lead in righteousness" (Ps. Sol. 17:28). "Them that walk in the righteousness of His commandments, in the law which He commanded us that we might live. The pious of the Lord shall live by it forever" (Ps. Sol. 14:1-2). Therefore, neither could Jesus be the Messiah, nor could his disciples be the people of the Messiah. If their claim was valid, the whole foundation of Judaism as a religion of the Law was invalid.[30] Thus the very existence of the church with its claim to be the people of the Messiah was a threat to Judaism. Saul the rabbi was certain that he was doing the will of God and standing firmly on the Word of God in trying to crush this new movement.

PAUL THE CHRISTIAN. Something happened to bring about a complete transformation in Paul's outlook. In trying to understand what this in-

30 See M. Dibelius and W. G. Kümmel, *Paul* (1953), p. 51.

volved, we will analyze the three most distinctive facts about his apostolic mission: he proclaimed the Christ whom he had previously persecuted; he was convinced that it was his distinctive mission to take the gospel to the Gentiles; and he preached justification by faith entirely apart from and in contrast to the works of the Law.

So far as we can determine from all of the data, this complete reversal of opinion did not occur as a gradual transformation as a result of study, reflection, debate, and argumentation, but occurred almost instantaneously in the Damascus Road experience. Paul's "conversion" has presented a problem for historical study, which attempts to explain such experience in terms of familiar human experience. The three accounts in Acts (9:1-9; 22:6-16; 26:12-18) disagree in details but agree that Saul saw a brilliant light in the sky, that he fell to the ground, that he heard a voice that identified itself as Jesus, that he was left blind.[31] Sometimes this experience has been explained in terms of an epileptic seizure,[32] more often in terms of the breakthrough of an intense inner conflict that Saul experienced as a Jew. Romans 7 has been interpreted by these scholars as describing Saul's inner turmoil under the Law. Outwardly he was the proud, irreproachable champion of the Law, but inwardly he was plunged in darkness and confusion. The conduct of Stephen in martyrdom further unsettled him, and down in his heart, whether in his consciousness or in his "subliminal self" (Goguel), he knew that the Christians were right. This inner conflict came to a head on the Damascus Road in a visionary experience that Paul attributed to the Lord, but which we, today, can understand in terms of religious psychology.[33] However, the psychological interpretation is refuted by Paul's own testimony that his devotion to the Law was a source of pride and boasting (Phil. 3:4, 7; Rom. 2:13, 23), and is reconstructed not so much on the basis of textual evidence as of supposed psychological necessity. Paul's own testimony paints no background of distress, despair, or wavering in his Jewish convictions. His conversion was an abrupt reversal of his previous attitude toward Jesus, his disciples, and the Law; and many scholars have abandoned the psychologizing explanation and have accepted the Pauline witness even if they cannot explain it.[34]

When one raises the question, What really happened? he must either be-

---

[31] The blindness is not mentioned in the third account.

[32] J. Klausner, *From Jesus to Paul,* pp. 326-30.

[33] For the psychological interpretation, see A. Deissmann, *Paul* (1926), p. 131; M. Goguel, *The Birth of Christianity* (1953), pp. 81-86; W. L. Knox, *St. Paul and the Church of Jerusalem* (1925), pp. 60, 98; W. Baird, *Paul's Message and Mission* (1960), pp. 57ff.; D. J. Selby, *Toward the Understanding of Paul* (1962), pp. 162f.

[34] W. G. Kümmel, *Römer 7 und die Bekehrung des Paulus* (1929), pp. 139-60; R. Bultmann, "Paul" in *Existence and Faith,* ed. by S. Ogden (1960), pp. 113-16; A. C. Purdy, "Paul the Apostle," *IDB* III, 684ff.; M. Dibelius and W. G. Kümmel, *Paul,* pp. 46ff.; J. Munck, *Paul and the Salvation of Mankind* (1959), pp. 11-35; H. G. Wood, "The Conversion of St. Paul," *NTS* I (1955), 276-82; H. J. Schoeps, *Paul,* pp. 53-55.

come a theologian or simply confess ignorance. The historian, as an historian, has no categories that allow for the resurrection, ascension, and glorification of Jesus, and the possibility of the appearance of such a glorious heavenly being to men in history. There is, however, no adequate historical, i.e., human explanation, of Saul's Damascus experience. To admit that we cannot trace the psychological background and still to insist that it is a psychic process[35] is to beg the question. An historian can only say, "We must conclude that the Damascus experience has made a disciple of Christ out of the Pharisee and persecutor of the Christians, without knowing anything about any sort of transition."[36] However, the same scholar goes on to say, "For the eye of faith, there is no question but that the sudden transformation of the enemy of the Christians into the apostle of Christ results from a special work of God, and that this work of God was experienced by Paul in serving the Lord. This is all we can say about the conversion of Paul."[37]

The existential interpretation identifies the appearance of Christ with the new understanding of the self. "Paul's conversion was the resolve to surrender his whole previous self-understanding, which was called in question by the Christian message, and to understand his existence anew."[38] Certainly, Damascus meant a new understanding of Paul's existence and of his relationship to God and the world; but this new understanding is not the content of the Damascus experience but its result. The recognition of Jesus as the Son of God preceded the utter reversal of Paul's previous understanding of himself.[39]

Paul himself insists that what happened at Damascus was an appearance to him of the risen, glorified Jesus, which he classifies with the appearance of Jesus during the forty days (I Cor. 15:8). He, like the other apostles, has seen Jesus the Lord (I Cor. 9:1). He has received a revelation of Jesus Christ (Gal. 1:12).[40] While Paul places Jesus' appearance to him on a par with the appearances of the forty days, he notes something abnormal about the appearance to him by the phrase, "as to one untimely born" (*ektrōmati,* I Cor. 15:8). Strictly speaking, the word does not mean a delayed birth but an early birth, and formally contradicts the expression, "last of all." However, the term may be understood generally to designate an abnormal birth, which in this case took place after Jesus had ceased

[35] R. Bultmann, "Paul" in *Existence and Faith,* p. 114. Bultmann is wrong in speaking of the "complete lack of biographical reports"; such references as Gal. 1:13-14; Phil. 3:4-8 provide specific biographical data.

[36] W. G. Kümmel, *Römer 7 . . .*, p. 158.

[37] *Ibid.,* pp. 159f. A Jewish scholar makes the amazing assertion, "We must accept fully the real objectivity of the encounter. . . . The historian of religion is expected to recognize the faith of Paul in the manifested Son of God to be the factual result of his encounter with the crucified and exalted Jesus of Nazareth. Hence he must accept the faith which inspired Paul." H. J. Schoeps, *Paul,* p. 55.

[38] R. Bultmann, "Paul" in *Existence and Faith,* p. 115. See also *Theology,* I, 300-2.

[39] H. G. Wood, in *NTS* I, 281.

[40] Objective genitive.

to appear to the other disciples.[41] It is of further significance that Paul distinguishes between this appearance of the resurrected Christ and his other ecstatic experiences (II Cor. 12). The Damascus experience was the latest and the last appearance of Christ; it is not repeatable, whereas the revelations of II Corinthians were not infrequent experiences. At Damascus he saw the Lord; in his visions he heard "things that cannot be told, which man may not utter" (II Cor. 12:4). Paul's conversion cannot be interpreted as the first true mystical experience of a great mystic.[42] The only real alternates for interpretating Paul's conversion are agnosticism—which is no solution—or the actual appearance of Jesus Christ to his senses on the way to Damascus, which is Paul's own interpretation. Nothing but his certainty of the reality of Jesus' appearance could have convinced him that Jesus was raised from the dead, and was therefore the Messiah and the Son of God. Nothing but the fact itself can, under the circumstances, fairly account for his certainty.[43]

"Conversion" is not the best word to describe Paul's experience, since this term in our idiom carries a load of psychological baggage. Furthermore, Saul was not converted from disbelief to faith, from sinfulness to righteousness, from irreligion to religion, nor even from one religion to another, since he considered Christianity to be the true Judaism. He was converted from one understanding of righteousness to another—from his own righteousness of works to God's righteousness by faith (Rom. 9:30ff.).[44] The appearance of Jesus proved to Paul that the Christian proclamation was correct; that Jesus had been raised from the dead; that he therefore must be the Messiah, and not only Messiah, but also Son of God (Acts 9:20). In all three accounts of Paul's conversion, the exalted Jesus identified himself with the Christians: "I am Jesus, whom you are persecuting" (Acts 9:5). This established that the church, which Saul had been persecuting, was indeed the people of the Messiah. But if a people who did not observe the Law as the Pharisees defined it were the people of the Messiah, then salvation could not be by the Law; it must be the gift of the Messiah. And it followed that if the messianic salvation had been bestowed on Jews apart from the Law, then this salvation must be universal in its scope and be the gift of God to all men. Here is the inner logic that lay behind Paul's call to be the apostle to the Gentiles, which came to him from the risen Jesus.

The realization that Jesus really was the Messiah was revolutionizing to Saul's evaluation of the entire meaning of the Law, for it was his very zeal for the Law that had made him hate the Christians and their alleged Messiah. Jesus had not been condemned by irreligious, immoral men, but by conscientious, devout Jews who believed they were defending God's

---

[41] See J. Schneider, *TDNT* II, 466. For other interpretations, see J. Munck, "Paulus Tanquam Abortivus" in *NT Essays,* ed. by A. J. B. Higgins (1959), pp. 180-93; T. Boman, "Paulus Abortivus," *StTh* 18 (1964), 46-50.

[42] As does W. Prokulski, "The Conversion of Paul," *CBQ* 19 (1957), 453-73.

[43] G. G. Findlay, "Paul the Apostle," *HDB* III, 703.

[44] G. Bornkamm, "Paulus," *RGG*³ V, 170.

Law. It was Judaism at its best that put Jesus on the cross.[45] If Paul's effort to establish righteousness by the Law had itself blinded him to the true righteousness of God in the Messiah (Rom. 10:3), then the Law could not be a way of righteousness. Judaism must be wrong in understanding the Law as the way of righteousness. It was this certainty that brought Paul to the conviction that Christ was the end of the Law as a way of righteousness (Rom. 10:4). Thus all the essentials of Paul's theology—Jesus as the Messiah, the gospel for the Gentiles, justification by faith as against works of the Law—are contained in his Damascus Road experience.

ALL THINGS NEW. The realization that Jesus was the Messiah promised in the Old Testament required a revision of Paul's understanding of redemptive history. He continued to look forward to the Day of the Lord, the appearance of the Messiah in power and glory, to establish his eschatological Kingdom. Paul does not surrender the Jewish scheme of the two ages and the evil character of the present age (Gal. 1:4). Demonic powers still oppose God's people (Eph. 6:12ff.), who are still subject to bodily evil, sickness (Rom. 8:35f.; Phil. 12:26f.), and death (Rom. 8:10). The physical world is still in bondage to decay (Rom. 8:21), and the spirit of the world of human society is opposed to the Spirit of God. The world stands under divine judgment (I Cor. 11:32). Believers still live in the world and make use of the world (I Cor. 7:31), and cannot avoid associating with the men of this world (I Cor. 5:11). Obviously, from the point of view of nature, history and culture, the Kingdom of God remains an eschatological hope.

Yet if Jesus is the Messiah and has brought to his people the messianic salvation, something has changed. The Kingdom of Christ must already be a present reality into which his people have been brought, even if the world cannot see it (Col. 1:13). His Kingdom is present, because Jesus has in some real sense entered upon his messianic reign; and in fact, Paul sees Jesus' messianic reign beginning with his resurrection and exaltation. His reign as King does not begin with his parousia and extend to the *telos;* it began with his resurrection and extends beyond the parousia to the *telos* (I Cor. 15:23-25). Then when he has conquered all his enemies, he will turn over the Kingdom to God.

These new implications of the messiahship of Jesus involve a radical modification of Paul's view of *Heilsgeschichte,* which is a radical departure from Judaism. Within history and the world as it exists in the old age, redemptive events have taken place *whose essential character is eschatological* in the sense that in all previous thought they belonged to the Age to to Come. How can Messiah be installed upon his throne while Caesar rules the world? Yet this is the conviction that Paul shared with the primitive Christian community, whose implications Paul understood better than others had done. Paul saw clearly that the resurrection of Jesus was an eschatological event. The resurrection of the dead remains an event at the

[45] G. B. Caird, *The Apostolic Age* (1955), p. 122.

end of the age when mortality will be exchanged for immortality (I Cor. 15:52ff.). However, the resurrection of Jesus means nothing less than that this *eschatological resurrection has already begun.*

Paul contrasts death, which entered into the world through a man, with the resurrection of the dead, which has entered into the world through a man. The resurrection takes place in different stages: Christ, the first fruits, is the first stage of the resurrection; the second stage will consist of those who belong to Christ at his coming (I Cor. 15:21-23). The important point here is that the resurrection of Christ is the beginning of *the* resurrection as such, and not an isolated event. Jesus' resurrection is in fact the beginning of the eschatological hope. The resurrection of the dead is no longer a single event taking place at one time at the end of the age; the resurrection has been divided into at least two stages, the first of which has already transpired. It is because *the* resurrection has already begun that the man in Christ knows that there is resurrection in the future for him. The first act of the drama of eschatological resurrection has been separated from the rest of the play and has been moved back into the midst of the present evil age.

This interpretation is supported by the word "first fruits." The first fruits constitute the beginning of the harvest itself. While they are not synonymous with the harvest in its totality, the first fruits are more than blossoms and leaves and green fruit; they are the fruit come to full growth, ready for harvest; and because they are the *first* fruits, they are also the promise and the assurance that the full harvest will shortly take place. The resurrection of believers is related to the resurrection of Jesus as the full harvest is related to the first fruits of that harvest. They are identical in kind; the only difference is quantitative and temporal.

In a similar manner Paul describes life in the Spirit as an eschatological reality. The Old Testament viewed the outpouring of the Spirit upon all flesh as an eschatological event that would attend the coming of the Day of the Lord and the messianic judgment and salvation (Joel 2:28-32). For Paul the full experience of the life of the Holy Spirit is a future eschatological event associated with the resurrection when the dead in Christ will be raised with "spiritual bodies" (I Cor. 15:44). A spiritual body is by no means a body made out of spirit, any more than a natural (*psychikos*) body is a body made out of *psychē*. The natural body is one designed for the experience of human life (*psychē*); the spiritual body will be a body so infused with the life-giving Spirit of God that it will be an imperishable, glorious, powerful body. In other words, the complete enjoyment of the life of the Spirit will result in the very transformation of the natural mortal order of bodily existence, so that mortality, weakness, will be swallowed up in the fullness of eternal life. The perfect experience of the Spirit will mean the redemption of the physical body (Rom. 8:23). It is against this background of the eschatological gift of the Holy Spirit that Paul interprets the present impartation of the Spirit. We already have the "first fruits of the Spirit" (Rom. 8:23). Here the indwelling of the Spirit, like the resurrection of Jesus, is the initial enjoyment of the eschatological event whose fullness yet lies in the future.

Paul elsewhere describes this same eschatological enjoyment of the Holy Spirit in terms of an initial payment. God has sealed us with the promised Holy Spirit "which is the down payment of our inheritance until we acquire possession of it" (Eph. 1:14; see also II Cor. 1:22; 5:5). Here the Holy Spirit is spoken of as an *arrabōn,* a word that means a down payment or security given to assure the consummation of a transaction. An *arrabōn* is promise, but it is more than promise; it is also realization. It is deposited money that both promises the full payment in the future and gives a partial payment in the present. Such is the gift of the Spirit in the present age; it is the deposit or down payment, which is at the same time the guarantee of the future eschatological inheritance that will be acquired in the resurrection. Here again the eschatological gift is divided into two portions, the first of which has become present experience, but the fullness of which remains an object of future eschatological realization. The resurrection is both history and eschatology; the life of the Spirit is both experience and hope; the Kingdom of God is both present and future; the blessings of the Age to Come remain in their fullness objects of hope and expectation; yet these very blessings have in part reached back into the present evil age because of the modification of the antithetical structure and have become in Christ the subjects of present Christian experience.

Paul's conversion meant for him the realization that in some real way the eschatological events had begun, but within history—within this present evil age. The Messiah has begun his reign; the resurrection has begun; the eschatological gift of the Spirit has been given; yet the coming of the Messiah, resurrection, and the eschatological salvation remain objects of hope. This conviction required a modification of the two-age structure, at least for believers. Christ gave himself to deliver us from this present evil age (Gal. 1:4). Those who are in Christ, although living in this age, are no longer to be conformed to this age. Their standards and motivations for conduct are different: the transforming power of the indwelling eschatological gift of the Spirit (Rom. 12:1-2). For the believer the "ends of the ages" have arrived (*ta telē tōn aiōnōn,* I Cor. 10:11).

It is possible that this unique expression is used precisely to designate the fact that the two ages—this age and the Age to Come—overlap, that the first part of the Age to Come reaches back into the last part of the old age, so that the period between the resurrection and the parousia is a period "between the times," or better, a period that belongs to two times. *Telē* "designates the ends of the two lines, in one case the end, in the other case, the beginning" of the two ages.[46] This view is very attractive and

[46] J. Weiss, *Der erste Korintherbrief* (1910), p. 254; see for this interpretation W. Bauer, *Griechisch-Deutsches Wörterbuch* (1937³), p. 45; J. Hering, *First Corinthians* (1962), p. 89, "We are at the point of intersection of the two worlds"; C. J. Craig, *IB* X, 111, "That isthmus of time between the ages"; O. Michel, *TDNT* III, 625; J. Marsh, *The Fulness of Time* (1952), p. 32; G. A. F. Knight,

actually corresponds to Paul's thought. However, since the context is concerned with the relationship of Old Testament history to Christians, it is better to understand *telē* in its teleological rather than its temporal sense, especially since *telē* is sometimes merely a formal plural.[47] The phrase designates the time introduced by Christ as the time in which the ages of history have found their fulfillment.[48] However, the nature of this fulfillment consists in the fact that Messiah has come and begun his reign, the resurrection has begun, the eschatological gift of the Spirit has been poured out. The amazing fact is that these eschatological events have occurred before the Day of the Lord, before the dawn of the Age to Come, in the midst of the present evil age. It is correct to say of Paul's thought as a whole, even if not of I Corinthians 10:11, "In a surprising way visible only to faith the end of the old aeon and the dawn of the new has come upon the community."[49]

We may not conclude that Paul interpreted this new age as being equivalent with the Jewish expectation of the Days of the Messiah that sometimes preceded the Age to Come. On the contrary, Jesus had appeared as the Messiah before the expected Days of the Messiah. His dying and rising were utterly unforeseen in the traditional eschatology. Through the resurrection of Jesus, the powers of the supernatural world, the Age to Come, are already at work in the created world. "With the resurrection of Jesus the supernatural world had already begun, though it had not yet been manifest."[50]

Paul's new understanding of redemptive history is summed up in II Corinthians 5:16-17. "From now on, therefore, we regard no one from a human point of view; even though we once regarded Christ from a human point of view, we regard him thus no longer. Therefore, if any one is in Christ, he is a new creation; the old has passed away, behold, the new has come." Because of the messianic work of Christ on his cross (vv. 15, 19), a new kind of existence has been opened up to men: existence "in Christ." This means existence in the realm of a new order. The very concept of newness is eschatological. The biblical perspective sees God's redemptive purpose accomplished in new heavens and a new earth (Isa. 65:17; Rev. 21:1; II Pet. 3:11) with its new Jerusalem (Rev. 3:12; 21:2), new wine

---

Law and Grace (1962), p. 83. Schoeps speaks of "this mingling of the two ages." H. J. Schoeps, *Paul,* p. 99. See also C. K. Barrett, *SJTh* 6 (1953), 147.

47 See Arndt and Gingrich, *A Greek-English Lexicon* (1957), p. 27. In the fourth and fifth German editions of Bauer's *Wörterbuch,* the view expressed in the preceding footnote was withdrawn.

48 See Heb. 9:26: *sunteleia tōn aiōnōn;* also Test. Levi 10:2. The precise phrase *ta telē tōn aiōnōn* occurs in Test. Levi 14:1 in one ms., designating merely the last days of history.

49 O. Michel, *TDNT* III, 625.

50 A. Schweitzer, *The Mysticism of St. Paul,* p. 99. At this point Schweitzer understood Paul, even though he drew unacceptable conclusions from this insight. See also W. D. Davies, *Paul and Rabbinic Judaism,* pp. 285ff.; H. J. Schoeps, *Paul,* pp. 97ff.

for the eschatological banquet (Mk. 14:25), a new name for the redeemed (Rev. 2:17; 3:12), a new song of redemption (Isa. 42:10; Rev. 5:9; 14:3). This redemption can be contained in the single phrase, "Behold, I make all things new" (Rev. 21:5; Isa. 43:19). It is Paul's assertion that in Christ *the new has come*, even though the old age has not yet passed away.[51]

Existence in the new age carries with it a fresh understanding and interpretation of all human experience. Before Paul became a Christian, when he was a Jewish rabbi, he knew all men *kata sarka*. His viewpoint, his values, his interpretation of other men was merely "from a human point of view" (RSV), according to fleshly, worldly standards. This is another way by which Paul describes his life in Judaism, a life according to the flesh.[52] As a zealous Pharisee, Saul was filled with pride because of his zeal for the Law; he boasted in his righteousness; he looked with pity and disgust upon the unclean among the Jews who neglected the Law (the *am haaretz*); he hated the Gentiles for their idolatry and immorality. He even looked at Christ from this same perspective. To know Christ *kata sarka*[53] meant to regard him as a blasphemous messianic claimant who transgressed the Law of God as the Pharisees understood it, and who deserved to be executed. This knowledge *kata sarka* refers to the time when Paul persecuted the church because he saw Jesus only through Jewish eyes.[54] Because of his Damascus Road experience, Paul sees things differently. He now knows that Jesus is the Messiah, the Son of God, who has inaugurated a new age that requires of Paul a new attitude toward all men. He sees them no longer as Jews and Greeks, slaves and free. Such distinctions, while real, no longer matter. They are all men whom God loves, for whom Christ died, to whom he must bring the good news of newness of life in Christ.

THE CENTER OF PAULINE THEOLOGY. Is there any unifying concept from which Paul's theology can be developed? Solutions to this problem have usually centered upon either justification by faith or the mystical experience of being in Christ. Under the influence of the Reformation, many scholars have seen justification by faith to be the central substance of Pauline thought. In recent scholarship a reaction has set in against the centrality of justification. Wrede insisted that the whole of Pauline religion could be expounded without mentioning justification, unless it be in the discussion of the Law.[55] Schweitzer, who rediscovered the importance of eschatology for Paul, felt that justification by faith as a starting point would lead to a misunderstanding of Paul, and that this doctrine

---

51 See J. Behm, *TDNT* III, 449; R. A. Harrisville, *The Concept of Newness in the NT* (1960).

52 See Gal. 6:14, 15, where circumcision belongs to the "world" whose standards are no longer binding because Paul has died with Christ to the world.

53 The phrase obviously modifies the verb "to know," not "Christ."

54 See A. Oepke, "Irrwege in der neueren Paulusforschung," *TLZ* 77 (1952), 454.

55 W. Wrede, *Paul* (1907), p. 123.

was only a side issue. The central concept was the mystical being-in-Christ conceived in quasi-physical terms.[56] Andrews follows Sabatier in describing justification as a "judicial and inferior notion" that renders it difficult to rise to the higher and finer idea of a righteousness that is imparted.[57] Stewart does not downgrade justification as radically as this, but he finds the real clue to understanding Paul's thought and experience in union with Christ rather than in justification.[58] Davies follows Wrede and Schweitzer in viewing justification as only a convenient polemic against the Judaizers that belongs to the periphery of Paul's thought. The central truth is found rather in Paul's awareness of the coming of the powers of the new age, the proof of which was the advent of the Spirit.[59]

The understanding of Paul outlined above agrees with Davies that the center of Pauline thought is the realization of the coming new age of redemption by the work of Christ. A Reformed scholar has pointed out that there is a danger in making justification by faith the central doctrine, namely, the danger of depriving Paul's message of its "redemptive historical dynamic" and making it into a timeless treatment of individual justification.[60] The unifying center is rather the redemptive work of Christ as the center of redemptive history. "The basic motif of the entire New Testament kerygma is that of the fulfillment of the historical redemption which began with Christ's coming."[61] Paul's theology is the exposition of new redemptive facts; the common characteristic of all his theological ideas is their relationship to God's historical act of salvation in Christ.[62] The meaning of Christ is the inauguration of a new age of salvation. In the death and resurrection of Christ, the Old Testament promises of the messianic salvation have been fulfilled, but within the old age. The new has come within the framework of the old; but the new is destined also to transform the old. Therefore Paul's message is one of both realized and futuristic eschatology.

A proper understanding of the new age in Christ offers a solution to the tension between justification and "mysticism," or the new life in Christ, for it includes them both. We shall show later that justification is essentially an eschatological reality; but even as the eschatological gift of the Spirit has been given in history because of the resurrection and glorification of Christ, so has the eschatological judgment in principle taken place in the death of Christ. Both justification—acquittal by the righteous judge—and the gift of the Holy Spirit belong to the Age to Come, but they have become matters of present experience to the man in Christ.

---

[56] A. Schweitzer, *The Mysticism of St. Paul,* p. 220.
[57] E. Andrews, *The Meaning of Christ for Paul* (1949), p. 65.
[58] J. S. Stewart, *A Man in Christ* (1935).
[59] W. D. Davies, *Paul and Rabbinic Judaism,* p. 222.
[60] H. N. Ridderbos, *Paul and Jesus* (1958), p. 63.
[61] *Ibid.,* p. 67. See the entire chapter for an excellent exposition of the *Heilsgechichte* interpretation.
[62] M. Dibelius and W. G. Kümmel, *Paul,* p. 123.

This understanding of Paul sets him in sharp contrast to Judaism. Paul as a Jew felt that revelation was embodied in its totality in the Law. Nothing more in this age was to be expected from God beyond the Law. God was no longer active in self-revelation, in the prophetic word or in historical events. The Law alone was the focus of revelation. Paul's Damascus Road experience made him realize that the message of the early Christians that he had vigorously rejected was true, that God had acted again to reveal himself and his salvation in a historical event—Jesus of Nazareth. In a word, Paul found a new understanding of revelation; or better, he recovered the prophetic understanding of revelation as divine redeeming events interpreted by the prophetic word. "God was in Christ reconciling the world to himself" (II Cor. 5:19). Paul's conversion meant a recovery of the sense of redemptive history that Judaism had lost. His experience of Christ forced him back beyond the Mosaic Law to rediscover the promise given to Abraham and to see its fulfillment in the recent events in the person and work of Jesus.

28

THE SOURCES OF PAUL'S THOUGHT

THE NATURE OF OUR SOURCES. We are fortunate to have a substantial collection of primary sources from Paul's own pen.[1] Nine of the thirteen traditional Pauline letters are usually accepted as authentic today. Many scholars think Ephesians is not from Paul's hand but written by a later disciple of Paul in imitation of Colossians.[2] Arguments against its authenticity are not overwhelming.[3] The problem of the three pastoral epistles is more acute, for the literary style varies widely from the acknowledged Pauline corpus, and the doctrinal emphasis is distinctly different from that in the accepted letters, especially in ecclesiology. However, those who reject direct Pauline authorship usually admit that the letters contain genuine Pauline material. Since there is a difference in theological emphasis, even though we accept the basic Pauline authorship,[4] our procedure will be to use the materials in the pastorals critically. References to this literature will be made when it supports or illustrates Pauline usage; but differences in doctrinal emphasis will be noted.

The student of Paul encounters distinct difficulties when he attempts to re-create his theological thought, for Paul's letters are not theological treatises nor formal literary productions but "unliterary," living, personal correspondence, written with deep feeling to Christian congregations that for the most part Paul himself had brought into being.[5] Some scholars have therefore discounted the importance of the theological element in Paul,

---

[1] This statement is not meant to refute the obvious fact that Paul usually employed an amanuensis or secretary to whom he dictated his letters, often concluding with a few words in his own hand. See Rom. 16:22; I Cor. 16:21; Gal. 6:11; Col. 4:18; II Thess. 2:17.

[2] See C. L. Mitton, *The Epistle to the Ephesians* (1951).

[3] See the introductions by W. G. Kümmel (1966), D. Guthrie (1961), and E. F. Harrison (1964).

[4] See in addition to the introductions in note 3, E. E. Ellis, "The Authorship of the Pastorals" in *Paul and His Recent Interpreters* (1961), pp. 49-57.

[5] For the "unliterary," informal character of the Pauline correspondence, see A. Deissmann, *Paul* (1926), pp. 8ff.; *Light from the Ancient East* (1922), pp. 234ff.

describing him as a religious genius rather than a theologian.[6] While it is obviously true that Paul has not left the church a systematic theology, and he cannot be called a systematic theologian in the sense that he deliberately tried to work out a consistent, balanced, coherent system like a modern theologian, it is equally true that Paul was a theologian from his Jewish origins,[7] and clearly tries to think through the implications of God's redemptive work in Christ so far as the needs of his churches demanded it. We cannot therefore speak of a Pauline theology as an abstract, theoretical, speculative system; but we can recognize a Pauline theology as an interpretation of the meaning of the person and work of Christ in its practical relevance for Christian life, both individual and collective. It is therefore improper to distinguish between Paul's theology and his religion, as though the former were speculative and the latter practical. For Paul, theology and religion are inseparable.[8] Paul was a theological thinker for whom theological "concepts" were facts about God, man, and the world that described the world's estrangement from God and God's deed in Christ to bring the world back to himself.

The fact that Paul's letters are *ad hoc* correspondence, usually called forth by specific situations in the Pauline churches, places certain limitations upon our study of his thought, the chief of which is that we do not have Paul's *complete* thought. Many studies in Paul have worked with the implicit assumption that his letters record all his ideas, and when some important matter was not discussed, they have assumed it was because it had no place in Paul's thought. This is a dangerous procedure; the argument from silence should be employed only with the greatest caution. Paul discusses many subjects only because a particular need in a given church required his instruction. The epistle to the Romans is the one letter that was not written to deal with a particular local need. Paul wrote this letter in anticipation of an expected visit to Rome (Rom. 15:22-33), and it is the nearest thing we have to a balanced statement of his message. However, it is clearly not a complete outline, but only the core of his gospel. Practically nothing is said about the church. Eschatology appears only in casual references. Important allusions occur to the person of Christ (e.g., 1:3-4), but any discussion of Christ similar to that in Philippians 2 is lacking.

This living, historical context of Paul's writings may account for some of the most difficult questions in the contemporary theological discussion. We would never know much about Paul's thought on the resurrection had this truth not been questioned in Corinth. We might conclude that Paul knew no tradition about the Lord's Supper had not abuses occurred in the Corinthian congregation. In other words, we may say that we owe whatever understanding we have of Paul's thought to the "accidents of history,"

6 A. Deissmann, *Paul,* pp. 6f.

7 M. Dibelius and W. G. Kümmel, *Paul* (1953), p. 103.

8 This is the point of J. Stewart's discussion "Paul or Paulinism" in *A Man in Christ* (1935), pp. 1-31.

which required him to deal with various problems, doctrinal and practical, in the life of the churches.

The result is that certain questions never were raised and never called forth Paul's reaction. Paul never discusses what he believes about the fate of the wicked. He has much to say about the destiny of those in Christ who are to share the likeness of Christ's resurrection, but only because the Thessalonians were perplexed about the fate of believers who had died before the return of the Lord (I Thess. 4:13), and because some in Corinth denied the resurrection of the body (I Cor. 15:12). However, the fate of those not in Christ apparently never became an important issue. How much more complete might be our knowledge of Pauline eschatology if, in one of his churches, a group of converts from the synagogue had carried over into their Christian faith the belief, held by some Jews, that a sort of purgatorial, cleansing fire awaited men who had been only moderately wicked,[9] and that some such way of salvation after death might avail for those who had not yet heard and therefore had not flatly rejected the salvation offered in Christ.

One question of vital importance for modern criticism apparently never became a problem in the Pauline churches—namely, the question of the historical career of Jesus. From this relative silence about Jesus, the existentialist theologians have concluded that Paul made little reference to Jesus because he really knew little about him and had no access to the gospel tradition about the life of Jesus.[10] However, the fact that Paul does not draw extensively upon the gospel tradition does not mean that he was unfamiliar with such a tradition, but only that the use of such tradition never became necessary. The facts of Jesus' earthly ministry, his teachings and mighty works, even his character and personality, were not a necessary part of the Pauline message of redemption,[11] and the validity of whatever tradition Paul was familiar with was never called into question. However, we may theorize that if a number of the disciples of the Qumranian Teacher of Righteousness had accepted the gospel but had perpetrated the teaching in Pauline churches that Jesus had spent several of his "silent years" at Qumran, and, as some modern scholars have held, that he was either himself in many ways a reincarnation of the Teacher of Righteousness[12] or was actually to be identified with the Teacher,[13] then we would very likely find in Paul's letters a corrective to such erroneous views and considerable information about the historical life and person of Jesus. But such questions never arose, and Paul is silent. We can only reconstruct Paul's thought from his expressed ideas; silence does not mean ignorance.

---

[9] See G. F. Moore, *Judaism* (1927), II, 318.

[10] R. Bultmann, *Theology,* I, 188.

[11] See below, p. 413, for an explanation of this fact.

[12] A. Dupont-Sommer, *The Jewish Sect of Qumran and the Essenes* (1954), pp. 160ff.

[13] J. L. Teicher, "Jesus and the Habakkuk Scroll," *Journal of Jewish Studies,* 3 (1951), 53-55.

Another problem that faces the modern interpreter is the loss of the historical setting for much that Paul says. In one of his earliest letters, he speaks in very enigmatic terms about the events that will precede the Day of the Lord: a rebellion, a man of lawlessness who sits in the temple of God, an obscure restraining power that is to be removed (II Thess. 2:3ff.). In the midst of this frustrating passage is the comment, "Do you not remember that when I was still with you I told you this?" (v. 5). The modern exegete cannot recover this background of oral teaching, and he can do little more than speculate what Paul's words really mean. Such enigmatic references as baptism for the dead (I Cor. 15:29) and Paul's instructions to "virgins" (I Cor. 7:36ff.) must remain problematical without the historical setting.

PAUL'S ATTITUDE TOWARD HIS OWN MESSAGE. Thus far we have been speaking solely from an historical point of view, evaluating Paul's thought as we must regard the thought of any ancient. This approach is unavoidable because the sources for Paul's thought are thoroughly historical situations and must be studied in context. The "proof-text" method of interpreting Paul's letters, which views them as direct revelations of the supernatural will of God conveying to men eternal, timeless truths that need only to be systematized to produce a complete theology, obviously ignores the means by which God has been pleased to give to men his Word. Admittedly, Paul's letters and thought are history, and they can be studied as nothing more than a segment of ancient religious history. This, however, raises the question, By what right can we speak of Pauline *theology?* Is "theology" only a descriptive discipline of what early Christians believed,[14] or has God been pleased to use Paul as the outstanding individual instrument in the early church to communicate to men authoritative, redemptive truth?

There can be little doubt about how Paul would answer this question, for his letters reflect a sense of authority in the light of which Paul's entire thought must be read. Paul lays claim to an understanding of the mind and will of God that on the purely human level is close to arrogance. In dealing with the question of marriage, he places his own authority on a level with that of the Lord himself (I Cor. 7:10, 12). He admonishes the Corinthians that those among them who consider themselves to be spiritual persons, i.e., those who are led by the Spirit of God, must recognize that what he is writing to them is the very will of God. If anyone does not recognize this fact, Paul pronounces the judgment that he is not to be recognized (I Cor. 14:37f.), probably meaning that such a person is not really known to God.[15] He boasts of his authority (II Cor. 10:8) and sets himself up over against other teachers in Corinth because of his knowledge of the will of

[14] See K. Stendahl, "Method in the Study of Biblical Theology" in *The Bible in Modern Scholarship,* ed. by J. P. Hyatt (1965), pp. 196ff.

[15] See II Tim. 2:19; Mt. 7:23. See J. Weiss, *Der erste Korintherbrief* (1910), p. 343; F. W. Grosheide, *First Corinthians* (1953), pp. 344f.

God (II Cor. 11:6). He calls down a curse on any who preach a gospel not in accordance with his message (Gal. 1:6ff.). He instructs the Thessalonians that any members of the congregation who do not submit to his instructions are to be excluded from fellowship (II Thess. 3:14). He expects his authority to be recognized and submitted to, and his many injunctions obeyed (II Cor. 2:9; 8:8), and he holds the conviction that God will eventually show even those who disagree with him that he is right (Phil. 3:15).

Interpreted solely in terms of human conduct, Paul seems indeed to be "boundlessly severe toward his opponents," speaking with "fanatical coarseness," "showing a classical instance of intolerance."[16] However, this superficial characterization ignores the fact that Paul writes with authority not as a private individual but with the consciousness of having been called by God to a position of apostolic authority. He is conscious that the Word of God has been committed to him and that he has been made a mouthpiece of the exalted Christ. He is aware of the difference between the will of God and his own opinions (I Cor. 7:6, 25; II Cor. 8:10), even though he has the leading of the Holy Spirit in his private opinions (I Cor. 7:40).

PAUL THE APOSTLE. Paul's sense of authority is not a private possession but has been conferred by the Lord upon him as an apostle.[17] Jesus had selected twelve of his disciples to be particularly close to him and sent them out to share the same mission and message in which he was engaged.[18] The use of the word *apostolos* for the twelve in the Gospels (Mk. 6:30 par.) designates their function as those sent by Jesus (Mk. 3:40) and is not yet a title.[19] In the early church, the twelve apostles constituted a college of authoritative leaders in the church. We are unable to reconstruct the exact historical situation, but it seems clear that the circle of the apostles was enlarged to include certain others, such as James the brother of Jesus (Gal. 1:19), Andronicus and Junias (Rom. 16:7), possibly Silvanus (I Thess. 2:6; cf. Acts 17:10), Barnabas and Paul (Acts 14:4, 14). It is also clear that other men who claimed to be apostles attempted to oppose Paul's work in Corinth (II Cor. 11:5, 13; 12:11), but Paul denies their claim to the position.

---

[16] A. Deissmann, *Paul,* p. 67.

[17] For the apostolate in the early church, see J. B. Lightfoot, "The Name and Office of an Apostle," *Galatians* (1865), pp. 92-101; K. H. Rengstorf in *TDNT* I, 407-47; R. N. Flew, *Jesus and His Church* (1943²), pp. 130-38; T. W. Manson, *The Church's Ministry* (1948), pp. 31-52; V. Taylor, "The Twelve and the Apostles," *Mark* (1952), pp. 619-27; H. F. von Campenhausen, "Der urchristliche Apostelbegriff," *StTh* 1 (1947), 96-130; H. Mosbech, "Apostolos in the NT," *StTh* 2 (1948), 166-200; J. Munck, "Paul, the Apostles and the Twelve," *StTh* 3 (1949), 96-110; E. Lohse, "Ursprung und Pragung des Christlichen Apostelates," *TZ* 9 (1953), 259-75.

[18] See K. H. Rengstorf in *TDNT* II, 321-28.

[19] The term is read back by Luke in several places. The word itself means "delegate" or "messenger, missionary" (II Cor. 8:23; Phil. 2:25) and becomes a technical term only in Christian usage.

It is as an apostle that Paul lays claim to a high authority. His experience on the Damascus Road not only brought him to a recognition of Jesus as the resurrected and exalted Messiah; it also contained a call from God to a particular mission. This fact is recorded in the conversion accounts in Acts (9:15-16; 22:15; 26:17-18) and is confirmed by Paul's own words. God had set him apart before his birth to preach the gospel to the Gentiles (Gal. 1:15f.). The consciousness of fulfilling a divinely ordained mission runs throughout his correspondence. He is an apostle to the Gentiles and magnifies his ministry to provoke Jews as well to faith (Rom. 11:13). He has a commission that he did not choose for himself and which lays upon him the inescapable necessity of preaching the gospel (I Cor. 9:16f.).[20] After his first mission in the Gentile world, when his gospel was challenged by the Judaizers, Paul's apostleship to the Gentiles was recognized and approved by the church in Jerusalem, including the other apostles—James, Peter, and John (Gal. 2:7-9).

As an apostle, Paul did not bear an exclusive authority but one that he shared with the other apostles. The unique factor in Paul's apostleship was his distinctive mission to the Gentiles. In his lists of leaders in the churches Paul ranks apostles as first (I Cor. 12:28; Eph. 4:11). The primary qualifications of an apostle were that he be an eyewitness of the resurrection (Acts 1:22; I Cor. 9:1) and receive a distinct call and commission from the risen Lord.[21] An apostle has the primary function of being a delegate of the risen Christ, going as his representative and in his authority. This idea of an authoritative representative derives from the Jewish institution of *sheluchim* or authorized messengers representing a person or a group of persons. "A man's representative (*shaliach*) is to be considered as the man himself."[22] This same concept of authoritative representation appears in Matthew 10:40: "He who receives you receives me"; and it is implicit in Mark 6:11 where Jesus tells the twelve to shake the dust from their feet against places that do not receive them. Thus the apostles are personal representatives of the risen Christ, called and commissioned by him to go in his authority to preach the gospel and to found churches. "Called to be an apostle" is to be "set apart to preach the gospel of God" (Rom. 1:1). To be an apostle is also to be a preacher (*kēryx,* I Tim. 2:7; II Tim. 1:11). As preachers of the gospel, apostles also founded churches. Paul reminds the Corinthians that he needs no letters of commendation to establish his apostolic authority, as certain recent teachers who had come to Corinth claimed to have. These teachers Paul labels "false apostles" (II Cor. 11:13), for all they have is human letters but no call from Christ. Paul has such a heavenly commission; and instead of human letters, the

---

[20] See also Rom. 15:16; I Cor. 3:10; II Cor. 3:6; Eph. 3:7; 6:20; Col. 1:25; I Thess. 2:4 for Paul's sense of mission.

[21] K. H. Rengstorf, *TDNT* II, 43. This is the note constantly resounded by Paul in his correspondence; "called to be an apostle" (Rom. 1:1 *et passim*).

[22] See H. L. Strack and P. Billerbeck, *Kommentar,* III, 2. See K. H. Rengstorf, *TDNT* II, 12ff.; H. Mosbech in *StTh* 2, 168f.

church in Corinth is itself a letter of commendation that confirms his apostolic call (I Cor. 2:17-3:3).

Another evidence of apostleship is the "signs of an apostle" (II Cor. 12:12)—the evidence of deeds in support of an apostle's words demonstrating the power of the Holy Spirit by signs and wonders (Rom. 15:19; Gal. 3:5).[23]

While Paul is conscious of sharing apostolic authority (*exousia,* II Cor. 10:8; 13:10), this is not an arbitrary or an automatic power that rendered the apostles omniscient and infallible.[24] We have already seen that Paul himself is conscious of a difference between his own opinions and the authoritative word of the Lord. The open conflict of opinion between two apostles —Paul and Peter (Gal. 2:11ff.)—illustrates that even an apostle can act contrary to his own best convictions (Gal. 2:7-9; Acts 15:7ff.). Furthermore, the authority of the apostles appears to have been exercised more at the moral and spiritual level and not to have been embodied in legal or institutional structures. The authority embodied in and through the apostolate was an authority to which the apostles themselves were subject. Their authority was that of God himself (I Thess. 2:13), but they were themselves subject to Jesus Christ (I Cor. 4:1). Apostolic authority was not an authority under the control of the apostles or at their disposal; they were controlled by the authority of the risen Lord and his Spirit. The mark of a false apostle is failure to be exclusively devoted to Christ. Self-seeking takes the place of selfless service (II Cor. 11:12). Such men take great pride in their position (II Cor. 5:12), and so exalt their apostleship that Paul ironically calls them "super-apostles" (II Cor. 11:5; 12:11). They delight in comparing themselves favorably with other people (II Cor. 10:12) and are domineering, arrogant, and greedy (II Cor. 11:20).[25] A true apostle, although a bearer of divine authority, does not lord it over the faith of his churches (II Cor. 1:24), does not exalt himself but preaches Christ as a servant of those to whom he ministers (II Cor. 4:5). The ultimate authority is so reposed in the gospel itself that even an apostle cannot proclaim another gospel (Gal. 1:6). Therefore even the apostles are in a real sense judged by the church. Believers are not slaves of the apostles (I Cor. 7:23; II Cor. 11:20); apostles are servants of Christ, stewards of the divine mysteries (I Cor. 4:1), and slaves of the churches (II Cor. 4:5). The authority invested in the apostles is, therefore, no external, worldly authority that can be arbitrarily wielded; it can be recognized only by those who are enlightened by the same Spirit who imparts to the apostles their authority (I Cor. 14:37). Therefore Paul's way of commending himself as an apostle is by no appeal to external authority but by a direct appeal to the conscience of his hearers (II Cor. 4:2).

[23] For the significance of these apostolic miracles, cf. K. H. Rengstorf, *TDNT* II, 46-47.

[24] See the discussion by H. von Campenhausen in *StTh* 1, 119-24.

[25] See K. H. Rengstorf, *TDNT* II, 62; F. V. Filson, "False and True Apostles," *IB* X, 271-72.

Thus Paul exercises his authority not to gain submission to his lordship over the churches, but to seek fellowship with them.[26]

THE APOSTLES AND REVELATION. In the study of Pauline theology, the most important aspect of his sense of apostolic authority is the consciousness of being the medium of revelation. A classic statement is that of Romans 16:25-26, where he speaks of "my gospel and the preaching of Jesus Christ . . . the revelation of the mystery which has been kept secret for long ages but is now disclosed and through the prophetic writings is made known to all nations." "Mystery" in the New Testament, particularly in Paul, has become a technical word associated with the divine revelation. Its background is not that of the Hellenistic mystery religions of esoteric rites or teachings disclosed only to initiates of the cult by which the initiates became perfect (*teleios*) or spiritual (*pneumatikos*). The background is found in the Old Testament concept of God disclosing his secrets to men—a concept that was further developed in Jewish literature.[27] This passage provides a clear understanding of the New Testament use of mystery. It is practically synonymous with the gospel[28] and the proclamation of Jesus Christ, but placed in the perspective of God's overall redemptive purpose. It is the divinely provided salvation, which though purposed by God for ages, has been hidden from men until the right time when it was revealed in Jesus Christ and proclaimed to all the nations. It is therefore a divine secret, but one designed by God to be revealed—an open secret.[29]

In correcting problems in the Corinthian church, Paul makes it clear that mystery as revelation involves three elements: the fact in history of Jesus Christ the crucified, his resurrection and exaltation as the glorified Lord, and the redemptive meaning of Jesus Christ crucified, raised, exalted. Dissensions and party spirit had arisen around the names of certain Christian leaders that threatened to disrupt the church. Apollos, an eloquent, well-trained Alexandrian, had come to Corinth after Paul had founded the church and had ministered there effectively (Acts 18:24-19:1). Apparently, Jewish Christians arrived from Palestine claiming special ties with the mother church at Jerusalem where Peter had been the first leader. The Corinthians aligned themselves around these several teachers, some retaining loyalty to Paul, others preferring Apollos' eloquence, still others boasting of an alleged superiority of Peter (I Cor. 1:10-12).

An analysis of Paul's language in refuting the problem in Corinth suggests that influential in these divisions was a distortion of the gospel by certain teachers of gnosticizing pneumatic tendencies who proudly claimed

---

[26] H. von Campenhausen in *StTh* 1, 124.

[27] See the present author's discussion in *Jesus and the Kingdom* (1964), pp. 218-20.

[28] Eph. 6:19 speaks of "the mystery of the gospel," meaning "the revelation contained in the gospel."

[29] C. F. D. Moule, "Mystery," *IDB* III, 480. See the discussion in Ch. 7.

access to a wisdom[30] that secured a perfected salvation (*teleioi,* I Cor. 2:6) and a quality of spirituality (*pneumatikoi,* I Cor. 3:1) that led to utter indifference to the flesh. This esoteric knowledge led to a haughty indifference to the scruples of the unenlightened (I Cor. 8:1). The deliverance from the flesh expressed itself in two different ways, both by indulgence and denial. "All things are lawful to me" (I Cor. 6:12) expressed the freedom of these *pneumatikoi;* and, as the context clearly shows, this freedom was understood to allow unhampered indulgence of bodily appetites, including sexual abuses. The same indifference could lead to a denial of the resurrection of the body (I Cor. 15).[31]

In correcting this distortion of the gospel, Paul almost appears himself to become a sort of gnostic. Although he speaks scornfully of these wise *pneumatikoi,* labeling such wisdom utter folly (I Cor. 1:20), he asserts that there is a wisdom of God known by the Christian *teleios,* unavailable and inconceivable to men, but revealed by the Spirit of God (I Cor. 2:6-10). It is a wisdom that the "unspiritual" (*psychikoi*) cannot receive, but which is known only by the true *pneumatikoi* (I Cor. 2:14-16). In contrast to the *pneumatikoi* are not only the *psychikoi*—men who do not have the Spirit—but also the *sarkikoi* (I Cor. 3:1ff.). This sounds as though the *pneumatikoi,* or *teleioi,* in Paul's thought are a special group of advanced Christians who, like Paul, have access to the mysteries of God, which are hidden from both the *psychikoi* and *sarkikoi.* This, however, is not Paul's meaning. The *sarkikoi,* indeed, act like men of this age, being only partially enlightened by the Spirit, because they substitute for the true *sophia* of God a human *sophia tou aiōnos toutou.* However, they are not *sarkikoi* because they have not received the Spirit, but because, although they have the Spirit,[32] they do not act like it. This deficiency is ethical and moral. Paul could not treat them as *pneumatikoi,* i.e., as those led by the Spirit, but only as babes (*nēpioi*), yet babes who are *in Christ* (I Cor. 3:1). Mature Christians will preserve the unity of Christ and will not be readily led into jealousy, strife, and party loyalty. In other words, the *pneumatikoi* are not an esoteric circle initiated into special inner secrets of spiritual truth; they are simply mature (*teleioi*) believers who understand the meaning of the cross[33] and live consistently with this truth. The basic fact of the gospel is the crucifixion of Jesus. The gospel is the message of the cross

---

[30] *Sophia logou,* I Cor. 1:17; *logos kai sophia,* I Cor. 2:1; *peithoi sophias logoi,* I Cor. 2:4.

[31] For this interpretation, see W. G. Kümmel, *Introduction to the NT* (1966), pp. 201ff.; S. M. Gilmour, "Corinthians, First," *IDB* I, 689f.; L. Goppelt, *Jesus, Paul, and Judaism* (1964), pp. 168ff.; *The Apostolic and Post-Apostolic Times* (1970), pp. 98ff. This is not the traditional understanding of the problem in Corinth, but it seems to the present author to be sound. The thesis of scholars like U. Wilckens, *Weisheit und Torheit* (1959), "Sophia," *TDNT* VII, 517ff., that the Corinthian "gnosticism" included the myth of a descending and ascending redeemer goes too far; there is no clear evidence for such a myth.

[32] Paul addresses them as men who are spiritually well-equipped (I Cor. 1:7).

[33] E. Schweizer, *TDNT* VI, 424.

(I Cor. 1:17), the only message that Paul preached among them (I Cor. 2:2). However, the cross is not a mere historical event; as such it is foolishness and offensive (I Cor. 1:23). To both Jews and Greeks, the idea that a man executed as a common criminal, suffering a degrading, humiliating death, could have anything to do with divine wisdom and salvation was utter folly.

At precisely this point, however, has been disclosed the wisdom and power of God. God in his wisdom has used the depth of humiliation and degradation as the means of salvation. This is the *meaning* of the cross, decreed by God ages ago (I Cor. 2:7), hidden in God's mind and heart, but now revealed in the proclamation of the gospel message. This redemptive meaning of the cross, although openly proclaimed (I Cor. 1:17, 23), is, from a purely human perspective, such foolishness[34] that men unaided by the Spirit cannot accept it or acknowledge its truthfulness. But those who believe are enlightened by the Holy Spirit to see in the cross the divine redemption (I Cor. 1:21, 24), as announced in the apostolic proclamation. The events in effecting salvation are the age-long hidden purpose of God, the historical fact of the crucifixion of Jesus, the revelation of the redemptive meaning of the cross in the apostolic kerygma, illumination by the Spirit in believing response to the proclamation issuing in salvation.

The gospel is, therefore, the proclamation of the *historical fact* and the *redemptive meaning* of the cross, which includes both present and future blessings. Man cannot conceive of what wonderful things God has prepared for those who love him; but God has revealed the blessings that await the eschatological consummation, for these are implicit in the cross (I Cor. 2:9-10). Thus, although Paul makes use of the language of the Corinthian pneumatics, his theology opposes the views of the mystery and gnostic cults and stands rather in the stream of late Jewish apocalyptic thought.[35]

Paul's sense of authority derives from his apostolic consciousness of being the bearer of revelation, i.e., the divinely given word that discloses the meaning of the cross and reveals an historical event to be what it really is, namely, the revelation of the wisdom and power of God. The fact of revelation through apostles is explicitly asserted in Ephesians. The "mystery of Christ," i.e., the divine purpose that was accomplished in the coming of Jesus Christ (Col. 4:3), was not made known to men in former generations, but now it has been revealed to the holy apostles and prophets by the Spirit (Eph. 3:5).[36] The particular aspect of revelation here in Paul's mind is the fact, undisclosed by the Old Testament prophets, that the salvation of the Gentiles would involve the creation of "one new man" (Eph. 2:15) by the incorporation of Jewish and Gentile believers alike, on the common ground of divine grace, as fellow-members of the body of Christ.

---

[34] This perspective is knowledge of Christ *kata sarka* (II Cor. 5:16).

[35] G. Bornkamm, "Mystērion," *TDNT* IV, 820.

[36] Many scholars think that the rather formal phrase "the holy apostles and prophets" is post-Pauline, reflecting later usage; but Paul elsewhere speaks of "the holy brethren" (Col. 1:2).

The disclosure of this truth came to Paul at his conversion when he was brought by divine call into the circle of the apostles (Eph. 3:3). The revelation imparted to the apostles and prophets did not have as its purpose the creation of a spiritually elite circle of men elevated above the rank and file of believers; the apostles are recipients of revelation that they in turn might "make all men see what is the plan of the mystery hidden for ages in God" (Eph. 3:9). Thus Paul can also say without inconsistency that the mystery hidden for ages and generations is "now made manifest to his saints" (Col. 1:26). The apostles are "administrators" (*oikonomoi*) of the mysteries of God (I Cor. 4:1), and have received this "divine office" (*oikonomian tou theou*) in order to bring the word of God to its completion (*plerōsai*) by making it fully known (Col. 1:25, RSV; cf. Rom. 15:19).

The mode of revelation cannot be reduced to any single pattern. For Paul himself, the revelation of Jesus Christ (Gal. 1:12, 16) on the Damascus Road was a unique experience, to be distinguished from frequent ecstatic experiences, which he also calls "revelations of the Lord" (II Cor. 12:1, 7), that have no immediate significance for salvation history.[37] Sometimes revelations were given by the Spirit to prophets in the form of immediate prophetic inspiration so that the prophet utters some disclosure of the mind of God (I Cor. 14:6, 30). Such prophecy differed from tongues in that the utterance was intelligible and not ecstatic (I Cor. 14:2-4). However, "revelation" is also the total Christian message without regard to the way it is made known to men (Rom. 16:25). In the gospel is revealed the righteousness of God (Rom. 1:17). All previous redemptive history focuses upon the revealing of faith as the only way of salvation (Gal. 3:23). In Jesus Christ, God has made known the mystery, i.e., the hidden purpose of his will to restore harmony to a disordered world (Eph. 1:9-10). Revelation, then, is the totality of the historical event of Jesus Christ plus the apostolic interpretation of the divine meaning of the event—the apostolic interpretation being itself a part of the event. This divinely initiated apostolic interpretation includes an eschatological dimension. The righteousness and the wrath of God that have already been revealed in God's redemptive acts in history (Rom. 1:17, 19) await their consummation at the revelation of Jesus Christ (I Cor. 1:7; II Thess. 1:7) in both glory (Rom. 8:18f.) and judgment (I Cor. 3:13; Rom. 2:5). In fact, the true locus of revelation is in eschatology.[38] This means that what God has done in history is inseparable from the eschatological consummation, for it is an anticipation of the eschatological redemption. This fact places the entire concept of revelation squarely in the stream of redemptive history.

REVELATION AND TRADITION. If the apostolic message consists of the proclamation of the historical facts of Jesus' death and resurrection and the redemptive meaning of these events, and if the apostles are the medium

[37] See A. Oepke in *TDNT* III, 585.
[38] A. Oepke, *TDNT* III, 583.

of revelation, we might easily conclude that revelation has to do only with the meaning of these events, not with the events themselves. This in turn could lead to the further conclusion that revelation did not take place in past historical events, but takes place in the preaching of the gospel. Only in the proclamation of the word does God confront man and reveal himself.

This conclusion has been drawn by modern existential theologians who see the event of revelation and salvation as "nowhere present except in the proclaiming, accosting, demanding, and promising word of preaching."[39] In Bultmann's view this salvation occurrence took place in the proclaimed word of the apostles, and continues to take place in the word as it is proclaimed today. From this point of view, the gospel is not the recital of past events; it is a present event. Revelation is not the disclosure of truths about God, the communication of knowledge; revelation is the confrontation with God that occurs in the proclaimed word.[40]

This view finds apparent support in the fact that there are sayings in Paul in which revelation seems to occur in the *kērygma* (preaching) and in the *euaggelion* (gospel) rather than in past events. Romans 16:25-26 appears to equate the gospel and the kerygma of Jesus Christ with the revelation of the mystery kept secret for long ages but now disclosed and made known to all nations. Furthermore, the gospel itself is the power of God unto salvation (Rom. 1:16). The gospel itself is "mystery" (Eph. 6:19), i.e., a secret purpose of God now made known to men. The gospel is not only of divine origin;[41] it is a divine activity performed for the benefit of men.[42] The gospel does not merely bear witness to salvation history; it is itself salvation history,[43] for it is only in the preaching of the gospel that salvation is accomplished. Bultmann is right, therefore, when he underlines the "existential" character of the gospel.[44]

However, the kerygma and the gospel cannot be limited to the activity of preaching; they designate also the message itself, the *content* of preaching. God's purpose to save men through the "foolishness of preaching" (I Cor. 1:21, KJV) does not refer to the activity but the content of preaching,[45] and this content is "Christ crucified"—an event in history that is offensive and foolishness to all but believers (I Cor. 1:23). Thus the gospel includes the proclamation of facts in history: the death of Christ, his resurrection, his appearances to his disciples (I Cor. 15:3ff.).[46] However,

---

39 R. Bultmann, *Theology,* I, 302.

40 R. Bultmann, "Revelation in the NT" in *Existence and Faith,* ed. by S. M. Ogden (1960), pp. 58ff.

41 Rom. 1:1; I Thess. 2:2. "The gospel of God" is subjective genitive.

42 O. Piper, "Gospel," *IDB* II, 414.

43 G. Friedrich, *TDNT* II, 731.

44 O. Piper, *IDB* II, 414.

45 See G. Friedrich, *TDNT* III, 716; C. H. Dodd, *The Apostolic Preaching* (1936), p. 3; C. T. Craig, *IB* X, 30; F. W. Grosheide, *First Corinthians,* p. 47.

46 Bultmann's one-sided emphasis upon the kerygma as proclamation and not content requires him to exclude arbitrarily I Cor. 15:3-8 from the kerygma. See *Kerygma and Myth,* ed. by H. W. Bartsch (1953), I, 112.

it is not the proclamation of mere events, but of events meaningfully understood. Christ died *for our sins*. The gospel is both historical event and meaning; and the meaning of the event is that God was acting in history for man's salvation. The historical facts must be interpreted to be understood for what they are: the redeeming, revealing act of God; and in the gospel, this redemptive event is proclaimed.

There exists a dynamic unity between the event and the proclamation of the event, for the proclamation is itself a part of the event. It is impossible to place primary emphasis upon events as past history, or as present proclamation; the two are inseparably bound together, for two reasons. Apart from proclamation (*kērygma, euaggelion*), the events in history cannot be understood for what they are: the redeeming acts of God. Furthermore, apart from proclamation, the events are mere events in past history; but in proclamation, they become present redeeming events. The past lives in the present through proclamation. This is why Paul can speak of the gospel as itself the power of God unto salvation.

This tension between the past and the present is confirmed by the concept of tradition in Paul.[47] Paul frequently refers to his preaching and teaching in the same terms that are used of the Jewish oral traditions: to deliver (*paradidonai*) and to receive (*paralambanein*) tradition (*paradosis*). Jesus had contrasted the Jewish traditions with the word of God (Mt. 15:6) and forbade his disciples to imitate the rabbis (Mt. 23:8-10), and yet Paul commends the Corinthians for maintaining the traditions he had delivered to them (I Cor. 11:2) and exhorts the Thessalonians to hold to the traditions they had been taught (II Thess. 2:15) and to shun those who ignored the tradition they had received from Paul (II Thess. 3:6). This idiom establishes a distinct similarity between Jewish rabbinic tradition and Christian tradition, for the terms are the same,[48] and they are used at times quite synonymously with preaching the gospel. The Corinthians received the gospel (*parelabete*) that Paul had preached to them (I Cor. 15:1). The gospel that the Galatians received (*parelabete*) is normative; there can be no other gospel (Gal. 1:9). The Thessalonians received (*paralabontes*) as the word of God the message that they heard from Paul, recognizing in Paul's words something more than human tradition—the word of God itself (I Thess. 2:13). In all of these passages, the idiom reflects the handing on and receiving of an oral tradition with a fixed content.

This tradition embodied the apostolic *kērygma* or *euaggelion*. Paul delivered (*paredōka*) to the Corinthians the gospel that he also received

---

[47] For literature see A. M. Hunter, *Paul and His Predecessors* (1961), ch. 2; O. Cullmann, "The Tradition" in *The Early Church*, ed. by A. J. B. Higgins (1956), ch. 4; B. Gerhardsson, *Memory and Manuscript* (1961), pp. 288-321; H. N. Ridderbos, *Paul and Jesus* (1958), pp. 46-53; L. Goppelt, "Tradition nach Paulus," *Kerygma und Dogma*, 4 (1958), 213-33; R. P. C. Hanson, *Tradition in the Early Church* (1962), ch. 1.

[48] See O. Cullmann in *The Early Church*, pp. 63ff.

(*parelabon*), that Christ died for our sins, that he was buried, that he rose on the third day, that he appeared to his disciples (I Cor. 15:1-5).[49] It is generally accepted that verses 3b-5 embody a primitive piece of pre-Pauline kerygma that Paul has received as a tradition from those who were apostles before him.[50]

The same idiom of oral tradition appears in connection with the preservation of a piece of tradition from Jesus' life, namely, the Lord's Supper. Paul received "from the Lord" the account that he delivered to the Corinthians of the institution of the Eucharist (I Cor. 11:23). Some scholars understand the expression "from the Lord" to mean that Paul received his knowledge of the Lord's Supper by direct illumination from the exalted Lord, as he received knowledge that Jesus was the Messiah on the Damascus Road.[51] However, in view of the language and the content of the tradition, this is highly unlikely. Most commentators think Paul means to assert that this tradition which he received from other apostles had its historical origin with Jesus. Paul says he received *apo,* not *para,* the Lord. The latter would suggest reception directly from the Lord, whereas the former indicates ultimate source.[52] In any case the words mean at least this: that the chain of historical tradition that Paul received goes back unbroken to the words of Jesus himself.[53] Thus Paul includes two things in the tradition handed down orally from earlier apostles: the good news of salvation in Christ and at least one piece of tradition from Jesus' life that found its way also into the Gospels.

While the oral gospel tradition is in some ways similar to Jewish oral tradition, in one all-important respect it is quite different. To receive the gospel tradition does not mean merely to accept the truthfulness of a report about certain historical facts, nor does it mean simply to receive instruction and intellectual enlightenment. To receive the tradition means to receive (*parelabete*) Christ Jesus as Lord (Col. 2:6). In the voice of the tradition, the voice of God himself is heard; and through this word, God himself is present and active in the church (I Thess. 2:13). Thus the Christian tradition is not mere instruction passed on like Jewish oral tradition from one teacher to another. The tradition handed on in the form of preaching (*euēggelisamen,* I Cor. 15:1) and the reception of the message involve a response of faith (*episteusate,* I Cor. 15:2). The tradition about the resurrection of Jesus must be believed in the heart and confessed with the mouth (Rom. 10:8-9), and issues in salvation. Such confession is possible only through the Holy Spirit (I Cor. 12:3).

---

49 Probably the appearances mentioned in vv. 6-8 were added by Paul to the tradition he received.

50 See J. Jeremias, *The Eucharistic Words of Jesus* (1955), pp. 129-30.

51 See F. Godet, *First Corinthians* (1890), II, 149. C. T. Craig thinks Paul may be asserting that his interpretation of the Lord's Supper was received from the risen Lord (*IB* X, 136).

52 See J. Hering, *First Corinthians* (1962), pp. 114f.; F. W. Grosheide, *First Corinthians,* p. 269.

53 J. Jeremias, *The Eucharistic Words of Jesus,* p. 129.

Thus the tradition has a twofold character: it is *both* historical tradition and kerygmatic-pneumatic tradition at one and the same time. It is historical because it is tied to events in history, and the tradition preserves the report of these events. It is kerygmatic because it can be perpetuated only as kerygma and received as a confession of faith. It is pneumatic because it can be received and preserved only by the enabling of the Spirit.[54]

A recognition of the kerygmatic-pneumatic character of the tradition provides the background for understanding Paul's statement that he received the tradition of the Lord's Supper "from the Lord" (I Cor. 11:23). The "Lord" designates the Jesus of history who is now the exalted Lord. The tradition had its origin with Jesus himself; but as the exalted Lord, Christ now stands behind the tradition and speaks to the church through it. The tradition that Paul received from men both comes from Jesus and is also the word of the exalted Lord to Paul. The tradition of the Lord's Supper also bears the dual character of being both historical and pneumatic at the same time.[55]

The kerygmatic-pneumatic character of the tradition is reflected most vividly in the fact that although it is the words of men mediated through the act of preaching, it is also the word of God (I Thess. 2:13). This word of God, which is received as tradition, is also the gospel (Eph. 1:13; Col. 1:5), the kerygma (I Cor. 1:18, 21), the mystery (Col. 1:25), which is not only proclaimed by the apostles but sounded forth from the churches unto all the surrounding region (I Thess. 1:8). While it is a word that can be taught and learned (Gal. 6:6), it is also a divine trust committed to men (II Cor. 5:19). While it is dependent upon human utterance for its propagation (Phil. 1:14), it is God's word, which cannot be fettered (II Tim. 2:9) and must speed on to triumph (II Thess. 3:1). The word of God is a word about a crucifixion (I Cor. 1:18); but the cross seen not as an isolated event in history but understood as the disclosure of the age-long redemptive purpose of God (Col. 1:25-26). This word is the subject of preaching (II Tim. 2:19), which is to be received by its hearers (I Thess. 1:6) and indwell them (Col. 3:16), bringing salvation (Eph. 1:13; Phil. 2:16).

Neither the historical nor the kerygmatic aspects of the word of God can be emphasized to the neglect of the other. Existentialist theologians emphasize the kerygmatic aspect of the word at the expense of its historical dimension, and the redemptive event becomes God's acting in the kerygma, not in events in history. Bultmann recognizes that the historical Jesus is the

---

[54] This has been best expounded by L. Goppelt, *Kerygma und Dogma,* 4, 216-17.

[55] *Ibid.,* p. 223. Cullmann finds even more in this passage. He believes that for Paul the exalted Lord is both the author and the content of the tradition, and that the Lord and tradition are practically identical. "There can be only one legitimate tradition, that which is transmitted by the apostles, and is designated as Kyrios" (O. Cullmann in *The Early Church,* p. 75). This appears to go further than the evidence allows. It has, however, been accepted by A. M. Hunter. See *Paul and His Predecessors,* p. 118.

origin of the word of God, but he says, "we must speak of God as acting only in the sense that He acts with me here and now."[56] This is contrary to the New Testament, which sees the acting of God to have occurred in the historical Jesus. However, the gospel is both past event and present proclamation. When the kerygmatic aspect is neglected, the kerygma becomes a recital of facts and events lying in the past and thereby loses its character as salvation event. Both aspects must be retained. "Since the revelation occurred in history, the gospel involves a report of historical events, yet the proclamation of the gospel is itself a powerful event."[57]

As the word of God, the gospel is indeed a divine communication, and it includes facts, truths, doctrines. However, if the gospel does no more than communicate facts and doctrines, it has been reduced to the level of human tradition. In the word, God communicates not only facts about redemption and truths about himself; God communicates himself, salvation, eternal life. The word of God is both the report about a redemptive event, and is itself a redemptive event, for in the word of the cross, the crucified himself confronts men to communicate to them the benefits of his redeeming death.

We may now draw certain conclusions about the Pauline concept of revelation. The focus of revelation is Jesus Christ. In the event in history of Jesus' life, death, resurrection, and exaltation, God has revealed himself redemptively to men. The revelation that occurred in the cross and resurrection is not complete; there yet awaits the revelation of the glory and salvation (Rom. 13:11) of God at thc parousia of Christ when faith will be exchanged for sight and we shall see face to face (II Cor. 5:7; I Cor. 13:12). Both the redemptive meaning of what God has done in the cross and resurrection and the disclosure of what God will yet do at the consummation (I Cor. 3:10) are revealed in the kerygma, the gospel, the word of God, which exists in the form of an historical kerygmatic-pneumatic tradition. This tradition is a complex of several streams including traditions from the life of Jesus (I Cor. 11:23), a summary of the Christian message expressed as a formula of faith and uniting facts of the life of Jesus and their theological interpretation (I Cor. 15:3f.), and also regulations or rules for practical Christian conduct (I Cor. 11:2; II Thess. 3:6).[58] The tradition has its origin with Jesus himself (I Cor. 11:23) and with the apostolic eyewitnesses (I Cor. 15:lff., 8). Among the primary apostolic functions is not only the propagation of the tradition, but also its preservation from corruption with human traditions (Col. 2:8), and from distortion by false apostles who preach a Jesus who is different from the Jesus of the apostolic

[56] R. Bultmann, *Jesus Christ and Mythology* (1958), p. 78. See G. E. Ladd, "What Does Bultmann Understand by the Acts of God?" *Bulletin of the Evangelical Theological Society,* 5 (1962), 91-97.

[57] W. Baird, "What Is the Kerygma?" *JBL* 76 (1957), 191. Baird studies the historical and the kerygmatic aspects of the gospel in C. H. Dodd and R. Bultmann and concludes that the Pauline gospel includes both.

[58] See O. Cullmann in *The Early Church,* p. 64.

tradition (II Cor. 11:3-5). The tradition is both a fixed and growing tradition; that is, the tradition cannot be changed, but it can be enlarged. That the gospel embodies a core of fixed tradition committed to the apostles is the explanation for Paul's passionate rejection of any message that diverges from the accepted tradition, even if it is propagated by an apostle himself (Gal. 1:8-9). On the other hand, the Spirit can add to the tradition by granting through the apostles and prophets an unfolding and outworking of the redemptive purpose of God that is already implicit in the redemptive work of Christ. This is seen in Paul's use of the term *mystērion,* or revealed secret. The "mystery" is the total meaning of God's redemptive purpose, which he has accomplished in Christ (Rom. 16:25-26). Particular disclosures of God's secret purpose revealed through the apostles include the fact of Christ as the embodiment of all wisdom and knowledge (Col. 2:2), the indwelling of Christ in the hearts of his people (Col. 1:27), the abolishing of the distinction between Jew and Gentile in the body of Christ, the church (Eph. 3:3-6), the intimacy established between Christ and his church (Eph. 6:19), the present rejection of the gospel by Israel, the salvation of the Gentiles, which will lead to the future salvation of Israel (Rom. 11:25-26), the translation of living saints into resurrection life at the parousia (I Cor. 15:51), and the final restoration of divine order in Christ to a disordered universe (Eph. 1:9-10). While all of these facets of the mystery of God's redemptive purpose embody new understandings and disclosures, they are all implicit in what God has done in the death, resurrection, and exaltation of Christ. Revelation is thus seen as an event that includes both deeds and words. The meaning of the events in history and their implications for Christian life are given in an historical tradition through which the exalted Christ himself speaks, and in direct disclosures by the Holy Spirit through the apostles and prophets.

In his letter to the Galatians, Paul seems to reject the role of tradition in revelation and to claim that revelation occurs only by direct illumination by the Holy Spirit. He appears to declare his complete independence from the primitive church. He asserts that he did not receive his gospel from men, that it did not come to him by tradition (*parelabon*) nor by instruction, but by direct revelation of Jesus Christ (Gal. 1:12). He declares his independence from the Jerusalem apostles. After his conversion, he did not go up to Jerusalem to receive the approval of the apostles but withdrew to Arabia. When he did go to Jerusalem three years later, it was not to establish an abiding relationship, but only to make a short visit to get acquainted with Peter and James (Gal. 1:17-19). Taken out of context, the assertions in this passage seem to contradict the statements of I Corinthians 11 and 15 that Paul handed on what he had received by tradition.

Various solutions to this apparent contradiction have been offered. Some have suggested that in Corinthians Paul refers only to the facts about Jesus that he learned from other Christians, while the meaning of these facts, i.e., their true interpretation, came to him not from men but only by the direct revelation of the exalted Lord.[59] This is, of course, true. Unquestionably, as Machen points out, Paul was familiar with many of the facts about Jesus' life and death, as well as the Christian claims for him as the Messiah, when he was still in Judaism. In fact, it was his Jewish understanding of the facts that made Saul a persecutor; what he gained on the Damascus Road was a new and correct understanding of the facts, namely, that Jesus was the Messiah. However, the tradition in I Corinthians 15 includes interpretation: "Christ died *for our sins";* and it includes also a fact that undoubtedly Paul as a Jew did not accept—the fact that Jesus was raised from the dead and appeared to his disciples.

Others have maintained that Paul received the form of his proclamation from men, but he received its essential content not from men but from the Lord. In its form, the Pauline kerygma was essentially the same as the tradition of the Jerusalem church; but in its essential dynamic nature, his gospel could not be transmitted by men but only communicated by direct revelation.[60] This solution is not satisfactory, for it contradicts the kerygmatic nature of the tradition and views it as though it were only a human tradition.

The apparent contradiction is due to the different purposes involved in the two passages. In Corinthians Paul is thinking of particular aspects of the substance of his gospel: the Lord's Supper, the saving death, the resurrection and the appearances of Jesus. These include both facts and at least something of the meaning of the facts. In the substance of his gospel, Paul stands in agreement with earlier Christians, and indeed he received information from them as to the gospel itself. However, in Galatians Paul is dealing with his apostolic authority and with the one central fact of the gospel, that Jesus was the resurrected and exalted Messiah. This he did not learn from other men, even though it was later corroborated by what he did learn from them. Paul was not converted by Christian preaching but by an immediate confrontation by the exalted Christ.[61] Neither did Paul receive his apostolic office from men. Both—his gospel and his apostolic office—came to him directly from the Lord, unmediated by men. The fact that subsequent to his conversion Paul consulted with Peter[62] and James and received from them both facts about Jesus and the gospel and their interpretation of it would in no way weaken his claim to complete independence in his reception of the gospel. The purpose of the passages is to argue that Paul enjoys the same apostolic authority as those who were

---

59 J. G. Machen, *The Origin of Paul's Religion* (1928), pp. 144ff.

60 W. Baird in *JBL* 76, 190f.

61 Here is an overlooked weakness in Bultmann's reconstruction of the kerygma, for Paul was not brought into "authentic existence" by the kerygma or Christian proclamation as Bultmann's interpretation requires. See "Paul" in *Existence and Faith,* ed. by S. M. Ogden (1960), p. 115.

62 G. D. Kilpatrick thinks that *historēsai Kēphan* (Gal. 1:18) means "to get information from Peter." See *NT Essays,* ed. by A. J. B. Higgins (1959), pp. 144-49. But see F. Büchsel in *TDNT* III, 395-96.

apostles before him (Gal. 1:17), because he, like them, received his commission and his gospel directly from the Lord.

PAUL AND THE OLD TESTAMENT. In addition to tradition and to the direct revelation of the Holy Spirit, an important source of Paul's theology was the Old Testament.[63] This is shown in two ways: in specific quotations and allusions to the Old Testament, and in the Old Testament foundation for Paul's theological ideas. The latter can be established only by a thorough study of Paul's thought; here we must limit the discussion to the former.

For Paul the Scriptures are holy and prophetic (Rom. 1:2; 4:3) and constitute the very oracles of God (*ta logia tou theou,* Rom. 3:1-2). Several times Paul uses the formula, "the Lord says" (*legei kyrios*),[64] and elsewhere *legei* presupposes *ho theos.*[65] The Scripture is the word of God[66] because it is spirit-inbreathed, i.e., inspired (II Tim. 3:16).

Paul frequently appealed to the Old Testament in support of his teaching, quoting from it ninety-three times.[67] His primary concern in using the Old Testament is not to gain biblical authority for specific doctrines so much as to show that redemption in Christ stands in direct continuity with the revelation in the Old Testament and is in fact the fulfillment of that revelation. It is significant that twenty-six of his quotations occur in Romans 9-11, where he is dealing specifically with the question of the *history* of salvation, showing that the church is directly continuous with Israel, and that the "word of God" (Rom. 9:6) given to Israel is not frustrated by Israel's unbelief but is fulfilled in the church. He is concerned to establish that justification by faith is taught in the Old Testament (Rom. 1:17; 4:3, 7-8; Gal. 3:6, 11), and that the gospel is the fulfillment of the promise given to Abraham (Rom. 4:17-18; Gal. 4:27, 30). Therefore the events of redemptive history in Christ have happened "according to the scriptures" (I Cor. 15:3, 4). The revelation of God's secret redemptive purpose, accomplished in Christ, is now made known to all nations "through the prophetic writings" (Rom. 16:26). Such a saying suggests that the Old Testament was widely used in the churches as a source of Christian truth. Because the Old Testament is inspired, it is profitable for Christian use in teaching, reproof, correction, and training in righteousness (II Tim. 3:16). That the Old Testament was the first Christian Bible is supported also by such statements as I Corinthians 10:11, that the events of Old Testament history happened for warning and instruction of Christians, for whom the preceding ages existed (see also Rom. 15:4).

Paul's use of the Old Testament is not so much to seek a one-to-one

---

[63] See H. N. Ridderbos, *Paul and Jesus,* pp. 59-62; E. E. Ellis, *Paul's Use of the OT* (1957).

[64] See I Cor. 14:21; II Cor. 6:17; Rom. 12:19; 14:11.

[65] See Rom. 9:15, 25; II Cor. 6:2, 16. See also G. Schrenk, *TDNT* I, 757.

[66] Paul does not call the Old Testament the word of God; but see Rom. 9:6.

[67] For a convenient list with the Greek and LXX, see E. E. Ellis, *Paul's Use of the OT,* pp. 156-85.

equating of prophecy and fulfillment as to place the new redemptive events squarely in the stream of Old Testament redemptive history. This leads him to find in the Old Testament meanings that do not readily appear in the quotations in their Old Testament setting. Thus he can apply to the church quotations that in the Old Testament refer only to Israel (Rom. 9:25-26; cf. Hos. 2:23; 1:10). This cannot be labeled a manipulation or misuse of the Old Testament; rather, it illustrates something essential in Paul's thought; that Jesus, even though crucified, is the Messiah foretold in the Old Testament, and that the people of the Messiah are the true people of God, continuous with the Israel of the Old Testament. The church is in fact the true Israel of God.

These Christian meanings in the Old Testament are not, however, self-evident but require the illumination of the Holy Spirit to be understood. When the Old Testament is read by unbelieving Jews, a veil of unbelief lies over their minds (II Cor. 3:15), and they cannot see that the Old Testament witnesses to the glory of God shining forth in Jesus Christ. The old covenant had its glory, but it was provisional and passing in contrast with the glory now revealed in Christ (II Cor. 3:7ff.). Therefore the Old Testament must be read in the light of its fulfillment in Christ[68] with the illumination of the Holy Spirit; otherwise the Holy Scripture becomes only a dead letter—a lifeless written code (II Cor. 3:6). The Holy Spirit does not reveal from the Scriptures mystical, esoteric truth; rather, the Spirit enables the believer to understand from the Old Testament the meaning of the redemptive event wrought in history in Jesus Christ. The new understanding of the Old Testament is controlled by the event of Jesus Christ.

Since Paul regards the Old Testament so highly as the word of God, we will not be surprised to find that his theological thought is grounded in Old Testament theology. His understanding of God, of anthropology, atonement, promise and Law, and eschatology cannot be understood apart from the Old Testament. This will emerge in the chapters that follow.

[68] See H. N. Ridderbos, *Paul and Jesus,* p. 60.

29

MAN OUTSIDE OF CHRIST

Paul's view of man and the world illustrates his basic eschatological outlook. Paul has often been interpreted against the background of Hellenistic dualism, which involved a cosmological dualism and closely associated with it an anthropological dualism.[1] Cosmological dualism contrasted two levels of existence: the earthly and the heavenly; and anthropological dualism contrasted two parts of man: his body and his soul. His body belonged to the earthly level while his soul belonged to the heavenly or spiritual level. In Plato the material world was not thought of as being actually evil, but it was considered an obstruction to the soul or mind by which man was related to the divine. The soul was pre-existent and by nature indestructible, immortal. In gnostic thought this dualism is sharpened to the point where matter is conceived to be the realm of evil. Thus redemption, both in Plato and in later gnostic thought, consisted of the escape of the soul from the realm of matter and of the body that it might take its flight to the world of ultimate reality.[2] The Greeks had no idea of a creating God. In Plato the Demiurge "begat" the world, but he did so by imposing form upon prior existing matter.

It is impossible to understand Paul in these terms. The basic structure of his thinking is not a cosmological but an eschatological dualism.[3] Paul is conscious of standing in an interval between two ages. The whole redemptive work of God moves toward the perfect realization of the Kingdom of God in the Age to Come and includes all creation. Until then, the old

---

1 The various forms of dualism may be listed in different ways. See D. E. H. Whiteley, *The Theology of St. Paul* (1964), pp. 32f.; M. Rist in *IDB* A-D, p. 873; G. E. Ladd, *Jesus and the Kingdom* (1964), pp. 83ff.

2 This is worked out in detail in Plato, Plutarch, and Philo in G. E. Ladd, *The Pattern of NT Truth* (1968), pp. 13-31. Philo was a Jew in his view of the Old Testament and cult, but philosophically he was a Greek dualist. The same dualism is found in the Egyptian movement that produced the Hermetic writings not long after New Testament times (see H. Jonas, *The Gnostic Religion* [1958], pp. 147-73), and in later gnosticism (see R. Bultmann, *Primitive Christianity in Its Contemporary Setting* [1956], pp. 162-71).

3 See above, p. 364.

age continues with its burden of sin, evil, and death. However, in the mission of Christ and the coming of the Spirit, the blessings of the new age have reached back to those who are in Christ. Meanwhile, the world and mankind as a whole remain in the grip of the old age.

Paul's view of creation is typically Hebrew and not Greek. God is the creator of all things in the world (Eph. 3:9; Col. 1:16), including man (I Cor. 15:45). While all things were created by God and through Christ (I Cor. 8:6), there is no room in Paul's thought for a Greek demiurge in the interests of holding God aloof from his creation.

Such expressions as "the foundation of the world" (Eph. 1:4) suggest *creatio ex nihilo* and not the structuring of pre-existent matter.[4] As creation, man has no more claim on God than the clay over the potter (Rom. 9:20ff.), whereas God lays claim to man's gratitude and worship (Rom. 1:21, 25). Both creation and man are fallen and therefore stand under divine judgment. Creation was subjected to futility and corruption (Rom. 8:20). Of itself creation has no goal but is subject to a gigantic circle of futility that leads to death. Because it is fallen, it is transitory and doomed to pass away (I Cor. 7:31).[5] This does not mean the annihilation of creation but its redemption to "obtain the glorious liberty of the children of God" (Rom. 8:21). However, Paul never views the creation as evil because it is matter in contrast to spirit. This is why he expressly refutes ascetic tendencies in the church.[6]

THE WORLD. In this connection, it is instructive to study Paul's view of the world (*kosmos*). *Kosmos* is a Greek word that has no Hebrew or Aramaic equivalent; the Old Testament speaks of "heaven and earth" or "the all" (Ps. 8:6, 15a; 44:24). However, the Hebrew word *olam,* which is strictly speaking a temporal word meaning "age," gained new nuances from the contact of Jewish thinkers with the Hellenistic world. The word assumed spatial connotations, and thus *olam* came to mean both age and the world.[7] This is the background for the interchange of *aiōn* and *kosmos* in Paul (I Cor. 1:20; 3:19; 2:6).[8] Ephesians 2:2 combines the two words to speak of "the age of this world."

Paul uses *kosmos* with a variety of meanings.[9] He uses it first of all to designate the universe—the totality of all that exists (Rom. 1:20; Eph. 1:4; I Cor. 3:22; 8:4, 5).

Second, Paul uses *kosmos* of the inhabited earth, the dwelling place of man, the scene of history. It is the scene into which men are born (I Tim.

---

4 See H. Sasse, *TDNT* III, 885.

5 *Kosmos* here means more than physical creation, although creation is included in the term. See below, p. 399.

6 See below, Ch. 36. See also W. Foerster, *TDNT* III, 1033.

7 See C. R. North, "World," *IDB* R-Z, p. 876; H. Sasse, *TDNT* I, 203-4.

8 Mk. 4:19 and Mt. 13:22 speak of the cares of the age; I Cor. 7:33 of the things of the world; Heb. 1:2 uses *aiōnas* to mean "world." See the RSV.

9 See H. Sasse, *TDNT* III, 884ff. C. R. North, "World," *IDB* R-Z, pp. 876f.; Arndt and Gingrich, *Lexicon, in loc.*

6:7), where the saints must of necessity mingle with immoral men (I Cor. 5:10b). The world was promised as an inheritance to Abraham (Rom. 4:13), and now is the scene of the proclamation of the gospel (Rom. 1:8; Col. 1:6). The world is the dwelling place of men who have no hope and who are without God (Eph. 2:12). In a few places the world in this sense is distinctly contrasted with heaven (I Tim. 1:15; 3:16; cf. Col. 1:20; Eph. 1:10).

Third, *kosmos* is used of mankind, humanity, the totality of the human society that inhabits the earth. When Paul describes his sincere conduct in the world (II Cor. 1:12), he might have said "among men." The apostles, as the refuse of the world (I Cor. 4:13), are viewed by other men as something to be despised. The foolish, the weak, the low and despised in the world (I Cor. 1:27f.) are men who come from the lowest social and cultural levels of human society. The accountability of the world to God (Rom. 3:19), the judgment (Rom. 3:6), and the reconciliation of the world (Rom. 11:15; II Cor. 5:19), all have in view mankind as a whole. In one reference (I Cor. 4:9), *world* includes both men and angels as the totality of created spiritual beings, a fact indicated in the translation of the RSV. The translation in the KJV, which sees three classes of beings, is quite difficult to interpret.

Fourth, when mankind is viewed in relationship to God, the word *kosmos* takes on a flavor that is absent from the preceding verses. Humanity in comparison to God is seen as fallen, as sunk in sin, and therefore as hostile to God. In this way *kosmos,* used of mankind, acquires overtones of evil. The world of men is not evil per se, for men are God's creatures and God's work is good. But when man is viewed as he actually exists, he is seen in rebellion against God; and as such the world is viewed as sinful. It is at this point that *kosmos* and *aiōn* approximate each other in usage. The Gentiles lived according to the course of this world (literally, "according to the age of this world"), following the prince of the power of the air (Eph. 2:2). The wisdom of this age or world is sharply contrasted with the divine wisdom (I Cor. 1:20f.). Intellectual attainment of knowledge and wisdom is not denied to this world; but the highest intellectual and rational achievements of mankind cannot attain to the knowledge of God and are therefore ultimately foolishness. There is no necessary deprecation of human wisdom and knowledge as such; but as a means of acquiring the knowledge of God, inasmuch as the very mind of the race is perverted by sin, it is folly; such knowledge can be acquired only through revelation. The "spirit of the world," that is, the whole outlook and orientation of the life of the world, is on a different level from that of the Spirit of God (I Cor. 2:12). Therefore, the wisdom of this world can never commend a man to God, for it is foolishness; and when a man depends solely on the attainments of human wisdom, he inevitably will be led astray from the knowledge of God (I Cor. 3:19). The principles of the world, which include human speculations and traditions and even religion, are antithetical to Christ (Col. 2:8). Outside of Christ, mankind, including God's people

Israel, is in a state of bondage to these worldly principles (Gal. 4:3). True freedom can be found only through the redemption that is in Christ. The world also has its religion, a religion that holds men in a bondage of asceticism and legalism that may have the appearance of wisdom and promote a kind of devotion and self-discipline; but it utterly fails to provide a solution for the moral dilemma with which man is faced (Col. 2:20ff.). Viewed from this point of view the world stands under the judgment of God (I Cor. 11:32) and is in need of reconciliation (II Cor. 5:19; Rom. 11:15).

Fifth, there is a final use of *kosmos* that is broader than man, and which includes the whole complex of human earthly relationships in which marriage, joy and sorrow, buying and selling, i.e., the totality of human activities, are included. It is not merely the world of men but the world system and complex of relationships that have been created by men. Paul writes that because of the strictures of the time, the believer should not permit himself to become inextricably involved in this world order. "Let those who have wives live as though they had none, and those who mourn as though they were not mourning, and those who rejoice as though they were not rejoicing, and those who buy as though they had no goods, and those who make use of the world as though they were not making complete use of it. For the form of this world is passing away" (I Cor. 7:29-31).[10] The key to the meaning of this passage is found in the last phrase; the form, the structure of this world is passing away. It is not evil in itself and therefore a life of physical detachment or asceticism is not required. The structure of worldly relationships is, however, transitory and is destined to pass away; and since the Christian belongs to the new and divine order, while he still finds himself in the world and must of necessity make use of the world, the goal of his life must not be that of making the fullest use of this world, that is, of finding his deepest motivations and satisfactions on the earthly, worldly level. Paul is not urging celibacy and poverty and emotional apathy to the experiences of life. Rather, he insists that the sources of one's true life stem from a higher level, and in the resources of this spiritual world and its objectives he finds the deepest meaning of existence. While continuing to live in the world, he is not to surrender to it or abandon himself to its enjoyment, for it can stand between man and God.

The ideal relationship of the Christian to this worldly order of human relationships is expressed in Galatians 6:14, "But far be it from me to glory except in the cross of our Lord Jesus Christ, by which the world has been crucified to me, and I to the world." The significance of this saying is found in the following verse, "For neither is circumcision anything, nor uncircumcision, but a new creation." Paul here includes circumcision as an element of the world. The Judaizers in Galatia were glorying in circumcision and making it the channel and means of the attainment of a

---

[10] Our interpretation of this passage follows the translation of the RV and NEB against the RSV.

higher spirituality. Such procedures appeal to human pride and are no longer of interest to Paul, for he has been crucified to the world. This does not mean that Paul opposed the practice of circumcision for Jews as Jews; he himself circumcised Timothy because his mother was a Jewess (Acts 16:3), and he took deliberate steps to frustrate the rumor that he had taught all Jews who lived among the Gentiles to abandon the practice of circumcision (Acts 21:21). Paul never ceased to recognize his Jewish heritage (Rom. 11:1) and the privileges and the glory of the divine calling of Israel (Rom. 9:4-5); but all such religious matters came to be viewed as part of the worldly system and no longer as an object of pride or glory. Paul was ready to sacrifice them all, together with all other human relationships, if their sacrifice would enable him to gain Christ (Phil. 3:4-9). The evil connected with the world resides not in the world itself, but in the attitudes the world engenders in men, which turn them aside from perfect worship of the Creator.

In summary, Paul's doctrine of the world is not analogous to Greek dualism. He views neither creation nor mankind *as such* as sinful, and does not give any support to ideas of asceticism, which seeks the good life in denial of nature or creation, or of commerce and intercourse with human society. "Worldliness" consists of worshipping the creature rather than the creator (Rom. 1:25), of finding one's pride and glory on the human and created level rather than in God. The world is sinful only insofar as it exalts itself above God and refuses to humble itself and acknowledge its creative Lord. Where men are redeemed, they cease to be part of the sinful world and become instead citizens of the Kingdom of God.

SPIRITUAL POWERS. A prominent element in Paul's thinking about the nature of the old age is the conviction that it is in the grip of evil supernatural powers. Paul conceives of both good and evil spirits.[11]

Angels are viewed as spiritual beings engaged in the service of God. The Law was given through the mediation of angels (Gal. 3:19). Angels are spectators of the human scene (I Cor. 4:9; 11:10; I Tim. 5:21). Angels are cited as witnesses of Jesus' ascension (I Tim. 3:16), and they will accompany the Lord Jesus in his revelation from heaven to inflict judgment upon the unrighteous (II Thess. 1:7). On the other hand, there are intimations that angels are also hostile to God and men; they would tend to separate men from God's love (Rom. 8:38); a day of judgment is awaiting them (I Cor. 6:3). Angels have become objects of worship and thus have turned men away from the worship of God (Col. 2:18).

Paul mentions demons as well as evil angels in connection with idolatry. While he recognizes that idols in themselves are nothing (I Cor. 8:4-6) and therefore have no power, there is nevertheless a power connected with

---

[11] See D. E. H. Whiteley, *The Theology of St. Paul,* pp. 18-31; G. H. C. MacGregor, "Principalities and Powers," *NTS* 1 (1954), 17-28; H. Schlier, *Principalities and Powers in the NT* (1961); G. B. Caird, *Principalities and Powers* (1956); J. Kallas, *The Satanward View* (1966).

idols that resides in demons. To worship idols therefore means to sacrifice to demons (I Cor. 10:19-21). Paul prophesies that in the last times deceitful spirits and demons will become increasingly active to turn men away from the truth (I Tim. 4:1-3); such a demonic activity is parallel with the climactic activity of Satan in the man of lawlessness who will appear just before the Day of the Lord (II Thess. 2:9).

The archenemy of God, however, is an evil spirit who is sometimes called the devil (Eph. 4:27; 6:11; I Tim. 3:7), but usually Satan. Satan is the ruler of the authority of the air (Eph. 2:2), the god of this age (II Cor. 4:4), whose objective is to blind the minds of men that they should not apprehend the saving power of the gospel. He is the tempter who seeks through affliction to turn believers away from the gospel (I Thess. 3:5), to hinder God's servants in their ministry (I Thess. 2:18), who raises up false apostles to pervert the truth of the gospel (II Cor. 11:14), who is ever seeking to overwhelm God's people (Eph. 6:11, 12, 16), and who is even able to bring his attacks in the form of bodily afflictions to God's choicest servants (II Cor. 12:7). Satan's main objective is to frustrate the redemptive purposes of God, and at the end of the age the satanic power will become incarnate in a man of lawlessness who will endeavor by one last final effort to overthrow the work of God and to turn men to the worship of evil (II Thess. 2:4-10). However, Satan's doom is sure; God will crush him under the feet of the saints (Rom. 16:20).

Paul refers not only to good and bad angels, to Satan and to demons; he uses another group of words to designate ranks of angelic spirits. The terminology is as follows:

"rule" (*archē*), I Cor. 15:24; Eph. 1:21; Col. 2:10
"rules" (*archai;* RSV, "principalities"), Eph. 3:10; 6:12; Col. 1:16; 2:15; Rom. 8:38
"authority" (*exousia*), I Cor. 15:24; Eph. 1:21; Col. 2:10
"authorities" (*exousiai;* RSV, "authorities"), Eph. 3:10; 6:12; Col. 1:16; 2:15
"power" (*dynamis*), I Cor. 15:24; Eph. 1:21
"powers" (*dynameis*), Rom. 8:38
"thrones" (*thronoi*), Col. 1:16
"lordship" (*kyriotēs;* RSV, "dominion"), Eph. 1:21
"lordships" (*kyriotētes*), Col. 1:16
"world rulers of this darkness," Eph. 6:12
"the spiritual (hosts) of evil in the heavenlies," Eph. 6:12
"the authority of darkness," Col. 1:13
"every name that is named," Eph. 1:21
"heavenly, earthly, and subterranean beings," Phil. 2:10

That this terminology designates supernatural beings is quite clear from Ephesians 6:11ff., where the believer's struggle is against the devil and against principalities, authorities, world rulers of this present darkness, spiritual hosts of wickedness. Usually they are conceived as being evil and opposing the Kingdom of God. Sometimes, however, these spiritual powers are not cast in an evil light but are represented as created beings who apparently exist to serve the divine glory (Col. 1:16). Christ is the head of all such rule and authority (Col. 2:10); the divine purpose will display to these principalities and powers in the heavenly places the manifold wisdom of God through the church (Eph. 3:10).

The data with reference to these spirits are similar to those which we have already discovered of the angels. They are created beings and like all creation exist for the purpose of serving the glory of God and of Christ. However, part of the angelic world has rebelled against God and has thereby become hostile to the divine purposes. The sovereign will has permitted Satan and the evil angels to exercise a large area of power over the course of this age. The rebellious state of the world is reflected not only in the fallen condition of mankind but also in the rebellious state of a portion of the angelic world.

A study of the language Paul uses to designate these angelic spirits suggests that Paul deliberately employed a vague and varied terminology. This is seen particularly in his alternation between the singular and the plural forms of several of the words. It is impossible successfully to group this terminology into clearly defined orders of angelic beings, nor is it at all clear that by the various words Paul purposes to designate different kinds or ranks of angels. Probably Paul was facing views that elaborated distinct orders of angels, and he purposed by his exceedingly flexible language, which may almost be called symbolic, to assert that all evil powers, whatever they may be, whether personal or impersonal, have been brought into subordination by the death and exaltation of Christ and will eventually be destroyed through his messianic reign.

STOICHEIA. A problem is found in the phrase *ta stoicheia tou kosmou*. In the older versions this phrase is translated "the rudiments of the world"; but in the RSV it is rendered, "the elemental spirits of the universe" (Gal. 4:3, 9; Col. 2:8, 20). The word *stoicheia* originally meant a series of things, such as the letters of the alphabet. Thus the word came to connote the A-B-C's of the subject, the basic elements necessary for a rudimentary knowledge (see Heb. 5:12). The word also came to refer to the basic materials of an organism, such as the elements of the physical world (II Pet. 3:10, 12). In later Greek of the third century A.D. the word was applied to the series of stars and astral deities that were supposed to be identified with the heavenly bodies. It is in this last meaning that the translators of the Revised Standard Version interpret the phrase in Paul to refer to an order of astral deities to whom false worship was addressed.

There are, however, serious difficulties to this interpretation, as popular as it may be. In the first place, the precise expression Paul uses is found nowhere else. Again, the evidence for the use of the word *stoicheia* of astral deities is much later than the first century; contemporary evidence is lacking. Third, it is difficult to conceive of Paul's asserting the Jews had been in bondage to heavenly star spirits as this interpretation would require (Gal. 4:3). The mediation of angels in the giving of the Law was not a bondage (Gal. 3:19), and we may say that it is quite impossible for Paul to class Jews together with Gentiles as being under the tyranny of star spirits before they became Christians.[12] The evidence being what it is, we must conclude that the enslavement to the rudiments of the world refers to the fifth use of *kosmos* discussed above.[13] Such a meaning certainly fits the context in each instance where the phrase occurs. The "world" in this expression means the whole system of earthly human relationships, including its wisdom and its religion. The system is transitory; but it can stand between a man and God. As Paul had been crucified to the world and was thus indifferent to circumcision (Gal. 6:14, 15) so far as he personally was concerned, so the Gentiles have with Christ died to the rudiments of the world and are no longer to practice the asceticism that the worldly system had required (Col. 2:20, 21). Since the Jewish institutions conceived as a legalistic system also belong to the world, Paul may speak of the Jews as having been slaves to the rudiments of the world (Gal. 4:9, 10).

From this discussion of Paul's view of the world, it becomes quite clear that the Pauline concept of angelic powers, even as the exorcism of demons in the Gospels, which manifested the presence of the Kingdom of God, is no peripheral element or the result of the influence of extraneous religious concepts upon Paul's view. It is rather something that belongs to the solid content of the New Testament faith.[14] This present evil age and the totality of human existence are under bondage to these evil powers, and the Kingdom of God can be realized only by their defeat and subjugation.

ADAM. Paul sees men outside of Christ not only as constituting the world that is in bondage to supernatural powers of evil; he sees them also as responsible sinners, whether they be Jews or Gentiles. The source of sin is traced to Adam. It is quite clear that Paul believed in "original sin" in the sense that Adam's sin constituted all men sinners.[15] When Paul says "in Adam all die" (I Cor. 15:21), he is expressing a common Old Testament idea of human solidarity,[16] which is very different from our modern individualistic thinking. The entire race is one with Adam, and his sin and death is the sin and death of the entire race. A crucial text is Romans 5:12: "Therefore as sin came into the world through one man and death through sin, and so death spread to all men because all men sinned." Grammatically, this can mean that all men died because they have personally sinned, or

---

[12] Cf. E. D. Burton, *The Epistle to the Galatians* (1920), pp. 510-18; H. St. John Thackeray, *The Relation of St. Paul to Contemporary Jewish Thought* (1900), pp. 156f. The spirit interpretation of *stoicheia* is also rejected by C. E. B. Cranfield, *NT Issues*, ed. by R. Batey (1970), pp. 164ff.; G. Delling, *TDNT* VII, 683-87; C. F. D. Moule, . . . *Colossians and* . . . *Philemon* (1957), pp. 91f.

[13] Cf. p. 399.

[14] G. H. C. MacGregor, "Principalities and Powers," *NTS* 1, 18-19.

[15] See D. E. H. Whiteley, *The Theology of St. Paul*, pp. 50ff.

[16] *Ibid*., p. 45 and literature cited.

it can mean that in Adam, all men sinned. Adam's sin became their sin and his death their death. In view of the context, the Augustinian interpretation is to be preferred rather than the Pelagian. This seems clear because of the statement in 5:19, "By one man's disobedience many were made sinners." This is balanced by the statement, "by one man's obedience [i.e., Christ's] many will be made righteous." In this context men are not righteous because they do righteous deeds; they are righteous in Christ. So in this context men are not sinners because they do sinful acts; they are sinners in Adam.[17]

NATURAL REVELATION. While Adam brought sin and death upon all men, they are guilty because they are themselves sinners. Paul argues this most forcibly when discussing the situation of Gentiles who do not have the Law. Men who have not known the revelation of the Law will be held accountable to God, for all men have available to them some knowledge of God. God's invisible nature, that is, his eternal power and deity, can be seen in the created world. This is not intended as a rational proof from nature that God exists; this is assumed. Paul wishes to assert that certain characteristics of God are revealed through nature: his power and his deity.[18] His main objective is a polemic against idolatry. Men are without excuse for substituting the worship of idols for the worship of God. "Although they knew God they did not honor him as God or give thanks to him" (Rom. 1:21). They exchanged the truth about God for a lie, and worshipped and served the creature rather than the Creator.

CONSCIENCE. Not only are men responsible to worship God, they are responsible to do the right because of conscience. God has implanted in all men a moral instinct that gives them a sense of right and wrong. "When Gentiles who have not the law do by nature what the law requires, they are a law to themselves, even though they do not have the law. They show that what the law requires is written on their hearts while their conscience also bears witness and their conflicting thoughts accuse or perhaps excuse them" (Rom. 2:14-15). Paul does not mean to say that conscience is an infallible guide in all questions or that conscience is a guide equal to the Law. He only means to say that all men have conscience, which gives them a sense of moral values,[19] and that pagans will be held

---

[17] For this interpretation, see F. F. Bruce, *Romans* (1963), p. 130; W. Manson in *NT Essays,* ed. by A. J. B. Higgins (1959), p. 159. Very close to this view is G. B. Stevens, *The Theology of the NT* (1906), p. 355; W. D. Davies, *Paul and Rabbinic Judaism* (1955), p. 32. For the other view, see C. K. Barrett, *Romans* (1957), p. 111; R. Scroggs, *The Last Adam* (1966), p. 78. The Vulgate renders the *eph' hō* by "in whom" (*in quo*), which Bruce understands to be a correct interpretation if not an accurate translation.

[18] B. Gärtner, *The Areopagus Speech and Natural Revelation* (1955), pp. 136f. See the entire discussion on pp. 133-44. For other points of view see H. P. Owen, "The Scope of Natural Revelation in Rom. 1 and Acts XVII," *NTS* 5 (1959), 133-43; M. D. Hooker, "Adam in Romans 1." *NTS* 6 (1960) 297-306.

[19] See R. Bultmann, *Theology,* I (1951), 218. On the whole subject, see C. A. Pierce, *Conscience in the NT* (1955).

accountable by God for that knowledge. Because men have the light of creation and the guidance of conscience and yet persist in idolatry and wrongdoing, they are sinners.

SIN. The nature of sin can be seen from a study of the several words Paul uses,[20] but the most profoundly theological word for sin is *asebeia,*[21] translated "ungodliness" in Romans 1:18. The most fundamental sin of the Gentiles is their refusal to worship God as God; all wickedness (*adikia*) arises from the perversion of worship.[22] The fundamental sin of the Jews who have the Law is "boasting," i.e., perverting the Law so that it becomes the basis of self-confidence that seeks glory before God and relies upon itself. Boasting is thus the antithesis of faith.[23] For both Gentile and Jew, the root of sin is not found in acts of sinfulness but in a perverted, rebellious will. This is supported by Paul's view of man as "flesh"—man standing in rebellious opposition to God.[24]

Sin is also missing the mark (*hamartia*) of the will of God. This is the most common Pauline word for sin. Sin came into the world through Adam (Rom. 5:12), and thus passed unto all men, bringing them into bondage, whose end is death (Rom. 6:23). Until Christ, sin reigned in death over man (Rom. 5:21) as a power from which he could not free himself.

Sometimes Paul speaks of sin almost as though it were an independent, hostile power, outside of man and alien to him. "But sin, finding opportunity in the commandment, wrought in me all kinds of covetousness" (Rom. 7:8). "For sin, finding opportunity in the commandment, deceived me and by it killed me" (Rom. 7:11). "So it is no longer I that do it [namely, the wrong], but sin which dwells within me" (Rom. 7:17). However, this in no way impinges on man's freedom or absolves him from guilt. "All have sinned and fall short of the glory of God" (Rom. 3:23).

Other terms for sin are transgression (*parabasis*)—a deliberate breach of law or morality (Rom. 2:23; 5:14); lawlessness (*anomia*)—contempt for and violation of law (Rom. 6:19); trespass (*paraptōma*)—indicating individual lapses (Rom. 4:25; 5:15; Eph. 2:1); and disobedience (*parakoē,* Rom. 5:19; II Cor. 10:6). Since three of these terms are used of Adam's sin in Romans 5:12-21, it is clear that, while each word carries its own shade of meaning, they are often basically interchangeable.

LAW. Paul does not regard the Law as merely the divine standard for human conduct, nor a part of Holy Scripture, although the Law is of divine origin and therefore good (Rom. 7:12, 14); but because of human weakness and sinfulness, the Law becomes an instrument of condemnation (Rom. 5:13), wrath (Rom. 4:15), and death (Rom. 7:19). The dis-

---

20 See S. J. DeVries, *IDB* R-Z, p. 371.
21 *Loc. cit.*
22 G. Schrenk, *TDNT* I, 156.
23 R. Bultmann, *TDNT* III, 649.
24 See below, pp. 471f.

pensation of the Law can be called a dispensation of death (II Cor. 3:17), of slavery to the world (Gal. 4:1-10), a covenant of slavery (Gal. 4:21-31). Life under Law is a bondage from which men need to be set free.[25]

FLESH. A final enemy of man outside of Christ, which need only be mentioned here, is the flesh. As we shall see in a later chapter,[26] "flesh" in Paul has a distinctive usage; it designates man in his fallenness, his sinfulness, and his rebellion to God. Sometimes Paul comes close to personifying the flesh (*sarx*) and viewing it as a hostile, alien power that has dominance over man, and from which he needs to be freed. The flesh is hostile to God's Spirit and cannot please God (Rom. 8:5-8). The flesh strives against the Spirit (Gal. 5:17) and leads to death (Gal. 6:8). This will be discussed in detail in Chapter 33.

ENEMIES. As sinners, men are estranged from God because they are hostile in their minds toward God (Col. 1:21; see also Eph. 2:12; 4:18). They are the enemies of God (Rom. 5:10). The word for "enemy" (*echthros*) can have two different meanings. The active meaning is that they are hostile to God, as in Colossians 1:21. The passive meaning is that God regards sinners as in a state of enmity toward him. As sinners, men are objects of the divine wrath, for God must be hostile to sin. Either interpretation is possible in this passage. The passive sense suits the context. Because men are enemies of God, they stand under the divine wrath (Rom. 5:9; Eph. 2:3). Because of their sins, men are not only sinful: they occupy the position of sinners. They are hostile in their minds toward God, and God must therefore look upon them as sinners, as his enemies.[27] The active meaning, "hating God," does not suit the passage, for the attitude of men was not changed by the death of Christ. *Echthros* in this context, then, does not refer to the feelings either of God or man but to the relation that exists between them.[28]

DEATH. Sinful men are also in a state of death: "You were dead through the trespasses and sins" (Eph. 2:1; Col. 2:13). While death usually includes physical dying (Rom. 5:12), it is obvious that here Paul must refer to "spiritual" death, which is equivalent to alienation from God. In a different idiom, Paul describes men in the old age as "those who are perishing" (I Cor. 1:18; II Cor. 2:15). This word (*apōleia, apollymi*) can designate both the final doom of the lost (Phil. 3:19; Rom. 2:12) and their present state outside of Christ. They are called "the perishing" not only because

---

[25] See Ch. 35 for a full discussion of the Law in Paul.

[26] See Ch. 33.

[27] For this interpretation, see J. Denney, *The Death of Christ* (1950), pp. 95-96; also "Romans," *Expositor's Greek Testament* (1900), II, 625; V. Taylor, *Forgiveness and Reconciliation* (1941), p. 75. See, for the entire problem, L. Morris, *The Apostolic Preaching of the Cross* (1955), pp. 193-98. Morris tends to see something of the passive idea in the word. See, however, W. Foerster, *TDNT* II, 814; F. F. Bruce, *Romans*, p. 124.

[28] D. E. H. Whiteley, *The Theology of St. Paul*, p. 70.

they are spiritually dead but also because they are on the way to final destruction.[29]

WRATH. The most vivid term Paul uses to describe the reaction of God to men of the old age is the wrath of God.[30] Wrath is primarily an eschatological concept. The day of judgment will be a day of wrath for the lost (Rom. 2:5; cf. I Thess. 1:10). The Lord Jesus is to be "revealed from heaven with his mighty angels in flaming fire, inflicting vengeance upon those who do not know God and upon those who do not obey the gospel of our Lord Jesus. They shall suffer the punishment of eternal destruction and exclusion from the presence of the Lord" (II Thess. 1:8-9). Probably Ephesians 5:6 and Colossians 3:6 refer to the impending wrath in the day of judgment.

However, this wrath is not only eschatological; it characterizes the present relationship between God and men. In the old age outside of Christ, men are children of wrath (Eph. 2:3). The wrath of God is revealed from heaven against all ungodliness and wickedness of men (Rom. 1:18). Here we have a bit of realized eschatology.[31]

The New Testament concept of the wrath of God is not to be understood as equivalent to the anger of pagan deities, which could be turned to good will by suitable offerings.[32] Neither can it be reduced to a natural impersonal interaction of cause and effect.[33] Rather, God's wrath is the "implacable divine hostility to everything that is evil, and it is sheer folly to overlook it or try to explain it away."[34] In Paul, the wrath of God is not an emotion telling how God feels; it tells us rather how he acts toward sin—and sinners.[35] "Wrath is God's personal . . . reaction against sin."[36] Sin is no trivial matter, and the plight of men is one from which they cannot rescue themselves. Wrath expresses what God is doing and what he will do with sin.

Such is the character of the old age and the condition of men who find themselves in it. Paul's view of the helpless plight of men outside of Christ is not due to Greek dualistic ideas but to an eschatological dualism that sees the old age as fallen, under the power of hostile spirits, rebellious against God, under doom to death and divine wrath.

---

29 C. K. Barrett, *I Corinthians* (1968), p. 51.

30 See D. E. H. Whiteley, *The Theology of St. Paul,* pp. 61-69 for an excellent discussion. See also R. V. G. Tasker, *The Biblical Doctrine of the Wrath of God* (n.d.); G. H. C. MacGregor, "The Concept of the Wrath of God in the NT," *NTS* 7 (1961), 101-209; A. T. Hanson, *The Wrath of the Lamb* (1957); L. Morris, *The Apostolic Preaching of the Cross* (1955), pp. 161-66; G. Stählin, *TDNT* V, 422-47.

31 D. E. H. Whiteley, *The Theology of St. Paul,* p. 67.

32 See H. Kleinknecht, *TDNT* V, 385-92.

33 C. H. Dodd, *Romans* (1932), p. 23.

34 L. Morris, *First and Second Thessalonians* (1959), p. 160.

35 D. E. H. Whiteley, *The Theology of St. Paul,* p. 65.

36 C. K. Barrett, *Romans,* p. 33.

30

THE PERSON OF CHRIST

Literature:

D. Somerville, *St. Paul's Conception of Christ* (1897); E. H. Gifford, *The Incarnation* (1897); S. N. Rostron, *The Christology of St. Paul* (1912); W. Bousset, *Kyrios Christos* (1913, 1970), pp. 153-210; A. E. J. Rawlinson, *The NT Doctrine of Christ* (1926), pp. 81-166; C. A. A. Scott, *Christianity According to St. Paul* (1927), pp. 244-79; E. Andrews, *The Meaning of Christ for Paul* (1949); V. Taylor, *The Names of Jesus* (1953); N. A. Dahl, "Die Messianität Jesu bei Paulus," *Studia Paulina* (de Zwaan Festschrift, 1953), pp. 83-95; W. D. Davies, *Paul and Rabbinic Judaism* (1955), pp. 177-226; V. Taylor, *The Person of Christ* (1958), pp. 32-79; L. Cerfaux, *Christ in the Theology of St. Paul* (1959); O. Cullmann, *The Christology of the NT* (1959); R. P. Martin, *An Early Christian Confession* (1960); R. Schnackenburg, *God's Rule and Kingdom* (1963), pp. 284-317; D. E. H. Whiteley, *The Theology of St. Paul* (1964), pp. 99-129; R. H. Fuller, *The Foundations of NT Christology* (1965); R. P. Martin, *Carmen Christi* (1967); F. Hahn, *The Titles of Jesus in Christology* (1968); C. F. D. Moule, "Further Reflections on Philippians 2:5-11," *Apostolic History and the Gospel,* ed. by W. W. Gasque and R. P. Martin (1970), pp. 264-276.

CHRIST: MESSIAH. The one all-important difference between Saul the Pharisee and the Apostle Paul was his evaluation of the person of Jesus. Everything else—his idea of salvation, the Law, the Christian life—was determined by this. Before the Damascus Road, Paul must have known the essentials of the Christian claim for Jesus, chief of which was the claim that he was the hoped-for Jewish Messiah. Damascus convinced Paul that this claim was correct. "It was at this one point that Paul parted company with Judaism, at the valuation of Jesus of Nazareth as the Messiah with all this implied."[1] At first glance Jesus' messiahship appears to play a small role in Paul's thought. It can be argued on the basis of the use of the term that the Pauline usage of *Christos* as compared to the Synoptics reflects a much later development. In the Gospels, *Christos* is almost always

[1] W. D. Davies, *Paul and Rabbinic Judaism* (1955), p. 324.

a title, seldom a proper name. In Paul, *Christos* has become exclusively a proper name. V. Taylor thinks there is only one place where *Christos* is used as a title: "and of their [the Jews] race, according to the flesh, is the Messiah" (Rom. 9:5).[2] Other scholars think that the titular meaning is possible in such references as Romans 10:6; I Corinthians 10:4, 15, 22; II Corinthians 4:4; 5:10.[3] However, for the most part *Christos* has become a proper name.

The simplest formula, "Jesus the Messiah," has altogether disappeared, while "Jesus Christ" and the full expression "our Lord Jesus Christ" are frequently used. Cullmann points out that Paul's occasional practice of putting Christ before Jesus shows that Paul is clearly aware that the title is not properly a proper name.[4] The transformation of *Christos* from a title into a proper name occurred probably in the Hellenistic church, where *Christos* would be a meaningless word, devoid of any religious connotations. Acts 11:26 reports that in Antioch believers were first called *Christianoi,* implying that Christos was already viewed as a proper name.

The fact that Paul does not frequently refer to Jesus as Messiah in no way minimizes the importance of the doctrine. The concept is much larger than the use of the term.[5] We have argued above that it was the recognition of the messiahship of Jesus that converted Saul the legalist into Paul the apostle.[6] However, the fact that it was as the glorified Lord that Paul recognized Jesus as Messiah led to a radical reinterpretation both of the person and function of Messiah. However, Jesus still retains traditional functions that belong to Messiah. His coming stands in the stream of the redemptive history of Israel, the covenants, the Law and the promises (Rom. 9:5). Messiah's coming fulfills the promises given in the prophets (Rom. 1:2) and his mission was accomplished "in accordance with the scriptures" (I Cor. 15:3). He preserves the functions of the expected Jewish eschatological redeemer. He is yet to appear in glory to establish his Kingdom (II Tim. 4:1; II Thess. 1:5); he will be the judge of men (I Cor. 5:10) and will destroy the wicked with the breath of his mouth (II Thess. 2:8). In fact, from one point of view, his primary mission is to establish the Kingdom of God in the world.

Paul says almost as little about the Kingdom of God as he does about the messiahship of Jesus, but both are fundamental doctrines to his thought. Probably the reason is to be sought in the fact that Paul's letters are addressed to Gentile audiences rather than to Jews. If we had Pauline correspondence addressed to Jews, we would probably find much more about Jesus' messiahship and his Kingdom. We must remember that these subjects

---

[2] See V. Taylor, *The Names of Jesus* (1953), p. 21.

[3] See J. Weiss, *The History of Primitive Christianity* (1937), II, 457.

[4] O. Cullmann, *The Christology of the NT* (1959), p. 134. See Rom. 3:24; 6:3, 11; 8:1, 11, *passim.* See also N. A. Dahl, "Die Messianität Jesu bei Paulus" in *Studia Paulina* (de Zwaan Festschrift, 1953), p. 84.

[5] N. A. Dahl in *Studia Paulina,* p. 84.

[6] See above, Ch. 28.

were capable of gross misinterpretation. To proclaim any king other than Caesar made one liable to the charge of sedition (Acts 17:3, 7).

However, in one passage Paul portrays the entire mission of Jesus in terms of his Kingdom or reign, and associates the Kingdom of God with the resurrection and salvation. Christ's reign as Messiah began with his resurrection. It will be concluded only when "he has put all his enemies under his feet" (I Cor. 15:25). By his reign, he will destroy every rule and every authority and power, the last of which is death. When his messianic reign is completed, he will turn over the Kingdom to God the Father (I Cor. 15:24).[7] Here the Kingdom of God is the redemptive, dynamic rule of God exercised in Christ's total messianic mission to bring order to a disordered universe, to accomplish God's total redemptive purpose.[8] This has both a positive and a negative side. Positively, it means resurrection—life for those who are in Christ. Negatively, it means the subordination and subjection of all spiritual powers and all hostile wills to the will of God. "The reign of the risen Christ is not only one of grace and blessing over the Church; it is one also of force and subjection over the spiritual powers."[9]

There is a polarity between present and future in Paul's teaching about the Kingdom of God.[10] In a number of places, God's Kingdom is an eschatological blessing that is to be "inherited" (I Cor. 6:9, 10; 15:50; Gal. 5:21). Jesus also had spoken of the Kingdom as an eschatological inheritance (Mt. 5:5). The background of this idiom is the prophetic idea of inheriting the promised land (Isa. 57:13; 60:21; 61:7; 65:9),[11] and in the New Testament the inheritance is the eschatological salvation of the Age to Come. The Kingdom is equated with "glory," which is also an eschatological concept (I Thess. 2:12); and the goal of salvation is set forth in terms of being called into God's Kingdom and glory. The Kingdom will become visible at the eschatological appearing of Jesus Christ (II Tim. 4:1). The sufferings God's people endure in this world are for the sake of the Kingdom of God (II Thess. 1:5). Now sufferings must be expected and endured; but those who patiently endure will be counted worthy of the gracious gift of the eschatological salvation. This suffering is not mere passive submission; it includes laboring for the Kingdom of God (Col. 4:11), i.e., devoted ministry in the service of the coming Kingdom by proclaiming it and helping other men to enter into it.

While the Kingdom of God is the eschatological salvation, it is also a present blessing. Already, because of what Christ has done, the saints have been delivered from the power of darkness—this fallen evil age—and have been transferred into the Kingdom of Christ (Col. 1:13). This "Kingdom

---

[7] For a further discussion of this passage, see Ch. 38.

[8] It is significant that both in the Synoptics and in Paul, the Kingdom of God has to do with the conquest of evil spiritual powers.

[9] R. Schnackenburg, *God's Rule and Kingdom* (1963), p. 301.

[10] *Ibid.*, pp. 284-317.

[11] *Ibid.*, p. 285.

of Christ" cannot be equated with the church; it is rather the sphere of Christ's rule, which is larger than the church.[12] Ideally, all who are in the church are also in the Kingdom of Christ; but even as the eschatological Kingdom of God is larger than the redeemed church and will include the subduing of everything hostile to the will of God, so the Kingdom of Christ here is the invisible sphere of Christ's reign into which men enter by faith in Jesus Christ. Thus God's Kingdom is not concerned primarily with physical things, necessary though they be, but with spiritual realities: righteousness and peace and joy—the fruits of the indwelling Holy Spirit (Rom. 14:17).

Paul's understanding of the messiahship of Jesus involves a transformation of traditional messianic categories, because it is not as an earthly monarch that Jesus reigns from a throne of political power, but as the resurrected, exalted Lord. He has been exalted to heaven (Rom. 8:34), where he has taken his seat at the right hand of God (Col. 3:1) and now reigns as king (*basileuein,* I Cor. 15:25). However, his enemies are no longer kingdoms and empires—the earthly enemies of God's people—but invisible, spiritual powers. The object of his reign is to subdue all of these rebellious enemies beneath his feet; the last enemy will be death (I Cor. 15:26). This corresponds to the fact that Jesus himself had refused an earthly kingdom (Jn. 6:15), had asserted that his rule came from a higher order and was not based on worldly powers (Jn. 18:31), and found the chief foes of God's Kingdom to be spiritual powers of evil (Mt. 12:28f.).

MESSIAH IS JESUS. There can be no question but that for Paul, the one who has been raised from the dead and exalted to heaven and who now reigns as Messiah at God's right hand is none other than Jesus of Nazareth. The modern debate about the historical Jesus and the exalted or kerygmatic Christ has often obscured Paul's thought by trying to make him answer questions he never raised. Modern scholars dwell much on the fact that Paul provides no biographical material about Jesus, that he is little interested in the life, words, and deeds of Jesus, indeed, that he has no interest in the historical Jesus at all, only in the "mythological,"[13] divine, incarnate Savior. One solution to this problem is that of radical criticism. The historical Jesus has been quite lost from sight behind the transforming power of Christian belief, which has changed a Jewish prophet into an incarnate deity. The other solution is that there never was an "historical" Jesus, i.e., one who is only man. The Jesus of the Gospels is represented as having a divine self-consciousness; and this is a true representation of the Jesus of history. Paul knows something of the tradition about the life of Jesus

---

[12] It is significant that the Catholic exegete, R. Schnackenburg, does not see the church here. *Ibid.*, pp. 298ff.

[13] It should be noted that in this context the word "mythological" designates any element that transcends ordinary human historical experience, i.e., the supernatural or miraculous.

(I Cor. 11:23ff.); but because his own experience with Jesus is not with the Jesus of history but with the exalted Lord, he is able under the leading of the Spirit to draw out the implications of the divine person of Jesus.

In any case, one thing is clear. For Paul the exalted Jesus is none other than Jesus of Nazareth. Paul knows that he is an Israelite (Rom. 9:5), of the family of David (Rom. 1:3), that he lived his life under the Law (Gal. 4:4), that he had a brother James (Gal. 1:19), that he was a poor man (II Cor. 8:9), ministered among the Jews (Rom. 15:2), had twelve disciples (I Cor. 15:5), instituted a last supper (I Cor. 11:23ff.), was crucified, buried, and rose from the dead (II Cor. 1:3, 4; I Cor. 15:4).

Paul is also familiar with traditions about the character of Jesus. He refers to his meekness and gentleness (II Cor. 10:1), his obedience to God (Rom. 5:19), his endurance (II Thess. 3:5), his grace (II Cor. 8:9), his love (Rom. 8:35), his utter self-abnegation (Phil. 2:9f.), his righteousness (Rom. 5:18), even his sinlessness (II Cor. 5:21). Andrews points out that these references must be historically sound, for this characterization is not derived from any known Jewish picture of the Messiah; "for no Jewish writings or expectations, not even that of the Servant of Yahweh, could have given Paul the outline of a being of such tenderness, sympathy, love, and grace."[14]

While these are authentic glimpses of the Jesus of history, perhaps it seems perplexing why they are so few and casual, why Paul appears so little concerned about the life, words, and deeds of Jesus. Bultmann's view that Paul's idea of the saving event must rest on the kerygma alone and not be at all dependent upon past historical facts shatters on I Corinthians 15:5-8, where Paul appeals to eyewitnesses to establish the factualness of the resurrection of Jesus.[15] The answer to the problem of the role of the Jesus of history for Paul is to be found in the nature of the gospel and the relative places of Jesus and Paul in redemptive history. The heart of the message of Jesus was the coming and presence of the eschatological Kingdom of God in his own person and mission. His words were important not because of their wisdom or ethical or religious content but because in them men were confronted by the dynamic rule of God. His deeds were important because they were the vehicle for God's acting among men to bring them deliverance and salvation. The Kingdom of God was active and present in his very person. The meaning of the person and mission of Jesus was that in him God was redemptively visiting men in history. In fact, he was conscious of a distinct oneness with God, both in his mission and person.

The kerygma of Paul is essentially the same as that of Jesus, namely, that in the person and mission of Jesus God has visited men to bring them the messianic salvation. But there is one great difference. Paul stands on

---

[14] E. Andrews, *The Meaning of Christ for Paul* (1949), p. 33.

[15] R. Bultmann, *Theology of the NT* (1951), I, 295. Bultmann recognizes the nature of Paul's argument but dismisses it as a passing apologetic device.

the other side of the cross and resurrection and is able to see something that Jesus had never been able to teach: the eschatological meaning of Jesus' death and resurrection. The death and resurrection of Jesus bear the same essential meaning as Jesus' life, words and deeds: the presence of the redemptive rule of God, a divine visitation. Paul understands that what was being accomplished in Jesus' life was incomplete apart from the cross and empty tomb. While the blessings of the Kingdom of God were present in Jesus' words and deeds, the greatest blessing of God's Kingdom was the conquest of death and the gift of life; and this was accomplished only by Jesus' death and resurrection. Furthermore, both in Jesus and Paul, as we have seen, the Kingdom is not a political power but the dynamic presence of God to overthrow the spiritual powers of evil and to deliver man from bondage to satanic enslavement. While this was being accomplished in the life and mission of Jesus, Paul sees that in this warfare the death and resurrection of Jesus provided an even greater victory.

This is true because during his earthly life the powers of the Age to Come were present in his historical person, and were therefore limited in their manifestation to his personal presence. The powers of the Kingdom were exercised only by Jesus and by those specifically commissioned by him to do so.[16] However, after Easter, when Jesus had been "designated Son of God in power according to the Spirit of holiness by his resurrection from the dead" (Rom. 1:4), when he who had been a Son of David (and of Adam) had by exaltation become a life-giving Spirit (I Cor. 15:45), the powers of the Age to Come that had been resident and operative in Jesus' historical person, now augmented by his ascension and the coming of the Holy Spirit, were released from historical *localization* and could be experienced by all believers regardless of the limitations of time and space. This is what Paul meant when he wrote, "The kingdom of God is righteousness and peace and joy *in the Holy Spirit*" (Rom. 14:17). No longer are such blessings limited by the bodily presence of Jesus on earth.

In other words, the total eschatological meaning of the person and deeds of the Jesus of history is not only perpetuated but greatly expanded by his death and resurrection. Therefore, when Paul proclaimed the eschatological meaning of Jesus' death, resurrection, and exaltation, he was proclaiming all that Jesus' life, deeds and words had meant, and far more. His relative silence about Jesus reflects neither historical nor theological disinterest in Jesus, but only the actual situation in the unfolding of redemptive history. All that Jesus in history had meant was included, and enlarged, in the preaching of the exalted one.

The question of Jesus and Paul must include an analysis of Paul's statement in II Corinthians 5:16: "From now on, therefore, we regard no one *kata sarka* (according to the flesh); even though we once regarded Christ *kata sarka,* we regard him thus no longer." Many scholars have seen in this

---

[16] See G. E. Ladd, *Jesus and the Kingdom* (1964), p. 267.

verse a deliberate contrast between the "historical Jesus" and the exalted Christ; between "the value of the earthly life of Jesus, the Christ, in contrast with his present rank."[17] More recently, Bultmann contrasts *Christos kata sarka* with Christ proclaimed in the kerygma. Bultmann thinks that the historical Jesus has been quite lost behind Christian tradition. Furthermore, his theological position leads him to say that Christian faith neither knows nor needs the historical Jesus. He speaks of the frantic efforts of conservative critics to rescue an historical Jesus from the flames of gospel criticism as comical, because theirs is the effort to recover *Christos kata sarka.* However, *Christos kata sarka* is of no concern for faith. Bultmann has no concern to know what went on in Jesus' mind,[18] for such a Christ is only a phenomenon of past history that can have no value for faith.[19] Relevant for faith alone is the Christ who confronts men in the kerygma; the *Christos kata sarka* must remain in the first century.

In this interpretation, we are in effect faced with two Christs: *Christos kata sarka*—the Jesus who lived in history in Palestine, and a completely different *Christos kata pneuma*[20] proclaimed by the church and by Paul as resurrected and exalted. Historical science is concerned with the former, Christian faith with the latter. Bultmann expressly says that there is no continuity between the historical Jesus and the Christ of the kerygma,[21] because the Christ of the kerygma seen both in the Gospels and in Paul is a divine, i.e., mythological being, not an "historical," i.e., merely human person. There is only continuity between Jesus and the preaching of the church; for Jesus is the ultimate source of this preaching.

This interpretation involves a modernization that obscures Paul's thought. Bultmann recognizes that the correct exegesis of II Corinthians 5:16 connects *Christos kata sarka* with the verb, not the noun. Paul is speaking of *knowing* after the flesh, not of a Christ who is after the flesh. But Bultmann insists that this really is not important, for " 'Christ regarded in the manner of the flesh' is just what a 'Christ after the flesh' is."[22] This may be true for the modern scholar, but it was not true for Paul. A critic of Bultmann has written, "The distinction between a *Christos kata sarka* and a *Christos kata pneuma* is not a desperate expedient (Verzweiflingsakt) of Paul but a desperate expedient of interpreters who have not understood him!"[23] The fact is that for Paul, *Christos kata sarka* is not the actual Jesus as he lived in history, as Bultmann thinks; *Christos kata sarka* for Paul is

---

[17] See C. von Weizsäcker, *The Apostolic Age* (1894), I, 142. C. A. A. Scott thinks this verse may be a claim to have known the historical Jesus (*Christianity According to St. Paul* [1927], p. 12).

[18] R. Bultmann, *Glauben und Verstehen* (1933), I, 101.

[19] *Ibid.*, p. 207.

[20] Bultmann does not usually use this phrase.

[21] R. Bultmann, "The Primitive Christian Kerygma and the Historical Jesus" in *The Historical Jesus and the Kerygmatic Christ,* ed. by C. E. Braaten and R. A. Harrisville (1964), p. 18.

[22] R. Bultmann, *Theology,* I, 239.

[23] A. Oepke, "Irrwege in der neueren Paulusforschung," *TLZ* 77 (1952), 454.

a complete misunderstanding and misrepresentation of the real Jesus. Christ, understood *kata sarka,* was a blasphemous claimant to messianic activity,[24] a transgressor of the Law. It was this wrong understanding of Jesus which led the Sanhedrin to ask for his crucifixion and which led Saul to persecute the church. Only when his eyes were opened by the Spirit could Paul understand who the Jesus of history really was: the messianic Son of God. For Paul, the modern understanding of the "historical Jesus," that of a Jewish apocalyptic prophet who preached the imminent end of the world, but who cannot be the Son of God who was put to death for our trespasses and raised for our justification (Rom. 4:25), is indeed a *Christos kata sarka*—a misunderstanding, a perversion of the Jesus who actually lived in history. For Paul, only the Holy Spirit could enable a man to understand correctly what had really happened in history.[25]

JESUS THE LORD. The predominant and most characteristic designation for Jesus is Lord (*Kyrios*), not only in Paul's epistles but in Gentile Christianity at large.[26] Men came into the fellowship of the church by believing in the resurrection and confessing the Lordship of Christ (Rom. 10:9).[27] The heart of the Pauline proclamation is the Lordship of Christ (II Cor. 4:5). The importance of this confession in the Pauline churches is vividly set forth in the words, "No one can say, 'Jesus is Lord' except by the Holy Spirit" (I Cor. 12:3). Paul obviously cannot mean that it is impossible to utter these words except by the inspiration of the Spirit (see Mt. 7:21). He means rather that a sincere confession of the Christian creed shows that the speaker is motivated by the Holy Spirit. Here is the most obvious mark of a Christian: confession of the Lordship of Christ (I Cor. 1:2; cf. Acts 9:14, 21; 22:16; II Tim. 2:22).

This confession has a twofold meaning. It reflects the personal experience of the confessor. He confesses Jesus as Lord because he has received Jesus Christ as his Lord (Col. 2:6). He has entered into a new relationship in which he acknowledges the absolute sovereignty and mastery of the exalted Jesus over his life. There are many other authorities in the world—both so-called gods and human authorities; but the believer recognizes only one final and ultimate authority over his life—one Lord, Jesus Christ (I Cor. 8:5-6). This is not an authority externally imposed but one gladly assumed by the confessor. By it he is brought into a personal relationship with the exalted Christ.

This relationship is not alone personal and individualistic; it is a relationship enjoyed by the church as a whole. This is seen in the frequent use of such idioms as "*our* Lord Jesus Christ" (28 times), "our Lord Jesus"

---

[24] See E. Schweizer, *TDNT* VII, 131, n. 263. Taylor says it is Jesus as he appeared outwardly to human eyes (*The Person of Christ* [1958], p. 39).

[25] See the discussion by O. Michel, "Erkennen dem Fleisch nach," *EvTh* 14 (1954), 22-29.

[26] V. Taylor, *The Names of Jesus,* p. 45. Taylor gives statistics on the use of *kyrios* in Paul.

[27] The idiom of the AV obscures the meaning of the passage.

(9 times), "Jesus Christ our Lord" (3 times).[28] In confessing Jesus as Lord, the confessor joins a fellowship of those who have already acknowledged his Lordship.

Confession of the Lordship of Christ is not simply an expression of personal devotion, for this personal devotion is itself grounded in a prior fact: the cosmic Lordship of Jesus. In the act of confession, the confessor not only acknowledges a new personal relationship to Christ, he also affirms an article of faith, namely, that by virtue of his death and resurrection, Jesus has been exalted to a place of sovereignty over all men, both living and dead (Rom. 14:9). He confesses Jesus as his Lord because Jesus has in fact been exalted and is the Lord exalted above all other gods and lords, whether real or imagined (I Cor. 8:5-6).

This is clearly affirmed in the great christological hymn in Philippians 2:5-11. Whatever the *morphē theou* is, whatever Jesus emptied himself of in his incarnation, one fact is clear in all interpretations of the passage: because of his self-emptying and obedience unto death, something new has been bestowed upon him—a new name indicating a new role and status: *Kyrios*. Before Jesus, now exalted as Lord, the entire universe of sentient beings must bow the knee. God's creation, hitherto rebellious, will be brought in submission at the feet of God's exalted one.

The significance of the title *Kyrios* is found in the fact that *Kyrios* is the Greek translation of the tetragrammaton *Yhwh,* the covenant name for God in the Old Testament. The exalted Jesus occupies the role of God himself in ruling over the world.[29] God is pleased to accomplish the restoration of a fallen universe in the person of his incarnate Son, Jesus Christ. As it worships Christ as Lord, the world will worship God.

Because Paul does not here make clear the time of the confession of Jesus' Lordship, some commentators believe that Paul saw this universal confession as occurring at the exaltation when cosmic homage was paid to him.[30] This would involve a different theology from that expressed in I Corinthians 15:25-26, where his reign begins at the ascension and is consummated at the parousia; and there is no reason for not understanding the Philippians passage in the light of Corinthians. Jesus' enthronement and the bestowal of the name occur at the ascension; but the universal acknowledgment of and submission to the sovereignty of the name await the parousia.[31]

This leads us to the basic significance of the title *Kyrios*. It is the ascription to Jesus of the functions of deity.[32] If confession of Jesus' Lordship

---

[28] See other formulae in V. Taylor, *The Names of Jesus,* p. 45.

[29] O. Cullmann, *The Christology of the NT,* pp. 180-217; R. H. Fuller, *The Foundations of NT Christology* (1965), p. 213.

[30] R. H. Fuller, *NT Christology,* p. 213; R. P. Martin, *An Early Christian Confession* (1960), pp. 36-37.

[31] G. R. Beasley-Murray in *Peake's Commentary on the Bible* (1962), p. 987; E. Schweizer, "Discipleship and Belief in Jesus as Lord from Jesus to the Hellenistic Church," *NTS* 2 (1955), 96.

[32] D. E. H. Whiteley, *The Theology of St. Paul* (1964), p. 106.

means salvation (Rom. 10:9), the background for this is the Old Testament concept of calling on the name of Yahweh. Paul himself makes this clear when he quotes from Joel 2:32: "For, 'every one who calls on the name of the Lord will be saved' " (Rom. 10:13). Thus we find that the Day of the Lord (I Cor. 5:5; I Thess. 5:2; II Thess. 2:2) has become the Day of the Lord Jesus (II Cor. 1:14), the Day of the Lord Jesus Christ (I Cor. 1:8), or even the Day of Christ (Phil. 1:6, 10; 2:16). As the Lord, the exalted Christ exercises the prerogatives of God. Thus the judgment seat of God (Rom. 14:10) is also the judgment seat of Christ (II Cor. 5:10). God will judge the world through Christ (Rom. 2:16); and until the end of his messianic reign, God rules the world through the exalted Lord.

It is clear that Lordship and messiahship are very similar categories, two ways of expressing the same reality. The reason for the predominance of Lordship over messiahship in Paul's letters is not that he did not understand messiahship or that he was unwilling to apply messianic categories to Jesus. It is that messiahship was strictly Jewish, and it was not wise in the Roman world to proclaim publicly the kingship of another than Caesar—even the rule of a crucified Jew. While in its Pauline content the idea of Christ's Lordship goes back to the Old Testament, it was a meaningful and acceptable category in the Hellenistic world, even though it was capable of misinterpretation in terms of cultic lords (I Cor. 8:5-6). Therefore when Paul writes that Jesus died and rose that he might be Lord (*kyrieusē*) of the dead and living (Rom. 14:9), he is saying nothing different from his assertion that Jesus must reign as king (*basileuein*) until he has subdued all his enemies (I Cor. 15:25).

JESUS AS SON OF GOD. Paul also speaks with some frequency of Jesus as the Son of God.[33] Jesus was God's Son, "descended from David according to the flesh and designated Son of God in power according to the Spirit of holiness by his resurrection from the dead" (Rom. 1:3-4). The conviction widely prevails that these words are not original with Paul but contain a familiar primitive confession. Critics speculate as to the pre-Pauline form of the confession and try to detect the specific Pauline additions. Some critics have seen here a primitive, pre-Pauline, adoptionist Christology. In the flesh Jesus was a Son of David; he became the Son of God by his resurrection from the dead.[34] Fuller has a rather novel interpretation: Jesus was predetermined from the time of the resurrection to be the eschatological Son of God at the parousia. Jesus was not adopted but predetermined to be the eschatological judge.[35] All of this is very speculative, and such conclusions rest upon the prior conclusion that Jesus did not think

[33] For references see V. Taylor, *The Person of Christ,* p. 44.

[34] E. Schweizer, *Lordship and Discipleship* (1960), p. 59; "The exaltation [is] the first beginning of Jesus' sonship to God." W. Kramer, *Christ, Lord, Son of God* (1966), p. 109.

[35] R. H. Fuller, *NT Christology,* p. 166.

of himself as the Son of God. This critical assumption, however, is not supported by the biblical data but rests on a theological assumption. In the passage under consideration, Paul designates Jesus as God's Son both according to the flesh and according to the resurrection. The key phrase is "with power." "According to the flesh," i.e., in the form of his earthly career, Jesus was Son of God in weakness; he was designated Son of God *in power* in the realm of the Spirit by his resurrection.[36] Paul's very language implies that pre-Pauline Christians knew that already in his earthly life, Jesus had been the Son of God in another way, that of humiliation.[37] It is significant that Paul concludes the passage by calling Jesus "Our Lord," for his becoming Son of God in power is precisely parallel to the bestowal of Lordship in Philippians 2:9.[38] Here are two spheres of existence of God's Son: earthly weakness, heavenly power. For Jesus was God's Son when God sent him to do by his death what the Law could not do (Rom. 8:3). He was God's Son who came in the fullness of time, born of a woman under the Law, sent by God to redeem those under the Law (Gal. 4:4).

The clue to the meaning of Jesus as God's Son can be found in the fact that his mission includes bringing others into the status of sons of God, and this is clearly a matter of relationship. God sent his Son that we might receive the adoption as sons (Gal. 4:5). However, Jesus' sonship is unique. He is God's *own* Son (Rom. 8:3, 31), the Son of his love (Col. 1:13). Jesus' sonship postulates a relationship that is independent of any historical experience that seems to involve "a community of nature between the Father and the Son."[39]

That Paul believed that Jesus was not only a man in history but also a divine person is clear from a number of references. He regards him as one who pre-existed before his earthly career and even as active with the Father in creation. "There is one God, the Father, from whom are all things and for whom we exist, and one Lord, Jesus Christ, through whom are all things and through whom we exist" (I Cor. 8:6). He is the image of the invisible God, the firstborn of all creation, the one in whom and for whom all things were created, and the one in whom all things hold together (Col. 1:15-17). "Firstborn" (*prōtotokos*) can have two meanings: temporal priority, or sovereignty of position. David, the youngest of eight sons, was to be made the firstborn, the highest of the kings of the earth (Ps. 89:27). Since Paul says nothing about the generation of the pre-existent Son, and since Christ himself is the one by whom creation itself came into existence, the second meaning, the status of primogeniture, appears to be

---

[36] Note that *kata sarka* has a distinctly different meaning here from what it has in II Cor. 5:16. See below, p. 467, for the several uses of *sarx*.

[37] A. M. Hunter, *Paul and His Predecessors* (rev. ed., 1961), p. 144.

[38] O. Cullmann, *The Christology of the NT*, p. 292.

[39] C. A. A. Scott, *Christianity According to St. Paul*, p. 256; followed by D. E. H. Whiteley, *The Theology of St. Paul*, p. 109.

Paul's meaning.[40] Christ is both the head over creation and the agent of creation. His creative activity includes not only the physical cosmos but all orders of spiritual beings, things both visible and invisible.

It is this pre-existent being, God's Son, who shared the creative activity of God, whom God sent into the world (Gal. 4:4; Rom. 8:3). This event is reflected in the saying, "For you know the grace of our Lord Jesus Christ, that though he was rich, yet for your sake he became poor, so that by his poverty you might become rich" (II Cor. 8:9). The classic passage is Philippians 2:6-11, which is at the same time one of the most important and most difficult Pauline passages to exegete.[41] The main statements are: Christ pre-existed in the *morphē* of God. He did not consider equality with God a *harpagmon*. He emptied himself. He took upon him the *morphē* of a slave, and was born in the likeness of men. In the *schēma* of men, he humbled himself in obedience to death on the cross. Therefore God has exalted him by elevating him to the status of Lord over all creation.

We have already discussed the meaning of his elevation and Lordship, and found that it refers to a rank or status of absolute sovereign in God's redemptive purpose that Christ had not previously enjoyed. In this connection, the discussion of the force of *hyper* in the term "exalted him" (*hyperhypsōsen*) is not important; it does not matter whether it means "he did *more* than exalt him,"[42] or "he raised him to the loftiest height."[43] The meaning of the word is expounded in the following words. Christ was elevated to the role of the Father himself.

The difficult questions are: What is the *morphē theou?* Is it divine essence—deity; or is it the mode of divine existence—God's glory? Is *morphē theou* something that Christ possessed, while he did not possess equality with God? Or is *morphē theou* to be identified with equality with God? *Harpagmon* can be either active or passive in meaning, but the active meaning, designating an act of seizing something, i.e., an act of robbery, is unlikely.[44] If the word is to be understood in a passive meaning, referring to the thing seized, two possibilities remain: something not possessed that is

---

[40] See F. F. Bruce in *Ephesians and Colossians,* by E. K. Simpson and F. F. Bruce (1957), p. 194.

[41] See R. P. Martin, *An Early Christian Confession;* V. Taylor, *The Person of Christ,* pp. 62-79. For older views see E. H. Gifford, *The Incarnation* (1897).

[42] O. Cullmann, *The Christology of the NT,* p. 180.

[43] W. F. Arndt and F. W. Gingrich, *Lexicon, in loc.*

[44] "The state of being equal with God cannot be equated with the act of robbery." Arndt and Gingrich, *Lexicon, in loc.* The difference between an active and passive noun can be seen in the words *psalmos*—the playing of a stringed instrument, and *psalma*—the tune played on the instrument. In form *harpagmon* should be active; but Hellenistic Greek tended to blur such distinctions. Thus *psalmos* comes to mean the song sung to the music of the harp. But see C. F. D. Moule, "Further Reflections on Philippians 2:5-11" in *Apostolic History and the Gospel,* ed. by W. W. Gasque and R. P. Martin (1970), pp. 267f. On the whole, see D. H. Wallace, "A Note on Morphē," *TZ* 22 (1966), 19-25.

seized (*res rapienda*), or something possessed that is held fast (*res rapta*). Between these two it is difficult to decide.

Another important question is, Of what did Christ empty himself? Of the *morphē theou?* If so, did he empty himself of his deity, as the classic kenotic theory holds,[45] or of the mode of the divine existence—his glory? Or, if *morphē theou* is equality with God, did he empty himself of equality with God?

The two most probable interpretations of the passage hinge on the rendering of *harpagmon.* If it is understood to designate *res rapta,* the probable meaning will be: Christ existed in the form and glory of God; but he did not consider this state of equality with God something to be forcibly retained but emptied himself of it by taking the form of a slave.[46]

The other interpretation understands *harpagmon* as *res rapienda.* He existed in the form and glory of God, but he did not possess equality of status with God. Yet he did not consider this equality a thing to be forcibly seized; instead, he poured himself out by taking the form of a slave and by humbling himself even unto death. Wherefore God has exalted him and made him equal with himself by bestowing on him his own name, Lord, that all creatures should worship the exalted Christ as they worship God himself.

It is very difficult on an objective exegetical basis to decide between these two renderings. Perhaps a point of departure may be taken from the fact that the text does not say that Christ emptied himself of *anything.* The self-emptying is qualified by the following participle: *morphēn doulou labōn*—"by taking the form of a slave." The text does not say that he emptied himself of the *morphē theou* or of equality with God. From other references we know that Paul regards Jesus incarnate as the embodiment of deity (Col. 1:19). All that the text states is that "he emptied himself by taking something else to himself, namely, the manner of being, the nature or form of a servant or slave."[47] By becoming man, by entering on a path of humiliation that led to death, the divine Son of God emptied himself.

A second guideline may be found from the implicit comparison between Christ and Adam.[48] The heart of the Adamic temptation was to grasp for equality with God (Gen. 3:5: "You will be like God"). Adam attempted to seize equality with God; Christ did not. By contrast, Christ chose the way of self-emptying rather than self-aggrandizement. For these two reasons the second rendition is to be preferred.[49]

---

[45] See the summary of this view by J. J. Müller, *Philippians and Philemon* (1955), pp. 83-85.

[46] V. Taylor, *The Person of Christ,* pp. 74ff.; A. Oepke, *TDNT* III, 161. A variant of this view distinguishes between *morphē theou*—deity, which he did not give up in his incarnation, and equality with God in glory, which he did give up. See J. J. Müller, *Philippians,* pp. 78ff.

[47] J. J. Müller, *Philippians,* p. 82. Müller has one of the best discussions of this passage. See also E. F. Scott, *IB* XI, 48.

[48] C. K. Barrett, *From First Adam to Last* (1962), pp. 69ff.

[49] See for this view E. Stauffer, *NT Theology* (1955), p. 284, n. 369; O. Cullmann,

In neither interpretation is there any intimation that Christ emptied himself of his deity. It is even possible that on rare occasions Paul calls Jesus "God." Romans 9:5 literally reads: "from whom is the Christ according to the flesh, the one being over all, God blessed forever." This can be translated by placing God in apposition with Jesus (AV, RV), or a period can be placed before God, making the last three words a doxology (RSV). Admittedly it is not Paul's style to call Jesus God; but a doxology here does not suit the context, and the style differs from Paul's frequent doxologies. Paul's view of the deity of Christ is so high he does everything but designate Christ as God, and it is likely that he actually does so here, although this can be only a tentative decision.[50] Titus 2:13 speaks of our great God and Savior Jesus Christ.

While Christ is the Son of God, the agent of both creation and redemption, and like the Father himself the object of universal worship, he does not usurp the position of God. It is difficult to deny that Paul does teach a kind of final subordination of the Son to the Father (I Cor. 15:28). If so, it is a subordination of economy and not of deity, of lordship and not of nature.[51]

While Christ as God's Son is God himself incarnate, this does not mean that Paul minimizes Jesus' humanity. He was born of a woman (Gal. 4:4) in the likeness and form of men (Phil. 2:7). Paul uses an interesting expression in Romans 8:3: God sent his Son "in the likeness of flesh of sin." To say that Christ came in the likeness of flesh would be docetic and suggest the unreality of Jesus' humanity. To say that he came in sinful flesh would make him a sinner. The Pauline expression asserts that he came in real flesh, like all flesh, with one exception—he did not share sinfulness.

CHRIST: THE LAST ADAM.[52] In two passages Paul speaks of Christ as the "last Adam." "Thus it is written, 'The first man Adam became a living being'; the last Adam became a life-giving spirit. But it is not the spiritual which is first but the physical, and then the spiritual. The first man was from the earth, a man of dust; the second man is from heaven" (I Cor. 15:45-47). Many commentators have found here in Paul reflections about ancient ideas of a primal man or *Urmensch* who descended from the heavenly world to free man from his incarceration in the world of matter and lead him back to the realm of light and life.[53]

Christology, pp. 176f.; E. Andrews, *The Meaning of Christ for Paul,* pp. 158-61; E. F. Scott, *IB* XI, 48f.; C. K. Barrett, *From First Adam to Last,* pp. 69ff.

[50] See F. F. Bruce, *Romans* (1963), pp. 186f.

[51] E. Andrews, *The Meaning of Christ for Paul,* p. 132.

[52] See R. Scroggs, *The Last Adam* (1966).

[53] For various treatments of the primordial man problem, see W. Bousset, *Kyrios Christos* (1921), pp. 140-43; C. H. Kraeling, *Anthropos and Son of Man* (1927); W. Manson, "The Heavenly Man Redemption Myth," *Jesus the Messiah* (1946), pp. 237-55; R. H. Fuller, *The Foundations of NT Christology,* pp. 76-78; O. Cullmann, *Christology,* pp. 166-81. Cullmann thinks that Paul drew on the Heavenly Man speculation in Judaism, but for *heilsgeschichtlich* rather than gnostic purposes.

We do find in contemporary religious thought the idea of a primal heavenly man. Philo sees in Genesis 1:27 and 2:7 two different Adams. The first is a heavenly Adam, the archetype of the earthly Adam, without participation in corruptible or terrestrial substance. The earthly Adam was made of clay animated by the divine creative breath.[54] However, the thought pattern of these two Adams is more platonic than religious.[55] The heavenly man belongs to the noumenal world and is only an object of thought. He serves as a pattern or archetype for the earthly Adam, as does the entire *noētos kosmos*. There must be a plan in the mind of God before there can be a tangible reality.[56] The earthly Adam is a twofold being, composed of body (clay) and mind or soul. The heavenly man in Philo has nothing to do with revelation or redemption. Salvation is achieved by the mastery of the mind over the bodily appetites, resulting in the release of the body from material world to return to the heavenly realm of the angels.[57]

The first tractate of the Hermetic writings, *Poimandres,* also has a primordial man.[58] He was not created but was the child of God, in the image of God, in that he, like God, is mind. This first man was set over all creation; but he fell in love with the created world and thus fell into the realm of materiality and consummated a union with nature. The fall of the heavenly man was also the origin of earthly man, who is thus twofold in nature: partly immortal (heavenly mind), partly mortal (body). The primal man in *Poimandres* serves in the interest of a dualistic cosmology.

Paul's reference to Christ as the man from heaven reflects no such ideas or tendencies, and can be adequately explained against the background of Adam and the eschatological Son of Man. "The man from heaven" (I Cor. 15:47) is not a primal being who pre-existed as man; he is the man who has been crucified, raised, and exalted, and whose coming is awaited from heaven. This is not a primal man but Paul's equivalent for the Son of Man—a term he never uses.[59] Paul nowhere talks about Jesus' pre-existence as a man; he pre-existed in the form of God (Phil. 2:6), and is the man from heaven "because he assumed our nature in his incarnation and retains it in his heavenly life."[60] He is the "last Adam" (v. 45) because by virtue of his resurrection and exaltation he has become a "life-giving spirit" (v. 45), the fountainhead of the people of God in the new age.

This interpretation is reinforced by Romans 5:12ff. where Adam and Christ are seen as the heads of two families: Adam the source of sin and death for all his descendants, Christ the source of righteousness and life for all who are in him.

---

[54] Philo, *On Creation,* 134-35; *Alleg. Int.*, I, 31-32.

[55] W. Manson, *Jesus the Messiah,* p. 242.

[56] Philo, *On Creation,* 16ff.

[57] Philo, *On the Giants,* 12ff.

[58] For the text in English, see R. M. Grant, *Gnosticism. An Anthology* (1961), pp. 211-19. See the discussion by C. H. Dodd in *The Bible and the Greeks* (1935), ch. VII.

[59] V. Taylor, *The Person of Christ,* p. 48.

[60] W. Manson, *Jesus the Messiah,* p. 250.

31

THE WORK OF CHRIST: ATONEMENT

Literature:

J. Denney, *The Death of Christ* (1903, 1950); C. H. Dodd, *The Bible and the Greeks* (1935) pp. 82-95; T. W. Manson, "Hilastērion," *JThS* 46 (1945), 170; V. Taylor, *The Atonement in NT Teaching* (1945), pp. 54-100; A. M. Stibbs, *The Meaning of the Word "Blood" in Scripture* (1947); L. Morris, *The Apostolic Preaching of the Cross* (1955), pp. 108-85; R. Nicole, "C. H. Dodd and the Doctrine of Propitiation," *WThJ* 17 (1955), 117-57; L. Morris, "The Meaning of Hilastērion in Romans 3:25," *NTS* 2 (1955), 33-43; L. Morris, "Atonement," *New Bible Dictionary*, ed. by J. D. Douglas (1962), pp. 107-10; D. E. H. Whiteley, *The Theology of St. Paul* (1964), pp. 130-50; L. Morris, *The Cross in the NT* (1965), pp. 208-59; D. Hill, *Greek Words and Hebrew Meanings* (1967), pp. 23-81.

The word "atonement" appears only once in the AV—at Romans 5:11; but in the RSV this word is properly translated: "through whom we have now received our reconciliation." While the word itself is not a New Testament word, the idea that the death of Christ dealt with the problem of human sin and brought men into fellowship with God is one of the central ideas in the New Testament.[1]

The subject of Christ's death plays so important a role in the structure of Pauline thought that it merits a thorough study. The centrality of the theme may be illustrated by its prominence in the first confessional statement of faith, a confession that was not created by Paul but which was received by him from the primitive church. "For I delivered to you as of first importance what I also received, that Christ died for our sins in accordance with the scriptures" (I Cor. 15:3). In almost every letter Paul refers in one form or another to the death of Christ. Paul uses considerable variety of expression, sometimes referring to Christ's death,[2] his blood,[3] his cross,[4] or his crucifixion.[5]

---

[1] See V. Taylor, *The Atonement in NT Teaching* (1945).

[2] Rom. 5:6ff.; 8:34; 14:9, 15; I Cor. 8:11; 15:3; II Cor. 5:15; Gal. 2:21; I Thess. 4:14; 5:10.

[3] Rom. 3:25; 5:9; Eph. 1:7; 2:13; Col. 1:20.

[4] I Cor. 1:17f.; Gal. 5:11; 6:12, 14; Eph. 2:16; Phil. 2:8; Col. 1:20; 2:14.

[5] I Cor. 1:23; 2:2; Gal. 3:1; II Cor. 13:4.

THE LOVE OF GOD. The first thing to be said about the death of Christ is that it is the supreme revelation of the love of God. While the New Testament as well as the Old has as its background for Christ's atoning work the wrath of God, this is in no way to be interpreted as turning God's wrath into love. In pagan Greek thought, the gods often became angry with men, but their anger could be placated and the good will of the gods obtained by some propitiatory sacrifice. Even in the Old Testament, the idea of atonement as the propitiating of an angry deity and transmuting his anger into benevolence is not to be found.[6] On the contrary, Paul repeatedly affirms that it was the very love of God that accomplished the atonement wrought by Jesus' death. Paul never deals with the cross as a mere event in human history, nor is he much interested in the historical circumstances that brought Christ to his death. For him the most ignominious and cruel form of human execution has become the place where God supremely displayed his love. This fact must not be construed to mean that Paul was not concerned with the death of Christ as an historical fact, or that the cross is a mere symbol for a subjective experience. He assumes its historicity but is interested primarily in the theological significance of that death.

The cross is not only the measure of the love of Christ but of God himself. "God was in Christ reconciling the world to himself" (II Cor. 5:19). "God shows his love for us in that while we were yet sinners Christ died for us" (Rom. 5:8). ". . . sending his own Son in the likeness of sinful flesh and for sin, he condemned sin in the flesh" (Rom. 8:3). "He did not spare his own Son, but gave him up for us all" (Rom. 8:32). "The love of God in the sacrifice of Christ is the undertone of his theology."[7] It is clear that for Paul, the final proof of God's love for men was the cross. Clearly, atonement is not an affair in which Christ takes the initiative while the Father adopts a passive role.

Paul does not differentiate between the love of God and of Christ. Both are seen in the cross. Indeed, the love of Christ is the love of God, and vice versa. "The life I now live in the flesh I live by faith in the Son of God, who loved me and gave himself for me" (Gal. 2:20). "For the love of Christ controls us, because we are convinced that one has died for all; therefore all have died" (II Cor. 5:14). "Christ loved us and gave himself up for us" (Eph. 5:25). The idea that the cross expresses the love of Christ for us while he wrings atonement from a stern and unwilling Father, perfectly just, but perfectly inflexible, is a perversion of New Testament theology.[8]

At the same time that we recognize the cross to be a work of a loving Father, we must acknowledge that the need for atonement is seen in the wrath of God against sin.[9] Paul introduces his line of thought in Romans, which leads to his most profound statement about atonement (Rom.

---

[6] L. Morris, *The Apostolic Preaching of the Cross* (1955), p. 155.
[7] V. Taylor, *The Atonement in NT Teaching*, p. 73.
[8] L. Morris, "Atonement," *New Bible Dictionary* (1962), p. 108.
[9] See above, p. 407.

3:21ff.), with the declaration, "The wrath of God is revealed from heaven against all ungodliness and wickedness of men" (Rom. 1:18). Whatever modern scholars may do with it, Paul clearly felt that there was neither contradiction nor incongruity between God's love and his wrath. Paul does not trace the consequences of sin to an impersonal principle; he ascribes them to the will of a personal God who is not mocked by wrongdoing (Gal. 6:7). While God in his love wills to redeem men, "he must fulfill this purpose in perfect fidelity to His own nature, without denying His righteousness, in conditions which are fully ethical."[10] Wrath is the judgment that falls upon sin in the moral order which God rules. Wrath is the divine reaction to sin. Atonement is necessary because men stand under the wrath and judgment of God. "Unless we give real content to the wrath of God, unless we hold that men really deserve to have God visit upon them the painful consequences of their wrongdoing, we empty God's forgiveness of its meaning."[11] The significance of this will be seen in the paragraphs that follow. The present point is that Christ's atoning work does not change God's wrath to love, for God's love is itself the source of atonement.

SACRIFICIAL. Paul views the death of Christ as a sacrificial death. In a number of references Paul distinctly associates the death of Christ with the Old Testament ritual and concept of sacrifice. Whether *hilastērion* (Rom. 3:25) is to be translated "mercy seat" as it is in the Septuagint or not, by the use of the word Paul makes a direct allusion to the sin-offering that was presented by the High Priest on the great Day of Atonement. Paul describes the death of Christ as "a fragrant offering and sacrifice to God" (Eph. 5:2). In Christ, God has done what the Law could not do with reference to sin: "sending his own Son in the likeness of sinful flesh and for sin, he condemned sin in the flesh" (Rom. 8:3). The words "for sin" (*peri hamartias*) probably refer to the sacrificial death of Christ, a fact that is recognized by the alternate reading of the Revised Standard Version, "and as a sin offering." Again Paul speaks of Christ as our paschal lamb who has been slain (I Cor. 5:7).

The sacrificial aspect of Christ's death is seen in the frequent references to his blood. God has made Christ to be the propitiation[12] by his blood (Rom. 3:25); we are justified by his blood (Rom. 5:9); we have redemption through his blood (Eph. 1:7); we are made near to God by the blood of Christ (Eph. 2:13); we have peace through the blood of his cross (Col. 1:20).

A moment's reflection suggests that such references are not primarily concerned with the actual physical blood of Jesus,[13] for, as a matter of fact, Jesus shed very little of his material blood. The idea of shed blood

---

[10] V. Taylor, *The Atonement in NT Teaching,* p. 76.
[11] L. Morris, *The Apostolic Preaching,* p. 185.
[12] See below, pp. 429ff.
[13] J. Behm, *TDNT* I, 174.

refers to the slaughter of the sacrificial lamb, whose throat was cut and whose blood gushed forth. Nothing like this happened to Jesus. The blood and water (Jn. 19:34) that came from Jesus' side did so after he had expired. In the New Testament, blood means life violently taken away, life offered in sacrifice.[14]

This view has been contested on the ground that the shedding of blood, instead of life given in sacrifice, means the presentation of life. "The significance of the sacrificial bloodshedding was twofold. The blood was regarded by the Hebrew as essentially the seat of life. . . . Hence the death of the victim was not only a death but a setting forth of life; the application of the blood was an application of life; and the offering of the blood to God was an offering of life. In this lay more especially the virtue of the sacrifice."[15] More recently, Taylor has espoused this view. "The victim is slain in order that its life, in the form of blood, may be released. . . . The aim is to make it possible for life to be presented as an offering to the Deity."[16]

This view has by no means carried the field. Speaking of the use of blood in Hebrews and John, James Denney said, "I venture to say that a more groundless fancy never haunted and troubled the interpretation of any part of Scripture than that which is introduced by this distinction. . . . There is no meaning in saying that by His death His life, as something other than His death, is 'liberated' and 'made available' for men."[17] We conclude that the "blood" in separation from the flesh does not mean life but death, life surrendered in sacrifice.[18]

VICARIOUS. In expounding the meaning of the death of Christ, theology has used the word "vicarious," meaning that Christ did not die merely as an event in history, nor did he die for his own sake. He "died for us" (I Thess. 5:9); "While we were yet sinners, Christ died for us" (Rom. 5:8). He was delivered up "for us all" (Rom. 8:32); he gave himself "for us" (Eph. 5:2); he became a curse "for us" (Gal. 3:13). Sayings of this sort reflect Jesus' own attitude toward his death: "The Son of man also came . . . to give his life as a ransom for many" (Mk. 10:45). Taylor has gone so far as to affirm that such sayings mean that Christ in his death was representative of men. "St. Paul believed that in some way, in some representative way, Christ acted for men, and that what happened to Him

---

14 J. Behm, *loc. cit.*

15 W. Sanday and A. C. Headlam, *Romans* (1902), p. 89. See also B. F. Westcott, *The Epistles of St. John* (1883), pp. 34-37.

16 V. Taylor, *Jesus and His Sacrifice* (1939), pp. 54f. See also *The Atonement in NT Teaching,* pp. 63f.; D. E. H. Whiteley, *The Theology of St. Paul* (1964), pp. 130ff.

17 J. Denney, *The Death of Christ* (1950), p. 149. The sacrificial interpretation is supported by Behm in *TDNT* and by Stibbs, Morris, and F. J. Taylor in *A Theological Word Book of the Bible,* ed. by A. Richardson (1950), p. 33. Barrett translates Rom. 3:25, "in his bloody sacrificial death." *Romans* (1957), p. 77.

18 L. Morris, *The Cross in the NT* (1955), p. 219.

was of supreme moment for them."[19] "What St. Paul means when he says of God that He made Christ to be 'sin on our behalf' is that Christ voluntarily came under the blight of sin, entered into its deepest gloom, and shared with men its awful weight and penalty."[20]

SUBSTITUTIONARY. Taylor, along with many modern scholars, resists the use of the word "substitutionary" to describe Jesus' death. To be sure, we must avoid all crude transactional interpretations. But is it enough to say that Jesus' death was only "representative" of men? If, as Taylor says, Christ voluntarily came under the blight of sin, entered into its deepest gloom, shared with men its awful weight and penalty, it is difficult to resist the conclusion that he not only died *for* me, he died *in my stead,* since because of his death, I shall not die, but shall live eternally with him. By suffering death, the penalty of sin, he delivers me from that very experience. In submitting to the judgment of God upon sin, he has delivered me from that same judgment. The rationale of this is difficult to understand unless Christ suffered the penalty and judgment of God in the stead of the sinner by virtue of which the sinner will never experience that awful penalty.

The universal presupposition that underlies the teaching about the death of Christ is that it was utterly unique. Of all men, Jesus alone knew no sin (II Cor. 5:21), and therefore being guiltless he did not have to die. His death was not the result of his own sin or guilt; it was suffered in the stead of others who were guilty and who deserved to die. By virtue of his unmerited death, sinners are delivered from the doom of death and from the experience of God's wrath that they eminently deserve. It is difficult to see how this can logically involve anything other than a substitutionary and vicarious experience. Proof for this point may be found in Paul's words that because Christ has died for all, "therefore all have died" (II Cor. 5:14). The truth in this saying is not the same as that in Galatians 2:20, which refers to the identification of the *believer* with Christ's death by virtue of which he has been crucified with Christ that he may live a new life of faith. The words in Corinthians refer to an objective event that took place in the historic death of Christ. In the death of Christ, all men died. The death of Christ was in some sense the death of all men. In the death of Christ I died; I experienced the doom of sin; everything that the guilt of sin merits from the wrath of God was fulfilled in the death I died in Christ. It is this objective fact which is the supreme manifestation of God's love and which is to be the controlling center of my life, and the quality of this love is derived from the fact that Christ's death was not his own; it was mine. He died not only as my representative; he died *in my stead,* for it is because of his death that I shall be spared that death. He has died my death in my behalf and in my place.

Many contemporary interpreters refuse to recognize this substitutionary element in the Pauline teaching on the ground that Paul does not use the

---

[19] V. Taylor, *The Atonement,* p. 60.
[20] *Ibid.,* p. 87.

preposition *anti,* which most explicitly expresses the thought of substitution. Aside from the passage in I Timothy 2:6 where Paul says that Christ gave himself a ransom for all (*antilutron huper pantōn*), Paul uniformly uses the preposition *huper;* and the significance of the passage in Timothy is discounted because the Pauline authorship of the pastoral epistles is widely denied.

However, the argument that rests on Paul's choice of prepositions does not exclude the substitutionary element. In Hellenistic Greek the preposition *huper* is often used in the place of *anti.*[21] In the papyri *huper* is used of a man who writes a letter in the stead of another.[22] In such instances a person serves not only as a representative but he is acting in the stead of the other. In such passages as II Corinthians 5:15, "He died for all," and Galatians 3:13 where it is said that Christ became a curse on our behalf, the idea of substitution is demanded and "only violence to the context can get rid of it."[23]

The objection that such a doctrine is repulsive because it is wrought entirely outside of and apart from ourselves so that we have nothing to do but to accept its benefits is the very crux of the argument. The Pauline teaching is precisely that God has done something outside of and apart from man that man does not merit but which man through faith can receive. "For by grace you have been saved through faith; and this is not your own doing, it is the gift of God—not because of works, lest any man should boast" (Eph. 2:8, 9). The objection Taylor raises becomes a serious problem only when the objective work of Christ is cut off from the accompanying subjective work and is made the totality of the doctrine of salvation. If the propitiatory death, justification, and reconciliation constituted the entirety of the work of Christ, then salvation would become an external transaction that is wrought outside of the believer and would have nothing to do with his own ethical and spiritual life. However, the substitutionary aspect of the death of Christ does not exhaust its significance. By the death of Christ the believer finds not only an objective atonement for sin; he finds also deliverance from the power of sin and the domination and bondage of the Law and of the world. There are also inseparable corollaries to the death of Christ that have to do with the subjective realm of Christian experience. The believer is to be identified with Jesus in his death that, being dead to sin, he may live in newness of life (Rom. 6:1ff.; Gal. 2:20). However, the substitutionary aspect of the death of Christ is in no way a subjective work; it is an objective accomplishment of God in the historic death of Christ by which God visited upon sin its just doom and penalty in him who is not only the sinner's representative but also his substitute, Jesus Christ.[24]

---

[21] L. Radermacher, *Neutestamentliche Grammatik* (1925), p. 139.

[22] A. Deissmann, *Light from the Ancient East* (1908), pp. 153, 335.

[23] A. T. Robertson, *A Grammar of the Greek NT in the Light of Historical Research* (3rd ed., 1919), p. 631. See also C. F. D. Moule, *An Idiom-Book of NT Greek* (1953), p. 64.

[24] See L. Morris, "Atonement," *New Bible Dictionary,* p. 109.

PROPITIATORY. The death of Christ has to do not only with man and his sin; it also looks Godward, and as such it is propitiatory. This truth is expressed in a single word that stands at the very center of Paul's teaching about the death of Christ. "They are justified by his grace as a gift, through the redemption which is in Christ Jesus, whom God put forward as a *hilastērion* by his blood, to be received by faith" (Rom. 3:24, 25). The word is *hilastērion,* which has traditionally been translated "propitiation" but which by many modern theologians has been rendered by "expiation."[25] This substantive is derived from the verb *exhilaskomai,* which throughout Greek literature means to propitiate or appease a person who has been offended. Traditionally, theology has recognized in these words of Paul a sense in which the death of Christ has effected an appeasing of the wrath of God against sin by virtue of which the sinner is delivered from God's wrath and made the recipient of his gracious gift of love. Modern theology has reacted against this traditional interpretation. The classic statement is that of C. H. Dodd in his *The Bible and the Greeks*[26] where the Hebrew terminology for atonement and the Greek equivalents in the Septuagint are carefully analyzed. Dodd points out that almost never is God the object of the verbs that describe the act of atonement. Linguistically, it is not God who is appeased, nor is his wrath assuaged; on the contrary, sin is atoned for. Dodd concludes that the linguistic phenomena in the Septuagint are not to be regarded "as conveying the sense of propitiating the Deity, but the sense of performing an act whereby guilt or defilement is removed." Assuming that the Septuagintal usage provides the background for Paul's thought, Dodd concludes that "the meaning conveyed (in accordance with LXX usage which is constantly determinative for Paul) is that of expiation, not that of propitiation. Most translators and commentators are wrong."[27] Dodd's view that the biblical concept of atonement involves the expiating of sin and not the propitiating of God has been widely accepted. "It cannot be right to think of God's wrath as being 'appeased' by the sacrifice of Christ, as some 'transactional' theories of the atonement have done . . . because it is God who in Christ reconciles the world to himself. . . . It cannot be right to make any opposition between the wrath of the Father and the love of the Son."[28]

In spite of the great influence Dodd has exercised and the prevalence of his view, his conclusions are not unassailable.[29] First, the word in non-biblical Hellenistic Greek authors, such as Josephus and Philo, uniformly

---

25 The RSV prefers this latter translation, relying apparently on the researches of C. H. Dodd.

26 (1935), pp. 82-95.

27 *Ibid.,* p. 94.

28 A. G. Hebert, in *A Theological Word Book of the Bible* (1950), ed. by A. Richardson, p. 26. See V. Taylor, *The Atonement in NT Thought,* p. 91.

29 See R. Nicole, "C. H. Dodd and the Doctrine of Propitiation," *WThJ* 17 (1955), 117-57, for a thorough examination and refutation. See also L. Morris, *The Apostolic Preaching of the Cross,* pp. 125-85.

means "to propitiate." This is also true of its use in the Apostolic Fathers.[30] As Morris has said, "If the LXX translators and the New Testament writers evolved an entirely new meaning of the word group, it perished with them, and was not resurrected until our own day."[31] Second, there are three places in the Septuagint where the word *exhilaskesthai* is used in the sense of propitiating or appeasing God (Zech. 7:2; 8:22; Mal. 1:9);[32] and Dodd's argument that there appears to be something exceptional about the usage of the word in these passages is not convincing. Third, if the verb in the Septuagint is infrequently used with God as its object, it is equally true that the verb is *never* followed by an accusative of sin in the canonical Scriptures of the Old Testament.[33] Fourth, and most significant, while the Old Testament does not speak of appeasing the wrath of God, it is nevertheless true that in many places where the word is used, the wrath of God provides the context for the thought. In many places atonement is necessary to save life that otherwise would be forfeited—apparently because of the wrath of God.

The context in Romans of Paul's statement about propitiation is the wrath of God, the guilt of sin, and the doom of death. A propitiation has been provided to rescue men from the wrath of God that is revealed from heaven against all ungodliness and wickedness of men (Rom. 1:18). It is certainly a distortion of Paul's thought to interpret the wrath of God merely in terms of natural retribution as Dodd attempts to do.[34] God is a living God who in the day of judgment will pour out his wrath upon men who merit his righteous judgment (Rom. 2:5). All men stand condemned as guilty sinners in the presence of a holy God. The main thrust of Paul's argument in Romans 1:18 through 3:20 is not to evaluate the degree of human sinfulness; it is to demonstrate the universality of sinfulness and of guilt before God. Both Gentile and Jew have been given illumination either through nature, conscience, or the Law; and both Gentile and Jew have abjectly failed to attain a righteousness before God and therefore are seen as the deserving objects of God's holy wrath. They stand condemned as guilty sinners. The ultimate doom merited by this guilt is death. It is God's righteous decree that those who practice the sins of the Gentiles deserve to die (Rom. 1:32). The destiny of sinners is to perish (Rom. 2:12), for the wages of sin is death (Rom. 6:23). God's wrath, poured out upon the guilty sinner, issues in his death.

This is the dark background of the New Testament doctrine of propitiation. By virtue of the death of Christ, man is rescued from death; he is acquitted of his guilt and is justified; a reconciliation is accomplished because of which the wrath of God no longer need be feared. The death of Christ has saved the believer from the wrath of God so that he may

---

[30] See F. Büchsel, *TDNT* III, 314; R. Nicole in *WThJ*, 131-32.
[31] L. Morris, "The Use of *Hilaskesthai* in Biblical Greek," *ET* 62 (1950-51), 233.
[32] C. H. Dodd, *The Bible and the Greeks*, pp. 86f.
[33] L. Morris in *ET* 62, 231.
[34] C. H. Dodd, *Romans* (1932), *in loc.*

look forward no longer to God's wrath but to life (I Thess. 5:9). The guilt and the doom of sin have been borne by Christ; the wrath of God has been propitiated.

It is not altogether clear precisely whether the word *hilastērion* is used as a noun or an adjective. In the other places where the word occurs in the Greek Bible (Heb. 9:5; Exod. 25:17-20), it is used of the lid of the ark, the mercy seat where the atoning blood was sprinkled. Many interpreters understand the word to bear this meaning in Romans 3:25. God set forth Jesus as a mercy seat in his blood.[35] However, this interpretation has been strongly opposed by Morris,[36] who argues for the adjectival use, "whom God put forward in propitiatory power," or "a propitiating thing."[37] We cannot here retrace the arguments, but one of the most forceful is that it seems harsh to think of Jesus being at once the priest who makes sacrifice, the victim, and the place of sprinkling. The New Testament regards the place of sprinkling of Christ's blood to be the cross. Furthermore, Romans is not moving in the sphere of Levitical symbolism. Therefore it seems best to translate it, "whom God put forward as a propitiatory (sacrifice)." In any case, the object of propitiation is the wrath of God, not merely the sin of men.

The objection has been raised that God is the subject of *hilastērion,* not its object.[38] This objection is met by the recognition that it is God who in Christ's death propitiates his own wrath. "If the propitiatory death of Jesus is eliminated from the love of God, it might be unfair to say that the love of God is robbed of all meaning, but it is certainly robbed of its apostolic meaning."[39] If *hilastērion* means only expiation, the question must be answered, Why should sin be expiated? What would be the result to man if there were no expiation? It is evident that if men die in their sins, they have the divine displeasure to face; and this is but another way of saying that the wrath of God abides on them.[40]

The propitiatory character of Jesus' death is further supported by the thought in verses 25 and 26. The death of Christ was an act of righteousness, a demonstration that God was indeed a righteous God. In times past he had seemed to pass over sin. This was due to the divine forbearance; but it appeared that he had not treated sin as it really deserved. In thus appearing to pass over sin, the righteousness and the justice of God seemed to be called into question. The death of Christ removed this apparent reproach against God by demonstrating his righteousness in visiting sin with the judgment it deserved. This was to prove at the present time that God is both just and the justifier of him who has faith in Jesus (v. 26).

---

35 T. W. Manson, "Hilastērion," *JTS* 46 (1945), 1-17; C. H. Dodd, *Romans,* pp. 21ff. See Luther's translation "Gnadenstuhl."

36 L. Morris, "The Meaning of *Hilastērion* in Romans 3:25," *NTS* 2 (1955), 33-43.

37 See also L. Morris, *The Apostolic Preaching,* p. 172.

38 F. Büchsel, *TDNT* III, 320.

39 J. Denney, *The Death of Christ* (1950), p. 152.

40 L. Morris, *The Apostolic Preaching,* p. 183.

Some interpreters attempt to render the word "and" (*kai*) as a correlative and interpret justification of the believer as the act of righteousness. It is God's nature to proffer forgiveness to sinful men, and therefore when God acts in accordance with his nature, he manifests his righteousness. Therefore the justification of the sinner is itself an act of righteousness, a manifestation of the essential character of God. Such an interpretation, however, violates the context of the passage. The just doom of sin is death; and God would have displayed his righteousness if he had visited upon every sinner the penalty of death. In this case condemnation would be the display of God's righteousness. Therefore the *kai* must be understood not as a copulative but as an adversative and is to be translated "it was to prove at the present time that he himself is just and *yet* the justifier of him who has faith in Jesus."[41] If there had been no death of Christ, God would have been unable to justify the sinner. Apart from the death of Christ, the only manifestation of righteousness is the sinner's condemnation in death. By virtue of Christ's death, the divine justice and mercy have both found their perfect realization. In justice God has dealt with sin as sin must be treated, and at the same time in mercy he has acquitted the sinner of all guilt and delivered him from its doom. We may therefore conclude, even though the Scriptures nowhere use this terminology, that Christ in his death in a real sense of the word experienced the wrath of God in the place of the guilty sinner.

Full recognition of the propitiatory, substitionary character of the death of Christ must not permit us to overlook or to underemphasize the companion teaching that the death of Christ as a demonstration of divine love is designed to kindle a loving response in the hearts of men. The objective and the substitutionary character of the death of Christ as the supreme demonstration of God's love should result in a transformation of conduct that is effected by the constraining power of that love. Those who recognize and acknowledge this love are to submit themselves to its controlling power; because Christ died for all, men are no longer to devote themselves to the satisfaction of their own desires but to him who for their sake died and was raised again (II Cor. 5:14, 15). The moral influence of Christ's death on the lives of men is not to be ignored because the teaching has been abused and wrongly made the central truth of the atonement. The love of Christ manifested in giving himself as a sacrifice to God is to be imitated by a walk of love (Eph. 5:2). The example of the utter humility of Christ in subjecting himself in perfect obedience to God even though that obedience led to the death of the cross, is to be emulated by the humble conduct of his disciples in their relationships one to the other (Phil. 2:5ff.). The main significance of Christ's death is to be found in its objective character as a propitiatory, substitutionary sacrifice, the benefits of which are to be received by faith as a gracious gift; but the subjective influence of his death in arousing the response of love in the hearts of men can

---

[41] B. F. Westcott, *St. Paul and Justification* (1913), p. 182.

be neither denied nor ignored. There is both an objective and a subjective significance in Christ's death.

REDEMPTIVE. Another objective of the death of Christ is redemption. This is expressed by two word groups: *lutron, apolutrōsis,* and *agorazō, exagorazō,* to buy or purchase. The noun *lutron,* meaning ransom or redemption, does not occur in Paul, but is found in Mark 10:45, which asserts that the Son of Man came to give his life as a ransom in the stead of many.[42] In both classical and Hellenistic Greek, this word group is used of the price paid to redeem something that is in pawn, of the money paid to ransom prisoners of war, and of money paid to purchase the freedom of a slave.[43] The same meaning is found of this word group in the LXX.[44] The verb *lutroō* is used in Titus 2:14: "who [Christ] gave himself to redeem us from all iniquity." This is a fairly obvious reference to Mark 10:45 and includes specific mention of the ransom price: he gave himself.[45]

A compound form of the noun is used in I Timothy 2:6: "who gave himself as a ransom (*antilutron*) for all." Here again is a specific reference to the price of ransom: he "gave himself." The use of *anti* suggests substitution. Christ's death was a substitute-ransom.

The most common word in Paul is *apolutrōsis*. This is a rare word, occurring only eight times outside the New Testament.[46] Several times the price of redemption is expressed in the context. We are justified by his grace "through the redemption which is in Christ Jesus, whom God put forward as a propitiation through his blood" (Rom. 3:24). "In him we have redemption through his blood" (Eph. 1:7).[47] In the light of such clear statements as these, it is hard to accept Büchsel's judgment that the original sense of the root *lutron* is watered down and only the general sense of "liberation" remains instead of ransom.[48] On the contrary, we can hardly resist the conclusion that the idea of *lutron* retains its full force, that it is identical with *timē* (price), and that both are ways of describing the death of Christ. The emphasis is on the *cost* of man's redemption.[49]

There are other passages where *apolutrōsis* is used eschatologically, of the day of redemption of the body (Rom. 8:23; Eph. 4:30). The use in Ephesians 1:14, obscured in the translation of the RSV, seems also to be eschatological. The passage in I Corinthians 1:30 is neutral: God has made Christ "our wisdom, our righteousness, and sanctification and redemption."

---

[42] See above, p. 187.

[43] See F. Büchsel, *TDNT* IV, 340; A. Deissmann, *Light from the Ancient East*. pp. 331f.

[44] L. Morris, *The Apostolic Preaching,* pp. 10ff.

[45] *Ibid.,* p. 35. The verb is also used in I Pet. 1:18, 19, where the price of ransom is clearly stated to be "the precious blood of Christ."

[46] *Ibid.,* p. 37.

[47] See also Heb. 9:15: "A death has occurred which redeems them from the transgressions under the first covenant."

[48] F. Büchsel, *TDNT* IV, 355.

[49] W. Sanday and A. C. Headlam, *Romans,* p. 86. See also C. K. Barrett, *Romans,* p. 76.

Redemption is also expressed by the verb *agorazō,* to buy or purchase. "You are not your own; you were bought with a price" (I Cor. 6:19, 20). "He who was free when called is a slave of Christ. You were bought with a price; do not become the slaves of men" (I Cor. 7:22, 23). While the cost of purchase is not stated, it is clearly in Paul's mind in view of the fact that both times he refers to the price. This can be nothing other than the death of Christ. This idea of purchase has a slightly different emphasis from the ransom words. The latter point more to the negative side—that from which men are redeemed: sin and death. The idea of purchase emphasizes a change in ownership. The believer now is the property of God by right of purchase. "You are not your own."

A compound form of purchase occurs once: "Christ redeemed (*exagorazō*) us from the curse of the law, having become a curse for us" (Gal. 3:13). The thought is that those who seek righteousness in law-keeping are under a curse, unless they perfectly fulfill the Law's demands. But Christ became a curse by hanging on a tree; and this he did "for us." This refers to deliverance from the plight of condemnation under the Law into which we had fallen because of our failure to keep it. It clearly involves the idea of substitution. It is "one of the clearest indications that St. Paul conceived of the death of Christ as both substitutionary and penal."[50] It also points to the cross as the cost of this redemption, for deliverance was achieved because Christ hung upon the tree. Galatians 4:4 adds little to this: "God sent forth his Son . . . to redeem those who were under the law." The emphasis of these verses is not so much redemption to become the possession of Christ, but redemption to freedom.

Morris adequately summarizes the doctrine of redemption, including both word groups.[51] (a) The state of sin out of which man is to be redeemed. This is likened to a slavery that man cannot break, so redemption involves intervention from an outside person who pays the price man cannot pay. (b) The price that is paid. The payment of a price is a necessary element in the redemption idea; and Christ has paid the price of our redemption. (c) The resultant state of the believer. This is expressed in a paradox. We are redeemed to freedom, as sons of God; but this freedom means slavery to God. The whole point of this redemption is that sin no longer has dominion. The redeemed are those saved to do the will of their Master.

TRIUMPHANT. Another end achieved by the death of Christ is triumph over the cosmic powers. We have seen that Paul's world-view includes the concept of an invisible world of both good and evil spirits. Men are in bondage not only to the Law, sin and death, but also to this evil spiritual world.[52] One of the purposes of the mission of Christ is to destroy "every rule and every authority and power. For he must reign until he has put all his

---

[50] H. W. Robinson, *Redemption and Revelation* (1942), p. 231.
[51] L. Morris, *The Apostolic Preaching,* pp. 58f.
[52] See above, pp. 400ff.

enemies under his feet" (I Cor. 15:24-25). In some unexplained way, the death of Christ constituted an initial defeat of these powers.[53] This is clearly set forth in Colossians. "He disarmed the principalities and powers and made a public example of them, triumphing over them in him" (Col. 2:15). Some exegetes interpret this differently. The word translated "disarmed" is *apekdusamenos*. Strictly speaking, this ought to mean "to strip off"; and some scholars take it to be a reference to the death of Christ in which he stripped off his flesh through which the powers of evil and death were able to attack men.[54] Another similar interpretation is that he stripped off the powers of evil that had clung to his humanity.[55] This understands the verb as a true middle. However, in Hellenistic Greek the middle may have an active meaning, and a more satisfactory translation is that of the RSV, which understands the verse to mean that Christ has disarmed the spiritual powers, stripping them of their insignia of rank or of their arms.[56] Thus the verse states that by his death Christ triumphed over his spiritual enemies, winning a divine triumph over the cosmic powers.

A problem is raised by the use of *archōn* as one of the terms for these spiritual powers. Satan is called the "prince (*archōn*) of the power of the air" (Eph. 2:2). In I Corinthians Paul speaks of "the rulers (*hoi archontes*) of this age who are doomed to pass away" (2:6). Again, speaking of God's wisdom, he says, "None of the rulers of this age understood this; for if they had, they would not have crucified the Lord of glory" (2:8). Many scholars understand the "rulers of this age" to carry a meaning parallel to the "principalities and powers" in Ephesians 3:10. According to this interpretation, it was really the spiritual powers that brought Christ to the cross, but they did this in ignorance, because they did not recognize who he was.[57] Cullmann sees this meaning in Romans 13:1-2, where Paul seems to be speaking of heads of the state—political rulers as "authorities" (*exousiai*) to whom the Christian should submit himself. He argues that the *exousiai* are indeed political rulers, but they are also angelic powers that stand behind the state. Christ, in conquering the spiritual powers, has brought under his rule both the angelic powers and through them the political rulers who are their executive agents. Thus Christ has in reality brought the state within the sphere of his reign, even though the state may not know it. This he calls "the Christological ground of the state."[58] However,

---

[53] We have seen above, pp. 65ff., that even Jesus' earthly mission, especially the exorcism of demons, constituted a victory over this spirit world.

[54] J. A. T. Robinson, *The Body* (1952), p. 41; G. H. C. MacGregor, *NTS* I (1954), 23.

[55] J. B. Lightfoot, *Colossians* (1876), p. 190. See also C. F. D. Moule, *Colossians* (1957), pp. 101-2.

[56] A. Oepke, *TDNT* II, 318-19; R. Leivestad, *Christ the Conqueror* (1954), p. 103; F. F. Bruce in E. K. Simpson and F. F. Bruce, *Ephesians and Colossians* (1957), p. 240.

[57] J. Hering, *First Corinthians* (1962), pp. 16-17; C. K. Barrett, *First Corinthians* (1968), p. 72.

[58] O. Cullmann, *Christ and Time* (1950), p. 193.

the more natural meaning of *exousiai* in Romans 13 is simply the political powers. There is no need nor clear intention to see spiritual powers standing behind the political rulers,[59] and it is easier to understand the *archontes* of I Corinthians 2:6, 8 as political rulers such as Pilate and Herod. Again, it is not at all clear that Paul intends to refer to ignorant angelic powers who brought Jesus to the cross.[60] We conclude that these passages in Corinthians and Romans add nothing to Paul's thought of Christ's victory over the spiritual powers.

[59] W. Foerster, *TDNT* II, 565; D. E. H. Whiteley, *The Theology of St. Paul,* p. 231. See C. D. Morrison, *The Powers That Be* (1960).

[60] A. Robertson and A. Plummer, *First Corinthians* (1911), p. 36; F. W. Grosheide, *First Corinthians* (1953), pp. 62-64.

32

THE WORK OF CHRIST: JUSTIFICATION AND RECONCILIATION

Literature:

W. Sanday and A. C. Headlam, *Romans* (1896), pp. 28-39; J. H. Ropes, "Righteousness in the OT and in St. Paul," *JBL* 22 (1903), 211-27; E. D. Burton, *Galatians* (1920), pp. 460-74; C. H. Dodd, *The Bible and the Greeks* (1935), pp. 42-59; G. Schrenk, "Dikaios, dikaiōsunē, dikaioō," *TDNT* II, 182-225; N. Snaith, *The Distinctive Ideas of the OT* (1944), pp. 51-78; V. Taylor, *Forgiveness and Reconciliation* (1947), pp. 29-69; R. Bultmann, *Theology of the NT* (1951), I, 270-84; E. C. Blackman, "Justification," *IDB* E-J, pp. 1027-30; E. R. Achtemeier, "Righteousness in the OT," *IDB* R-Z, pp. 80-85; D. E. H. Whiteley, *The Theology of St. Paul* (1964), pp. 156-65; J. Jeremias, *The Central Message of the NT* (1965), pp. 51-70; D. Hill, *Greek Words and Hebrew Meanings* (1967), pp. 82-162; E. Käsemann, "The Righteousness of God in Paul," *NT Questions of Today* (1969), pp. 168-82; E. Käsemann, "Justification and Salvation History" in *Perspectives on Paul* (1969), pp. 60-78; H. Conzelmann, "Current Problems in Pauline Research," *NT Issues,* ed. by R. Batey (1970), pp. 130-47; M. Barth, *Justification* (1971); J. A. Ziesler, *The Meaning of Righteousness in Paul* (1972).

Paul employs many terms to set forth the work of Christ. One of the most important, which dominates the letters to the Galatians and Romans, is justification. The verb "to justify" is *dikaioō,* built on the same root as righteous (*dikaios*) and righteousness (*dikaiōsunē*). The idea expressed by *dikaioō* is "to declare righteous," not "to make righteous." As we shall see, the root idea in justification is the declaration of God, the righteous judge, that the man who believes in Christ, sinful though he may be, is righteous—is viewed as being righteous, because in Christ he has come into a righteous relationship with God.

THE IMPORTANCE OF THE DOCTRINE. The importance of justification in Paul's theological thinking has been debated. While Paul used the verb "to forgive" (*aphiēmi*) only once (Rom. 4:7), the noun (*aphesis*) twice (Eph. 1:7; Col. 1:14), and another verb "to forgive" (*charizomai*) twice (Eph. 4:32; Col. 2:13), he used the verb "to justify" (*dikaioō*) fourteen times, and righteousness (*dikaiōsunē*) fifty-two times.[1] It is, however, a fact that these terms are concentrated in Romans and Galatians. Thus the verb "to justify" is found outside of Galatians and Romans only in I Corinthians 6:11 and in Titus 3:7.

This fact has led many scholars to the conclusion that the doctrine of justification was by no means central to Paul's theological thought but was only a polemic that he created for the purpose of dealing with the Judaizing controversy. He never would have formulated the doctrine of justification by faith apart from the works of the Law had he not been required to answer the Judaizers who insisted that Gentiles must keep the Law in order to be saved. "In fact, the whole Pauline religion can be expounded without a word being said about the doctrine, unless it be in the part devoted to the law."[2] Albert Schweitzer, who rediscovered the importance of eschatology for Paul, felt that to take justification by faith as a starting point would lead to a misunderstanding of Paul, and that this doctrine was only a "subsidiary crater" formed within the rim of the main crater—the mystical doctrine of redemption through being in Christ.[3] Andrews follows Sabatier in describing justification as a "judicial and inferior notion," which makes it difficult to rise to the higher and finer idea of a righteousness that is imparted.[4] Stewart does not downgrade justification as radically as this, but he finds the real clue to the understanding of Paul's thought and experience in union with Christ rather than in justification.[5] Davies follows Wrede and Schweitzer in viewing justification as only a convenient polemic against the Judaizers, which belongs to the periphery of Paul's thought. The central truth is found rather in Paul's awareness of the coming of the powers of the new age, the proof of which was the advent of the Spirit.[6] Schoeps is able to devote a large book to Pauline theology with no section on justification and no discussion of such an important verse as Romans 3:26.[7]

Many students, especially those who move in the tradition of the Reformation, make the doctrine of justification central in Pauline thought, and recent continental theology has recognized that it is an indispensable element in Paul's thinking.[8] We shall try to show that it is a false antithesis to contrast justification with the life in Christ or the inbreaking of the powers of the new age. On the contrary, justification is the verdict by the

[1] See V. Taylor, *Forgiveness and Reconciliation* (1941), p. 29.
[2] W. Wrede, *Paul* (1907), p. 123.
[3] A. Schweitzer, *The Mysticism of St. Paul* (1931), p. 225.
[4] E. Andrews, *The Meaning of Christ for Paul* (1949), p. 65.
[5] J. S. Stewart, *A Man in Christ* (1935).
[6] W. D. Davies, *Paul and Rabbinic Judaism* (1955), p. 222.
[7] H. J. Schoeps, *Paul* (1961).
[8] See in Literature the references to Bultmann, Conzelmann, Käsemann, and Jeremias. See also G. Bornkamm, *Paul* (1969), p. 116: "His whole preaching, even when it says nothing expressly about justification, can be properly understood only when taken in closest connection with that doctrine and related to it."

righteous Judge, "Guiltless," which belongs to the eschatological day of judgment but which has taken place in history in the Christ-event. Justification is one of the blessings of the new age that have come to us in Christ. Justification is one way of describing the objective work of Christ for us. The life in Christ is the subjective or experiential side of this same redemptive work, and both of them are essentially eschatological blessings.

THE BACKGROUND OF JUSTIFICATION. The Pauline doctrine of justification can be understood only against an Old Testament background. Among the Greeks, righteousness was an innate human quality. Plato designated *dikaiōsunē* as one of the four cardinal virtues: justice, wisdom, temperance, and courage or fortitude. These virtues were emphasized by the Stoics and sometimes found their way into Hellenistic Judaism.[9] However, in the Old Testament righteousness is a distinctly religious doctrine. The verb translated "to justify" is *tsadaq.* If the true meaning of the root is lost, scholars generally agree that the basic idea is conformity to a norm.

The Greek word "to justify" is *dikaioō.* The noun *dikaiōsunē* can be translated by the word "justification" (Gal. 2:21) but it is usually translated "righteousness." The adjective *dikaios* may be translated either "just" or "righteous." Some scholars, especially in the Catholic tradition, have insisted that the meaning of *dikaioō* is "to make righteous," and *dikaiosunē* designates the ethical quality of righteousness.[10] However, the majority of contemporary scholars understand justification to involve a relationship rather than an ethical quality, and the distinctive Pauline meaning is "to be right with God."

The background for the Pauline doctrine is the Old Testament. Righteousness (*tsedeq, tsedaqa*) in the Old Testament is not primarily an ethical quality. The basic meaning of the word is "that norm in the affairs of the world to which men and things should conform, and by which they can be measured."[11] The righteous man (*tsaddiq*) is the man who conforms to the given norm. The verb "to be righteous" (*tsadaq*) means to conform to the given norm, and in certain forms, especially in the hiphil, it means "to declare righteous" or "to justify."

The word complex is used in many contexts. Sometimes the norm consisted of the demands imposed by family relationships. Thus Tamar, who played the harlot, was more righteous than Judah because she fulfilled these demands, which Judah did not (Gen. 38:26). David is said to be righteous because he refused to slay Saul, with whom he stood in a covenant relationship (I Sam. 24:17; 26:23), and he condemned those who murdered Ishbosheth, Saul's son (II Sam. 4:11). But after the downfall of Saul's

---

9 See IV Macc. 1:6.

10 See R. Schnackenburg, *NT Theology Today* (1963), p. 80. See also E. J. Goodspeed, "Justification," *JBL* 73 (1954), 86-91.

11 See N. Snaith, *Distinctive Ideas of the OT* (1944), p. 73. See also D. Hill, *Greek Words and Hebrew Meanings* (1967), p. 83.

house, Mephibosheth had no right to expect kindness from the new king (II Sam. 19:28). The demands of righteousness changed with the relationship.

Basically, "righteousness" is a concept of *relationship*. He is righteous who has fulfilled the demands laid upon him by the relationship in which he stands.[12] It is not a word designating personal ethical character, but faithfulness to a relationship.

As such, righteousness becomes a word of great theological significance. Righteousness is the standard God has decreed for human conduct. The righteous man is he who in God's judgment meets the divine standard and thus stands in a right relationship with God. He would agree with Snaith that the norm of righteousness depends entirely on the nature of God.[13] Ultimately it is only God who can decide if a man has met the norm that he decreed for human righteousness. The background of righteousness and justification is finally *theology:* the concept of God as the ruler, lawgiver and judge of the world. "Shall not the judge of all the earth do right?" (Gen. 18:25).

The idea of righteousness is often understood in a forensic context: the righteous man is he whom the judge declares to be free from guilt. It is the business of the judge to acquit the innocent and condemn the guilty (Deut. 25:1; see also I Kings 8:32). God is often pictured as the judge of men (Ps. 9:4; 33:5; Jer. 11:20). The verb appears almost exclusively in the forensic sense. He is righteous who is judged to be in the right (Exod. 23:7; Deut. 25:1), i.e., who in judgment through acquittal thus stands in a right relationship with God. Some Old Testament scholars feel that this is the primary connotation of the term. "When applied to the conduct of God the concept is narrowed and almost exclusively employed in a forensic sense."[14]

In Judaism righteousness came to be defined largely in terms of conformity to the Torah—to the Law of Moses as exemplified by the oral scribal tradition. The rabbis did not believe that God demands flawless obedience to the Law; that exceeded the human ability. The rabbis recognized two impulses in men: an impulse toward good (*yetzer hatob*) and an impulse toward evil (*yetzer hara*). The righteous man was he who nurtured the good impulse and restrained the evil impulse so that in the end his good deeds outweighed his evil deeds. "God's justice was committed to requite men strictly according to their deeds. . . . Judaism had no hesitation about recognizing the merit of good works, or in exhorting men to

---

[12] E. R. Achtemeier, *IDB* R-Z, p. 80.

[13] N. Snaith, *Distinctive Ideas of the OT*, p. 77.

[14] W. Eichrodt, *Theology of the OT* (1961), I, 240. Von Rad thinks Eichrodt has overemphasized the forensic aspect (*OT Theology* [1962], I, 370); but the forensic meaning is important for the New Testament. See also the article by G. Schrenk in *TDNT* II, 176f. For other aspects of righteousness, see the article by Achtemeier in *IDB* R-Z, pp. 80ff. We can here only trace the aspect of the word that is most significant for Pauline usage.

acquire it and to accumulate a store of merit laid up for the hereafter."[15] Sometimes man's standing toward God is pictured as a kind of current account kept by the Almighty regarding every Israelite. The credit and debit columns in this divine account book are balanced up every day. If the balance is on the credit side, a man is justified before God; if it is on the debit side, he is condemned. Therefore it is said that a man is judged "according to that which balances."[16] The things above all that go to balance the credit side of a man's account are the study of the Torah, almsgiving, and deeds of mercy.

The striking—indeed to a Jew, the shocking—thing about Paul's use of the word is his affirmation that in Christ God justifies the ungodly (Rom. 4:5). If the ungodly were treated as they deserve, they would be condemned. A judge in Old Testament times who justified or acquitted the wicked would prove himself to be an unrighteous judge. Righteousness means upholding the norms of right conduct—the acquittal of the innocent and the condemnation of the guilty. Paul asserts that in the very act of justifying the ungodly, God has shown himself to be righteous (Rom. 3:26). Furthermore, this acquittal comes entirely apart from the works of the Law (Gal. 2:16; 3:11)—by faith alone (Gal. 2:16). Little wonder that Paul found himself in conflict with many Jewish Christians.[17]

JUSTIFICATION IS ESCHATOLOGICAL. One of the most important facts that will provide an understanding of the Pauline doctrine is that justification is an eschatological doctrine.[18] We have seen that in Judaism men will be judged according to their works in the last judgment. God is the righteous lawgiver and judge; and it is only in the final judgment when God will render a judicial verdict upon each man that his righteousness or his unrighteousness will be finally determined. Only God, who has set the norm for human conduct, can determine whether a man has met that norm and is therefore righteous. The issue of the final judgment will be either a declaration of righteousness that will mean acquittal from all guilt, or conviction of unrighteousness and subsequent condemnation. The

---

15 G. F. Moore, *Judaism* (1927), II, 89, 90. See also I, 494-95.

16 W. O. E. Oesterley, *The Religion and Worship of the Synagogue* (1927), p. 249. See the picture of final judgment as the weighing of a man's deeds in Test. Abr. 13. See also G. Schrenk, *TDNT* II, 197.

17 It has been contended that certain passages in the Qumran writings are close to the Pauline doctrine. See M. Burrows, *The Dead Sea Scrolls* (1955), pp. 334f. But the context of the Qumran idea of "justification" is "radical submission to the law and not liberation from it." H. Conzelmann, *NT Issues* (1920), p. 141.

18 This is recognized by G. Schrenk, *TDNT* II, 217; L. Morris. *The Apostolic Preaching of the Cross* (1955), p. 258; V. Taylor, *Forgiveness and Reconciliation,* pp. 33, 36; D. E. H. Whiteley, *The Theology of St. Paul* (1964), p. 160; D. Hill, *Greek Words and Hebrew Meanings,* p. 151; J. Jeremias, *The Central Message of the NT* (1965), p. 64. While all of these authors recognize the eschatological dimension of justification, they do not all emphasize the significance of this fact.

essential meaning of justification, therefore, is forensic and involves acquittal by the righteous judge.

This eschatological significance of justification is seen in several uses of the word *dikaioō*. When Paul says, "Who shall bring any charge against God's elect? It is God who justifies; who is to condemn?" (Rom. 8:33, 34), he is looking forward to the final judgment when God's verdict of acquittal cannot be set aside by anyone who would bring an accusation that might result in condemnation. When we read that it is not the hearers of the Law who in God's sight are righteous but only the doers of the Law who *will be* justified, we must look forward to a day of judgment when God will issue a verdict on the conduct of man in terms of obedience or disobedience to the Law (Rom. 2:13). The temporal orientation of the words "by one man's obedience many will be made righteous" (Rom. 5:19) is the future judgment when God will pronounce the verdict of righteousness on the many. The *"hope* of righteousness" for which we wait is the judicial pronouncement of righteousness, that is, of acquittal in the day of judgment (Gal. 5:5).

The eschatological setting of justification is seen even more clearly in one of the sayings of our Lord: "I tell you, on the day of judgment, men will render account for every careless word they utter; for by your words you will be justified, and by your words you will be condemned" (Mt. 12:36, 37).

In the eschatological understanding of justification, as well as in its forensic aspect, the Pauline doctrine agrees with that of contemporary Jewish thought. However, there are several points at which the Pauline teaching is radically different from the Jewish concept; and one of the essential differences is that the future eschatological justification has *already taken place*. "Since therefore we have now been justified by his blood, much more shall we be saved by him from the wrath of God" (Rom. 5:9). "Since we have been justified by faith, we have peace with God" (Rom. 5:1). "You were justified in the name of the Lord Jesus Christ" (I Cor. 6:11). In these instances the verb is in the aorist tense, expressing an act that has been accomplished. Through faith in Christ, on the ground of his shed blood, men have already been justified, acquitted of the guilt of sin, and therefore are delivered from condemnation. Here again we find a further illustration of the modification of the antithetical eschatological structure of biblical thought. Justification, which primarily means acquittal at the final judgment, has already taken place in the present. The eschatological judgment is no longer alone future; it has become a verdict in history. Justification, which belongs to the Age to Come and issues in the future salvation, has become a present reality inasmuch as the Age to Come has reached back into the present evil age to bring its soteric blessings to men. An essential element in the salvation of the future age is the divine acquittal and the pronouncement of righteousness; this acquittal, justification, which consists of the divine absolution of sin, has already been effected by the death of Christ and may be received by faith here and now. The future judgment has thus become essentially a present experience. God in Christ has acquitted the believer; therefore he is certain of deliverance from the wrath of God (Rom. 5:9), and he no longer stands under condemnation (Rom. 8:1).

Recognition of the eschatological character of justification nullifies the criticism that what is central in Pauline thought is the awareness of the coming of the powers of the new age. Justification is one of the blessings of the inbreaking of the new age into the old. In Christ the future has become present; the eschatological judgment has in effect already taken place in history. As the eschatological Kingdom of God is present in history in the Synoptics, as the eschatological eternal life is present in Christ in John, as the eschatological resurrection has already begun in Jesus' resurrection, as the eschatological Spirit is given to the church in Acts (and in Paul), so the eschatological judgment has already occurred in principle in Christ, and God has acquitted his people.

JUSTIFICATION IS FORENSIC.[19] Many scholars recognize that the basic idea in justification is forensic. This term has, however, fallen into some disrepute. Forensic means that God is conceived as the ruler, lawgiver, and judge, and justification is the declaration of the judge that a man is righteous. Some who avoid the term "forensic" emphasize that justification does involve a new status—a new relationship.[20] This amounts to the same thing. The unrighteous man stands in relationship to God as a sinner, and must finally experience the condemnation of the righteous judge. The justified man has, in Christ, entered into a new relationship with God. God now views him as righteous and treats him as such. Justification is the pronouncement of the righteous judge that the man in Christ is righteous; but this righteousness is a matter of relationship and not of ethical character. We must not conclude that *dikaiōsunē* never carries the connotation of personal ethical righteousness; sometimes it does (II Cor. 9:9). But "it is almost universally agreed that the word justify (*dikaioō*) does not mean 'make righteous.' "[21] Rather, it designates the status—the relationship of righteousness.

Long ago, Sanday and Headlam in their great commentary on Romans raised a logical objection. Recognizing the forensic aspect of justification, they interpreted it in terms of a fiction. Justification by faith means that the believer, by virtue of his faith, is accounted or treated as if he were righteous in the sight of God. The person who is thus accounted righteous is, however, in reality not actually righteous but is in fact ungodly (Rom. 4:5), an offender against God. Since God treats a man as though he were

---

19 See G. Schrenk, *TDNT* II, 215-16; L. Morris, *The Apostolic Preaching,* pp. 249ff.; D. Hill, *Greek Words,* pp. 152, 160.

20 D. E. H. Whiteley, *The Theology of St. Paul,* p. 159; K. Käsemann, *NT Questions Today* (1969), p. 172.

21 D. E. H. Whiteley, *The Theology of St. Paul,* p. 159.

righteous when in fact he is ungodly, "the Christian life is made to have its beginning in a fiction."[22]

Vincent Taylor, feeling the incongruity of such an interpretation, denies that justification can be regarded as fictitious and interprets the doctrine in terms of a real imparted righteousness. Justifying faith must issue in a real righteousness, not a righteousness that is merely imputed. "Righteousness can be no more imputed to a sinner than bravery to a coward or wisdom to a fool. If through faith a man is accounted righteous, it must be because, in a reputable sense of the term, he is righteous, and not because another is righteous in his stead."[23] "In Pauline thought, in the spiritual moment when a man is justified, he is no longer ungodly or a sinner; in a sense proper to the justifying act of God, he is truly righteous." By this Taylor means that "he really is righteous in mind and in purpose, although not yet in achievement." "He is righteous because, through faith in Christ the Redeemer, he gains a righteous mind." By justification God in Christ "does for us what we cannot do for ourselves and thus creates in us a righteous mind for which we can claim no credit."[24]

Norman Snaith criticizes Taylor for not going far enough when he removes justification from the sphere of a forensic righteousness. Snaith agrees with Taylor that justification has nothing to do with an imputed righteousness; but he thinks that Taylor has not entirely emancipated himself from confusion in interpreting justification as the impartation of a righteous mind. Snaith insists that justification has nothing to do with righteousness at all, and that righteousness is not a condition of salvation. Both the Reformed view and Taylor's view are erroneous in assuming that God must require some kind of righteousness as the condition of salvation. Righteousness is a result of salvation and not a condition of it. Snaith says that to make righteousness a condition of salvation is to make God subservient to a Necessity outside of himself; both God and man must bow to Righteousness. "As long as we insist upon Righteousness, in whatever way, as a condition of salvation, we do not recognize God as Sovereign Lord. Though we honor him as such with our lips, we still tend in our theology to insist that he must satisfy Righteousness before he can be Mercy. Even a fictional Righteousness will do, but he must satisfy some Righteousness. Either it is a Righteousness to which God and man alike must bow, or it is one half of God which must first be satisfied before the other half can accomplish its (his) saving work."[25] Snaith insists that justification is a salvation word *that requires no righteousness as its condition,* either imputed or imparted. The only thing required for justification (salvation) is faith; and Paul spent most of his life combating the error that salvation is by righteousness. "To assume that ethical righteousness,

---

[22] W. Sanday and A. C. Headlam, *Romans* (1896), p. 36.

[23] V. Taylor, *Forgiveness and Reconciliation,* p. 57.

[24] *Ibid.,* pp. 58, 59, 60.

[25] N. H. Snaith, *The Distinctive Ideas of the OT,* p. 165.

whether actual, imputed, or imparted (infused), is a necessary condition of salvation is a travesty of Paul's teaching."[26]

These distortions of the biblical teaching of justification must be answered on two grounds: theological and exegetical. Justification is theologically grounded, for it involves the basic question of the character of God and his relationship to mankind. When Snaith insists that we should abandon the idea that the Pauline justification terminology is primarily or even mainly forensic and judicial because "with Paul also the court is mostly the whole world of human affairs, and the jury is the whole world of man,"[27] he strikes at the very center of theology properly speaking, that is, at the doctrine of God. The uniform biblical view is that God is at the same time the lawgiver, the judge, and the jury. In fact, the idea of a jury is a modern one that ought not to intrude itself into the biblical view. God is a just and holy judge who himself and himself alone renders the decision about man's righteousness or guilt. When Snaith speaks of Righteousness as though it were some Necessity outside of God to which God himself must be subservient, he is guilty of emptying the biblical doctrine of God of its judicial content. God is the Redeemer and Savior; God is also a just and holy judge; and it is a sub-biblical view that minimizes or subordinates the second element to the first. Righteousness is no necessity external to God; God is righteousness; God is *holy* love. It is a caricature of the biblical doctrine of God to speak of him as part love and part justice as though God were divided; God is perfect love and perfect justice; and all of God is love and all of God is justice.

The theological difficulty raised by both Taylor and Snaith rests on a misunderstanding. The description of justification as involving a fictitious righteousness is erroneous. The forensic righteousness of justification is a *real righteousness,* because a man's relationship to God is just as real as his subjective ethical condition. A man's relationship to God is no fiction. God does not treat a sinner *as though* he were righteous; he is in fact righteous. Through Christ he has entered into a new relationship with God and is in fact righteous in terms of this relationship. The impartation of ethical righteousness, the righteous mind and will described by Taylor, belongs to the category of regeneration in its broadest connotations. As we shall see, the subjective aspect and the objective must not be confused; and the doctrine of justification has to do with a man's standing, his relationship to God and God's attitude toward him.[28] When Jesus uttered an encomium on John the Baptist, "all the people and the tax collectors justified God, having been baptized with the baptism of John" (Lk. 7:29), this can hardly mean that any quality of righteousness is added to God but that the people attributed righteousness to God and vindicated the divine conduct through John. That Christ was manifested in the flesh, and justified

---

26 *Ibid.*, p. 171.

27 *Ibid.*, p. 167.

28 This interpretation of righteousness is splendidly asserted by Bultmann, *Theology of the NT* (1951), I, 270-79.

(RSV, "vindicated") in the Spirit (I Tim. 3:16) means that his sinlessness and deity were vindicated through the resurrection. When Paul speaks of the justification of God by his words (Rom. 3:4), he means that the righteousness of God must be recognized and acknowledged by men. It is as though God were on trial before mankind and God is to be shown to be just by his words. When the sinner who offered a prayer of humility and contrition went down to his house justified rather than the Pharisee (Lk. 18:14), he had not acquired a new quality of subjective righteousness, but through his humility and contrition he had received the vindication of God.

The theological use of the word in Paul further reinforces the contention that justification is a matter of relationship to God and not of ethical righteousness. "It is God who justifies; who is to condemn?" (Rom. 8:33, 34). Justification is the opposite of condemnation. Condemnation is not sinfulness of character or life; it is the *decree* of condemnation pronounced against a guilty man. Similarly, justification is not subjective ethical righteousness; it is the decree of acquittal from all guilt and issues in freedom from all condemnation and punishment. The forensic concept of righteousness is further illustrated in the contrast between the dispensation of condemnation and the dispensation of righteousness (II Cor. 3:9). It is further reinforced by Paul's saying "For our sake he [God] made him to be sin who knew no sin so that in him we might become the righteousness of God" (II Cor. 5:21). This verse clearly asserts that in some sense of the word Jesus was a sinner; and at the same time it asserts that he knew no sin. His "sinfulness" must then be a forensic sinfulness by virtue of which he stood in the place of sinners, bearing their sin, their guilt, and the doom of their sin. In the same way those who are in him have become the righteousness of God. Righteousness in this context is not an ethical subjective righteousness any more than the "sinfulness" of Christ is ethical subjective sinfulness; it means rather that the man in Christ now stands in the position of a righteous man and sustains a relationship to God that only the righteous can enjoy. He is in fact in terms of his relationship to God a righteous man.

The doctrine of justification means that God has pronounced the eschatological verdict of acquittal over the man of faith in the present, in advance of the final judgment. The resulting righteousness is not ethical perfection; it is "sinlessness" in the sense that God no longer counts a man's sin against him (II Cor. 5:19). The righteous man is not "regarded as if he were righteous"; he really is righteous, he is absolved from his sin by God's verdict. When Christ was made to be sin (II Cor. 5:21), God did not merely treat him "as if" he were a sinner. Rather, God made the (ethically) sinless one *to be* a sinner (forensically). Thus the man in Christ is actually righteous, not ethically but forensically, in terms of his relationship to God. Righteousness is both an ethical quality and a relationship; and the latter is no more a fiction than the former. The latter has to do with justification; the former with sanctification. Justification, therefore, is not an ethical quality nor anything that a person has of his own. Nor is it a matter that can be subjectively experienced. It is a righteousness that he possesses by virtue of the favorable verdict of the divine law court to which he is accountable. Nor is it the equivalent of innocence, for it goes beyond the stage of innocence. When all the evidence is in and the case has been adjudicated, the God of the universe who is both lawgiver and righteous judge pronounces the verdict of acquittal. Therefore, in the sight of God a man is not a sinner but a righteous man.

THE GROUND AND THE MEANS OF JUSTIFICATION. Contemporary Jewish thought agrees with Paul in viewing justification as an eschatological forensic act. In the final judgment God will vindicate the righteous. The ground of this final vindication in Jewish thought would be conformity to the Law of God; and sometimes acceptance of and obedience to the Law was described in terms of faith. The Gentiles will be condemned because they have despised the Law and "believed not his commandments" (IV Ez. 7:24). The acceptance of the Law by Israel was an act of faith that issued in good works of conformity to the Law (IV Ez. 9:7; 13:23; cf. also Apoc. Bar. 59:2).

At this point Paul's doctrine of justification differs radically from that of Jewish thought. As the preceding references show, the very acceptance of the Law and its acknowledgment by Israel as God's Law was an act of "faith" that contributed to their righteousness. This Jewish concept of faith makes it a meritorious work. Perfect conformity was not expected but only a righteousness sufficient to outweigh the debit of one's sins. The Pauline doctrine does not balance a man's sins against his righteousness; vindication in terms of the Law could be found only by a perfect conformity to its demands, "for it is not the hearers of the Law who are righteous before God, but the doers of the law who will be justified" (Rom. 2:13). In the first chapters of Romans Paul's argument, which shuts up all men to sin, does not follow the line that their sinfulness outweighs their righteousness; it is rather that all men are sinful and guilty before a holy God because they have sinned. It is the fact of sin, not the degree of sin, that constitutes their guilt as sinners. Since a man is unable to render the perfect obedience required by the Law, "no human being will be justified in his sight by the works of the law" (Rom. 3:20). The Law, rather than bringing justification, brings condemnation since it is through the Law and its elucidation of the holy will of God that sin is defined (Rom. 3:20). While the Law itself is holy and just and good, it is the means by which a man realizes that he has come short of the will of God and by which he is convicted of his sinfulness (Rom. 7:7-12). Paul's contention with the Judaizers in Galatia was over the means and the ground of justification. It is utterly impossible for a man to be justified by the works of the Law (Gal. 2:16; 3:11). The man who has once believed in Christ only to turn away to seek justification by obedience and conformity to the Law has fallen away from grace (Gal. 5:4), that is, he has relinquished the gracious means of salvation for one that can only end in condemnation.

The ground of justification is not obedience to the Law; it is the death of Christ. His death is both the supreme manifestation of God's love for sinners and the ground on which justification is secured; "We are now justified by his blood" (Rom. 5:9). The ground of our acceptance is not our works nor our faith, nor is it the work of Christ within us; it is what he has done for us objectively. Thus, if it were possible for a man to be justified through the Law, the death of Christ would have been to no purpose (Gal. 2:21).

The death of Christ as the ground of justification is set forth in greatest detail in Romans 3:21-26. Men are "justified by his grace as a gift, through the redemption which is in Christ Jesus, whom God put forward as a propitiation by his blood to be received by faith" (vv. 24, 25). The shedding of Christ's blood, i.e., his sacrificial death, provides the means of propitiation on the ground of which acquittal or justification can be bestowed upon man as a free gift. This propitiatory death of Christ was an act of divine righteousness (v. 25). Previous to the death of Christ God had appeared to pass over sins, that is, he had appeared to be more benevolent than just in failing to require the penalty of death that sin merited. In the death of Christ, God is no longer passing over sins but is dealing with them as a righteous God ought to do. Thus the death of Christ is a demonstration in the present time that God is both righteous and that he declares righteous him who has faith in Jesus (v. 26). The righteousness of God would be sustained inviolate if God visited every sinner with the doom that sin deserves, the condemnation of death. This is what the sinner merits, and God's righteousness could not be called into question if in the final judgment he visited wrath and condemnation upon the sinner, issuing in death (Rom. 6:23a). However, God is not only righteous; he is also mercy and love; and in mercy he would vindicate the sinner and acquit him of his guilt to deliver him from the doom of sin. By the death of Christ, God has both demonstrated and effected this justification of undeserving sinners. The death of Christ was an act of righteousness on God's part; and we can only conclude that this act of righteousness consisted in visiting upon Christ, who was ethically sinless, the guilt and doom that sin deserves, namely, death. The death of Christ was not merited because of his own sinfulness, for he knew no sin; and unless his death involved a voluntary forensic experience of the sinfulness of man so that his death was the just doom that human sinfulness merited, his death is the most monstrous instance of injustice history has ever seen. It is because God manifested both his righteousness and his love by visiting upon Jesus the guilt and the doom of sin that he can now in perfect righteousness bestow the vindication of acquittal upon the sinner.

Thus while the *ground* of justification is the death of Christ, the *means* by which justification becomes efficacious to the individual is faith.[29] Justi-

---

[29] The word "means" is here used to designate the agency, instrumentality or medium by which the benefits of justification become efficacious to the individual. Some scholars use "means" synonymously with "ground."

fication is a gift bestowed to be received by faith (Rom. 3:24, 25). Faith means acceptance of this work of God in Christ, complete reliance upon it, and an utter abandonment of one's own works as the grounds of justification. Vincent Taylor in his effort to avoid the forensic character of justification at times seems to identify faith and righteousness. He holds that God counts a man righteous because a man is in reality righteous; "in virtue of his faith resting upon the work of Christ, he really is righteous in mind and in purpose, although not yet in achievement."[30] "The attitude of mind which makes this relationship possible is faith."[31] These words identify the righteousness of mind that a man must possess for justification by faith; faith is of itself the righteousness on the basis of which God justifies. If this were so, faith would be the ground and not the means of justification, and it would in effect come close to being a meritorious work. However, Paul argues emphatically that a man is justified on the principle of faith, which is the opposite of the principle of works (Rom. 3:28). The ground of my justification is nothing within me, either righteousness of mind or attitude or will; it is the objective work of Christ in his death. Faith is the means by which the work of Christ is personally appropriated. It means the relinquishing of any effort to justify oneself and a complete reliance on the work of God in his behalf. It thus excludes any boasting; faith is in fact the absolute contrary of boasting. Boasting means the exaltation of self and of one's own attainments; this is in its essence sinfulness. Faith is complete and utter reliance on God and the divine provision for salvation.

JUSTIFICATION AND SUBSEQUENT SINS. The question has been frequently raised about the relationship of the doctrine of justification to sins committed after justification. It might appear that justification acquits the believer only of those sins which have been committed prior to justification and that some other means must be provided to care for sins committed afterward. The solution to this problem is found in the eschatological character of justification. Since justification is an eschatological event, it belongs at the end of life when men will stand before the final judgment of God to answer for the entire course of their conduct. Its temporal location, therefore, is not really the point of belief; it is in fact no less than the final judgment that has in Christ thrust itself forward into the stream of history. As the final judgment, it retains its orientation toward the believer's entire life. He is justified not only from the sins committed before the time of belief; he is justified from *all* guilt.

IMPUTATION. In classical Reformed theology, a corollary of justification is the doctrine of the imputation of Christ's righteousness to the believer.[32] However, Paul never expressly states that the righteousness of Christ is imputed to believers. His words are, "And to one who does not work but

---

30 V. Taylor, *Forgiveness and Reconciliation,* p. 59.
31 *Ibid.,* p. 54.
32 See Calvin, *Institutes* II, xvi, 6.

trusts him who justifies the ungodly, his faith is reckoned as righteousness" (Rom. 4:3).

These words could be taken to mean that God regarded faith as the most meritorious human achievement, and therefore God accounts faith as the equivalent to full righteousness. This, however, would ignore the context of Pauline thought. In contemporary Jewish thought, faith was considered a meritorious work;[33] and it is Paul's main concern to refute the idea that salvation is based in any way on human works or merit. Faith is clearly excluded from the category of human achievement. Righteousness is reckoned "to one who does not work" (Rom. 4:5). What is reckoned is not faith but righteousness on the basis of faith. David committed notorious sins (Rom. 4:8). It is clear that what is reckoned (imputed) is righteousness entirely apart from human merit.

Paul answers the question when he says, *"In him* we might become the righteousness of God" (II Cor. 5:21). Christ was made sin for our sake. We might say that our sins were reckoned to Christ. He, although sinless, identified himself with our sins, suffered their penalty and doom—death. So we have reckoned to us Christ's righteousness even though in character and deed we remain sinners. It is an unavoidable logical conclusion that men of faith are justified because Christ's righteousness is imputed to them.

RECONCILIATION

Literature:

J. Denney, *The Death of Christ* (1903, 1950); *idem, The Christian Doctrine of Reconciliation* (1917); F. Büchsel, "Katallassō," *TDNT* I, 255-59; V. Taylor, *Forgiveness and Reconciliation* (1946), pp. 70-108; L. Morris, *The Apostolic Preaching of the Cross* (1955), pp. 186-223; E. C. Blackman, "Reconciliation," *IDB* R-Z, pp. 16-17.

Reconciliation (*katallassō, katallagē*) is a doctrine closely allied with that of justification. Justification is the acquittal of the sinner from all guilt of sin; reconciliation is the restoration of the justified man to fellowship with God. While the teaching of reconciliation does not play a large role in Paul's thought in terms of space devoted to the doctrine, it nevertheless is an essential and integral doctrine in his pattern of thought. The very idea of reconciliation suggests estrangement. Reconciliation is necessary between two parties when something has occurred to disrupt fellowship and to cause one or both parties to be hostile to the other. Sin has estranged man from God. It has broken fellowship and become a barrier. Thus explained, there would appear to be no problem in the biblical teaching. However, the difficult question is raised, Who is estranged, and who needs to be reconciled? It needs little proof that man has been estranged from God, that he is rebellious in heart and mind, and that his rebellion needs to be changed into a willing and glad submission to God. But is God estranged from man? Does God as well as man need to be reconciled? Is

[33] C. K. Barrett, *Romans* (1957), p. 87.

reconciliation exhausted in the subjective sphere of human experience, or is reconciliation also an objective accomplishment outside of man's experience? Is it possible that reconciliation means that God's anger must be turned into love before a man can be saved? Some interpretations of reconciliation have suggested that precisely this is needed, that God's anger must be appeased that his hostility may be converted into love. Other scholars deny that any such element can adhere in the biblical doctrine of reconciliation. "A God who needs to be reconciled, who stands over against offending man and waits till satisfaction is forthcoming and his hostility is appeased, is not the apostolic God of grace. He is certainly not the God and Father of Jesus Christ."[34] Stewart finds no objective element in the doctrine of reconciliation; it is only man's rebellious and hostile attitude toward God that needs to be reconciled to God. Such are the problems that are raised by the doctrine of reconciliation.

THE EXEGETICAL DATA. When we examine closely the Pauline language about reconciliation, it at once becomes clear that Paul nowhere expressly speaks of God reconciling himself to men or of God being reconciled to men. God is always the subject of reconciliation and man or the world is the object. "God was in Christ reconciling the world to himself" (II Cor. 5:19). "We were reconciled to God by the death of his Son" (Rom. 5:10). "And you, who were once estranged and hostile in mind, doing evil deeds, he has now reconciled in the body of flesh by his death" (Col. 1:21, 22). Christ through the cross has reconciled both Jew and Gentile to God (Eph. 2:15, 16). Reconciliation is thus the work of God and man is its object. Man cannot reconcile himself to God; he must be reconciled to God by the divine action.

These data lead us to one inescapable conclusion, which must be strongly emphasized: whatever else the doctrine involves, it is God who has both initiated and in Christ accomplished reconciliation. We are not to think either of a bifurcation within the character of God by virtue of which one part of him is love and the other part enmity and that his enmity must be appeased before his love can be active; nor are we to suppose that there is an antithesis between God the Father and Christ the Son and that the Son through his death has appeased the anger of God and turned his hostility into friendship and his hatred into love. It is God the Father who is the author of reconciliation. Perhaps the correct translation of II Corinthians 5:19 should be, "God, in Christ, was reconciling the world to himself." Reconciliation is initiated by the love of God; and while, as we shall see, the doctrine of reconciliation does have a Godward direction so that we shall be compelled to conclude that there is a sense in which God himself is reconciled to man, this is not to be construed to mean that God's hostility must be changed into love. God is everlasting love. The death of Christ was a manifestation and proof of God's love for men even while they were sinners and in a state of hostility against him (Rom. 5:8). No

[34] J. Stewart, *A Man in Christ* (1935), p. 212.

interpretation of the doctrine of reconciliation can be satisfactory that says that God's anger must be transformed into love or his hostility converted into friendliness. It is God's very love that is the source and ground of reconciliation.

RECONCILIATION IS OBJECTIVE. A closer examination of the passages in Romans 5 and II Corinthians 5 leads to the inescapable conclusion that reconciliation is not primarily a change in man's attitude toward God; it is, like justification, an objective event that is accomplished by God for man's salvation. Reconciliation was wrought first by God *for* men, not *in* men. It is while we were enemies that we were reconciled to God by the death of his Son (Rom. 5:10). The death of Christ itself accomplished a reconciliation while we were in a state of enmity to God. The same thought is earlier expressed in different words: "While we were yet sinners Christ died for us" (Rom. 5:8). The love of God manifested in reconciliation is not here focused upon the moment when the individual believes on Christ and finds his attitude toward God changed from enmity to love; the manifestation of God's love took place while we were still sinners, in the objective, historical event of the death of Christ. Reconciliation was accomplished by that death. Therefore reconciliation is a gift that is to be received (Rom. 5:11). It comes to man from God and is not directly or indirectly due to any act of his own.

The objective character of reconciliation is further illustrated by the fact that it is a message given to the apostle to proclaim to men. God in Christ has reconciled men to himself and has given unto the apostles the ministry of reconciliation. God has given man a message to proclaim to man; it is a message that reconciliation has been accomplished. It is the proclamation that God has done something for man. It is by virtue of an accomplished work that Paul would beseech men to be reconciled to God. Because God has effected a work of reconciliation for them, men are in turn to respond in loving submission to the gracious overture of a loving God and so are to be reconciled to God. We would quote the classic words of James Denney: "The work of reconciliation, in the sense of the New Testament, is a work which is *finished,* and which we must conceive to be finished *before the gospel is preached.* It is the good tidings of the gospel with which the evangelists go forth that God has wrought in Christ a work of reconciliation which avails for no less than the world, and of which the whole world may have the benefit. The summons of the evangelist is—*'receive* the reconciliation; consent that it become effective in your case'. The work of reconciliation is not a work wrought upon the souls of men though it is a work wrought in their interest, and bearing so directly upon them that we can say God has reconciled the world to himself. It is a work . . . *outside of us* in which God so deals in Christ with the sin of the world, that it shall no longer be a barrier between himself and men . . . reconciliation, in the New Testament sense, is not something which is being done; it is something which is done."[35]

THE NEED OF RECONCILIATION. The objective character of reconciliation will be further illustrated when it is seen that the need of reconciliation rests not only in the subjective hostility of sinners toward God but primarily in the objective relationship of alienation and hostility in which sinners stand toward God. It was "while we were enemies" (*echthroi*) that we were reconciled to God by the death of his Son (Rom. 5:10). We have already seen[36] that this term can be rendered actively—man's active hostility toward God—or passively—man's situation of being in a state of hostility, and therefore of being so regarded by God. Because men are hostile in their minds toward God (Col. 1:21), God must look upon them as sinners, as his enemies. In Romans 5:10, Paul "has in mind the attitude of God rather than men."[37] Because sinners are God's enemies, they stand under his wrath.[38] At the same time, God loves those who are his enemies. The wonder of reconciliation is that while we were still in this state of enmity, God wrought the work of reconciliation so that he could bestow on men all the gifts of his love.

THE CHARACTER OF RECONCILIATION. The objective character of reconciliation is strongly confirmed by the words in which Paul most specifically describes its specific content: "not counting their trepasses against them" (II Cor. 5:19). Reconciliation primarily has to do, not with men's attitude toward God, but with God's attitude toward men and their sins. Men are ethically sinful; and when God counts their trespasses against them, he must view them as sinners, as enemies, as the objects of the divine wrath; for it is an ethical and religious necessity that the holiness of God manifest itself in wrath against sin. Reconciliation is an act of God, initiated by his love, by virtue of which God no longer counts men's trespasses against them; it has to do with the divine attitude toward men as the result of which God no longer looks upon them as enemies, as occupying a hostile status. The barrier of sin has been swept away. God has made men free from the guilt and debt of sin, and this has been accomplished entirely through the divine initiative, not by human attainment. Thus reconciliation makes a difference to God as well as to men.

Denney points out that a father's readiness to forgive an offense is not the same as the actual forgiveness. When he actually forgives, he not only loves his penitent child as he always loved him, but his attitude toward him is changed. It is actually different from what it was when he was only waiting for the opportunity to forgive. The only natural way to express the difference is to say that the father is reconciled to the offender. "In the

---

35 J. Denney, *The Death of Christ* (1950), pp. 85, 86.

36 See above, Ch. 29. See also J. Denney, "Romans," *Expositor's Greek Testament* (1900), II, 625.

37 W. Foerster, *TDNT* I, 814.

38 See above, Ch. 29.

experience of forgiveness, as a matter of fact, not only are we reconciled to God, but God is reconciled to us. He is not reconciled in the sense that something is won from him for us against his will, but in the sense that his will to bless us is realized, as it was not before, on the basis of what Christ has done, and of our appropriation of it."[39] Many scholars refuse to follow Denney's affirmation that God in fact is reconciled to men; they refuse to go any further than the actual words Paul employs. However, we must attempt to enter into the mind of Paul, and not only use his terminology but draw the necessary implications of his statements. Perhaps Paul refrained from flatly asserting that God was reconciled because of the danger of misunderstanding and misinterpretation of such a statement in a pagan world where the anger of the gods must be appeased by bribery just as the anger of men had to be assuaged. In spite of the lack of explicit verbal expression at this point, it appears to be a necessary inference that there is a sense in which God has reconciled himself;[40] and it is this very act of reconciliation, of self-reconciliation, at the cost of the death of his Son, which is the stupendous illustration of the magnitude of God's love for hostile sinners.

THE SUBJECTIVE ASPECT OF RECONCILIATION. Reconciliation is primarily a divine, objective act by which God has removed the barrier of sin that had separated man from God, and has made possible man's restoration to fellowship with God. This act was accomplished when men were objectively enemies of God and subjectively hostile to him. However, reconciliation does not become efficacious, fellowship is not restored in the case of any individual, until he has received the divine act of reconciliation, that is, until *he is reconciled to God.* God has wrought the objective work and has committed to the apostles the proclamation of the good news; they in turn appeal to men to accept God's proffered reconciliation and to "be reconciled to God" (II Cor. 5:20).

We are quite ready to agree with Hodge that this verse does not suggest that man can reconcile himself to God, and that it involves merely an exhortation to embrace the offer of reconciliation. "All men have to do is not to refuse the offered love of God."[41] But the mind of the flesh, that is, of unregenerate human nature, is hostile toward God (Rom. 8:7). So long as a man is "hostile in mind" (Col. 1:21), he will reject God's proffered reconciliation and will himself remain unreconciled. The very words of Hodge, "embrace," "not to refuse," indicate a subjective reaction on the part of man; and it is difficult to see why the very act of "embracing" or "not refusing" God's proffered love does not involve a change of attitude from one of hostility toward God to one of willing submission. Our present

39 J. Denney, *The Christian Doctrine of Reconciliation* (1917), p. 238.

40 L. Morris, *The Apostolic Preaching of the Cross,* p. 220.

41 C. Hodge, *Corinthians* (repr. 1950), p. 147. In his discussion of reconciliation in his *Systematic Theology* (1873, II, 514-15), Hodge excludes any discussion of the subjective aspect of reconciliation, thereby apparently denying that the doctrine contains a subjective element.

concern is not to pursue the question of precisely what this change in attitude involves and whether it is analogous to faith or a result of regeneration. We would only insist that until God's offer of objective reconciliation has been received in an attitude of glad surrender, no man is in fact reconciled to God; he is still a sinner and in the last day he will suffer the full and awful outpouring of the wrath of a holy God. The content of reconciliation, therefore, while first of all the objective act of God, is also the affirmative reaction of men to the proffer of reconciliation.[42] Only then does reconciliation become effective for the sinner; only then is he reconciled to God.

This inward reconciliation appears to be the object of reference in Colossians 1:21, 22. As sinners, men are estranged and hostile *in mind;* and the description of hostility in terms of the human attitude requires the active meaning of the word *echthroi* and suggests the subjective interpretation of reconciliation.[43] Those who were openly hostile toward God have been reconciled through Christ's death. The hostile minds of the Colossian Christians have been turned into a willing and glad subservience; and the ultimate result of this inner change of attitude toward God will be perfection in sanctification (v. 22).

Here again, in the doctrine of reconciliation, we are brought face to face with the inseparable relationship between the objective and the subjective aspects of the work of Christ, which is analogous to the inseparable relationship between justification and the life in Christ. Reconciliation is both objective and subjective; and it is impossible for a man to accept the objective act of reconciliation as God's gift without at the same time experiencing a reconciliation within his own mind toward God that starts him out upon a sanctified life that will be brought to its consummation in the eschatological day when Christ will present the redeemed, perfected in holiness, unto God.

THE RESULTS OF RECONCILIATION. Justification is the divine pronouncement of acquittal upon the sinner; reconciliation is the restoration to fellowship that results from justification. Justification is the ethical condition of reconciliation, the gift to the sinner of that standing by which alone he can enter into fellowship with God.[44] Once the sinner has been restored to fellowship, certain wonderful results accrue, the first of which is *peace with God.* The concept of peace is a very rich, many-sided concept that cannot here be elucidated. We can only indicate some of the most important aspects of peace as it results from the blessing of reconciliation, which is grounded upon justification. "Therefore, since we are justified by faith, we

---

[42] H. A. W. Meyer, who insists strongly on the objective side of reconciliation, comments on II Cor. 5:20, "do not, by refusing faith, frustrate the work of reconciliation in your case, but through your faith bring about that the objectively accomplished reconciliation may be accomplished subjectively in you." *Corinthians* (1881), II, 294.

[43] Cf. H. A. W. Meyer, *Colossians, in loc.,* for the contrary view.

[44] V. Taylor, *Forgiveness and Reconciliation,* p. 65.

have[45] peace with God, through our Lord Jesus Christ" (Rom. 5:1). The peace that is here indicated is not a subjective experience of peace; it is rather the obverse of the enmity or hostility discussed above. The justified man has been reconciled and therefore has peace with God. God's wrath no longer threatens him; he is accepted in Christ. We have peace with God in that God is now at peace with us; his wrath is removed. Peace here refers not to a state of mind but to a relationship to God.[46] We are no longer his enemies but the objects of his favor. While it is recognized that the result of this status is an inward peace of heart, it is not the inward peace but the outward objective relationship that is here described. In fact, inward peace of mind is unthinkable from the biblical point of view until a man first of all sustains peace with God, the peace of reconciliation. Peace with God, therefore, is grounded upon the redemptive work of Christ.

A second blessing that accrues from reconciliation with God is a *reconciliation between men* who had been estranged. Because men have been reconciled to God both objectively and subjectively, the human enmities that had raised barriers between men are done away, and those who are reconciled to God are to enjoy peace with one another. The classic passage is Paul's discussion of the relationship between Jew and Gentile in Ephesians 2. The Gentiles were at one time alienated from the people of God, strangers to the covenants of promise, having no hope and without God in the world. They who were once afar off have been brought near in the blood of Christ, "for he is our peace, who has made us both one, and has broken down the dividing wall of hostility . . . that he might create in himself one new man in place of the two, so making peace, and might reconcile us both to God in one body through the cross, thereby bringing the hostility to an end" (Eph. 2:14-16). The hostility that existed between Jew and Gentile may be taken as typical of all barriers that break fellowship between men. Because of reconciliation to God in Christ, men who have been estranged from one another are to be reconciled and every dividing wall of hostility removed, because Christ is our peace. Instead of two men, Jew and Gentile, who were separated by hostility, there is one new man created in peace because reconciliation to God is in one body through the cross. Thus hostility between man and man is brought to an end. The reconciliation of the hostility between Jew and Greek may be taken as representative of every sort of interpersonal hostility. In Christ there is peace among men.

---

45 A strongly supported variant in the Greek text reads "let us have peace"; and if it is followed, the verse becomes an exhortation to enjoy the peace with God achieved by justification. The essential meaning of the passage is not changed.

46 See C. K. Barrett, *Romans,* p. 102; L. Morris, *The Apostolic Preaching,* p. 216; W. Foerster, *TDNT* II, 415.

33

THE PAULINE PSYCHOLOGY

Literature:

E. D. Burton, *Spirit, Soul, and Flesh* (1918), pp. 186-98; H. Wheeler Robinson, *The Christian Doctrine of Man* (1926), pp. 104-35; R. Bultmann, *Theology of the NT,* I (1951), 190-245; J. A. T. Robinson, *The Body* (1952); W. D. Stacey, *The Pauline View of Man* (1956); W. G. Kümmel, *Man in the NT* (1963); D. E. H. Whiteley, *The Theology of St. Paul* (1964), pp. 31-44; E. Schweizer, "Sarx," *TDNT* (1964, 1971), VII, 125-38; E. Schweizer, "Pneuma," *TDNT* VI, 375-451; H. Conzelmann, *An Outline of the Theology of the NT* (1969), pp. 173-83; R. Jewett, *Paul's Anthropological Terms* (1971).

Paul employs a rich vocabulary in speaking about man, but he seldom speaks of man as such. His perspective is man as a Christian.

Paul's view of man has been interpreted in three ways. Scholars of an older generation understood I Thessalonians 5:23, where Paul prays for the preservation of the spirit, soul, and body, to be a psychological statement and understood Paul in terms of trichotomy; spirit, soul, and body are three separable parts of man.[1] Other scholars have interpreted Paul against the background of Greek dualism and have seen a dichotomy of soul and body.[2] Recent scholarship has recognized that such terms as body, soul, and spirit are not different, separable faculties of man but different ways of viewing the whole man.

BACKGROUND. In order to appreciate Pauline psychology, we need to have in mind the chief elements in the Greek and Hebrew concepts of man. One of the most influential thinkers for the subsequent history of Greek philosophy was Plato. Plato held to a dualism of two worlds, the noumenal and the phenomenal, and to an anthropological dualism of body-soul. The body was not *ipso facto* evil, but it was a burden and hindrance to the soul. The wise man cultivated the soul so that it might rise above the body and

---

[1] See F. Delitzsch, *A System of Biblical Psychology* (1867), pp. 103-19.

[2] G. H. C. MacGregor and A. C. Purdy, *Jew and Greek: Tutors Unto Christ* (1936), pp. 335f.

at death be freed from the body and escape to the world above.[3] In Hellenistic times, the body, belonging to the world of matter, was thought to be *ipso facto* evil by the gnostics. Stacey has pointed out that most of the philosophers of Greece followed Plato in his view of soul and body, and that it was so impressed upon the civilized world that "no man can discuss the relation of soul and body today without encountering some resurgence of the Platonic view."[4]

The Hebrew view of man is very different from the Greek view. There is no trace of dualism. The Hebrew word for body occurs only fourteen times in the Old Testament[5] and never stands in contrast to the soul (*nephesh*). More often, the word for flesh (*basar*) is used to designate the body (23 times). This word carries primarily a physical meaning. One significant usage is "flesh" as a symbol of human frailty in relation to God. *Basar* appears as something that men and animals possess in their weakness, which God does not possess. "My spirit shall not abide in man for ever, for he is flesh" (Gen. 6:3). "The Egyptians are men, and not God; and their horses are flesh, and not spirit" (Isa. 31:3). *Basar* refers to human beings in their frailty and transience, to man in his limitations, as distinct from the infinite God.[6]

Soul (*nephesh*) is not a higher part of man standing over against his body but designates the vitality or life principle in man. God breathed into man's nostrils the breath of life, and man became a living *nephesh* (Gen. 2:7). Body and the divine breath together make the vital, active *nephesh*. The word is then extended from the life principle to include the feelings, passions, will, and even the mentality of man.[7] It then comes to be used as a synonym for man himself. Families were numbered as so many souls (Gen. 12:5; 46:27). Incorporeal life for the *nephesh* is never visualized. Death afflicted the *nephesh* (Num. 23:10) as well as the body.

A third term is spirit (*ruach*). The root meaning of the word is "air in motion," and it is used of every kind of wind. The word is often used of God. God's *ruach* is his breath—his power—working in the world (Isa. 40:7), creating and sustaining life (Ps. 33:6; 104:29-30). Man's *ruach*—his breath—comes from God's *ruach* (Isa. 42:5; Job 27:3). Thus man is conceived of as possessing *ruach,* inbreathed from God, as an element in his personality (Gen. 45:27; I Sam. 30:12; I Kings 10:5). God is the supreme spirit (Gen. 6:3; Isa. 31:3). *Ruach* in man is expanded to include the whole range of emotional and volitional life, thus overlapping with *nephesh*.[8] The difference between *nephesh* and *ruach* in man is that

---

[3] See G. E. Ladd, *The Pattern of NT Truth* (1968), pp. 13-20; W. D. Stacey, *The Pauline View of Man* (1956), pp. 72-74.

[4] W. D. Stacey, *The Pauline View of Man,* p. 74. Stacey gives an excellent brief history of the Greeks' view of man.

[5] *Ibid.,* p. 94.

[6] *Ibid.,* p. 93.

[7] Illustrations in *ibid.,* p. 87.

[8] Illustrations in *ibid.,* pp. 89-90.

nephesh designates man in relation to other men as man living the common life of men, while *ruach* is man in his relation to God.[9] However, neither *nephesh* nor *ruach* is conceived of as a part of man capable of surviving the death of *basar*. They both designate man as a whole viewed from different perspectives.

In the intertestamental period, a distinct development is to be noted; both *pneuma* and *psychē* are conceived as entities capable of separate existence. I Enoch speaks of the souls of men who have died (9:3, 10) and also of their spirits (13:6; 20:3). In describing Sheol, it speaks of "the spirits of the souls of the dead" (22:3) and thereafter refers to their spirits (22:5, 7, 9, 11, 13). The Wisdom of Solomon uses soul and spirit interchangeably (1:4-5; 15:11; 16:14; cf. I En. 98:12) and refers to the pre-existence of the soul (8:19), and to its existence after death (16:14). Furthermore, the body is seen to be a burden to the soul (9:15). Several times the words body and soul are used together to refer to man as a whole (II Macc. 6:30; 7:37), and the Wisdom of Solomon 8:19f. speaks of the coming together of two dissimilar parts, body and soul, to form man. In Wisdom, *psychē* is used several times where it seems to be a separate entity of man (2:22; 3:1), and in one place the soul is imprisoned after death (16:14). After death, the soul that was "lent" to man must be returned, presumably to God (15:8). While Wisdom seems to reflect Hellenistic influences, "This idea of pre-existence . . . was not the highly developed belief which Philo took into his Judaism from the Greek philosophers."[10] In Wisdom 15:16, man is said to borrow his spirit for the duration of his life, which implies that his *pneuma* existed in the presence of the Lord's spirit before he was born.[11]

Another development in the intertestamental literature is that while in the Old Testament *ruach* is the power of God at work in the world, in the later writings the personal use of *pneuma* is primary. The origin of spirit in the divine breath is forgotten and the spirit is regarded as a constituent element in man. This does not necessarily imply Greek influence, only that the development of *ruach* was completed in the *pneuma* of the intertestamental writings.[12] God, the Lord of all, is the "Lord" of spirits (I En. 49:2, 4; 67:8). Spirit is often used of God; soul is never so used. This suggests that *pneuma* represents man in his Godward side,[13] while *psychē* represents man in his human side. Another aspect of this development is that *pneuma* is frequently used of supernatural spirits who can affect man for good or bad.[14]

PSYCHĒ. The Pauline usage of *psychē* is closer to the Old Testament than is the intertestamental literature. Paul never uses *psychē* as a separate entity

---

9 *Ibid.*, p. 90.
10 *Ibid.*, p. 98.
11 *Ibid.*, p. 101.
12 Illustrations in *ibid.*, p. 100.
13 *Loc. cit.*
14 Illustrations in *ibid.*, pp. 99-100.

in man, nor does he ever intimate that the *psychē* can survive the death of the body. *Psychē* is "life" understood against a Hebrew background.[15] In Romans 11:3, Paul quotes from the Old Testament where Elijah complains that "they seek my *psychē*." *Psychē* here is clearly his life. When Epaphroditus risked his soul for Paul, he nearly died (Phil. 2:30). When Aquila and Priscilla risked their necks for Paul's *psychē*, they nearly lost their lives on behalf of his.

There are one or two examples where *psychē*, like the Old Testament usage, is used of an individual person. "Every soul of man that works evil" (Rom. 2:9) is correctly translated by the RSV, "every human being who does evil." When "every soul" is exhorted to be subject to the governing authorities, Paul obviously refers to "every person" (Rom. 13:1, RSV).

Frequently *psychē* goes beyond mere physical life and refers to man as a thinking, working, and feeling person. When Paul is willing gladly to spend and be spent for the souls of his converts (II Cor. 12:15), he refers to something far more than their bodily life. We do not need to recognize here a distinct contrast between the soul and the body; Paul is concerned for the welfare of the whole man and everything life involves; but the emphasis is upon the inner life. Paul's desire to share with the Thessalonians not only the gospel but also his very soul (I Thess. 2:8) suggests more than a willingness to die for them; it means a sharing of his whole being including all that is involved in a redeemed personality. To strive for the gospel with one's soul is very close to standing firm in one spirit (Phil. 1:27); here *psychē* is nearly interchangeable with *pneuma*. To do the will of God from the heart (Eph. 6:6; *ek psychēs*) means to serve God with all of one's being and personality. However, *psychē* and *pneuma* are not strictly interchangeable but refer to man's inner life viewed from two points of view. *Pneuma* is man's inner self viewed in terms of man's relationship to God and to other men; *psychē* is man as a living being, as a human personality, the vitality of man viewed from the point of view of his body and flesh. Paul never speaks of the salvation of the soul, nor is there any intimation of the pre-existence of the soul. "*Psychē* is that specifically human state of being alive which inheres in man as a striving, willing, purposing self."[16] He never uses the obvious Hellenistic summary of man: body and soul.[17]

---

[15] R. Bultmann, *Theology of the NT* (1951), I, 207.

[16] *Ibid.*, p. 205.

[17] It should be noted that other New Testament writings diverge from Paul in their use of *psychē* and regard it as an entity in man standing over against his body and capable of salvation. Jesus contrasted the death of the body and the destruction of the soul (Mt. 10:28). The preservation of the soul (Heb. 10:39) refers to something more than physical life (see also Jas. 1:21; I Pet. 1:9). John saw the souls of the martyrs under the altar (Rev. 6:9), and at the glorious advent of Christ, the souls of the martyrs will be raised in resurrection life to share the millennial reign (Rev. 20:4). In such references as these, *psychē* is man's essential self, which is capable of continued existence after the dissolution of

There is one difference between Paul and the Old Testament. The central term for man in the Old Testament, in the intertestamental literature, and in the rabbis was *nephesh* or *psychē*. In Paul it is *pneuma*. "Spirit" has made a dramatic advance, *psychē* a dramatic retreat. Stacey thinks that this was not due to Hellenistic influences but to Paul's Christian experience in which his knowledge of the *pneuma hagion* set the basis for his anthropology, and *pneuma* took the leading role.[18]

SPIRIT. The most important Pauline use of *pneuma* is as a designation for God's Spirit. He often speaks of the *pneuma* of God (Rom. 8:14; I Cor. 2:11; 3:16; II Cor. 3:3, etc.), of the Holy Spirit (I Thess. 4:8; Eph. 1:13; 4:30), and of the Spirit of Christ (Rom. 8:9; Gal. 4:6; Phil. 1:19). We have already seen that Paul in some real sense identifies Christ and the Spirit in the work of salvation. The second Adam became a life-giving Spirit (I Cor. 15:45).[19]

The sphere of the Spirit's activity is humanity, and it is with the spirit of man that God's Spirit is largely concerned.[20]

It is with the spirit that man serves God (Rom. 1:9). Man as spirit is able to enjoy union with the Lord (I Cor. 6:17). Prayer (I Cor. 14:14) and prophecy (I Cor. 14:32) are exercises of man's spirit. Grace bestowed by God upon man is in the sphere of the spirit (Gal. 6:18). Renewal is experienced in the spirit (Eph. 4:23). The divine life imparted to man is in the realm of the spirit even while the body is perishing (Rom. 8:10). God through the Spirit witnesses to man's spirit that he is a child of God (Rom. 8:16). While Paul never asserts it explicitly, there is little doubt but that he could have said, in the words of Jesus, "God is spirit" (Jn. 4:24). It is because man also is spirit that he is able to enter into relationships with God, to fellowship with God, and to enjoy the blessings of God.

A further important significance of *pneuma* is found in contexts where it is set over against his body as the inner dimension of man in contrast with the outer. It is necessary to seek sanctification in both body and spirit (I Cor. 7:34; II Cor. 7:1).[21] A clear contrast between the inner and outer aspects of man is found in Romans 8:10. When the Spirit indwells a man, although his body is dying ("dead" potentially) because of sin, his spirit is alive because of righteousness. In this age the Holy Spirit imparts life only to the spirit of man; in the Age to Come it will also infuse with life

---

the body. This is a usage that does not contradict, but which complements the Pauline use of the term.

[18] W. D. Stacey, *The Pauline View of Man*, pp. 126-27.

[19] See above, p. 422; W. D. Stacey, *The Pauline View of Man*, pp. 129-30 for a summary of this. See also E. Schweizer, "Pneuma," *TDNT* VI, 420-34. Schweizer regards Paul's thought about the divine *pneuma* to designate a celestial matter or substance; but this is not at all clear. Cf. W. D. Stacey, *The Pauline View of Man*, p. 177. Schweizer's discussion of the human spirit is very inadequate. *TDNT* VI, 434-37.

[20] W. D. Stacey, *The Pauline View of Man*, p. 132. Elsewhere he speaks of it as the "Godward side of man"—a usage not found in the Old Testament (p. 137).

[21] In the latter reference *sarx* is used as the equivalent of body.

the mortal body (v. 11). Bultmann recognizes a seeming difficulty in this passage and solves it by interpreting *pneuma* to refer not simply to the self, the person, but to the divine *pneuma* that has become the subject self of the Christian.[22] Such an interpretation appears to fit the data to a theory and not deduce the theory from the data. The contrast between the mortal body and the spirit is not that of man versus the Spirit of God, but that of the material part of man versus the immaterial or spiritual part. The one is dying, mortal; the other has been made alive.

The contrast between the inner and the outer is very clear where the spirit refers to a quality or element diametrically opposite to the flesh. Worship of God in spirit (Phil. 3:3) is the opposite of worship in purely material form. Circumcision "in the spirit" is the opposite of literal physical circumcision (Rom. 2:28f.)

In the discussion of glossolalia, man's spirit is even differentiated from his mind (I Cor. 14:14). "For if I pray in a tongue, my spirit prays but my mind is unfruitful." There is a realm of fellowship with God in which spirit enjoys fellowship with Spirit, a realm that transcends the processes of the mind because man is spirit. He may enjoy immediate fellowship with God in a "mystical" relationship that does not contradict but which transcends the cognitive faculty. Bultmann attempts to avoid the embarrassment of this verse by understanding "my spirit" to be the Spirit of God bestowed upon man. The contrast is therefore between the human mind and the divine Spirit.[23] This, however, is rather devious exegesis; for when one interprets this expression in the light of the same or similar expressions elsewhere,[24] the conclusion is unavoidable that the spirit is man's spirit, man's true inner self that enjoys direct fellowship through prayer with God.

Since *pneuma* is man's true inner self, the word is naturally used to represent man as such in terms of his self-consciousness as a willing and knowing self.[25] To act in the same spirit (II Cor. 12:18) means to act with the same attitude and intention. To stand firm in one spirit (Phil. 1:27) means to share the same outlook and judgment and refers to a common orientation of the will. When Paul speaks of finding refreshment or rest for his spirit (I Cor. 6:18; II Cor. 2:13; 7:13), he means that he has found inner rest. There is, however, a contrast[26] between rest of mind (II Cor. 2:13) and rest of the flesh (II Cor. 7:5). The former reference places the emphasis solely upon inner distress while the latter includes the outward afflictions that Paul encountered.[27]

---

[22] R. Bultmann, *Theology of the NT,* I, 208.
[23] *Ibid.,* p. 207.
[24] See Rom. 1:9; 8:16; I Cor. 5:4; 16:18; II Cor. 2:13; 7:13; Phil. 4:23.
[25] Bultmann brilliantly works out this use of *pneuma,* and at this point we may cordially agree with his conclusions (*Theology,* I, 206f.). We disagree with Bultmann in his insistence that this meaning exhausts the significance of the concept.
[26] Against Bultmann (*Theology,* I, 206).
[27] Cf. R. Bultmann, *Theology,* I, 203, 204.

The question has been raised whether all men possess *pneuma,* or whether it is a distinct possession of Christians by virtue of their having received God's *pneuma.*[28] A key verse is I Corinthians 2:11: "For what person knows a man's thoughts except the spirit of man which is in him." This seems to be a psychological statement that is universal in its application. *Pneuma* is used here of man's self-awareness or self-consciousness.[29] Although Paul does not affirm it, it follows logically that because all men are *pneumata,* they are capable of enjoying a distinctive relationship to each other. Furthermore, because God too is *pneuma,* the human *pneuma* is the "organ which receives the Spirit of God."[30] It is because man possesses *pneuma* that he is capable of being related to God. Kümmel may be right in insisting that this verse does not mean that man stands in a position particularly close to God;[31] but it does suggest that because man is *pneuma,* he is capable of receiving the divine *pneuma* and thus coming into a close living relationship with God. We would agree with Stacey that all men possess *pneuma,* but the reception of the divine *pneuma* means the renewal of the human *pneuma* so that it acquires new dimensions.[32] In Romans 8:10, to which Stacey refers, Paul says that though your bodies are dead (i.e., mortal, dying), your spirits are alive because of righteousness. We cannot follow those scholars who understand *pneuma* in this verse to refer to the divine *pneuma.*[33] The thought seems to be that while the body is still mortal and dying, the divine *pneuma* has imparted to man the gift of life, but this life is experienced on the level of the human *pneuma.*[34] When Paul says that men are in their human situation dead but made alive in Christ (Eph. 2:1), he must mean that they were spiritually dead, i.e., their spirits did not enjoy a living relationship with God. To be made alive means to be quickened in spirit so that men enter into living fellowship with God.

Although Paul never speaks of the survival of either soul or spirit after the death of the body, the question must be raised whether death means extinction, as Stacey suggests,[35] or whether Paul does believe in some sort of survival of the self after death. Here we must agree with Whiteley, who speaks of Paul's "modification of the unitary view" of man.[36] In two places

---

28 See the excellent discussion in W. D. Stacey, *The Pauline View of Man,* pp. 141ff.
29 E. Schweizer, *TDNT* VI, 435.
30 *Ibid.,* p. 436. The German uses the word "organ," which Bromiley translates "vehicle."
31 W. G. Kümmel, *Man in the NT* (1963), p. 44.
32 W. D. Stacey, *The Pauline View of Man,* p. 135.
33 C. K. Barrett, *Romans* (1957), p. 17, translates it "the Spirit (of God) is life-giving." See also F. F. Bruce, *Romans* (1963), p. 164.
34 See commentaries by W. Sanday and J. Denney *in loc.* See also R. P. Martin in *The New Bible Commentary* (1970), p. 1031.
35 W. D. Stacey, *The Pauline View of Man,* p. 126.
36 D. E. H. Whiteley, *The Theology of St. Paul* (1964), p. 38. See also S. Laeuchli, "Monism and Dualism in the Pauline Anthropology," *Biblical Research,* 3 (1958), 15-27.

Paul refers to survival after death. To be away from the body is to be at home with the Lord (II Cor. 5:8). To be sure, Paul shrinks from the idea of being "naked," i.e., of being a disembodied spirit,[37] for full existence must always be bodily existence; and what Paul longs for is the resurrection body. However, he comforts himself with the thought that he will be with the Lord. The same thought is expressed in Philippians 1:23-24: "my desire is to depart and be with Christ, for that is far better." We may not attribute this modification of the monistic view of man to outside Hellenistic dualism, but to Paul's own conviction that even death cannot separate the believer from the love of Christ (Rom. 8:38).

SŌMA. As obvious and simple a subject as "body" (*sōma*) ought not to involve difficulties of interpretation; but problems have been raised that make this a most complex problem. As indicated above, Bultmann has vigorously defended the position that the Pauline concept of man does not conceive of him as a person of two constituent parts, an inner spiritual life and the outer material body. Bultmann insists that man cannot be partitioned but is viewed as an indivisible entity; and that *sōma, pneuma,* and *psychē* constitute merely different ways of looking upon man in his entirety. Pursuing this interpretation, Bultmann insists that *sōma* is not something that outwardly clings to man's real self (to his soul, for instance), but belongs to its very essence so that we can say, "Man does not have a *sōma*; he is *sōma*."[38] Bultmann admits that there are sayings where there appear to be reflections of the naive, popular usage in which *sōma* is contrasted with the soul or spirit; but such passages do not reflect the essential Pauline thought. Man, his person as a whole, can be denoted by *sōma.* If I give my body to be burned (I Cor. 13:3) I deliver *myself* to death. When Paul says that he pummels his body and subdues it (I Cor. 9:27), he means that he is bringing *himself* under control. That a woman is not to rule over her own body (I Cor. 7:4) means that she is not to have control of herself, but rather to submit to her husband. The offering of the body as a living sacrifice (Rom. 12:2) means the surrender of one's self to God. The magnification of Christ in my body (Phil. 1:20) means the honoring of Christ in my person, in myself. Taking his point of departure from such references, Bultmann interprets the body to mean "man in respect to his being able to make himself the object of his own action, or to experience himself as the subject to whom something happens."[39] As *sōma,* man can be the object of his own control.

There is a truth here that merits emphasis. Clearly, *sōma* is an essential element in man, and from this point of view *sōma* can stand as an equivalent for "I." I have no experience with myself except in a bodily form of existence. "I," "self" must always be expressed in bodily terms, and therefore the control of my body is the control of myself. The important truth

---

[37] See below, pp. 552f.
[38] *Theology,* I, 194.
[39] *Theology,* I, 195.

that emerges is this: somatic existence is conceived as being the normal and proper mode of existence. *Sōma* is an *essential,* not an unimportant element in human existence. The life of the soul or spirit is not contrasted with bodily life in terms of true and essential life over and against that which is extraneous or incidental or as though the body of itself were an obstacle standing in the way of the realization of man's true life. We shall see that the body can *become* an obstacle, but it is not a hindrance of itself. There is no depreciation of the body per se.

The import of this may be seen from the fact that redeemed, glorified existence will be somatic existence, not a "spiritual," i.e., nonmaterial mode of being. Glorification will include the redemption of the body (Rom. 8:23). The coming of Christ will mean the transformation of our lowly bodies into the likeness of his glorious body (Phil. 4:3-21). The basic argument of I Corinthians 15 is directed against a Greek view of the survival of personality apart from any form of bodily existence. Paul's argument rests upon the necessity of a body for full, rich life. The resurrection will involve somatic existence, although not *fleshly* existence. "Flesh and blood," that is, our present fleshly bodies, cannot inherit the Kingdom of God (I Cor. 15:50). This impossibility does not inhere in the intrinsic evil of the body as such but in the mortal character of the fleshly body. There are, however, different kinds of bodies; resurrection life will be bodily life and Paul describes it as a "spiritual body" (I Cor. 15:44). The one point to be emphasized here is that this involves a real body, however different it may be from our mortal physical bodies.[40] The work of redemption does not mean merely the salvation of the soul or spirit; it includes the redemption of the body. The ultimate and perfect mode of life designed by God that his people may enjoy the fullness of the divine blessings will be a somatic existence. The survival of personality that is often presented as the essence of the Christian hope is a Greek teaching and is not the equivalent of the biblical hope of a fulfilled redemption.

We now turn to a brief statement of Paul's positive teaching about the Christian's attitude toward his body. First, although the body is an integral part of man's being, the body of flesh is corruptible and mortal (Rom. 6:12; 8:11; II Cor. 4:11) and therefore is not the realm in which one now finds his true life. It is in fact a "body of death" (Rom. 7:24). Second, the body is not only weak and mortal but also an instrument of the flesh. Sin and death do not, however, reside in corporeality itself or in the natural body but in the flesh.[41] Since sin can reign in the mortal body (Rom. 6:12), the body viewed as the instrumentality of sin can be called a sinful body (Rom. 6:6); and therefore the man indwelt by the Spirit must put to death the deeds of the body (Rom. 8:13). This, however, is not mortification of the body itself, but of its sinful acts.

---

40 For a further discussion of the resurrection body, see Ch. 38.

41 As indicated below, "flesh" is to be understood ethically and not physically. In such contexts it refers to fallen human nature and not the material constituting the body.

Third, the body must be kept in subjection. Although it is an integral part of human existence, since the body is mortal and capable of sin it must be disciplined and prevented from gaining domination over a man's spiritual life. This life is found in the inner man, in the realm of the spirit when it is quickened and energized by the Spirit of God. The outward man, the body, slowly wastes away and it succumbs to death (II Cor. 4:16). The highest object of one's existence is to be found in the spiritual realm, and the body, therefore, must become the servant of the spirit, the true self. The body cannot become master, for of itself it is not one's true life. Paul sets forth this truth very clearly in I Corinthians 9. In the first part of the chapter he contrasts the spiritual and physical realms. Because he is a minister in spiritual things, Paul insists that he has a right to physical rewards and enjoyments. Nevertheless he refuses to exercise his liberty lest the material realm become his master. The "perishable wreath," that is, bodily, material satisfactions, is not his goal. Therefore he exercises rigorous self-control, like an athlete in training, holding his body in check that it may not gain the upper hand over his spiritual life. The material realm must be made subservient to the spiritual lest Paul be disqualified and lose the crown. There is no hint here that physical satisfactions in themselves involve any evil or degrading influence; on the contrary, it is implied that they are perfectly natural and good. The danger is that they become the end of one's life and thus defeat the higher spiritual goals. It is when the body would frustrate spiritual ends that it must be disciplined.

Fourth, self-control over the body is attained by its consecration to God. The body is to be presented to God as a living sacrifice (Rom. 12:1). This is not achieved by asceticism and mortification of the body itself. On the contrary, the Christian is to recognize that his body is indwelt by the Spirit of God (I Cor. 6:19) and is a member of Christ (I Cor. 6:15). The body is to be an instrument in the service of Christ. Since the body shares in sanctification even while it is mortal, it follows that the Christian must exercise a cultivation and care for the body and use it as a means of the fullest realization of his spiritual life. So intimate is the relationship between the body and the spirit that sins of the body touch the very springs of personality. Therefore bodily enjoyments are not an end in themselves but are to be made subservient to spiritual ends.

Fifth, as we have already pointed out, the bodies of believers are themselves to be redeemed in the day of consummated salvation (Rom. 8:23; Phil. 3:21).

SARX. The most difficult and complicated aspect of the Pauline psychology is his doctrine of *sarx*. The difficulty arises both because of the complexity of Paul's use of the word, and because of one usage that is characteristic of Paul but which is rarely found elsewhere; and this peculiarly Pauline doctrine of flesh has been subject to diverse interpretations. We may first trace briefly the various meanings that are given to the word in the Pauline terminology.

SARX IS THE BODILY TISSUES. *Sarx* is frequently used to describe the tissues that constitute the body and is thus contrasted with bones and blood. There are different kinds of flesh, of men, of animals, of birds, of fish (I Cor. 15:39). Pain and suffering may be experienced in the flesh (II Cor. 12:7); circumcision was wrought in the flesh (Rom. 2:28). Jesus' body was a body of flesh (Col. 1:22). Flesh, however, is corruptible and cannot inherit the Kingdom of God (I Cor. 15:50).

SARX IS THE BODY ITSELF. By a natural transition, the part is used for the whole, and in many places *sarx* is synonymous with the body as a whole rather than designating the fleshly part of the body. Paul may thus speak either of being absent in the body (I Cor. 5:3) or in the flesh (Col. 2:5). "The one who joins himself to a harlot is one body (with her), for it says, the two shall be one flesh" (I Cor. 6:16, 17). Paul can say that "the life of Jesus may also be manifested in our bodies" or "in our mortal flesh" (II Cor. 4:10, 11).[42]

SARX IS MAN WITH REFERENCE TO HIS ORIGIN. Following the Old Testament usage, *sarx* is used to refer not merely to the material of the body or to the body itself, but concretely to man who is constituted of flesh. In this usage the word may refer particularly to man's human relationships, his physical origin and the natural ties that bind him to other men. Paul speaks of his kinsmen "according to the flesh," his fellow-Jews (Rom. 9:3). The "children of the flesh" (Rom. 9:8) are those born by natural generation in contrast with those born as a result of divine intervention. Israel "after the flesh" (I Cor. 10:18) is natural Israel, those who are physically Jews. Paul can even use "my flesh" (Rom. 11:14) as a synonym for his kinsmen, fellow-Jews. Christ was descended from David according to the flesh (Rom. 1:3). The phrase does not designate merely the source of his *bodily* life but of his entire human existence including both his body and human spirit.

SARX IS MAN IN TERMS OF HIS OUTWARD APPEARANCE AND CONDITIONS.[43] A further extension of *sarx* reaches beyond man in his bodily life to include other factors that are inseparable elements to human existence. "Confidence in the flesh" (Phil. 3:3ff.) does not mean confidence in the body, but confidence in the whole complex of the outward realm of human existence. It includes Paul's Jewish ancestry, his strict religious training, his zeal and his prominence in Jewish religious circles. The phrase "boasting according to the flesh" is rendered "boasting of worldly things" in II Corinthians 11:18 (RSV). A good showing "in the flesh" is practically synonymous with worldly prominence (Gal. 6:12-14).

---

[42] For other illustrations see Eph. 5:28-31; II Cor. 7:1; Col. 2:1; Gal. 4:13; Eph. 2:15.

[43] See E. Schweizer, *TDNT* VII, 126ff.

The Judaizers insisted upon circumcision to promote a sense of prideful attainment in the religious life that they might have a ground of glorying. But these external distinctions and grounds of glorying no longer appealed to Paul because the world had been crucified to him and he to the world.

In the three references cited above, "the flesh" refers to the sphere of societal relationships in which a man is compared with his fellow men, and the emphasis rests particularly upon religious attainments and their appeal to human pride. The word is also used of outward relationships in describing the social ties existing between slave and master (Phlm. 16; Col. 3:22; Eph. 6:5). *En sarki* describes also the realm of marital relationships, which entails certain troublesome problems (I Cor. 7:28).

This usage illuminates an otherwise difficult passage: "from now on, we regard no one according to the flesh; even though we once regarded Christ according to the flesh, we regard him thus no longer" (II Cor. 5:16). The RSV correctly renders the phrase, "from a human point of view." This verse cannot be used to support the view that Paul has no interest in the historical Jesus; and it provides no evidence to answer the question as to whether Paul had ever personally known the historical Jesus. Paul is referring to a transformation in his own outlook on all the relationships of life. At one time the "human viewpoint" predominated Paul's outlook and it was then of the greatest importance whether a man practiced a legal righteousness and devoted himself to a perfect obedience to the Jewish torah. From this point of view, Jesus who had sought out publicans and sinners and who had been crucified as a common criminal could not possibly be the Messiah but must be an impostor. However, now Paul's viewpoint is completely transformed and these matters of human relationships and religious pride are quite irrelevant. To be in Christ is to be a new creation by virtue of which an entirely different interpretation is given to life and its relationships (v. 17).

This usage in a few passages is extended to describe the whole state or sphere in which men naturally live, the way of life that characterizes ordinary human existence. Paul had been accused in Corinth of seeking his own selfish ends and of conducting himself for his own self-advantage. Such people accused him of acting "according to the flesh"; but Paul replies that though he lives "in the flesh," he is not carrying on a warfare "according to the flesh," for his weapons are not fleshly but divine (II Cor. 10:1-3). Here the expression "to live in the flesh" cannot refer to bodily existence per se; that is too obvious to be mentioned. Paul admits that he lives in the midst of a *world system,* but insists that his ministry is not performed by resources that are derived from this worldly system or are in accordance with worldly principles. The emphasis is not upon the *sinfulness* of the worldly order; in fact, a Christian must of necessity live in its midst. Such a system is, however, impotent to provide the resources to reach a divine goal. The same use appears where Paul says that "not many wise according to the flesh, not many powerful, not many of noble birth were called" (I Cor. 1:26). The realm "according to the flesh" is the sphere of life that characterizes human existence; it has its wisdom, its nobility, and its power. It is not sinful intrinsically, but it is impotent to attain to the wisdom and the knowledge of God. A new and higher level of existence is necessary to enter into the world of divine realities.

THE ETHICAL USE OF SARX. There remains a group of references that are distinctly Pauline, which are usually called the "ethical" use of the term.[44] The most important feature about this usage is that man as flesh is contrasted with Spirit, is sinful, and without the aid of the Spirit cannot please God. The most vivid passage is the first part of Romans 8. Paul sharply contrasts those who are "in the flesh" and "in the Spirit." Those who are in the flesh cannot please God. "But you are not in the flesh but in the Spirit, if the Spirit of God really dwells in you" (Rom. 8:8, 9). Formally, the statement "Those who are in the flesh cannot please God" is contradicted by Galatians 2:20: "The life I now live in the flesh I live by faith in the Son of God." Obviously, Paul is using the same phrase to designate two very different things. To be "in the flesh" (Gal. 2:20) is to be in the physical body, which can be existence in faith. "In the flesh" in Romans 8:8 means, according to verse 9, not to be indwelt by the Spirit, i.e., to be an unregenerate man. Those who are unregenerate, not indwelt by the Spirit, cannot fulfill the Law of God and thereby please him. This statement surely does not mean that they can do no deed that pleases God. Romans 2:15 affirms that even Gentiles have the Law of God in some way written in their hearts; and so far as they obey the inner Law, they must be pleasing to God. Romans 8:8 means that unregenerate man cannot please God by loving him and serving him as God desires. Thus the Law was unable to make men please God because the flesh is weak (Rom. 8:2). To live after the flesh is death; to live after the Spirit is life (Rom. 8:6). Elsewhere Paul says, "I know that nothing good dwells within me, that is, in my flesh" (Rom. 7:18). Flesh here cannot be the physical flesh, for the body of flesh is the temple of the Spirit (I Cor. 6:19) and a member of Christ (I Cor. 6:15), and is to be the means of glorifying God (I Cor. 6:20). Paul means that in his unregenerate nature there dwells none of the goodness that God demands.

The flesh is something that stays with the believer even after he has received the Spirit. Writing to Christians, Paul says that the flesh and the Spirit are opposed to each other "to prevent you from doing what you would" (Gal. 5:17). There is a conflict that rages in the Christian's breast. Reception of the Spirit does not mean that the problem of the flesh is dis-

---

[44] See H. W. Robinson, *The Christian Doctrine of Man* (1926), p. 114; W. D. Davies, *Christian Origins and Judaism* (1926), p. 153. The following list, which is close to that of Davies, represents this usage: Rom. 6:19; 7:5, 18, 25; 8:3, 4, 5, 6, 7, 8, 9, 12, 13; I Cor. 5:5; II Cor. 1:17; 11:18; Gal. 3:3; 5:13, 16, 17, 19, 24; 6:8; Eph. 2:3; Col. 2:11, 13, 18, 23.

posed of. There is a conflict between the flesh and the Spirit in which the believer must learn how to let the Spirit have dominance.

DIFFERENT VIEWPOINTS. We have followed the RSV in capitalizing Spirit, believing that it refers to the divine Spirit that is given and not intrinsic to man. However, many scholars have interpreted Paul's doctrine of the flesh in terms of Hellenistic dualism in which the flesh is the actual body, which is viewed as essentially sinful.[45] The source of evil is materiality itself. This dualistic interpretation has been given a classical statement in Pfleiderer, who understands Paul's concept of sin to be that a demonic spiritual being finds its residence in the physical flesh; and while therefore the flesh itself is not identical with sin, it is nevertheless the seat and organ of the demonic sinful principle. Because man physically consists of flesh, he has become enslaved to the sinful power that dwells in his material substance.[46]

Against this dualistic interpretation, there stands the incontrovertible fact that Paul did not view the body as sinful per se; and therefore when *sarx* is viewed as sinful, it must refer to something other than the physical material that constitutes my body. The body is made for the Lord (I Cor. 6:13) and is to be joined with Christ (v. 15). The body is indwelt by the Spirit of God (I Cor. 6:19) and is to be the means by which God is glorified (v. 20). The body shares the experience of sanctification (I Cor. 7:34) and is to be presented to God as a living sacrifice that is holy and well-pleasing to God (Rom. 12:1).[47]

A second view interprets *sarx* in the light of an alleged ethical dualism innate in man's nature. Within man there are two principles: the higher and the lower, *pneuma* and *sarx,* and between these two an incessant conflict is waged. The Christian is the man who by divine help has found victory for the higher spiritual principle. The spirit of man is the true ego, the better self, the spiritual nature in which he is most kindred to God, that imperishable part which relates him to the eternal and imperishable world. In Christians this higher life has become the predominant element, and in them the human spirit is developed and assumes dominance in the conduct of life.[48] This innate ethical dualism is vividly depicted in the words of Beyschlag, "But none of the apostles has described, like Paul, the overpowering strength of the flesh, the sensuous, selfish nature, or has emphasized the feebleness of the divine in man, which is like a smoking flax or a latent germ; and no one, like him, has made the whole work of salvation bear upon this evil element in man and nature; for salvation, founded by Christ as the ideal spiritual man, consists in breaking the power of the

[45] See W. Morgan, *The Religion and Theology of Paul* (1917), pp. 17ff.

[46] See O. Pfleiderer, *Primitive Christianity* (1906), I, 280; see also Pfleiderer's *Paulinism* (1891), I, 47-67.

[47] J. A. T. Robinson goes so far as to say that *sōma* stands for man as made for God (*The Body* [1952], p. 31). This seems to go too far; *pneuma* is man in his relationship to God.

[48] See G. B. Stevens, *The Theology of the NT* (1899), pp. 343f.

flesh and kindling the smoking flax of the spirit into a clear, holy flame through supplies from above; and that flame first of all transfigures the heart and the conduct, and, finally, it changes the mortal body also into the image of the perfected Christ."[49]

The objection to this interpretation rests in the fact that the conflict Paul finds between the flesh and the spirit is not between the flesh and the human spirit, but between human flesh and the Spirit of God. That the higher side of the conflict in Romans 8:4-8 is the Holy Spirit and not man's spirit is indubitably clear from verse 9, "But you are not in the flesh, you are in the Spirit, if the Spirit of God really dwells in you" (Rom. 8:9). In this state the human spirit is indeed alive, but it is due to the fact that the Spirit of God who raised Jesus from the dead dwells within man (Rom. 8:10, 11). Paul does frequently speak of the human spirit, as we have already seen, but he does not contrast it with *sarx*. The conflict that is depicted in Galatians 5:16-26 is not found in the unregenerate man but only in the man in whom the Spirit of God has come to dwell. Within such a man, there arises a conflict between the Spirit and *sarx* that is resolved only when the "flesh is crucified" and the Spirit obtains complete mastery of his life.

A third interpretation is that of Rudolf Bultmann, who insists that Paul's concept of the flesh does not extend beyond that of the preceding discussion in which flesh is viewed as the realm of man's earthly-natural existence, which, in contrast to God, is weak and transitory. When this realm of the external and the natural becomes the objective of man's pursuit, it becomes not merely the earthly-transitory in contrast with the transcendent-eternal, but is viewed as being positively sinful and opposed to God. That conduct or attitude which directs itself toward the flesh, taking flesh for its norm, is sinful. The pursuit of the merely human, the earthly-transitory, is sinful, because man should find his true life in God.[50]

This interpretation is far more attractive and consonant with the exegetical data than either of the two already discussed. But these data require a position that goes further than Bultmann. Bultmann is himself compelled to recognize that sometimes *sarx* is personified and becomes practically equivalent to "I."[51] Furthermore, the "works of the flesh" are not primarily directed to the world of externality and the outward realm of the earthly-natural; such sins as enmity, jealousy, selfishness, and envy are "sins of the spirit," which may or may not have their manifestation in the realm of external relationships (Gal. 5:19-21). They are self-centered rather than God-centered, and the flesh is myself seeking its own ends in opposition to the Spirit of God. Bultmann's interpretation requires him to exegete the phrases "when we were in the flesh" (Rom. 7:5) and "you are not in the flesh, you are in the Spirit" (Rom. 8:9) proleptically to refer in a promis-

[49] W. Beyschlag, *NT Theology* (1895), II, 46f.

[50] R. Bultmann, *Theology*, I, 233-38. See also H. Conzelmann, *Theology of the NT* (1969), p. 179; J. A. T. Robinson, *The Body*, p. 25.

[51] R. Bultmann, *Theology*, I, 245.

sory manner to the glorified state.[52] This, however, does not appear to be Paul's meaning. He is not looking forward to future deliverance from the flesh but affirms a present state of existence that is in the Spirit and not in the flesh. The man who is "in the Spirit" in fact continues to live "in the flesh" (Gal. 2:20); but while he continues to live in the body and in the natural world, he is no longer "in the flesh" but "in the Spirit" because the Spirit of God really dwells within him. We can only conclude that the expression, to be "in the flesh," means to live as an unregenerate man, to be a man who is not indwelt by the Spirit of God. *Sarx* ethically conceived is human nature, man viewed in his entirety apart from and in contrast with the righteousness and holiness of God. As such, man is not only weak and impotent, he is also sinful and rebellious against God. Paul differentiates absolutely between the realms "in the Spirit" and "in the flesh" in Romans 8:4-11. A man belongs either to one realm or to the other; and a man's status is determined by whether or not he is indwelt by the Spirit of God. Those who are indwelt by the Spirit *are* "in the Spirit"; the natural man is "in the flesh." The latter lives out his entire life in the humanness that will issue in death. Man is able to serve God only when God's Spirit has indwelt and quickened him in the realm of the spirit (v. 10).

A fourth view is that of W. D. Davies, who sees the background for the conflict between flesh and spirit in the rabbinic doctrine of two inclinations, the good inclination (*yetzer hatob*) and the evil inclination (*yetzer hara*), which indwell all men and struggle for supremacy.[53] However, there is one distinct difference between Paul and the rabbis: for them the good inclination was an innate possession of all men, while the Spirit that opposes the flesh in Paul is not the human spirit but the divine Spirit, possessed only by believers.[54]

SARX IS UNREGENERATE HUMAN NATURE. We follow those scholars who understand this "ethical" use of *sarx* to refer neither to man's physical materiality nor to a lower element in man, but to man as a whole, seen in his fallenness, opposed to God. This usage is a natural development of the Old Testament use of *basar,* which is man viewed in his frailty and weakness before God. When this is applied to the ethical realm, it becomes man in his ethical weakness, i.e., sinfulness before God. *Sarx* represents not a part of man but man as a whole—unregenerate, fallen, sinful man. "In the case of *sarx* the predominant thought [is] of man standing by himself over against God—in other words, the natural man conceived as not

---

[52] *Ibid.,* p. 236.

[53] W. D. Davies, *Paul and Rabbinic Judaism* (1955), pp. 17-35.

[54] Certain parallels exist between Paul and the Qumran community (K. G. Kuhn, "New Light on Temptation, Sin, and Flesh in the NT" in *The Scrolls and the NT,* ed. by Krister Stendahl [1958], pp. 94-113). However, Davies has pointed out that the similarities are largely those of language and not of substance or theology. See W. D. Davies, "Paul and the Dead Sea Scrolls; Flesh and Spirit," *Christian Origins and Judaism* (1962), pp. 145-78. For other views see W. D. Stacey, *The Pauline View of Man,* pp. 41-55, 163-73.

having yet received grace, or as yet not wholly under its influence."[55] "The Apostle does not identify *sarx* with the material body or outward bodily substance of man."[56] "Gal. 5:19f. makes it clear that when 'flesh' is used in a moral sense it does not necessarily have any physical meaning, since most of the sins ascribed to the lower nature *(sarx)* could well be practiced by a disembodied spirit."[57] "It was not only in the physical desires, but in every department of the life, that sin was manifested. . . . The persistence of sinful acts suggests a principle of sin in each man, a lower sinful nature; it was identified with the flesh. The flesh became a synonym for the lower nature in general in contrast to the higher self. . . . The lower nature was so much an entity that it had a mind (Col. 2:18, Rom. 8:6) of its own."[58] We cannot follow Stacey if he means that the "lower nature" is identified with the physical flesh. As indicated above, many of the "ethical" references have no physical connotations. "The evidence is against the view that Paul found in the flesh as a physical thing a compelling force for evil. The flesh that makes for evil is not the body or matter as such, but an inherited impulse to evil."[59]

While Paul makes a sharp and absolute contrast between being "in the flesh" (unregenerate) and being "in the spirit" (regenerate), there remains in the believer a struggle between the flesh and spirit. If "flesh" means unregenerate human nature, the believer still possesses this nature even though he has received the Spirit. Even in the Christian the flesh struggles against the Spirit so that he cannot be the (perfect) man that he would wish to be (Gal. 5:17).[60]

This same situation is reflected in I Corinthians 2:14-3:3, where Paul describes three classes of people: *psychikos,* the natural man (2:14); *sarkikos,* the fleshly man (3:3); and *pneumatikos,* the spiritual man (3:1). In this passage the "natural man" is the unregenerate man, the man who is "in the flesh" (Rom. 8:9), that is, the whole realm of his life is devoted to the human level and as such he is unable to know the things of God. The "spiritual man" is the man whose life is ruled by the Holy Spirit. Between these two is a third class of those who are "fleshly" yet who are babes *in Christ.* They must therefore be "in the Spirit," yet they do not walk "according to the Spirit." Because they are babes in Christ, we must conclude that the Spirit of God dwells in them; yet the Holy Spirit does not exercise full control over their lives, and they are still walking "like men" (v. 3), manifesting the works of the flesh in jealousy and strife. The man who is "in the Spirit" and no longer "in the flesh," that is, a regenerate

---

55 W. P. Dickson, *St. Paul's Use of the Terms Flesh and Spirit* (1883), p. 271. This old book remains a classic study of this theme.

56 *Ibid.*, p. 310.

57 D. E. H. Whiteley, *The Theology of St. Paul,* p. 39.

58 W. D. Stacey, *The Pauline View of Man,* p. 163.

59 E. D. Burton, *Spirit, Soul, and Flesh* (1918), p. 197.

60 For the interpretation of the conflict in Rom. 7, see the chapter on the Law. In this chapter Paul does not speak of a conflict between the flesh and the Spirit, but between the flesh and the Law.

man indwelt by the Spirit of God, has yet to learn the lesson of walking by the Spirit and not by the flesh.

VICTORY OVER THE FLESH. While a struggle remains in the Christian between the Spirit and the flesh, Paul knows the way of victory for the Spirit. The flesh of the body comes within the orb of sanctification (I Thess. 5:23). But the flesh as unregenerate human nature can only be put to death.

Here we meet the familiar Pauline tension between the indicative and the imperative.[61] Paul views the death of the flesh as something that has already happened in the death of Christ. Those who belong to Christ have crucified the flesh with its passions and desires (Gal. 5:24). They have put off the body of flesh[62] in the circumcision of Christ, that is, in the circumcision of the heart, which is accomplished by Christ (Col. 2:11). Paul says, "I have been crucified with Christ" (Gal. 2:20), and "our old self was crucified with him" (Rom. 6:6). The identity of the flesh and the self is further supported in this teaching of crucifixion, for Paul means the same thing by the crucifixion of the flesh as he means when he says, "How can we who died to sin still live in it?" "We have been united with him in death." "We are buried with him by baptism into death" (Rom. 6:2-4). It is I, myself, who have died with Christ.

The same idea is expressed in a different idiom in Colossians 3:9: "Do not lie to one another, seeing that you have put off the old nature (*anthrōpon*) with its practices and have put on the new nature (*anthrōpon*)." This views a change as already having taken place. The "old man" "denotes the sinful being of the unconverted man."[63] This is another way of saying that the old self (*anthrōpon*) has been crucified with Christ (Rom. 6:6).

This death of the flesh is not, however, something that works automatically. It is an event that must be appropriated by faith. This involves two aspects. Believers are to recognize that the flesh has been crucified with Christ, and therefore "consider *yourselves* dead to sin and alive to God in Christ Jesus" (Rom. 6:11). One cannot consider himself dead with Christ unless he has actually died and been crucified with Christ; but because this has happened, it can be put into practice in daily experience. Because I have died with Christ, I am to "put to death the deeds of the body" (Rom. 8:13). "Body" is here used as a vehicle for the works of the "flesh"—the sensual life of the unregenerate nature. Because I have been brought from death into life, I am to "yield my members to God as instruments of righteousness" (Rom. 6:13). Because I have died with Christ, I am to "put to death what is earthly . . . : immorality, impurity, . . ." (Col. 3:5). Because I have already put off the old nature and put on the new nature, I am to put on compassion, kindness, lowliness, and the like (Col. 3:12).

---

[61] See below, pp. 524ff.

[62] The phrase, "the body of flesh," cannot here refer to the fleshly body, but to "the personality as dominated by sensuality," a self-centered, sensual self. C. F. D. Moule, *Colossians* (1957), p. 95.

[63] J. Jeremias, *TDNT* I, 365.

Another way of describing victory over the flesh is "to walk in the Spirit." "Walk in the Spirit, and do not gratify the desires of the flesh" (Gal. 5:16; cf. Rom. 8:4). Walking in the Spirit means to live each moment under the control of the Holy Spirit. Walking involves living a step at a time, moment by moment; and to walk in the Spirit means to take each step of my earthly walk under the direction and control and leadership of the Holy Spirit.

HEART.[64] There are several other words used by Paul to characterize man, the most important of which is the heart (*kardia*). The Pauline usage is essentially the same as the Hebrew word *lēb*[65] and designates the inner life of man from various points of view. The heart or inner aspect of man is contrasted to the outward and visible. True circumcision is a matter of the heart (Rom. 2:29), not of the flesh. Physical absence can mean presence in heart (I Thess. 2:17). Outward glory is vanity compared to that of the heart (II Cor. 5:12). The heart holds secrets that only the Holy Spirit can reveal (I Cor. 4:5; 14:25). True knowledge of man can be found only by searching the heart (Rom. 8:27).

The heart is the seat of the emotions, both good and bad. The heart can lust for evil things (Rom. 1:24); but Paul can say that his heart's desire is for the conversion of his fellow-Jews (Rom. 10:1). Paul wrote to the Corinthians in "anguish of heart" (II Cor. 2:4); he was pained in his heart because the Jews had rejected Christ (Rom. 9:2). His plea to the Corinthians to "open your hearts to us" (II Cor. 7:3) means to receive them in love.

A word bearing a similar meaning is *splangchna,* wrongly translated "bowels" in the KJV. The *splangchna* were the nobler organs—the heart, liver, and lungs—[66] and in Paul the word is used of Christian affection (II Cor. 6:12; 7:15; Col. 3:12; Phlm. 7, 12, 20). In Philippians 1:8 and 2:1 it means love.

Kardia can also be used for man's intellectual activity. In Romans 1:21, the heart of ungodly men is without understanding.[67] In II Corinthians 9:7 Paul exhorts his reader to give liberally "as he has made up his mind" (RSV). The "eyes of the heart" must be enlightened (Eph. 1:18) to understand the Christians' hope.

Kardia can be used of the seat of the will. The heart has purposes or intentions that only God knows (I Cor. 4:5). The heart can be impenitent because it is willful in wrongdoing (Rom. 2:5). The heart can be obedient (Rom. 6:17), i.e., supported by the will.

The *kardia* is the organ of ethical judgment. The "senseless hearts" of ungodly men are those whose sin has made them incapable of sound judg-

---

64 R. Bultmann, *Theology*, I, 220-26; W. D. Stacey, *The Pauline View of Man*, pp. 194-97.

65 H. W. Robinson, *The Christian Doctrine of Man*, p. 106.

66 H. Köster, *TDNT* VII, 548.

67 The RSV translates *kardia* by "minds."

ment (Rom. 1:21). The Gentiles possess a law, written in their hearts, that enables them to distinguish between good and evil (Rom. 2:14). The heart can be corrupt (Rom. 2:5) or enlightened (II Cor. 4:6).

The *kardia* is the seat of religious experience. God can shine in the heart (II Cor. 4:6); the heart receives the down payment of the Spirit (II Cor. 1:22); the heart experiences the outpouring of God's love (Rom. 5:5); Christ can dwell in the heart (Eph. 3:17); the peace of Christ can reign in the heart (Col. 3:15).

MIND. Paul often speaks of the mind *(nous),*[68] by which he designates man as a knowing, thinking, judging creature. *Nous* is not used of man engaged in speculative, reflective reason; the word can be used of practical judgment.

That *nous* is the organ of understanding is obvious in Paul's discussion of tongues. When one prays in a tongue, his spirit prays but his mind is unfruitful (I Cor. 14:14), i.e., he does not understand his own words. The peace of God surpasses all thought (Phil. 4:7). Paul exhorts the Thessalonians not to be shaken in their minds (II Thess. 2:2), i.e., confused in thought.

That *nous* is not speculative reason but moral judgment is clear from the fact that godless men have a "base mind" (Rom. 1:28). They live in "the futility of their minds" (Eph. 4:17). Even the flesh can be said to have its mind (Col. 2:18), which leads to vain pride. In believers the mind must be constantly renewed (Rom. 12:2; Eph. 4:23). Clearly, the *nous* is a human faculty that can be dominated either by evil or by God.

The religious aspect of the word is seen in that Paul can speak of the mind of God (Rom. 11:34), and of the mind of Christ (I Cor. 2:16), which means insight into the very mind of God himself. The "mind of the Lord" is undoubtedly his hidden plan of salvation, now revealed.[69]

Nous can also designate "the moral consciousness as it concretely determines will and action."[70] In Romans 7, the *nous* approves of the Law of God, recognizes its spiritual character, and desires to obey it (Rom. 7:23). But the flesh dominates the mind in the unregenerate man, so that although he serves the Law of God with his mind, with the flesh he serves the law of sin (Rom. 7:25).

THE INNER MAN.[71] Paul uses the phrase *ho esō anthrōpos* in two different ways: of the unregenerate man and of the regenerate man. In Romans 7:22, the "inmost self" is used synonymously with the "mind," which can approve of the Law of God and will to obey it, but finds itself impotent. Behm describes this as "the spiritual side of man, or man him-

---

[68] See R. Bultmann, *Theology,* I, 211-16; E. Würthwein, *TDNT* IV, 958-59; W. D. Stacey, *The Pauline View of Man,* pp. 198-205.

[69] E. Würthwein, *TDNT* IV, 959.

[70] *Ibid.,* p. 958.

[71] See J. Behm, *TDNT* II, 698-99; W. D. Stacey, *The Pauline View of Man,* pp. 211-14.

self in so far as he enjoys self-awareness, as he thinks and wills and feels."[72] In II Corinthians 4:16, the inner man is contrasted with the "outer man"—man as a corruptible earthly being. While the outer man is wasting away, the inner man is being renewed every day. "The inward man is the real self that passes from the body of flesh to the body of resurrection."[73] In both instances, "the inner man" is the higher, essential self, either redeemed or redeemable, made for God and opposed to sin.[74]

CONSCIENCE.[75] Paul uses another word that has no Hebrew equivalent: *syneidēsis*. However, while the term was widely used by Greek philosophers, especially the Stoics, the idea is included in the Hebrew word for heart, *lēb*.[76] Conscience is a universal faculty. Paul speaks of his own conscience (Rom. 9:1), the conscience of Christians (I Cor. 8:1-13; 10:23-11:1), and the conscience of Gentiles (Rom. 2:15). The conscience is the faculty of moral judgment. The word *syneidēsis* means knowledge shared with one's self. It is man's consciousness of his conduct as his own,[77] and his judgment as to whether it is right or wrong. When Paul says, "I am not aware of anything against myself" (I Cor. 4:4),[78] he means that his conscience is clear; it does not condemn him of having done anything wrong. However, conscience is not the court of last appeal. It is not an autonomous, self-sufficient guide. He goes on to say, "but I am not thereby acquitted. It is the Lord who judges me." Conscience at best is, therefore, a guide of relative value. One could have a clear conscience, and yet be guilty of wrong in the sight of God. In Romans 9:1, he links the verdict of conscience with the Holy Spirit; but he nowhere develops the relation between these two guides.

He challenges the Corinthians to judge his conduct in the light of their conscience. He commends himself to every man's conscience "in the sight of God" (II Cor. 4:2). This means that conscience is to judge Paul's conduct in the light of the revelation that God has given. He again asserts that God knows the motivations for his conduct, and he hopes the consciences of the Corinthians will agree (II Cor. 5:11). In I Timothy 1:5 and 19, he links a good conscience with sincere faith. However, conscience is not an absolute guide. When men depart from the faith, their conscience can become seared (I Tim. 4:2), i.e., hardened so that it is not a safe guide. All this suggests that the conscience of the Christian must always be exercised in the light of the divine revelation in Jesus Christ.

In the question of eating meats offered to idols he speaks of those who

72 J. Behm, *TDNT* II, 699.
73 W. D. Stacey, *The Pauline View of Man*, p. 211.
74 *Ibid.*, p. 212.
75 C. Maurer, *TDNT* VII, 914-17; C. A. Pierce, *Conscience in the NT* (1955); W. D. Stacey, *The Pauline View of Man*, pp. 206-10; W. D. Davies, *IDB* A-D, pp. 674-75; R. Bultmann, *Theology*, I, 216-20.
76 W. D. Stacey, *The Pauline View of Man*, p. 206.
77 R. Bultmann, *Theology*, I, 217.
78 Here he uses the verb *sunoida*. See also II Cor. 1:12.

have a "weak conscience" because they do not all possess correct knowledge (I Cor. 8:7). They do not understand that "everything is indeed clean" (Rom. 14:20). However, even for such, the conscience is a guide that must not be violated; and Paul exhorts those who have a strong conscience, i.e., who understand that "the earth is the Lord's and everything in it" (I Cor. 10:26), so to conduct themselves that they do not by example encourage the weak to defile their conscience (I Cor. 8:9-13).

Unbelievers, as well as Christians, have a conscience. When the Gentiles who do not have the Old Testament Law to guide them do the right, "they show that what the law requires is written on their hearts, while their conscience also bears witness and their conflicting thoughts accuse or perhaps excuse them" (Rom. 2:15). Paul does not intimate that conscience is a guide that can lead to salvation; he only says that because they have conscience, they know the difference between right and wrong.

34

THE NEW LIFE IN CHRIST

Literature:

C. A. A. Scott, *Christianity According to St. Paul* (1927), ch. IV; J. S. Stewart, *A Man in Christ* (1935), chs. IV and VI; E. Wahlstrom, *The New Life in Christ* (1950); E. Best, *One Body in Christ* (1955); W. D. Davies, "The Lord the Spirit," *Paul and Rabbinic Judaism* (1955), pp. 177-226; A. Wikenhauser, *Pauline Mysticism* (1956); N. Q. Hamilton, *The Holy Spirit and Eschatology in Paul* (1957); R. A. Harrisville, *The Concept of Newness in the NT* (1960); M. Bouttier, *Christianity According to Paul* (1966); R. C. Tannehill, *Dying and Rising with Christ* (1966); D. Hill, *Greek Words and Hebrew Meanings* (1967), pp. 265-93; G. Bornkamm, "Baptism and New Life in Paul," *Early Christian Experience* (1969), pp. 71-86; E. Schweizer, "Dying and Rising with Christ" in *NT Issues,* ed. by R. Batey (1970), pp. 173-90; E. Schweizer, "Pneuma," *TDNT* VI, pp. 415-437; L. B. Smedes, *All Things Made New* (1970).

THE NEW LIFE IN CHRIST is summarized in Paul's classic statement, "If any one is in Christ, he is a new creation; the old has passed away, behold, the new has come" (II Cor. 5:17).[1] This verse is popularly interpreted in terms of subjective experience. All of the desires and appetites of this unregenerate man have passed away and have been replaced by an entirely new set of desires and appetites. However, this statement must be interpreted in the context of Pauline thought in particular and New Testament thought in general.

The idea of newness is distinctly eschatological. The prophets looked forward to the day when God would do a new thing (Isa. 43:19; cf. Jer. 31:21). When God completes his redemptive work, he will make a new covenant with his people (Jer. 31:31ff.; cf. Ezek. 34:25; 37:27); he will implant a new heart and a new spirit within them (Ezek. 11:19; 18:31; 36:26); he will call them by a new name (Isa. 62:2), give them a new song (Ps. 96:1), and create new heavens and a new earth (Isa. 65:17; 66:22).[2]

---

1 The reading of the AV, "all things are become new," is based on the Textus Receptus and is a distinctly inferior reading.

2 F. F. Bruce, "New," *IDB* K-Q, p. 542.

The idea of newness preserves its eschatological character in the New Testament. God will create new heavens and a new earth (Rev. 21:1; II Pet. 3:13); the new Jerusalem will come down out of heaven and be planted among men (Rev. 21:2; cf. 3:12); God will provide new wine for the eschatological banquet (Mk. 14:25); he will give to his people a new name (Rev. 2:17; 3:12) and a new song (Rev. 5:9; 14:3); he will make all things new (Rev. 21:5). A new creation is the glorious end of the revelation of God's salvation;[3] it is the supreme goal of the entire biblical *Heilsgeschichte*.

The Pauline statement that in Christ the old has passed away and the new has come is an eschatological statement. "The new aeon, which has dawned with Christ, brings a new creation, the creation of a new man."[4] This must be understood within Paul's total eschatological perspective. The "new creation" obviously does not refer to a renovation of the physical world; this new creation awaits the eschatological consummation (Rom. 8:21). The statement must be defined in terms of what Paul sees new in Christ. The passing of the old does not mean the end of the old age; it continues until the parousia. But the old age does not remain intact; the new age has broken in. In Christ there is deliverance from the present evil age (Gal. 1:4). In Christ men need no longer be conformed to the old age (Rom. 12:2). The new covenant with God has already come into existence (I Cor. 11:25). God has wrought a new creation in Christ that should express itself in good works (Eph. 2:10). He has created "one new man" that is constituted of all who are in Christ, whether Jews or Gentiles (Eph. 2:15). That this new creation does not refer primarily to a new inner moral nature is shown by the fact that Paul tells those who are in Christ that they are to live upright lives because they have already put off the old man[5] and have put on the new man, "which is being renewed in knowledge after the image of its creator" (Col. 3:9-10). The putting on of the new man is something deeper than moral renewal, but it demands moral conduct. The renewal of the new man[6] does not designate gradual renewal of the character, but that the new humanity, already existing in Christ, is progressively actualized in the Christian church.[7] While the putting on of the new man is viewed as something that has already happened in Christ, it is not a once-and-for-all event, for Paul exhorts to put off the old man that manifests itself in pagan conduct and to put on the new man that is created after the likeness of God (Eph. 4:22-24). The underlying idea is that while believers live in the old age, because they are in Christ they belong to the new age with its new creation (indicative), and they are to live a life that is expressive of the new existence (imperative).

---

[3] See J. Behm in *TDNT* III, 449.
[4] *Loc. cit.*
[5] The RSV translates it "nature," but the word is *anthrōpos.*
[6] The Greek has a present participle.
[7] C. F. D. Moule, *Colossians* (1957), p. 120.

IN CHRIST. The expression "in Christ" is one of Paul's most characteristic formulations and its precise meaning has been vigorously debated.[8] Deissmann brought the theological significance of the phrase to the attention of the scholarly world by emphasizing its "mystical" dimension. Basic to Deissmann's interpretation is the identification of Christ and the Spirit (II Cor. 3:17). The "Spirit-Christ" has a body that is not earthly or material, but consists of the divine effulgence.[9] The Spirit-Christ is the Christian's new environment. It is analogous to the air. As we are in the air and the air is in us, so we are in Christ and Christ is in us. Something similar to this is expressed by Johannes Weiss, who understands the Pauline doctrine of the Christ-Spirit as "a fluid which surrounds and also penetrates us . . . a formless, impersonal, all-penetrating being."[10] This very idea will seem intolerable to people unfamiliar with ancient ways of thought who conceive of "spiritual" as *ipso facto* nonmaterial. However, the ancient world had different thought categories. "Spirit" could be understood in terms of fine invisible matter that could interpenetrate all visible forms of matter.[11]

Deissmann's central contention, namely, that the basic meaning of "in Christ" is one of mystical fellowship, has been accepted by many scholars. "In Christ" designates conscious communion with him.[12] Nothing shall be able to separate us from the love of God in Christ Jesus (Rom. 8:39). The new life means righteousness and peace and joy in the Holy Spirit (Rom. 14:17).[13] There is encouragement in Christ (Phil. 2:1) and in humble service (Phil. 2:5). The peace of God guards the hearts and minds of those who are in Christ (Phil. 4:7). Paul can be content in every kind of human situation in Christ (Phil. 4:13).

Other scholars do not deny the fundamental truth of Deissmann's view of personal mysticism but point out that there are many passages that have a collective emphasis. "In Christ" is practically equivalent to being in the church.[14] The churches of Judea are in Christ (Gal. 1:22).[15] Those who

---

8 One of the best surveys is that of E. Best, *One Body in Christ* (1955), pp. 8-19. See also A. Wikenhauser, *Pauline Mysticism* (1956), pp. 95ff.

9 A. Deissmann, *Paul* (1926), p. 142.

10 J. Weiss, *The History of Primitive Christianity* (1937), II, 464, 405.

11 See H. Kleinknecht, *TDNT* VI, 339, 358; E. Schweizer, *TDNT* VI, 392.

12 See for instance A. Wikenhauser, *Pauline Mysticism*, pp. 25ff.; J. Stewart, *A Man in Christ* (1935), pp. 158ff. Stewart takes this as the center of the Pauline theology. C. A. A. Scott, *Christianity According to St. Paul* (1927), pp. 153f.; E. Andrews, *The Meaning of Christ for Paul* (1949), p. 83; W. D. Davies, *Paul and Rabbinic Judaism* (1958), p. 87.

13 For our present purpose, we will not try to distinguish between "in Christ" and "in the Spirit." For a discussion, see A. Wikenhauser, *Pauline Mysticism*, pp. 49-64.

14 Cf. R. N. Flew, *Jesus and His Church* (1943), p. 152; C. H. Dodd, *Romans* (1932), pp. 87f. This meaning is also recognized by W. D. Davies, *Paul and Rabbinic Judaism*, p. 86; C. A. A. Scott, *Christianity According to St. Paul*, pp. 151f.

15 The RSV obscures this verse.

lead the church as ministers do so in Christ (I Cor. 4:15). There is one body in Christ (Rom. 12:5). All believers are one in Christ Jesus (Gal. 3:28). Gentiles and Jews partake of the same promise in Christ (Eph. 3:6). The saints and believing brethren in Colossae are together in Christ (Col. 1:2). In such sayings, there is an unmistakable corporate emphasis. Believers are in Christ not only as individuals but as a people.

The centrality of the "mystical" interpretation has waned in recent scholarship.[16] In addition to sayings that can be interpreted mystically and ecclesiologically, there are numerous statements involving objective facts stating what God has done in Christ. Such statements cannot be subsumed either in the mystical or ecclesiological categories. God has chosen us in Christ (Eph. 1:4), and foreordained us (Eph. 1:7). Both redemption (Rom. 3:24) and sanctification (I Cor. 1:2) have been wrought in Jesus Christ. Reconciliation of the world has been accomplished in Christ (I Cor. 5:19). Justification comes to men in Christ (Gal. 2:17). Access to God is available in him (Eph. 2:12). Forgiveness of sins occurs in him (Eph. 4:32). The totality of salvation is in Christ (II Tim. 2:10). In addition to such "juridical" sayings[17] are many sayings that have to do with everyday Christian life and service. Paul speaks the truth in Christ (Rom. 9:1). He is proud in Christ (Rom. 15:17); his whole life is conducted in Christ (I Cor. 4:17); his imprisonment in Rome is in Christ (Phil. 1:13); believers even die in Christ (I Thess. 4:16).

The clue to this dismaying diversity of usage may be found in the parallel phrase "in Adam." As in Adam all die, so also in Christ shall all be made alive (I Cor. 15:22). This involves a twofold idea: that of solidarity and of the eschatological contrast between the two ages.[18] Paul conceives of two races of men. Natural men are in Adam; renewed men are in Christ. As Adam is the head and representative of the old race, so Christ is the head and representative of the new humanity. In Adam came sin, disobedience, condemnation, and death; in Christ comes righteousness, obedience, acquittal, and life (Rom. 5:12ff.). Those who are in Adam belong to the old aeon with its bondage to sin and death; those who belong to Christ belong to the new aeon with its freedom and life. Best expresses it in terms of the history of redemption. "The phrase 'in Christ' is the phrase for the salvation-historical *(heilsgeschichtlich)* situation of those who belong to Christ in virtue of their existential union with the death and resurrection of Christ."[19] The same idea can be expressed in terms of eschatology. "It is best explained as originating neither in mysticism nor in the realistic ideas of sacramental communion, nor in the idea of the Church as an institution, but in primitive Christian eschatology. The death and resurrec-

[16] See A. Oepke, *TDNT* I, 541f.; R. Schnackenburg, *NT Theology Today* (1963), p. 83; H. Conzelmann, *Theology of the NT* (1969), p. 210. For an extended criticism, see E. Wahlstrom, *The New Life in Christ* (1950), pp. 89-94.

[17] See H. Conzelmann, *Theology of the NT,* p. 209.

[18] For the idea of solidarity "in Adam," see above, p. 403.

[19] E. Best, *One Body in Christ,* p. 18.

tion of Jesus were eschatological events, effecting the transition from this age to the Age to Come. Believers could take advantage of this transition, but the transference from the one age to the other could take place only 'in Christ.' Those who belonged to him by faith passed through death and resurrection and so came to be alive to God."[20] Therefore to be "in Christ" means to be in the new sphere of salvation. To be in Christ means to experience the newness of the new aeon. In the realm of faith, if not in the realm of nature and society, the old has passed away, the new has come (II Cor. 5:17). In a sense, even believers are still in Adam, for they die; they are still in the old aeon, for they live in a sinful world and share the fallenness of creation. But redemptively, *heilsgeschichtlich,* they have entered into a new existence in Christ—the life of the new aeon.[21]

IN THE SPIRIT. The man in Christ is also "in the Spirit." If the opposite of "in Christ" is to be in Adam, the opposite of "in the Spirit" is to be "in the flesh" (Rom. 8:9). We have seen that the idiom "in the flesh" can have several meanings.[22] It has only a physiological and social meaning when it designates merely human existence in the body (Gal. 2:20), but here it carries a religious connotation and designates life that is lived solely on the human level, to the exclusion of everything related to God. It is synonymous with life in the old aeon of sin, bondage, and death. Those who are "in Adam" are also "in the flesh." However, the man who is "in Christ," in the aeon of life and freedom, is also in the Spirit. At this point it is difficult to find any meaningful difference between the two terms.[23] To be "in the Spirit" means to be in the realm that the Spirit has created, where the Spirit blesses and gives new life. It is difficult to see in this verse anything of the inner experience of the believer;[24] it appears to have the full local sense.[25] Life "in the Spirit" is not a blessing bestowed on a particular category of believers; it is true of them all. To be a Christian means to have received life by the Holy Spirit. The two go together: inner life granted by the Holy Spirit, and life in the new realm of the Holy Spirit. "Any one who does not have the Spirit of Christ [i.e., the indwelling of the Holy Spirit] does not belong to him" (Rom. 8:9).

Life in the Spirit means eschatological existence—life in the new age.

---

[20] C. K. Barrett, *Romans* (1957), p. 127.

[21] See A. Oepke, *TDNT* I, 542. "*En christo* is not a formula of mystical fellowship but means that the believer belongs to Christ. The new creation in Christ (II Cor. 5:17) designates not a mystical but an eschatological fact. In Christ man has righteousness (II Cor. 5:21; Gal. 2:17), freedom (Gal. 2:4); he belongs to the new aeon, to the new humanity which has come into being with the salvation event." R. Bultmann, *Glauben und Verstehen* (1933), I, 257f. Of course Bultmann interprets this existentially and not *heilsgeschichtlich.*

[22] See above, p. 467.

[23] On the basis of II Cor. 3:17, Deissmann identified Christ and the Spirit. For efforts to distinguish between "in Christ" and "in the Spirit," see E. Best, *One Body in Christ,* pp. 11f.; A. Wikenhauser, *Pauline Mysticism,* pp. 49ff.

[24] Against E. Best, *One Body in Christ,* p. 11.

[25] See A. Oepke, *TDNT* I, 540.

This is established by the fact that the presence of the Holy Spirit in the church is itself an eschatological event.[26]

This *heilsgeschichtlich* meaning of "in the Spirit" is supported by I Corinthians 6:11: "You were washed, you were sanctified, you were justified . . . in the Spirit of our God." Washing may include the symbolic act of baptism, but its primary meaning is cleansing from sin. Justification is the act of acquittal, sanctification the fact of dedication to God.[27] These are all viewed as facts that have already occurred in the life of those who are in the Spirit. In the same way, Gentiles who were formerly unclean have been sanctified in the Holy Spirit (Rom. 15:16). In the Holy Spirit, believers are sealed for the day of redemption (Eph. 4:30). Through Christ, but in the Spirit, men have access to God the Father (Eph. 2:18). It is in the Spirit that believers are built together so as to form a dwelling place for God (Eph. 2:22).[28] The affirmation that the Kingdom of God means "righteousness and peace and joy in the Holy Spirit" (Rom. 14:17) is probably to be taken in the same sense. Righteousness and peace usually designate an objective relationship to God.[29] To be "in the Spirit" has the same meaning as being in the Kingdom of Christ (Col. 1:13), for it was in the coming of the Holy Spirit into the world, first in the ministry of Jesus (Mt. 12:28) and then at Pentecost, that the new age was inaugurated. To be in the Spirit means to be in the sphere of God's redemptive reign, which is mediated through the Spirit.

Other sayings about those who are in the Spirit are concerned with matters of the Christian life. Prayer should be in the Spirit (Eph. 6:18) as well as love (Col. 1:8). The ministry of the gospel is carried out in the Spirit (I Thess. 1:5). Worship of Christ is carried out in the Spirit (I Cor. 12:3). Other passages carry a more instrumental meaning: Ephesians 3:5; I Corinthians 12:9; and probably I Corinthians 12:13.[30]

NOT IN THE FLESH. Corresponding to the fact that believers are in the Spirit is the fact that they are no longer in the flesh. "You are not in the flesh, you are in the Spirit" (Rom. 8:9). It is difficult to understand this proleptically, referring in a promissory manner to the glorified state.[31] The same idea is found in Romans 7:5: "when we were in the flesh," clearly indicating that those in the Spirit are no longer in the flesh. Here again is the contrast between two modes of existence—two realms of life: the old

---

[26] See above, pp. 370f. This has been carefully worked out by N. Q. Hamilton, *The Holy Spirit and Eschatology in Paul* (1957).

[27] See above, Ch. 32.

[28] This phrase could be taken as an instrumental or a phrase qualifying God; but it may also qualify the whole statement and mean, "It is by your being in the Spirit that this is taking place." S. D. F. Salmond, *The Expositor's Greek Testament,* III, 301. See also J. A. Robinson, *Ephesians* (1904), p. 166.

[29] C. K. Barrett, *Romans,* p. 265.

[30] See below, p. 542. Some of the passages that Oepke takes to be instrumental may well be locative. *TDNT* I, 541.

[31] R. Bultmann, *Theology* (1951), I, 245.

aeon—in the flesh—of sin and death; the new aeon—in the Spirit—of righteousness and life. The man who is in the Spirit continues to live in his human, mortal flesh (Gal. 2:20), but he has entered a new realm of life in the Spirit. In the old aeon, the concerns of the flesh, of the world, of natural life were the focus and chief end of his existence; in the new aeon, the things of God and of Christ have become his chief love. Every man is in one realm or the other. The determining factor is whether the Spirit of Christ dwells in a man. One does not pass from one realm to the other by gradual growth or progress, but by receiving Jesus Christ as Lord.

DEAD TO THE FLESH. Another way Paul expresses the same truth is the idiom of dying and of crucifying the flesh. When one comes to be in the Spirit, he is delivered from the realm of the flesh. It is viewed as dead; it has been crucified (Gal. 5:24). Paul can express the same truth by saying that *he* has died. "I have been crucified with Christ" (Gal. 2:20). This is not a subjective statement of something that happens in the Christian consciousness but a theological statement of one's position in Christ; but it has great consequences for the Christian consciousness and life. The same idea is expressed when Paul says that he has been crucified to the world and the world to him (Gal. 6:14). That Paul can say that the world has been crucified to him proves that this is no subjective experience. He lives in the world, but he no longer belongs to the world, for he has entered a new existence. These are not mystical experiential statements but affirmations of theological fact that the believer is to accept by faith as the whole basis of his life. They are different ways of expressing the one eschatological fact: the man in Christ—or in the Spirit—is a new creature for whom the old life of bondage to sin and death has passed away and the new life of freedom and righteousness has come.

DEAD-ALIVE WITH CHRIST. Again, Paul uses the idiom of dying and rising with Christ to express the same truth (Rom. 6:1-11). Baptism into Christ (v. 2) means union with him in his death, burial with him, which in turn means death to sin, the crucifixion of the old man, the destruction of the "body of sin" (v. 6). On the positive side, it means freedom from sin and life unto God. In this passage resurrection with Christ is future and eschatological (vv. 5, 7), but Ephesians 2:5-6 speaks of a present resurrection with Christ, and the statement that we are alive unto God (v. 11) shows that the idea is in his mind in Romans 6.

This passage has often been interpreted in terms of individualistic mysticism of inner personal experience, or of the contemporizing of the benefits of the past events of Christ's death and resurrection through the sacrament of baptism. However, recent studies[32] have shown that the passage is to be interpreted in terms of Paul's eschatological thought. Dying and rising with Christ means death to the old aeon of sin and death, and participation

[32] See R. C. Tannehill, *Dying and Rising with Christ* (1967); E. Schweizer, "Dying and Rising with Christ" in *NT Issues,* ed. by R. Batey (1970), pp. 173-90.

in the new aeon of life and righteousness. The death and resurrection of Christ were not merely events in past history but eschatological events. By death and resurrection Christ introduced a new aeon. "Paul thinks of an aeon or dominion as a unified sphere which is ruled by certain powers which determine the character of existence there."[33] Adam, who introduced sin and death, is determinative of existence in the old aeon, and Christ is the inclusive man "who represents and embodies the whole of the new aeon because he determines the nature of existence there."[34] This death and resurrection is not a mystical experience that *ipso facto* changes one's inner nature when he believes, nor is it a transformation accomplished by the sacramental efficacy of baptism. It is rather an eschatological fact that has happened in the mission of Jesus Christ but which can only be perceived by faith. Since Christ, there exist two dominions: of Adam and of Christ. "The new world and its salvation are already present, but they are hidden in the midst of the old world."[35] Since God's act in Christ, man is faced with the choice of standing within one of two dominions. He may remain indifferent and so go the way of sin and death; or he may decide for Christ and by faith be brought into the new dominion of life and righteousness. This is an eschatological fact that every believer should know (Rom. 6:2, 6), and on whose basis he is to consider himself alive to God. It means a change in dominion. In the old aeon, sin reigned (v. 12); but in the new aeon, the dominion of sin has been broken (v. 14). Believers are to recognize this change of dominions, and *for this reason* they are to change their alliance from sin to God (vv. 17, 18, 22). It is because this change has occurred in Christ that believers are exhorted to yield themselves to righteousness (v. 19).

CIRCUMCISION. The metaphor of death and resurrection is coupled with circumcision in Colossians 2:11-12. "In him also you were circumcised with a circumcision made without hands, by putting off the body of flesh in the circumcision of Christ; and you were buried with him in baptism, in which you were also raised with him through faith in the working of God, who raised him from the dead."[36] This is a notoriously difficult passage to exegete. Many commentators understand the circumcision of Christ to be a metaphor for his death, and "putting off the body of flesh" to refer to Christ in his crucifixion.[37] However, since Paul has referred to a circumcision of the heart, it is easier to understand the circumcision made without hands to refer to this "spiritual" circumcision (cf. Rom. 2:29), especially since circumcision is an unusual metaphor to refer to Christ's death.[38] Following this, "putting off the body of flesh" is equivalent to putting off

---

[33] R. C. Tannehill, *Dying and Rising with Christ*, p. 39.
[34] *Loc. cit.*
[35] *Ibid.*, p. 74.
[36] See C. F. D. Moule, *Colossians*, pp. 94-96.
[37] This is Moule's conclusion. See also J. A. T. Robinson, *The Body* (1952), pp. 43ff.
[38] See R. Meyer, *TDNT* VI, 83.

the old man (Col. 3:9).[39] This group of metaphors—circumcision, putting off the flesh, burial in baptism, resurrection with Christ—are expounded in verse 13 where Paul changes the idiom to say that outside of Christ men were dead in trespasses, and, as Gentiles, were alienated from the covenants of Israel (see Eph. 2:11-12); yet God has made them alive with Christ. Death,[40] burial, and resurrection with Christ; a state of death and making alive—these are two different ways of stating the same eschatological truth. Again, they do not refer first of all to a subjective experience of the individual believer but to an event that has occurred in the death and resurrection of Christ. The believer enters into this new realm of life by faith and baptism.

The life into which the believer has been introduced is explicated in terms of the forgiveness of our trespasses (v. 13), and the canceling of "the bond which stood against us with its legal demands" (v. 14). A "bond" is a legal statement of indebtedness—an IOU signed by the debtor. The Jew is in debt to God because he has not fulfilled the Law; the Gentile is in debt to God because he has followed neither the light of creation (Rom. 1:20) nor that of conscience (Rom. 2:15). Christ in his crucifixion took this bond of debt, of sin, of condemnation and discharged the debt by assuming its penalty—death. Thus Christ's death avails to transfer the believer from the realm of indebtedness, of condemnation and death—the old aeon—to the realm of life in the new aeon.

DEATH TO THE WORLD. This union of the believer with Christ in his death means that he has also died to the elements of the world (Col. 2:20).[41] This is not an experience but a fact on the basis of which the Christian is to live his life. Since he has died to the world, he is no longer to live as though he were a mere worldling. In the context, this is defined as submitting oneself to legalistic rules of ascetic practices to achieve a higher level of holiness rather than experiencing the freedom that is in Christ. The pursuit of such perversions of the gospel is a denial of true Christian existence. Christ has been raised and seated in heaven at the right hand of God. He is Lord over the new aeon of redemption. The believer has been raised with Christ, exalted to heaven, and his "life is hid with Christ in God" (Col. 3:3). Again, it should be obvious that this is no subjective experience; it affirms the new sphere in which the believer carries on his life. Because he has been exalted to heaven, the believer is to set his mind "on things that are above, not on things that are on earth" (Col. 3:2). Obviously this command does not mean complete indifference to human affairs and the details of everyday existence. While this language sounds quite dualistic, it embodies neither a platonic dualism nor a gnostic doctrine of matter as evil. The dualism is religious and not cosmological.[42] The "things that

[39] See E. Schweizer, *TDNT* VII, 136.
[40] Rom. 6:5.
[41] For *ta stoicheia tou kosmou,* translated "the elemental spirits of the universe" in the RSV, see p. 402.
[42] F. Büchsel, *TDNT* I, 377.

are above" represent the realm of God that has already invaded human history in the person and mission of Jesus and brought to men[43] the new realm of life.

The same theology of deadness, being made alive with Christ, and being exalted with him to sit in the heavenly places is found in Ephesians 2:5-6 with no mention of baptism unto Christ's death or resurrection. This new life is further described as a new creation of God, designed for good works (v. 10).

THE INDWELLING OF CHRIST. Not only is the renewed man in Christ and in the Spirit; both Christ and the Spirit dwell in him. That these are two aspects of the same reality is seen in Romans 8:9-10: "But you are not in the flesh, you are in the Spirit, if the Spirit of God dwells in you. . . . But if Christ dwells in you. . . ." Here are the objective and the subjective sides of the same reality. It is, however, surprising, in view of the frequency of the phrase "in Christ," that Paul only infrequently refers to the indwelling of Christ but speaks often of the indwelling of the Spirit. He does make it clear that he conceives of Christ indwelling the believer. The believer has been crucified with Christ, but he has a new life because Christ lives in him (Gal. 2:20). It is Christ in the believer that assures him of the hope of final redemption (Col. 1:27). Christ himself is our life (Col. 3:4). This is not a once-and-for-all experience, for Paul prays that believers may be strengthened in the inner man, "and that Christ may dwell in your hearts through faith" (Eph. 3:17).

Much more frequently does Paul speak of the indwelling of the Holy Spirit. God has poured out his Spirit (Rom. 5:5; II Cor. 1:22; 5:5; Gal. 3:5; 1 Thess. 4:8), and Christians have received the Spirit (Rom. 8:15; I Cor. 2:12; 12:13b; II Cor. 11:4; Gal. 3:2) and have the Spirit (Rom. 8:23), who indwells them (Rom. 8:9, 11; I Cor. 3:16; 6:19; II Tim. 1:14). The Spirit works in Christians, witnessing to them (Rom. 8:16), helping them in weakness (Rom. 8:26), guiding them (Rom. 8:14). The Spirit is the Spirit of Christ (Rom. 8:9), the "Spirit of his Son" (Gal. 4:6).

THE LORD IS THE SPIRIT. The close relationship between Christ and the Spirit is affirmed in II Corinthians 3:17: "The Lord is the Spirit." Some scholars have taken this to mean that Paul completely identifies the risen Christ with the Holy Spirit, drawing upon Hellenistic ideas in which Spirit is conceived of as a fluid that surrounds and penetrates us, and the exalted Christ is thought of as "formless, impersonal, all-penetrating being." However, the saying is to be taken in a Christian and not a gnostic context.[44]

Christian thought conceives of two worlds: the world of God and the world of men. The whole history of New Testament thought is to be understood as the invasion of God's world into the realm of history to secure man's redemption.[45] While Paul may often use language similar to that of

[43] See G. E. Ladd, *The Pattern of NT Truth* (1968), ch. 4.
[44] See above, p. 481.
[45] See G. E. Ladd, *The Pattern of NT Truth.*

gnostic dualism, the basic theology is fundamentally different.[46] Salvation does not mean flight and escape from the lower material world to a higher spiritual world; it means the redemption of the realm of human history by the invasion of the spiritual realm of God, so that the historical realm is lifted to a new and higher level of existence. The "spiritual bodies" of the resurrection are not bodies composed of a fine ethereal substance—*pneuma*—but are *bodies* adapted for new redeemed existence governed by the *pneuma theou*.[47] It is impossible to understand in concrete terms basically what Paul meant, either in terms of ancient comparative religions or of modern chemistry. He conceives of a real *body* but one that has been transformed by *pneuma* so that it is quite different in substance from physical bodies.

This world view of Paul is fundamental for his understanding of the relationship between the Jesus of history and the ascended Lord. Jesus was "descended from David according to the flesh and designated Son of God in power according to the Spirit of holiness by his resurrection from the dead" (Rom. 1:4). This does not reflect two ways of looking at Jesus but two stages in his ministry. On the human level he was a Son of David; after his resurrection he entered a new realm of existence in which he was shown to be the Son of God *in power* "in the sphere of the Holy Spirit."[48] This is not adoptionist Christology but an affirmation that "after the Resurrection, that Spirit becomes the mode or manner of Jesus' existence as Lord: the limitations and infirmity of the flesh have given way to *power* in the Spirit. By the resurrection there has been brought into being the age of the Spirit, the age of power, in which the impact of Christ becomes effective upon all believers."[49]

This truth is more clearly affirmed in Paul's statement that "the first man Adam became a living being; the last Adam became a life-giving spirit" (I Cor. 15:45). There is no Adamic speculation here of a heavenly and earthly man. In Philo the first man was the ideal man in the mind of God—the archetype of creation; the second man was the actual human Adam.[50] The first Adam does not descend to earth as Savior or Redeemer but remains the ideal man in the mind of God. For Paul, the last Adam is Christ in his resurrected glory who has entered into a transformed realm of existence. Paul does not speculate as to the nature of this existence. "Paul, unlike the gnostics, never speaks of the spiritual substance of the pre-existent Lord."[51] The ascended Christ has not only entered the realm of spirit; he

---

[46] See E. Schweizer on Spirit, *TDNT* VI, 415-34. Schweizer's view is a bit confusing, for he does conceive of Paul as thinking of *pneuma* in terms of celestial substance.

[47] E. Schweizer, *TDNT* VI, 421.

[48] See C. K. Barrett, *Romans*, p. 18.

[49] D. Hill, *Greek Words and Hebrew Meanings* (1967), p. 281.

[50] See J. Jeremias, *TDNT* I, 143 and references.

[51] E. Schweizer, *TDNT* VI, 420. Schweizer insists that while Paul uses Hellenistic vocabulary, the substance is Jewish (*ibid.*, p. 421).

has become a life-giving spirit, able because of his new mode of existence to impart life to men as he could not do in the days of his flesh.

This background enables us to understand the much-debated saying where Paul verbally identifies the risen Lord and the Spirit: "Now the Lord is the Spirit, and where the Spirit of the Lord is, there is freedom" (II Cor. 3:17). This cannot mean complete personal identification, for Paul speaks *both* of the Lord as the Spirit and the Spirit *of the Lord.* In the context, Paul is contrasting the old order of the Mosaic Law with the new order in Christ. The old order was a "dispensation of death" (II Cor. 3:7); the new order a dispensation of the Spirit that means life. This new order has been inaugurated by the risen Lord, who has entered into the realm of spirit. The Lord and the Spirit are not personally identified, but the Spirit is the mode in which the Lord works in the new dispensation. The Spirit is Christ himself present in his church.[52] This is why Paul can exchange so freely the idioms "in Christ—in the Spirit"; "Christ in you—the Spirit in you." Probably the precise idiom would be, "Christ indwells his people in the Spirit."

When we seek more closely the meaning of the indwelling of Christ and of the Spirit, there is no question but that Paul conceives of this as a new inner power and dynamic by which God accomplishes a renewal of the "inner man." Christ dwells in the inner man, giving him strength (Eph. 3:16-17) and renewing him day by day (II Cor. 4:16).

The first work of the Spirit is to enable men to understand the divine work of redemption. This is affirmed in gnostic-sounding language that sets forth a very ungnostic theology. Paul speaks of a hidden wisdom of God—of the revelation through the Spirit of divine truths—of being enabled by the Spirit to think the thoughts of God—of a wisdom that transcends all human wisdom (I Cor. 2:6-13). All this can be understood only by the inner illumination of the Spirit. "The unspiritual [*psychikos*—natural] man does not receive the gifts of the Spirit of God, for they are folly to him, and he is not able to understand them because they are spiritually discerned" (I Cor. 2:14). Taken out of context, this language could refer to heavenly mysteries of the spiritual world that are perceived only by an esoteric circle who are spiritually illuminated. However, the context of the passage is the proclamation in preaching of an event in history together with its inner meaning. It is the word of the cross (I Cor. 1:18)—the execution of the Jesus of history. This was an event whose meaning was folly to Greeks and an offense to Jews. But to those enlightened by the Spirit, it is the wisdom of God. In other words, Paul recognizes a hidden meaning in the historical event of the death of Christ ("God was in Christ reconciling the world to himself," II Cor. 5:19) that is not evident to the human eye but which can be accepted only by a supernatural illumination. The Spirit does not reveal heavenly realities but the true meaning of an historical event. He does not

---

[52] See E. Schweizer, *TDNT* VI, 433-34; D. Hill, *Greek Words,* pp. 278-81; N. Q. Hamilton, *The Holy Spirit and Eschatology in Paul,* pp. 12-15.

impart some kind of "gnostic" esoteric truth but the real meaning of an event in history. Only by the illumination of the Spirit can men understand the meaning of the cross; only by the Spirit can men therefore confess that Jesus who was executed is also the Lord (I Cor. 12:3). This is why Paul can call the Spirit "a spirit of wisdom and of revelation in the knowledge of him" (Eph. 1:17).[53] "Revelation" does not mean abstract theological truth but the meaning of the person and work of Jesus—what God "accomplished in Christ when he raised him from the dead and made him sit at his right hand in the heavenly places" (Eph. 1:20). The Spirit is also the "spirit of faith," i.e., the Spirit who imparts faith (II Cor. 4:13).[54] Possessing the "earnest" (*arrabōn*) of the Spirit means to walk by faith (II Cor. 5:5, 7).[55] An apparent contradiction to the idea that it is the Spirit who enables men to believe is found in Galatians 3:2, where Paul seems to say that faith precedes the reception of the Spirit. "Did you receive the Spirit by the works of the law, or by hearing with faith?" (Gal. 3:2). However, Paul is not here primarily concerned to present the relationship between faith and the reception of the Spirit; he is concerned with the contrast between the era of the Law and the gospel. The former was an era of works in the flesh, the latter of faith in the Spirit.[56]

Not only does the Spirit create faith, enabling men to accept the saving significance of the cross; he indwells the believer enabling him to live "according to the Spirit." He creates a spirit of sonship giving to the believer an inner conviction that he is a child of God (Rom. 8:15-16; Gal. 4:6), and enabling him to have direct access to the Father (Eph. 3:16-17). He enables men to offer true worship to God (Phil. 3:3).[57] He enables them to grasp something of the vastness of the love of God (Eph. 3:16-17). He helps in prayer (Rom. 8:26; Eph. 6:18). He brings hope that is not merely an optimistic attitude toward the future or a stance of the emotional life but the deep conviction of the certainty of the eschatological consummation of God's redemptive purpose (Rom. 15:13; Gal. 5:5). He produces the fruit of the Spirit, the chief of which is love. God's love is poured into the believer's heart through the Holy Spirit (Rom. 5:5). The "love of the Spirit" (Rom. 15:30) may well be translated, "love created by the Spirit" (see Col. 1:8).[58] This love manifests itself primarily in its relationship to other people; it is patient, kind, good, trustworthy, gentle, and self-disciplined (Gal. 5:22-23).

Coupled with love are joy and peace (Gal. 5:22; Rom. 14:17; 15:13). These terms may be easily misunderstood and interpreted in terms of

---

53 The RSV does not understand this to be a reference to the Holy Spirit, but see Arndt and Gingrich, *Lexicon,* p. 683; E. Schweizer, *TDNT* VI, 444.

54 Again, the RSV does not translate this as a reference to the Holy Spirit, but see Arndt-Gingrich, *loc. cit.;* E. Schweizer, *TDNT* VI, 426.

55 E. Schweizer, *loc. cit.*

56 *Loc. cit.*

57 See Arndt-Gingrich, *Lexicon,* p. 682 (5a).

58 C. K. Barrett, *Romans,* p. 279.

human emotional experience: joy is emotional happiness and peace is emotional tranquility. However, these are theological words that carry profound implications for the emotional life but which in themselves convey a far deeper meaning. Joy is primarily a religious sentiment that finds its deepest satisfaction in the Lord. Therefore one can rejoice even when he is sorrowing (II Cor. 6:10) or experiencing physical sufferings (Col. 1:24). One can rejoice in the gospel in the midst of severe afflictions (I Thess. 1:6). It is significant that the eschatological gift of the Spirit is given while we groan inwardly because of the curse of sin and decay in the world (Rom. 8:23) and "sigh with anxiety" in the face of death (II Cor. 5:4).[59]

In the same way peace is not primarily emotional tranquility but a term encompassing the salvation of the whole man. The "gospel of peace" (Eph. 6:15) is the good news that God has made peace with man that we may now have peace with God (Rom. 5:1). Peace is practically synonymous with salvation (Rom. 2:10) and is a power that protects man in his inner being (Phil. 4:7) and which rules in his heart (Col. 3:15).[60]

SUMMARY. In summary, we conclude that union with Christ in his death and resurrection, the indwelling of Christ in the Spirit, and the blessing of eternal life[61] are different ways of describing the same reality: the situation of the man of faith who has become a new creation in Christ and entered the new era of salvation and life.

We would seek further what this new life in Christ—the indwelling of Christ in the Spirit—means in terms of Paul's anthropology. We have seen that it involves a definite cognitive element. Only by the inner illumination of the Holy Spirit can one understand the real meaning of the cross.[62] However, there is no idea that a renewed mind possesses higher intellectual faculties than it did before.

The new life is experienced in the realm of the spirit.[63] When Paul says that outside of Christ men are dead (Eph. 2:1), he must mean spiritually dead. He cannot mean that unredeemed men have no spirits—that spirit is a gift of the new life in Christ. That men are dead in their spirits means that they are not living in fellowship with God. That they have been made alive means that they have been brought into fellowship with the living God.

This is affirmed in a verse whose exegesis is disputed, but which bears full and lucid meaning in this context. "If Christ is in you, although your

---

59 On the whole subject, see R. Bultmann, *Theology,* I, 339.

60 See W. Foerster, *TDNT* I, 413-14.

61 It is probably only a coincidence that Paul, unlike John, never clearly speaks of "eternal life" as a present reality. The phrase usually designates life in the eschatological consummation (Rom. 2:7; 6:22; Gal. 6:8; I Tim. 1:16; Tit. 1:2; 3:7). In its immediate context (Rom. 5:21 and 6:23), the phrase could be understood as eschatological. However, since the new aeon in Christ is the aeon of life (Rom. 5:18; 6:4; 8:2; Col. 3:4; II Tim. 1:10), it is clear that Paul conceives of eternal life as a present possession even though he does not emphasize it in the way John does.

62 See above, p. 490.

63 See above, p. 483.

bodies are dead because of sin, your spirits are alive because of righteousness" (Rom. 8:10). Furthermore, if our spirits have been made alive by the indwelling of the Holy Spirit, this same Spirit will one day give life to our dying bodies. While this verse is often interpreted in terms of the Holy Spirit indwelling man,[64] it fits the Pauline context better to understand it of the quickened human spirit.[65] The body is still mortal and stands under the doom of death, but the human spirit has been made alive.

Another way of saying the same thing is in terms of the renewal of the mind (Rom. 12:2).[66] While *nous* can sometimes refer to the cognitive faculty in man, here it refers to man in terms of "the inner direction of [his] thought and will and the orientation of [his] moral consciousness."[67] The internal work of Christ is to be understood not in terms of a complete transformation of the human personality or the displacement of something human by something divine, but in terms of an influx of divine power accomplishing a reorientation of the will toward God. Now a man is enabled to do what the Law could not accomplish; he is enabled to love and worship and serve God and thus fulfill the highest demand of the Law (Rom. 8:4).

The practical outworking of this new life is, however, one of tension—the tension between the indicative and the imperative. Because the man of faith *is* a new creation and has entered the new aeon of salvation, he has died with Christ (Rom. 6:5); he has been crucified with Christ (Gal. 2:20); the old man has been crucified with him (Rom. 6:6); the flesh has been crucified (Gal. 5:24); the body of flesh has been put off in circumcision of the heart (Col. 2:11). This is the indicative. This is not something subjective and automatic and spontaneous; it indicates a new state of existence that must manifest itself in a new life. Negatively, one must put to death the deeds of the body (Rom. 8:13)—"what is earthly in you" (Col. 3:5). It is clear that Paul is not advocating physical asceticism;[68] the deeds of the body—"what is earthly"—are synonymous with the flesh—the old, natural, rebellious human nature with its sinful deeds: "immorality, impurity, passion, evil desire, and covetousness" (Col. 3:5). Paul changes the idiom from death to clothing: "Put off your old nature [the old man] which belongs to your former manner of life" (Eph. 4:22). The "old man" denotes "the sinful being of the unconverted man."[69] The important thing to note is the tension between the indicative and the imperative: the old man—the old nature—the old self has been put to death—it has been put off in principle; yet believers are exhorted to do in practice what has already been done in principle. Paul does not say that sin is dead but that the believer has died to sin. He does not say that the flesh is done away, but that we no

64 See C. K. Barrett, *Romans,* p. 159; F. F. Bruce, *Romans* (1963), p. 164.

65 W. Sanday and A. C. Headlam, *Romans* (1896), *in loc.;* G. W. H. Lampe in *IDB* E-J, p. 636; W. D. Stacey, *The Pauline View of Man* (1956), p. 135.

66 See above, p. 476.

67 J. Behm, *TDNT* IV, 958.

68 See above, p. 466.

69 J. Jeremias, *TDNT* I, 365.

longer live in the flesh and therefore are not to walk according to the flesh. He never says, "Do not sin," but rather, "Do not let sin reign over you."[70]

The positive side of the outworking of the new life is expressed in several ways. "Be renewed in the spirit of your minds, and put on the new nature [new man]" (Eph. 4:23-24). This can be done only because it has already been accomplished in principle in Christ (Col. 3:10). The same idea is expressed in the idiom of walking in newness of life (Rom. 6:4), walking after the Spirit (Rom. 8:4; Gal. 5:16). The power of the indwelling Spirit is not a spontaneous, all-possessing power; it requires a human response. Walking after the Spirit means to live each moment and to make each decision under the guidance of the indwelling Spirit.

Walking in the Spirit is walking in tension between the Spirit and the flesh. While the flesh has been crucified with Christ in principle, it can still be an active power in the Christian's life and he must be constantly vigilant to keep the flesh under the control of the Spirit. "The desires of the flesh are against the Spirit, and the desires of the Spirit are against the flesh; for these are opposed to each other, to prevent you from doing what you would" (Gal. 5:17). The crucifixion and death of the flesh does not mean that it need no longer be reckoned with in Christian experience. The Christian will never be the man he wishes to be—free from temptation, struggle, tension. The old self is ever with him; only by a constant walking after the Spirit can the dominance of the flesh be broken.

[70] See G. Bornkamm, *Early Christian Experience* (1969), pp. 80-82.

35

THE LAW*

Literature:

W. G. Kümmel, *Römer 7 und die Bekehrung des Paulus* (1929); C. H. Dodd, "The Law," *The Bible and the Greeks* (1935), pp. 25-41; C. L. Mitton, "Romans VII Reconsidered," *ET* 65 (1953/54), 78-81; W. D. Davies, *Paul and Rabbinic Judaism* (1958), pp. 147-76; H. J. Schoeps, *Paul* (1961), pp. 168-218; G. A. F. Knight, *Law and Gospel* (1962); W. Kleinknecht and W. Gutbrod, "Nomos," *TDNT* IV, 1022-91; see also *Bible Key Words: Law* (1962); W. G. Kümmel, *Man in the NT* (1963); R. N. Longenecker, *Paul, Apostle of Liberty* (1964); D. E. H. Whiteley, *The Theology of St. Paul* (1964), pp. 76-85; G. von Rad, "The Law," *OT Theology* (1965), II, 388-409; H. L. Ellison, "Paul and the Law" in *Apostolic History and the Gospel*, ed. by W. W. Gasque and R. P. Martin (1970), pp. 195-202.

Paul's thought about the Law is difficult to understand because he seems to make numerous contradictory statements. He asserts that those who do the Law shall be justified (Rom. 2:13) and shall find life by the Law (Rom. 10:5; Gal. 3:12); but at the same time he affirms that no man shall be justified by the Law (Rom. 3:20) but is only brought to death by the written code of the Law (II Cor. 3:6), for the Law cannot give life (Gal. 3:21). He claims that he was blameless in his obedience to the Law (Phil. 3:6) and yet asserts that no man can perfectly submit to the Law (Rom. 8:7).

Paul's teaching about the Law is often approached from the perspective of the historical experience either of Paul himself as a Jewish rabbi, or of a typical first-century Jew under the Law. However, Paul's thought must be seen neither as a confession of his spiritual autobiography, nor as a description of the legalistic character of first-century Pharisaism, but as a theological interpretation by a Christian thinker of two ways of righteousness: legalism and faith. This is made clear in Romans 10, where Paul bemoans the fate of Israel in having failed to recognize Jesus as her Messiah and

*This chapter was first published in *Soli Deo Gloria*, ed. by J. McDowell Richards. © M. E. Bratcher 1968. Used by permission of John Knox Press.

embrace the divine gift of a free salvation. Why was Israel blind to the claims of Christ? Paul's answer is that there are two ways of righteousness, and because Israel pursued one way, they missed the other. Israel followed the "law of righteousness" (Rom. 9:31), i.e., the Law that revealed the will of God and showed what a right relationship with God was; but Israel failed to attain to that goal because they misused the Law by making it a means of attaining righteousness by their own works instead of through faith (Rom. 9:32). Thus they showed themselves to be ignorant of the righteousness that comes from God and is received by faith; instead, they tried to establish their own righteousness of works and did not submit to the righteousness of God through faith (Rom. 10:1-3). In these words, Paul makes the fundamental issue clear: the establishing of one's own righteousness (by works), or submission to the righteousness of God (by faith).

In writing as he does about the Law, Paul is writing from a distinctly Christian viewpoint. His experience of justification through faith in Christ and the subsequent conflict with the Judaizers led him to insights he could not have held as a Jew, and to a fundamental reinterpretation of the role of the Law in redemptive history.

THE BACKGROUND OF PAUL'S THOUGHT ABOUT THE LAW. To understand Paul's thought on the role of the Law, we must interpret it against the threefold background of Old Testament religion, Judaism, and his own experiences. The heart of Old Testament religion cannot be characterized as legalism, nor was the Law given as the means of achieving a right relationship with God by obedience. On the contrary, the context of the Law was the covenant that preceded and underlay the Law; and the covenant was initiated by the gracious act of God. Israel was constituted God's people not because of merit gained by obedience to the Law, but because of God's free election.[1] Israel belongs to God because he has revealed himself by delivering his people out of Egypt. The Law was given as the means of binding Israel to her God. Obedience to the Law did not constitute Israel God's people; rather, it provided Israel with a standard for obedience by which the covenant relationship must be preserved. "Thus the object of the law is to settle the relationship of the covenant-nation and of the individual to the God of the covenant and to the members of the nation who belong to the same covenant."[2] The reward for obedience to the Law was preservation of the positive relationship to Yahweh. This is the meaning of Leviticus 18:5: "The man who obeys the law shall live," i.e., enjoy the blessings of God.[3] However, life was not a reward earned by

---

[1] See W. Eichrodt, *Theology of the OT* (1961), I, ch. 2; G. A. F. Knight, *Law and Gospel* (1962), pp. 25f.

[2] H. Kleinknecht, *Bible Key Words: Law* (1962), p. 27. "The Law of Moses in itself was originally given not as a code, the observance of which was necessary to salvation, but as a set of principles for the guidance of the people of God." R. McL. Wilson, "Nomos," *StTh* 5 (1952), 39.

[3] The primary concept of "life" in the Old Testament is not the life of the Age to

good works; it was itself God's gift. This is illustrated by Deuteronomy 30:15-20 where Moses lays before the people the choice of life or death, which is determined by whether or not Israel chooses the Word of God. "Only by faith, i.e., by cleaving to the God of salvation, will the righteous have life (cf. Hab. 2:4; Am. 5:4, 14; Jer. 38:20). It is obvious that life is here understood as a gift."[4] Furthermore, the obedience demanded by the Law could not be satisfied by a mere legalism, for the Law itself demanded love for God (Deut. 6:5; 10:12) and for neighbor (Lev. 19:18). Obedience to the Law of God was an expression of trust in God; and only those who offered God such trust were really his people.

One of the most important factors in the old covenant was the twofold character of the people of God. On the one hand, they constituted a theocracy—a nation; but they were also a spiritual people. Membership in the nation required obedience to external commands, for example, circumcision; but circumcision of the flesh did not make a man right with God; there must also be a circumcision of the heart (Jer. 4:4; Deut. 10:16). When the nation proved disobedient to the demands of the covenant, the prophets announced that God had rejected the nation as a whole and would raise up in her place a faithful remnant that was righteous in heart as well as in deed. Thus there is found even in the Old Testament the distinction between the nation and the "church," between physical Israel and the true, spiritual Israel,[5] who have the Law written on their hearts (Jer. 31:33).

In the intertestamental period a fundamental change occurred in the role of the Law in the life of the people. The importance of the Law overshadows the concept of the covenant and becomes the condition of membership in God's people. Even more importantly, observance of the Law becomes the basis of God's verdict upon the individual. Resurrection will be the reward of those who have been devoted to the Law (II Macc. 7:9). The Law is the basis of the hope of the faithful (Test. Jud. 26:1), of justification (Apoc. Bar. 51:3), of salvation (Apoc. Bar. 51:7), of righteousness (Apoc. Bar. 57:6), of life (IV Ez. 7:21; 9:31). Obedience to the Law will even bring God's Kingdom and transform the entire sin-cursed world (Jub. 23). Thus the Law attains the position of an intermediary between God and man.

This new role of the Law characterizes rabbinic Judaism; and for this reason, "the basic starting point of the Old Testament is characteristically and decisively altered and invalidated."[6] The Torah becomes the one and

---

Come, as in Dan. 12:2, but the enjoyment of the good gifts of God in fellowship with God in this life.

[4] G. von Rad, *TDNT* II, 845. See also his essay on "Law" in *OT Theology* (1965), II, 388ff., where he shows that the apostasy of Israel consisted not in breaking individual commandments, but in failing to respond to God's saving acts for his people.

[5] See J. Bright, *The Kingdom of God* (1953), p. 94.

[6] H. Kleinknecht, *Bible Key Words: Law*, p. 69.

only mediator between God and man; all other relationships between God and man, Israel, or the world are subordinated to the Torah. Both righteousness and life in the world to come are secured by obeying the Law. "The more study of the law, the more life. . . ." "If (a man) has gained for himself words of the law, he has gained for himself life in the world to come" (Pirke Aboth 2:7).[7]

This does not mean that the Judaism out of which Paul came was utterly destitute of any spiritual values. There were circles in Judaism where the higher elements of inner devotion and piety were coupled with strict obedience to the Law.[8] Nor are we to forget that at the heart of first-century Jewish personal devotion as well as the synagogue worship was the recital of the *Shema* with its call to love God with the whole heart.[9] However, the tendency to externalism is evident even at this point, for the very repetition of the *Shema* was seen as a submitting to the reign of God.[10]

It is true that repentance played a large role in Jewish piety. While the Jews never despaired about the "fulfillability of the law," it was nevertheless a real problem.[11] All of the commandments, both written and oral, must be kept. "To violate one of them was equivalent to rejecting the whole law and refusing God's yoke (*Sifre on Num.* 15:22)."[12] However, salvation did not depend upon faultless conformity to the Law. Man is indwelt by an evil impulse as well as a good impulse, and therefore no man can attain to sinless perfection.[13]

Therefore the "righteous" man is not he who obeys the Law flawlessly, but he alone who *strives* to regulate his life by the Law. The sincerity and supremacy of this purpose and the strenuous endeavor to accomplish it are the marks of a righteous man.[14] Because God knew that man could not perfectly keep the Law because of the evil impulse God himself had implanted in his creature, God provided repentance as the way by which his sins could be forgiven. Repentance therefore must be coeval with the

---

7 For other references see H. Kleinknecht, *Bible Key Words: Law,* p. 76; Strack and Billerbeck, *Kommentar,* III, 129ff., 237. Schoeps recognizes the change in the concept of the Law in apocryphal writings and the LXX, but not in classical Judaism. He maintains that Paul's opposition to the Law was based in part upon this distortion and misrepresentation of the Law in Hellenistic Judaism. *Paul* (1961), pp. 215ff.

8 See such writings as *The Testaments of the Twelve Patriarchs, The Hymns of the Qumran Community.* See also R. Longenecker, *Paul, Apostle of Liberty* (1964), ch. III, who differentiates between "legalism" with its emphasis on law-keeping as a human action, and "nomism," which offers obedience to the Law as the reaction to the goodness and saving acts of God—an expression of trust in God.

9 E. Schürer, *A History of the Jewish People in the Time of Jesus Christ* (1890), II, ii, pp. 77-115; G. F. Moore, *Judaism* (1927), I, 291.

10 G. F. Moore, *Judaism,* II, 465.

11 See H. J. Schoeps, *Paul,* pp. 177, 193.

12 J. Bonsirven, *Palestinian Judaism in the Time of Jesus Christ* (1964), p. 95.

13 See G. F. Moore, *Judaism,* I, 467f. We are dependent on Moore for the following summary.

14 *Ibid.,* I, 494.

Law, and is one of the seven things pre-existent before creation.[15] Repentance plays such a large role in Judaism that Moore calls it "the Jewish doctrine of salvation."[16] The righteous man, therefore, is not the man who actually succeeds in keeping the Law, but the man who intends to, strives to do so, and is repentant when he fails. This repentance is the sole but inexorable condition of God's forgiveness, and is efficacious however great the sin may have been, or however late a man comes to repentance.[17] Repentance is purification of the inner man, and so annuls the sinner's past that he is in effect a new creation.[18] Sacrifices were carried out because the Law commanded them; but Judaism had no theory of atonement. It was repentance that secured the efficacy of the sacrifices.[19]

It is this background in Jewish thought that leads Schoeps to say that whether a man actually fulfills the Law or not, the mere intention to fulfill it brings a man close to God. This good intention is "an affirmation of the covenant which precedes the law."[20] Paul, however, was fatally ignorant of the Jewish doctrine of repentance. He failed to understand the relationship between the covenant and the Law, and isolated the Law from the controlling context of God's covenant with Israel.[21]

Schoeps bases his argument on the Old Testament view of the relationship between covenant and Law, attributing this understanding to Judaism. However, the reverse appears to be the historical fact: namely, that Judaism had in reality substituted the Law for the covenant, or identified the covenant with the Law. Schoeps in effect admits this when he says, "By covenant is meant nothing other than the Torah."[22] It is significant that the concept of the covenant plays a very small role in rabbinic writings,[23] and tends to be identified with circumcision and the sabbath.[24] Moore on the basis of Mishnah Sanhedrin 10.1 argues that eternal life is ultimately assured to every Israelite[25] "on the ground of the original election of the people by the free grace of God, prompted not by its merits, collective or individual, but solely by God's love."[26] This conclusion is difficult to sustain, if for no other reason than that of the exclusion of certain classes of Israelites from eternal life in the paragraphs that follow. It is refuted by the discussion of the fate of the righteous, the wicked, and the middle class whose

[15] *Ibid.*, I, 266, 526.
[16] *Ibid.*, I, 114, 117, 500.
[17] *Ibid.*, I, 520-21.
[18] *Ibid.*, I, 532f.
[19] *Ibid.*, I, 500-4, 508.
[20] *Paul*, p. 196.
[21] *Ibid.*, p. 213.
[22] *Ibid.*, p. 216.
[23] See J. Behm in *TDNT* II, 128-29.
[24] See G. F. Moore, *Judaism*, II, 16-21.
[25] "All Israelites have a share in the world to come." See H. Danby, *The Mishnah* (1933), p. 397.
[26] *Judaism*, II, 95. Krauss interprets this saying in light of San. 6:2, which assures extreme sinners of a share in the world to come, providing they make confession of their sin. S. Krauss, *Die Mischna* (1933), IV, iv and v, p. 264.

righteousness and sins balanced each other. The righteous enter at once into eternal life. Certain extremely wicked classes of people will be locked up to punishment in hell forever. Others less wicked, together with the wicked of the nations, are thrown into hell to be punished for twelve months and then destroyed.[27] As to the great majority of Israelites who were "half righteous and half sinful," the Schools of Hillel and Shammai differed. The School of Hillel maintained that God in mercy would incline the balance to the side of mercy and not send them into hell at all, while the School of Shammai held that they would be plunged into hell but would come up healed.[28] While it is true that it was God's kindness that gave the Law to Israel, thus providing a basis for salvation, salvation itself is dependent on good works, including the good work of repentance. This conclusion is strongly supported by the numerous references in Jewish literature to the books in which the good works of the righteous are recorded,[29] treasuries in which good works are stored up,[30] scales on which the merits and demerits are weighed.[31] God's grace grants forgiveness to the repentant man who has transgressed the Law, but the devout man who fulfills the Law, insofar as he fulfills it, does not need grace.

In any case, it is clear that Paul's life as a Jew was one of legalistic obedience to the Law. He himself tells us that he was a committed Jew, a Pharisee who was blameless in his obedience to the letter of the Law (Phil. 3:5-6). He was outstanding in his zeal not only for the written Law but also for the oral scribal traditions (Gal. 1:14).

In view of these clear statements, it is impossible to accept the autobiographical interpretation of Romans 7[32] that pictures Paul torn by an inward struggle that plunged his soul in darkness and confusion, making him feel that the Law had broken him and hope was almost gone.[33] In fact, the key to Paul's understanding of the Law lies in the fact that his very devotion to the Law had led to pride (Phil. 3:4, 7) and boasting (Rom. 2:13, 23). Boasting is the very antithesis of faith (Rom. 4:2), for it means the effort to establish a human righteousness of works (Rom. 3:27) that seeks glory before God and which relies on itself rather than on God. This human

---

27 *Judaism,* II, 387.

28 *Ibid.,* II, 318. The text from Tosefta Sanhedrin 13.3ff. is quoted by J. Bonsirven, *Palestinian Judaism,* p. 250.

29 En. 47:3; 81:4; 89:61-70; 90:20; 98:7-8; 104:7; Apoc. Bar. 24:1; IV Ez. 6:20; Asc. Isa. 9:22; Jub. 30:22; Aboth 3:17.

30 IV Ez. 7:77; 8:33; Apoc. Bar. 14:12; Ps. Sol. 9:9.

31 Test. Abr. 13; En. 41:1; 61:8; Ps. Sol. 5:6; Pesikta 26. See J. Bonsirven, *Palestinian Judaism,* p. 239; F. Weber, *Jüdische Theologie* (1897), pp. 279ff.

32 W. Gutbrod, *Bible Key Words: Law,* p. 119.

33 See C. H. Dodd, *The Meaning of Paul for Today* (1920), pp. 71, 73. Others who follow this autobiographical interpretation of Rom. 7 are A. Deissmann, *Paul* (1926), pp. 92ff.; W. D. Davies, *Paul and Rabbinic Judaism* (1955), pp. 24ff.; J. Klausner, *Paul* (1944), pp. 498f.; A. C. Purdy, *IDB* III, 685, 692. J. Murray, *Romans* (1959), I, 255 sees an unregenerate man under conviction of sin. J. Knox, "Romans," *IB* IX, 499 thinks Paul describes both past and present experience.

pride and boasting is an affront to the very character of God, who alone must receive glory and before whom no human being may boast (I Cor. 1:29). The only object for man's boasting is God himself (I Cor. 1:31); II Cor. 10:17).[34]

Here is the shocking fact that compelled Paul to a complete re-evaluation of the Law. It was his very zeal for the Law that had blinded him to the revelation of God's righteousness in Christ. What he as a Jew had thought was righteousness, he now realizes to be the very essence of sin, for his pride in his own righteousness (Phil. 3:9) had blinded him to the revelation of the divine righteousness in Christ. Only the divine intervention on the Damascus Road shattered his pride and self-righteousness and brought him to a humble acceptance of the righteousness of God.

THE LAW IN THE MESSIANIC AGE. Many features of Paul's interpretation of the Law not only find no parallel in Judaism, but in fact so differ from Jewish thought that modern Jewish scholars refuse to accept his claim to have been a Palestinian rabbi but insist that he represents a distorted Judaism of the Diaspora.[35] On the contrary, Paul represents a fresh Christian interpretation that can be understood only from Paul's eschatological perspective. With Christ the messianic age has been inaugurated. In Christ, "the old has passed away, behold, the new has come" (II Cor. 5:17). Before he was in Christ, Paul understood the Law *kata sarka,* from a human point of view, in terms of the standards of the old aeon, even as he interpreted all his experience (II Cor. 5:16). Viewed *kata sarka,* the Law was the basis of good works, which led to pride and boasting. Viewed *kata pneuma,* from the perspective of the new age in Christ, the Law assumes an entirely different role in God's redemptive purpose. The prophets had foretold a day when God would make a new covenant with his people, when the Law would be no longer primarily an outward written code, but a Law implanted within men, written on their hearts (Jer. 31:33). This promise of a new dimension of inwardness does not carry with it the complete abolition of the Mosaic Law. On the basis of such Old Testament promises, the Jews debated the role the Law would play in the messianic age and in the world to come. Moore concludes that in the messianic age the Law would be more faithfully studied and better applied than in this world; and in the Age to Come, although much of the Law will be no longer applicable because of the changed conditions on the new earth, the Law will continue to express the will of God, but God himself will be the teacher.[36]

---

34 On the theological significance of boasting, see R. Bultmann, *TDNT* III, 649; *Theology,* I, 242.

35 See C. G. Montefiore, *Judaism and St. Paul* (1914), p. 93; S. Sandmel, *A Jewish Understanding of the NT* (1956), pp. 37-51; H. J. Schoeps, *Paul,* pp. 198, 206, 218.

36 G. F. Moore, *Judaism,* I, 271f. See also W. D. Davies, *Torah in the Messianic Age and/or the Age to Come* (1952), who cites some evidence for the expectation of a modified Torah in the messianic age. Schoeps cites rabbinic sayings that anticipated the cessation of the Law in the messianic Kingdom as a basis

With Christ a new era has come in which the Law plays a new and different role. Paul designates these two eras of the Law and the gospel as two covenants. The old covenant is one of the "letter" (*gramma*), and is a dispensation (*diakonia*) of condemnation and death, while the new covenant is one of the Spirit, a dispensation of life and righteousness (II Cor. 3:6ff.). These words do not refer to two ways of interpreting Scripture: a literal and a spiritual or allegorical approach. They contrast the ages of the Law and of Christ as two different forms of the Law. Under the old covenant, the Law was an external written code that set before men the will of God. When they failed, it condemned them to death. The new covenant in this passage says nothing explicitly about the permanence of the Law. The difference in the new age is that the Holy Spirit has been given to men to write the Law upon their hearts, as Jeremiah foretold, and thus the Law is no longer merely an external written code but an inward, life-giving power that produces righteousness.[37]

Most interpreters of this passage have overlooked the fact that since the Holy Spirit is an eschatological gift, the entire passage has an eschatological orientation. The new age, which is the age of Christ and the Spirit, has come in fulfillment of Jeremiah 31,[38] even while the old age goes on.

While this passage in II Corinthians says nothing about the permanence of the Law, Paul tells the Romans, *"telos gar nomou Christos eis dikaiosunēn panti tō pisteuonti"* (For Christ is [the] end of [the] Law unto righteousness to everyone who believes, Rom. 10:4). This verse can be rendered in two different ways. "Christ is the end of the Law with the objective of righteousness for everyone who believes." That is, Christ has brought the Law to its end in order that a righteousness based on faith alone may be available to all men. Another rendering is, "Christ is the end of the Law so far as righteousness is concerned for everyone who believes." That is, the Law is not itself abolished, but it has come to its end as a way of righteousness, for in Christ righteousness is by faith, not by works.

In view of the fact that Paul has just contrasted the righteousness of God with that of the Law, and continues immediately with the righteousness of the Law (v. 5), the latter rendering is preferable.[39] Paul does not affirm the total abrogation of the Law, that by its abrogation righteousness might come to believers.[40] He affirms the end of the Law in its connection with righteousness in Christ apart from the Law, with the result that the Law has

---

for Paul's view of the abolition of the Law (*Paul,* pp. 171-72). However, this is not the prevailing Jewish view, and Paul does not teach the complete *abolition* of the Law. See also R. N. Longenecker, *Paul, Apostle of Liberty,* pp. 128-32.

[37] See G. Schrenk in *TDNT* I, 765ff.

[38] R. A. Harrisville, *The Concept of Newness in the NT* (1960), p. 60. It is recognized by W. D. Davies, *Paul,* p. 225. Davies points out that this emphasis is largely missing in rabbinic Judaism.

[39] See R. N. Longenecker, *Paul, Apostle of Liberty,* pp. 144ff.

[40] See below, p. 509, for the permanence of the Law.

come to an end for the believer as a way of righteousness. This is not true historically; the Jews continue to practice the Law. It is true *heilsgeschichtlich*—for men of faith.

This is true because Christ is the end of the Law. *Telos* can mean both end and goal, and both meanings are to be seen here. Christ has brought the era of the Law to its end because he has fulfilled all that the Law demands.

Paul expounds the life of the believer in the new age in several different ways. The new age is the age of life; and since the believer has been identified with Christ in his death and resurrection, he is dead to the old life, including the rule of the Law. Paul uses the metaphor of a woman being freed from her husband when he dies, and applies it by saying that it is the believer who has died with Christ who is therefore free from the Law (Rom. 7:4). Therefore we no longer serve God under bondage to a written external code but with the new life of the Spirit (Rom. 7:6). It was the Law itself, which had become a basis of boasting, and therefore of sin, that convinced Paul that he must die to the reign of Law (Gal. 2:19).

An apparent contradiction appears in Paul's thought when he insists, on the one hand, that the believer is no longer under Law, but at the same time, according to the Acts, approves of the Law for Jewish Christians (Acts 21:20ff.), and even circumcised Timothy when he joined Paul in missionary work because he was half Jewish (Acts 16:3). However, this contradiction corresponds with Paul's eschatological perspective. While believers have experienced the freedom of the new age in Christ, they still live in the present evil age. The Law with its ceremonial demands belongs to this world—the old order. The proper attitude for men of the new age toward the old age is not a negative one but neutral: "For neither circumcision counts for anything, nor uncircumcision, but a new creation," because circumcision belongs to the world, and the man in Christ has been crucified to the world (Gal. 6:15).

An application of this principle is that Paul himself as a Jew observed the Law when he was in a Jewish environment (I Cor. 9:20). As a man in Christ, he was no longer under Law, and therefore, where the human situation required it for his ministry to the Gentiles, he "became as one outside the law" (I Cor. 9:21). This involves, admittedly, an inconsistency in conduct; but the very inconsistency rests upon the consistent application of a profound theological truth: that Christians belong to two worlds at once and have obligations to both orders.[41]

THE LAW AS THE WILL OF GOD. Paul never conceived of the claims of the Law coming to their end because of any imperfection in the Law itself. The Law is and remains the Law of God (Rom. 7:22, 25). The Law is not sinful (Rom. 7:7) but is holy and just and good (Rom. 7:12) because it comes from God ("spiritual," Rom. 7:14).

---

[41] See R. N. Longenecker, *Paul, Apostle of Liberty*, pp. 245ff., who comes to similar conclusions from the perspective of Paul's doctrine of liberty.

At this point it is important to note that Paul can speak of the Law from several different points of view. The Greek word *nomos* is not equivalent to the Hebrew *torah. Nomos* is fundamentally "custom," hardening into what we call "law," and is human in its perspective. *Torah* means "instruction" and is used not only of the legislation God gave to be obeyed but also divine instructions and teachings. In its broadest sense it designates the divine revelation as a whole.[42] Under the influence of the Old Testament, Paul uses *nomos* not only to designate legislation—"the law of commandments and ordinances" (Eph. 2:15), but, like *torah,* also to refer to the Old Testament where no legislation is involved.[43] In still other places Paul uses *nomos* in a Greek way to designate a principle (Rom. 3:27; 7:23, 25; 8:2).[44]

Thus we can understand how Paul can reflect the Jewish point of view that the Law is a standard for life by which he as a Pharisee lived blamelessly (Phil. 3:6). This level of interpretation had led him to pride and boasting in his own righteous achievements. At the same time, there is a deeper demand of the Law, for the Law expresses the total will of God. The Law itself witnesses to the righteousness of God (Rom. 3:21). The Law's demand is such that only love can satisfy it (Rom. 13:8).

When Paul says that the mind set on the flesh "is hostile to God; it does not submit to God's law, indeed it cannot" (Rom. 8:7), he is referring to more than legal statutes. Hostility to God is in reality rejection of the Law of God; what God's Law requires is not merely outward obedience but an obedient and submissive heart. Israel's problem lay at precisely this point. Pursuing a "law of righteousness," i.e., a Law that would make men right with God, they failed to attain this very righteousness because they refused to submit to God's righteousness by faith but instead sought a righteousness by works, which is no true righteousness at all (Rom. 9:31-32; 10:1-2). The human righteousness that is achieved by works (Phil. 3:6) is itself a denial of true righteousness; it is "a righteousness of my own" (Phil. 3:9), and is therefore a ground of boasting (Rom. 2:23; Eph. 2:9); and this very boasting is the essence of sin, for it is the exaltation of self against God. Boasting in one's own righteousness is equivalent to having confidence in the flesh (Phil. 3:3). Legal righteousness leads to this selfish, sinful pride and frustrates the true righteousness demanded by God. When the Jews boast in the Law and sit in prideful judgment on those who do not have the Law, they show by this very fact that they do not know true righteousness (Rom. 2:17-21). The very act of judging convicts them of being sinners (Rom. 2:1). Sin is man's ambition to put himself in the place of God and so be his own lord. This is precisely what the judge does when he assumes the right to sit in judgment on his fellow creatures.[45]

---

[42] H. Kleinknecht, *Bible Key Words: Law,* p. 46.

[43] Rom. 3:10-18 cites passages from Isaiah and Psalms as utterances of the *nomos* (3:19). I Cor. 14:21 quotes Isa. 28:11 as *nomos.*

[44] See C. H. Dodd, "The Law" in *The Bible and the Greeks* (1935), pp. 25-41.

[45] C. K. Barrett, *The Epistle of the Romans* (1957), p. 44.

When Paul accuses the Jews of inconsistency for breaking the Law at the very points where they condemn others—stealing, adultery, temple robbing—he must have the higher demand of the Law for an inner righteousness in mind, for instances of such flagrant conduct did not characterize first-century Jews, who were in fact recognized by the Gentiles for their high moral standards. Paul must be referring to robbing God of the honor due him, spiritual adultery, and profaning the devotion due God alone by exalting themselves as judge and lord over their fellow creatures (Rom. 2:17ff.).[46] Paul immediately goes on to say that circumcision—the symbol of all law-keeping—is really of the heart and not of the flesh, and to be a true Jew is to have a right heart toward God (Rom. 2:25-29).

If, then, the Law in fact embodies the full will of God, it follows ideally that full conformity to the Law would lead to life (Rom. 7:10). Those who do the Law will be justified (Rom. 2:13). But at this point Paul goes beyond Judaism. Judaism based salvation on conformity to the Law, but recognized that most men really did not keep the Law. Therefore it had to mix its doctrine of salvation by obedience to the Law with a doctrine of forgiveness and repentance, by which God in his mercy grants salvation to men who are partly righteous and partly sinners.[47]

Paul sees that this involved the confession of two contradictory principles: works and grace. He therefore insists upon something that no Jewish rabbi would accept,[48] namely, that if righteousness is obedience to Law, then obedience must be perfect—without a single flaw. One who submits to the Law must keep the *whole* Law (Gal. 5:3). Any man who does not do *all things* written in the Law is cursed (Gal. 3:10). Paul would assent to the words of James that whoever obeys the entire Law but fails in a single point is guilty of being a lawbreaker and stands under condemnation (Jas. 2:11).

The problem of perfect fulfillment of the Law is most acute at the point where the Law demands more than conformity to outward regulations. This is revealed when Paul says that a man may accept circumcision and yet not keep the Law (Rom. 2:25). On the surface this is a nonsensical statement, for the very act of circumcision is obedience to the Law. When Paul goes on to say that true circumcision is a matter of the heart and not something external and physical (Rom. 2:28-29), it is clear that "obedience to the law does not mean carrying out the detailed precepts written in the Pentateuch, but fulfilling that relation to God to which the law points; and this proves in the last resort to be a relation not of legal obedience but of faith."[49]

THE FAILURE OF THE LAW. Although the Law remains for Paul the righteous and holy expression of the will of God, the Law has failed to

---

46 *Ibid.,* pp. 56ff. See for a similar interpretation L. Goppelt, *Jesus, Paul and Judaism* (1964), p. 137.

47 See above, p. 498.

48 See G. F. Moore, *Judaism,* III, 150-51.

49 C. K. Barrett, *Romans,* p. 58.

make men righteous before God. It is impossible for a man to be justified by the works of the Law (Gal. 2:16). In fact, there is no possible law that can make a man right with God (Gal. 3:21). The reason for this failure is twofold.

The most fundamental reason is that the weakness and the sinfulness of man render him incapable of giving the obedience the Law demands. The condition of the human heart is such that no law could help it. The weakness of the flesh (Rom. 8:3) and the sinfulness of human nature (Rom. 7:23) could not be changed by the Law. The idea of some rabbis that man's evil impulses could be overcome by study of the Law,[50] Paul would firmly reject.

The reason why the Law cannot make sinful men righteous is that it is an external code, whereas the sinful hearts of men need a transforming inward power. The Law is a written code, not a life imparted by God's Spirit (Rom. 7:6). This idea is extended in the contrast between the new and the old covenant. The old covenant of Law consisted of commands written on tables of stone, which could only declare the will of God but not provide the power to sinful men to obey God's will. Therefore, even though it was glorious, the written code condemns men as sinners and places them under the judgment of death. "The written code kills," whereas what men need is life (II Cor. 3:6).

THE REINTERPRETATION OF THE LAW. In reflecting on the failure of the Law in contrast with the work of Christ to bring him to a knowledge of the righteousness of God, Paul achieves a new interpretation of the role of the Law in God's overall redemptive purposes. First, he explains the inability of the Law to procure salvation by showing that this was not the divine intention. The Law is secondary to the promise, and God's way of salvation by faith is found in the promise.

To the Galatians, Paul argues that God made a covenant of promise with Abraham long before he gave the Law to Moses (Gal. 3:15-18). Making a play on the word *diathēkē,* which can mean both will-testament and covenant, Paul points out that as a valid human testament cannot be contested or altered by additions, so the promise of God given to Abraham cannot be invalidated by the Law, which came later.[51] And since this covenant with Abraham was one of promise, the possibility of righteousness by works is excluded, for promise and Law are mutually exclusive. The promise is no longer promise if it has anything to do with the Law.[52]

This idea is further supported in Romans by the argument that Abraham did not have the Law but was accounted righteous by faith (Rom. 4:1-5). Paul points out that this righteousness was attained by faith even before the sign of circumcision had been given. Circumcision, then, in its true sig-

---

[50] G. F. Moore, *Judaism,* I, 491.
[51] See J. Behm, *TDNT* II, 129.
[52] J. Schniewind, *TDNT* II, 582.

nificance does not belong to the Law but is a sign and seal of justifying faith (Rom. 4:9-12).

It is disappointing to the modern student of Paul and Judaism that Paul does not work out a consistent pattern of the relationship between covenant and Law. Thus he uses *diathēkē* for the covenant of promise made with Abraham (Gal. 3), but he also uses it for the covenant of the Law (II Cor. 3:14), as well as for the covenant in Christ. Quite certainly, while Paul says that the Law was a dispensation of death, he would not maintain that the old covenant of the Law meant death to all who were under that covenant. On the contrary, the implication of the line of thought in Galatians 3 and Romans 4 is that all Israelites who trusted God's covenant of promise to Abraham and did not use the Law as a way of salvation by works were assured of salvation. This becomes explicit in the case of David, who, though under the Law, pronounced a blessing on the man to whom God reckons righteousness apart from works (Rom. 4:6-7). When Paul speaks of the *coming* of faith (Gal. 3:25), he does not mean that no one had previously ever exercised saving faith. On the contrary, for Paul faith appeared with Abraham; but faith could be frustrated when the Law was made a basis of human righteousness and boasting.

If salvation is by way of promise and not Law, what was the role of the Law in God's redemptive purpose? In answering this question, Paul comes to conclusions that were both novel and quite unacceptable to Judaism.[53] The Law was added (*pareisēlthen*) not to save men from their sins but to show them what sin was (Rom. 3:20; 5:13, 20; Gal. 3:19). By declaring the will of God, by showing what God forbids, the Law shows what sin is. By forbidding coveting, it shows that coveting is sin (Rom. 7:7). Thus the power of sin is the Law (I Cor. 15:56), for only by the Law is sin clearly defined. Sayings about the Law making sin to increase (Rom. 5:20) do not mean that it was the Law that actually brought sin into being and made man more sinful than he was without the Law. The Law is not itself sinful nor sin-producing (Rom. 7:7). Rather, the Law discloses man's true situation, that his accountability to God as a sinner may be revealed (Rom. 3:19).

Thus the Law is an instrument of condemnation (Rom. 5:13), wrath (Rom. 4:15), and death (Rom. 7:19; II Cor. 3:6). It is not the Law itself that produces this tragic situation; it is sin in man that makes the Law an instrument of death (Rom. 7:13). The dispensation of the Law can be called a dispensation of death (II Cor. 3:7), of slavery to the world (Gal. 4:1-10), a covenant of slavery (Gal. 4:21-31), a period of childhood when one is under the control of guardians (Gal. 3:23-26).[54]

---

53 H. J. Schoeps, *Paul,* pp. 174, 183. However, this reinterpretation is due to his Christian perspective and not to the Hellenistic background that Schoeps assumes.

54 These verses describe a time of immaturity and subjection in contrast to maturity and freedom. *Eis Christon* (v. 24) should therefore be rendered "until Christ" (RSV), not "to bring us to Christ" (KJV).

Certainly Paul does not mean to suggest that all men who lived between Moses and Christ were in such bondage to sin and death that there was no salvation until Christ came. His reference to David (Rom. 4:6-8) disproves that. The promise antedates the Law and was valid both before and after its fulfillment in Christ. Nor does Paul mean that this was his experience as a Jew under the Law. This is his understanding of what the Law, apart from the promise, really accomplishes. Paul's argument in both Romans and Galatians is not designed to instruct Jews how they should understand the Law, but to keep Gentile Christians, who had no racial tie to the Law as Jewish Christians did, from exchanging salvation by grace for salvation by the works of the Law.[55]

It is from this same Christian perspective that the much contested passage in Romans 7:13-25 is to be interpreted. The older autobiographical interpretation is very difficult in the light of Paul's own descriptions of his Jewish life in Galatians 1:14 and Philippians 3:5-7.[56] It is equally difficult to understand the passage to describe the experience of the defeated Christian who still relies on the flesh in contrast to the victorious Christian who has learned to rely on the Spirit (Rom. 8).[57] Paul's concern in this passage is not life in the flesh but the nature of the Law. "Is the law sin?" (Rom. 7:7). No; but because sin dwells in man, the holy Law shows sin to be sin and thus becomes an instrument of death. But it is sin, not the Law, that brings death (Rom. 7:10-11).

This theme is further expanded in verses 13-24. The entire chapter embodies a Christian understanding of the actual plight of man under the Law, whether this corresponds to his conscious experience or not. As a Pharisee, Saul was quite satisfied with his obedience to the Law and found therein a cause for pride and boasting. But as a Christian, Paul understands that he was deceived because he had misused the Law. Only in the light of his life in Christ can he understand what his situation under the Law really was; and only as a Christian can he understand why the Law can in fact only condemn a man to death when it is itself holy and just and good. The reason is not the sinful nature of the Law but the sinful nature of man. Thus Romans 7 is a picture of existence under the Law understood from a Christian perspective.[58] The will of God therefore is a

---

[55] See L. Goppelt, *Jesus, Paul and Judaism,* p. 147. Also G. F. Moore, *Judaism,* III, 151.

[56] See above, p. 366, for this interpretation.

[57] See W. Sanday and A. C. Headlam, *Romans* (1896), pp. 184ff.; W. D. Stacey, *The Pauline View of Man* (1956), p. 212. C. L. Mitton, "Romans VII Reconsidered," *ET* 65 (1953/54), pp. 78ff., 99ff., 132ff. considers it to be the Christian who falls back into reliance on the Law. F. F. Bruce, *Romans* (1963), p. 150, the Christian who lives in two ages at once.

[58] This viewpoint was supported by J. Denney, *Romans: Expositor's Greek Testament,* III, 639. The basic work today is W. G. Kümmel, *Römer 7 und die Bekehrung des Paulus* (1929), who has been followed by the majority of German scholars. See references cited in Kümmel's *Man in the NT* (1963), pp. 51f. See also C. K. Barrett, *Romans,* pp. 140, 152; L. Goppelt, *Jesus, Paul and Judaism,*

delight to man, and he desires to fulfill the highest demand of the Law to love both God and neighbor. As Paul looks back on his life as a Jew under the Law, he realizes, contrary to his previous conviction, that he had not fulfilled the Law. Because of sin residing in his flesh, he was incapable of providing the righteousness God requires, for the good demanded by the Law is not mere outward, formal obedience, but the demand of God for true righteousness.[59] Of this man is incapable—so incapable, in fact, that it is as though his own will was overcome completely by sin, which rules his life (vv. 17, 20). Freedom from this bondage to sin and death is found only in Jesus Christ.

THE PERMANENCE OF THE LAW. By fulfilling the promise given to Abraham, Christ has ended the age of the Law and inaugurated the age of Christ, which means freedom from bondage and the end of the Law for the believer. However, it is clear that inasmuch as Paul always regards the Law as holy and just and good, he never thinks of the Law as being abolished. It remains the expression of the will of God.

This is evident from his frequent assertion that redemption in Christ enables believers in some real sense to fulfill the Law. In Christ, God has done what the Law could not do, namely, condemned sin in the flesh, that the just requirement of the Law might be fulfilled in those who walk by the Spirit (Rom. 8:3-4). Here is paradox: by being freed from the Law, we uphold the Law (Rom. 3:31). It is obvious that the new life in Christ enables the Christian to keep the Law not as an external code but in terms of its higher demand, i.e., at the very point where the Law was powerless because it was an external written code. Thus Paul repeats that the essential Christian ethic of love, which is a gift of the Holy Spirit (I Cor. 13; Gal. 5:22), is the fulfilling of the Law. The whole law is fulfilled in one word, "You shall love your neighbor as yourself" (Gal. 5:14). In place of the Law as a written code is now the law of Christ. This "new law" cannot be reduced to specific rules but goes far beyond legislation. No set of rules can tell one how to bear the burdens of another (Gal. 6:2); only love can dictate such conduct. However, the law of Christ, which is the law of love, does fulfill the Law. Love will not commit adultery, or lie or steal or covet, or do any wrong to one's neighbor (Rom. 12:8-10).

Probably Paul refers to this same law of Christ when he expounds his own personal relationship to Law. As a man in Christ, he is no longer under the Law, and therefore he can minister to Gentiles as though he were a Gentile who had no Law (*anomos*). Yet he is not therefore an antinomian (*anomos theou*) but *ennomos Christou*—"subject to the law of Christ."[60]

---

p. 146. R. N. Longenecker, *Paul, Apostle of Liberty,* pp. 114ff. includes with this interpretation "the human cry . . . of the spiritually sensitive."

[59] R. Bultmann, "Romans 7 and the Anthropology of Paul" in *Existence and Faith,* ed. by S. Ogden (1960), pp. 145ff.

[60] Cf. Arndt and Gingrich, *Lexicon,* p. 266.

Because he is motivated by love, he adapts himself to men of all kinds of conditions to bring them the gospel.[61]

The permanence of the Law is reflected further in the fact that Paul appeals to specific commands in the Law as the norm for Christian conduct. He appeals to several specific commandments (*entolai*) of the Decalogue that are fulfilled by love (Rom. 13:8-10). His reference to "any other commandment" designates everything in the Law that relates to one's neighbor. Yet it was the character of the Law as *entolai* that marked its externality. Again, Paul quotes the command to love father and mother as the first commandment with a promise (Eph. 6:2). It is clear that the Law continues to be the expression of the will of God for conduct, even for those who are no longer under the Law.

It is quite clear, however, that the permanent aspect of the Law is the ethical and not the ceremonial. "For neither circumcision counts for anything nor uncircumcision, but keeping the commandments of God" (I Cor. 7:19). Most of the studies on Paul emphasize the fact that Paul does not explicitly distinguish between the ethical and ceremonial aspects of the Law. This is of course true; but the implicit distinction is unavoidable and should be stressed. Although circumcision is a command of God and a part of the Law, Paul sets circumcision in contrast to the commandments, and in doing so separates the ethical from the ceremonial—the permanent from the temporal. Thus he can commend the *entolai theou* to Gentiles, and yet adamantly reject the ceremonial *entolai,* such as circumcision, foods, feasts, and even sabbath keeping (Col. 2:16), for these are but a shadow of the reality that has come in Christ.

Thus Christ has brought the Law as a way of righteousness and as a ceremonial code to its end; but the Law as the expression of the will of God is permanent; and the man indwelt by the Holy Spirit and thus energized by love is enabled to fulfill the Law as men under the Law never could.

---

[61] C. H. Dodd, "Ennomos Christou" in *Studia Paulina* (de Zwaan Festschrift, 1953), pp. 96-110, followed by R. N. Longenecker, *Paul, Apostle of Liberty,* pp. 183-90, feels that the law of Christ is not the law of love but a body of traditional sayings of Jesus that provided an objective basis for Christian conduct. While the existence of such a tradition is established, we do not feel that the "law of Christ" is this tradition conceived as a new law for the Christian community.

36

THE CHRISTIAN LIFE

Literature:

C. H. Dodd, "The Ethics of the Pauline Epistles," *The Evolution of Ethics,* ed. by E. H. Sneath (1927); M. S. Enslin, *The Ethics of Paul* (1930); C. A. A. Scott, *NT Ethics* (1930); F. V. Filson, *St. Paul's Conception of Recompense* (1931); M. E. Andrews, *The Ethical Teaching of Paul* (1930); L. Dewar, *An Outline of NT Ethics* (1949); E. H. Wahlstrom, *The New Life in Christ* (1950); J. Murray, *Principles of Conduct* (1957); W. A. Beardslee, *Human Achievement and Divine Vocation in the Message of Paul* (1961); W. D. Davies, "Ethics in the NT," *IDB* E-J (1962), pp. 167-176; D. E. H. Whiteley, *The Theology of St. Paul* (1964), ch. 9; R. Schnackenburg, *The Moral Teaching of the NT* (1965); M. Bouttier, *Christianity According to Paul* (1966); R. C. Tannehill, *Dying and Rising with Christ* (1967), pp. 77-83; V. P. Furnish, *Theology and Ethics in Paul* (1968) with extensive bibliography; V. P. Furnish, *The Love Command in the NT* (1972).

We have already outlined Paul's view of the situation of the man in Christ. We must now ask about Paul's view of the Christian life, of Christian conduct, of Christian ethics. What is his concept of the good life? How does the new life in Christ manifest itself in practical conduct?

We are defining "ethics" in the broadest sense of the word to include both personal conduct and the Christian attitude toward social ethics.

When one reads Paul with this question in mind, it becomes at once obvious that he has no ethical system. This can easily be illustrated by the most casual reading of Paul's lists of virtues. The "fruit of the Spirit" in Galatians 5:22, 23 is often taken as normative for Paul's concept of the good Christian life, but these virtues must be compared with the similar lists in Philippians 4:8 and Colossians 3:12-15.[1] There is no overlapping between the list in Philippians and the other two lists; and there are only four virtues that occur more than once: love, kindness, meekness, and longsuffering. Such lists do not offer a formal ethic, nor are they designed to portray the pattern of the good man or the Christian ideal toward which

[1] See L. Dewar, *NT Ethics* (1949), p. 143.

all are to strive.[2] They are rather different ways Paul addresses himself to concrete historical situations to explain how the new life in Christ is to express itself.

SOURCES. Closely related to the nature of the Pauline ethic is the question of the sources upon which he drew, and the influences that formulated his thinking about Christian conduct. It is highly improbable that his ethical instruction is his original creation, or that he received it by divine revelation. On the contrary, several different influences can be detected if they cannot be clearly isolated.[3] It seems beyond question that one of the strongest influences was the Old Testament. While Paul strongly affirms that for those in Christ the Law has come to its end (Rom. 10:4), yet he regards the Old Testament as the revelation of the will of God.[4] He appeals to several specific commands of the Decalogue that the Christian fulfills by love (Rom. 13:8-10). He refers to the command to love father and mother as a standard of Christian conduct (Eph. 6:2). As a Christian, he continued to regard the Old Testament as a book "written for our instruction" (Rom. 15:4). However, it is significant that Paul never quotes the Old Testament at length for the purpose of developing a pattern of conduct. "There is no evidence which indicates that the apostle regarded it as in any sense a source book for detailed moral instruction or even a manual of ethical norms."[5] He never attempts to codify or interpret in a formal way the ethical and moral teachings of the Old Testament. No direct influence from the intertestamental literature can be established.

Some scholars detect a strong influence from Paul's rabbinic background. Indeed, W. D. Davies thinks that Paul would describe himself as a "Christian Rabbi," teaching a new Torah.[6] While we would expect to find rabbinic influences, it is going too far to say that Paul is a self-conscious bearer and interpreter of that tradition, or that his ethical teaching embodies substantial reformulation of rabbinic materials.[7]

Clear evidences of Hellenistic influence can be detected in the Pauline terminology and style.[8] Once Paul quotes a Greek proverb, "Bad company ruins good morals" (I Cor. 15:33), but this does not prove literary dependence. Greek influence is seen in Paul's use of the metaphors of warfare (II Cor. 10:3ff.; I Thess. 5:8) or of athletic competition (I Cor. 9:25); in the use of the idioms "what is fitting" (Phlm. 8; Col. 3:18; Eph.

---

[2] V. P. Furnish, *Theology and Ethics in Paul* (1968), p. 87.

[3] See particularly Furnish, *Theology and Ethics in Paul*, part I; M. Enslin, *The Ethics of Paul* (1930), part I.

[4] See above, p. 394.

[5] V. Furnish, *Theology and Ethics in Paul*, p. 33.

[6] W. D. Davies, *Paul and Rabbinic Judaism* (1955), p. 145.

[7] V. Furnish, *Theology and Ethics in Paul*, p. 42.

[8] See *ibid.*, pp. 45-49; R. Schnackenburg, *The Moral Teaching of the NT* (1965), pp. 303-6. For efforts to detect direct literary influence from Greek writers, see the literature in V. Furnish, *Theology and Ethics in Paul*, p. 45. For parallels with stoicism, see J. B. Lightfoot, "St. Paul and Seneca," *Philippians* (1878), pp. 270ff.

4:5), "what is seemly" (Eph. 5:3), "what is shameful" (Eph. 5:12); and particularly in the virtues listed in Philippians 4:8. The words for "lovely" (*prosphilēs*), "gracious" (*euphēmos*), "excellence" (*aretē*, which means moral excellence or virtue), and "praiseworthy" (*epainos*) are drawn from Hellenistic ethical vocabulary. While there can be no doubt that Paul used the language drawn from the vocabulary of Hellenistic popular philosophy, he uses it differently from contemporary Greek teachers. He is not concerned to portray the ideal of perfect humanity; he is altogether concerned with the new life in Christ and how it should manifest itself. Thus he makes use of two common Hellenistic concepts: "freedom" (*eleutheria*) and "contentment" (*autarkeia*) but gives them a very different meaning. The free man is he who is a slave of Christ, and contentment does not mean self-sufficiency but contentment with God's provision for life.

Hellenistic thought is detected at two particular points. Paul frequently refers to the conscience (*suneidēsis;* eleven times in the Corinthian correspondence). The important fact here is that there is no word for conscience in Hebrew. The one place where the word appears in the LXX with the same meaning it has in Paul is the Wisdom of Solomon 17:10, which was influenced by Greek philosophy. Conscience for Paul, as in the Hellenistic world, was the universal human capacity to judge one's own actions.[9] However, Paul does not conceive of the conscience as an authoritative guide for moral action or a norm for conduct. Conscience tells man that there is right and wrong; it is not a safe guide to give him the content of the right.[10]

Another term of distinctive Hellenistic philosophy is "nature" (*physis*). Paul asserts that Gentiles who do not have the revealed Law of God are able "by nature" to do what the Law demands (Rom. 2:14). Some scholars understand this to be a reflection of popular Greek philosophy.[11] However, while the language may be borrowed from Greek thought, Paul uses it in a non-Greek way. His thought is not that there is a universal natural law intrinsic to human nature, but that God the Creator has implanted in man a knowledge of right and wrong. When any man obeys the positive leadings of conscience, he does "by nature," i.e., instinctively, the right thing. However, the reason for Paul's appeal to nature and conscience is not primarily to suggest that men have an intrinsic inner guide for correct ethical conduct. It is rather to assert that even those who do not have the revealed Law do have an inner sense of right and wrong, but have failed to be obedient to the light they have even as the Jews have failed to keep the Law.

Another important source for Paul's ethical teaching is the teaching of Jesus. Some scholars have felt that Paul's ethic was basically a fresh interpre-

---

[9] See V. Furnish, *Theology and Ethics in Paul,* p. 229. See also R. Schnackenburg, *The Moral Teaching of the NT,* pp. 287ff.; C. A. Pierce, *Conscience in the NT* (1955); W. D. Davies, *IDB* A-D, pp. 671-76.

[10] R. Bultmann, *Theology of the NT* (1951), I, 218.

[11] For references see M. Enslin, *The Ethics of St. Paul,* pp. 102ff.; V. Furnish, *Theology and Ethics in Paul,* p. 49.

tation of Jesus' ethical teaching in a completely different setting,[12] while others feel that the Pauline ethic was a radical distortion of Jesus' teaching.[13] The question is by no means an easy one. On a few occasions Paul appeals directly to the authority of the Lord: in the matter of divorce (I Cor. 7:10-11), concerning the support of Christian workers (I Cor. 9:14), concerning conduct of the Lord's Supper (I Cor. 11:22ff.), concerning the coming of the Lord (I Thess. 4:15), and in general (I Cor. 14:37). In other places Paul clearly echoes teachings of Jesus without referring to them: Rom. 12:14=Mt. 5:44; Rom. 12:17=Mt. 5:39ff.; Rom. 13:7=Mt. 22:15-22; Rom. 14:13-14=Lk. 17:1-2; Rom. 14:14=Mk. 7:15: I Thess. 5:2=Mt. 24:34; I Thess. 5:13=Mk. 9:50; I Thess. 5:15=Mt. 5:39-47. Such references make it clear that Paul was familiar with a body of ethical tradition coming from Jesus. His statement that he has no word of the Lord concerning those who are not married (I Cor. 7:25) confirms this. That he is careful to distinguish between his own opinion and the word of the Lord (I Cor. 7:12) reinforces this conclusion.

However, we cannot but be impressed by the fact that Paul appeals to the ethical teaching of Jesus very infrequently and even less frequently directly quotes him. "One must regard with some surprise the fact that the teaching of the earthly Jesus seems not to play as vital, or at least as obvious, a role in Paul's concrete ethical instruction as the Old Testament."[14] Furthermore, Paul never refers to Jesus as a teacher or to his followers as disciples.

A few scholars have interpreted Paul's reference to the "law of Christ" (Gal. 6:2) to refer to a more or less fixed body of tradition coming from Jesus;[15] and when Paul asserts that he is "under the law of Christ" (*ennomos Christou,* I Cor. 9:21), he means that he is bound by an ethical tradition coming from Jesus.[16] This conclusion is difficult to sustain.[17] There is no proof that Paul knew a fixed body of ethical tradition coming from Jesus. It is far more likely that the law of Christ is the law of love that Jesus said embodied the totality of the Old Testament Law (Mt. 22:40).[18]

From this survey of the possible sources for Paul's ethical thought, several conclusions emerge. It is clear that Paul is no legalist. He does not try to substitute a new Christian code of ethics to replace the Old Testament Law. On the other hand, he has strong convictions about correct Christian conduct. The sources of his ethical thinking are complex. The substructure of his thought is the Old Testament. He does not hesitate to

---

[12] C. A. A. Scott, *NT Ethics* (1930).

[13] J. Knox, *The Ethic of Jesus and the Teaching of the Church* (1961).

[14] V. Furnish, *Theology and Ethics in Paul,* p. 55.

[15] See W. D. Davies, *Paul and Rabbinic Judaism* (1953), pp. 136ff.; *IDB* E-J, p. 175. For the existence of pre-Pauline oral *didachē,* see D. E. H. Whiteley, *The Theology of St. Paul* (1964), pp. 207f.

[16] C. H. Dodd, "Ennomos Christou" in *Studia Paulina* (1953), pp. 96ff.

[17] Cf. the thorough criticism by V. Furnish, *Theology and Ethics in Paul,* pp. 56-65.

[18] See *ibid.,* p. 64 and references.

make use of Hellenistic concepts, but these are always interpreted in terms of the new life in Christ. Paul draws upon all the ethical ideals available to him to express his convictions about how the Christian should live.

MOTIVATIONS. What are the motivations for Christian living?[19] A popular view is that the central motivation is the indwelling of the Holy Spirit. Paul is said to have taught that "The Spirit of God in action in a man's heart was an adequate ethical guide, and that a man under the sway of the Spirit knew from within what the will of God was and was enabled both to will and to do it. . . ."[20] Marshall does go on to say that Paul recognized that few Christians were mature and that the majority were babes. However, such a sweeping statement is misleading, for Paul appeals not only to the indwelling of the Spirit as a motivating power but to many other principles as well. Furthermore, it is not altogether clear to what extent Paul considered the Spirit to impart to believers an intuitive knowledge of the right; and we shall see that his doctrine of the indwelling of the Spirit is not thought of as an inner spontaneous power but involves the tension between the indicative and the imperative. Nor is it clear that the indwelling of the Spirit is thought of as the most important motivation.

Sometimes Paul simply appeals to reason and good sense.[21] Drunkenness is debauchery and ruin (Eph. 5:18). Christians should so live as to command the respect of outsiders (I Thess. 4:12) and the approval of men (Rom. 14:18). Christians should shun anything that brings shame (Eph. 5:12). The list of virtues in Philippians 4:8-9 is self-commending, and Paul's appeal here is simply to the good judgment of his readers.

IMITATION OF CHRIST. Such motivations are, however, quite secondary; the primary motivations are profoundly theological. Paul does make some use of the motivation of the imitation of Christ, but he refers explicitly to such imitation only once. The Thessalonians had become "imitators of us and of the Lord" in the way they received the gospel (I Thess. 1:6). The emphasis appears to rest on the fact that they received it "in much affliction." The same idea appears in Corinthians: "Be imitators of me, as I am of Christ" (I Cor. 11:1). The context of this *imitatio Christi* is sacrificial service. Paul did not pursue his own personal ends but sought the welfare of those to whom he ministered. "I try to please all men in everything I do, not seeking my own advantage" (I Cor. 10:33). The same idea is behind the great christological passage in Philippians 2:5ff., where Paul holds up the example of Christ's sacrificial obedience to the Father to show that

---

19 For some of the older points of view, see M. E. Andrews, "The Problem of Motive in the Ethics of Paul," *JR* 13 (1933), 200-15. See C. A. A. Scott, *NT Ethics,* ch. IV.

20 L. H. Marshall, *The Challenge of NT Ethics* (1947), p. 220. Wahlstrom thinks that the indwelling Christ enables the Christian to know of himself what is right or wrong. See E. H. Wahlstrom, *The New Life in Christ* (1950), p. 152.

21 C. A. A. Scott calls this "The Intuition of an Educated Conscience." *NT Ethics,* p. 101.

Christians should not seek their own interests but the interests of others. By inference, Paul points to the example of Christ, who, though he was rich, "yet for your sake . . . he became poor" in his incarnation (II Cor. 8:9) that the Corinthians might serve their fellow Christians in Jerusalem by making a generous gift to them in their poverty. It is true that Paul does not hold up the *earthly life* of Jesus as a standard of moral excellence.[22] Christ is, however, to be imitated in his self-effacing love and in the giving of himself in suffering and death.[23]

It has been frequently recognized that the Pauline ethic is firmly rooted in his theology. Paul saw the root of all wickedness in irreligion.[24] The black picture Paul paints of pagan society with its corruption and vices stems from the fact that they did not see fit to acknowledge God (Rom. 1:28). Ungodliness precedes wickedness and is its ultimate source (Rom. 1:18). Rejection of God led to darkness and all kinds of ethical folly.

UNION WITH CHRIST. On the positive side, one of the main theological motifs is that of union with Christ. This truth is expressed in several ways. Paul had to deal with a very lax morality in Corinth, apparently because of gnostic influences, which led certain of the Corinthians to claim that what was done with the body was a matter of indifference to the spirit; for the body was of no consequence to the spiritual man. Their call was "All things are lawful to me" (I Cor. 6:12), even sexual license. Paul answers this aberration by reminding the Corinthians that they were united to Christ, not only in their spirits but in their total being. "Do you not know that your bodies are members of Christ?" (I Cor. 6:15). Here emerges the tension between the indicative and the imperative. Because of certain redemptive facts, certain results inevitably accrue. I have been joined to Christ (indicative); therefore I must live in a certain way (imperative). I have been joined to Christ; therefore I cannot enter into illicit relationships with prostitutes.

That this way of thinking stands at the heart of Paul's theology is proven by Romans 6, where the same truth of union with Christ is expressed in a somewhat different idiom. If a man has been acquitted in justification from all guilt in the eyes of God, is he therefore not free to sin with impunity? This Paul says is impossible. "We were buried therefore with him by baptism unto death, so that as Christ was raised from the dead by the glory of the Father, we too might walk in newness of life" (Rom. 6:4). Baptism is a representation of union with Christ in his death and resurrection. "You were buried with him in baptism, in which you were raised with him through faith in the working of God, who raised him from the dead" (Col. 2:12). By faith men are united with Christ in his death and raised up into a new

---

[22] W. Michaelis, *TDNT* IV, 672.

[23] See V. Furnish, *Theology and Ethics in Paul,* pp. 218-24; L. Dewar, *NT Ethics,* p. 134.

[24] L. H. Marshall, *The Challenge of NT Ethics,* p. 234; see also L. Dewar, *NT Ethics,* pp. 122ff.; D. E. H. Whiteley, *The Theology of St. Paul,* pp. 205-9.

life (indicative); therefore they should walk in newness of life (imperative), and this new life cannot be one in which the believer is indifferent to sin. Therefore the position reflected in the question, "Are we to continue in sin that grace may abound?" (Rom. 6:1) embodies a patent internal contradiction.

The ethical significance of union with Christ is again illustrated in Ephesians 2, where this union is expressed in terms of new life through identification with Christ in his resurrection and ascension. The believer is raised into newness of life, and even exalted to heaven to be seated with Christ at the right hand of God. The contrast between the old life and the new life is expressed primarily in ethical terms. Outside of faith in Christ, men are dead—but dead through trespasses and sins, living under the domination of "the passions of [the] flesh, following the desires of body and mind" (Eph. 2:3). The new life in Christ, which is a new creation, expresses itself in good works (Eph. 2:10). Here again are the indicative and the imperative: the believer who was dead in sins is now alive with Christ (indicative); he is therefore to live a life of good works (imperative).

INDWELLING OF CHRIST. Another motivation for conduct well pleasing to God is the indwelling of Christ and the Holy Spirit.[25] As we have seen, some interpreters of Paul feel that this is for him the most important motivation. Marshall places great emphasis upon the contrast Paul makes between the old economy and the new age with its inner dynamic of the Spirit. Paul insists that for the Christian the code-method is no more and the spirit-method has taken its place. The Law has been abolished both as a principle of salvation and as the principle of conduct. "Paul insists that Christianity is not a Code (an external control), but a 'Spirit' (an internal control)."[26] Paul found the secret of the good life in a good disposition, and the secret of a good disposition is the sway of the Spirit of God over the inner life of man.[27] This interpretation of Paul is flatly contradicted by the fact that Paul appeals to the statutes of the Law as the revealed will of God normative for Christian conduct.[28] His contrast between the external written code and the new life of the Spirit (Rom. 7:6; II Cor. 3:3) does not mean that Paul views the indwelling of the Spirit as a spontaneous power that will enable men to do the right automatically, nor does Paul set aside the Old Testament Law *in toto*. The Law has come to an end as a way of righteousness (Rom. 10:4). But Paul distinguishes between the Law as legal code and as the abiding revelation of God,[29] and more than once he asserts that it is the new life of the Spirit that enables the Christian truly to fulfill the Law (Rom. 8:3-4; 13:10; Gal. 5:14).

It is clear that Paul conceives of the Spirit as a new indwelling power

---

[25] See above, p. 488.
[26] L. H. Marshall, *The Challenge of NT Ethics*, p. 229.
[27] *Ibid.*, p. 231.
[28] See above, p. 504.
[29] See p. 509.

that manifests itself in conduct. The new life is the gift of the Spirit (II Cor. 3:6; Gal. 6:25), and this life evidences itself in the "fruit of the Spirit" (Gal. 5:20), which Paul interprets in terms of Christian virtues. An obvious contrast is intended between works and fruit: between human effort and an inner spiritual dynamic. The indwelling of the Spirit means a new experience of love (Rom. 5:5), freedom (Rom. 8:2), and service (Rom. 7:6).

However, it is not clear that Paul conceives of the indwelling of the Spirit as an inner spontaneous power that issues in gradual progress and growth in Christian virtues.[30] That Paul expects growth in moral character is clear. "And we all, with unveiled face, beholding the glory of the Lord, are being changed into his likeness from one degree of glory to another; for this comes from the Lord who is the Spirit" (II Cor. 3:18). However, in this passage the Spirit is not the indwelling power of the new life but is identified with the ascended, glorified Lord. The Christian's preoccupation with his exalted Lord will mean that he will be more and more conformed to the image of Christ. However, the context of the passage is that of ministry. "Therefore, having this ministry by the mercy of God . . ." (II Cor. 4:1). "What is described is the *doxa* of the office, of proclamation, of *kērussomen* (4:5),"[31] not general moral excellence.

It is striking that Paul does not appeal to the Spirit as a direct source of moral enlightenment. Paul is conscious that the Holy Spirit reveals the things of God (I Cor. 2:10), but this does not mean that Paul feels himself to be independent of the Old Testament and the teaching of Jesus.[32] There is only one place where Paul appeals to the Spirit as a moral guide, and here, while he claimed to have the Spirit, he only gives his opinion (I Cor. 7:40). In his most extended hortatory passage (Rom. 12:1-15:13), there are only three passing references to the Spirit (Rom. 12:11; 14:17; 15:13), none of which suggests that the Spirit is a moral guide. It is doubtful whether Paul conceives of the Spirit as a source of the spontaneous knowledge of right and wrong. In fact, he never propounds any theory about how the right is known.[33] The Spirit is an indwelling power to enable the believer to live in accordance with the will of God.

Even here we find the tension between the indicative and the imperative. "If we live by the Spirit [indicative: the new life is from the Spirit], let us also walk by the Spirit [imperative]" (Gal. 5:25). However, this new life of the Spirit is not a free, inner, spontaneous power but one that finds itself in tension with the flesh. The flesh and the Spirit are opposed to each

---

[30] V. Furnish, *Theology and Ethics in Paul,* pp. 240-41; M. Bouttier, *Christianity According to Paul* (1966), pp. 22ff. In his discussion of "Progress, Growth, and Perfection," W. A. Beardslee makes very little reference to the transforming power of the indwelling Spirit. See *Human Achievement and Divine Vocation in the Message of Paul* (1961), pp. 66-78.

[31] G. Kittel, *TDNT* II, 251. P. Ramsay understands this to refer to fully obedient love. *Basic Christian Ethics* (1950), p. 259.

[32] See the claim by E. F. Scott, *The Spirit in the NT* (1923), pp. 172-73.

[33] V. Furnish, *Theology and Ethics in Paul,* pp. 231-33.

other, "to prevent you from doing what you would" (Gal. 5:17). This dialectic is solved only by a life of sustained decision. This requires a constant denial of the flesh and an equally constant "walking in the Spirit." "As you have always obeyed, so now . . . work out your own salvation with fear and trembling; for God is at work in you" (Phil. 2:12). This is what it means to be led by the Spirit (Rom. 8:14; Gal. 5:18).

SANCTIFICATION. Closely associated with the indwelling of the Spirit is the doctrine of sanctification.[34] A widely prevailing view is that justification is the term designating the beginning of the Christian life, while sanctification designates development of that life through the internal work of the Spirit.[35] This, however, is an oversimplification of the New Testament teaching and it obscures an important truth. In fact, the idea of sanctification is soteriological before it is a moral concept.[36] The very idea of "holiness" is first of all cultic, and secondarily moral. Procksch goes so far as to say that holiness in the New Testament does not refer to ethical conduct but to a condition of ethical innocence.[37] Sanctification is not a synonym for moral growth.[38] What is holy is dedicated to God or in some way belongs to the service of God. Israel as a people even in disbelief remains a holy people for the patriarchs' sake (Rom. 11:16). The children of mixed marriages are holy because of one believing parent (I Cor. 7:14). The church as a whole is a holy temple (Eph. 2:21). When Paul says that the unmarried girl or woman is anxious about the affairs of the Lord, how to be holy in body and spirit (I Cor. 7:34), he cannot be referring to an ethical state, or else marriage itself is unclean; and this completely contradicts Paul's thought. Holiness here is complete, undisturbed dedication to the things of God. The RSV does well to render the verb "consecrated" where Paul speaks of foods that some people regarded as unclean for cultic reasons but which cannot be considered cultically unclean when consecrated to God (I Tim. 4:5; see also II Tim. 2:21).

When applied to Christians, holiness or sanctification is not in the first place an ethical concept although it includes the ethical aspect. It denotes first of all a soteriological truth that Christians belong to God. They are God's people. This is why the most common use of *hagios* in Paul is to designate all Christians as saints[39]—the people of God. Christians are holy even in their bodily existence when they give themselves to God (Rom. 12:1). Believers from among the Gentiles come into the holy people of God, "sanctified by the Holy Spirit" (Rom. 15:16). Even more important

---

[34] See articles by O. Procksch, *TDNT* I, 107-15; E. C. Blackman in *IDB* R-Z, pp. 212f.; V. Taylor, *Forgiveness and Reconciliation* (1941), section V; V. P. Furnish, *Theology and Ethics in Paul,* pp. 153ff.

[35] See G. B. Stevens, *The Theology of the NT* (1906), p. 437.

[36] See V. Furnish, *Theology and Ethics in Paul,* p. 155.

[37] See O. Procksch, *TWNT* I, 110. The German at this point is very difficult and the English translation (*TDNT* I, 109) is not altogether clear.

[38] See E. Blackman, *IDB* R-Z, p. 212.

[39] See below, p. 544.

than this is the fact that all believers are viewed as already sanctified in Christ. In this sense, sanctification does not designate growth in ethical conduct but is a redemptive truth. Paul addresses the Corinthians among whom existed scandalous sins not only as saints but as those sanctified in Christ Jesus (I Cor. 1:2; see also 1:30). Cleansing, sanctification, justification are factual events of the past. Sanctification here means inclusion in the people whom God claims as his own.[40] "Sanctification consists not in a particular moral quality which has been attained but in a particular relationship to God which has been given."[41] Sanctification has an eschatological goal. It is God's purpose that the church should be finally presented to him in splendor, "without spot or wrinkle or any such thing, that she might be holy and without blemish" (Eph. 5:27; see Col. 1:22; I Thess. 3:13; 5:23).

Because believers do belong to God—because they have been sanctified—they are called upon to experience sanctification and to shun uncleanness. While sanctification is the work of the Holy Spirit (II Thess. 2:13), it also involves a human response. Paul calls upon the Corinthians to cleanse themselves from every defilement of body and spirit, and to make holiness perfect in fear of God (II Cor. 7:1). Believers are no longer to yield themselves to impurity but to righteousness for sanctification (Rom. 6:19). God has not called us for uncleanness but in holiness (I Thess. 4:7).

It should be noted that when the ethical aspect of sanctification is stressed, it is concerned primarily with purity. The opposite of holiness is uncleanness (*akatharsia*) (I Thess. 4:7). Sanctification is particularly concerned with sexual purity (I Thess. 4:4), but closely associated with sexual impurity is covetousness (lit., "a desire to have more"). The idea of covetousness is greediness, possessiveness, acquisitiveness. Immorality is sinful because a man seeks to possess something that does not belong to him, to which he has no right or claim. Both immorality and covetousness are viewed as uncleanness or filthiness. Covetousness means in the ultimate issue insatiableness, to the final exclusion of all spiritual values.[42]

Paul's emphasis on moral purity was undoubtedly due to the prevalence of sexual sins in the Hellenistic world, particularly in the practice of pagan religions. The man who is completely devoted to God will manifest his Christian devotion by separation from typical pagan sinfulness. Sanctification is not a term designating the totality of the good life as such, but one that denotes the dedication of Christians to God in contrast to the prevailing evils of their society.

The important point to note is that there is a tension between the indicative and the imperative. Sanctification is a factual past event (indicative); therefore it is to be experienced here and now (imperative). Believers have been sanctified; therefore they are to cleanse themselves from all that

[40] C. K. Barrett, *First Corinthians* (1968), p. 142.
[41] V. Furnish, *Theology and Ethics in Paul*, p. 155.
[42] Cf. C. A. A. Scott, *NT Ethics*, pp. 112ff.; G. Delling, *TDNT* VI, 271-73.

defiles. Therefore it is not correct to say that justification is the beginning and sanctification the continuation of the Christian life. Both involve the tension between indicative and imperative. Since we have been justified by faith, we have[43] peace with God (Rom. 5:1). Since we have been sanctified—set apart to be God's people, we are to live as God's people and shun all that would defile. Therefore the fact of accomplished sanctification is one of the motivations to which Paul appeals for ethical conduct, particularly in the sexual sphere.

ESCHATOLOGY. Another strong motive influencing conduct is the eschatological. Christians as well as the world must stand before the judgment seat of God (Rom. 14:10) and of Christ (II Cor. 5:10) "so that each one may receive good or evil, according to what he has done in the body." While believers have not received the spirit of bondage to fear (Rom. 8:15), they are nevertheless exhorted to "make holiness perfect in the fear of God" (II Cor. 7:1). Slaves are exhorted to exercise obedience in fear and trembling (Eph. 6:5), and Christians are to work out their salvation in fear and trembling (Phil. 2:12); wrongdoers will be paid back for the wrong they have done (Col. 3:25).

Two different questions are raised in consideration of the eschatological motive: those of rewards and punishment for believers.[44] As to rewards, Paul's thought is fairly clear. He uses the motivation of rewards more as an incentive to faithful and effective ministry than to ethical living; but the two cannot be completely separated. The day of judgment will test every man's service for Christ. Those who have built upon the foundation of Christ will receive a reward. "If any man's work is burned up, he will suffer loss, though he himself will be saved, only as through fire" (I Cor. 3:15). Those who have a proper foundation but produce an unworthy work will not experience exclusion from the Kingdom but the loss of privilege and position in the Kingdom. We must conclude that Paul thought of graded positions in the Kingdom, which would be bestowed on the basis of Christian faithfulness.[45]

A more difficult question is whether Paul thinks that believers will lose their salvation if they deny their profession by grossly sinful lives. Several passages sound like it. When Paul writes the Galatians that he who "sows to his own flesh will from the flesh reap corruption" (Gal. 6:8), it is difficult to think that this is only of theoretical interest to Christians but that all believers will *ipso facto* sow to the Spirit. The stern warning of destruction upon those who destroy the church by false teaching and schism (I Cor. 3:17) certainly refers to leaders in the church. Paul's admonition to the Corinthians not to emulate the fall of the Israelites in the wilderness (I Cor. 10:6ff.) by immoral conduct suggests that salvation must evidence itself in moral living if it is to be real. The warning that immoral or impure

---

[43] A strongly attested reading is "let us have."
[44] See F. V. Filson, *St. Paul's Conception of Recompense* (1931), pp. 83-115.
[45] *Ibid.*, pp. 108, 115.

men or idolaters will not inherit the Kingdom of God (Eph. 5:5) is addressed to Christians. It is difficult to avoid the conclusion that when Paul describes his own self-discipline because he is engaged in a race to win an imperishable prize (*brabeion*) that is the goal of all Christians, he is referring to the prize of eternal life. In another passage the same word is used to refer to the resurrection (Phil. 3:11).[46] The crown he hopes to win at the end of the race is the crown of life—the eschatological gift of God.[47] Therefore when Paul contemplates the possibility that if he should "run aimlessly" he would be "disqualified" (*adokimos,* I Cor. 9:27), it is difficult to avoid the conclusion that he is thinking of the possible failure to reach the goal of the Christian life.[48]

From these passages and others like them, we must conclude that Paul uses the motivation of the final attainment of salvation in the Kingdom of God as a motivation to faithful and devoted Christian living. It is significant that Paul does not use the ethical sanction in any theoretical way that leads him to discuss the possibility of losing salvation; he uses it as a sanction to moral earnestness to avoid having the gospel of grace distorted into Hellenistic enthusiasm, libertinism, or moral passivity.[49] There is a deliberate tension in Paul's ethical exhortations: work out your own salvation . . . for it is God who works in you (Phil. 2:12). Eternal life is a free gift of God (Rom. 6:23), but it is at the same time a reward bestowed on those who have manifested steadfast loyalty in persecutions and afflictions (II Thess. 1:4ff.). Those who sow to the Spirit will reap the harvest of eternal life (Gal. 6:8).

LOVE. The most important motivation for Christian living is love. Love is the law of Christ (Gal. 6:2).[50] This means that the whole of ethical conduct can be subsumed in the principle of love, as Jesus taught (Mk. 10:30-31). Love fulfills the demands of the Law.[51] The Spirit is the Spirit of love (Rom. 15:30; Col. 1:8) who has shed abroad the love of God in our hearts (Rom. 5:5). The fruit of the Spirit is nothing but a commentary on the first fruit, showing how love acts (Gal. 5:22-23). The most excellent *charisma,* which all should covet, is love (I Cor. 13). "It is love which activates all human conduct (Col. 3:14). . . . The noble hymn of I Cor. 13 is at the centre of all Paul's teaching both for individual and social ethics."[52]

---

[46] See E. Stauffer, *TDNT* I, 638-39.
[47] See W. Grundmann in *TDNT* VII, 630.
[48] See F. V. Filson, *St. Paul's Conception of Recompense,* pp. 93, 103; C. K. Barrett, *First Corinthians,* p. 218.
[49] H. Preisker, *TDNT* IV, 722.
[50] V. Furnish, *Theology and Ethics in Paul,* p. 64 and references in n. 111; R. N. Flew, *Jesus and His Way* (1963), pp. 104ff.; L. Dewar, *NT Ethics,* pp. 27ff., 128. For a different interpretation of the "law of Christ," see above, p. 514.
[51] See p. 509.
[52] A. S. Herbert, "Biblical Ethics," *A Companion to the Bible,* ed. by H. H. Rowley (1963), p. 434.

One of the most vivid illustrations of how love should work out in Christian fellowship is seen in the problem raised by foods offered to idols. Every Hellenistic city had a large quota of temples, and most of the meat sold in the *macellum* or market (I Cor. 10:25) had come from a temple where it had first been sacrificed to a pagan deity, part of it possibly eaten at a feast in the temple, the rest sold to the public in the market. Jews were forbidden to eat foods that had been sacrificed to idols. The early church advised Gentile Christians in Asia Minor to abstain from these meats, not as a ground of salvation but as a *modus vivendi* with Jewish Christians who were deeply offended by the practice (Acts 15:20).

In such cities as Rome and Corinth (Rom. 14:1-23; I Cor. 8:1-13; 10:14-33), the situation was different. Paul seems not to have imposed the terms of the Jerusalem decree beyond Asia Minor. Christians in European cities were divided over the issue. Some felt that such food was unclean because it had been in association with pagan worship, while others felt that the food itself was not cultically contaminated and could be freely eaten. This created dissension in the churches. Those who ate these foods despised the narrow scruples of those who did not, while those who abstained sharply criticized and condemned those who ate (Rom. 14:2-4).

Paul's solution to the problem embodies a tension between freedom and love. He expressly forbids active participation in feasts in the temple (I Cor. 8:10). However, he clearly sides with those who feel that such foods are not unclean, and Christians are free in Christ to partake of any foods; nothing is unclean of itself (Rom. 14:14). He characterizes those who have strong scruples in such matters as weak in faith (Rom. 14:1). He clearly advises Christians to eat whatever they buy in the market without raising questions of conscience (I Cor. 10:25). Furthermore, if a Christian has a pagan friend who invites him to dinner, he is free to engage in such social intercourse and to eat what is served without asking questions (I Cor. 10:26). Those who have scruples against such food are to exercise love by not condemning those who have no such scruples (Rom. 14:3). On the other hand, those who feel free to eat are to show love by not despising those with strong scruples (Rom. 14:3). Those whose conscience offends them must not eat (Rom. 14:22); those whose conscience is clear are free to eat. However, love requires that when the free man finds himself in a situation where the exercise of his freedom would really offend a brother and cause him to violate his conscience and thus lead him to sin, in love he is to abstain. It would seem obvious that such abstinence is recommended only in cases where the weaker brother would be actually caused to sin; otherwise the whole standard of conduct in such matters would be decreed by the rigorism of the weakest Christians. "If the weaker brother's conscience is to govern the behavior of Christians generally, then Christian morality is inevitably bound in the fetters of rigorism."[53] The basic principle

---

[53] L. Dewar, *NT Ethics,* p. 173.

is clear: personal freedom must be tempered by love for the brethren. It is clear that such love is not an emotion but Christian concern in action.

INDICATIVE AND IMPERATIVE. We have found in several of the Pauline motivations for Christian living a tension between the indicative and the imperative. This is a reflection of the fundamental theological substructure of the whole of Pauline thinking: the tension between the two ages.[54] The Christian lives in two ages. He is a citizen of the new age while he still lives in the old age. The new has come (II Cor. 5:17) while the old remains. The indicative involves the affirmation of what God has done to inaugurate the new age; the imperative involves the exhortation to live out this new life in the setting of the old world. The new is not wholly spontaneous and irresistible. It exists in a dialetical tension with the old. Therefore the simple indicative is not enough; there must always be the imperative—man's response to God's deed.

This has profound significance for Pauline ethics,[55] and it can be explicitly illustrated from the hortatory portion of Paul's most theological letter: Romans 12:1-15:21.[56] "I appeal to you therefore, brethren, by the mercies of God, to present your bodies as a living sacrifice, holy and acceptable to God, which is your spiritual worship. Do not be conformed to this world (*aiōn*), but be transformed by the renewal of your mind, that you may prove what is the will of God, what is good and acceptable and perfect" (Rom. 12:1-2). The mercies of God (indicative) mean all that has been accomplished in the revelation of the righteousness of God (Rom. 1:17, indicative). On the basis of what God has done, Paul summons Christians to the ultimate act of worship by offering themselves to God (imperative).

This meaning of the imperative is further expanded in the exhortation not to be conformed to this age. Christians live in this age, but their life pattern, their standard of conduct, their aims and goals are not those of this age, which are essentially man-centered and prideful. The aim of the man who has experienced the life of the new age is to conform to the will of God. However, the will of God is not a decision that arises from within in answer to each moral decision that must be made; it must be "proven"—discovered, affirmed. The will of God here is not proper conduct in specific situations; it is the redemptive purpose of God for man. "God's will is that one should put his whole being at God's disposal. In this total 'belonging' to him he is to apply himself to what is good."[57]

This is accomplished only by an inner renewal of the mind. Only by a renewal of the mind can one prove what the will of God is. In biblical thought mind (*nous*) is not a term representing man's emotions or simply

---

[54] See above, pp. 369ff.

[55] It is the merit of V. Furnish to have accomplished this theological basis of the Pauline ethic as no previous scholar had done. See *Theology and Ethics in Paul.*

[56] See C. E. B. Cranfield, *A Commentary on Romans 12-13* (1965).

[57] V. Furnish, *Theology and Ethics in Paul,* p. 189.

his intellectual and rational capacity; it designates particularly his will. "By it (*nous*) is meant not the mind or the intellect as a special faculty, but the knowing, understanding, and judging which belong to man as man and determine what attitude he adopts."[58] The Christian's newness does not mean, as the AV has it, that "old things are passed away; behold, all things are become new" (II Cor. 5:17). It means rather that the new has broken into the context of the old. What is renewed—or made alive—is man's spirit (Eph. 2:1; Rom. 8:10) and his mind or will. He now wills to do the will of God; he now has dedicated himself to God as a living sacrifice in an act of spiritual worship. The renewed mind stands in obvious contrast to the "base mind" (*adokimon noun*) of Romans 1:28, which obviously does not refer to erroneous ideas or false theology but to a perverse will that manifests itself in all kinds of evil and corrupt conduct. Conversely, the renewed mind is conformable to the will of God. That this does not mean total inner ethical renewal is evident from the fact that Paul devotes three chapters to the exposition of proper Christian ethical conduct. "Even the renewed mind needs a good deal of motivation."[59]

ASCETICISM. This nonconformity to the world has often been understood in terms either of asceticism or of social disengagement. Paul does indeed teach self-discipline and the rigorous control of his body. "I pommel my body and subdue it, lest after preaching to others I myself should be disqualified" (I Cor. 9:27). This does not mean that Paul tried to smother his bodily appetites as though they were in themselves evil. On the contrary, God is to be glorified through the body (I Cor. 6:20), and the Christian is to eat and drink to the glory of God (I Cor. 10:31). However, since the body is a medium in which sin can function, the believer must control his body so that sin does not have the ascendancy (Rom. 6:12). The "deeds of the body"—its potential sinful activities—are to be put to death (Rom. 8:13; Col. 3:5). On the other hand, Paul expressly rejects ascetic practices. He rebukes the Colossians for following a dualistic teaching that sought to disparage the sacredness of bodily appetites by such regulations as "Do not handle, Do not taste, Do not touch," because they have an appearance of promoting a religious life of deep devotion to spiritual realities by treating the body with severity, when in reality "they are of no value in checking the indulgence of the flesh" (Col. 2:23). It is clear that "flesh" here is not bodily existence but the prideful human self that finds status in the externals of religion rather than in devotion and trust in God.[60] In fact, Paul designates this very ascetic interpretation of religion as an element of the world, because its appeal is to human pride and attainment rather than to humble trust in the salvation in Christ. The Christian view is that "the earth is the Lord's, and everything in it" (I Cor. 10:26). Paul was himself an ascetic in sexual matters (I Cor. 7:7), but he recognized that this was a special gift

58 R. Bultmann, *Theology of the NT,* I, 211.
59 C. K. Barrett, *Romans* (1957), p. 233.
60 For "flesh," see pp. 469ff.

given him that he might devote himself without distraction to the ministry of the gospel. He further wishes that all Christians could possess the same gift (I Cor. 7:1), but not because there is anything sinful in sex or because the celibate has achieved a higher level of morality and holiness than married people. His concern is entirely practical: "The unmarried man is anxious about the affairs of the Lord, how to please the Lord, but the married man is anxious about worldly affairs, how to please his wife, and his interests are divided" (I Cor. 7:33-34). Paul feels that the ideal would be for every Christian to be like him—a full-time missionary with no distractions; but this is to promote the gospel, not to achieve greater sanctification.

SEPARATION. In social relationships, Paul does command that the believer should not be mismated (literally, "unequally yoked") with unbelievers (II Cor. 6:14). This cannot mean the breaking of all ties and relationships that ordinarily relate believers and unbelievers in social intercourse. Paul expressly approves of a Christian fellowshiping with pagans on a social level; and in such a situation, the believer is not to raise questions of scrupulosity about whether the meat on the table has come from an idol temple (I Cor. 10:27). On the other hand, he expressly forbids joining with pagans in feasts in an idol temple (I Cor. 8:10), because his conduct might be interpreted as indifference to idolatry. The warning against the "unequal yoke" is directed against close ties that link Christians with unbelievers in pagan ways of thought and action. The fact that Paul interprets this prohibition in terms of idols (v. 16) and defilement of the body (7:1) suggests that he has in mind primarily the worship in pagan temples with the accompanying licentious revels and flagrant immorality. Nonconformity to this age means neither asceticism nor a rejection of the social mores of the world, but a rejection of its idolatry and sinful conduct. The Christian is both a citizen of his own culture and a citizen of the Age to Come at one and the same time.

VICES. The kind of life to which the new man is not to be conformed is set forth in several lists of vices (Rom. 1:29-32; I Cor. 5:11; 6:9; II Cor. 12:20; Gal. 5:19-21; Eph. 4:31; 5:3-4; Col. 3:5-9). These sins compose five groups: sexual sins—fornication, uncleanness, lasciviousness, adultery, sodomy, homosexuality; sins of selfishness—covetousness, extortion; sins of speech—whispering, backbiting, railing, boastings, shameful speaking, foolish talking, jesting, clamor; sins of attitude and personal relations—enmity, strife, factiousness, jealousy, wrath, dissension, heresies, envy; and sins of drunkenness—drunkenness, reveling, as well as idolatry.[61] If sexual sins predominate, it is not because such sins were considered worse than others, but because of the notorious immorality of the Graeco-Roman world. A famous saying illustrates this: "We have harlots for our pleasure, concu-

[61] For these lists, see L. Dewar, *NT Ethics,* pp. 147-48. See also L. H. Marshall, *The Challenge of NT Ethics,* pp. 278ff. Full lists are given in E. Wahlstrom, *The New Life in Christ,* pp. 281-87.

bines for daily physical use, wives to bring up legitimate children and to be faithful stewards in household matters."[62] Furthermore, temple prostitution was commonplace. The temple of Aphrodite in Corinth had a thousand sacred prostitutes. Fornication heads each list in which it appears. However, covetousness and idolatry occur in five of the lists, while wrath appears in four. Paul was greatly concerned about how Christians conducted their business affairs. Selfish ambition expressed in covetousness (lit., "the desire to have more") should have no place in the Christian's life.

It is of considerable interest that similar lists of vices are to be found in the pagan philosophical texts.[63] In his concept of sins to be avoided, Paul was not original, but is similar to the best in pagan thought. However, the fundamental motivation is radically different. The Greeks were interested in how the virtuous man might avoid that which would impair his moral stature; the vices Paul lists, on the other hand, belong to the old age and are antithetical to the newness that has been introduced by Christ. The one exalts human achievement; the other is centered in the redemptive act of God in Jesus Christ.

SOCIAL ETHICS. Paul does have a good bit to say about the Christian's relationship to the social institutions of his day. In our modern Christian outlook, social ethics commands a predominant place in our ethical thinking. By social ethics, we mean a concern that social structures should be based upon principles of humanity and concern for human well-being. It is difficult to find a clear social ethic in Paul. It is impossible to avoid the conclusion that Paul's eschatological perspective affected his attitude toward social structures. He seems to have no genuinely historical perspective nor to be concerned about the impact of the gospel on contemporary social structures. In fact, he expressly says, "In view of the impending distress, it is well for a person to remain as he is" (I Cor. 7:26). Married people should not seek to break the marriage bond, Jews should not try to appear like Gentiles and vice versa, slaves should not seek to be free even if the opportunity presents itself.[64] However, the context of the passage is one of indifference to one's situation in the social structures of the old age. "Every one should remain in the state in which he was called" (I Cor. 7:20) because "the form of this world is passing away" (I Cor. 7:31). The "impending distress" (I Cor. 7:26) and the shortness of the time (I Cor. 7:29) have been differently interpreted. The present distress may refer to the inevitable tension that arises between the new creation in Christ and the

---

[62] See *TDNT* I, 778.

[63] See A. Deissmann, *Light from the Ancient East* (1911), pp. 320ff.; M. Enslin, *The Ethics of Paul,* pp. 160ff.

[64] The language of I Cor. 7:21 is ambiguous. The RSV, "avail yourselves of the opportunity," i.e., to be free, is one interpretation of the Greek, and simply says, "Make use of it." This could mean, "Make use of your freedom if you have the opportunity to be free," but in the context it probably means "Make good use of your servitude" (NEB mg.). See L. H. Marshall, *The Challenge of NT Ethics,* p. 328; D. E. H. Whiteley, *The Theology of St. Paul,* pp. 226-27.

old age,[65] or to the idea that the eschatological woes (the great tribulation) are immediately impending and are already anticipated in the sufferings of Christians.[66] In any case, Paul clearly is dominated by a sense of the imminence of the parousia and the end of the world that rendered questions of social ethics comparatively irrelevant. "In the NT perspective, the inter-adventual period is short, however long it may be from our historically oriented viewpoint."[67] From this Murray draws the conclusion, "The eschatological perspective should always characterize our attitude to things temporal and temporary."[68] This is difficult in our modern world if it means indifference to the impact of the gospel on social structures. The cultural situation and structure of the church are very different from that of first-century Christianity, and the modern Christian cannot apply the teachings of Scripture in a one-to-one relationship but must seek the basic truth underlying the particular formulations in the New Testament.

WOMEN. This principle is obvious in the Pauline teaching about the status of women. Paul does indeed state a new Christian principle about the place of women in the eyes of God. "There is neither male nor female; for you are all one in Christ Jesus" (Gal. 3:28). Before God, women stand in a position not at all inferior to men. Furthermore, Paul admonishes men to love their wives with a concern analogous to the love of Christ (Eph. 5:25). In view of the low regard for women both in Judaism[69] and the Graeco-Roman world,[70] this was a revolutionary principle. However, Paul retains the Jewish idea of the subordination of woman to man. The head of every man is Christ, and the head of every woman is her husband (I Cor. 11:3). As man is the image and glory of God, so woman is the glory of man (I Cor. 11:7). This means that "the origin and *raison d'être* of woman are to be found in man."[71] Women are to show their subordination by never participating in public worship without having their heads veiled; only men may pray with bare heads (I Cor. 11:4ff.).[72] Furthermore, Paul says that he does not allow women to speak publicly in the gatherings for worship (I Cor. 14:34ff.).[73]

---

[65] See W. Grundmann, *TDNT* I, 346.

[66] C. K. Barrett, *First Corinthians,* p. 175; see R. Schnackenburg, *The Moral Teaching of the NT,* p. 190.

[67] J. Murray, *Principles of Conduct* (1957), p. 72.

[68] *Loc. cit.*

[69] J. Jeremias, *Jerusalem in the Time of Jesus* (1969), pp. 359ff.

[70] A. Oepke in *TDNT* I, 777-80.

[71] H. Schlier, *TDNT* III, 679.

[72] The entire problem of praying with covered or uncovered heads involves a social situation in Corinth that we cannot precisely recover. One fact is clear: a veiled head was a sign of the subordinate position of women. See W. Foerster, *TDNT* II, 573ff. and commentaries.

[73] For the apparent contradiction between this and I Cor. 11:4, see C. K. Barrett, *First Corinthians,* pp. 331f. Whiteley thinks the prohibition is directed against women addressing the assembly. D. E. H. Whiteley, *The Theology of St. Paul,* p. 223.

MARRIAGE. While Paul was himself a celibate and considered celibacy a gift of God that all should desire,[74] he recognized that not all men possessed this gift, and he expressly recommends that men marry rather than be consumed with unsatisfied sexual desires (I Cor. 7:9). This obviously takes a rather low view of marriage, but it is clearly non-ascetic. Within the marriage bond, Paul counsels unselfishness and self-giving. Neither husband nor wife should withhold sexual pleasure from the other (I Cor. 7:4-5), but each should be concerned to provide satisfaction for the other. Sex is here regarded not merely as a means of procreation but of mutual pleasure.

Paul flatly refuses to countenance divorce on the authority of the Lord himself. If a separation occurs, the woman must not marry again, and the husband may not divorce his wife (I Cor. 7:10-11). If one partner in a marriage becomes a Christian and the unbeliever does not wish to continue this relationship, the separation is admissible (I Cor. 7:12-15): "in such a case, the brother or sister is not bound" (I Cor. 7:15). This phrase is ambiguous and has been interpreted to mean "is not bound to continue to live with an unbeliever" or "is not tied to the marriage bond" and is therefore free to marry again. However, in view of Paul's clear refusal to recognize divorce, the former meaning is probably correct. If a man dies, the wife is free to marry again, providing the mate is a believer (I Cor. 7:39). Paul does not discuss whether a husband may marry if his wife dies; presumably it would be permitted.[75]

SLAVERY. One of the most evil institutions in the Graeco-Roman world was that of slavery. Slavery was universal and inseparable from the texture of society. It has been estimated that in the time of Paul there were as many slaves as free men in Rome, and the proportion of slaves to free men in Italy has been put as high as three to one.[76] In the fortunes of war, the population of entire cities were sold into slavery, and slaves were often more educated and cultured than their masters. While they were often treated with kindness and consideration, legally they were the property of their owners—things and not human beings. Their fate rested altogether on the whim and fancy of their masters.

Paul has no word of criticism for the institution as such. In this sense, he was unconcerned about "social ethics"—the impact of the gospel on social structures. In fact, he admonishes slaves to be indifferent to their social status (I Cor. 7:21), because a human slave is really a freedman of the Lord. The Christian faith is to be lived out within the context of existing social structures, for they belong to the form of this world, which is passing away (I Cor. 7:31). Therefore slaves as Christians are to be obedient and loyal to their masters, giving a full measure of service (Col.

---

[74] See above, p. 525.

[75] For a discussion of the difficult passage in I Cor. 7:31-38, which has little modern relevance, see D. E. H. Whiteley, *The Theology of St. Paul,* pp. 218-22.

[76] G. H. C. MacGregor and A. C. Purdy, *Jew and Greek: Tutors unto Christ* (1936), p. 264.

3:22-25; Eph. 6:5-8), while masters are to treat their slaves with justice and consideration (Col. 4:1; Eph. 6:9). When a runaway slave, Onesimus, met Paul in Rome and became a Christian, Paul sent him back to Philemon, his owner, with instructions to Philemon to welcome him as a brother in Christ (Phlm. 16). There is no word of setting the slave free. However, within the fellowship of the church, such social distinctions have been transcended (I Cor. 12:13; Gal. 3:28), even though they cannot be avoided in society.

Paul's attitude toward the state is set forth in the letter to the Romans.[77] Even though it was an authoritarian structure in whose functioning pagan religion played an important role, it was the agent of law and order, and as such is "the servant of God to execute his wrath on the wrongdoer" (Rom. 13:5). Even Christians—indeed, especially Christians—must be subject to the state because it is divinely ordained, and support it by paying the duly levied taxes. Support of law and order rests upon physical force: "he does not bear the sword in vain" (Rom. 13:4). It is probable that Paul's reference to a restraining power holding back the lawlessness of antichrist (II Thess. 2:6) is to the Roman government as an instrument of law and order.[78]

It is clear that Paul was not concerned about social structures but only with how the Christian should live out his Christian life within the contemporary social situation. He did indeed introduce Christian principles which, if faithfully practiced, would inevitably make a profound impact on social structures once the Christians became an influential people in society. But in his view social structures belong to the old age that is passing away. There is no evidence that Paul looked upon the church as a structure that would take its place with other social structures and change them for the good.

---

[77] See G. E. Ladd, "The Christian and the State," *His* (Dec. 1967), pp. 2ff.

[78] See below, p. 560.

37

THE CHURCH

Literature:

K. L. Schmidt, "Ekklēsia," *TDNT* III, 501-36; F. J. A. Hort, *The Christian Ecclesia* (1897); G. Johnston, *The Doctrine of the Church in the NT* (1943); S. Hanson, *The Unity of the Church in the NT: Colossians and Ephesians* (1946); J. R. Nelson, *The Realm of Redemption* (1951); J. A. T. Robinson, *The Body* (1952); E. Best, *One Body in Christ* (1955); R. P. Shedd, *Man in Community* (1958); L. Cerfaux, *The Church in the Theology of Paul* (1959); P. S. Minear, *Images of the Church in the NT* (1961); E. Schweizer, *Church Order in the NT* (1961); G. Johnston, "The Constitution of the Church in the NT," "The Doctrine of the Church in the NT," *Peake's Commentary on the Bible* (1962), pp. 719-27; N. A. Dahl, *Das Volk Gottes* (1963); C. W. Dugmore, "The Organization and Worship of the Primitive Church" in *A Companion to the Bible*, ed. by H. H. Rowley (1963[2]), pp. 546-69; A. Cole, *The Body of Christ* (1964); E. Schweizer, *The Church as the Body of Christ* (1964); B. Gärtner, *The Temple and the Community in the NT* (1965); R. Schnackenburg, *The Church in the NT* (1965); P. Richardson, *Israel in the Apostolic Church* (1969).

FORM. The outward form of the church as reflected in the Pauline epistles is basically the same as that reflected in Acts, with a few notable differences in emphasis. The church was made up of groups of believers scattered throughout the Mediterranean world from Antioch to Rome with no external or formal organization binding them together. The one obvious point of external or formal organization binding them together was apostolic authority. Paul as an apostle claimed an authority, especially in teaching, that he insisted must be recognized by all the churches.[1] However, this authority was that of spiritual and moral suasion, not formal and legal. Acts pictures Paul exercising his authority at the Jerusalem council in terms of persuasion rather than official authority. The final decision was made by the "apostles and the elders, with the whole church" (Acts

[1] See above, pp. 379ff.

15:22ff.). While Paul utters an anathema upon false teachers (Gal. 1:8), he took no formal or legal action against them. James exercised great authority in Jerusalem and was later thought to have been the first bishop of that city,[2] but it is not clear to what extent his authority extended beyond the city. "Those from James" (Gal. 2:12; cf. Acts 15:1) may have formally represented him, or may only have claimed his authority. In any case, the idea that the unity of the church found expression in some kind of external organization or ecclesiastical structure finds no support in the New Testament. Furthermore, the idea of denominations would be abhorrent to Paul. The nearest thing to denominations was the sects in Corinth that Paul heartily condemned (I Cor. 1:12ff.).[3]

The form of the church in a given city is not clear. The Corinthian correspondence suggests that all believers in Corinth gathered together in one place (I Cor. 14:23). Acts refers to gatherings in upper rooms in private houses (Acts 1:13; 12:12; 20:8), but it is difficult to believe that such a meeting place would be large enough to accommodate all the Christians in a given city. Archaeology confirms that for the first three centuries, the meeting place of Christians was private homes, not distinctive church buildings. Sometimes an entire house would be set aside for the Christian gathering.[4] On the other hand, Paul refers to "house churches," i.e., to groups of believers who gathered together in a particular house (Rom. 16:5; I Cor. 16:19; Col. 4:15; Phlm. 2; see also Rom. 16:14, 15).[5] There were probably enough Christians in each of the large Pauline cities to constitute several house churches. These facts leave the outward form of the local church rather unclear.

The organization of the local church is somewhat unclear in the major Pauline epistles, although a clearer picture emerges in the pastorals. Acts says that Paul appointed elders in the churches he founded (Acts 14:23), thereby extending into the Hellenistic churches the same structure that had developed in the Jerusalem church (Acts 11:30). The language of Acts suggests that the elders (*presbyteroi*) could also be called overseers or bishops (*episkopoi,* Acts 20:17, 28). In Paul's major epistles, elders are never mentioned; bishops and deacons provided leadership for the Philippian church (Phil. 1:1). That the Pauline churches had a formal leadership is clear from Paul's appeal to the Thessalonians to respect those who "are over you (*proistamenoi*) in the Lord and admonish you" (I Thess. 5:12). The same participle is used of church leaders in Romans 12:8. In view of the fact that the same participle is used in the pastorals of bishops (I Tim. 3:4), deacons (I Tim. 3:12), and elders (I Tim. 5:17), there is good

---

[2] See W. A. Beardslee, "James," *IDB* E-J, p. 793.

[3] See A. Richardson, *Theology of the NT* (1958), p. 286.

[4] See J. Finegan, *Light from the Ancient Past* (1946), pp. 399-409.

[5] See F. V. Filson in *JBL* 58 (1939), 105-12; L. Goppelt, *Apostolic and Post-Apostolic Times* (1970), p. 205.

reason to conclude that *proistamenoi* designates the office of elder-bishop and deacon.[6]

In Ephesians Paul refers to evangelists and pastor-teachers (Eph. 4:11). Evangelists are preachers who carry on the missionary task of preaching the gospel but without the authority of the apostles. The term denotes a function rather than an office.[7] Teaching is also mentioned as being next to apostles and prophets among the gifts of the Spirit (I Cor. 14:28f.). Since prophets were pneumatics, it is likely that teachers were nonpneumatics.[8] Teachers are also coupled with prophets in Acts 13:1. The language of Ephesians 4:11 suggests that pastor-teacher is a single office embodying a twofold function: that of shepherding or overseeing the flock, and of teaching. It is probable that this term designates leaders in the local church and is basically the same as *presbyteroi* and *episkopoi.*[9]

Paul also lists one of the gifts of the Spirit as "administration" (I Cor. 12:28). The word literally means "steersman," "helmsman," and must refer to the gift of leadership in the churches, "a true director of its order and therefore of its life." It is highly probable that this is the gift exercised by the *episkopoi* and the *proistamenoi.*[10]

The organization of the church appears in clearer outline in the pastoral epistles. The functions of deacons are not specifically described (I Tim. 3:8-12) because they were well known, but their qualifications are emphasized. Like elders, they must have the ability to rule well and be devoted to the gospel, but no reference is made to teaching. They must not be double-tongued or avaricious since they have access to many homes and are entrusted with the administration of funds.[11] Paul refers to women in the same context; these women obviously assisted the deacons and were probably deaconesses (see Rom. 16:1).

Both the qualifications and duties of elders are set forth in I Timothy 5:17-22. They exercise a threefold function: ruling, preaching, and teaching. The wording of the passage suggests that all elders rule but not all engage in preaching and teaching. This coincides with the injunction of Paul to the Ephesian elders to shepherd the flock, oversee it, and feed it (Acts 20:28). The duties of bishops are outlined in I Timothy 3:1-5. Aside from qualities of personal excellence, they must manifest gifts of teaching and ruling. The same qualities are listed in Titus 1:5-9, with the addition of hospitality and ability to defend the gospel against false teachers.

In the apostolic fathers, especially in Ignatius, the bishop emerges as distinct and superior to the elders, giving rise to the office of monarchical bishop. Many have contended that the pastorals reflect the beginning of

---

[6] Hebrews 13:7, 17 also refers to church leaders without calling them elders or bishops.
[7] G. Friedrich in *TDNT* II, 737.
[8] K. H. Rengstorf in *TDNT* II, 158.
[9] See J. Jeremias in *TDNT* VI, 498.
[10] H. W. Beyer in *TDNT* III, 1036.
[11] *Ibid.,* II, 90.

this development. Menoud points out that the bishop is always spoken of in the singular while deacons and elders are invariably mentioned in the plural. He concludes that there was only one bishop to a community and that he was responsible for duties distinct from those of the elders.[12] However, Lightfoot's famous essay[13] has persuaded many scholars that the two terms are interchangeable. Both elders and bishops engage in ruling and teaching, and the two words are used to describe the one office in Titus 1:5, 7.[14] However, the variety of scholarly opinion suggests that one can hardly be dogmatic in his understanding of the organization of the Pauline churches. Even if presbyter and bishop are two words for the same office, the picture is less than clear. That the presbyters acted as a college is clear from I Timothy 4:14, where Timothy was ordained by "the laying on of hands of the presbytery." However, it is not clear whether there was a single elder-bishop over each local congregation or a college of elders as in the Jewish synagogue; and in a large city with several congregations, it is not clear whether the elders of the several congregations constituted a single presbytery for the Christian community of the entire city. It appears likely that there was no normative pattern of church government in the apostolic age,[15] and that the organizational structure of the church is no essential element in the theology of the church. In view of the central theological emphasis on the unity of the church, it is important to understand that unity does not mean organizational uniformity.

CHARISMATA. Another important fact in the visible form of the Pauline churches was the exercise of spiritual gifts or *charismata.* The table below provides a survey of the several lists of spiritual gifts.

	I Cor.			*Rom.*	*Eph.*
	12:28	*12:29-30*	*12:8-10*	*12:6-8*	*4:4*
1. Apostle	1[16]	1			1
2. Prophet	2	2	5	1	2
3. Discernment of spirits			6		
4. Teacher	3	3		3	4

[12] P. H. Menoud in *IDB* A-D, p. 624. But see H. W. Beyer in *TDNT* II, 617. M. H. Shepherd also holds that elders and bishops represent two different orders. Bishops were elders appointed to the distinctive ministerial office, while elders enjoyed a position of honor, not of ministerial office. See *IDB* K-Q, p. 391.

[13] See J. B. Lightfoot, "The Christian Ministry," *Saint Paul's Epistle to the Philippians* (1890), pp. 181-269.

[14] See H. W. Beyer in *TDNT* II, 617. Goppelt believes that the local church leaders were called elders in Jewish Christianity and bishops in the Pauline churches, and that these two terms later conflated. L. Goppelt, *Apostolic and Post-Apostolic Times,* pp. 186-89.

[15] See W. D. Davies, "A Normative Pattern of Church Life in the NT" in *Christian Origins and Judaism* (1962), pp. 199-230. For an effort to interpret the New Testament data, see C. W. Dugmore, "The Organization and Worship of the Primitive Church," *A Companion to the Bible,* ed. by H. H. Rowley (1963), pp. 549-59.

[16] The numbers indicate the order of the gifts in the several passages.

5. Word of wisdom-knowledge			1		
6. Evangelists					3
7. Exhorters				4	
8. Faith			2		
9. Miracles	4	4	4		
10. Healings	5	5	3		
11. Tongues	8	6	7		
12. Interpretation		7	8		
13. Ministry				2	
14. Administration	7				
15. Rulers				6	
16. Helpers	6				
17. Mercy				7	
18. Giving				5	

Some scholars have argued that the leadership of the Pauline churches was altogether charismatic and not official. However, a careful study of these several gifts makes it clear that while some of them are truly charismatic, others are obviously natural gifts used by the Holy Spirit. Such functions as ministry, administration, ruling, helping, showing mercy, and giving employ the natural talents of men, while prophecy, miracles, healings, and tongues are supernatural endowments beyond the control of the individual. The noncharismatic functions were probably those exercised by elder-bishops, teachers, and deacons. However, Paul is discussing functions and not formal positions in the church. He writes I Corinthians not out of an interest in correct organization but proper ordering of the entire Christian fellowship. He conceives of every Christian as an active member of the body of Christ—"to each is given the manifestation of the Spirit for the common good" (I Cor. 12:8). The *charisma* granted to each is not so much a supernatural gift as the call of the Spirit to serve the church, so when Paul enumerates the *charismata,* he refers partly to offices and partly to functions.[17]

It is obvious that, apart from the priority of apostles and prophets, Paul attaches no special order of importance to the several gifts. Apostles and prophets were of primary importance because they were the vehicles of revelation (Eph. 3:5) and thereby provided the foundation for the church (Eph. 2:20). All apostles were prophets but not all prophets were apostles. Apostles were commissioned with an authority in the churches that the prophets did not possess. Prophets spoke by direct illumination of the Spirit (the Word of God). We must remember that the early churches did not possess the New Testament Scriptures that preserve for successive generations the prophetic witness of the meaning of the person and work of Christ. We do not know, although we can assume, that they possessed a fixed body

[17] L. Goppelt, *Apostolic and Post-Apostolic Times,* p. 183.

of catechetical tradition. In any case, it is clear from I Corinthians 12 and 14 that prophets were men inspired by the Spirit to speak in intelligible language a revelation from God. Their purpose was to edify the church (I Cor. 14:3). Prophecy was not an office but a gift that the Spirit could bestow on any member of the congregation. Christian prophets were concerned about future events so far as they involved the consummation of redemptive history, as the Revelation of John indicates (Rev. 1:3); but this element is not emphasized in the Pauline writings. Prophecy is the medium for disclosing the mysteries of God (I Cor. 13:2).

The gift of the Spirit most coveted in Corinth was the gift of tongues or glossolalia. The person experiencing this gift would utter praises to God in language that was intelligible neither to him nor to his hearers. The person speaking experienced great exaltation of spirit but had no rational communication of the will of God (I Cor. 14:14) as did the prophets. The experience was altogether meaningless to the hearers unless a gift of interpretation was given either to the speaker himself (I Cor. 14:13) or to another, who would then translate the unintelligible jargon into rational speech. Then the hearers would understand what was said and join in saying "Amen" (I Cor. 14:16). However, the Corinthians felt that tongues was the superlative evidence of the Spirit, and excesses in the exercise of this gift had introduced disorder and strife in the church. Paul declares the proper order. The goal is not personal ecstasy but the edifying of the church (I Cor. 14:26). No more than two or three may speak in a tongue in a single meeting, and only then in turn, and only if someone is present to interpret. Tongues are to be subordinate to prophecy, but prophetic utterance must also be conducted in an orderly manner (I Cor. 14:29).

It is important to note that some of the *charismata* are distinctly supernatural and can be exercised only by the sovereign activity of the Spirit, while others, such as helping, showing mercy, and giving are gifts that should be exercised by all Christians. The question as to whether all the *charismata* should be normative for the life of the entire church receives different answers. Since the gifts of apostleship and prophecy were given for the founding of the church (Eph. 2:20), it is possible that the distinctly supernatural gifts belong primarily to the apostolic period. In any case, Paul makes it clear that the highest manifestation of the Spirit is love. It is not always noted that I Corinthians 13 is a part of Paul's discussion of the *charismata*. Other gifts such as prophecy and tongues will cease, but love abides as the highest evidence of a Spirit-endowed believer.

EKKLĒSIA. The theology of the church can best be approached by surveying Paul's use of the word *ekklēsia*. The word in its Hellenistic setting can designate an assembly gathered as a political body (Acts 19:39) or an assembly as such (Acts 19:32, 39). However, in Paul the background of the word is the Old Testament use of *ekklēsia* of Israel as the people of God.[18]

---

[18] See above, pp. 109f. Acts 7:38 reflects this usage.

Implicit in the word is the claim that the church stands in direct continuity with the Old Testament people of God.

Ekklēsia can designate a meeting of Christians for worship; *en ekklēsia* (I Cor. 11:18; 14:19, 28, 35) can best be rendered simply "in church." This does not mean in a building called a church; *ekklēsia* is never used of a building as is the English word "church." It is the assembling of the saints for worship. As such, *ekklēsia* can designate the believers who gather in a particular home as a house-church (Rom. 16:5; I Cor. 16:19; Col. 4:15; Phlm. 2); it can designate the totality of believers living in one place—in Cenchrea (Rom. 16:1), Laodicea (Col. 4:16) or in the cities of Judaea (Gal. 1:22) and Galatia (Gal. 1:2). The most significant use, as in Acts,[19] is of the universal or catholic church. It is clearly used of the totality of all believers twice in Colossians (1:18, 24) and nine times in Ephesians (1:22; 3:10, 21; 5:23, 24, 25, 27, 29, 32). This usage probably appears also in I Corinthians 12:28; 15:9; Galatians 1:13; and Philippians 3:6, but this is contested.[20]

The very usage of *ekklēsia* is suggestive of Paul's concept of the church. The local congregation is the church; the totality of all believers is the church. This leads to the conclusion that the church is not conceived of numerically but organically. The church universal is not thought of as the totality of all the local churches; rather, "each community, however small, represents the total community, the Church."[21] The correct rendering of such verses as I Corinthians 1:2 and II Corinthians 1:1 is not "the Corinthian congregation standing side by side with other congregations," but "the congregation, church, assembly, as it is in Corinth." The local church is not part of the church but is *the church* in its local expression. This means that the whole power of Christ is available to every local congregation, that each congregation functions in its community as the universal church functions in the world as a whole, and that the local congregation is no isolated group but stands in a state of solidarity with the church as a whole.[22]

PEOPLE OF GOD. The church is the new people (*laos*) of God. The term "people" in biblical thought often has a technical sense designating those who stand in a special relationship to God. This usage is by no means unique to Paul but appears frequently in the New Testament. In the old dispensation, Israel was the people of God. Israel's rejection of her Messiah leads Paul to the question, "Has God rejected his people?" (Rom. 11:1). No further qualifier is necessary to designate Israel as God's people.[23] Paul devotes a long discussion to the problem of Israel (Rom. 9-11) in the course of which he makes it clear that the church is God's new people. This

---

[19] See above, p. 353.
[20] See D. E. H. Whiteley, *The Theology of St. Paul* (1964), p. 187.
[21] K. L. Schmidt, *TDNT* III, 506.
[22] D. E. H. Whiteley, *The Theology of St. Paul,* p. 190.
[23] See H. Strathmann, *TDNT* IV, 52.

is most vividly expressed in the use of quotations from Hosea. The prophet speaks of the present apostasy of Israel and her eschatological salvation. Hosea was directed to name one of his sons "Not my people," for apostate Israel was no longer God's people and he was not their God (Hos. 1:9). However, in the day of salvation, this situation will be changed; they will be called "Sons of the living God" (Hos. 1:10). "And I will say to Not my people, 'You are my people'; and he shall say, 'Thou art my God' " (Hos. 2:23). In Hosea these prophecies clearly refer to Israel, but Paul applies them to the church, which consists of both Jews and Gentiles (Rom. 9:24).[24] This does not mean that the title *laos* is taken from Israel, but that another people is brought into being along with Israel on a different basis. That Israel in some real sense remains the people of God is seen in Paul's affirmation that the Jewish people are still a "holy" people (Rom. 11:16), a people belonging to God. The fate of the Jews is seen in the light of the whole history of *Heilsgeschichte*. If the patriarchs—the first fruits and the root—are holy, so is the whole people. They are still "beloved for the sake of their forefathers, for the gifts and the call of God are irrevocable" (Rom. 11:28f.).

ISRAEL. This opens up the whole question of the relationship between the church and Israel. Paul clearly distinguishes between empirical Israel and spiritual Israel—between the people as a whole and the faithful remnant. "For not all who are descended from Israel belong to Israel" (Rom. 9:6). Here Paul sets over against the Israel according to natural descent the true Israel who have been faithful to God. While the nation as a whole has rejected her Messiah, there is a remnant chosen by grace (Rom. 11:5) who have believed. A real Jew is not one who is outwardly a Jew; he is a Jew who is one inwardly; and circumcision is not a thing of the flesh but of the heart (Rom. 2:28f.). This may not refer to all believers but only to those Jews who have truly fulfilled the Law.

To this believing remnant have been added believing Gentiles. Paul's metaphor of the olive tree suggests the unity of the old people of God—Israel—and the church. The olive tree is the one people of God. Natural branches—unbelieving Jews—were broken off, and wild branches—believing Gentiles—were grafted onto the tree. "This makes it perfectly clear that the church of Jesus Christ lives from the root and the trunk of the Old Testament Israel."[25]

Thus, while God has not finally and irrevocably cast away his people Israel, the church consisting of both Jews and Gentiles has become the branches of the olive tree—the people of God—the true Israel. Not only faithful Jews, but all believers, including Gentiles, are the true circumcision who worship God in spirit and glory in Christ Jesus (Phil. 3:3). All such have been circumcised in heart (Col. 2:11). As the spiritually circumcised, they are the children of Abraham (Gal. 3:7), their father (Rom.

[24] See also II Cor. 6:16; Tit. 2:14.
[25] H. J. Kraus, *The People of God in the OT* (1958), p. 89.

4:11, 16, 18); they are the offspring (Gal. 3:29) and descendants of Abraham (Rom. 4:16). Those who formerly were alienated from the commonwealth of Israel and strangers to the covenants of promise (Eph. 2:12) have now been brought near to the God of Israel. In view of such statements, it is highly probable that when Paul speaks of the "Israel of God" (Gal. 6:16) he is referring to the church as the true spiritual Israel.[26] This is also implied when Paul speaks of "Israel after the flesh" (I Cor. 10:18), which is implicitly contrasted with "Israel after the spirit."[27]

This does not mean that Paul shuts the door to Israel after the flesh.[28] The whole tenor of Paul's use of the metaphor of the olive tree is that while natural branches—Jews—have been broken off the olive tree and wild branches—Gentiles—grafted into the people of God, it is God's sovereign pleasure yet to bring the natural branches to faith and so graft them back into the tree (Rom. 11:23-24). Paul's argument is circular. Israel did not stumble in unbelief so as finally to fall (Rom. 11:11), but that through their unbelief salvation might come to the Gentiles. The salvation of the Gentiles will in turn provoke Israel to jealousy. "If their trespass means riches for the world, and if their failure means riches for the Gentiles, how much more will their full inclusion mean?" (Rom. 11:12). Even in unbelief, Israel remains a "holy" people (Rom. 11:16) and will finally be grafted back into their own olive tree (Rom. 11:24). In this manner—by provocation by the Gentiles—"all Israel will be saved" (Rom. 11:26). This is the language of *Heilsgeschichte* and does not mean that every last Israelite will be saved but the people as a whole.[29] Paul does not speculate when or how the salvation of the Jews will take place, but it is probably an eschatological event to occur at the end of the age.[30] Whatever form the salvation of Israel takes, it is clear that the terms of salvation must be the same as those for the Gentiles: faith in Jesus as the crucified and risen Messiah.

THE TEMPLE OF GOD. Another metaphor Paul uses that shows that the church is the true Israel is that of the temple. Both the Old Testament and Judaism anticipated the creation of a new temple in the Kingdom of God

---

26 So W. Gutbrod, *TDNT* III, 387; A. Richardson, *The Theology of the NT,* p. 353; P. Minear, *Images of the Church* (1961), p. 71; E. Schweizer, *Church Order in the NT* (1961), p. 89; it is contested by P. Richardson, *Israel in the Apostolic Church* (1969), pp. 74ff. Richardson insists in a detailed study that the phrase designates the believing remnant in Israel. "Israel" is not applied to the church, though all Christians become a part of Israel by virtue of their faith in Christ (p. 147).

27 The RSV omits "after the flesh."

28 "Christianity could not pre-empt the title 'Israel' without shutting the door to Judaism." P. Richardson, *Israel in the Apostolic Church,* p. 201.

29 W. Gutbrod, *TDNT* III, 387. See P. Richardson, *Israel in the Apostolic Church,* pp. 126ff.

30 See J. Munck, *Christ and Israel* (1967), pp. 136f. O. Piper suggests that the salvation of Israel does not mean that the Jews will be transformed into a Gentile church. Rather, they will form a distinct type of Christianity in which they will preserve everything in their heritage compatible with their dedication to the Messiah. "Church and Judaism in Holy History," *TT* 18 (1961), 70-71.

(Ezek. 37:26ff.; 40:1ff.; Hag. 2:9; En. 90:29; 91:13; Jub. 1:17, 29). Jesus had spoken of the formation of his church as the erection of a building (Mt. 16:18). He was also reported as uttering an enigmatic prophecy: "I will destroy this temple that is made with hands, and in three days I will build another, not made with hands" (Mk. 14:58). It is possible that this was understood by the early Christians to mean the establishment of the new messianic community.[31] While the primitive community continued as Jews to worship in the temple (Acts 2:46), Stephen was the first to realize that temple worship was irrelevant for Christians (Acts 7:48f.). Paul sees the Christian community taking the place of the temple as the eschatological temple of God, as the place where God dwells and is worshipped.

This metaphor had a threefold emphasis. The individual believer has become a temple of God because the Spirit of God indwells him (I Cor. 6:19). As the temple of God, the believer is holy; he belongs to God. Therefore he is not his own and may not dispose of his life as he may desire. Immorality is a contradiction of the essential character of the believer. There was a libertine tendency in Corinth that disparaged the body under the slogan, "All things are lawful for me" (I Cor. 6:12), even sexual license. Paul corrects this view by the affirmation that the body is the temple of God's Spirit.

Not only the individual believer but also the local congregation is the temple of God because the Spirit indwells the corporate fellowship. This again has a very practical application. As the dwelling place of God, the congregation is a holy people. The community in Corinth was rent by schisms that clustered around four prominent names: Paul, Apollos, Cephas, and Christ. This seems not to have been mere sectarianism but to have resulted from the impact of gnosticizing Judaism[32] that had in turn disrupted the church. This situation Paul condemns in frightening language. Because the local church is God's dwelling place, whoever "destroys," i.e., brings ruin upon, the local congregation by false teaching and destroys its unity, him will God destroy (I Cor. 3:17).

The fact that the church is the temple where God dwells excludes the logical possibility of becoming "mismated with unbelievers" (II Cor. 6:14). This must refer to relationships with idolatrous pagans of such a sort that it compromised one's Christian testimony. It is clear that Paul does not mean to prohibit all social contacts with unbelievers, "since then you would need to go out of the world" (I Cor. 5:10). The clue to Paul's meaning is found in the words, "what agreement has the temple of God with idols?" (I Cor. 6:16). Any yoke with unbelievers that compromised one with idolatrous and unusual practices (I Cor. 6:15) was excluded because of the holiness of the church.

Paul applies the same metaphor to the universal church (Eph. 2:19-22). Gentile believers are no longer aliens from God's people; they are God's

[31] See O. Michel, *TDNT* IV, 883, 886.
[32] See L. Goppelt, *Apostolic and Post-Apostolic Times,* pp. 98ff.

true household; they are in fact a temple built upon the foundation of Christ, the apostles, and the prophets, who grow into a holy temple in the Lord. Here in the church rather than in Judaism is the dwelling place of God to be found. The presence of God has removed from the Jerusalem temple to the new temple, the Christian church.[33]

The fact that Paul uses the metaphor of the temple to designate both the local and the universal church reinforces a fact already evident in the use of *ekklēsia,*[34] namely, the unity of the church in its diversity. The local congregation is not part of the church; the universal church is not thought of as the sum and total of its parts; rather, the local congregation is the church in its local expression.

AN ESCHATOLOGICAL PEOPLE. This leads us to the idea that the church is an eschatological people. We have found that the expectation of a new temple was an eschatological concept that was applied to the church. The church is also the people of the Kingdom of God and therefore an eschatological people. This means two things. They are destined to inherit the Kingdom in its eschatological consummation (I Thess. 2:12; Rom. 8:17; Eph. 1:18), because they have already experienced that same Kingdom (Col. 1:13; Rom. 14:17).[35]

This fact is expressly affirmed in Philippians 3:20, where Paul affirms that the Christians' true homeland (*politeuma*)[36] is heaven; and we await the coming of the Lord, who will fulfill the eschatological hope by the transformation of our lowly bodies. This statement had particular significance to the Philippians, who constituted a Roman colony in the heart of Greece. The word *politeuma* designates a colony of foreigners whose organization reflects their native homeland. "We have our own home in heaven and are here on earth a colony of citizens of heaven."[37] The life and fellowship of Christians in history is to be a foretaste of life in the Kingdom of God and is to reflect in the world something of what the eschatological reality will be.

This truth is affirmed also in Galatians 4:24f., where Mount Sinai as the mother of children of slavery is contrasted with the heavenly Jerusalem as the mother of children of freedom—Christians.

THE HOLY SPIRIT. The eschatological character of the church is seen in the fact that the church is created by the Holy Spirit. We have seen above[38]

---

[33] See B. Gärtner, *The Temple and the Community in Qumran and the NT* (1965), p. 65; see also S. Hanson, *The Unity of the Church in the NT* (1946), p. 133. The fact that the new temple grows proves that it is an organic and not a static concept.

[34] See above, p. 537.

[35] The eschatological nature of the church is a theme pervading S. Hanson's work (*The Unity of the Church in the NT*), but he applies it primarily to the concept of unity, which is an eschatological concept already realized in the church.

[36] The translation of the AV, "conversation," is utterly misleading.

[37] See M. Dibelius, *An die Thessalonicher I. II. An die Philipper* (1937), p. 93.

[38] See pp. 370f.

that the presence of the Holy Spirit is an eschatological fact. It is the coming of the eschatological Spirit in history that created the church. The church is therefore the product of the powers of the Age to Come. While the Holy Spirit works diversely in the church bestowing different gifts upon different individuals (I Cor. 12:7), the Holy Spirit himself is the possession of all believers. Peter said on the day of Pentecost that all who repent and are baptized would receive the gift of the Holy Spirit (Acts 2:38; appositive genitive). Paul affirms that possession of the Spirit is necessary to belong to Christ (Rom. 8:9). While Paul places great emphasis on the work of the Spirit in individual Christian experience, it also has a corporate side: it is the work of the Holy Spirit to create the church. "By one Spirit we were all baptized into one body—Jews or Greeks, slaves or free—and were all made to drink of one Spirit" (I Cor. 12:13). Most contemporary scholars believe that baptism here refers to water baptism as the means by which the Spirit is imparted to believers. "Baptism in water is baptism in the Spirit."[39] This, however, is not self-evident and should not be taken for granted. It makes considerable difference whether Paul means to say that water baptism is "the means of incorporation into the Christian community,"[40] or that an act of the Holy Spirit is the means of incorporation into the Christian community. It appears highly probable that "the baptism of I Cor. 12:13 . . . is not water baptism but baptism in the Spirit. Water baptism is the sign and seal of this latter baptism."[41] If Paul has water baptism in mind, he does not emphasize it; the entire emphasis is on the work of the Spirit. Both John the Baptist (Mt. 3:11) and the resurrected Lord (Acts 1:5) distinguished between water baptism and Spirit baptism, and Paul's central thought is the work of the Holy Spirit in forming the church.

It can be debated whether baptism *en heni pneumati* should be understood as a dative of agent or of sphere. If we use Matthew 3:11 and Acts 1:5 as an analogy, the Spirit is the sphere of baptism in contrast to water; but the analogy of the context in I Corinthians 12:9 suggests that the Spirit is the agent of the baptism.[42] In either case, the role of the Spirit is emphasized; it is the work of the Holy Spirit to form the body of Christ. This remains true even if water baptism is also in Paul's mind, although few commentators emphasize this fact. When a person believes in Christ and is baptized, he becomes a member of the body of Christ. This fact is not to be confused with the New Testament teaching about the indwelling of the Spirit or the gifts of the Spirit for service (I Cor. 12:5); it is viewed as an objective fact. In New Testament thought there can be no such thing as an isolated believer—a Christian who stands remote from other Christians. When he believes in Christ, he is made a member of Christ's

---

[39] G. R. Beasley-Murray, *Baptism Today and Tomorrow* (1966), p. 56.

[40] W. F. Flemington, "Baptism," *IDB* A-D, p. 350.

[41] E. Best, *One Body in Christ* (1955), p. 73; J. D. G. Dunn, *Baptism in the Holy Spirit* (1970), pp. 127-31.

[42] See G. R. Beasley-Murray, *Baptism in the NT* (1962), pp. 167ff.; H. Oepke, *TDNT* II, 541.

body; he is joined to Christ himself and therefore to all others who in union with Christ constitute his body. In the biblical sense of the word, it is true that *extra ecclesiam nulla salus*. The Holy Spirit has been given by the exalted Christ to form a new people in history who constitute his body.

The eschatological character of this new people carries with it the fact that it cuts across our normal human sociological structures. Race does not matter; social status does not matter; by Spirit baptism all kinds of people are equally members of the body of Christ because we have all experienced the eschatological outpouring of the Spirit.[43]

FELLOWSHIP. One of the most notable features in this eschatological people is that of fellowship (*koinōnia*).[44] Fellowship was one of the distinctive marks of the Jerusalem church (Acts 2:42). This is something more than human fellowship or the pleasure people of like mind find in each other's presence. It is more than a fellowship in a common religion. It is an eschatological creation of the Holy Spirit. Probably II Corinthians 13:14 should be rendered "the fellowship created by the Holy Spirit"; and Philippians 2:1 may be rendered "if the Spirit has really created a fellowship."[45] This relationship exists between people because they share a common relationship to Christ (I Cor. 1:9). A bond exists between all who are in Christ that is unique and transcends all other human relationships.

From the divine side, those who have entered this fellowship do so because they have been called of God (I Cor. 1:9). The church is a fellowship of the elect (Eph. 1:4; I Thess. 1:4), regardless of social status, education, wealth or race (I Cor. 1:27). The church can be designated simply as the elect of God (Rom. 8:33; Col. 3:12; II Tim. 2:10; Tit. 1:1). This emphasizes the fact that the church is not primarily a human institution nor a religious movement founded on good works or even allegiance to a great teacher or leader; it is a creation of God based on his gracious purpose (Rom. 9:11; 11:5-6). It can never be a people, like Israel, formed upon natural or racial lines. There is in the church, indeed, a nucleus of Jews; but they are a remnant, chosen by grace (Rom. 11:5). The idea of election is not primarily that of the individual to salvation, but a *Heilsgeschichte* concept of the election of the people of God. The background of

---

43 The phrase rendered "all were made to drink of one spirit" is taken by many scholars to refer to the cup at the Lord's Supper (L. Goppelt, *TDNT* IV, 160, 147), but the idea of drinking the Spirit is not a New Testament idea. The word (*epotisthēmen*) can also mean "we were immersed in one Spirit . . . and were saturated in His outpouring" (G. R. Beasley-Murray, *Baptism in the NT*, p. 170).

44 See C. A. A. Scott, *Christianity According to St. Paul* (1927), pp. 158ff.; A. R. George, *Communion with God* (1953), pp. 169ff.

45 See C. A. A. Scott, *Christianity According to St. Paul*, p. 160; see also E. Schweizer, *TDNT* VI, 434. Other scholars interpret these verses as objective genitives. A. R. George, *Communion with God*, pp. 17ff.

the term is Israel as the elect people of God,[46] and it designates the church as the successors of Israel. It is primarily a corporate concept.[47]

SAINTS. Again, from the divine side, the church is a fellowship of the saints (*hagioi*) or the sanctified (*hagiasmenoi*). This is one of Paul's most common terms for Christians. The root idea of holiness is carried over from the Old Testament and designates anything set apart for divine use. Jerusalem is the holy city (Mt. 4:5; 27:53); the temple is the holy place (Mt. 24:15; Acts 6:13); the altar is holy as well as the gift offered on the altar (Mt. 23:19); the Law is holy (Rom. 7:12); Israel is a holy people (Isa. 62:12); the church as the new Israel is the fellowship of holy ones or saints.[48]

Almost never is *hagios* used in the singular designating individual members of the church.[49] That the term carries primarily a *Heilsgeschichte* rather than an ethical connotation is proven by Paul's address to the Corinthians as "those sanctified in Christ Jesus, called to be saints" (I Cor. 1:2). The congregation in Corinth was anything but a "holy" people in terms of life and conduct; false teaching, schisms, and immorality marred the church. Still, it was a congregation of saints, of the sanctified, because in spite of the sinful conduct of many of its members and the worldly character of the church itself, it was still the church of God in Corinth. As such, Christ has become its sanctification (I Cor. 1:30; 6:11) as well as its redemption. Paul's challenge to his churches was that they should realize in life and conduct what was already theirs in Christ. Because they were the saints of God, they were to live holy lives.

BELIEVERS. If from the divine side the church is a fellowship of elect saints, from the human side it is a fellowship of those who respond to the proclaimed Word of God and who believe in Jesus Christ and confess him as Lord (Rom. 10:9). The church consists of those who call upon the name of the Lord Jesus Christ (I Cor. 1:2) and can be designated by the term "believers" (*hoi pisteuontes*) (I Cor. 1:21; 14:22; Gal. 3:22; I Thess. 1:7; II Thess. 2:13). That personal faith in Jesus Christ is constitutive of the church is clear from Romans 4, where Paul argues that the salvation wrought by Christ is effective only to those who, like Abraham, believe. Abraham was not accepted by God because of good works of religious rites (circumcision) but because he believed God. Circumcision was the sign or seal of the righteousness that he had by faith. Thus he is the father of all who believe apart from the rites of Judaism but who emulate the faith of Abraham (Rom. 4:11f.).

The indispensable role of saving faith is again illustrated in Romans 9:30-32. Israel according to the flesh was rejected because they sought

[46] See references in Arndt-Gingrich, *Lexicon,* p. 242.

[47] See A. Richardson, *The Theology of the NT,* pp. 274f.; P. Minear, *Images of the Church in the NT,* pp. 81f.

[48] References in Arndt-Gingrich, *Lexicon,* p. 10.

[49] P. Minear, *Images of the Church,* p. 136.

righteousness by works, whereas Gentiles attained unto righteousness and were brought into the true Israel because they sought it by faith. Here is an outstanding difference between participation in the old and the new Israel. Membership in the old Israel required circumcision and acceptance of the Law; membership in the new Israel requires individual personal faith and confession of Christ as Lord (Rom. 10:9).

THE BODY OF CHRIST. The most distinctive Pauline metaphor for the church is the body of Christ. Scholars have debated the source of this concept and numerous theories have been propounded.[50] However, the background for the idea is not important. What is important is the use Paul makes of it. Possibly Paul may have formulated the idea of the body of Christ out of his own creative mind.[51]

Paul never speaks of the church as a body per se; it is the body *in Christ* (Rom. 12:5) or the body of Christ (I Cor. 12:27). As his body, the church is in some sense identified with Christ (I Cor. 12:12). This is an amazing statement. "For just as the body is one and has many members, and all the members of the body, though many, are one body, so it is with Christ." We would have expected Paul to say, "so it is with the church." Paul uses the metaphor of the body to express the oneness of the church with her Lord. The church is not a body or society of believers but the body of Christ. The primary emphasis of the metaphor is the unity of believers with Christ;[52] but Paul introduces the concept both in Romans and Corinthians to deal with the problem of Christians' relations to one another.

This truth of the solidarity of believers with the Lord has a background in the teaching of Jesus and in Paul's conversion experience. "He who receives you receives me" (Mt. 10:40); "as you did it to one of the least of these my brethren, you did it to me" (Mt. 25:40). The voice Paul heard on the Damascus Road where he was journeying to persecute the church asked him, "Saul, Saul, why do you persecute me?" (Acts 9:4).

This close relationship falls short of being one of complete identity. Paul does say once that "your bodies are members of Christ" (I Cor. 6:15). But in the discussion in I Corinthians 12, Christians are thought of as members of Christ's body rather than members of Christ. It is too much to say that Paul thought of the church as an extension of the incarnation—that just as God was incarnate in Christ, Christ is incarnate in the church. Paul preserves a clear distinction between Christ and his church.

The reason Paul draws upon the metaphor of the church as the body of Christ in Romans and Corinthians is, as already noted, to establish the proper relationship of Christians to each other. There is one body but it has many members, and these members differ greatly from one another. There was a tendency, particularly in Corinth, to make distinctions among

---

[50] See E. Best, *One Body in Christ,* pp. 83-93, where he discusses seven different theories.

[51] *Ibid.,* p. 94.

[52] *Ibid.,* p. 93; C. F. D. Moule, *Colossians and Philemon* (1957), p. 6.

Christians and to covet the more spectacular gifts of the Spirit. This led to tensions and dissensions in the congregation. Paul argues that there are admittedly great differences in the roles of different members of the body, but they all belong to the body, and the least member is important. Since it is God who has arranged the members of the body as it has pleased him, there should be no discord but only mutual love and concern among the several members of the church (I Cor. 12:24f.). Indeed, the inferior members should receive the greater honor.

Paul carries the metaphor a step further in the prison epistles and speaks of Christ as the head of the body—an idea not found in Romans or Corinthians (Eph. 4:15; Col. 1:18). This makes it clear that Paul does not completely identify Christ and his church. He is the Savior of the body (Eph. 5:23). Paul obviously goes beyond the ordinary analogy of the physical body and its head, for the body is pictured as deriving its nourishment and unity from the head (Col. 2:19); and the body is to grow up in every way into him who is the head (Eph. 4:15).[53] This emphasizes even more than the earlier epistles the complete dependence of the church upon Christ for all of its life and growth. This also means that the church is the instrument of Christ in the world. It is "the fullness of him who fills all in all" (Eph. 1:23). "Fullness" (*plērōma*) has two different meanings. Some take it to mean that the church completes Christ—fills him up. However, it is easier to take it to mean that the church as the body of Christ is filled with his life and power,[54] which are to work through Christ in the world. The church is a "partaker of all that He owns and is for the purpose of continuing his work."[55]

This metaphor emphasizes also the unity of the church, especially since *ekklēsia* in Ephesians and Colossians refers to the universal church rather than the local congregation. The final goal of Christ's redemptive ministry is to restore order and unity in the whole universe, which has been disrupted by sin. God's plan is "to unite all things in him, things in heaven and things on earth" (Eph. 1:10). This cosmic unity in Christ has already been achieved in principle. He has already been exalted far above every hostile power and has been made head over all things for his church (Eph. 1:22). In this context, "head" is not analogous to the head of the body but represents primacy.[56] Probably the goal stated in Ephesians 4:13 is eschatological: "until we all attain to the unity of the faith and of the knowledge of the Son of God, to mature manhood, to the measure of the stature of the fulness of Christ."[57] However, the very certainty of the eschatological unity de-

[53] Some scholars think that Paul is here making use of the gnostic concept of a heavenly *anthrōpos* who is the head of the universe, which is his body (H. Schlier, *TDNT* III, 680). However, this is quite unlikely (G. Delling, *TDNT* VI, 304; S. Hanson, *The Unity of the Church,* pp. 113ff.).

[54] E. Best, *One Body in Christ,* p. 142; G. Delling, *TDNT* VI, 304.

[55] S. Hanson, *The Unity of the Church,* p. 129.

[56] So I Cor. 11:3, where man is the head of woman.

[57] H. Chadwick in *Peake's Commentary* (1962), p. 984; O. Michel, *TDNT* III, 624. In I Cor. 13:11-12, Paul uses the same contrast of childhood-maturity to

mands the effort to realize this unity in Christ in history. This unity is not something to be created; it is given in Christ, although it can be disrupted (Eph. 4:3). There is and can be only one church because there is only one Christ, and he cannot be divided (I Cor. 1:13). "There is one body and one Spirit . . . one hope . . . one Lord, one faith,[58] one baptism, one God and Father of all" (Eph. 4:4-6). This unity is not a static thing consisting of outward structure or formal organization. Indeed, in outward form the church of A.D. 50-60 consisted of many scattered autonomous communities.[59] There does not seem to have been a single prevailing form of church government. The unity is one of Spirit and life, of faith and fellowship. It is a unity that is realized in considerable diversity. It is a unity that should exclude schism in the local congregation (I Cor. 1:13), which expresses itself in humble preference of one another (Rom. 12:3) and in mutual love and affection (I Cor. 12:25-26), which means the end of racial distinctions (Eph. 2:16) and which should exclude doctrinal and religious aberrations (Col. 2:18-19).

THE EUCHARIST. The unity of the body of Christ is further illustrated by the Eucharist. "Because there is one loaf [*artos*—bread], we who are many are one body, for we all partake of the same loaf" (I Cor. 10:17). Paul here uses the symbolism of a loaf of bread broken in pieces and distributed among the worshippers to illustrate the oneness of the individual members (see *Didachē* 9:4). Unity must exist among the participants of the Eucharist because they have a prior unity with Christ. The drinking of the cup is participation in the blood of Christ, and the eating of the bread is participation in the body of Christ (I Cor. 10:16). Believers find their unity in Christ. The question of how realistically these words should be taken is widely debated. The cup and the bread are indeed a memorial of the death of Christ, and are used in memory of Jesus' death (I Cor. 11:25). But eating and drinking involve more than a memory of a past event; they also represent participation in the body and blood of Christ, and therefore participation in his body. "The bread and the wine are vehicles of the presence of Christ. . . . Partaking of bread and wine is union (sharing) with the heavenly Christ."[60] However, the Eucharist mediates fellowship with Christ in the same sense that the altar in the Old Testament economy mediated fellowship with God, and sacrifices to idols mediated fellowship with demons (I Cor. 10:18-21). Some interpret these words in a very realistic, sacramental sense, others in a more symbolic, metaphorical sense. It is faith by which one is identified with Christ in his death and becomes a member of his body; partaking of the bread and cup constitutes an event in which faith apprehends Christ. "The real presence

illustrate life in this age in contrast to life in the Age to Come when we shall see face to face.

58 Objective, meaning a single confession of faith. B. F. Westcott, *Ephesians* (1906), p. 59; S. Hanson, *The Unity of the Church,* p. 154.

59 See above, pp. 352f.

60 F. Hauck, *TDNT* III, 805.

of Christ in the Lord's Supper is exactly the same as his presence in the Word—nothing more, nothing less."[61]

BAPTISM also symbolizes union with Christ. Unless I Corinthians 12:13 refers to water baptism,[62] baptism does not have the same corporate emphasis as the Eucharist. Baptism is the rite of admission into the church, but it represents the identification of the believer with Christ. Men are baptized "into Christ Jesus" (I Cor. 6:3). Baptism "into Christ" means to put on Christ (Gal. 3:27). Baptism means union with Christ in his death and resurrection (Rom. 6:1-4; Col. 2:12). It is not a repetition of the death and resurrection of Christ, nor does it symbolize his death and resurrection. It symbolizes the believer's union with Christ in which he dies to his old life and is raised up to walk in newness of life. It is a symbol of spiritual death and resurrection. Paul does not speak of baptism as a cleansing, unless I Corinthians 6:11, Ephesians 5:26, and Titus 3:5 are oblique references to the baptismal waters.

As with the Eucharist, it is widely debated to what extent baptism is sacramental and to what extent symbolic. The question cannot be finally resolved, for in the early church saving faith and baptism were practically synonymous. However, in New Testament terms, "we should never of course say 'baptism' without also thinking 'faith.' "[63] Without faith, baptism has no meaning. "You were buried with him in baptism, in which you were also raised with him through *faith* in the working of God" (Col. 2:12). In I Corinthians 10:1-13 Paul combats a materialistic and genuinely sacramental view of baptism and the Lord's Supper.[64] Certainly Paul did not think that the Israelites were united with Moses in any truly sacramental sense when they were baptized in Moses in the cloud and in the sea (I Cor. 10:2). Furthermore, it is doubtful whether Paul would have written about baptism as he does in I Corinthians 1:13-16 if he had considered it a true sacrament. This is not to minimize the importance of baptism and the Lord's Supper. Surely Paul could not have conceived of any believer who did not partake of the two Christian rites.

It is not at all clear that Paul conceived of baptism as the Christian equivalent of circumcision.[65] The "circumcision of Christ" (Col. 2:11) is easiest to understand as the circumcision of the heart that Christ performs.[66] This is an altogether spiritual event, one "made without hands,"

---

61 E. Schweizer, *The Lord's Supper According to the NT* (1967), p. 37. Schweizer includes an extensive bibliography. See also an older book, J. C. Lambert, *The Sacraments in the NT* (1903), which still is of great value.

62 See above, p. 542.

63 D. E. H. Whiteley, *The Theology of St. Paul,* p. 170.

64 A. Oepke, *TDNT* I, 542.

65 "He can even call baptism the *peritomē Christou.*" R. Meyer, *TDNT* VI, 83.

66 The alternative view is that the circumcision of Christ is his putting off his body of flesh in his death on the cross. See G. R. Beasley-Murray, *Baptism in the NT,* p. 153.

and is synonymous with dying to sin. Circumcision then stands in contrast to baptism, not in correlation with it.[67]

[67] See R. E. O. White, *The Biblical Doctrine of Initiation* (1960), p. 212. For bibliography on baptism, see G. R. Beasley-Murray, *Baptism in the NT*, pp. 396-406. See also R. Schnackenburg, *Baptism in the Thought of St. Paul* (1964).

38

ESCHATOLOGY

Literature:

H. A. A. Kennedy, *St. Paul's Conception of the Last Things* (1904); R. H. Charles, *A Critical History of the Doctrine of a Future Life* (2nd ed., 1913), pp. 437-75; J. Lowe, "An Examination of Attempts to Detect Development in St. Paul's Theology," *JTS* 42 (1941), 129-42; G. Vos, *The Pauline Eschatology* (1952); J. H. Sevenster, "Some Remarks on the *Gumnos* in II Cor. v. 3," *Studia Paulina* (de Zwaan Festschrift, 1953), pp. 202-14; C. K. Barrett, "NT Eschatology," *SJTh* 6 (1953), 136-55, 225-43; W. D. Davies, "The Old and New Hope: Resurrection," *Paul and Rabbinic Judaism* (1955), pp. 285-320; J. Jeremias, "Flesh and Blood Cannot Inherit the Kingdom of God," *NTS* 2 (1956), 151-59; N. Q. Hamilton, *The Holy Spirit and Eschatology in Paul* (1957); R. F. Hettlinger, "2 Corinthians 5.1-10," *SJTh* 10 (1957), 174-94; O. Cullmann, *Immortality of the Soul or Resurrection of the Dead?* (1958); E. E. Ellis, "The Structure of Pauline Eschatology," *Paul and His Recent Interpreters* (1961), pp. 35-48; H. J. Schoeps, *Paul* (1961), pp. 88-125; D. E. H. Whiteley, *The Theology of St. Paul* (1964), pp. 233-73; H. M. Shires, *The Eschatology of Paul* (1966); F. F. Bruce, "Paul on Immortality," *SJTh* 24 (1971), 457-72; C. F. D. Moule, "St. Paul and Dualism: The Pauline Concept of Resurrection," *NTS* 12 (1966), 106-23.

INTRODUCTION. We have already seen that the framework of Paul's entire theological thought is that of apocalyptic dualism of this age and the Age to Come.[1] It is clear that this was no Pauline creation, for we find it emerging in Judaism in the first century; and the Synoptics represent it as providing the basic structure for Jesus' teachings.

However, we have seen that Paul as a Christian made a radical modification in this temporal dualism. Because of what God has done in Jesus' historic mission, the contrast between the two ages does not remain intact. On the contrary, the redemptive blessings brought to man by Jesus' death and resurrection and the giving of the Holy Spirit are eschatological events.

---

[1] See above, p. 364.

This means that the Pauline eschatology is inseparable from Paul's theological thought as a whole.[2]

The events of the eschatological consummation are not merely detached events lying in the future about which Paul speculates. They are rather redemptive events that have already begun to unfold within history. The blessings of the Age to Come no longer lie exclusively in the future; they have become objects of present experience. The death of Christ is an eschatological event. Because of Christ's death, the justified man stands already on the age-to-come side of the eschatological judgment, acquitted of all guilt. By virtue of the death of Christ, the believer has already been delivered from this present evil age (Gal. 1:4). He has been transferred from the rule of darkness and now knows the life of the Kingdom of Christ (Col. 1:13). In his cross, Christ has already defeated the powers of evil that have brought chaos into the world (Col. 2:14f.).

The resurrection of Christ is an eschatological event. The first act of the eschatological resurrection has been separated from the eschatological consummation and has taken place in history. Christ has already abolished death and displayed the life and immortality of the Age to Come in an event that occurred within history (II Tim. 1:10). Thus the light and the glory that belong to the Age to Come have already shined in this dark world in the person of Jesus Christ (II Cor. 4:6).

Because of these eschatological events, the believer lives the life of the new age. The very phrase describing the status of the believer, "in Christ," is an eschatological term. To be "in Christ" means to be in the new age and to experience its life and powers. "If any one is in Christ, he is a new creation; the old has passed away, behold, the new has come" (II Cor. 5:17). The believer has already experienced death and resurrection (Rom. 6:3-4). He has even been raised with Christ and exalted to heaven (Eph. 2:6), sharing the resurrection and ascension life of his Lord.

Yet the experience of this new life of the Age to Come is not a secular event of world history; it is known only to believers. This good news of the new life is hidden to unbelievers. Their eyes are blinded so that they cannot behold it (II Cor. 4:4). They are still in the darkness of this present evil age.

Furthermore, the new life of the believer is an ambiguous experience, for he still lives in the old age. He has been delivered from its power, yet he must still live out his life in this age, although he is not to be conformed to its life but is to experience the renewing powers of the new age (Rom. 12:1-2). The believer's new life is only "in the Spirit." He still has to make use of the world, but he is no longer concerned to make full use of it (I Cor. 7:31), for this world is transitory. Although Christ is in him, and his Spirit has been made alive by the powers of the new age, his body is dying (Rom. 8:10).

[2] The eschatological character of Paul's theology is emphasized by C. K. Barrett, N. Q. Hamilton, and H. M. Shires.

Therefore the transition from the sin and death of the old age to the life of the new age is as yet only partial, although it is real. All that the new age means cannot be experienced in the old age. It must pass away and give place to the Kingdom of God in the Age to Come when all that is mortal is swallowed up in life (II Cor. 5:4). Thus the believer lives in a tension of experienced and anticipated eschatology. He is already in the Kingdom of Christ (Col. 1:13), but he awaits the coming of the Kingdom of God (I Cor. 15:50). He has already experienced the new life (II Cor. 2:16), but he looks forward to the inheritance of eternal life (Gal. 6:8). He has already been saved (Eph. 2:5), but he is still awaiting his salvation (Rom. 13:11). He has been raised into newness of life (Rom. 6:4), yet he longs for the resurrection (II Cor. 5:4).

The present ambiguity of the new life in Christ demands the return of Christ to complete the work of redemption already begun. The central theme of the Pauline eschatology is the consummation of God's saving purpose. Apart from the return of Christ and the inauguration of the Age to Come, God's saving work remains unfinished.

THE INTERMEDIATE STATE. Paul's eschatology is concerned mainly with the events that will mark the transition from this age to the Age to Come: the return of Christ and the resurrection of the dead. However, before these themes are considered, a prior question must be raised: the state of the dead between death and the resurrection. We have already seen that while the Old Testament usually conceives of the shades of the dead existing in Sheol, the Psalms contain intimations of life beyond the grave. Judaism developed the idea of Sheol as a place of both punishment and blessing, which is reflected in Jesus' parable of the rich man and Lazarus (Lk. 16:19-31). Jesus assured the dying thief that they would both enter Paradise after death.[3]

The question of the intermediate state in Paul rests largely upon the interpretation of II Corinthians 5:1-10. The most natural way to interpret the passage is to understand it in the light of Paul's strong emphasis on the resurrection of the body. According to this view, Paul affirms that after the dissolution of this earthly, tentlike body, the believer will receive from God an eternal, heavenly body at the resurrection. In this earthly body we groan because of its weakness and frailty. What we desire is to put on the new body, not to be a naked, disembodied soul or spirit. The frailties of this body bring anxieties; even so, the idea of being unclothed, i.e., a disembodied spirit, is repugnant; we long for the resurrection body so that what is mortal may be swallowed up in life. Nevertheless, in spite of Paul's natural abhorrence of being disembodied, he finds courage in the fact that to be away from the body—a disembodied spirit—means to be at home with the Lord.[4]

---

[3] See above, pp. 194f.

[4] This interpretation will be found in H. A. A. Kennedy, *St. Paul's Conception of the Last Things* (1904), pp. 264ff.; A. Plummer, *Second Corinthians* (1915),

One of the chief difficulties in this interpretation is the word "we have," which suggests that we have this body at death, not at a future resurrection. However, the present tense may be Paul's way of simply expressing the complete certainty that we are to have it.[5] The tense need not be pressed.

In this interpretation, Paul has no light on the mode of existence in the intermediate state. He has the conviction, beginning to emerge in the Psalms, and expressed by Jesus to the dying thief, that "death could not bring the believer into any situation which meant separation from the Lord."[6] So far as he knows, the death of the body means the survival of the spirit,[7] although in a disembodied, "naked" state; and his view of the role of the body in human existence leads him to shrink from this. But his Christian conviction overcomes his natural aversion to this disembodied state, for nothing, not even death, can separate from the love of Christ (Rom. 8:38); and if one is closer to the Lord, he will be in a blessed state.

This interpretation is confirmed by a passing allusion in Philippians 1:23: "My desire is to depart and be with Christ, for that is far better" than the frustrations and frailties of mortal existence. "With Christ"—this is all Paul knows about the intermediate state. It does not surpass what Jesus said to the dying thief (Lk. 23:43).

Many scholars have rejected this interpretation. Long ago R. H. Charles traced four stages in the development of Pauline thought, the third of which is reflected in II Corinthians 5, where Paul expects to receive an immortal body at death.[8] He emphasizes the word "we have." When we die, we come into possession of an immortal body in heaven. W. L. Knox believed that this change of view was due to "a complete revision of Pauline eschatology in a Hellenistic sense."[9] W. D. Davies has rejected the thesis of Hellenistic influence and has tried to show that the dual expectation of a body at death and a body in the Age to Come could be understood against rabbinic backgrounds. He accepts, however, the thesis that Paul experienced a significant change of mind between the writing of First and Second Corinthians.[10] This thesis has also been supported with differing arguments by several recent scholars.[11]

---

pp. 140ff.; P. E. Hughes, *Second Corinthians* (1962), 160ff. (excellent discussion); F. V. Filson, "II Corinthians" in *IB* X, 326; J. Hering, *Second Corinthians* (1967), pp. 39ff.; J. N. Sevenster, "Some Remarks on the *Gumnos* in II Cor. v. 3" in *Studia Paulina* (de Zwaan Festschrift, 1953), pp. 212-14.

5 F. V. Filson in *IB* X, 326.

6 H. A. A. Kennedy, *St. Paul's Conception of the Last Things,* p. 269.

7 In view of Paul's use of soul and spirit (see above, Ch. 33), he would probably speak of the spirit rather than the soul, even though in this passage he refers neither to soul nor spirit.

8 R. H. Charles, *A Critical History of the Doctrine of a Future Life* (1913), pp. 455-61.

9 W. L. Knox, *St. Paul and the Church of the Gentiles* (1931), p. 128.

10 W. D. Davies, *Paul and Rabbinic Judaism* (1955), pp. 309ff.

11 See C. H. Dodd, *NT Studies* (1953), pp. 122ff.; R. F. Hettlinger, "2 Corinthians

As foreboding an array of scholarship as this may be, it seems difficult to understand why, if the believer puts on a heavenly, eternal body at death, there remains a need for the "resurrection and redemption of the Body [to be] achieved [at] the end of the age."[12] This criticism is all the more pointed because there is no hint in Paul's other writings of an intermediate body, and it is easier to interpret II Corinthians 5 in the light of his extensive references to resurrection at the parousia. It would seem, therefore, that this interpretation definitely diminishes the significance of the coming consummation, in spite of the denial of this fact.[13]

THE SLEEP OF THE DEAD. The thesis that between death and the resurrection the soul is in a condition of sleep has recently received the weighty support of Cullmann.[14] Cullmann is of course right that Paul, and all other biblical writers, look upon the final destiny of man in terms of resurrection of the body and not immortality of the soul. At this point Paul's expectation of the state of the dead in II Corinthians 5 is very Hebraic, for he abhors the idea of existing as a disembodied spirit, while the Greeks welcomed it. In fact, the very essence of the Greek idea was the flight of the soul from its imprisonment in the body, that it might find its true freedom in the heavenly world.[15] Paul's view stands in sharp contrast to the Greek view. What he longs for is the new body to be received at the resurrection. His expectation of being disembodied in the intermediate state is not due to Greek influence.

It is true that Paul often describes the state of death in terms of sleep (I Thess. 4:13; I Cor. 15:16, etc.). However, sleep was a common term for death both in Greek and Hebrew literature[16] and need not carry any theological significance. To interpret Paul's references to depart and be with Christ (Phil. 1:2), to be absent from the body but at home with the Lord (II Cor. 5:8), as a state in which we "continue to live with Christ . . . in the condition of sleep,"[17] and thus are nearer to God, although in an unconscious state, is difficult in spite of what Cullmann says about the pleasure of dreams.[18]

THE RETURN OF CHRIST. In the Old Testament "the Day of the Lord" could designate a day in the immediate historical future when God would visit his people in judgment (Amos 5:18; cf. Isa. 2:12ff.). It could also designate the final visitation of God when he would establish his Kingdom in the world, bringing salvation to his faithful people and judgment to the

5.1-10," *SJTh* 10 (1957), 174-94; F. F. Bruce, "Paul on Immortality," *SJTh* 24 (1971), 457-72; H. M. Shires, *The Eschatology of Paul* (1966), pp. 89-91.

12 R. F. Hettlinger in *SJTh* 10, 193.

13 F. F. Bruce in *SJTh* 24, 472.

14 O. Cullmann, *Immortality of the Soul or Resurrection of the Dead?* (1958).

15 See G. E. Ladd, *The Pattern of NT Truth* (1968), pp. 13-37.

16 R. Bultmann, *TDNT* III, 14.

17 O. Cullmann, *Immortality,* p. 56.

18 For a strong refutation of this view, see D. E. H. Whiteley, *The Theology of St. Paul* (1964), pp. 262-69.

wicked (Zeph. 1:14ff.; Joel 3:14ff.).[19] In the New Testament the term has become a technical expression for the day when God will visit the world to bring this age to its end and to inaugurate the Age to Come.[20] The term is not to be thought of as a single calendar day but as the entire period that will witness the final redemptive visitation of God in Christ.

The expression assumes different forms: the Day of the Lord (I Thess. 5:2; II Thess. 2:2; cf. also Acts 2:20; II Pet. 3:10); the Day of the Lord Jesus (I Cor. 5:5; II Cor. 1:14); the Day of the Lord Jesus Christ (I Cor. 1:8); the Day of Jesus Christ (Phil. 1:6); the Day of Christ (Phil. 1:10; 2:16); that Day (II Thess. 1:10; II Tim. 1:18).[21] In view of the fact that the exalted Christ is for Paul as for the early church the Lord (Phil. 2:11; Rom. 10:9), it should be obvious that efforts to distinguish between the Day of the Lord and the Day of Christ and to find in them two different eschatological programs, one for Israel and one for the church, are misguided.[22] The coming of Christ to gather his people, both living and dead, to himself (I Thess. 4:13-17) is called the Day of the Lord (I Thess. 5:2), as is his coming to judge the man of lawlessness (II Thess. 2:2).

Paul uses three words to describe the return of the Lord. The first is *parousia,* which may mean both "presence" (Phil. 2:2) and "arrival" (I Cor. 16:17; II Cor. 7:7). The word was used in a semi-technical sense of the visit of persons of high rank, especially of kings and emperors visiting a province. Since his ascension, Christ is pictured seated at the right hand of God in heaven. He will visit the earth again in personal presence (see Acts 1:11) at the end of the age (see Mt. 24:3) in power and glory (see Mt. 24:27) to raise the dead in Christ (I Cor. 15:23), to gather his people to himself (II Thess. 2:1; cf. Mt. 24:31), and to destroy evil (II Thess. 2:8; see also I Thess. 2:19; 3:13; 4:15; 5:23).

The coming of Christ will also be an *apokalypsis,* an "unveiling" or disclosure." The power and glory that are now his by virtue of his exaltation and heavenly session must be disclosed to the world. Christ has already been elevated by his resurrection and exaltation to the right hand of God, where he has been given sovereignty over all spiritual foes (Eph. 1:20-23). He now bears the name that is above every name; he is now the exalted Lord (Phil. 2:9). He is now reigning as King at God's right hand (I Cor. 15:25). However, his reign and his Lordship are not evident to the world. His *apokalypsis* will be the revealing to the world of the glory and power that are now his (II Thess. 1:7; I Cor. 1:7; see also I Pet. 1:7, 13). Thus the second coming of Christ is inseparable from his ascension and heavenly session, for it will disclose his present Lordship to the world and be the

---

19 See H. H. Rowley, *The Faith of Israel* (1956), pp. 177ff.

20 See Acts 2:20. It is curious that while Jewish apocalyptic often speaks of an apocalyptic "day," it does not use the full technical term "the Day of the Lord." See P. Volz, *Die Eschatologie der jüdischen Gemeinde* (1934), pp. 163-65.

21 See also the Day of God in II Pet. 3:12.

22 See J. D. Pentecost, *Things to Come* (1958), pp. 229-32, who relates the Day of the Lord to Israel, and the Day of Christ to the church.

means by which every knee shall finally bow and every tongue acknowledge his Lordship (Phil. 2:10-11).

A third term is *epiphaneia,* "appearing," and indicates the visibility of Christ's return. Although this term is limited largely to the pastoral epistles, Paul tells the Thessalonians that Christ will slay the man of lawlessness by the breath of his mouth and destroy him "by the *epiphaneia* of his *parousia*" (II Thess. 2:8). The return of the Lord will be no secret, hidden event but a breaking into history of the glory of God.

The inseparable connection between the two acts in Christ's redemptive work is illustrated by the twofold use of *epiphaneia* to designate both the incarnation and the second coming of Christ. God has already broken the power of death and displayed the reality of life and immortality within history through the appearing (*epiphaneia*) of our Savior Christ Jesus in the flesh (II Tim. 1:10). However, this is not the final term of redemption. Hope still awaits us in the future in the "appearing (*epiphaneia*) of the glory of our great God and Savior Jesus Christ" (Tit. 2:13). In view of this twofold usage, the objections sometimes made against speaking of a "second" coming of Christ are overly critical.[23]

Dispensational theology separates the return of Christ into two parts: a secret coming of Christ before the great tribulation for the church, and a glorious appearing at the end of the tribulation to bring salvation to Israel and to establish his millennial kingdom. These two comings have usually been called the rapture and the revelation.[24] While dispensationalist theologians retain the view of a twofold return of Christ, many of the usual exegetical arguments have been surrendered. In fact, Walvoord goes so far as to admit that "pretribulationism," i.e., a coming of Christ before the great tribulation for the church, is not explicitly taught in Scripture.[25] This is a significant admission. The fact is that the hope of the church is not a secret event, unseen by the world. The Christian hope is the visible appearing of the glory of God in Christ's return (Tit. 2:13), the *revelation* to the world of Jesus as Lord when he comes with his mighty angels (II Thess. 1:7).

It has often been argued in defense of a twofold coming of Christ that if he is to come "with all his saints" (I Thess. 3:13), he must of necessity have come first "for" them.[26] His coming for his saints is the rapture at the beginning of the great tribulation; his coming "with his saints" is a later event at the end of the tribulation. This phrase, however, provides no proof for such a view of two comings of Christ. If the "saints" (*hagioi,* "holy ones") of I Thessalonians 3:13 are redeemed men, this says no more

---

[23] See Heb. 9:28, "Christ . . . will appear a second time."

[24] See W. E. B., *Jesus Is Coming* (1908), ch. IX; C. L. Feinberg, *Premillennialism or Amillennialism?* (1954), pp. 162ff.; J. D. Pentecost, *Things to Come,* pp. 206-7.

[25] J. Walvoord, *The Rapture Question* (1957), p. 148. This admission, which appears in the first printing of the book, was deleted from later printings.

[26] G. B. Stanton, *Kept from the Hour* (1950), p. 265.

than I Thessalonians 4:14, where Paul says that at the coming of Christ to rapture the church, "God will bring with him those who have fallen asleep." However, the "holy ones" of I Thessalonians 3:13 may be another reference to the holy angels who will accompany the Lord at his return.[27]

The background of this language of the coming of Christ in glory is the Old Testament language of theophany. The Old Testament conceives of God working in history to accomplish his redemptive purposes; but it also looks forward to a day of divine visitation when God will come in judgment and salvation to establish his Kingdom.[28] In the New Testament this divine theophany is fulfilled in the coming of Christ; and the glorious return of the Lord is necessary to bring salvation to his people (I Thess. 5:8-9) and judgment upon the wicked (II Thess. 1:7-8) and to establish the Kingdom, which is now his, in the world (II Tim. 4:1).

The theology of the coming of Christ is the same in Paul as in the Synoptics. Salvation is not a matter that concerns only the destiny of the individual soul. It includes the entire course of human history and mankind as a whole. The coming of Christ is a definitive event for *all* men; it means either salvation or judgment. Furthermore, salvation is not merely an individual matter; it concerns the whole people of God, and it includes the transformation of the entire physical order.

This redemption is altogether the work of God. The coming of Christ is a cosmic event in which God, who visited men in the humble historical Jesus, will visit them again in the glorified Christ. The goal of redemption is nothing less than the establishment of God's rule in all the world, "that God may be everything to every one" (I Cor. 15:28).

THE KINGDOM OF GOD. In our discussion of the messiahship of Jesus, we have had occasion to outline Paul's teaching about the Kingdom of God. We have seen[29] that the Kingdom of God is the messianic rule of God in Christ that began at his resurrection and ascension and will continue "until he has put all his enemies under his feet" (I Cor. 15:25). The Kingdom of God—the perfect rule of God in the world—is the eschatological goal of redemption; but it is a goal the achievement of which reaches back to Easter.

Here we must deal with the question of the eschatological aspect of the Kingdom—in particular, whether Paul looked for an interim messianic kingdom before the inauguration of the Age to Come.

Background for this idea is found in the prophecy of Ezekiel. The prophet looks forward to the restoration of a believing remnant to whom God has given a new heart and a new spirit (Ezek. 33-37). This is not, however, the goal of God's redemptive purpose. Before the era of peace

---

[27] The word *hagioi* is used of angels in the LXX in Ps. 89:5, 7; Dan. 4:13 (Theodotion; see RSV); 8:13; Zech. 14:5. Angels are frequently called "the holy ones" in the Qumran literature. See F. M. Cross, Jr., *The Ancient Library of Qumran* (1957), p. 73; M. Mansoor, *The Thanksgiving Hymns* (1961), p. 82.

[28] See Isa. 2:12-22, esp. v. 21; 26:31; 35:4; 40:10; 66:15ff.; Zech. 14:5.

[29] See above, p. 410.

is completely established, there will occur the final terrible war with the barbarous, unrepentant forces of evil from the distant places of the world (Ezek. 38-39). Only after this battle will the world be completely purified and ready for the new Jerusalem to which the glory of God shall return.[30]

Judaism had a great variety of ideas about the nature of the Kingdom of God. In addition to those already discussed,[31] sometimes we find a temporal kingdom preceding the coming of the Age to Come, similar to the pattern in Ezekiel. This temporary messianic kingdom is found in Enoch (91:13-14), in IV Ezra (7:28), and the Apocalypse of Baruch (29:3ff.). Similar ideas are to be found in rabbinic literature, which sometimes distinguishes between the temporary "days of the Messiah" and the eternal "Age to Come."[32] This pattern is also found in Revelation 20. Because of this passage, the "days of the Messiah" are often spoken of as the millennium by Christian theologians.

In I Corinthians 15:23-26, Paul pictures the triumph of Christ as being accomplished in several stages. The resurrection of Christ is the first stage (*tagma*). The second stage will occur at the parousia when those who are Christ's will share his resurrection. "Then comes the end, when he delivers the kingdom to God the Father after destroying every rule and every authority and power. For he must reign until he has put all his enemies under his feet. The last enemy to be destroyed is death."

Vos thinks that by proving that Christ's messianic reign began with his resurrection-ascension, he has established that Christ's Kingdom must lie in its entirety before the parousia.[33] Schoeps takes a similar view, arguing that Paul adapted the scheme of a temporal messianic kingdom to his conviction that the resurrection had already begun and Christ was already the Exalted One. He holds that Paul probably knew a rabbinic tradition that the days of the Messiah would last forty years. Therefore Paul expected the heavenly reign of Christ to be very short, and looked for the parousia and the Age to Come within forty years at most.[34]

We agree with both Vos and Schoeps that Paul views Jesus' messianic reign as beginning at his resurrection-ascension. But this does not exclude the natural sense of the passage cited. The adverbs translated "then" are *epeita, eita,* which denote a sequence: "after that." There are three distinct stages: Jesus' resurrection; after that (*epeita*) the resurrection of those who are Christ's at his parousia; after that (*eita*) the end (*telos*). A few scholars understand *to telos* to designate the end of the resurrection, i.e., the resurrection of unbelievers;[35] but this seems impossible.[36] The natural meaning

---

[30] G. E. Wright, "The Faith of Israel," *IB* I, 372.
[31] See above, pp. 60ff.
[32] See J. Klausner, *The Messianic Idea in Israel* (1955), pp. 408-19.
[33] G. Vos, *The Pauline Eschatology* (1952), p. 246.
[34] H. J. Schoeps, *Paul* (1961), p. 101.
[35] J. Weiss, *The History of Primitive Christianity* (1937), p. 532.
[36] J. Hering, *First Corinthians* (1962), p. 166.

of *to telos* is the consummation, which will see the inauguration of the Age to Come. An undefined interval falls between Christ's resurrection and his parousia; and a second undefined interval falls between the parousia and the *telos*.[37]

THE MYSTERY OF LAWLESSNESS. The coming of Christ is to be preceded by certain eschatological events. In his first letter to the Thessalonians, Paul spoke only of the return of Christ to gather the saints, both dead and living, to be with him (I Thess. 4:13-18). He wrote with earnest anticipation, admonishing the Thessalonians to live with an attitude of expectancy of that day so as not to be taken by surprise (I Thess. 5:1-11). As a result, believers in Thessalonica became upset and excited, and some claimed to have revelations from God or a special word from Paul indicating that the end was upon them and the events of the Day of the Lord had actually begun (II Thess. 2:1-2). Paul corrects this erroneous view of imminency by saying that before the end comes, there will appear an evil ruler, the man of lawlessness, who will arrogate to himself all authority, both secular and sacred, and will demand the total submission of men to his rule, including worship (II Thess. 2:3-4). The statement that he will take his seat in the temple of God is a metaphorical way of expressing, in Old Testament language, his defiance of God (see Ezek. 28:2; Isa. 14:13-14). He will be satanically empowered to deceive men and turn them away from the truth (vv. 9-10). The essence of his character is his "lawlessness." He defies both the Law of God and the laws of man, insisting that his will alone is law.

This "man of lawlessness" is called the Beast in Revelation 13, but he is usually spoken of as the antichrist. His appearance will be accompanied by "the rebellion" (II Thess. 2:3). The word *apostasia* is sometimes translated "falling away" and is understood to designate an apostasy within the Christian church. It is better translated "rebellion" or "revolt" as in the RSV. The idea is not so much that of drifting away from the Lord into apathy as a deliberate setting of oneself in violent opposition to God. This rebellion is to be a definite event, an apocalyptic happening.[38] Antichrist not only will oppose all divine authority, but will be supported by a general rebellion against God.

The "revealing" of the man of lawlessness will not be a new thing in human history, but only the final manifestation of a principle that was operative even in the days of Paul (v. 7). Paul could see the spirit of opposition and rebellion against God already at work. However, this evil principle is at present held in check. There is something that is restraining the appearance of the man of lawlessness (v. 6). Paul does not tell us what

---

37 This interpretation is found in H. St. John Thackeray, *The Relation of St. Paul to Contemporary Jewish Thought* (1900), pp. 120-28; O. Cullmann, "The Kingship of Christ and the Church in the NT" in *The Early Church,* ed. by A. J. B. Higgins (1956), pp. 111ff.; C. T. Craig, *IB* X, 236ff.; N. A. Dahl, "Die Messianität Jesu bei Paulus" in *Studia Paulina* (de Zwaan Festschrift, 1953), pp. 94f.

38 W. Neil, *Thessalonians* (1950), p. 160.

this restraining principle is. Again, Paul indicates that this restraining principle is embodied in a person; "only he who now restrains it will do so until he is out of the way" (v. 7). When the restraining one is removed the lawless one will be revealed.

There are no darker words in the entire Pauline corpus than these, and any interpretation must be at best a hypothesis. In many evangelical circles, the only interpretation that is considered possible is that the restraining power is the Holy Spirit; and this verse is often cited in support of the rapture of the church before the tribulation. The Holy Spirit will be taken out of the world when the church is raptured. When this divine restraining power is removed, then lawlessness is free to break out.[39] It is true that some early fathers saw the restraining principle in the Holy Spirit,[40] but this view has little to commend it. There is no hint of the teaching that the Holy Spirit, who was given at Pentecost, will leave the world at the parousia.

Recently the view has been propounded that the passage must be understood in the light of Paul's missionary work. Paul believed that the whole world must be evangelized before the parousia of Christ, and he was the chief missionary in carrying out this mission to the Gentiles. Until this mission should be complete, the end could not come. Therefore the missionary mission is the restraining principle and Paul himself is the person restraining.[41]

The traditional view has been that the restraining principle is the Roman empire and the restrainer the Emperor.[42] This view, or a modification of it, fits best into the Pauline theology. In Romans 13:4, Paul affirms that the ruling authority (even though it be pagan Rome) is "God's servant for your good." God has ordained human authorities to preserve order, i.e., to approve those who do good, and to punish those who do wrong. The antithesis of this is the lawlessness of II Thessalonians 2:4: the deifying of the state so that it no longer is an instrument of law and order but a totalitarian system that defies God and demands the worship of men. This is the demonic state. "The coming of the lawless one by the activity of Satan will be with all power . . . and with all wicked deception" (v. 8). This is the same demonic, totalitarian state pictured in Revelation 13. In Paul's day, God had invested this authority in the Roman empire and its head, the Emperor. Paul sees a day when the rule of law will collapse, when political order will be swept away and be unable any longer to restrain the principle of lawlessness. Then the last defenses that the Creator has erected against the powers of chaos will break down completely.[43]

---

[39] J. D. Pentecost, *Things to Come,* pp. 204f.; G. B. Stanton, *Kept from the Hour,* ch. 5.

[40] B. F. Westcott, *Thessalonians* (1908), p. 101.

[41] O. Cullmann, *Christ and Time* (1964), pp. 164f.; J. Munck, *Paul and the Salvation of Mankind* (1959), pp. 31-39.

[42] R. H. Charles, *A Critical History of the Doctrine of a Future Life,* p. 440.

[43] See E. Stauffer, *NT Theology* (1955), p. 214; L. Morris, *Thessalonians* (1959), pp. 225-27.

This can well be understood in the principle of the deification of the state in defiance of the divine ordinance. The principles of both order and lawlessness can be at work at the same time, even in the same state. These two principles will be in conflict during the course of the age. At the very end, law and order will break down, demonic lawlessness will burst forth, and the church will experience a brief period of terrible evil that will be quickly terminated by the return of Christ (v. 8).

THE MYSTERY OF ISRAEL'S HARDENING AND FINAL SALVATION

Literature:

See commentaries on Romans 9-11; J. Munck, *Christ and Israel* (1967); P. Richardson, *Israel in the Apostolic Church* (1969), pp. 126-47.

Another event Paul expects to occur in connection with the consummation is the salvation of Israel. This truth Paul expounds in Romans 9-11. The rejection of Christ by Israel and their subsequent fall was not a mere accident of history but a factor in God's redemptive purpose—an event in *Heilsgeschichte*. Even in the rejection of Israel, God had a purpose: that by Israel's fall, salvation might come to the Gentiles (Rom. 11:11). Then Paul makes a key statement: "Now if the fall of them be the riches of the world, and the diminishing of them the riches of the Gentiles, how much more their fulness?" (11:12).

In this statement is embodied Paul's theology of the future salvation of Israel. If the fall of Israel has brought salvation to the Gentiles, in how much larger measure will salvation come to the Gentile world if the "fulness," i.e., full salvation of Israel, comes? Israel was God's chosen instrument to bring salvation to the world. This was the heart of the promise given to Abraham. He was to be the father of many nations, and in him would all families of the earth be blessed (Gen. 12:1-3; 17:6). This is why Christ came into the world as an Israelite. Israel's rejection of her Messiah and her subsequent fall were the means used by God to bring salvation to the Gentiles. But this is not the last chapter of the story. The church age as we know it is not the end. Two things must yet happen: the fullness of literal Israel must come in, and by her salvation greater riches be brought to the Gentile world.

Paul further develops this truth in the following verses. Israel is still the chosen people. She is still the special object of God's care and will yet be the instrument of salvation. This is asserted in Romans 11:15-16. The first fruits of Israel (the patriarchs) were holy, i.e., the objects of God's election and care; and the entire lump (Israel as a people) is also holy. If the root of the tree is holy, so is the entire tree. The people Israel continues to be a "holy" people—a people whom God has designated for his redemptive purpose in the world. This future purpose is indicated in the following words: "For if the casting away of them be the reconciling of the world, what shall the receiving of them be, but life from the dead?" (v. 15).

Here is the twofold contrast: the present rejection of Israel bcause of unbelief is contrasted with a future receiving of Israel in belief. The other contrast is even more significant. The present rejection of unbelieving Israel means that the message of reconciliation has gone out to all the world; Israel's future restoration will mean much more than this—a state of blessedness that Paul describes by the phrase "life from the dead." The balanced structure of the sentence shows that this is a blessing that comes upon the Gentile world. The balance of the sentence is the key to its interpretation, and the following diagram illustrates this balance.

I	II
a. Present rejection of Israel	a. Reconciliation of the world
b. Future restoration of Israel	b. Life from the dead

Israel is the subject of the two members in I; and the Gentile world is the subject of the two members in II. "Life from the dead" (IIb) is not a parallel member with "Israel" (Ib) but with "the world" (IIa). It stands in contrast with Israel (Ib). "Life from the dead" does not refer to Israel's restoration but to the results for the Gentiles of Israel's restoration. Israel's future salvation will issue in a new order of blessedness and happiness for the Gentile world that is likened to the emergence of life from the dead. There remains in the future for the world an enjoyment of the reality of the life in Christ extending far beyond anything we have now experienced; and this will be accomplished through the instrumentality of Israel's conversion. Paul does not here tell us when or how this era of blessing will occur.[44]

Paul sums up the entire matter in verses 25-27. Israel is now hardened. The Gentiles are now being brought in. Finally "all Israel shall be saved." "All Israel" does not need to mean every single Israelite but the people as a whole.[45] Paul does not here add the thought that through this salvation of Israel a new wave of life will come to the whole world; his concern at this point is only the destiny of Israel.

Paul does not explain how the salvation of Israel is accomplished. One thing, however, is clear: it must take place in fundamentally the same terms as the salvation of the Gentiles, namely, through saving faith in Jesus as the crucified Messiah. The words of Romans 11:26, "Then shall come out of Zion the Deliverer, and shall turn away ungodliness from Jacob," may refer to the second coming of Christ, but not necessarily so. This is a composite quotation from Isaiah 59:20 and 27:9, neither of which refers to the Messiah. So far as the passage in Romans 11 is concerned, the salvation of Israel could occur by a great evangelistic movement that would bring Israel into the church; however, Paul says nothing about Gentile Christians evangelizing the Jews.

[44] See W. Sanday and A. C. Headlam, *Romans* (1906), p. 325. They also consider the possibility that Paul is referring to the first resurrection of the dead. See also J. Murray, *Romans* (1965), II, 82-84.

[45] W. Gutbrod, *TDNT* III, 387.

Whatever the means of Israel's salvation, it appears to be an eschatological event in Paul's thought. It is impossible that Israel should be saved in any way but by faith in Jesus as her Messiah. Saul of Tarsus was brought to faith by a special vision of the glorified Christ; yet he was saved by faith like any believer and was brought into the church. Literal Israel, temporarily rejected, is yet to come to faith and be grafted back into the olive tree—the true people of God (Rom. 11:23). Piper has suggested that in God's plan of redemptive history, converted Israel may become for the first time in history a *truly Christian nation.*[46]

THE RESURRECTION AND THE RAPTURE. Paul has more to say about the resurrection than any other writer in the New Testament. Redemption applies to the whole man, including the body (Rom. 8:23). Paul often contrasts the sufferings of earthly existence with the future glory (Rom. 8:18), but he never considers bodily life in itself an evil thing from which he longs to be freed. Rather than being discarded, the body, which often humiliates us, is to be transformed and glorified (Phil. 3:21). The Holy Spirit who has quickened our spirits will also give fullness of life to our mortal bodies in the resurrection (Rom. 8:11). Paul's doctrine of the resurrection is grounded in his unitary view of man.

We have seen, however, that as Paul reflected on death, he could not conceive that even death could separate the believer from the love of God. To be absent from the body means to be at home with the Lord, apparently as a disembodied spirit.[47] However, this is not what Paul longs for. The intermediate state, although one of blessing, is not the goal of salvation. The consummation of salvation and the full possession of our inheritance at the resurrection (Eph. 1:14) await the return of Christ when God will "bring with him those who have fallen asleep" (I Thess. 4:14). Then the spirits of the dead will be reunited with their bodies, but transformed, glorified. Paul knows nothing of glorified spirits apart from the body. The problem that called forth his long discussion of the resurrection was some form of denial of the resurrection of the body (I Cor. 15:12, 35). If Paul had taught some form of blessed immortality of the soul or resurrection of the spirit out of its entanglement in the world of matter into the realm of God, the Corinthians would have had no problem. They have difficulty accepting the idea of bodily resurrection. The resurrection body as described by Paul transcends present historical experience. A body suited to the life of the Kingdom must be different from the bodies of this age. That there can logically be such a body Paul establishes by pointing to the fact that there is a difference between a kernel of grain and the shoot that comes from it (I Cor. 15:35-38). There are also different kinds of flesh—of men, beasts, fish, birds (v. 39), and there are different kinds of bodies—earthly and heavenly, which differ in their glory (vv. 40-41). Therefore it should

---

[46] O. Piper, "Church and Judaism in Holy History," *TT* 18 (1961), 60-71.
[47] See above, pp. 552f.

not be surprising that God has a new and different kind of body adapted to the life of the Age to Come.

However, Paul does not attempt to describe the nature of the resurrection body. He knows nothing of its constitution; but he can speak of some of the qualities in which it differs from the physical body. The latter is perishable, dishonoring and weak. The new body will be imperishable, glorious and powerful (vv. 42-43). The contrast is summarized in the words *psychikon* versus *pneumatikon* (v. 44). The former word is impossible to translate literally. While *psychē* can mean "soul," it often means the totality of natural life,[48] and this is the meaning here. The *psychikon sōma* is the "natural" (KJV) or "physical" (RSV) body adapted to life in this age. It is clearly not a body whose substance is *psychē*. The resurrection body will be *pneumatikon,* i.e., not constituted of *pneuma,* but adapted to all that the life of the *pneuma,* God's *pneuma,* means.[49]

Echoes of this idea are found elsewhere. It is the indwelling Holy Spirit who will give life to our mortal bodies (Rom. 8:11). The present experience of the Holy Spirit is the initial "down payment" (*arrabōn*) that guarantees the final swallowing up of mortality by the life of the resurrection body (II Cor. 5:4-5; see also Eph. 1:14). The Holy Spirit is also called the first fruits (*aparchē*) of the completed eschatological harvest, which will be the redemption of the body (Rom. 8:23). Paul's "spiritual body," then, is a new body that stands in some kind of real continuity with the physical body, which will yet be different because it has been transformed by the Holy Spirit and made like the glorious body of the resurrected Jesus (Phil. 3:21). The physical body was of dust, like Adam's body; the spiritual body will be heavenly, like Christ's body (I Cor. 15:45-49); but it is still a body.

Paul inseparably associates the resurrection of the saints with the resurrection of Christ. The same power that raised Christ will raise up his people (I Cor. 6:14; II Cor. 4:14). In fact, Christ's resurrection was itself the first act of the final resurrection. It is the "first fruits" of which the eschatological resurrection will be the harvest (I Cor. 15:20). Therefore Paul is concerned only with the resurrection of "the dead in Christ" (I Thess. 4:16). Paul has no word in his epistles as to the resurrection of those who do not stand in solidarity with Christ—the unsaved. Luke quotes him in Acts 24:15 asserting resurrection of both the just and the unjust; and we may well believe this, for Paul does teach the judgment of all men (Rom. 2:6-11). But he says nothing about the time or the nature of the resurrection of any except Christians. Neither does Paul refer to the state of the unsaved after death. He does not even mention Hades in his letters.[50]

---

[48] See above, pp. 459f.

[49] See D. E. H. Whiteley, *The Theology of St. Paul,* p. 252.

[50] Hades in I Cor. 15:55 (KJV) reflects the inferior Textus Receptus. The reference in Eph. 4:8 to "the lower parts of the earth" does not refer to a descent into Sheol. See E. K. Simpson and F. F. Bruce, *Ephesians and Colossians* (1957), p. 91.

The resurrection will occur instantaneously at the coming of Christ (I Thess. 4:16; I Cor. 15:52). The change that will occur for the dead in Christ will also overtake the living in Christ. Those "who are left until the coming of the Lord" will have no advantage over those who have fallen asleep (I Thess. 4:15). The same transformation will overtake both the living and the dead (I Cor. 15:51). The living will, as it were, put the new resurrection body on over the mortal body (*ependusasthai,* II Cor. 5:4) without the dissolution of the latter. This is what Paul means by the so-called "rapture"[51] of the church. The "catching up" of living believers, immediately after the resurrection, to meet the Lord in the air is Paul's vivid way of expressing the sudden transformation of the living from the weak, corruptible bodies of this physical order to the powerful, incorruptible bodies that belong to the new order of the Age to Come. It is the sign of passing from the level of mortal existence to immortality. The important words are "so shall we always be with the Lord" (v. 17).

Paul is referring to the rapture, i.e., the transformation of the living saints, when he says, "We shall not all sleep [in death], but we shall all be changed" (I Cor. 15:51). He has just asserted that "flesh and blood cannot inherit the kingdom of God, nor does the perishable inherit the imperishable" (v. 50). In these words he is probably referring to the saints who are living at the parousia, who will put on their resurrection bodies without experiencing death. He calls this a "mystery" (v. 51)—the revelation of a new truth, namely, that the change of the living as well as of the dead will take place immediately at the parousia.[52]

JUDGMENT. While Paul refers frequently to judgment, he nowhere develops this doctrine as he does the resurrection. He speaks of those who store up "wrath for themselves" on the day of wrath when God's righteous judgment will be revealed (Rom. 2:5). In that day God will judge the secrets of men by Christ Jesus (Rom. 2:16). Other passing references to judgment are found in Romans 13:2; I Corinthians 11:32; Romans 3:6; I Corinthians 4:5; II Thessalonians 2:12; and II Timothy 4:1. In some way not explained to us, the saints are to assist God in the judgment of the world, even to the point of judging angels (I Cor. 6:2-3).

The most developed passage on judgment is Romans 2. There will be a day of judgment (Rom. 2:5) when God will judge all men according to their works. To the righteous he will give eternal life, to the wicked wrath and fury (vv. 6-10). Furthermore, men will be judged by the light they have. All men have the light of nature by which they should recognize the existence of the true God and worship him alone (Rom. 1:18ff.). The Jews will be judged by the Law (Rom. 2:12), and those who have not had the Law will be judged by the law of God written on their hearts—by conscience (vv. 14-16). While these verses suggest theoretically that men

---

51 "Rapture" comes from the Latin *raptus.* "We . . . shall be caught up" in I Thess. 4:17 is *rapiemur* in the Latin.

52 See J. Jeremias in *NTS* 2 (1956), 151-59.

can survive the day of judgment on the basis of good works, Paul states clearly that men have not lived up to their light. The Gentiles have perverted the light of general revelation (Rom. 1:21ff.), and the Jews have failed to keep the Law (Gal. 3:10-12). However, God in his mercy has provided a way of salvation in the redeeming work of Christ, and the final basis of judgment will be the gospel (Rom. 2:16; II Thess. 1:8). God's final judgment will be absolutely just and not arbitrary.

There is another important element in the Pauline teaching of judgment. The constant New Testament tension between experienced and futuristic eschatology is found in the doctrine of judgment. Justification is an eschatological fact that has occurred in history. It means acquittal from the guilt of sin by a favorable decision of the Judge. This decision has already been rendered for believers on the ground of the death of Christ (Rom. 3:21-26). Because of present justification, we shall be saved from wrath on the day of judgment (Rom. 5:9).

Nevertheless, judgment remains an eschatological fact, even for believers. The righteousness we hope for (Gal. 5:5) is acquittal at the final judgment.[53] "We must all appear before the judgment seat of Christ" (II Cor. 5:10), which is also the judgment seat of God (Rom. 14:10, RV, RSV). However, because of the justification in Christ, the day of judgment has lost its terror for the man in Christ (Rom. 8:1, 33-34). Nevertheless, the believer will be judged for his works. Our life will be laid bare before the divine scrutiny that each one may receive the proper recompense for the things done through the life of the body, in accordance with the things that he has done, whether that life record is good or bad.[54] This judgment is not "a declaration of doom, but an assessment of worth,"[55] involving not condemnation or acquittal, but rewards or loss on the basis of the worthfulness or worthlessness of the Christian's life. The same principle of judgment is expounded in I Corinthians 3:12-15. Paul is here speaking of the work of Christian leaders, but the principle is valid for all believers. The only foundation upon which anything permanent can be built is Jesus Christ. However, not all build alike. Some erect structures with gold, silver, or precious stones; others will build worthless houses of wood, hay, or stubble. Clearly, Paul is applying his metaphor rather loosely, for these materials were not usually used in ancient construction. Paul is deliberately using a radical metaphor to contrast great value with worthlessness. Some Christians will live worthless lives; their works, like wood, hay, and stubble, will be consumed in the flames of judgment so that nothing remains as a result of their life on earth. This does not mean the loss of salvation: "he himself will be saved," but he will suffer loss of the "well done, good and faithful servant." Those who have built faithfully and effectively will be rewarded for their love and devotion. Paul does not indicate what the reward will be. The principle involved in this judgment is that while salva-

---

[53] See G. Schrenk, *TDNT* II, 207.
[54] See F. V. Filson in *IB* X, 332.
[55] See P. E. Hughes, *Second Corinthians,* p. 182.

tion is altogether of grace, the Christian is left in no doubt that he is regarded by God as fully answerable for the quality of his present life in the body.

THE CONSUMMATION. The goal of God's redemptive purpose is the restoration of order to a universe that has been disturbed by evil and sin. This includes the realm of human experience, the spiritual world (Eph. 1:10), and, as we shall see, even nature itself. God will finally reconcile all things to himself through Christ (Col. 1:20). All things were originally created through Christ and for him (Col. 1:16), and he will finally enjoy the pre-eminence that is his due (Col. 1:18). The very cosmos, which has been rent by conflict and rebellion against God, will be restored to peace with its Creator. This eschatological reconciliation will be accomplished through the blood of his cross (Col. 1:20). Paul sees in the death of Christ a triumph over evil spiritual powers (Col. 2:14-15), although he nowhere explains what this involves; and the final eschatological reconciliation is but the effective extension of the victory won on the cross.

This same emphasis on universal reconciliation is repeated elsewhere. In the great kenosis hymn, Jesus is now exalted as Lord; and because of the exaltation, every knee is yet to bow and every tongue confess that Jesus Christ is Lord, to the glory of God the Father (Phil. 2:10-11). No rebellious will can finally remain outside the sway of Christ's Lordship.

The final subjection of every hostile will is also asserted in I Corinthians 15 as the extension of Christ's kingly rule in the universe. He is to reign as king (*basileuein*) until he has subdued every enemy, the last of which is death (I Cor. 15:25). When he has subdued every hostile spiritual power, he will deliver the Kingdom to God the Father (v. 24). In view of the Pauline emphasis that Jesus has now been exalted and is reigning as Lord at God's right hand (Eph. 1:20-23; Phil. 2:9), we must think of Christ as beginning his kingly reign at his ascension. Lord and king are interchangeable concepts expressing Christ's exalted sovereignty. His sovereignty rests in this passage on his resurrection.

The final restoration includes the very material world. Creation itself awaits the disclosure of the sons of God when they shall experience the redemption of their bodies, for creation shall be freed from the bondage to decay and shall experience freedom from the burden of evil to which it has been subjected (Rom. 8:19-23). While Paul does not develop this truth of the redemption of nature, there is profound biblical theology underlying it. The redemption of the natural world from evil and decay is the corollary of the redemption of the body. The prophets constantly described the establishment of God's Kingdom in terms of a redeemed world (Isa. 11:6-9; 65:17-25); and the New Testament shares the same theology. Creation is never viewed as something evil that must be escaped. Man as body is a creature of God. Man is not sinful because he is a creature but because he has rebelled against God. In the final consummation, the whole man and the world of which he is a part will be delivered from the curse of evil.

Some interpreters have seen in the language of this final reconciliation a "universal homecoming," interpreted in terms of a universal salvation of all sentient creatures, both human and angelic.[56] Such an interpretation can indeed be read into such verses as Colossians 1:20 if they are taken out of the context of the total Pauline teaching. However, the universal reconciliation means that peace is everywhere restored. The universal acknowledgment of Christ's Lordship (Phil. 2:10-11) is not synonymous with universal salvation. There is a stern element in Paul's eschatology that cannot be avoided. There remain recalcitrant wills that must be subdued and which will bow before Christ's rule, even though unwillingly. How they will be dealt with Paul does not say except in very general terms.

Paul describes the final state of those who have not obeyed the gospel of Christ by saying they "shall suffer the punishment of eternal destruction and exclusion from the presence of the Lord and from the glory of his might" (II Thess. 1:9; see I Thess. 5:3). The rebellious and impenitent store up for themselves wrath on the day of wrath when God's righteous judgment will be revealed (Rom. 2:5, 8; see 5:9; I Thess. 1:10; 5:9). Paul also describes the fate of the unsaved by the concept of perishing (*apollumi*). This is both a present condition (I Cor. 1:18; II Cor. 2:15; 4:3) and a future doom (Rom. 2:12; II Thess. 2:10). This eschatological doom is also destruction (*apōleia,* Phil. 3:19; Rom. 9:22). A companion idea is that of death. Death, in the full inclusiveness of the term, is the penalty of sin (Rom. 5:12; 6:16, 23). While this death is the death of the body (Rom. 8:38; I Cor. 3:22), the term includes much more. This is shown by the fact that death is the opposite of eternal life (Rom. 6:23; 7:10; 8:6; II Cor. 2:16). It is both a present fact (Rom. 7:10f.; Eph. 2:1) and a future fate (Rom. 1:32; 6:16, 21, 23; 7:5). The central idea is exclusion from the presence of the Lord in his consummated Kingdom (II Thess. 1:9) and the subsequent loss of the blessings of life that come from the enjoyment of the divine presence. However, the terms Paul uses make it clear that the final judgment will issue in a fearful condemnation that is the just desert of sin and unbelief; but he nowhere describes what this doom involves.

However, the judgment of the wicked is not an end in itself, but only a necessary act in the establishment of God's reign in his world. God has done all things possible to bring men to himself; if they reject his will, they must face his judgment, for in the end God can brook no opposition to his holy will. The divine purpose is that men may be gathered in willing subordination to the divine rule, that in the end "God may be everything to every one" (I Cor. 15:28).

---

[56] See E. Stauffer, *NT Theology,* ch. 57.

PART 5

THE GENERAL EPISTLES

39

HEBREWS

Literature:

G. B. Stevens, *The Theology of the NT* (1906), pp. 483-522; B. F. Westcott, *The Epistle to the Hebrews* (1906); E. F. Scott, *The Epistle to the Hebrews, Its Doctrine and Significance* (1922); J. Moffatt, *The Epistle to the Hebrews* (1930), pp. 30-49; W. Robinson, *The Eschatology of the Epistle to the Hebrews* (1950); W. F. Howard, "The Epistle to the Hebrews," *Int* 5 (1951), 80-91; A. C. Purdy, "The Epistle to the Hebrews," *IB* XI (1955), 583-89; C. K. Barrett, "The Eschatology of the Epistle to the Hebrews," *The Background of the NT and Its Eschatology*, ed. by W. D. Davies and D. Daube (1956), pp. 363-93; O. Cullmann, *The Christology of the NT* (1959), pp. 89-104; A. Wikgren, "Patterns of Perfection in the Epistle to the Hebrews," *NTS* 6 (1960), 159-67; E. Dinkler, "Hebrews," *IDB* E-J (1962), pp. 573-75; F. V. Filson, *"Yesterday," A Study of the Hebrews in the Light of Chapter 13* (1967); F. F. Bruce, "The Kerygma of Hebrews," *Int* 23 (1969), 3-19.

INTRODUCTION. The questions of the authorship and the destination of the epistle to the Hebrews are unsolved problems. The traditional view has been that Hebrews is correctly named,[1] and that it was written to a community of Jewish Christians, probably in Rome (13:24), who in the face of threatening persecution were apostatizing from Christ and going back into Judaism. However, there is no reference to the Jewish-Christian controversy; Christ is made superior to the Old Testament, not to Judaism; furthermore, the warning against "falling away from the living God" (3:12) points to Gentile-Christian rather than to Jewish-Christian readers.[2] For the purpose of discussing the theology of Hebrews, we may leave this question open. In either case, the epistle[3] was written to a group of Christians who were facing persecution (10:32; 12:4), with whom the author was acquainted (13:18, 19, 23), who were on the point of falling away from Christ. The author writes to warn them against apostasy. This pur-

[1] The title, "To the Hebrews," is not original but came into use at an early date.
[2] For this problem, see the introductions by W. G. Kümmel and D. Guthrie.
[3] Hebrews sounds more like a sermon than a letter.

pose is clear from the several hortatory passages scattered throughout the book.[4] The author tries to steady his readers' loyalty to Christ by the line of argument that the blessings that have come to men in Christ are superior to all that has preceded him: Christ is superior to the old revelation (1:1-3), to angels (1:4-2:18), to Moses (3:1-19), to Joshua (4:1-13), to the Old Testament priesthood (4:14-10:31). If the readers are Gentile Christians, they must be former Jewish proselytes who would be very familiar with the Old Testament. We may study the theology of Hebrews without deciding whether the readers were Jewish or Gentile Christians. The problem faced by the author would be basically the same in either case.

DUALISM. The basic world view of Hebrews has been much debated. There is a twofold dualism in Hebrews: a dualism of the above and below—the real heavenly world and the transient earthly world; and there is an eschatological dualism: the present age versus the world to come. It has been often argued that the spatial dualism of two worlds—above and below—reflects platonic thought as mediated through Philo, while the eschatological dualism is a remnant of primitive Christian eschatology.

Some scholars have insisted that the spatial dualism of two worlds is the real center of the theology of Hebrews, and the eschatological dualism is an unassimilated leftover from tradition. "Whereas Jewish and Christian Apocalyptists envisaged the difference between imperfection and perfection primarily under the categories of *time,* distinguishing between this age and the age to come, the language of Hebrews suggests categories of *space,* distinguishing between this world and the heavenly world of spiritual realities. For the author of Hebrews, the present reality of the heavenly sphere into which Christ has passed and to which we are anchored, is the fundamentally important fact."[5] "Like Philo, our author accepts a kind of philosophical and cosmological framework which is more Platonic than biblical. Two successive aeons . . . are replaced by two co-existent, superimposed planes—the suprasensible world and the phenomenal world. The former contains the eternal ideas, which the second one attempts to embody materially. The former is 'heaven' for Philo, as it is in our epistle."[6] Other scholars have given greater weight to the role of eschatology but have concluded that the writer was unable to assimilate two utterly diverse theologies. "Our author is content to leave the two presentations side by side. He tries to find room for both of them in a theology which is at once primitive and Hellenistic, and which therefore suffers, in spite of its grandeur and suggestiveness, from a lack of inner harmony."[7] Other scholars have disagreed with these conclusions and have recognized that the eschatological

---

[4] 2:1-4; 3:7-4:11; 5:11-6:12; 10:19-39.
[5] F. D. V. Narborough, *Hebrews* (1930), p. 43.
[6] J. Hering, *Hebrews* (1970), p. xii.
[7] E. F. Scott, *Hebrews* (1922), p. 121.

perspective is fundamental to the theology of Hebrews.[8] This problem must be carefully examined.

The idea of two worlds appears in chapters 8 and 9 in the discussion of the priestly institution of the Old Testament. The Israelite priests offered gifts and sacrifices in an earthly temple. These, however, did not embody ultimate realities; "they serve as a copy and shadow of the heavenly sanctuary" (8:5). The Old Testament tabernacle was made in accordance with the pattern of the real in heaven. The earthly copies were purified with animal sacrifices; the heavenly realities must be purified with better sacrifices (9:23). Christ after his ascension entered into the real heavenly sanctuary (9:24). The institution of the Law provided only a shadow of the good things to come, not the true form of the heavenly realities (10:1). Faith is the means by which the believer can now lay hold of this invisible world of heavenly realities (11:1).

This indeed sounds very much like Philonic dualism. Philo believed that the entire phenomenal world was transitory and ephemeral—only a copy of the real, invisible, spiritual world of ideas in heaven, which are apprehended by the mind. Philo has entirely displaced the Jewish hope for the future with the Greek hope of the flight of the soul after death to the invisible world of eternal reality.[9]

Hebrews has not, however, displaced eschatology. Elements of it are found throughout the book. The object of all of God's dealings with men is "the world to come" (2:5). This future world will not be subject to angels but to Christ. However, Christ has been seated at the right hand of God, already crowned with glory and honor, but not yet being made Lord over all things (2:8). He is waiting until his enemies are made the footstool of his feet (1:11; 10:13).[10] This will occur at "the day" (10:25), i.e., the Day of the Lord that is drawing near. Christ "will appear a second time, not to deal with sin but to save those who are eagerly waiting for him" (9:28). This passage makes it unmistakably clear that Christians will receive the promised salvation (10:36) only at the parousia of Christ. "For yet a little while and the coming one shall come and shall not tarry" (10:37). This provides the clue for understanding the rest that remains for the people of God (4:9), the promised eternal inheritance (9:15), the promised homeland (11:14) or better country (11:16) promised the Old Testament saints. The use of the word "heavenly" to describe this Kingdom (11:16) does not look away from an eschatological future to a present world of invisible reality. Paul describes the eschatological resurrection in terms of heavenly bodies (I Cor. 15:40). "The *epourania*

---

8 See W. Robinson, *The Eschatology of the Epistle to the Hebrews* (1950); W. Manson, *Hebrews* (1950), pp. 9, 125, 142, 184, 189-91; C. K. Barrett, "The Eschatology of the Epistle to the Hebrews," *The NT and Its Eschatology*, ed. by W. D. Davies and D. Daube (1956), pp. 363-93; F. V. Filson, *Yesterday* (1967), pp. 69-70.

9 See G. E. Ladd, *The Pattern of NT Truth* (1968), pp. 25-31.

10 See the parallel eschatological passage in Paul in I Cor. 15:23-28.

are what is truly real, what is eschatologically future."[11] The longed-for homeland of 11:16 and the heavenly Jerusalem of 12:22 are also eschatological: the final aim of God's community.[12] The unshaken Kingdom (12:28) and the city to come (13:14) belong to this same futuristic perspective.[13] It is the new order that will emerge after God shakes the present order (12:26; cf. 1:11). Hebrews conceives of an invisible Kingdom already existing in heaven. When the present is shaken by a cosmic catastrophe, God's Kingdom will be left unimpaired and will stand out in its supreme reality and permanence.[14] Hebrews does not here say explicitly that God's Kingdom must come; but its coming is implicitly bound up with the second coming of Christ (9:28). The theology here is the same as that of Revelation 20:11; 21:1, where earth and heaven flee away from the face of the Judge on the great white throne, to be replaced by a new heaven and a new earth.[15] In the light of this eschatological perspective, the passing references to resurrection (6:2; 11:35) and to judgment (6:2; 10:27, 31; 12:23) are no accidental allusions but belong to his expectation of the end. It is also possible that the two references to faithfulness "to the end" (3:14; 6:11) are eschatological references, designating the end of the age, not the end of life. This age will end with a cosmic catastrophe by which the present world order will be shaken (1:11-12; 13:26) and the true eternal Kingdom of God, now invisible, will become visible.

The eschatological perspective alone accounts for the comparatively frequent emphasis on hope. We must hold fast our confidence and pride in our hope (3:6; 10:23); we must realize the full assurance of hope until the end—apparently the end of the world (6:11); we must seize the hope set before us (6:18); Christ has introduced a better hope than the Old Testament saints had because we have experienced its partial fulfillment.

Furthermore, it is not accurate to say that Hebrews, like Philo, contrasts the phenomenal world with the noumenal, regarding the former as unreal and ephemeral. Hebrews applies the idea of two worlds primarily to the Old Testament cult. The tabernacle with its priests was a copy and shadow of the heavenly sanctuary. *The real has come to men in the historical life and death of Jesus of Nazareth.* History has become the medium of the eternal. There is nothing ephemeral or transitory about Jesus' life and work. The Christ-event was history with an eternal significance. What Jesus did, he did *once for all* (*ephapax,* 7:27; 9:12; 10:10).

No New Testament book emphasizes the humanity of Jesus more emphatically than does Hebrews. He showed the same nature as those whom he came to save (2:14). He had to be made like them in every respect (2:17). Like them, he has suffered and has been tempted (2:18). Hebrews does emphasize Jesus' sinlessness, but he was tempted in every respect like

---

11 H. Traub, *TDNT* V, 540.
12 *Ibid.,* p. 541. See also H. W. Montefiore, *Hebrews* (1964), pp. 229f.
13 F. V. Filson, *Yesterday,* p. 70.
14 J. Moffatt, *Hebrews* (1924), p. 222.
15 F. F. Bruce, *Hebrews* (1964), p. 383.

other men (4:15). His sufferings were real; they wrung from him loud cries and tears (5:7). His humanity was real; he had to learn the meaning of obedience (5:8).

To be sure, Hebrews represents Christ as entering into the Holy Place in heaven, taking his own blood (9:12). "For Christ has entered, not into a sanctuary made with hands, a copy of the true one, but into heaven itself, now to appear in the presence of God on our behalf" (9:24). However, it is difficult to think that the author of Hebrews conceived of Jesus after his ascension realistically entering a literal Holy Place in heaven. To be sure, he does say, "Thus it was necessary for the copies of the heavenly things to be purified with these [animal] rites, but the heavenly things themselves with better sacrifices than these" (9:23). It is self-evident that the heavenly things experience no defilement or sin and therefore require no cleansing. One commentator says, "We cannot explain verse 23 in a satisfactory manner."[16] A statement like this should make it clear that Hebrews is describing heavenly things in earthly, symbolic language. What Christ did on the cross, although an event in time and space, was itself an event in the spiritual world. Eternity at this point intersects time; the heavenly is embodied in the earthly; the transcendental occurs in the historical. Christ's entrance into the Holy Place and sprinkling of his blood to effect cleansing and an eternal salvation occurred when "he . . . appeared once for all at the end of the age to put away sin by the sacrifice of himself" (9:26). Christ offered himself on the cross to purify his people (9:14). Sanctification was secured when Jesus sacrificed his body "once for all" (10:10). By dying, he "offered for all time a single sacrifice for sins" (10:12). Hebrews uses the liturgical language of the Old Testament cult to depict the spiritual meaning of what Jesus accomplished by his death on the cross. Here in history on earth is no shadow, but the very reality itself.

Furthermore, Hebrews places Christians in the same eschatological tension as did primitive Christianity. Christ has come "at the end of the age(s)" (9:26). This idiom is similar to the Pauline expression, "the ends of the ages" (I Cor. 10:11), and is an eschatological expression indicating that Christ's coming marked the time of fulfillment of the Old Testament hope. Because he has introduced the time of fulfillment, the present era is described as "the last days" (1:2). This idiom was sometimes used by the Old Testament prophets to designate the messianic age of fulfillment (Isa. 2:2; Ezek. 38:16; Hos. 3:5; Mic. 4:1). Thus Hebrews recognizes the present as the time of eschatological fulfillment (realized eschatology), while the consummation awaits the second coming of Christ.

This tension between the "already" and the "not yet" is evident at numerous points throughout the book. It first appears in the discussion of the rest God promised his people. Although Joshua led Israel into the

---

[16] J. Schneider, *Hebrews* (1957), p. 90.

promised land, this could not be equated with the promised rest. "So then, there remains a sabbath rest for the people of God" (4:9) in the eschatological consummation. We must not take it for granted but "strive to enter that rest" by obedience (4:11). However, because the present is the time of fulfillment, believers already enter God's rest (4:3). There is a proleptic experience of the eschatological blessing. "The 'rest,' precisely because it is God's, is both present and future; men enter it, and must strive to enter it. This is paradoxical, but it is a paradox that Hebrews shares with all primitive eschatology."[17]

Realized eschatology appears again incidentally in the expression of tasting the heavenly gift and the powers of the Age to Come (6:4-5). "The age to come" is a distinct eschatological idiom, even though Hebrews never uses the contrasting idiom, "this age." The heavenly gift, like the heavenly call (3:1) and the heavenly city (12:22), is eschatological—"the final aim for God's community."[18] Yet the eschatological blessing may already be "tasted," i.e., experienced in part.

Believers may also be said to enter the sanctuary by the blood of Jesus, by the new and living way that he opened for us through the curtain, that is, through his flesh (10:19-20). We can, therefore, now draw near to God. The Old Testament cult was marked by difficulty of access to God. As long as the outer tent is still standing, the way into the sanctuary is not yet opened (9:8). Since Christ has opened the way into the true spiritual sanctuary, believers everywhere may experience true access to God. "The heavenly tabernacle in Hebrews is not the product of Platonic idealism but the eschatological temple of apocalyptic Judaism, the temple which is in heaven primarily in order that it may be manifested on earth."[19] But since Christ has already appeared as the great High Priest, believers already have access to the sanctuary and God's presence. This is one of the main themes of Hebrews: through Christ's atoning work alone may be found entrance into God's presence. If this is rejected, there remains no other way.

Realized eschatology is found in the discussion of the heavenly Jerusalem and Mount Zion. While on earth, Christians are like the Old Testament saints, who "were strangers and exiles on earth" (11:13). They have here "no lasting city, but we seek the city which is to come" (13:14). This is Mount Zion, the heavenly Jerusalem (12:22). However, while this Jerusalem will come to earth only in the eschatological consummation, it can also be said that Christians in their conversion have come to this city (12:22).[20] This is another way of describing the present access to God won by Christ. We may now draw near to the throne of grace (4:16); we may draw near to God (7:19); we come near to the heavenly Jerusalem, but we do not yet enter it.

---

[17] C. K. Barrett in *The NT and Its Eschatology,* p. 372.
[18] H. Traub, *TDNT* V, 541.
[19] C. K. Barrett in *The NT and Its Eschatology,* p. 389.
[20] *Ibid.,* p. 376.

The threefold tension between the Old Testament forms, the New Testament realization, and the heavenly reality is evident in 10:1: "For since the law has but a shadow of the good things to come instead of the true form of these realities. . . ." The Old Testament provided only a shadow of the realities; the New Testament provides more—the "true form" (*eikōn*) of these realities. Yet the realities themselves remain in the future. The image is far more than a shadow. It is an exact replica, "not an imperfect, partial reproduction but a manifestation adequate to the reality itself." The possession of the reality awaits the eschatological consummation.[21]

If Hebrews makes use of Philonic dualistic language, it is thoroughly assimilated to a Christian world view of redemptive history with an eschatological consummation. However, it is not a strictly futuristic eschatology; it has broken into history in the person and work of Christ. Thus believers already experience the heavenly realities; yet they await their fullness at the end of the age.

CHRISTOLOGY. Hebrews has an explicit high Christology. The preexistence of Christ is mentioned at the very beginning. It was through Christ that God created the world (1:2).[22] Also, Christ by the word of his power upholds the universe (1:3). He reflects the glory of God and bears the very stamp of his nature (1:3). We find no discussion of the incarnation, but it is clearly in the author's mind when he speaks of Christ's coming into the world (10:5; cf. also 2:9).

Hebrews' favorite designation for Christ is "Son of God" (1:2, 5; 4:14; 5:5; 6:6; 7:3, etc.). As the Son, he is the heir of all things (1:2). As the Son of God, he shares in deity. The angels worship him (1:6). Hebrews even calls Jesus God by applying to him Psalm 45: "Thy throne, O God, is for ever and ever" (1:8). The deity of Christ is also seen in the use of Lord (*Kyrios*). Several times passages are quoted from the Old Testament in which God is referred to as the Lord (7:21; 8:8, 11; 10:16, 30). But Jesus is also *Kyrios*. The Jesus of history is twice called the Lord (2:3; 7:14); and once, a passage that in the Old Testament refers to God is applied to Christ (1:10). In some undefined sense, Jesus is God.[23]

Perhaps it is not particularly significant, but Hebrews refers to Jesus more often by his human name (10 times) than by his messianic name, Christ (9 times). The compound name, Jesus Christ, occurs three times. "Christ" is used without the usual Old Testament messianic implications. The use of "Jesus" illustrates that the author was very concerned with the actual Jesus of history.

Hebrews mentions Jesus' resurrection only once (13:20), but it emphasizes the heavenly session of Christ. The ascension is clearly in mind when it speaks of Jesus passing through the heavens (4:14). There he

---

[21] F. F. Bruce, *Hebrews,* p. 226.
[22] Literally "ages," meaning all that is contained in time.
[23] See O. Cullmann, *Christology,* pp. 310-11.

is crowned with glory and honor (2:9), and is seated at the right hand of God (1:3, 13; 12:2), where he waits until all his enemies are subdued beneath his feet. As the exalted Christ he continues forever, and ever lives to represent his people in the presence of God (7:24).

While Christ is called the "pioneer and perfecter of our faith" (12:2) and the forerunner into the inner shrine (6:19), it does not speak of the flight of the soul at death to join Jesus in heaven. One reference does speak of "the spirits of just men made perfect" (12:23), but this is not dwelt on. Resurrection is mentioned twice (6:2; 11:35), and Jesus must appear a second time to bring to his saints the fullness of salvation (9:28).

The emphasis on the full deity of Jesus in no way minimizes the author's view of his humanity. We have already seen that Hebrews emphasizes the full and real humanity of Jesus more than any of the other epistles.[24] His real humanity, his temptations and his sufferings were necessary for Jesus to feel at one with his people, to understand them, and to help them. He has identified himself with those he would save at every point except one—he was without sin (4:15).

THE HIGH PRIEST. The central theme in the Christology of Hebrews is the High Priesthood of Christ. The main argument of the book is that the Old Testament priestly institution was only a shadow of reality and could not deal with the problem of sin. The heavenly reality has come near in the death of Jesus by which he put away sin once for all. Therefore apostasy from Christ means doom, for there is no other way.

The author's thought in which he contrasts Christ's priesthood with the Aaronic priesthood is woven throughout the argument of chapters 5-10. He argues that the Old Testament cult really accomplished nothing in dealing with the real problem, that of purifying the conscience (9:9). It involved only the sacrifice of dumb animals, and this cannot touch the real problem of sin (10:4). All it can accomplish is an external ceremonial purity (9:13), and it is therefore weak and useless (7:18). In fact, the structure of the Old Testament tabernacle served to keep men away from God rather than open the way into his presence (9:8). The sacrifices are constantly repeated (10:1) and are impotent to take away sins (10:11). In fact, the very repetition of the sacrifices serves only as a reminder of sin (10:2-3). The Old Testament priests were inadequate, because they were mortal men (7:24) who must offer sacrifice for their own sins as well as for the people (5:3; 7:27).

On four different occasions, Hebrews describes the inadequacy of the Old Testament era in terms of its failure to bring men to perfection. "Gifts and sacrifices are offered which cannot perfect the conscience of the worshiper" (9:9; cf. 7:11, 19; 10:1). The idea of perfection (*teleioō*) is one of the repeated themes of Hebrews. It is the goal of the Christian life (6:1, *teleiotēs*), and was a goal that even Jesus had to achieve. He had to attain perfection through suffering (2:10). It is obvious that since Jesus

[24] See above, pp. 574f.

was the pre-existent Son of God, and also sinless in his humanity, "perfection" cannot designate moral perfection or a state of sinlessness. The RSV translates the noun by the word "maturity" (6:1). In 5:8, Jesus' perfection is parallel to his obedience. "He learned obedience through what he suffered; and being made perfect. . . ." The perfection of Jesus must therefore refer to his complete adequacy and effectiveness as the Redeemer of men.[25] Applied to men, it designates their complete consecration to God. Perfection and sanctification are closely related. "For by a single offering he has perfected for all time those who are sanctified" (10:14). As a man, although sinless, Jesus had to learn complete trust and dependence on God. Perfect manhood cannot be realized apart from dependence upon and communion with God. Jesus fulfilled this in himself, and opened the way for all men to enter into the same experience of complete consecration to God.[26] This perfection was utterly unattainable in the Old Testament system; therefore it had to be displaced (7:11). The Old Testament priesthood and sacrificial system was only a shadow of the future reality; it did not embody the reality itself (10:1); therefore it had to be displaced by a better priesthood and sacrifice that embodied reality.

This perfect priesthood was fulfilled by Jesus. He had the qualifications that set him apart from the Aaronic priesthood and enabled him to bring men to perfection. He did not choose the role for himself but was appointed by God (5:5). He took upon himself complete humanity. He shared the same nature as other men in every respect essential to humanity (2:17). He suffered all the temptations they suffer; therefore he is able to feel for those he came to save (4:15). As a man, he was different at only one point; he was sinless (4:15), and therefore did not have to offer sacrifice for himself as did the Old Testament priests (7:27). Through his human sufferings, he learned perfection—complete dedication and trust in God (2:10; 5:9; 7:28). In contrast to the Aaronic priests who died, Jesus holds his priesthood permanently, because he continues forever (7:23). Thus the true High Priest is "holy, blameless, unstained, separated from sinners, exalted above the heavens" (7:26).

Hebrews explains the superiority of Jesus' High Priesthood in terms of the order of Melchizedek. Melchizedek was a priest of Salem (Jerusalem) whom Abraham met after returning from successful battle. Abraham recognized Melchizedek as a true priest, and consequently gave him a tithe of all he possessed. Melchizedek appears in the Old Testament Scriptures suddenly and departs abruptly. No record was left of his birth, his ancestry, or his death. Hebrews seizes upon the silences of Scripture to interpret them to mean that "he is without father, mother, or genealogy, and has neither beginning of days nor end of life, but resembling the Son of God he continues a priest for ever" (7:3). This is an imperfect analogy, for Jesus had a human mother, and Hebrews is aware of his ancestry

---

25 See J. Y. Campbell, "Perfection," *IDB* K-Q, p. 730.
26 See B. F. Westcott, *Hebrews* (1906), pp. 64-68.

(7:14). The main point is that Abraham gave tithes to Melchizedek and received his blessing. This proves that Abraham recognized that Melchizedek was greater than he. Since Aaron was as yet unborn and was yet in the loins of Abraham, Levi in Abraham gave tithes to Melchizedek, thus proving the superiority of the latter. Christ is a High Priest after the order of Melchizedek, and is therefore superior to the Aaronic priesthood (5:6, 10; 6:20; 7:1-17). This would not be a kind of reasoning appealing to the modern critical mind, but it was persuasive in its own day. Hebrews uses this as scriptural support for Jesus as a priest who, as the Son of God, continues a priest forever.

The service that the new High Priest wrought is, as we have already seen, viewed from two points of view: the historical and the heavenly.[27] Jesus is himself both the High Priest and the sacrifice that the High Priest offers to God. He "offered himself without blemish to God" (9:14; cf. 7:27). He put away sin by the sacrifice of himself (9:26); by his death he made purification for sins (1:3). His death is efficacious; he tasted death for everyone (2:9). His death accomplished expiation for the sins of the people (2:17). It is clear that the author of Hebrews has in mind the historical death of Jesus, for he speaks of "the offering of the body of Jesus Christ once for all" (10:10; cf. 7:27). The author of Hebrews has no "theory of the atonement." He does not reflect on why it was necessary for Jesus to die, or how his death accomplishes salvation. He merely affirms that "without the shedding of blood there is no forgiveness of sins" (9:22).

As we have already seen, Hebrews views the death of Jesus on the cross both as an event in history and as an event in the spiritual world. If we were to take the language of Hebrews literally, we would have to think that after his death and resurrection Jesus ascended to heaven, passing "through the heavens" (4:14), where he entered the heavenly Holy Place, taking his own blood (9:12), which had already been shed on the cross, and purified the heavenly sanctuary (9:23-24). It is, however, self-evident that the heavenly sanctuary needs no purification. The author of Hebrews is applying the language of the Old Testament cult to the work of Christ on the cross. He is in reality blending the atoning and cleansing work of Christ on the cross with his heavenly work as mediator.

This is another aspect of the service Christ has rendered. By his ascension he has become the forerunner of all who follow him (6:20). Saints of the new era have a way opened for them into the presence of God that men of the old economy could not know. Although Jesus is pictured as messianic King, seated at the right hand of God (8:1; 10:12; 12:2), he is also pictured as the heavenly priest ministering as mediator in the presence of God. "He is able for all time to save those who draw near to God through him, since he always lives to make intercession for them" (7:25). He has entered into the heavenly sanctuary not only to cleanse it with his own blood (9:12), but also "to appear in the presence of God on

[27] Cf. above, pp. 572ff.

our behalf" (9:24). The picture is of Christians still in the world, weak and tempted, but helped through their temptations by a heavenly intercessor who effectively prays on their behalf.

The mission of the High Priest is effective. Three words, which appear frequently in Hebrews, describe his achievement for men: he has wrought their purification, their sanctification, and their perfection, none of which the Old Testament order was able to do. The perfect offering of Christ on the cross avails to "purify your conscience from dead works to serve the living God" (9:14). The Old Testament was unable to accomplish this; the constant repetition of the Old Testament sacrifices served as a reminder that they really accomplished nothing of eternal value. "If the worshipers had once been cleansed [purified], they would no longer have any consciousness of sin" (10:2). But in the work of Christ, the believer is assured that Christ has put away sin by the sacrifice of himself (9:26). Therefore we may "draw near to God with a true heart in full assurance of faith, with our heart sprinkled clean from an evil conscience and our bodies washed with pure water" (10:22). The last phrase is probably a reference to the waters of baptism; but it is only symbolic of the true reality—the cleansing of the conscience. Because of the work of Christ, believers may have the assurance that they are no more sinners but men who have been cleansed and purified from all stain and guilt of sin. Forgiveness of sins (10:18) is a synonym for this purification.

Christ's work is effective also in accomplishing the sanctification of the redeemed. "We have been sanctified through the offering of the body of Jesus Christ once for all" (10:10). Jesus "suffered outside the gate in order to sanctify the people through his own blood" (13:12). Sanctification does not have the connotation of sinlessness but of dedication to God.[28] The Old Testament sacrifices "sanctified for the purification of the flesh" (9:13), i.e., they effected ceremonial holiness and dedication to God; but only the sacrifice of Christ can avail to accomplish a true dedication.

Hebrews sums up the total work of Christ in terms of "perfection," which was unattainable under the old covenant (7:11). "By a single offering he has perfected for all time those who are sanctified" (10:14). He has enabled those who have been purified and dedicated to God to realize all that manhood ought to mean—complete reliance and trust in God.

The death of Christ is effective not only for those who come to faith in him. Because it is also an event in the spiritual world, he has become "the mediator of a new covenant, so that those who are called may receive the promised eternal inheritance, since a death has occurred which redeems them from the transgressions under the first covenant" (9:15).

Thus Christ is the inauguration of a new covenant. "Where there is a change in the priesthood, there is necessarily a change in the law as well" (7:12). This is one of the central themes of Hebrews, sounded in the first words of the book. The old covenant conveyed an inadequate revelation

---

[28] See above, p. 519.

of God. "In many and various ways God spoke of old to our fathers by the prophets" (1:1). The English is much weaker than the Greek: *polymerōs* and *polytropōs*. The Old Testament revelation was fragmentary, coming in many pieces. No single point of revelation transmitted all revelation together as a whole. The Old Testament revelation was also diverse, coming to men in different ways: through visions, dreams, theophanies, angelic appearances, and prophets, no one of which was adequate to convey the full revelation.

In these days of messianic fulfillment, God has spoken in a different way: through the one who is his Son. In Jesus, perfect Son of God and perfect man, God is able to say what he wants men to hear. In these opening words, the author of Hebrews does not refer to the old or to the new covenant, but the contrast is obviously in his thought. This becomes explicit later in the book, particularly in connection with Christ's priestly work.

Because Jesus abides a High Priest forever, he is "the surety of a better covenant" (7:22). "He is the mediator of a new covenant, so that those who are called may receive the promised eternal inheritance" (9:15), something that the old covenant was unable to accomplish. "If that first covenant had been faultless, there would have been no occasion for a second" (8:7). The significance of the new covenant is expounded by a prophecy from Jeremiah 31:31-34. The old covenant had proved ineffective to create a faithful people. "They did not continue in my covenant" (8:9). The new covenant will be different from the old, in that it will put God's laws into their minds and write them on their hearts. Then will be fulfilled the repeated goal of God's dealings with his people: "I will be their God and they shall be my people" (8:10).[29] The new covenant will bring with it a new dimension of inwardness. God's people will obey his will because of an inner motivation, not because of a written external law. They will experience an immediate knowledge of God. There was a sense in which Old Testament Israel had a knowledge of God, but it was impermanent. Israel repeatedly slid into apostasy and forgot her God (Judg. 2:10; Hos. 4:1, 6). The new covenant will bring an abiding, permanent knowledge of God. "All shall know me, from the least of them to the greatest" (8:11). This will be accomplished because "I will be merciful toward their iniquities, and I will remember their sins no more" (8:12). The Old Testament covenant with its repeated sacrifices served only as a constant reminder of sins. The new covenant made in the blood of Christ will enable God to forget the sins of his people and thus provide a way for the cleansing of their consciences from sin (10:22). In sum, the new covenant will provide two things: a better sacrifice that accomplishes a perfect forgiveness for sins, and a new heart in the worshipper so that he may be enabled to do the will of God. This theme of a new heart, parallel to the Johannine idea of a new birth and the Pauline idea of the indwelling

[29] See Exod. 6:7; 29:45; Lev. 21:12; Jer. 7:23; 30:22; Ezek. 11:20; Hos. 2:23; Zech. 8:8; 13:9; Rev. 21:3.

of Christ in the Spirit, is not a prominent theme in Hebrews. The author refers to it only in this quotation from Jeremiah. His chief concern is the provision made by the new covenant for the worshipper to draw near to God, to have real access to the holy Presence that the old covenant did not provide.

As the inauguration of a new covenant, Christ abolishes the old covenant. This is one of the main themes of Hebrews. If anyone who has professed allegiance to Christ turns in apostasy away from him, he cannot go back to the old way of worship, for it has been superseded—abolished. "In speaking of a new covenant, he treats the first as obsolete, and what is becoming obsolete and growing old is ready to vanish away" (8:13). Whether or not this is meant to say that the temple service in Jerusalem was about to disappear, it means at least that for the Christian the old order had no more validity. All that the old order symbolized was fulfilled in the reality of Christ, and therefore the old had fulfilled its mission and had no further place in the divine economy. This fact is repeated: "He abolishes the first in order to establish the second" (10:9). Because Christ has opened a new and living way for us through the curtain, that is, through his flesh (10:20), it is obvious the old order, which served only to keep men away from the presence of God (9:8), must be abolished. Thus Christ as the better Priest has fulfilled all that the old order promised: a better hope, because it is already partially realized in our access to God (7:19); a better covenant (7:22), which is based on better promises (8:6); better sacrifices (9:23)—all because of his shed blood (12:24).

The author of Hebrews mentions another achievement of Christ in his death that he does not dwell on. Through his death he has destroyed him who has the power of death, that is, the devil, that he might deliver men who through fear of death were subject to lifelong bondage (2:14-15). This theme of the Christus Victor has also appeared in John and in Paul.[30] Hebrews does not indicate in what way Christ's death accomplished a defeat of satanic power; but this is a strand of theology running throughout the New Testament, from Jesus' conflict with demons and victory over Satan (Lk. 10:18) to the final destruction of Satan in the lake of fire (Rev. 20:10). The word translated "destroy" (*katargeō*) is the same word used of Christ abolishing "death" (II Tim. 1:10) in his death and resurrection. It does not designate the complete destruction of the devil, but the fact that his power is broken, his grip on men who lived in fear of death torn loose.

It is in the context of Jesus' priestly work that Hebrews speaks of his second coming. He has appeared "once for all" in the eschatological hour to put away sin by the sacrifice of himself, but he must "appear a second time, not to deal with sin but to save those who are eagerly waiting for him" (9:27). The high-priestly work of Christ goes on in his intercession in heaven; it will be completed only when he comes again. Here "sal-

[30] See pp. 227f., 434ff.

vation" is eschatological, and will be the work of the returning Christ.[31] What he wrought on the cross is once for all (*ephapax,* 9:12; 10:10); his present work in heaven as priestly intercessor is "forever" (*eis to diē-nekes*), i.e., so long as this age lasts. There is an aspect of salvation that awaits his second coming: the final homecoming of a redeemed people into the heavenly city.

THE CHRISTIAN LIFE. The primary prerequisite for the Christian life in Hebrews is faith. Faith in Hebrews has a distinctly different emphasis from that in John and Paul. The latter conceive of faith as personal trust and commitment to Jesus that brings union with Christ and therefore salvation. In Hebrews faith is the faculty to perceive the reality of the unseen world of God and to make it the primary object of one's life, in contrast to the transitory and often evil character of present human existence. Hebrews gives us what amounts to a definition of faith as the term is used in this book: "Now faith is the assurance of things hoped for, the conviction of things not seen" (11:1). This statement involves both the transcendental and the eschatological character of the divine blessings. Faith is that which makes real to the believer the unseen world of God. "For whoever would draw near to God must believe that he exists and that he rewards those who seek him" (11:6), not in this life but in the fulfillment of the promised salvation. The man of faith is he who does not consider the visible world of human experience to be the world of ultimate values. He recognizes that above are the spiritual realities of God's Kingdom, which he cannot perceive with his physical senses but which to him are more real than the phenomenal world.

This is the context of the statement that Jesus is "the pioneer and perfecter of our faith" (12:62). He led the way and he perfectly filled the demands of a true faith. It is obvious that this cannot mean a personal commitment to God that resulted in Jesus' salvation. It meant rather that he who was faced with a cross and its shame could see beyond his human experience of suffering and death to the "joy that was set before him" (12:2). Jesus set the perfect example of a man who endured all the evils life could heap upon him because he lived his life in full confidence in him who is invisible.

Faith also knows that this invisible world will finally be the goal of those who trust God. It is "the assurance of things hoped for" (11:1). The invisible world will one day become a visible reality; the heavenly Jerusalem will come down to men. Faith is the faculty that makes these promises real.

The people of the Old Testament era who failed did so because they did not possess this faith. They could not see beyond their immediate situation in history; and if it was adverse, they had nothing to cling to. They did not understand the promises of God. God promised a rest to the people of the Old Testament, "but the message which they heard did not benefit them, because it did not meet with faith in the hearers" (11:2). All they could

[31] O. Cullmann, *Christology*, pp. 103f.

see was the rest in Palestine; they were oblivious to the true rest of God. By way of contrast, "we who have believed enter that rest" (4:3), but it is a spiritual and not a human, earthly blessing.

This note resounds through the great chapter of the heroes of faith (ch. 11). Those who had faith looked beyond their immediate situation and trusted the promise of God. By faith Abraham and his sons entered the land of promise, but they looked beyond it to the promise of God—to "the city which has foundations" (11:10). The Old Testament saints "all died in faith, not having received what was promised, but having seen it and greeted it from afar, and having acknowledged that they were strangers and exiles on the earth" (11:13). They were seeking a homeland (11:14), a better country, that is, a heavenly one (11:16). This confidence rested on the promise of God, who "has prepared for them a city" (11:16). Moses refused a high position in Egypt, choosing to suffer with the people of God because "he looked to the reward" (11:26).

The roll call of the heroes of faith in Hebrews 11 might suggest that faith is the faculty to lay hold of God to see demonstrations of his power and deliverance. However, while mighty deliverances are cited, they are not the central theme, for "some were tortured, refusing to accept release, that they might rise again to a better life" (11:35). This is followed by a roll call of men of faith who saw no deliverances but only sufferings, violence, and death. "And all these, though well attested by their faith, did not receive what was promised" (11:39). Faith is a laying hold of the promise of God for his ultimate salvation whether this life brings physical blessings or evils.

Hebrews was written to encourage believers to stand true in a faith that would hold fast to the promises of God and to the blessings that have already come in Christ. They had already met mild persecution. The Christian life was proving to be no guarantee against evil and affliction. They had already "endured a hard struggle with sufferings, sometimes being publicly exposed to abuse and affliction" and had experienced the plundering of their property (10:33-34). However, they had not yet suffered to the point of shedding their blood (12:4), i.e., martyrdom. Most of them had held fast to their faith, knowing that they "had a better possession and an abiding one" (10:34). The author writes because they need endurance so that they may do the will of God and receive what is promised (10:36), and in faith keep their souls (10:39).

The numerous exhortations throughout the book reflect the practical situation to which the author addresses himself. In his introductory paragraphs, after expounding the superiority and the deity of Christ, the author asks: "How shall we escape if we neglect such a great salvation?" (2:3). His hearers are in danger of "drifting away" from the message they have heard (2:1).

The problem is most vividly expressed when the author asserts that it is impossible to restore again to repentance those who have heard the gospel, have professed to receive it, but then "commit apostasy" (6:1-8).

Although the verb used is not the usual verb for apostasy (*aphistēmi;* cf. 3:12), the context clearly suggests deliberate and willful apostasy, not ordinary sin or what is now called "back-sliding." The RSV correctly renders the idea. Men who have embraced the gospel and entered the Christian life and the fellowship of the Christian church may become disillusioned because God is not protecting them from evil and suffering as they had expected. They may, therefore, deliberately turn their back on Christ and deny the profession they have made. For those who have been thus enlightened but who have willfully rejected the light, there can remain no way of salvation, for there can be no salvation except in Christ.

This same danger is expressed in 3:12: "Take heed, brethren, lest there be in any of you an evil, unbelieving heart, leading you to fall away (*apostēnai*) from the living God." This is the usual verb for to commit apostasy.

The passage in 10:26 has led many interpreters to think that the author of Hebrews is talking about post-baptismal sin in general. "For if we sin deliberately after receiving the knowledge of the truth, there no longer remains a sacrifice for sins, but a fearful prospect of judgment" (10:26-27). However, modern commentators generally admit that they (the sinners in view) are apostates, that is to say, those who deny Christianity after embracing it, in full knowledge of what they are doing.[32] There is a parallel in the apostates in the wilderness who "fell away from the living God" (3:12). They hardened their hearts and were rebellious. Hebrews can describe them simply as "those who sinned" (3:17). Such apostasy as Hebrews' readers were facing means nothing less than spurning the Son of God, profaning the blood of the covenant by which they were sanctified, and outraging the Spirit of grace (10:29).[33] The author of Hebrews is not interested in questions the systematic theologian asks: Were such people really saved people, only to lose their salvation? He is facing the actual situation where people gave all the evidences of conversion, separating themselves from their former pagan ways and identifying themselves with the Christian community, only to deny their faith in Christ in the face of persecution. For those who deliberately turn their backs on Christ, "there no longer remains a sacrifice for sins." Christ is the only way. To deny him means to close the door of salvation. In the face of persecution, the Christian has need of endurance, so that "[he] may do the will of God and receive what is promised" (10:36). That such apostasy seems not yet to have been widespread is evident from the words, "we are not of those who shrink back and are destroyed, but of those who have faith and keep their souls" (10:39).

In the concluding paragraphs, Hebrews has some practical exhortations for Christian conduct. The readers are exhorted to a life of love and purity. Elders or bishops are not mentioned; the church is guided by

[32] J. Hering, *Hebrews,* p. 93.

[33] Note that the sanctification of these people designates their apparent dedication to God.

"leaders" (*hēgoumenoi*) who speak the word of God and watch over the church (13:7, 24). The custom of extending hospitality to traveling Christian brethren is encouraged (13:2). The author closes with a personal note: Timothy has been released from prison, and the author hopes to accompany Timothy to visit his readers. This sounds quite Pauline, but the theology as well as the structure and style of Hebrews is so different from Paul's epistles that Paul can hardly have been the author.

40

JAMES

Literature:

There is a dismaying lack of good studies on the thought of James. The chapter in G. B. Stevens, *The Theology of the NT* (1906), is still valuable. See "Ideas of the Epistle," J. H. Ropes, *James* (1916), pp. 28-39; A. T. Cadoux, *The Thought of St. James* (1944); A. E. Barnett, *IDB* K-Q, pp. 795-99.

In addition to Hebrews, the New Testament includes several shorter letters that are called "Catholic," meaning universal, because, with the exception of II and III John, they are addressed to the church at large. The main ideas of these epistles need be only briefly summarized, for they add little to the main theological thought of the New Testament.

New Testament theology need not be primarily concerned with questions of introduction such as author, date and provenance, but these questions cannot be altogether ignored. Radically different answers have been given to the authorship and date of James. Scholars of an earlier generation, especially in Great Britain, often viewed James as one of the earliest of the New Testament epistles, and to have been written by James the brother of Jesus.[1] They emphasized the Jewishness of the book, its affinities with the Old Testament and Jewish Hellenistic literature.[2] The pendulum of criticism has swung to the opposite extreme so that A. E. Barnett can say that there is nothing in the letter that suggests the Jewish origin of the readers.[3] He dates the book around A.D. 125-150. This seems to be an ill-founded judgment in view of the fact that one of the classic interpretations of James is that it was originally a Jewish writing and was made Christian simply by the interpolation of the name "Christ" in two places (1:1; 2:1).[4]

---

[1] See the commentaries by J. B. Mayor, R. J. Knowling, and F. J. A. Hort.

[2] See W. Montgomery, "James," *Hastings' Dictionary of the Apostolic Church,* I, 632.

[3] A. E. Barnett, "James," *IDB* E-J, p. 795-99.

[4] See W. G. Kümmel, *Introduction* (1966), p. 286.

The work is thoroughly Jewish in tone. Moule has taken a judicious position in assuming that James may have been written by a Jewish Christian to conciliate non-Christian Jews. He must have belonged still to their synagogues. If not, the alternative is that the book was written when an antinomian interpretation of Christian liberty had already set in, whether or not it be through Paul's epistles.[5]

Conservative scholars have been able to make a good case for the traditional Jacobean authorship.[6] There are striking similarities between James and the teaching of Jesus.[7] Shepherd thinks his allusions reflect a knowledge of the Gospel of Matthew,[8] but there are no direct quotations, and it is equally possible that James drew upon an early tradition instead of the written Gospel and his allusions are never identical in language.[9] The major problem for the Jacobean authorship is that it makes no clear references to Jesus and his teaching, which one might expect James to do if he were in fact the author of the epistle. However, it is a psychologically sound principle that he may have deliberately chosen to keep altogether in the background the fact that he was the brother of our Lord. We know from I Corinthians 15:7 that James became a believer as a result of a special appearance of the risen Jesus and became the leader of the church in Jerusalem (Acts 15:13; 21:12; Gal. 1:19), filling a role as the head of the Jerusalem church that was unique in the apostolic age. The reference to the early and late rain (5:7) clearly reveals a Palestinian provenance. Later tradition confirms this, and tells us that James was martyred by hostile Jews in A.D. 62.[10] We may conclude that the epistle was written by James, the brother of Jesus, from Jerusalem, to Jewish Christians who were being oppressed by their fellow Jews.

James' purpose is altogether practical. It is impossible to conclude from the contents of the epistle that he was not interested in theology; a theologian can write practical homilies. James is writing to encourage fellow Jewish Christians who for the most part came from the lower level of society and who were being oppressed by wealthy fellow Jews. There is no clear evidence that they were suffering persecution because they were Christians. It is clear, however, that James writes as a Christian to fellow Christians. Jesus is designated "the Lord Jesus Christ" (1:1), and elsewhere he is called "the Lord of glory" (2:1). While this is the most striking christological phrase in the epistle, it clearly involves faith in the glorification, i.e., in the resurrection and ascension of Jesus—and even in his deity. James lives in anticipation of the last days—a time, James implies,

---

5 C. F. D. Moule, *The Birth of the NT* (1962), p. 166.

6 See D. Guthrie, *NT Introduction* (1962), III, 61ff.; G. W. Barker *et al., The NT Speaks* (1969), pp. 325ff.; R. H. Gundry, *A Survey of the NT* (1970), pp. 342ff.; E. F. Harrison, *Introduction to the NT* (1964), pp. 363ff.

7 See D. Guthrie, *NT Introduction,* p. 67.

8 M. H. Shepherd, *JBL* 75 (1956), 40-51.

9 See E. M. Sidebottom, *James, Jude, and I Peter* (1967), p. 15.

10 Eusebius, *Church History,* II, xxiii, 4-15.

when accumulation of earthly treasures will be meaningless.[11] The imminent return (parousia) of the Lord is still a living hope (5:7, 8); "the Judge is standing at the doors" (5:9). Such a hope argues strongly for an early date. It is obviously at the parousia that salvation will be complete—an experience described as receiving "the crown of life" (1:12), the saving of the soul from death (5:20), or inheriting the Kingdom of God (2:5). Such passing references make it clear that eschatology plays an important role in James' thinking.

James reveals little about the nature and structure of the church. It is striking that he uses the Jewish term "synagogue" to designate the Christian meeting (2:2). He refers to elders of the church (5:14) and instructs them in Christian pastoral duties: visiting the sick and anointing them with oil. This is to be accompanied by the confession of sins (5:16). He is probably referring to the ministry of elders who regain a man who has wandered away from the truth into error, and who will thus "save his soul from death" (5:20). In the churches with which James was familiar, teachers played an important role, and teaching apparently was a position warmly coveted—so much so that James warns his readers against seeking the position (3:1). It would probably be too much to say that teaching represented a formal office; neither is the relationship between elders and teachers clear. The fact that James follows his warning about teachers with a condemnation of sins of the tongue (3:2) suggests that he was aware of the practical problems of teachers who were intemperate and unwise in their use of language and who were more interested in the eloquence of words than soundness of conduct.

James is interested in temptation, which in turn reflects something of his idea of the nature of man. Apparently he was acquainted with Christians who shunned personal responsibility for their sins, blaming them on the situation into which God had thrust them, and so in fact blaming God. James insists that God can neither be tempted nor does he tempt anyone to sin. Each person is tempted when he is lured and enticed by his own desire (1:14). This translation of the AV, "lust," is unfortunate, for it generally connotes temptation to sexual sins. Such is not James' thought. The word for "desire" (*epithumia*) is not of itself a word bearing any evil connotation; in fact, Paul uses it of desire to be with Christ (Phil. 1:23). It is not clear whether James means desire for evil things. It would be possible to interpret desire here in a natural sense, desire for things that in and of themselves are not evil—somewhat analogous to our psychological understanding of the human drives. There is nothing wrong with them, until a man is "lured and enticed by his own desire." Their attainment becomes an end in itself so that one hungers to fulfill certain desires more than he wants the will of God. This may be illustrated by the rich farmer whose great ambition to accumulate earthly treasures led him to put his love for them ahead of his obligation to God (Lk. 12:16ff.). When

[11] See C. L. Mitton, *James* (1966), p. 178.

desires, good in themselves, lure and entice a man away from seeking the will of God, sin is conceived, and death is the final end. It seems clear that in James' thought, desire itself is not sinful or evil; it becomes such only when man is "lured and enticed" by it.

James has little to say about the nature of the Christian life, but what he says is important. One enters upon the Christian life when he is "brought . . . forth by the word of truth that we should be a kind of first fruits of his creatures" (1:18). The word, as is usual in the New Testament, is the proclaimed gospel. When it is received—when it is "implanted" within the heart (1:21), man enters upon salvation. The word "he brought us forth" (*apekuēsen*) means "to give birth to." James has already used it in saying that sin gives birth to death (1:15). The word is a common medical word designating physical birth. This is James' way of saying what other New Testament writers mean by analogous expressions such as to receive the Kingdom of God as a child (Mk. 10:15); to be born from above (Jn. 3:3); to be buried and raised with Christ (Rom. 6:1ff.; Eph. 2:1ff.); to become a new creation (II Cor. 5:13); and regeneration (Tit. 3:3). All of these expressions, including James', indicate that an inner change must take place by the Holy Spirit—by Christ—by the word, for one to enter the Christian life. Those who are thus born again and enter new life become in a special sense God's people. They represent the fact that in reality God as the Creator has a rightful claim on the entire human race. His redeemed people are first fruits of his creation.

It is interesting that while James sees the source of temptation to be the inner nature of man, he recognizes the existence of the devil, and implies that he too is a source of temptation; for he warns his readers to "resist the devil and he will flee from you" (4:7). This resistance may have reference not only to temptation to sin but to every wile by which Satan tries to turn men from the truth. The same word "to resist" is used in Ephesians 6:13: "take the whole armor of God, that you may be able to withstand in the evil day, and having done all, to stand." But it must include temptation to sin. James obviously shares the Jewish-Christian view of the existence of demons, although he refers to them only in passing (2:19). He does not reflect at all on the problem of how temptation can come both from the inner man and from the devil.

It is clearly implicit in James that the Christian lives in a tension between the "already" and the "not yet."[12] By the divine will one is born again; he has become one of God's redeemed people (1:18), with God's word planted in his heart (1:21). In spite of this fact, the Christian is subject both to temptations to sin of many sorts and to the pressure of trials (1:2) that may cause him to wander from the faith (5:19); yet he looks forward to the parousia of Christ when he will inherit the Kingdom of God (2:5) and enter into eternal life (1:12).

James' idea of the essence of Christian living clearly reflects the words of

---

[12] R. Bultmann denies this. See *Theology of the NT* (1935), II, 163.

Jesus. He expresses himself in Jewish idiom but pours into it a distinctly Christian content. It is the Christian's duty to fulfill the royal Law (2:7). The Law is royal because its author is none other than the King of the universe.[13] Obedience to the royal Law bestows freedom (1:25). In the day of judgment God will judge the works of men according to this Law of liberty (2:12). It is clear that James has the Old Testament Law in mind from his discussion of the weight of various sins (2:9-11). "Whoever keeps the whole law but fails in one point has become guilty of all of it" (2:10). The point that James is making is most interesting in view of the prevalent view that sexual sins outweigh all others. What seems to matter most to James is showing partiality, and that to non-Christians. The context of the whole discussion that precedes his statement about relative sins is the sin of currying the favor of a rich unbeliever who happens to attend a Christian synagogue (2:1ff.), and is showered with attention, while an obviously poor, shabbily dressed man is thrust aside. However, the essential content of the Law is summarized in Christian terms: "You shall love your neighbor as yourself" (2:8; see Mt. 22:39). If one really fulfills the Law, he will show love equally to the poor man and to the rich man.

James does present one theological problem in which he has been held to be in flat contradiction to the Pauline doctrine of justification. To be sure, the admission of a verbal contradiction is unavoidable. The heart of the Pauline doctrine of justification was the divine acquittal entirely through grace on the basis of faith without the works of the Law. No human being will be justified in God's sight by works of the Law (Rom. 3:20). James seems to contradict Paul. "What does it profit, my brethren, if a man says he has faith but has not works? Can his faith save him? . . . So faith by itself, if it has no works, is dead. But some one will say, 'You have faith and I have works.' Show me your faith apart from your works, and I by my works will show you my faith" (2:14-18). Scholars have argued that the author is familiar with Romans and Galatians and is deliberately refuting them. There is, however, a more judicious solution.[14] While the words are similar, the concepts are very different. It is probable that James is refuting perversions of Pauline teaching, whether the Pauline epistles were known or not. In fact, Paul and James have different meaning for the words faith and works. By faith, Paul means acceptance of the gospel and personal commitment to the one proclaimed. James means something different. "You believe that God is one; you do well. Even the demons believe—and shudder" (2:19). James is using the concept of faith in accordance with the rabbinic assertion of *'emuna,* which means the assertion of monotheism! Faith for Paul is personal, cordial trust; for James it is orthodox opinion.[15]

Furthermore, by works Paul designates Jewish deeds of formal obedience

[13] See K. L. Schmidt, *TDNT* I, 591.
[14] See J. Jeremias, "Paul and James," *ET* 66 (1954-55), 368-71.
[15] *Ibid.,* p. 370.

to the Law that provide man a basis for boasting in his good achievements.[16] For James, works are deeds of Christian love—deeds that fulfill the "royal law" of love for the neighbor. This is evident in his illustration of "works." A complacent word to Christian brethren who are in dire need is not love; only loving provision for their need really expresses love (2:15). Probably James' summation of pure religion—to visit orphans and widows in their affliction and to keep oneself unstained from the world (1:27)—means to avoid a spirit of greed and acquisitiveness, but on the contrary to minister substantially to the material need of helpless widows and orphans. This the primitive Jerusalem church had done (Acts 2:45; 6:1). In brief, James and Paul are dealing with two different situations: Paul with the self-righteousness of Jewish legal piety and James with dead orthodoxy.

There is an additional wealth of material in James about practical Christian living, but it hardly demands the attention of the theologian. The reader is referred to New Testament introductions and commentaries.[17]

---

[16] *Ibid.*, p. 371.
[17] See especially C. L. Mitton, *James.*

41

FIRST PETER

Literature:

G. B. Stevens, *The Theology of the NT* (1906), pp. 293-311; C. Bigg, "Doctrine, Discipline, and Organization in I Peter," *St. Peter and St. Jude* (1909), pp. 33-50; E. G. Selwyn, "Theology and Ethics," *The First Epistle of Peter* (1947), pp. 64-115; J. P. Love, "The First Epistle of Peter," *Int* 8 (1954), 63-87; W. C. van Unnik, "The Teaching of Good Works in I Peter," *NTS* 1 (1954-55), 92-110; R. Bultmann, *Theology of the NT* (1955), II, 180-83; D. G. Miller, "Deliverance and Destiny. Salvation in First Peter," *Int* 9 (1955), 413-25; W. C. van Unnik, "Christianity in I Peter," *ET* 68 (1956-57), 79-83; E. G. Selwyn, "Eschatology in I Peter," *The Background of the NT and Its Eschatology,* ed. by W. D. Davies and D. Daube (1956), pp. 394-401; F. V. Filson, "Partakers with Christ. Suffering in First Peter," *Int* 9 (1959), 400-12; W. C. van Unnik, "Main Theological Ideas," *IDB* K-Q, pp. 765-66.

The epistle of Peter claims to be written by the Apostle Peter (1:1), an "elder" who was an eyewitness of the sufferings of Christ (5:1). He has as a companion his "son," Mark (5:13). A strong tradition attributes this letter to the Apostle Peter, who used as his amanuensis or secretary Silvanus (Silas; 5:12).[1]

It was quite certainly written from Rome—designated as Babylon (5:13)—just before the outbreak of the Neronian persecution.[2] The letter is written in substantial part to encourage Christians in the face of persecution at the hands of the pagan populace (4:12; see 5:9), with the possibility that they might face official persecution because they were Christians (4:15ff.). This is what happened in the time of Nero. The letter is addressed "to the exiles of the dispersion" in the provinces of Asia (1:1), but it is clear that these are Gentiles (2:10; 4:3). Probably Peter is a circular

[1] The role of Silvanus in the composition of the letter is not clear. See E. G. Selwyn, *I Peter* (1947), pp. 9-17. Filson thinks the letter was written by Silvanus shortly after the death of Peter (*Int* 9 [1955], 403). For an entirely different view, see F. W. Beare, *Peter* (1959).

[2] Note the positive references to the Emperor: 2:13, 17.

letter like Ephesians. Many scholars, recent[3] as well as older,[4] see in Peter an excellent example of a relatively primitive Christian theology, recognizing striking parallels to Peter's sermons in Acts[5] and to the gospel tradition.[6] Although Peter is written to meet practical needs, to strengthen Christians in suffering[7] and not to give doctrinal instruction, it has rightly been called "a teaching epistle" because the Christian life is grounded in Christian truth.[8] Therefore the book is especially rich in truth. However, since these ideas embody little that is theologically different either from Peter in Acts or from Paul,[9] they need be here only summarized without extensive exposition.

DUALISM. Recent scholarship has emphasized the similarity in the world view of Peter and the sermons in Acts.[10] The language expressing the dualism found in the Gospels and in Paul—this age and the Age to Come—as well as all reference to the Kingdom of God is lacking. Present, however, is the eschatological tension between the present and the future, which is not merely chronological but also soteriological.[11] The death of Christ is not merely an event that promises an eschatological salvation; it is itself the object of messianic prophecy. The eschatological glory is inseparably related to the sufferings of Christ (1:11). This strong emphasis on the fulfillment of prophecy means that in some real sense the messianic age has begun.[12] The death of Christ was no mere historical event, but an event predestined by God before the foundation of the world (1:20). By his death, Christ has inaugurated the "end of the times" (1:20).

THE RESURRECTION OF CHRIST partakes of this eschatological character, for the resurrected Christ has gone into heaven and is now "at the right hand of God, with angels, authorities, and powers subject to him" (3:22). This language parallels that of Paul (Eph. 1:22). This means nothing less than that Christ has already entered upon his messianic rule at God's right hand, where he must reign "until he has put all enemies under his feet" (I Cor. 15:25). In Christ's messianic reign there is the tension between the already and the not yet. That Peter regards the present as the beginning of the eschatological (messianic) era is seen from the fact that

3 See the commentaries by E. G. Selwyn, A. M. Hunter in *IB*, B. Reicke, C. E. B. Cranfield.

4 G. B. Stevens, *The Theology of the NT* (1906), pp. 293-311.

5 E. G. Selwyn, *I Peter*, pp. 33-36. "I Peter reflects very closely the mind of the primitive Christian community" (p. 22).

6 See A. M. Hunter in *IB* XII, 83.

7 F. V. Filson, *Int* 9, 410. "The central theme is suffering."

8 E. G. Selwyn, *I Peter*, p. 64.

9 C. Bigg, *St. Peter and St. Jude* (1909), p. 36.

10 E. G. Selwyn, *I Peter*, p. 73.

11 Cf. R. Bultmann, *Theology*, II, 180f.

12 See E. G. Selwyn, "Eschatology in I Peter," *The Background of the NT and Its Eschatology*, pp. 394-401; *I Peter, loc. cit.* Love calls it "realized eschatology" (*Int* 8 [1954], 82). Van Unnik describes it as the situation "between the times" (*ET* 68 [1956-57], 82).

salvation is an eschatological inheritance to be revealed in the last time (1:5), and the historical appearance of Jesus is called "the end of the times" (1:20; see Acts 2:17; Heb. 1:2).

Christ's resurrection is not simply an event of the past; it is an event by virtue of which all who believe can, in subsequent time, enter into newness of life through the proclamation of the good news (1:23). God, who has wrought a work of newness of life in Christ's resurrection, brings newness of life to all who respond to his word. It is clear that Peter regards the Christian life as the inner transforming power of Christ.

Yet the world remains an evil place. The devil "prowls around like a roaring lion, seeking some one to devour" (5:8). By this vivid metaphor, Peter describes the situation of the Christian in the world—open to persecutions and sufferings; therefore salvation is also a matter of hope. In fact, "we have been born anew to a living hope" (1:3). What happens in the new birth is only the first word; the last work will be an inheritance—a salvation that is kept in heaven for you (1:5). "Hope" is an important key word in Peter.

ESCHATOLOGY. Thus eschatology plays a large role in the epistle. Peter does not use the word *parousia* but speaks several times of the revelation (*apokalypsis*) of Christ (1:7, 13; 4:13; see also 5:4). God has already bestowed the messianic glory on the ascended Christ (1:21); and it is nothing less than this messianic glory which will be disclosed at the revelation of Christ (4:13) and which Christians, afflicted in this world, will share (5:1, 10). This eschatological blessing is called an inheritance (1:4), a salvation ready to be revealed in the last time (1:5), the salvation of your souls (1:9) that is the goal of all prophetic teaching (1:10), a crown of glory (1:4). Negatively, it will be a day of visitation (2:12), i.e., of judgment (see also 4:17). All of this is similar to primitive Christian eschatology. While the eschatological inheritance is represented as already existing and being kept in heaven (1:4), it is not thought of as a blessing entered at death when the soul leaves the body, in spite of the fact that Peter speaks of the "salvation of your souls" (1:9); it is a blessing that will be *revealed* from heaven at the return of Christ from heaven.[13]

Peter says nothing more definitive about the eschatological state than is contained in this traditional Christian idiom. He does not mention the resurrection of believers, although we must assume it, and he says nothing to describe the nature of the eschatological Kingdom. His main concern is not with eschatology as such, but with the importance of the Christian hope to enable believers to meet suffering in this life victoriously. Peter regards the end as near (4:7); Christians have only a little while to suffer before Christ will deliver them (5:10). In brief, we find in Peter, as elsewhere,[14] a twofold dualism: a contrast between the present evil situation and the future eschatological era, and a contrast between the present

---

[13] See the same idea in Phil. 3:20-21.

[14] See the chapter on Johannine dualism (Ch. 17).

evil world and heaven above. The eschatological salvation will mean in effect the descent of the present heavenly blessings to believers on earth. As in John, there is a tension between the present and the future and between the below and the above.

The contrast between the evil world and heaven is particularly strong and plays an essential role in Petrine thought. Peter speaks of the world (*kosmos*) only twice, and there it means creation (1:20) or the inhabited world (5:9). But the idea of an evil world, hostile to Christ and therefore to Christians, is the setting of his thought. However, the world is the world of men who are devoted to sinful lives (4:3). He has in mind the degraded, corrupt pagan society in the midst of which Christians find themselves. From licentiousness, drunkenness, revels, and carousing his readers have been delivered, and their friends are surprised that they no longer pursue such sinful practices (4:4). This is the setting for the note of world denial in Peter; it is not denial of the world as such, but denial of the evil society whose practices they once shared, and from which they have been ransomed (1:18, 14). Against this background of sharp contrast, Christians are to regard themselves as aliens and exiles in the world (2:11). Peter could have added, with Paul, "Our commonwealth is in heaven" (Phil. 3:20). As the people of God, they are to regard themselves as "holy" (1:15), a holy priesthood (2:5), a chosen race and a holy nation (2:9). They have been made holy by the sprinkling of Christ's blood (1:2; cf. Exod. 24:8). When Peter quotes Leviticus 11:44-45: "You shall be holy, for I am holy" (1:15), the root idea is that as Israel was set apart from all the nations to be the people of God, so the church is the new people of God and stands in contrast to the world. Holiness means basically dedication, separation to God. The church is in the world but regards it and its evil customs and mores as hostile to the Christian life. Yet he exhorts submission to the institutions of the world—citizens to the state (2:13-14), wives to their husbands (3:1), and slaves to their masters (2:18).

GOD. Peter's concept of God contains the raw materials of trinitarian theology, but his expression is altogether practical rather than theoretical. His emphasis on God has particular reference to the Christian's evil plight in the world and the sufferings he must endure. His introduction contains references to God the Father, the Holy Spirit, and Jesus Christ (1:2). He has a strong emphasis on the sovereignty and transcendence of God. Men have come into the new people of God not primarily because they have chosen to do so but because they are Christians, because they have been chosen and predestined by the Father; sanctified—set apart—by the Holy Spirit, that they might live in obedience to Jesus Christ (1:2), being sanctified—set apart—by sprinkling with his blood.

HUMAN SUFFERING. The most important emphasis in Peter's thought about God is that of the divine providence in human suffering. The sufferings of which Peter speaks are not those of physical afflictions, natural evils, or accidents, or the sort of ordinary tragedy that besets all men. It is the sufferings men are called upon to endure because they are Christians. The trials they are called upon to endure (1:6) are false accusations of wrongdoing (1:12), which may be so strong as to be called a fiery ordeal (4:12). They may suffer simply because they are Christians (4:16). However, this is to be regarded as nothing strange (4:12), but is the normal experience of believers in an evil society (5:9). Although such trials may be attributed to Satan (5:8), Peter emphasizes that they happen according to the will of God. "For it is better to suffer for doing right, if that should be God's will, than for doing wrong" (3:17). God is the righteous judge both of the world and of his people. Therefore, those who suffer according to the will of God are to persist in well-doing and entrust their souls to a faithful Creator (4:19).

Furthermore, in such suffering Christians are doing no more than following Christ's example and participating in his sufferings (4:13). This is indeed an essential element in the Christian life. "For to this you have been called, because Christ also suffered for you, leaving you an example, that you should follow in his steps" (2:21). In this connection Peter emphasizes the meekness of Christ. "When he was reviled he did not revile in return . . . but trusted to him who judges justly" (2:23). We are reminded of the words of Jesus, that every man who would be his disciple must be willing to take up his cross (Mk. 8:34). This means a willingness to share Jesus' sufferings, and even his death.

Because Christian suffering is according to the will of God and only follows the example of Christ, the Christian response should be not merely one of passivity but rejoicing. Suffering under the hand of God has a salutary effect; it proves the validity and reality of Christian faith. It demonstrates that the believer's faith is genuine, even though it be tried by fire; and this is a subject for rejoicing (1:6-7). Furthermore, suffering in some way has a sanctifying influence. "Whoever has suffered in the flesh has ceased from sin" (4:1). Some take the verb to be a passive (*pepautai*), meaning that such persons are freed from the dominion of sin.[15] However, the verb may be a true middle and be quite intelligible in its context. Anyone who has suffered because he is a Christian has obviously broken with his old sinful life and suffers precisely because he no longer participates in the flagrant evils of his erstwhile friends (4:3-4). Such suffering is a testimony to the change in a man's life from pagan evil to Christian conduct. In view of all this, Peter exhorts his readers to "humble yourselves, therefore, under the mighty hand of God . . . cast all your anxieties on him, for he cares for you" (5:4-7). Thus Peter desires his readers to face the evils that are befalling them not with stoic pessimism or mere passive fatalism, but with an affirmation that they play a positive role in God's will for the Christian life.

[15] J. N. D. Kelly, *Peter and Jude* (1969), p. 166; see also A. M. Hunter, *IB* XII, 135, who cites Rom. 6:7: "He who has died is freed from sin." See 2:24: "that we might die to sin."

CHRISTOLOGY. Peter clearly holds a high Christology, although it appears only incidentally. Although he does not speak of Christ as "the Son," his opening statement placing Christ on a par with the Father demands a belief in his unique sonship. Some interpreters see a reference to Christ's pre-existence in the statement that he was predestined before the foundation of the world (1:20), but that is by no means necessary. Christians also have been predestined (1:1). Peter basically regards Christ as "the Lord" (1:3, 13; 3:15). His concern is practical more than theological: the relationship of believers to Christ as their Lord. The Father is also the Lord (1:25; 3:12). Peter applies to Jesus as Lord statements that in the Old Testament refer to God the Father (2:3; see Ps. 34:8). The position Peter assigns to Christ is "one which needs the doctrine of the Incarnation to set it forth."[16]

ATONEMENT. Although Peter sets forth no clear view of the atonement, the death of Christ and its redemptive meaning are important in his thought. In his introductory sentence reference is found to the blood of Christ (1:2), which in this case effects the believer's sanctification and participation in the people of God. In another reference, the "precious blood of Christ" (1:19) is the means of ransoming men from their sinful lives. In his death, Christ "bore our sins in his own body on the tree" (2:24). This appears to be an allusion to Isaiah 53:12: "he bore the sin of many." This must mean nothing less than that Christ took the blame for our sins, suffering the curse that is the penalty of sin, namely, separation from God. He endured the penal consequences of our sins.[17] Peter's main concern is practical. The effect of the atoning death of Christ is "that we might die to sin and live to righteousness" (2:24). The word for "die" (*apoginomai*) is different from the usual Pauline word and in this context means to be done with, not to partake of. Peter is not so much concerned with the removal of guilt as with the change in the life of these erstwhile pagans.

Again, Peter says that Christ died for (*peri*) sins "once for all," the righteous for (*hyper*) the unrighteous, that he might bring us to God (3:18). It is only by the death of Christ that sinful men may be constituted the people of God. The word "once for all" (*hapax*) is important. It indicates that an event in history has been invested by God with atoning and efficacious power.

THE CHURCH. Peter's concept of the church is prominent, even though he does not use the word *ekklēsia*. He regards the church as the true Israel. The old Israel has stumbled at the one whom God designed to be the cornerstone for his spiritual temple. "They stumble because they disobey the word" (2:8). Yet this is no historical accident; it has occurred under the providential hand of God. "They stumble . . . as they were destined to do"

[16] E. G. Selwyn, *I Peter,* p. 249.
[17] *Ibid.,* p. 180.

(1:8). Israel's place has been taken by the church, who are "a chosen race, a royal priesthood, a holy nation" (2:9). They constitute the true temple of God, as living stones being built into a spiritual house (2:5). They are also a holy priesthood, replacing the Old Testament priesthood, who minister to God by offering "spiritual sacrifices acceptable to God" (2:5). That Peter regards the church as the true Israel is further supported by the fact that he, like Paul (Rom. 9:25-26), applies to the church words that in their Old Testament context refer to the future conversion of literal Israel (Hos. 1:10), "Once you were no people, but now you are God's people; once you had not received mercy, but now you have received mercy" (2:10; cf. also Hos. 2:23).

Peter reflects a simple organization of the church. It is ruled by elders (5:1), whom Peter exhorts to "tend the flock of God" (5:2) in discipline and doctrine. Peter does not refer to them as "bishops" although he is familiar with the word in a religious context. Christ is the "Shepherd and *episkopos* of your souls" (2:25).

There is no reference to the Lord's Supper, and a single reference to baptism. After referring to Noah's ark, in which eight persons were saved from the flood, he says, "Baptism, which corresponds to this, now saves you. Not as a removal of dirt from the body but as an appeal to God for a clean conscience, through the resurrection of Jesus Christ" (3:21). This brief verse is beset by difficult exegetical questions that cannot be here discussed.[18] While Peter says that in some sense or other baptism may be said to save us, the context makes it clear that Peter emphatically denies that the external elements of baptism constitute either its essence or its power.[19] The meaning of baptism is not the external cleansing of the flesh with water; it is the appeal[20] to God for a cleansed conscience. Its power is not found in water but in the resurrection of Jesus Christ. Baptism may be said to save only "through the resurrection."

ESCHATOLOGY. We have discussed Peter's eschatology at the beginning of the chapter in connection with Peter's world view. There remains one difficult verse. The resurrection of Christ was not a mere revitalization of his physical body. He was "put to death in the flesh but made alive in the spirit" (3:18). It is difficult to decide whether "spirit" should be capitalized (AV) or not (RSV), depending on whether the spirit is Christ's spirit in contrast to his body, or whether it is the Holy Spirit. If it is the former, we may have the idea of an altogether "spiritual resurrection" in contrast to the resurrection of the body. This, however, is contrary to primitive Christian belief, which always thought of the resurrection of the *body*, although of a body transformed by the Holy Spirit. It is better, therefore, to take flesh and spirit not as two parts of Christ, but two different ways of viewing the whole

---

[18] For a careful discussion, see G. R. Beasley-Murray, *Baptism in the NT* (1962), pp. 258-62.

[19] *Ibid.*, p. 262.

[20] The word can also mean "pledge." See *ibid.*, p. 261.

Christ. Flesh is the human sphere of existence; Spirit is Christ in his heavenly sphere of existence.[21] This can include his bodily resurrection, but the body glorified by the Holy Spirit.

Our problem is with the words that follow: "in which [i.e., in the Spirit] he went and preached to the spirits in prison, who formerly did not obey, when God's patience waited in the days of Noah, during the building of the ark" (3:19-20). We can do little more than outline the three major interpretations.[22] The older patristic interpretation is that in the intermediate state, Christ in the Spirit went and preached the gospel to the spirits of dead men imprisoned in Hades, who either lived in the days of Noah or in the time before Christ.[23] This view soon lost favor, for it opened the door to the possibility of salvation after death. A second view, held by Augustine and many Reformers, holds that Christ in his pre-existent state of being preached the gospel through Noah to Noah's living contemporaries. The third view, most widely accepted today, is that in the intermediate state Christ proclaimed the victory of the gospel to fallen angels imprisoned in Hades.[24] The "preaching" involved may not mean an offer of salvation, but the triumphant announcement that through his death and resurrection, Christ had broken the power of the spirit world.[25]

THE CHRISTIAN LIFE. There are two outstanding emphases in Peter as to the Christian life, which we need here only refer to briefly,[26] for they have already entered into our discussion. The first is steadfastness in suffering. Suffering is the normal experience of Christians because the world is to them an alien land. It must be borne patiently and steadfastly, even with rejoicing, for it occurs under the providential hand of God, brings added blessings with it, and gives assurance of sharing Christ's future glory (4:13).

The second is that of good behavior (the verb *agathopoieō,* "to do good," occurs four times in Peter—2:15, 20; 3:6, 17—but nowhere in Paul). This doing of good is not the good works of Jewish legalism, but involves righteous conduct in contrast to pagan sinfulness (4:2). This good behavior is itself a witness to unbelievers and will frustrate their hostility (2:15), and possibly win them to Christ (3:1). It includes a right relationship to other men, and submissiveness to the established institutions of the state (2:13, 15), family (3:1, 6), and even of slaves to their masters (2:18). The Christian life is to express itself in true love toward the brethren (1:22) and in tenderness and humble-mindedness (3:8; 5:6).

---

21 See J. N. D. Kelly, *Peter and Jude,* p. 151. See the parallel thought in Rom. 1:3.

22 See B. Reicke, *Disobedient Spirits and Christian Baptism* (1946).

23 This view is supported by A. M. Hunter in *IB* XII, 132.

24 See Jude 6: "And the angels that did not keep their own position but left their proper dwelling have been kept by him in eternal chains in nether gloom until the judgment of the great day."

25 See J. N. D. Kelly, *Peter and Jude,* p. 156; A. M. Stibbs, *First Peter* (1959), p. 142.

26 W. C. van Unnik, "Peter," *IDB* K-Q, p. 765.

42

SECOND PETER AND JUDE

Literature:

There is very little literature in English dealing with the theology of II Peter. See E. Käsemann, "An Apologia for Primitive Christian Eschatology," *Essays on NT Themes* (1964), pp. 149-168; E. M. B. Green, *2 Peter Reconsidered* (1961); D. Guthrie, *NT Introduction* (1962), III, 164-68.

THE SECOND EPISTLE OF PETER claims to come from the pen of the apostle, Simon Peter (1:1), who was an eyewitness of Jesus' majesty at the transfiguration (1:16-18), shortly before his death (1:14). If this claim is trustworthy, the Second Epistle must have been written shortly after I Peter. There are admittedly difficulties in accepting the apostolic authorship of the book, but conservative scholars have not found these difficulties insurmountable and therefore continue to defend the Petrine authorship.[1]

The occasion for the writing of the letter determines its contents. II Peter was written for an entirely different purpose than I Peter; this is the reason for the striking difference in the substance of the two letters. If I Peter was written to encourage his readers in the face of persecution, II Peter was written to warn them against false teachers (2:2). They are clearly teachers within the church who have apostatized from the sound faith (2:21). We can determine from Peter's strong emphasis on "knowledge," by which he counters these false teachers, that they were gnostics who claimed to have special access to divine truth.[2] It is clear that they claimed to have achieved the true freedom (2:19), but it is equally clear that their freedom was freedom from Christian discipline and freedom to give free

[1] See the introductions by E. F. Harrison (1964), D. Guthrie (1962), R. H. Gundry (1970), G. Barker *et al.* (1969), and especially E. M. B. Green, *2 Peter Reconsidered* (1961) and *Second Peter and Jude* (1968). Barker *et al.* think it was composed by one of Peter's disciples shortly after his death and therefore contains genuine Petrine material.

[2] He mentions knowledge of God or Christ seven times in this short letter, thus emphasizing the true knowledge through the gospel in contrast to the pseudo-knowledge of these "gnostics."

vent to their bodily appetites. We know that ancient gnosticism moved in two directions: either ascetic control of the appetites or antinomian freedom; and Peter's oppenents followed the latter course. One of their primary doctrinal heresies was denial of the parousia of Christ; and Peter devotes most of the third chapter to this problem.

Many scholars reject the apostolic authorship of II Peter on the ground that its theology reflects second-century Christianity in contrast to the authentic apostolic form. It is said to have a degenerate Christology, a sub-Christian eschatology, and an unsatisfactory ethic that considers evil as imprisonment in the world of sense.[3] All this is reinforced by Käsemann's argument that the world view of the author is that of Hellenistic dualism rather than that of the Christian eschatological tension. Käsemann finds this dualism in the contrast between escaping the corruption that is in the world because of passion and partaking of the divine nature (1:4). "It would be hard to find in the whole New Testament a sentence which, in its expression, its individual motifs and its whole trend more clearly marks the relapse of Christianity into Hellenistic dualism."[4] This is further supported by the argument that "faith" in Peter (1:1, 5) means acceptance of orthodox tradition rather than personal commitment to Christ.[5] Faith is acceptance of orthodox doctrine, by which a man is enabled to escape his imprisonment in sensuality and finally to attain to a world without death.

This is indeed one possible exegesis of the passage cited (1:1-4), but it is improbable. In the first place, a possible Hellenistic dualism is shattered by the vivid apocalyptic eschatology of 3:10ff. Entrance into God's eternal Kingdom (1:11) is not the apotheosis of the soul at death but entrance into the new heavens and new earth (Isa. 65:17; 66:22).

Furthermore, it is not at all clear that faith is acceptance of apostolic doctrine. Peter does unquestionably place strong emphasis on the apostles as conveyors of truth (3:2; cf. 1:12) in refutation of the claim of gnostics that they have a new and fresh access to divine truth. However, faith, while not defined, is paralleled by knowledge (1:2, 3 *et passim*); and knowledge in Peter is not knowledge of theological truth nor mystical union with God as in gnosticism, but it is knowledge of God and Jesus our Lord (1:2). As in the Gospel of John, it is a personal relationship to God in Christ.[6] Furthermore, the idea that ordinary Christians have obtained a faith of equal standing with that of the apostles "in the righteousness of our God and Savior Jesus Christ" (1:1) suits the idea of saving faith in Christ better

---

[3] The most vigorous recent statement of this position is that of E. Käsemann, "An Apologia for Primitive Christian Eschatology," *Essays on NT Themes* (1964), pp. 169-95.

[4] *Ibid.*, pp. 179-80. If this is true, it is worth remarking that the epistle has adopted the basic world view of the very gnostic heresy it is refuting.

[5] *Pistis* does indeed mean that which is believed in Jude 3, 20.

[6] For this view of faith as trust, see the commentaries by C. E. B. Cranfield (*Torch Bible Commentaries*) and E. M. Sidebottom (*Century Bible*), *in loc.*

than a correct theology. Such faith is not a human attainment but is the gift of God.

Admittedly, the idiom of partaking of the divine nature is probably deliberately taken over from gnostic idiom. However, such language can be found in the middle of the first century A.D.[7] And it is not at all clear that Peter means the same thing as the gnostics, namely, apotheosis. In its context the thought seems to be that of entering the Christian life rather than the goal of the Christian life after death.[8] Escaping the corruption that is in the world and partaking of the divine nature are two sides of the Christian experience. Peter calls it "life" in verse 3; and life here is in parallelism with godliness and refers to a present experience of life. While Peter uses gnostic idiom, he does so to refute the gnostic claim. By it he means the same thing that Paul means by union with Christ.

Furthermore, there is no reason to understand Peter's idea of the "corruption that is in the world" (1:4) to mean imprisonment in the world of the senses. In fact, this cannot be the case, for escape from the defilements of the world has already occurred "through the knowledge of our Lord and Savior Jesus Christ" (2:20) for the true "gnostic." Gnostics taught that *gnōsis* was the destiny of man after death; in this life the body doesn't matter, so one is free to give full expression to all bodily appetites. Peter says, on the contrary, that this very immoral conduct constitutes the defilement of the world from which the Christian "gnostic" has been delivered.

If this is the correct interpretation of II Peter, we find in him, as in other apostolic expressions of Christianity, the tension between the already and the not yet. Christians have already been delivered from the corruption that is in the world; yet they await the new heavens and new earth in which dwells righteousness. They have already entered life; they have shared the divine nature in the sense of having received the gift of the Spirit of God and of sonship;[9] yet they await entrance into "the eternal kingdom of our Lord and Savior Jesus Christ" (1:11).[10]

II Peter is of special interest because of Peter's teaching about Scripture. He does indeed emphasize the importance and the primacy of the apostolic norm of truth. This is because many in the church have departed from the truth and propagated heretical teachings, reviling the way of truth (2:1-2). In reality, the truth is "a holy commandment" delivered to the church through the apostles (3:2). However, this does not stand in contradiction to personal commitment and relationship to Christ. It is by no means a mere formal orthodoxy. Paul claims with equal vigor the authority of the apostles as vehicles of divine truth (Rom. 16:26; Eph. 3:5).

---

[7] See E. M. B. Green, *2 Peter Reconsidered,* p. 23.

[8] See the commentaries by Cranfield and Sidebottom for this interpretation; see also B. Reicke (*Anchor Commentary, in loc.*).

[9] E. M. Sidebottom, *James, Jude and 2 Peter* (1967), p. 106.

[10] On this see E. M. B. Green, *2 Peter Reconsidered,* p. 18. This is one of the points contradicted by Käsemann in *Essays on NT Themes,* p. 170.

Peter has one of the classic statements about inspiration in the entire Bible. "No prophecy of scripture is a matter of one's own interpretation, because no prophecy ever came by the impulse of man, but men moved by the Holy Spirit spoke from God" (1:20-21). Peter's primary reference is to the Old Testament Scriptures. The first part of the passage is difficult. It may stand in refutation of gnostic enthusiasts who claimed to have a new word from God that supplemented the received gospel. It then means that the interpretation of Scripture is not a private matter but belongs to the church as a whole, which is the custodian of the apostolic truth. However, this would not explain why Peter places inspiration and interpretation so close together, the latter being the logical issue of the former. Peter is referring to the authentication of Scripture rather than to its interpretation.[11] To be sure, Peter is contrasting the truth of Scripture with the "myths" (1:16) of the gnostics; but he does so by authenticating Scripture because of the inspiration of its authors. "The true prophets did not prophesy out of their own heads according to their own caprice."[12] He implies that the only source of divine truth is Scripture, because its authors were inspired, and therefore able to write the divine truth.

Peter's concept of the prophetic word is significant. It is entirely trustworthy, but it is likened to a lamp shining in a dark place. An ancient lamp was vastly different from modern electric lights; at best it gave only limited light. However, it provided sufficient light for the bearer to make his way through dark streets. In other words, the prophetic word is the truth of God, but only partial truth. The full truth will be disclosed when "the day dawns and the morning star rises in your hearts" (1:19)—at the parousia. Prophecy, then, is light shining from the future upon the dark present to enable God's people to make their way in the world. It is in no way a full blueprint of the future.

II Peter gives us the earliest reference to the fact that the apostolic church regarded the Pauline writings—or at least some of them—as Scripture. Peter refers to letters of Paul with which his readers were familiar that were sometimes hard to understand, "which the ignorant and unstable twist to their own destruction, as they do the other scriptures" (3:16). The word translated "scriptures" (*graphai*) may not have a technical meaning here,[13] but it probably does designate the Old Testament Scriptures, placing Paul's writings on the same level. There is no need to think that Peter was familiar with a collection of Pauline writings, only that he was familiar with some of them.

Peter, probably following Jude 6,[14] tells us something about angels, a subject that pervades such apocryphal books as I Enoch but is not found

---

[11] M. Green, *Second Peter* (1968), p. 90.

[12] C. E. B. Cranfield, *I and II Peter and Jude* (1960), p. 182.

[13] *Graphai* can designate noncanonical writings. See G. Schrenk, *TDNT* I, 756.

[14] There is a clear interdependence of some sort between II Peter and Jude, but its precise nature is disputed. Probably Jude is prior to Peter. See D. Guthrie, *NT Introduction* (1962), III, 240-48.

in the rest of the New Testament, except Jude. There is a class of angels who sinned (Jude says they left their proper dwelling, v. 6) and who were therefore cast down into Sheol,[15] where they are imprisoned until the day of judgment (2:4). This is the New Testament source of the idea that evil spirits are fallen angels.

We must conclude from the contents of II Peter that one of the chief doctrinal errors of the gnostics was denial of fundamental Christian eschatology and the coming of the Lord. This can be the only reason that Peter devotes so much attention to eschatology. Whereas I Peter speaks of Christ's *apokalypsis* (1:7, 13), II Peter speaks of his *parousia* (3:4). This should cause no problem, for Paul uses both terms interchangeably. The gnostics denied the teaching of Christ's return. It is obvious from verse 4 that II Peter was written late in the apostolic age when the delay of the parousia could be felt to be a problem. The gnostics ridiculed the idea of the parousia, probably favoring the idea of salvation at death. They mocked, "Where is the promise of his coming? For ever since the fathers fell asleep, all things have continued as they were from the beginning of creation" (3:4). Many scholars understand the "fathers" to be the Christian fathers and use this as an argument for a second-century date.[16] But the word is never used of Christians in the New Testament, and it is more likely that the Old Testament fathers are meant. The mention of creation takes us back into Old Testament times.

Peter answers that God does not count time as men count time. One day is as a thousand years and a thousand years as one day. That is, Christ's parousia could be delayed as men reckon time. In reality, the delay of the parousia has a merciful purpose: it gives sinful men more time to repent (3:9). However, Christ will return at an unexpected time, like a thief in the night.[17] The parousia can be hastened by proper Christian conduct. The universal proclamation of the gospel must precede the end, and will hasten its coming.[18] The Day of God is not for the Christian a day of terror but of entrance into his eternal Kingdom (1:11) and therefore is an object of eager expectation.

The two aspects of the Day of God that Peter emphasizes are the fact of judgment, and the coming of a new righteous order. He emphasizes judgment because in the last analysis only divine judgment can deal with the apostate teachers and mete out their due. The day will be a day of judgment and destruction of ungodly men (3:7). The importance of the divine judgment is seen in the fact that in chapter 2 this is a central theme. If God did not spare the angels that sinned, if he did not spare the ancient world when it became corrupt in the days of Noah, if he did not

---

[15] The Greek word is *tartaros,* which embodies a Greek idea of the underworld; but this word is also used in Jewish literature as a synonym for Sheol. See Arndt and Gingrich, *Lexicon, in loc.*

[16] See Arndt and Gingrich, *Lexicon,* p. 640.

[17] Cf. Mt. 24:43; I Thess. 5:2.

[18] A. E. Barnett, *IB* XII, 203. See Mt. 24:14; Acts 3:19.

spare Sodom and Gomorrah, he can be counted on to bring the corrupt apostates to judgment (2:4-10).

The coming of the Day of God, which is synonymous with the "day of the Lord" (3:10) and "the day of judgment" (2:9), will witness a complete transformation of the present fallen order. It will occur in a fiery conflagration (3:10, 12) that will purge the universe of its corruption, including the corrupt apostates, and witness the establishment of new heavens and a new earth (3:13). It has often been argued that Peter here reflects the stoic idea of world conflagration; but this is doubtful, for the fundamental theology is entirely different. The stoic view of *ekpryōsis* held that an invisible fire was the essence of things and interpenetrated all the world and all beings. The world was destined to be dissolved into the primal fire, only for a new cycle of existence to occur and a new world order to emerge. This cycle of fire-world-fire was to go on indefinitely. Peter's theology is more in line with the biblical idea of fire as an agent of divine judgment.[19]

The prophets always view the Kingdom of God as being established on the *earth,* but they describe the relationship between the old and new orders in different ways. Sometimes continuity is emphasized; the new order is much like the old, except that the curse is removed (Amos 9). Sometimes discontinuity is emphasized, and the redeemed order is called new heavens and a new earth (Isa. 65:17; 66:22). Zephaniah sees a total destruction of the old order. "In the fire of his jealous wrath all the earth shall be consumed; for a full, yea, sudden end he will make of all the inhabitants of the earth" (Zeph. 1:18). Yet he sees a new order freed from the curse of evil (3:20). The prophet does not reflect on the relationship between the new order and the old order that is destroyed; there is both continuity and discontinuity.

Peter emphasizes the element of discontinuity to the greatest degree, envisaging the total destruction of the old order in a judgment of fire. Yet destruction is not the end; it is the emergence of new heavens and a new earth freed from the corruption that has plagued the old order. He does not reflect further on the character of this new order or the kind of existence it promises.

However, the hope of the new order is not an end in itself. It promises judgment for the apostates; but it provides the basis for Peter's ethical exhortation, "Since all these things are thus to be dissolved, what sort of persons ought you to be in lives of holiness and godliness" (3:11). "Since you wait for these, be zealous to be found by him without spot or blemish, and at peace" (3:14).[20]

JUDE. There is little of theological interest in Jude that is not found in II Peter. Jude is addressing himself to the same problem of libertine gnostics as II Peter, and writes to encourage his readers to contend for an orthodox

---

19 See E. M. Good, "Fire," *IDB* F-J, p. 269.

20 This fact is overlooked in Käsemann's criticism of Peter's eschatology and ethics. See C. Maurer, *TDNT* VI, 726.

faith (v. 3). False teachers have come into the church who "deny our only Master and Lord, Jesus Christ" (v. 4), who reject authority and revile angels (v. 8), who are scoffers (v. 18) of the accepted Christian way. Jude does not say that they scoff at the idea of Christ's parousia, as does II Peter (3:3). They claim special illumination by the Spirit but are in fact devoid of the Spirit (v. 19). Their error manifests itself in sensual license (vv. 4, 12). "The false teachers were claiming to be so Spirit-filled that there was no room for law in their Christian lives."[21] Jude, like II Peter, emphasizes the fact of the eschatological judgment of these apostates (v. 14). It is clear from the reference to the predictions of the apostles that Jude, like II Peter, must have been written late in the apostolic age (v. 17).

The two items of theological interest are Jude's reference to "the angels that did not keep their own position but left their proper dwelling [who] have been kept by him in eternal chains in the nether gloom until the judgment of the great day" (see II Pet. 2:4), and his use of apocryphal literature. He quotes verbally from "Enoch in the seventh generation from Adam" (v. 14). These exact words are found in the apocalypse of Enoch, usually designated I Enoch.[22] This raises a twofold problem: Did Jude consider the apocalypse of Enoch to be canonical Scripture, and did Jude think that the words came from the Enoch of antiquity? It is clear that Jude regards Enoch to be a writing of great value, but he does not call it Scripture (*graphē*). Furthermore, the apocalypse of Enoch refers twice to Enoch as the seventh generation from Adam.[23]

It is probable that Jude made use of another apocryphal book, the Assumption of Moses, in verse 9. Although this book is lost to us, both Clement and Origen assumed that Jude was using such a book with which they were familiar. However, this raises no problem different from the quotation from Enoch. It is not at all clear that Jude uses this book because he regarded it as inspired Scripture.

These two instances of the use of noncanonical literature are not unique. Paul makes use of a rabbinical midrash in I Corinthians 10:4 about the rock following the Israelites in the wilderness. He even quotes a pagan poet in his speech in Athens (Acts 17:28) and again in I Corinthians 15:33. He names the magicians who withstood Moses as Jannes and Jambres (II Tim. 3:8), probably drawing upon some noncanonical source.[24]

---

21 M. Green, *Second Peter and Jude*, p. 181.

22 See I En. 1:9.

23 I En. 37:1ff.; 60:8.

24 D. Guthrie, *NT Introduction*, III, 239.

43

JOHANNINE EPISTLES

Literature:

B. F. Westcott, *The Epistles of St. John* (1883), numerous brief theological essays; Robert Law, *The Tests of Life* (1909); A. E. Brooke, *The Johannine Epistles* (1912), pp. xxxviii-lii; C. H. Dodd, *The Johannine Epistles* (1946), pp. xxvii-lvi. Excellent for historical setting.

The majority of critics agree that the Johannine epistles share a common authorship with the Fourth Gospel.[1] The First Epistle is clearly addressed to a church or churches in which "false prophets" (4:1) have appeared who have initiated a schismatic movement in the church (2:19). They claimed a special illumination by the Spirit (2:20, 27) that imparted to them the true *gnōsis theou*. This explains John's strong emphasis on the real knowledge of God.[2] He opposes the apostates' claim to knowledge with the knowledge that can come only in the Christian tradition. Through this spiritual illumination, these schismatics claimed to have attained a state beyond ordinary Christian morality in which they had no more sin but attained moral perfection (1:8-10). It is clear that their ethical error was different from that of the opponents attacked in II Peter, who had given themselves over to gross immorality. No such immoral excess appears in I John. Their chief ethical error appears to be a spiritual pride and haughtiness that led them to despise ordinary Christians who did not claim to have attained the same level of spiritual illumination as had the gnostics. This is why John places so much emphasis upon the love of the brethren.

Their chief theological error, in contrast to II Peter, was christological; they denied the incarnation (2:22; 4:1). We know from patristic literature that an early form of gnosticism was docetism. The gnostic docetics held to the typical Greek contrast between spirit and matter, and thought that

[1] See for parallels of idiom A. E. Brooke, *The Johannine Epistles* (1912), pp. ii-xix. This has been contested by C. H. Dodd, *The Johannine Epistles* (1946), pp. xlviiff., lxviff., but he has not won many scholars to his views.

[2] See 2:3, 5; 3:16, 19, 24; 4:2, 6, 13; 5:2.

since matter was *ipso facto* evil, God could not possibly have come into direct contact with the phenomenal world in Christ. Therefore they either denied the incarnation in general terms, or else taught that the body of Christ was only an appearance (*dokeō*) and not real. The heavenly Christ only *seemed* to take a human form. Many scholars have felt that the particular form of the heresy opposed by John was that taught by Cerinthus, one of the earliest Christian heretics.[3] They went further to deny the reality of Christ's sufferings. They accepted his baptism but refused to accept the passion as part of the messianic work of salvation. He came by water but not by blood (5:6). In refuting the gnostic denial of Jesus' passion, John emphasizes the atoning effect of Jesus' death. He says nothing about the resurrection—this was apparently not in question; but he alludes several times to the efficacy of the cross. It is by the blood of Jesus that we are cleansed from sin (1:8). He laid down his life for us (3:16). By his death, he has wrought a work of propitiation[4] for our sins, even for the sins of the whole world (2:2). His propitiatory death is the supreme proof of the love of God (4:10).

John writes to urge his readers to "test the spirits to see whether they are of God" (4:1). That is, they are to measure the charismatic utterances of all so-called prophets by the norm of the sound Christian tradition, at the center of which is the real incarnation of Christ (4:2-3). Second John is a true letter to a particular church, called the "elect lady and her children" (v. 1), to warn them not to give hospitality, as the custom was, to an alleged itinerant Christian teacher who does not proclaim sound doctrine (vv. 8-11). Such are not true prophets but deceivers, because they "will not acknowledge the coming of Jesus Christ in the flesh" (v. 7). Third John was written to advise one Gaius how to deal with Diotrephes (v. 9), a schismatic. It is not clear whether his divisiveness was due to his adherence to gnostic doctrine, or was primarily personal. It may well have been the latter.[5]

One passage, taken out of context, might suggest a Christian mystical perception of truth with which John counters gnostic enthusiasm. "But you have been anointed by the Holy One, and you all know" (2:20). This means at least that one does not have to pursue the gnostic separatist movement to attain to true knowledge of God. The gift of the Holy Spirit is itself an anointing that enables the Christian to enter into true knowledge. The question is whether this means direct, unmediated illumination by the Spirit or whether it is an inner work of the Spirit that enables a man to perceive the truthfulness of the Christian tradition. In view of John's strong emphasis on correct doctrine, the latter would seem to be the correct interpretation.[6] The emphasis is upon the phrase "you *all* know." The Spirit is

---

[3] For references see A. E. Brooke, *The Johannine Epistles,* pp. xlvff.

[4] For the problem of propitiation-expiation, see above, pp. 429ff.

[5] See A. N. Wilder in *IB* XII, 210.

[6] C. H. Dodd (*The Johannine Epistles,* p. 61) thinks this refers to Christian initia-

given to all believers; all share the true knowledge of God, not a few who have been specially enlightened.

John repeats this idea: "but the anointing which you have received abides in you, and you have no need that any one [such as gnostic pneumatics] should teach you; as his anointing teaches you about everything . . ." (2:27). We are reminded of the words in the Gospel, "when the Spirit of truth comes, he will guide you into all the truth" (Jn. 16:13). The scope of this knowledge (everything) must be all that pertains to the Christian gospel. The truth is not merely an intellectual matter; it requires an inner work of the Spirit to be effective.

The denial that Christ has come in the flesh is also a denial that Jesus is the Son of God (4:15; 5:5). The reason for such a denial again is that God belongs to the realm of light and could not by definition dwell among men. Therefore Christ would not be God's Son in the sense of the Christian understanding of that term.

Another facet of the heretical gnostic Christology is reflected in John's statement, "Who is the liar but he who denies that Jesus is the Christ?" (2:22). In a Jewish context, this would have a definite meaning: Jesus could be a prophet but certainly not the Messiah of Old Testament prophetic hopes. In a Hellenistic context, Christ carries a different meaning. It distinguishes between the divine Christ, conceived as an emanation from the eternal Deity, and the man Jesus. Their dualistic view of the universe prevented the gnostics from accepting a real union between the heavenly Christ and the human Jesus. On the contrary, the two were only temporarily, externally connected. At some point in Jesus' life, e.g., his baptism, the divine Christ descended upon him, but left him again before his passion. John is refuting some such view as this,[7] and insisting on a real incarnation of God's Son. Jesus and Christ are one and the same.

In meeting this heresy, John does not attack the false teachers as II Peter does. His concern is not only polemical but also pastoral. He is concerned to encourage his readers to abide in a sound Christian faith and to live consistently with a true Christian conduct.

Near the beginning of his tractate, John refutes the gnostic error by using gnostic language. "God is light and in him is no darkness at all" (1:5). The gnostics believed that God was light but the visible material world was the realm of darkness. The way of salvation consisted in obtaining *gnōsis,* which was not simply intellectual apprehension but involved direct mystical experience[8] by which man's soul could escape the bondage to darkness and at death take flight to the world of light. John, however, says that the Christian gospel has it the other way: "The true light is already shining" (2:8). Rather than escape from the darkness, men are to welcome the light that has already shined in the darkness of this world (Jn. 1:9).

---

tion at baptism; but most scholars think the anointing is that of the Holy Spirit (cf. 3:24; 4:2).

[7] See C. H. Dodd, *The Johannine Epistles,* p. 55.

[8] See pp. 455, 460.

However, darkness for John is not the physical world; it is altogether ethical. "He who says he is in the light and hates his brother is in darkness still" (2:9). "He who hates his brother is in the darkness and walks in darkness, and does not know where he is going, because the darkness has blinded his eyes" (2:11). Because the true light is already shining, the darkness is passing away (2:8). Here is a bit of realized eschatology. With the coming of Christ into the world, "a new age has dawned; night is yielding to day, darkness to light."[9] The realms of light and darkness are not two static realms of the above and below as in gnosticism. The light is indeed the world of God, but darkness characterizes the "world." The world in I John, as in the Gospel,[10] is not creation but the world of men seen in their rebellion and hostility to God. Believers are still in the world (4:17); but "the whole world is in the power of the evil one" (5:19). Several times John speaks of the world as mankind. Christ is the propitiation for our sins; "and not for ours only but also for the sins of the whole world" (2:2). Again, "many false prophets have gone out into the world" (4:1). "The Father has sent his Son as the Savior of the world" (4:14; see 4:9). But the prevailing usage is the world of the contemporary pagan society, addicted to the pursuit of the satisfaction of gross sensual pleasures (which John characterizes as "the lust of the flesh"), to a materialistic view of life and values ("the lust of the eyes"), and to self-glorification ("the pride of life," 2:16). John strikes an absolute contrast between this evil world and the new order inaugurated by Christ. Whatever is of the world is not of God (2:16). The false prophets are of the world, and the world listens to them (4:5). The world does not understand Christians any more than it understood Christ (3:1). In fact, the world hates them (3:13). In response, the Christian is not to love the world. He is to set his affections upon an entirely different set of values than sensual pleasure, materialism, and self-glorification (2:16). It is obvious that the negation of love for the world cannot mean a denial of love for the people who make up the world, for Christ came to be the Savior of all men, even of the world (4:14); and even though the epistle, like the Gospel,[11] exhorts love only for the "brethren," i.e., for those within the Christian fellowship, yet love is the essence of Christian conduct. Because Christ has introduced Christians into a new order where the light shines, through the power of faith in Christ as the Son of God the believer is to conquer the world (5:4). The evil world is indeed an impermanent and transient situation. "The world passes away and the lust of it" (2:17). Only he who does the will of God (2:17), i.e., who walks in the light that has shined forth in Christ, will abide forever.

While John uses dualistic language—light and darkness, God and the world—he is not dualistic in thought but stands squarely in the center of Christian tradition. His theology is structured in the dualism of the past

[9] C. H. Dodd, *The Johannine Epistles,* p. 34.
[10] See above, pp. 225f.
[11] See pp. 279f.

and the future—the already and the not yet. The heart of the gospel is something the church has possessed "from the beginning" (2:7). It is that which occurred in the historical event of Jesus Christ. Here John uses the same Logos theology that appears in the Gospel, although the epistle speaks of "the word of life" (1:1). This divine word, like the Logos of John 1:1, "was from the beginning" yet was made manifest in history in the person of Jesus. John emphasizes the objective historical reality of the incarnation. It meant the appearance in flesh of a life that could be seen and touched and heard (1:1-3).

This life was made manifest to bring life to men. Like the Gospel, the epistle concentrates on the present experience of eternal life. It mentions eternal life at least ten times, always with emphasis upon the present. "We know that we have passed out of death into life" (3:14). One of the purposes of the epistle is to reassure the Christians who have rejected the gnostic higher light that they may know that they have eternal life (5:13). In Christ, God has already given us eternal life; he who has the Son has life (5:11-12).

However, this experience of eternal life has a future cast. He who does the will of God abides forever (2:17). John looks forward to the realization of all that Christ means at his eschatological parousia (2:28). Although we have received life, although we have been born again (2:29), we are not yet like Christ. We await his parousia, when we shall experience an unimaginable change. "It does not yet appear what we shall be, but we know that when he appears we shall be like him, for we shall see him as he is" (3:2). This is a purifying hope. "Every one who thus hopes in him purifies himself as he is pure" (3:3). It is clear that John lives in expectation of an imminent parousia, for "it is the last hour" (2:18).

One of the phenomena that characterize the last hour is the appearance of antichrists. The word *antichristos* occurs only in the Johannine epistles in the New Testament (2:18, 22; 4:3; II Jn. 7), but the idea is found elsewhere. Antichrist is the adversary of the Messiah, either opposing him or replacing him. A similar expression is found in the Olivet Discourse. "False Christs and false prophets will arise . . . so as to lead astray, if possible, even the elect" (Mt. 24:24). John's thought about antichrists is the same; they are false prophets who deny that Jesus is the Messiah (2:22) and who separate themselves from the church (2:19) and, presumably, try to lead astray all who will listen to them.

Another interpretation of antichrist (although the word is not used) appears in II Thessalonians 2 and Revelation 13: a single antichrist who flagrantly opposes the worship of Christ and sets himself up as an object of worship. We may conclude that the spirit of antichrist manifests itself everywhere in heretical, schismatic teachers, but will be climactically embodied in a single evil person at the end of the age.

That John has a good deal to say about sin is undoubtedly due to a gnostic teaching that the one who has been spiritually enlightened may attain a perfection that places him beyond temptation and sin. This is the first step toward antinomianism, which had proceeded much further in the gnostic heresy addressed in II Peter. In refutation of such an idea, John asserts, "If we say we have no sin, we deceive ourselves, and the truth is not in us" (1:8). Not even the most mature Christian can attain sinless perfection in this life. Perfection will not be achieved until we become like him at his parousia (3:2). Again, it is heresy to make light of sin. "If we say that we have not sinned, we make him a liar, and his word is not in us" (1:10). God has made provision for the sins a Christian commits. "If we confess our sins, he is faithful and just, and will forgive our sins and cleanse us from all unrighteousness" (1:9). "If we walk in the light . . . , the blood of Jesus his Son cleanses us from all sin" (1:7).

John is concerned that his opposition to the gnostic idea of sinless perfection should not itself lead to a soft attitude on the part of his readers toward sin. Therefore he hastens to say, "I am writing this to you that you may not sin" (2:1). Complete victory over sin is the Christian ideal. Yet he at once adds, "If any one does sin, we have an advocate with the Father, Jesus Christ the righteous; and he is the propitiation for our sins" (2:2). Here John uses a word appearing only in the First Epistle and the Gospel: *paraklētos*. In the Gospel the Holy Spirit will be sent to Jesus' disciples to be their Helper.[12] Here Jesus is our *paraklētos* in heaven in the presence of God. Here the word fits the more technical meaning of advocate: one who represents another and pleads his case. Salvation from sin in the present tense is based not only upon the propitiatory work of Christ upon the cross, but also upon his exalted status in the presence of God. The idea includes intercession for believers on earth as in Hebrews 7:25; 9:24; and Romans 8:34.

Later John seems flatly to contradict what he has already written about sin in the Christian life. "He who commits sin is of the devil" (3:8). "No one born of God commits sin; for God's nature abides in him, and he cannot sin because he is born of God" (3:9). "We know that any one born of God does not sin, but He who was born of God keeps him, and the evil one does not touch him" (5:18). These verses indeed constitute a formal verbal contradiction to what John says in 1:8 and 2:1. There are two possible solutions to the problem. The translation of the RSV, quoted above, may well overtranslate the passage. In 3:8 and 9, a literal translation says, "He who practices sin is of the devil." The verbs are in the present tense throughout, and the meaning may well be that the one who is born again cannot continue to live in sin because a new principle of life has been implanted in him. There *must* be an obvious change in his conduct. When one follows Christ, he will of necessity break with his pagan past. This idea is expressed in the New Testament elsewhere. "A sound tree cannot bear evil fruit, nor can a bad tree bear good fruit" (Mt. (7:18). Paul expresses the same idea with a different metaphor. "For he who has died [with Christ] is free from sin" (Rom. 6:7). "Let not sin, there-

---

[12] See above, pp. 292ff.

fore, reign in your mortal bodies" (Rom. 6:12).[13] This is a very plausible and consistent interpretation and cannot be rejected because it is based on grammatical subtleties.[14] Tenses in Greek did mean something. The tense of 2:1 is aorist; the goal of the Christian life is that one shall commit no sin. In experience the dominance and practice of sin is broken; but this does not mean sinless perfection.

Another interpretation, less satisfactory, goes back to Augustine. "Insofar as one abides in him, to this extent he does not sin."[15] The saying, "No one who abides in him sins" (present tense, 3:6) lends credibility to this view.

John has another word to say about sin that is to us rather enigmatic. "If any one sees his brother committing what is not a mortal sin, he will ask, and God will give him life for those whose sin is not mortal. There is sin which is mortal; I do not say that one is to pray for that" (5:16). We can do no more than interpret "sin which leads to death" in the context of the whole epistle, and understand it to be the sin of apostasy in deliberate and defiant repudiation of one's Christian faith.[16] It is curious that John neither forbids nor commands prayer for such; he only discourages it. He does not expressly say that such sin places a man beyond redemption, but only expresses a clear conviction that such radical sin excludes one from the prayers of the church.

The epistle, like the Gospel (Jn. 3:3), speaks of entrance into the Christian life as a new birth, being begotten by God, having the seed of God implanted in one's inner being (2:29; 3:9; 4:7; 5:1, 4, 18). Here John, like II Peter 1:4, employs language familiar to gnostics to express Christian truth. That this is metaphorical language that is difficult to interpret in psychological terms is seen from the fact that another way of expressing the same truth is to speak of "having Christ" (5:12), even as the Gospel speaks of receiving Christ (Jn. 1:12). By the new birth, we have entered into a new relationship; we have become the children of God (3:1, 2, 10; 5:2). Paul conceives of believers as children of God, but by adoption rather than by new birth (Rom. 8:15). However, by the new birth and the implanting of the divine seed, John clearly means something more than a new relationship. It means that a new dynamic, a new power, has entered the human personality, which is reflected in a change of conduct. In modern times, we would probably think of a change in the orientation of man's will. Whereas the non-Christian is content to pursue sinful ways and to ignore the claims of God, the child of God has found a new orientation of his will—to do the will of God, to love and serve him, to break with sin and follow righteousness.

---

[13] C. H. Dodd (*The Johannine Epistles,* pp. 78-79) expands this view, but expresses doubts about it. However, he appeals to this interpretation in his exposition of 5:18 (see p. 138).

[14] See *ibid.,* p. 79.

[15] A. E. Brooke, *The Johannine Epistles,* p. 86.

[16] C. H. Dodd, *The Johannine Epistles,* pp. 136-37.

John uses language to describe the Christian life that sounds mystical. One of his characteristic words is "abide."[17] God abides in believers (4:16); Christ abides in them (3:24); God's word abides in them (2:14); life abides in them (3:15); love abides in them (3:17); truth abides in them (II Jn. 2); the anointing (of the Spirit) abides in them (2:27). Believers, in turn, abide in God (2:24); in Christ (2:5, 6, 24, 27); in light (2:10); in sound doctrine (II Jn. 9). By way of contrast, unbelievers abide in death (3:14).

John's meaning does not belong to mystical experience but to Christian conduct, particularly to the manifestation of love. "He who says he abides in him ought to walk in the same way in which he walked" (2:6). "He who loves his brother abides in the light" (2:10). "No one who abides in him practices sin" (3:6). "He who does not love remains in death" (3:14). "All who keep his commandments abide in him and he in them" (3:24). Abiding in Christ means to be living a life of love in unbroken fellowship with fellow believers. Abiding, then, means obedience to the law of love.

Abiding in Christ also means remaining in the true Christian tradition —a thing the gnostics have not done. "Let what you have heard from the beginning abide in you. If what you have heard from the beginning abides in you, then you will abide in the Son and in the Father" (2:24). False teaching that ruptures the fellowship of God's people means a rupture with God and with Christ.

John's ethic is a repetition of what is found in the Gospel; it is the new commandment of love (Jn. 13:34). The verb "to love" (*agapaō*) occurs at least twenty-eight times. The totality of the Christian life is summed up in shunning love for the world (2:15), in loving God (4:21), and expressing this love for God by loving the brethren (4:20). This is the message heard from the beginning, that we should love one another (3:11). This is both the old commandment, and a new commandment (3:7-8). This new love means following Christ's example of love to the point of being willing to "lay down one's life for the brethren" (3:16). Love is proof that we have passed from death to life (3:14), that we have been begotten by God (4:7), that we know God (4:7), that God abides in us (4:12). This love is not a mere human achievement; it is the human response to the love of God. "In this is love, not that we loved God, but that he loved us and sent his Son to be the propitiation for our sins. Beloved, if God so loved us, we ought to love one another" (4:10-11). "We love, because he first loved us" (4:19). "This commandment we have from him, that he who loves God should love his brother also" (4:21).

---

[17] *Menō* (23 times).

PART 6

THE APOCALYPSE

44

THE APOCALYPSE

Literature:

There is very little literature on the theology of the Revelation; one must turn largely to commentaries. Among the most helpful books are H. Lilje, *The Last Book of the Bible* (1955); M. C. Tenney, *Interpreting Revelation* (1957); M. Rissi, *Time and History* (n.d.); L. Morris, *The Revelation of John* (1969); G. E. Ladd, *The Revelation of John* (1972); G. R. Beasley-Murray, *Highlights of the Book of Revelation* (1972); M. Rissi, *The Future of the World* (n.d.). See also the footnotes.

INTRODUCTION. The book of Revelation purports to be a revelation of the events that will attend the end of the age and the establishing of the Kingdom of God. The primary theology of the book, therefore, is its eschatology. It claims to be a prophecy of the things that must soon take place (1:2-3), whose central event is the second coming of Jesus Christ (1:7).

However, the interpretation of this book has been the most difficult and confusing of all the books of the New Testament. Out of the history of interpretation have emerged several distinct approaches. The easiest approach to the Revelation is to follow one's own particular tradition as the true view and ignore all others; but the intelligent interpreter must familiarize himself with the various methods of interpretation that he may criticize and purify his own view.

THE CONTENTS OF THE REVELATION. Since the book must be interpreted as a whole, we must have an outline of its contents in mind. The following outline is based on the literary structure of the book, which is indicated by the expression "in the Spirit" (1:10; 4:1; 17:3; 21:10).

The first vision (1:9-3:22) consists of the exalted Christ and his letters to the seven churches. Christ is seen standing in the midst of seven lampstands (1:12f.), symbolizing his superintendence of the life of his church on earth. The letters to the seven churches (2-3) are seven actual letters to seven churches in Asia Minor. The fact that other churches existed in Asia at this time suggests that seven of them are chosen to be representative of the entire church. Here in these letters is Christ's message to his church in all times.

The second vision (4:1-16:21) pictures the heavenly throne room with a seven-sealed scroll resting in the hand of God. This can only be opened by the Lion of the tribe of Judah, who is the slain Lamb of God (4:1-11). There follows a threefold series of seven: the breaking of the seven seals (5:1-8:1), the blowing of seven trumpets (8:2-9:21), and the emptying of seven bowls (15:1-16:21). Each seal, trumpet, and bowl is followed by a symbolic representation of something that happens on earth. Before the sounding of the seven trumpets, two multitudes are seen: the first, 12,000 from twelve tribes of Israel, is sealed on their foreheads (7:3) that they might not be hurt by the plagues of the trumpets (9:4). The second multitude is an innumerable body of redeemed gathered from all races of men (7:9-17) who have "come out of great tribulation" (7:14).

A central theme in this second vision is the conflict between God and Satan, who is pictured in mythological colors as a fierce red dragon (12:3-4). The Dragon is frustrated in his efforts to destroy the Messiah (12:5), and after being defeated in a battle with Michael and the angels (12:7ff.) devotes his efforts to destroying the church on earth (12:17). In pursuing this purpose, the Dragon calls up two beasts (12:17-13:1; 13:11), who defy God (13:6), turn the hearts of men away from God (13:4, 14), and persecute the church (13:7, 15). This Beast and his False Prophet (19:20) are permitted to succeed in their purposes and force their rule on all men (13:7-8, 16-17).

The third vision (17:1-21:8) is the great harlot, Babylon (17:1, 5), the great city that has dominion over the kings of the earth (17:18). The judgment and destruction of Babylon are then announced and portrayed (18:1-24), followed by a hymn of praise for her destruction (19:1-5).

The remainder of the third vision pictures the final victory of God over the powers of evil. First comes a hymn of praise celebrating the marriage of the Lamb and his Bride (19:6-10). This is followed by scenes of the conquering Christ riding to judgment and victory (19:11-16) and his destruction of the Beast and the False Prophet (19:17-21). This in turn is followed by the victory over the Dragon, who is not, however, at once destroyed as were the Beast and False Prophet. First, he is bound and locked up in the "bottomless pit" for a thousand years (20:1-3) while Christ with his saints and martyrs who "came to life" (*ezēsan*) reign over the earth (20:4-6). This is called the "first resurrection" (20:5). At the end of this interim kingdom, Satan (the Dragon) is loosed from his incarceration and once again deceives the nations, rousing them to battle against the saints (20:9). Satan is now destroyed along with the Beast and the False Prophet in the lake of fire (20:10). Then follow the second resurrection, the final judgment (20:11-15), and the coming of the new heaven and earth to take the place of the old (21:1-8), in which the redeemed enjoy perfected fellowship with God (21:3-4).

A final vision pictures the heavenly Jerusalem, which is the Bride, the wife of the Lamb (21:9-22:5). The book closes with an Epilogue (22:6-21) inviting men to receive God's gift of life (22:17).

METHODS OF INTERPRETATION. 1. *The Preterist Interpretation.* The prevailing interpretation of the Revelation in critical scholarship treats the book as a typical example of the genre of apocalyptic literature and interprets it in the same way as the apocalypse of Enoch, the Assumption of Moses, IV Ezra, and Baruch are interpreted.[1] Apocalypses are "tracts for bad times." They arise out of times of unusual evil and persecution. God's people cannot understand the problem of evil in history or why such fearful sufferings and persecutions befall them. The apocalypses were written to answer this problem and to encourage a distressed people. The solution is found in the view that God has turned this age over to the powers of evil but is soon to intervene to destroy evil and establish his Kingdom. The message of the apocalypses is addressed to their own contemporaries and in no way contains prophecies of the future, but pseudo-prophecies of history rewritten under the guise of prophecy.[2] All allusions to historical events or personages must be sought in the historical environment of the book itself.

This interpretation assumes that the Revelation was produced by a church facing the threat of fearful persecution at the hands of Rome, perhaps in the province of Asia where Emperor-worship flourished. Therefore the Beast is one of the Roman Emperors, and the False Prophet is the cult of the worship of the Emperor. The author assures Christians that even though a great martyrdom may ensue, Christ will shortly return, destroy Rome, and establish his Kingdom on earth.[3]

There must be an element of truth in this approach, for surely the Revelation was intended to speak to its own generation. But for the Preterist interpretation, the Revelation is no more a true prophecy than is its contemporary apocalypse, IV Ezra. There are, however, some distinct differences between the Revelation and Jewish apocalypses,[4] the most important of which is its consciousness of standing within the stream of *Heilsgeschichte* or redemptive history, which is wanting in Jewish apocalyptic. Therefore, while we may recognize the shadows of contemporary events in the Revelation, we must conclude that the elaborate symbolism of Jewish apocalyptic

---

[1] See M. Stuart, *A Commentary on the Apocalypse* (1845; 2 vols.); F. C. Porter, *The Messages of the Apocalyptical Writers* (1905); H. H. Rowley, *The Relevance of Apocalyptic* (1947).

[2] See G. E. Ladd, "Apocalyptic, Apocalypse," *Baker's Dictionary of Theology*, ed. by E. F. Harrison (1960), pp. 50-54.

[3] See H. C. Kee and F. W. Young, *Understanding the NT* (1957), pp. 335-37, 453-62. Most modern critical commentaries are written from this point of view. See R. H. Charles (*ICC*); J. Moffatt (*Expositor's Greek Testament*); I. T. Beckwith; C. A. Scott (*Century Bible*); A. S. Peake; H. B. Swete (in part); M. Rist (*IB*).

[4] See G. E. Ladd, "The Revelation and Jewish Apocalyptic," *EQ* XXIX (1957), 94-100.

literature was employed in the interests of a prophetic forecast of the consummation of God's redemptive purpose.[5]

2. *The Historical Method.* This interpretation, which was favored by the Reformers, sees in the Revelation a prophecy of the history of the church. Specific events, nations, personages are sought in church history that fit the seals, trumpets, bowls, etc. The most important identification in this interpretation is the identification of the Beast and the False Prophet with Papacy in its political and religious aspects. This method can be millenarian (I. Newton, Bengel, H. Alford), nonmillenarian (Luther, Hengstenberg), or postmillenarian (D. Brown). A major difficulty with this view is that no consensus has been achieved as to what the outline of history foreseen in the Revelation really is.

3. *The Symbolical or Idealist Method.* One of the most attractive methods is that which sees in the Revelation only symbols of spiritual powers at work in the world. The message of the book is the assurance to suffering saints of God's final triumph without the prediction of concrete events either in the past or future. William Milligan is an outstanding exponent of this view (*Expositor's Bible*). The objection to this view is that the genre of apocalyptic literature always used apocalyptic symbolism to describe events in history; and we must expect the Apocalypse to share at least this feature with other books of its character.

4. *The Extreme Futurist Interpretation: Dispensationalism.*[6] A view that has become deeply rooted in many American Evangelical churches interprets the Revelation in terms of its dispensationalist premise of two different divine programs: one for Israel and one for the church. All of the seals, trumpets, and bowls belong to the great tribulation; and since this is the time of "Jacob's trouble" (Jer. 30:7), by definition it has to do with Israel and not with the church. In chapters 2 and 3 the church is seen on earth, but "church" never occurs again in the book, except in 22:16. The twenty-four elders seen around the throne of God are thought to be the church, raptured and rewarded (4:4). Therefore the rapture of the church must occur at 4:1; and the people of God on earth are the Jews, twelve thousand from each of the twelve tribes (7:1-8), who proclaim the "gospel of the Kingdom" during the tribulation and win a great host of Gentiles (7:9-17). The Beast is the head of the Roman empire, which is to be restored in the last days.[7] The prophecy in Daniel 9:27 is also understood to refer to the head of this restored empire. The last seven years will begin with a covenant between the Beast (antichrist) and Israel[8] that the Beast will break after

---

[5] A few interpreters have tried to adapt the preterist view to a conservative approach. See A. Pieters, *Studies in the Revelation of St. John* (1943, 1954); R. Summers, *Worthy Is the Lamb* (1951). The best effort is that of G. R. Beasley-Murray in *The New Bible Commentary* (ed. by F. Davidson; 1953), who combines the Preterist and Futurist methods. See also L. Morris, *Revelation* (1969); G. E. Ladd, *Revelation* (1972).

[6] The most recent commentary is that by J. Walvoord (1966).

[7] See J. D. Pentecost, *Things to Come* (1958), ch. 19.

[8] *Ibid.*, p. 295.

three and a half years, and then turn in anger to persecute the Jews. The great conflict in the Revelation is between antichrist and Israel, not antichrist and the church. Since chapters 4-19 have to do with the tribulation period, chapters 2-3 alone are for the church and the church age. The usual view has been that the seven churches represent seven successive periods of church history, the final period being one of apostasy and spiritual apathy.[9] This view is, however, being surrendered by contemporary dispensational theologians.[10]

5. *The Moderate Futurist View.*[11] The Revelation claims to depict the consummation of God's redemptive purpose, involving both judgment and salvation. One of the key problems in the interpretation of the book is the relationship between the seals, trumpets, and bowls. In the solution of this problem may lie the key to the interpretation of the book. John sees a book in the form of a scroll, sealed with seven seals along its outer edge, resting in the hand of God. No creature was found able to break the seals and open the book, except the Lion of the tribe of Judah, who was the slain Lamb. This strikes the keynote of the book. The conquering Lion, who alone can disclose the hidden purposes of God, is the Jesus who died on the cross.

The little book is in the form of an ancient will, which was usually sealed with the seals of the seven witnesses. The book contains God's inheritance for his people, which is founded upon the death of his Son.[12] The saints' inheritance is the Kingdom of God; but the blessings of God's Kingdom cannot be bestowed apart from the destruction of evil. In fact, the very destruction of all evil powers is one of the blessings of God's kingly rule. Here is the twofold theme of the Revelation: the judgment of evil and the coming of the Kingdom.

The successive breaking of the seals does not gradually open the book. Its contents cannot be disclosed until the last seal is broken. However, as each seal is broken, something happens. After the first seal, conquest rides forth over the earth; after the second, war; then famine, and death, and martyrdom. The sixth seal brings us to the end of the age and the coming of the great Day of the Lord and of the wrath of the Lamb (6:16-17). This suggests that the events attending the breaking of the seals do not constitute the end itself but events leading up to the end. This structure is paralleled in Matthew 24, where wars, famines, and other evils are but the "beginning of woes," not the end itself (Mt. 24:8). Furthermore, the conquering white horse parallels Matthew 24:14, and pictures the victories to be won by the preaching of the gospel in the world. Many commentators feel that the four horsemen must be alike in kind, and that the white horse must therefore

[9] *The Scofield Reference Bible,* pp. 1331ff.; J. D. Pentecost, *Things to Come,* p. 152.

[10] See A. J. McClain, *The Greatness of the Kingdom* (1959), p. 419; C. C. Ryrie, *Biblical Theology of the NT* (1959), p. 355.

[11] See H. Lilje, *The Last Book of the Bible* (1955); L. Morris, *The Revelation of St. John;* G. E. Ladd, *The Revelation of St. John.*

[12] The idea occurs also in Heb. 9.

represent some evil power. However, no woe is mentioned as with the other horsemen, and white in the Revelation is always associated with Christ or with spiritual victory.[13] That the preaching of the gospel is associated with plagues is here no more incongruous than it is in Matthew 24:1-14. It is no effective objection to say that the gospel in this present order will never be triumphant.[14] This is true; but the gospel does win victories. Both the sword (Heb. 4:12; Rev. 2:12) and the bow (Isa. 49:2-3) are symbols of God's working among men.[15] In the breaking of the five seals are disclosed the agencies God uses before the end to lead up to the fulfillment of salvation and judgment: the preaching of the gospel and the evils of war, death, famine, and martyrdom. These are, as it were, anticipations of the consummated salvation and judgment that are contained within the sealed book.

The sixth seal brings us to the end; but with the breaking of the seventh seal, when the book itself can at last be opened and its contents disclosed, nothing happens (8:1). There is no woe. While it is in accordance with the flexibility of apocalyptic symbolism that the actual book now drops out of sight and its contents are never explicitly mentioned, the fact that the seventh seal is given no specific content suggests that all that follows, beginning with the seven trumpets, constitutes the contents of the book. Here then begins the actual unfolding of the judicial and redemptive events that constitute the consummation.

We may conclude that a moderate futurist interpretation understands the seven letters to be addressed to seven historical churches that are representative of the entire church. The seals represent the forces in history, however long it lasts, by which God works out his redemptive and judicial purposes in history leading up to the end. The events beginning with chapter 7 lie in the future and will attend the final disposition of the divine will for human history.

THE THEOLOGY OF THE APOCALYPSE

We cannot deal with all of the theology of the book but only summarize its central message in three parts.

THE PROBLEM OF EVIL. The Revelation foresees a short period of terrible evil in history at the end time. Like Matthew 24:15ff. and II Thessalonians 2:3ff., it tells of an evil personage who will be satanically inspired and empowered, who openly defies God and demands that men worship him rather than God. He will be permitted to wage effective war against the church and will exercise a worldwide rule (Rev. 13:1-10). His purposes will be reinforced by a False Prophet who successfully prostitutes religion to direct the worship of men to the Beast. The False Prophet is able to com-

[13] See 1:14; 2:17; 3:4, 5, 18; 4:4; 6:11; 9:7, 13; 14:14; 19:11, 14; 20:11.

[14] J. A. Seiss, *The Apocalypse* (1913), I, 310.

[15] This interpretation is followed by T. Zahn, *Die Offenbarung des Johannes* (1926), II, 352f. H. Alford, *The Greek Testament* (1877), IV, 613f.; J. Schneider, *Die Offenbarung Jesu Christi* (1942), pp. 56f.

bine the powers of religion and economic exchange so as to control the entire social order in the interests of Beast-worship (13:11-18). Here is a satanically inspired deification of the state, which dictates even the worship of its subjects. The apostate civilization is portrayed as Babylon, the great whore, who has beguiled the kings of the earth by her evil allures of a luxurious but godless materialism (17-18), so that they too have turned against Christ (17:14) to worship the Beast.

This short interval[16] will witness terrible martyrdom. A man will have his choice of denying Christ or dying. A great, innumerable number from many nations will be martyred because they have been loyal to the Lamb (7:9-17). In fact, their martyrdom will be their victory. John sees "those who had *conquered* the beast and its image" standing beside the sea of glass before God's throne (4:6) singing a hymn of victory (15:1-4). In the day when the eternal destiny of men is at stake, martyrdom will itself be a victory.

However, this struggle between the Beast and the Lamb for the souls of men is nothing new, nor is the last manifestation of satanic hatred for the church limited to the end time. The vision of Revelation 12, which explains the last terrible persecution, is one of the most important visions of the book. John sees a vision of the powers that operate in the spiritual world behind the scenes of human history. The church is pictured as a gloriously adorned woman (Rev. 12:1). She is not the historical church on earth but the ideal church in heaven. As such, she is to be identified directly with neither Israel nor the church, yet includes both. As the heavenly, ideal people of God, she gives birth both to the Messiah (12:2, 5) and to the empirical church in history (12:17). The idea of an ideal heavenly people of God is not unique with John. Paul speaks of the Jerusalem above who is the mother of all believers on earth (Gal. 4:26; see also Heb. 12:22). Furthermore, the last vision of the Revelation is a vision of the heavenly Jerusalem descending to earth; but she is the Bride of Christ, the wife of the Lamb, the people of God (Rev. 21:9-10). Thus the efforts of the red dragon (Satan) to destroy the woman represent in vivid, picturesque terms an age-long battle between Satan and the people of God.

Satan's effort to destroy the Messiah is frustrated (12:4-5). Instead, he is himself cast down from his place of power as a result of a spiritual conflict that is pictured as a battle between the Dragon and Michael. The language in which this victory over Satan is described (12:10-12) suggests that we should interpret this victory not as an eschatological event but as the victory won by Christ over satanic evil. When Jesus himself once said, "I saw Satan fall like lightning from heaven" (Lk. 10:18), he was referring in symbolic terms to the defeat of Satan effected by his own presence among men and the powers of the Kingdom of God brought to

---

[16] The number 3½ (11:2; 12:6, 14; 13:5) is probably symbolic of a very short period of time.

them (Lk. 10:17; cf. Mt. 12:28-29). Because of this defeat of the Dragon, he is more infuriated and tries even harder to destroy the woman.

This vision pictures the unrelenting enmity of Satan against the people of God, an enmity that bursts out in historical expression. This appears to be the meaning of John's words that the Dragon went off to make war with "the rest of her offspring" (12:17), the church on earth. It is this conflict in heaven between the Dragon and the woman that explains the evil the church experiences throughout its entire history (12:11), first at the hands of the Roman empire, and in its final, most intense eschatological manifestation in antichrist. It is the Dragon who stands[17] on the seashore to call for the Beast in a final effort to destroy God's people. The Beast, the final embodiment of satanic evil, is a composite of the four beasts of Daniel 7 (13:2). This suggests that the persecution of the end times has been manifested throughout the course of history. Therefore the only unique thing about the last time of tribulation is its intensity; but Jesus spoke of the same evil (Mt. 24:21-22). The modern evangelical fear of suffering in the great tribulation has forgotten the biblical teaching that the church in her fundamental character is always a martyr church (Acts 14:22). The true victory consists in conquering the Beast by loyalty to Christ to death (15:2).

THE VISITATION OF WRATH. The Revelation pictures something that is taught nowhere else in the Bible: that the time of the great tribulation will also be a time when God pours out anticipatory judgments upon men. This is the meaning of the seven trumpets and the seven bowls. They are symbolic representations of some sort of judgments or woes that God will pour out in the last climactic hour of the struggle between the Lamb and the Dragon. We cannot say what these plagues are. The descriptions are highly symbolic. They are anticipations of the wrath of God (16:1), which will be consummated with the return of Christ.

Three facts are to be noted. First, the woes are directed against the men who bore the mark of the Beast and worshipped its image (16:2). In this last terrible hour, men will have to stand on one side or the other. Martyrdom may await the followers of the Lamb, but the wrath of a holy God awaits those who submit to the Beast.

Second, the plagues have a merciful purpose. They are designed to drive men to their knees, as it were, in repentance before it is irrevocably too late. This merciful purpose in God's judgments is clearly suggested in such verses as 9:20; 16:9 and 11, where it is reiterated that in spite of God's hand falling upon them heavy in wrath, they did not repent and give God glory. Even the fearfulness of God's wrath in these last awful moments before the dawn of the new age has a merciful objective.

Third, there is a sealed company who are sheltered from these plagues and who do not suffer God's wrath. Just before the sounding of the trumpets, John hears the sealing of a host of people who are described as

---

[17] *Estathē,* "he stood," is the better reading in 12:28, with Papyrus 47, Sinaiticus, and Alexandrinus.

twelve thousand from each of twelve tribes of Israel (7:1-8). These are sealed that they may be protected from the plagues God is about to pour out upon the Beast and his followers (7:3; 9:4). The seal of God or the mark of the Beast will distinguish men in this last hour, whether they are on God's side or on Satan's.

Many commentators see in this sealed host the final salvation of Israel that Paul anticipated in Romans 11 (see also Mt. 10:23; 23:39). So it might seem, except for one fact: these twelve tribes cannot be literal Israel, because they are not the twelve tribes of Old Testament Israel. The tribes here listed nowhere appear in the entire Bible. Three irregularities appear that make it difficult if not impossible to see in these sealed ones literal Israel. Judah is named first, and thus the Old Testament order of the tribes is ignored. Dan is omitted with no explanation whatsoever.[18] Furthermore, Joseph is mentioned instead of Ephraim. These two facts suggest that John means by this deliberate irregular listing of the twelve tribes to designate the Israel that is not the literal Israel.

That John conceives of a spiritual Israel is shown by other references. Twice he speaks of those "who say that they are Jews and are not, but are a synagogue of Satan" (2:9; 3:9). By this John means that there are people who are Jews by race but are not spiritually Jews, but are rather dupes of Satan. A real Jew, then, is not one who is racially or religiously a Jew, but one who acknowledges the claims of Christ and therefore recognizes the church as the true people of God. This the pseudo-Jews refuse to do.

With this as a clue, we may understand the twelve tribes in Revelation 7 as the true Israel, the elect of God whether Jew or Gentile. This seems to be the deliberate reason for the utterly irregular listing of the twelve tribes. Here is true Israel, which is not literal Israel but the church. On the threshold of the last day, God's people are sealed on their foreheads that they might not suffer the wrath outpoured upon the Beast and his followers. Undoubtedly John recalled the mark of the blood over the doors of every Israelite house in Egypt, which was thereby spared from the plague of death that visited the household of every unmarked door. Here is a company who pass through the tribulation but who do not suffer the wrath of God.

The two groups in Revelation 7 picture the same people of God from two perspectives. From the divine perspective, this is an ideal number; twelve thousand of each of twelve tribes. God's people will be complete, and will be safely preserved through this terrible time of wrath. However, from the human perspective the church is a great unnumbered throng from all nations who will suffer martyrdom but who will emerge from the tribulation triumphant and stand before the throne of God in victory because they have washed their robes in the blood of the Lamb (7:14).

---

[18] Note that Dan is the first tribe mentioned in Ezekiel's vision of the Kingdom (Ezek. 48:1).

THE COMING OF THE KINGDOM. The coming of God's Kingdom is pictured in two-tone colors: the destruction of evil and the blessing of eternal life. The destruction of evil occurs in several stages. The second coming of Christ, pictured in 19:11-16, has as its primary purpose the destruction of evil. His coming is pictured in terms of ancient warfare. He rides a battle horse and wears garments blood-stained from battle. He is accompanied by the armies of heaven, apparently angels; but they do not join in the conflict. The one weapon with which he wages war is a sharp sword proceeding out of his mouth—his naked word. No military conquest is this. His victory over evil is in the power of his word. He shall speak and the victory will be his.

He first conquers the Beast, the False Prophet, and their followers (19:17-21). This victory is pictured in terms of bloody carnage, but the picture is obviously symbolic. Their doom is not to be slain in battle but to be cast into the lake of fire and brimstone.

Attention is now turned to the Dragon who inspired the Beast. The Conqueror surprisingly disappears from the scene, and in his place appears an angel who descends from heaven to overcome the Dragon. We would expect him to be thrown at once into the lake of fire, but this doom is delayed. First, the Dragon is bound and shut up in a "bottomless pit" for a thousand years. Only at the end of the thousand years, when he is released and is again able to entice men to rebel against Christ and the saints, is he finally destroyed. Then the Dragon, who is the Devil, is cast into the lake of fire along with the Beast and the False Prophet.

The positive aspect of the coming of God's Kingdom also occurs in stages, not in a single great event. First is a temporal kingdom of a thousand years when the resurrected saints reign with Christ (20:4). This is followed by what we may call the eternal Kingdom with its new heaven and new earth. Each of these two aspects of God's Kingdom is preceded by a resurrection. The resurrection before the millennial kingdom is called "the first resurrection" (20:5). Some commentators feel that this resurrection is limited to the martyrs of the tribulation. They are indeed given special mention; but the rather rough language of the Greek is well rendered in the RSV: "Then I saw thrones, and seated on them were those to whom judgment was committed" (20:4). This group is all the saints of God, who are now raised up and share Christ's reign. The promise that the saints will share Christ's rule and judgment is one that occurs not infrequently in Scripture (Dan. 7:9, 22; Mt. 19:28; I Cor. 4:8; 6:2, 3; II Tim. 2:12; Rev. 2:26, 28; 3:12, 21; 5:9-10, RSV). A second group is the martyrs, particularly those of the recent tribulation. "Also, I saw the souls of those who had been beheaded for their testimony to Jesus and for the word of God." They are singled out for special attention. There is a third group consisting of those "who had not worshiped the Beast or its image and had not received its mark on their foreheads or their hands." That this is indeed a third group does not appear in most English translations, but the syntax of the Greek sentence changes at this point. This third group designates those who survive the persecution of the tribulation and who are living when Christ returns. Of all of these three groups, it is said that they "came to life" and reigned with Christ during the millennium. If the third group designates the living saints,[19] the word *ezēsan* includes both the resurrection of dead saints and the rapture of the living, as in I Thessalonians 4:16f. and I Corinthians 15:51f.[20]

The first resurrection is a partial resurrection, for "the rest of the dead did not come to life until the thousand years were ended" (20:5). The "second resurrection," although it is not so designated, occurs at the end of the millennium (20:11-15), when all the rest of the dead are raised for the final judgment. No judgment had been mentioned in connection with the first resurrection, but now the dead stand before the great white throne of God to be judged. This company includes apparently all of the unsaved of all ages together with all who have died during the millennium.[21] The basis of judgment is twofold: works, and the book of life. The destiny of men will be decided in accordance with their works (Rom. 2:6-11) and in accordance with their relationship to Jesus.

One of the most hotly debated questions in the conservative interpretation of Revelation is that of the millennium. The doctrine is usually rejected not on exegetical but on theological grounds. The Revelation nowhere expounds the theology of the millennial kingdom. Why must there be a temporal kingdom on this earth before the eternal Kingdom on the new earth? An answer frequently offered is that the Revelation simply reflects contemporary apocalyptic ideas and adapts the twofold Jewish concept of the temporary "days of the Messiah" and the final "Age to Come" to Christian theology.[22] Whatever historical background lies behind the concept, we must still ask the question of its theological significance in the New Testament. Here we are shut up to inferences, for the New Testament nowhere explains the need for this temporal kingdom, except to indicate that in some undisclosed way it is essential in the accomplishment of the reign of Christ (I Cor. 15:24ff.).

There should be no objection to the idea of such a temporal kingdom in principle, for the New Testament is quite clear that we are already experiencing a temporal reign of Christ in the church age. Christ is already exalted as Lord (Phil. 2:9) and reigning at the right hand of God (Acts

19 See W. H. Simcox, *The Revelation* (1893), pp. 182f.; G. R. Beasley-Murray in *The New Bible Commentary*, p. 1195; M. Rissi, *Zeit und Geschichte in der Offenbarung* (1952), p. 155.

20 See G. R. Beasley-Murray, *loc. cit.* We cannot here discuss the many attempts to interpret this first resurrection in other than literal terms. The various views are discussed in the author's book, *Crucial Questions About the Kingdom of God* (1952), ch. 7.

21 That there will be death during the millennium is suggested by the fact that death is not destroyed until after this temporal kingdom (20:13).

22 See IV Ez. 7:28ff. where a temporal kingdom of four hundred years precedes the Age to Come. See S. Mowinckel, *He That Cometh* (1956), pp. 326f.; J. Klausner, *The Messianic Idea in Israel* (1955), pp. 408-19.

2:33-36; Heb. 1:3, 13; 8:1; 10:12-13; 12:2). He is already enthroned as King (Rev. 3:21; I Cor. 15:24-26) and has brought the blessings of his Kingdom to men (Rom. 14:17) and men unto his Kingdom (Col. 1:13). One of the unifying centers in the diversity of New Testament theology is the tension between experienced and futuristic theology.[23] If then in the present age there is a real overlapping of the two ages so that while we live in the old age we experience the powers of the Age to Come, there should be no objection in principle to the idea that God in his redemptive purpose may yet have an age in which there is an even further interaction between the powers of the new age and the present evil age.

In fact, it is at this point that we find one of the theological reasons for such a kingdom. Christ is now reigning as Lord and King, but his reign is veiled, unseen and unrecognized by the world. The glory that is now his is known only by men of faith. So far as the world is concerned, Christ's reign is only potential and unrealized. Nevertheless, contrary to appearances, he is reigning and "he must reign until he has put all his enemies under his feet" (I Cor. 15:25). Then his reign must become public in power and glory and his Lordship universally recognized (Phil. 2:10-11).

The Age to Come will not be the time of Christ's reign but the age of the Father's glory. When Christ has reigned as King and has subdued every hostile will, he will turn over the Kingdom to God the Father and will himself become finally subjected to the Father "that God may be everything to every one" (I Cor. 15:27f.). If then the present age is the time of Christ's veiled reign and hidden glory, and the Age to Come is the time of the Father's all-encompassing dominion, the millennial kingdom will be the age of the manifestation of Christ's glory when the sovereignty, which he now possesses but does not openly manifest, and which he will turn over to the Father in the Age to Come, will be displayed in the world.[24]

The idea of a temporal reign of Christ has further theological relevance. During this interval Satan is bound and locked up in a "bottomless pit" (20:2-3) that he cannot deceive the nations. At the end of this period of unparalleled righteousness, when Satan is released from his incarceration, he goes about to deceive the nations once again (v. 8). Even after Christ has ruled over men for a thousand years, the human heart is still responsive to satanic enticements.

The Word of God has much to say about the justness and righteousness of God's judgments (Rom. 3:4; II Thess. 1:5-6; II Tim. 4:8; Rev. 16:5, 7; 19:2; I Pet. 2:23; see esp. Rom. 2:1-16). Furthermore, it is God's concern so to deal with men in righteousness and judgment that "every mouth may be stopped, and the whole world held accountable to God" (Rom. 3:19). If then there is yet to be in the sovereign wisdom of God an era in

---

[23] See G. E. Ladd, "Eschatology and the Unity of NT Theology," *ET* 68 (1957), 268-72.

[24] See G. E. Ladd, "The Revelation of Christ's Glory," *Christianity Today* (Sept. 1, 1958), pp. 13-14.

history when evil is restrained, when righteousness prevails as it never has before in this age—if there is to be a time of social and political and economic justice when men dwell together under the government of Christ in peace and prosperity—if before the final judgment God grants to men a time when their social environment is as nearly perfect as possible, and yet after such a period of righteousness, the hearts of unregenerate men prove still to be rebellious against God, in the final judgment of the great white throne every mouth will indeed be stopped and every excuse voided, to the vindication of the glory and the righteousness of God. There are theologians today who insist that the love of God demands that hell be evacuated of every human being, that God cannot be a righteous and just God if a single soul finally perishes. The very idea of eternal punishment is utterly repugnant to the modern mind. There is indeed a need to vindicate the judgment of God as well as to display his unlimited love. The "sterner aspects of God's love" cannot be diluted into sentimentality that does not take sin seriously. The millennial reign of righteousness is the backdrop for the last judgment, that when the final terrible doom of the wicked is pronounced, God may be justified in his acts and his righteousness vindicated in his judgments.[25]

The final state of the Kingdom of God is a new heaven and a new earth (21:1ff.). This expresses a theology of creation that runs throughout the Bible. The Old Testament prophets picture the Kingdom of God in terms of a redeemed earth (Isa. 11:6-9; Joel 3:18; Amos 9:13-15). This is described in terms of a new heaven and new earth even in the Old Testament (Isa. 65:17; 66:22). However, this picture of a new order is in the Old Testament less than perfect, for Isaiah still speaks of sin and death in the new earth (Isa. 65:20). However, a fundamental theology underlies these expectations, even though they must be clarified by progressive revelation: that man's ultimate destiny is an earthly one. Man is a creature, and God created the earth to be the scene of his creaturely existence. Therefore, even as the redemption of man in the bodily aspect of his being demands the resurrection of the body, so the redemption of the very physical creation requires a renewed earth as the scene of his perfected existence. Man never ceases to be God's creature. The New Testament does not outstrip this theology, although it reveals more than the Old Testament does by showing that the newness of the eternal order is much more radical than God had disclosed to the prophets. Jesus spoke of the regeneration of the world (Mt. 19:28), and Paul spoke of the redemption of the created order (Rom. 8:20-21). The new earth of Revelation 21 is the final term in the revelation of how this redemption is to take place. Just as we can speak of the resurrection of the body even though the resurrection body will be very different from the physical bodies of this order, so we can

---

[25] For other interpretations of Revelation 20, see G. E. Ladd, *Crucial Questions About the Kingdom of God*, pp. 135-83.

speak of the redemption of the creation even though the new order is indeed a new earth.[26]

The new earth is the scene of the final goal of redemption: "Behold, the dwelling of God is with men. He will dwell with them, and they shall be his people, and God himself will be with them" (Rev. 21:3). This feature —the fact that God will be God to his people—is the central element of God's covenant with his people throughout the entire course of redemptive history. That Yahweh should be God to his people was the continuing element in the covenant made with Abraham (Gen. 17:7), with Moses (Exod. 6:7; Deut. 29:13), and with David (II Sam. 7:24f.), and it is the abiding feature of the new covenant that God promised to make in the future Kingdom (Jer. 31:1, 33; Ezek. 37:23; 36:28). Now at last, this covenant promise finds its perfect fulfillment in the new earth of the Age to Come.

The center of the new earth is the holy city, the new Jerusalem, which is pictured as the Bride of the Lamb, magnificently arrayed (21:9-11). The description of the city is highly symbolic. Its inhabitants include the redeemed from both Old Testament (21:12) and New Testament (21:14) times. There will be no temple in the city, for there will be immediate fellowship between God and his people, unmediated by cult or ritual (21:22). Death and disease are banished (22:1-2). The most important word of all—that which contains every other blessing of the new order—is subsumed in the words, "They shall see his face" (22:4). This is the goal of redemption. No man has seen God at any time; the only Son is the sole mediator bringing the knowledge of God to men (John 1:18). When Christ's redeeming mission is completed, the redeemed will enjoy the glory of the beatific vision. They will see God's face. All else is secondary and contained in this greatest of all blessings.

And so the Bible ends, with a redeemed society dwelling on a new earth that has been purged of all evil, with God dwelling in the midst of his people. This is the goal of the long course of redemptive history. Soli Deo gloria!

[26] II Pet. 3:12-13 describes the new earth in terms of a dissolution of the element of the present order and the emergence of a new order.

Index of Authors

Index of Scriptures

OLD TESTAMENT

Jeremiah

Lamentations

Ezekiel

INTERTESTAMENTAL LITERATURE

Luke

I Corinthians

Galatians

Ephesians

Philippians

Colossians

I Thessalonians

II Thessalonians

CORPUS HERMETICUM